Trade and Exchange
in Prehistoric Europe

Proceedings of a Conference held at the
University of Bristol, April 1992

Edited by Chris Scarre and Frances Healy

Published by
Oxbow Bocks
in association with
The Prehistoric Society and the Société Préhistorique Française

Published by
Oxbow Books, Park End Place, Oxford OX1 1HN

ISBN 0 946897 62 X

This book is available from
Oxbow Books, Park End Place, Oxford OX1 1HN
(Phone: 0865–241249; Fax: 0865–794449)

and

The David Brown Book Company
PO Box 5605, Bloomington, IN 47407, USA
(Phone: 812–331–0266; Fax: 812–331–0277)

*The cover shows bronze amphorae from Veii and Gevlinghausen
(after Jockenhövel 1974, Abb. 2 & 4)*

Printed in Great Britain by
The Short Run Press, Exeter

Contents

List of Contributors

A. J. AMMERMAN
Department of Anthropology, Colgate University,
Hamilton, New York 13346, U.S.A.

J. BRIARD
U.P.R. 403 du C.N.R.S., Laboratoire Anthropologie,
Université de Rennes 1, 35042 Rennes Cedex, France

P. BRUN
Centre de Recherches Archéologiques, 3 Rue Michelet,
75006 Paris, France

C. DU GARDIN
U.P.R. 403 du C.N.R.S., Laboratoire Anthropologie,
Université de Rennes 1, 35042 Rennes Cedex, France

C.M. EDENS
Department of Anthropology, Wellesley College,
Wellesley, Massachusetts 02181, U.S.A.

M. EDMONDS
Department of Archaeology and Prehistory, University of
Sheffield, Sheffield S10 2TN, U.K.

A.P. FITZPATRICK
Wessex Archaeology, Portway House, South Portway Estate,
Old Sarum Park, Salisbury, Wiltshire SP4 6EB, U.K.

C. GAMBLE
Department of Archaeology, University of Southampton,
Southampton SO9 5NH, U.K.

A.F. HARDING
University of Durham, Department of Archaeology, 46
Saddler Street, Durham DH1 3NU, U.K.

F. HEALY
Oxford Archaeological Unit, 46 Hythe Bridge Street,
Oxford OX1 2EP, U.K.

J. GOMEZ DE SOTO
52 rue Fontaine-du-Lizier, B.P. 310, 16008 Angoulême,
France

F. JEUDY
37 rue Charles Nodier, F25000 Besançon, France

C. JEUNESSE
DRAC, Service Régionale de l'Archéologie, Palais du
Rhin, 2 Place de la République, 67082 Strasbourg Cedex,
France

P.L. KOHL
Department of Anthropology, Wellesley College,
Wellesley, Massachusetts 02181, U.S.A.

K. KRISTIANSEN
Ministry of the Environment, the National Forest and
Nature Agency, Haraldsgade 53, DK-2100 Copenhagen Ø,
Denmark

M.A. LEVINE
The McDonald Institute for Archaeological Research, 62
Sidney Street, Cambridge CB2 3JW, U.K.

J.V.S. MEGAW
Discipline of Visual Arts and Archaeology, The Flinders
University of South Australia, GPO Box 2100, Adelaide,
South Australia 5001, Australia

M.R. MEGAW
Discipline of Visual Arts and Archaeology, The Flinders
University of South Australia, GPO Box 2100, Adelaide,
South Australia 5001, Australia

S. MCGRAIL
Institute of Archaeology, 36 Beaumont Street, Oxford OX1
2PG, U.K.

S. NEEDHAM
Department of Prehistoric and Romano-British Antiquities,
British Museum, London WC1B 3DG, U.K.

P. PÉTREQUIN
69 Grande Rue, 70100 Gray, France

C. POLGLASE
Department of Anthropology, Colgate University,
Hamilton, New York 13346, U.S.A.

A.C. RENFREW
University of Cambridge, Department of Archaeology,
Downing Street, Cambridge CB2 3DZ, U.K.

M. RICQ-DE BOUARD
Centre de Recherches Archéologiques, Sophia Antipolis,
06565 Valbonne, France

C. J. SCARRE
The McDonald Institute for Archaeological Research, 62
Sidney Street, Cambridge CB2 3JW, U.K.

E. SHEE TWOHIG
Department of Archaeology, University College Cork,
Cork, Ireland

A. SHERRATT
Department of Antiquities, Ashmolean Museum, Oxford
OX1 2PH, U.K.

R. SKEATES
The Queen's College, Oxford OX1 4AW, U.K.

Z. STOS-GALE
University of Oxford, Department of Physics, Particle and
Nuclear Physics, Nuclear Physics Laboratory, Keble Road,
Oxford OX1 3RH, U.K.

G. WOOLF
Brasenose College, Oxford OX1 4AJ, U.K.

Preface

THE MAJORITY of the papers in this volume are based on those delivered at the conference *Trade and Exchange in Prehistoric Europe* held at Bristol in April 1992. The conference theme was chosen to coincide with the inauguration of the Single European Market which came into operation on 1 January 1993. The conference was itself a collaboration within the field of European prehistory, organised by the Prehistoric Society in conjunction with the Société Préhistorique Française.

Acknowledgements

THANKS ARE DUE to Christiane Eluère and Jean-Pierre Mohen, who undertook the bulk of the conference organisation on the French side, and to Peter Chowne, Bryony Coles, and Judith Harris, who shared the organisation in England. We would also like to thank Jean-Claude Blanchet, then President of the Société Préhistorique Française, for helping to promote closer relations between our two societies. Financial support from the British Academy, the British Council and the University of Bristol is warmly acknowledged, as is the provision of office facilities by the McDonald Institute and Wessex Archaeology.

We are particularly grateful to all those who have contributed to this volume. Thanks are also extended to Professor D.R. Harris for his help and support during its production, to Laurent Olivier and Nathalie Haudecour for their translations of and improvements to the French abstracts of articles written in English, to Ruth Daniel for bringing a fresh and expert eye to proof-reading and to the McDonald Institute and the Oxford Archaeological Unit for the use of their equipment. Lastly, thanks are extended to David Brown and Oxbow Books for publishing this book.

1

Introduction

Chris Scarre

In Book IV of his *Histories*, the Greek writer Herodotus breaks off his account of the Scythians to tell us the following strange story about the Hyperboreans, the people dwelling in the extreme north of Europe:

> But the Delians tell much more concerning them than do any others. They say that offerings wrapped in wheat straw are brought from the Hyperboreans to Scythia. When they have passed Scythia, each nation in turn receives them from its neighbours till they are carried to the Adriatic sea, which is the most westerly limit of their journey. Thence they are brought on to the south, the people of Dodona being the first of the Greeks to receive them. From Dodona they come down to the Melian gulf, and are carried across to Euboea, and city sends them on to city until they come to Carystus. After this, Andros is left out of their journey, for it is Carystians who carry them to Tenos, and Tenians to Delos. Thus (they say) these offerings come to Delos.

> But on the first journey the Hyperboreans sent two maidens bearing the offerings, to whom the Delians give the names Hyperoche and Laodice, sending with them for safe conduct five men of their people as escort, those who are now called the Bearers and greatly honoured at Delos. But when the Hyperboreans found that those whom they sent never returned, they were very ill content that it should be their fate not to receive their messengers back; wherefore they carry the offerings, wrapped in wheat straw, to their borders, and charge their neighbours to send them on from their own country to the next; and the offerings, it is said, come by this conveyance to Delos.
> (Herodotus: *Histories* IV.33)[1]

Taken at face value this story appears to describe a long distance transport mechanism in which certain items travelled many hundreds of miles, at first perhaps brought by a travelling delegation, but later entrusted to a string of peoples none of whom moved beyond the limits of their home territory. What the sacred offerings were Herodotus omits to tell us. It is however just the kind of mechanism which prehistorians have often considered must have lain behind long-distance transport of amber in Bronze Age Europe.[2] And note that we use the word 'transport' rather than 'trade' advisedly here, since nowhere in Herodotus' story is there any hint of anything given by the Greeks in exchange; these were sacred offerings, donated without any expectation of reciprocity at a shrine of widespread repute. Whether its fame was sufficient to attract dedications from such a distance, or whether Herodotus' Greek-centred view of the importance of Delos blinded him to the true nature of the undertaking – whether indeed the offerings really came from as far away as he believed – we cannot now be sure. But the story demonstrates that the peoples of the literate Mediterranean world in the mid first millennium BC had a hazy idea of a series of routes and trade links spreading far to the north into the heart of temperate Europe, and that along these and other routes items moved to and fro, sometimes over long distances and for quite specific commercial and non-commercial reasons.

It is these movements of materials and artefacts which are the subject of the present volume.

Herodotus' story encapsulates a number of key elements which must be borne in mind in studying and assessing the evidence for prehistoric trade and transport in Europe: that items themselves could travel long distances without the need for people to move as far; that many of these exchanges would not have been purely commercial but would have incorporated a strong symbolic or conceptual element; that the nature of contacts will often have changed over time (in this case from long-distance bearers to down-the-line trade); and that they will have been surrounded by a mythology which may have entirely obscured their true origins but may have greatly enhanced their value and prestige. These are all points which will re-surface frequently in the papers which follow.

Herodotus' story of the Delian offerings is an excellent example of an anthropological account of artefact or material transport. It is indeed anthropology rather than archaeology which has thrown most light on the kinds of trade mechanism which operated in pre-industrial societies. A justly renowned example of the anthropological contribution to this subject, dating from early in the present century, is Marcel Mauss' *Essai sur le don, forme archaïque de l'échange* (1925). He defined his subject matter as 'prestations which are in theory voluntary, disinterested and spontaneous, but are in fact obligatory and interested. The form usually taken is that of the gift generously offered; but the accompanying behaviour is formal pretence and social deception, while the transaction itself is based on obligation and economic self-interest' (Mauss 1966 [1925], 1).

The importance of Mauss' work was twofold: it situated exchanges within a social context, and it showed how a purely economic approach to exchange would fail to appreciate the full significance of these transactions. A similar message had been conveyed three years earlier by Malinowski's *Argonauts of the Western Pacific*, where the exchange of valuables in the Trobriand Islands was based on a socially ascribed value rather than their 'real' economic value, and depended as much on the fame and associations of the valuables as on their workmanship and raw material (Malinowski 1922). Voyages for the exchange of kula valuables were also the pretext for exchanges of a more purely economic nature (Brookfield & Hart 1971, 324–7; Irwin 1983). The practical importance of exchange in eastern New Guinea and adjacent islands was well brought out by Harding's study of the Vitiaz Straits, where exchange was so frequent and so important that the Siassi islanders were able to derive considerable wealth from their role as middlemen (Harding 1967; Sahlins 1972).

The foregoing discussion serves to emphasise the variety of expressions in which trade and exchange can occur. Sahlins distinguished a range of possibilities based on the degree to which an equivalent return was expected or required, from generalised reciprocity at one end of the spectrum (where no immediate return is expected), through balanced reciprocity, to negative reciprocity (warfare, piracy, theft) at the other extreme (Sahlins 1972). It is open to question whether all these manifestations may properly be termed exchange, but at the same time it is difficult for the archaeologist to distinguish between them without the benefit of written records. The problem is one of equifinality: that a number of different processes can lead to the same resulting pattern. This is a difficulty emphasised by Hodder & Orton, who point out that different spatial processes may produce the same spatial form, but argue that careful simulation studies sometimes enable the specific dispersal mechanism to be identified (Hodder & Orton 1976, 126–54, 239–40).

At a minimalist level, what archaeology provides is evidence for the movement of goods and materials. Here, advances in source attribution have added greatly to our knowledge over the last 30 years, and a whole battery of techniques is now available to the analyst wishing to establish the origin of particular materials, ranging from amber and marine shell to pottery and metals (Renfrew & Bahn 1991, 314–20). It is on the basis of this information, coupled with distribution patterns, modes of transport, and cultural context, that the archaeologist seeks to comprehend the nature of prehistoric exchange in social and economic terms. The

success with which archaeologists now do this may be gauged from several of the papers in this volume.

The importance of trade in early societies is hardly to be questioned. A whole series of monographs and edited volumes have been devoted to the subject of prehistoric trade and exchange (e.g. Sabloff & Lamberg-Karlovsky 1975; Earle & Ericson 1977; Ericson & Earle 1982; Renfrew & Shennan 1982), and the provenance of any foreign materials is one of the first questions which the excavator asks of the material he uncovers. But were trade and exchange marginal phenomena, or causative factors in the development of particular human societies? The cost of transport meant that bulk carriage of heavy goods such as foodstuffs was never an attractive option, save sometimes by sea. In the 3rd century AD it cost as much to ship grain from one end of the Mediterranean to another as to cart it 75 miles inland (Finley 1985, 126). Most items traded over any great distance were in any case rare and valuable: *Biens Fortement Valorisés*, to use the term coined by Féblot-Augustins & Perlès (see Gamble, this volume). Their exotic character seems itself to have given them value in many cases, and control over the supply and distribution of exotics is one of the regular attributes of social elites. Prestige goods economies, in which political power is associated with access to foreign commodities, have been much discussed in both the anthropological and archaeological literature since the 1960s (e.g. Dupré & Rey 1968; Sahlins 1968; 1972; Ekholm 1972; Frankenstein & Rowlands 1978). Helms has expanded this point and shown how not only objects from distant places but knowledge about far away lands has been a source of power for individuals in many societies (Helms 1988).

Archaeological studies have interpreted the role of imported exotics in a number of different ways. Frankenstein & Rowlands have emphasised the importance of prestige goods from the Mediterranean in the increasing power of the Heuneburg chieftains during the 7th to 5th centuries BC; here the exotic goods seem to aid and accelerate a process of development which had already begun at a more local level (Frankenstein & Rowlands 1978). A somewhat different emphasis on the role of exchange in social change is given by Rathje in his theory of the rise of civilisation in the Maya lowlands. Here economic need was seen as the driving force, the lack of crucial raw materials in the Maya lowlands obliging communities to organize themselves so as to obtain them by trade with communities of the neighbouring uplands. This need to organize fostered the emergence of local elites. These consolidated their hold by monopolizing control over imports, which came to include exotic display items as well as material essentials (Rathje 1971). Though the model may not be accepted as a general explanation for the rise of Maya polities, the chain of causation which it embodies may well have been powerful in many different times and places in prehistory.

The model put forward by Frankenstein & Rowlands

emphasises the social significance of exotic imports while Rathje's lays greater stress on the economic importance of raw materials. In reality these two aspects would have been difficult to disentangle, since the distinction between symbolic and economic is a peculiarly modern western concept. Whether stemming from economic need or social strategy, however, the use of objects and materials from distant sources seems to be an integral part of human behaviour which can be traced back at least as far as the Middle Palaeolithic. Middle Palaeolithic groups were the first to gather and transport raw materials over significant distances, frequently from over 30 km away and sometimes as much as 100 km (Mellars 1991; Gamble, this volume). The scale of transport increased dramatically during the Upper Palaeolithic, when chocolate-coloured flint from the Holy Cross Mountains of central Poland was travelling up to 400 kilometres across the North European Plain (Schild 1976), while in the Ukraine sea shells from the Black Sea were found at Kostienki on the Don, some 450 km inland (Klein 1969). This increase in scale shows that between Middle and Upper Palaeolithic there was an important change. Middle Palaeolithic communities may well have travelled to the sources of raw materials and directly exploited them for what they needed. The long-distance transport of raw materials during the later part of the European Upper Palaeolithic was however clearly the result of exchange between different social groups. As with several other features of human cultural behaviour (e.g. Mellars 1991), it is perhaps at this important transition from Middle to Upper Palaeolithic that we may place the beginnings of exchange between prehistoric European communities.

Since the Upper Palaeolithic, mechanisms of trade and exchange have come to play a key role in social and economic development throughout Europe, and have attracted considerable attention from European archaeologists. Some have concentrated on the identification of traded items, using increasingly sophisticated analytical techniques to trace them back to their sources. Others have studied the social significance of trade between communities, drawing heavily on anthropological models. Both approaches are represented in this volume.

Some thirty-five years ago, Gordon Childe put forward the idea that particular forms of trade and technology were a key element in the development of a distinctive European character. He drew this conclusion from the contrast between the Bronze Age societies of the Near East, where craftsmen worked under the close control of rulers, and Europe, where he envisaged itinerant bronze-smiths selling their skills to local chiefs but retaining their independence. This freedom, he thought, lay at the heart of European technological progress (Childe 1958). Few would follow this line today, and while trade and exchange must inevitably have bound European communities together there is no implication here that they did so at the expense of contacts with adjacent non-European areas,

nor that the nature of that trade and exchange conferred on European society an especially innovative character. The concept of Europe itself may date back only to the 5th century BC [3], and it was not for many centuries that the peoples of Europe developed any special awareness of being 'European'; even today, the term is geographical rather than cultural, ethnic or economic.

Nor should we forget that throughout prehistoric times many European communities were regular recipients of non-European artefacts and raw materials: threads of Chinese silk in the Hallstatt princely burial at Hohmichele being one of the more spectacular examples which springs to mind (Riek & Hundt 1962, 206 ff.). Furthermore, the practice of archaeology in Europe today is characterized by theoretical diversity rather than by any single widely held viewpoint or approach, as a recent survey amply illustrates (Hodder 1991). It is hence in their simple geographical sense that the terms 'Europe' and 'European' are used in these pages. The shifting patterns and processes of trade and exchange which are documented in the studies which follow played a crucial role in the formation and character of European societies; but these were societies of such richness and diversity in cultural terms as would defy any attempt to reduce them to a single 'European' type or model, or to attribute to them a specifically 'European' identity.

Notes

1. Passage from Herodotus reprinted by permission of the publishers and the Loeb Classical Library from Herodotus, Volume 2, Translated by A.D. Godley, Cambridge, Mass.: Harvard University Press, 1982.

2. This passage was referred to by Professor J.L. Myres in the discussion following de Navarro's famous paper to the Geographical Society on the prehistoric amber routes in 1925. De Navarro's paper is notable also for its early use of chemical analysis to establish the provenance of the amber found at Mediterranean sites and to differentiate Baltic from Sicilian amber (de Navarro 1925).

3. The concept and name of Europe first appear in wiritings of Greek geographers of the sixth and fifth centuries BC. Herodotus, in the later fifth century, argued for a tripartite division of the habitable world into Europe, Asia and Libya (Africa). This was generally followed by later Classical authors who placed the boundary between Europe and Asia along the River Don, and that between Libya and Asia along the Nile or the Isthmus of Suez. It was not until 1833 that Volger in his *Handbuch der Geographie* located the boundary between Russia in Europe and Russia in Asia at the River Ural and the Ural mountains, so fixing the eastern frontier in its present position (Hay 1957).

References

Brookfield, H.C., & Hart, D., 1971. *Melanesia: A Geographical Interpretation of an Island World*. London: Methuen

Childe, V.G., 1958. *The Prehistory of European Society*. Harmondsworth: Penguin

de Navarro, J.M., 1925. Prehistoric routes between northern Europe and Italy defined by the amber trade. *Geographical Journal* 66, 481–507

Dupré, G., & Rey, P.P., 1968. Réflexions sur la pertinence d'une théorie de l'histoire des échanges. *Cahiers Internationaux de Sociologie* 46, 133–62

Earle, T.K., & Ericson, J.E., (eds) 1977. *Exchange Systems in Prehistory*. New York & London: Academic Press

Ekholm, K., 1972. *Power and Prestige: The Rise and Fall of the Kongo Kingdom*. Uppsala

Ericson, J.E., & Earle, T.K., (eds) 1982. *Contexts for Prehistoric Exchange*. New York & London: Academic Press

Finley, M.I., 1985. *The Ancient Economy*. Harmondsworth: Penguin Books

Frankenstein, S., & Rowlands, M.J., 1978. The Internal structure and regional context of early Iron Age society in south-western Germany. *University of London Institute of Archaeology Bulletin* 15, 74–112

Harding, T.G., 1967. *Voyagers of the Vitiaz Strait. American Ethnological Society Monograph 44*. Seattle: University of Washington Press

Hay, D., 1957. *Europe: The Emergence of an Idea*. Edinburgh: Edinburgh University Press

Helms, M.W., 1988. *Ulysses' Sail. An Ethnographic Odyssey of Power, Knowledge, and Geographical Distance*. Princeton, N.J.: Princeton University Press

Hodder, I., (ed.) 1991. *Archaeological Theory in Europe. The Last Three Decades*. London: Routledge

Hodder, I., & Orton, C., 1976. *Spatial Analysis in Archaeology*. Cambridge: Cambridge University Press

Irwin, G.J., 1983. Chieftainship, kula, and trade in Massim prehistory, in *The Kula. New Perspectives on Massim Exchange*, eds. J.W. Leach & E. Leach. Cambridge: Cambridge University Press, 29–72

Klein, R.G., 1969. *Man and Culture in the Late Pleistocene: A Case Study*. San Francisco: Chandler

Malinowski, B., 1922. *Argonauts of the Western Pacific*. London: Routledge & Kegan Paul

Mauss, M., 1966. *The Gift. Forms and Functions of Exchange in Archaic Societies*. London: Routledge & Kegan Paul

Mellars, P., 1991. Cognitive changes and the emergence of modern humans in Europe. *Cambridge Archaeological Journal* 1, 63–76

Rathje, W.L., 1971. The origin and development of lowland Classic Maya civilization. *American Antiquity* 36, 275–85

Renfrew, C., & Bahn, P., 1991. *Archaeology. Theories, Methods and Practice*. London: Thames & Hudson

Renfrew, C., & Shennan, S., (eds) 1982. *Ranking, Resource and Exchange: Aspects of the Archaeology of Early European Society*. Cambridge: Cambridge University Press

Riek, G., & Hundt, H.J., 1962. *Der Hohmichele. Ein Fürstengrabhügel der späten Hallstattzeit bei der Heuneburg*. Römisch-Germanische Forschungen 25

Sabloff, J., & Lamberg-Karlovsky, C.C., (eds) 1975. *Ancient Civilization and Trade*. Albuquerque: University of New Mexico Press

Sahlins, M., 1968. *Tribesmen*. Englewood Cliffs: Prentice Hall

Sahlins, M., 1972. *Stone Age Economics*. Chicago: Aldine

Schild, R., 1976. The final Palaeolithic settlements of the European plain. *Scientific American* 234, 88–99

2

Trade Beyond the Material

Colin Renfrew

Archaeological approaches to trade and exchange are reviewed: the early phase of diffusionism, the development of characterization studies and the influence of substantivist economists. Careless and ill-defined applications of the 'world systems' approach to prehistoric trade are criticized. The role of trade as a social and symbolic rather than purely economic activity is emphasized. Questions relating to reasons for early travel are posed, and consideration of the role of the individual, without recourse to hermeneutic obscurantism, advocated.

Dans cet article, les différentes approches archéologiques de la question des échanges dans la préhistoire sont soumises à une analyse critique. Elles se rattachent à une phase initiale d'inspiration diffusionniste, puis au développement des études de provenance des matériaux, et enfin à une série de travaux influencés par les économistes de l'école 'substantialiste'. Les transpositions approximatives et mal définies de l'approche des 'world systems' ('systèmes mondiaux') au problème du commerce préhistorique sont critiqués. Le rôle joué par les échanges dans le domaine sociale et symbolique, au delà d'une simple activité économique, est mis en relief. Les questions relatives aux causes des premiers déplacements à longue distance sont envisagées, de même que le rôle des individus est abordé, sans tomber pour autant dans l'obscurantisme de l'herméneutique.

Introduction

'Trade and Exchange' constituted an admirable subject for the first joint meeting of the Société Préhistorique Française and the Prehistoric Society. My hope in presenting the first paper was to indicate some of the shifts in emphasis which have taken place over the past 30 or so years in this field. It seems appropriate to suggest that, although we are now good at conducting some parts of the archaeological enterprise, and some aspects of trade have shown themselves very much open to systematic investigation, we are less good at dealing with other aspects, with what one might term cognitive aspects. I shall argue later that this is not necessarily because these are inherently more difficult to consider, nor that they demand some different, possibly 'post-processual' kind of logic. It is rather that our frameworks of inference are still underdeveloped in some areas.

We have certainly learnt to cope with some of the material aspects of trade, exchange and interaction. Increasingly we can undertake successful characterization studies. We are however less competent at understanding how goods work in society, what role the traded materials played in the societies in question. It is only relatively recently that such notions as 'commodity' and 'value' have been regarded by prehistorians as anything other than obvious. Now we can see that they are complicated and sophisticated concepts whose working is still not completely understood (Appadurai 1986).

Part of the success of characterization studies springs from the circumstance that much of the procedure and reasoning is available already, ready-made, in the field of science or of archaeological science. The physics of radiocarbon determination or of neutron activation analysis is now well understood, but it should not be forgotten that the appropriate application of that physics to the subject materials of archaeology has taken some 40 years to put on a sound basis. Likewise, characterization studies have had teething troubles in their application in the early stages. One thinks here of the monumental failure of the Studien zu den Anfängen der Metallurgie project in so far as it relates to the elucidation of the trade in copper or bronze (Junghans *et al.* 1960; 1968; Coles & Harding 1979, 13 & 18). So even here, with the considerable experience of the natural sciences at one's disposal, it has been difficult to find the correct path without uncertainties and errors. But it is now widely recognized that the successful application of such techniques represents only one component of fruitful archaeological science. To apply them to give useful information about human behaviour in the past often requires a different and more complicated research design. This point has been well made by Albert Ammerman (this volume) in showing how, to analyse a trading system, the raw characterization data must be broken down to give a well-defined chronological structure, and attention given to function as well as to presence or absence.

A first, necessary step in our enterprise is to be clear that we are talking about rather more than 'trade' in a strict economic sense. Polanyi's useful definition of trade (Polanyi 1957, 266) as 'the mutual appropriative movement of goods between hands' expresses well what the economist means by the term. But for the archaeologist it is the movement of goods which is instantly recognizable, rather than the transfer of ownership or possession. What we have to deal with first is movement, or 'displacement', to use Stuart Needham's useful term (this volume).

Secondly, it is necessary to take a broader view of exchange, and to go beyond the material sphere, in order to consider the full range of possible human interactions. That wider sense was already implied in the title of an earlier paper, 'Trade as action at a distance' (Renfrew 1975). The full range of human interactions can be the subject of scrutiny. Those which result in the transport or displacement of material goods may only be a minority. But they are not adequately understood unless we consider the wider context.

The early phase

Already in the 1930s there was an acute awareness of the importance of cultural contact, of the sometimes determining significance of the intercourse between one region and another. For the prehistorian, it had long been understood, such contacts could be documented by:

(a)   notable similarities between the forms of artefacts seen in one region and another, and
(b)   direct evidence afforded by recognizably traded materials.

In the 1930s it was not common to seek to demonstrate in great detail that the traded goods derived from some specific source. It was often sufficient that their exotic character should be recognized and asserted.

The view offered by Gordon Childe of the Vinča culture of the Balkans is a case in point (Childe 1957, 92). Initially there was a tendency to follow a migrationist model: to see the persons using the supposedly traded objects as settlers, as immigrants, who would in some cases have brought the exotic objects (for example the copper tools) with them, or in other cases would have obtained them through continuing trade with the parent area. Gradually this model was replaced by one where the changes were not the results of the influx of new people, but rather the result of contact. The recognition of similarities, and where possible of actual traded goods, was thus used to allow the recognition of what in modern parlance would be termed a 'world system'. Implicit in the approach was the notion of a civilized homeland, a hearth of civilization, a 'centre'. This centre would despatch manufactured goods to, and receive raw materials from, secondary locations on the 'periphery'. Childe described such a situation well in his work *Man Makes Himself* (Childe 1936). Indeed many of the ideas were present already in his earlier book *The Bronze Age* (Childe 1930).

The approach was one of the 'diffusion' of culture: diffusion implied a 'dependency model', and dependency models were seen to work in terms of diffusion.

Systematic application to the material

Although in the early days traded goods were sometimes supposedly recognized by simple inspection, there were already pioneering applications of more scientific studies. Already by 1740 Edmund Halley was using the microscope to examine the stones of Stonehenge (Stukeley 1740, 5). And by the later nineteenth century such innovators as Heinrich Schliemann were commissioning petrological studies on supposedly imported artefacts. It was in the 1920s and 1930s that such studies became more systematic and more common. Already in 1923, Halley's insights at Stonehenge were being followed up in the light of the more extensive petrological knowledge then available (Thomas 1923). The establishment of the Implement Petrology Sub-Committee of the South-Western Group of Museums and Art Galleries in England for the study of the Neolithic axe trade was a significant step (Keiller *et al.* 1941; Stone & Wallis 1947). In Austria the very systematic investigations by Pittioni (1951) applied new techniques of trace element analysis to the metal artefacts themselves (Otto & Witter 1952), and considered the source areas – the mines and quarries of Alpine copper – in a systematic way not superseded for at least 30 years.

In Britain, the work of Stone & Thomas (1956) on the faience beads of the Wessex culture, although not entirely conclusive, was novel in using trace element analysis (in this case by means of optical emission spectroscopy) for an archaeological characterization study, although they had in this been anticipated by Pittioni. Some years later the same techniques were applied to obsidian, which proved a very suitable material for characterization (Cann & Renfrew 1964). Subsequently a whole battery of techniques became available (Renfrew & Bahn 1991, ch. 9), among them neutron activation analysis. The developing technical competence in physical and chemical analysis was matched by the use of suitable statistical techniques, such as discriminant analysis. Patterns of 'fall off' in quantity, plotted spatially, gave further insights into the movement of goods (Hodder & Orton 1976).

Polanyi and the substantivist economists

Along with the growing competence in the handling of traded goods as materials came a marked interest in considering various modes of trade, considered now largely in social terms. Grahame Clark devoted a chapter to trade in his pioneering work *Prehistoric Europe: the Economic Basis* (Clark 1952). And Karl Polanyi (1957) laid the foundations for a new approach by his careful consideration of the early development of markets, which he situated (so far as Europe is concerned) very late in prehistoric times, with the emergence of a coinage in Greece.

Polanyi's work on 'reciprocity' was undoubtedly influenced significantly by both the pioneering study of Malinowski (1922) on the *kula* exchange system of Melanesia, and by the seminal work of Marcel Mauss (1925) *The Gift*. Clark (1965) was later one of the first to use the notion of gift exchange in the discussion of the British Neolithic axe trade. It was, however, Polanyi's work on redistribution which was the most influential, coinciding as it did with an interest in chiefdoms (Service 1962). A typology of social forms (tribe-chiefdom-state) could now notionally be equated, at least in part, with a typology of modes of trade. These ideas were further developed by Sahlins (1972) in his *Stone Age Economics*. They were influential also for George Dalton (Dalton 1977), with his careful consideration of 'primitive valuables'.

Early attempts to reconstruct whole systems

As already noted, Childe was one of the first to consider entire trading systems and their effects, although in the main he did so before the development of detailed characterization studies, and without the benefit of the substantivist school of economic anthropologists. It was, however, within the framework of the new processual archaeology, with its aspiration for more general models, that some of the most influential analyses of early trading systems were formulated. Kent Flannery offered a study for the rise of complex society among the Olmec (Flannery 1968) in which the development of interregional trade played a major role. Rathje (1973) offered a model for the development of complex society among the Maya, in which trade again played a significant causative role. And in Europe, Frankenstein & Rowlands (1978) applied a very similar approach to the south German Iron Age. Here once again the control of exotic prestige goods in the hands of a local elite was identified as of determining significance for the development of a more highly structured hierarchical system. Pires Ferreira (1976) integrated a considerable variety of characterization methods into her analysis of Mesoamerican trading systems during the Formative period.

In recent years the 'world system' approach of Immanuel Wallerstein (1974) has proved an attractive one to many. Although his own application of that term was to West Indian trade with Europe in the eighteenth century AD, the concept was appropriated by various prehistorians (Kohl 1987; Rowlands *et al.* 1987).

I have myself always been sceptical of the very ready projection of Wallerstein's model back into the prehistoric period, as indeed has Wallerstein himself. In the first place the term 'world system' seems an unduly grandiose one, where the area in question is inevitably very much sub-global in scale. Why 'world'? But more significantly, the practitioners of this concept in prehistoric times very rarely stop to ask themselves precisely what evidential basis would be appropriate for its invocation. If region A imports just a few minor items from Region B, do A and B together constitute a 'world system', with B as centre and A as periphery? The objection to the way the model has been employed hitherto is that it is used simply by assertion. What might simply be regarded as a local trading system is *named* a 'world system' – that is to say the assertion is made, generally without further elucidation, that it is a 'world system', and all manner of consequences are inferred. It may well be the case, as Andrew Sherratt has recently asserted, that in the Iron Age Europe became part of a wider 'world system' which involved the East Mediterranean region also. And it may well be that the trading systems seen in the Neolithic period in Europe are best viewed as interlinked local systems not so closely coupled together as to merit the title of a 'world system'. But even in the Iron Age, to apply a centre/periphery vocabulary in this way may not be helpful, and to identify Europe in the Bronze Age as 'marginal' rather than 'peripheral' may not be a particularly helpful step. The merit of the 'world system' approach is certainly that it brings up for consideration the question as to whether various regions are so highly coupled together in their trading networks that their economies can no longer be considered separately, but should rather be considered as a single functioning whole. The question is a useful one, but unfortunately it has rarely been posed other than rhetorically, nor have the archaeological criteria for defining a 'world system' been adequately defined.

In the last analysis, in my view, most of those who have applied the term to the field of European prehistory have simply been treading in the footsteps of Childe, and adding very little to his own influential and plausible analysis for prehistoric Europe. But Childe's analysis, as we now know, was wrong. It was based upon a chronology itself based upon diffusionist principles which the advent of radiocarbon dating has served to undermine. Those who have used centre/periphery models recently have in general employed the same methodology as Childe, but without the excuse that, in a pre-radiocarbon era, he had little option but to think in diffusionist terms. Had these practition-

ers considered carefully under precisely which circumstances the concept might be appropriate and under
which it would not be valid, they might have progressed
beyond Childe's perhaps inevitably diffusionist position. In the main they have failed to do this. There is
an acute need to examine precisely when dependency
models are appropriate and when they are not.

It was in an attempt to break out of the sometimes
sterile dichotomy between 'diffusion' and 'independent
invention' that the concept of 'peer-polity interaction'
was developed (Renfrew & Cherry 1986). The simple
point here is that the different participants in a trading
system are significantly influenced in a number of ways
by the continuing interactions taking place, without the
development of either centre or periphery, or indeed of
a margin. The invitation is there, moreover, to investigate more carefully the precise nature of the interactions and their effects upon the individuals and communities in question. But simply to invoke 'peer-polity
interaction' as an explanatory formula naturally risks
that same automatism and sterility which has tended to
characterize the prehistoric applications of the 'world
system' approach. Further analysis is needed.

The present situation

At present, as noted earlier, we have available a wide
range of varied characterization techniques. One good
example is offered by lead isotope analysis, which has
given a way out of the impasse in metal studies brought
about by the difficulties with the trace element analysis
of metals (Stos-Gale, this volume). Another example of
a technique now proving its worth is infra-red absorption spectroscopy, as applied to amber (Beck & Shennan
1991). The recent publication of a definitive treatment
of prehistoric amber finds in Britain is a conspicuously
successful application of a characterization technique.

Modern studies in general also develop techniques for
the quantitative handling of the data obtained, so that the
nature of the fall-off from source is carefully examined
by such methods as trend surface analysis. There is
scope here for the application of the further techniques
of spatial analysis already used for the investigation of
gene frequency distributions (Barbujani & Sokal 1990).

Secondly, it may be asserted that while earlier
studies focused mainly upon the distribution of the
traded material, significant advances have been made
in the study of the production which precedes distribution, and (perhaps to a lesser extent) of the consumption
which accompanies and succeeds it.

An outstanding case of the study of the production
of the material at the sources themselves is offered by
Robin Torrence's study of the Melian obsidian quarries
(Torrence 1986), and other important studies in Australia (McBryde 1979; 1984) and in California (Ericson
1982) may be cited. In Britain the axe trade has been
studied anew by Bradley & Edmonds (1993). But few
studies have yet succeeded in studying the consumption

of goods with the same coherence as has been applied
to their production.

It cannot yet be claimed, however, that a great deal
more has been achieved in studying the role of trade
within whole economic systems than has been undertaken by Flannery (1968), by Rathje (1973) or by
Frankenstein & Rowlands (1978) some two decades
ago. The monograph by Wells (1980) on the Iron Age
of southern France and Germany also gives a clear
account within what is in essence the same genre as
those just cited.

What has to some extent been lacking is a more
sustained analysis of the role of each commodity, of
each class of traded material or finished object within
the society in question. To discuss that role requires
some more sensitive understanding of how that material
was valued by its users, and how it was regarded in the
society in question. This is a point already very well
made by Hodder (1982, 4) in stressing the active role
played by material culture in the social world within
which we live. The same point was already clearly
perceived by Thorstein Veblen (1925; cf. Renfrew
1972, 497). But the emphasis that human social reality
is a *construct*, in which value and meaning are ascribed
to material objects, is one which we have not yet fully
assimilated, even though it was implied by Childe
already in 1936 with the prescient title of his book on
this subject, *Man Makes Himself*. It is not, I believe,
possible to reach an understanding of the inception and
development of metallurgy in Europe without some
insight into the social impact of early objects, and a
clear realization that even gold is not *intrinsically*
valuable in any absolute sense (Renfrew 1986). What
is needed at this point, in my view, is not some 'post-
processual' abandonment of scientific method, some
retreat to a relativist or 'hermeneutic' position where
each worker is encouraged to invent his or her own
'meaning', to develop some personal 'reading' of the
prehistoric 'text'. I have tried to argue that in order to
understand the working of objects in society with regard to their symbolic value it is not at all necessary to
abandon the well-established frameworks of inference
employed by earlier generations of archaeologists.
Cognitive-processual archaeology (Renfrew & Bahn
1991, ch.10; Renfrew, in press) seeks to discuss these
matters without any radically new epistemological
claims. It may be enough to ask some new questions in
a fairly straightforward way, and to seek to answer
them in adequate detail. It is because we have been
overlooking the use of artefacts as agents of communication that our analyses have sometimes seemed excessively utilitarian. It is this aspect of 'action at a distance' which requires much closer consideration.

Travel as a social activity

Economic man, it may be argued (and no apology is
needed for the gender-oriented terminology, since the

concept itself is as dated as the form of expression), does not travel very much. This is certainly the case for the basics of present life. Many farms can be virtually self-sufficient, and an economic analysis can quite reasonably proceed in terms of von Thünen's *Die isolierte Stadt* (von Thünen 1875). The traditional analysis of the economic geographer with its hexagonal lattice and hierarchy of centres rarely envisages that the individual would need to travel further than the nearest third or second-order centre, and just occasionally the primary organizational centre. Trade in such a construction fulfils the supply needs of economic units and is undertaken, so far as long-distance trade is concerned, between entrepreneurs or administrators.

It must be admitted that the reality in some cases does not depart too far from this stereotype. In the recent past there were indeed farmers (and also town dwellers) who had never in their lives travelled more than a few tens of kilometres from their birthplace. There were people in Britain who never travelled far enough to see the sea.

But this picture, while perhaps validly stressing some sedentary aspects of farming life (in contrast with the often greater mobility of hunter-gatherers), overlooks a range of social and symbolic patterns of travel. For while it may be true that 'human social organization is segmentary in nature: human spatial organization is therefore cellular and modular' (Renfrew 1974, 102), it is also the case that 'Basic groups do not exist in isolation, but affiliate into larger groups, meeting together at periodic intervals' (Renfrew 1974, 103). In nearly all human societies there are gatherings of people, some from very distant places, which are difficult to explain in terms of the basic needs of 'economic man' (although the opportunity is certainly taken at such meetings to conduct what may be regarded as economic transactions).

Such meetings can be regarded in the terms of the above statement as meetings of groups, but they can more readily be understood as meetings of individuals who happen to be members of a number of different social groups or segmentary units. Such meetings are common, perhaps general, among hunter-gatherers, where the smaller bands which constitute hunter-gatherer society meet together for talk, for ritual, for exchange, to prepare for or conduct the exchange of marriage partners, in short to conduct a very full range of human interactions. Such meetings are generally on peaceful terms, so that warfare is not one of the modes of interaction practised, although it cannot necessarily be excluded.

If we seek to gain an insight into the range of interactions, it is more appropriate to do so under the rubric of 'communication' than of 'trade', since the underlying motivation and functional role may not primarily be the acquisition of goods. It is of course possible to put these periodic meetings, and the communication which takes place at them, in purely functional terms. Among hunter-gatherers, information about the up-to-the-minute availability of plant and animal resources over a wide area may be of crucial significance, and such periodic meetings may fulfil a well-defined functional requirement. The same may be so for exchange of marriage partners, which more efficiently takes place with the availability of a larger gene pool than may be possible between neighbouring bands. But the functional explanation is not enough.

It is the case that such meetings nearly always involve singing and dancing. They involve the exchange of gifts. They may involve competition within a broadly non-hostile environment. They certainly involve a series of rituals, secular as well as religious. Such comments apply as much to the Olympic Games and other periodic meetings in the pan-Hellenic world as to the corroborees of Australian hunter-gatherers. For they are also an affirmation of faith, of a shared world view, involving belief systems which are powerfully reinforced by their visible acceptance by a much wider group than the basic segmentary social unit.

There are of course political connotations here. Such social interactions inevitably have to function in relation to the existing structures of power. But in general they also manage to transcend these, so that the reach of social interaction generally far exceeds that of the individual polity. Only in the more extensive empires does political power extend as far as or further than the areas of shared symbolism and belief which these periodic meetings reflect and encourage. Here, then, is a different kind of 'world system', and one that is often overlooked by Marxist economic historians, a symbolic system in which economic factors may not take first place. It is only by recognizing that 'trade' is not the primary motivation, nor economic processes the dominant ones, that we can hope to begin to understand the context in which trade and exchange in fact operate.

Travel, generally with the aim of a shared social and religious experience, is a near-universal among human societies. Certainly the *kula* cycle of Melanesia can be regarded more effectively in this light. The ritual and the range of symbolic activities involved are not merely 'feather waving', as the more materialist Marxist historians might argue. These are not activities which mask the underlying exchanges of material goods. On the contrary, the exchange of goods can sometimes be seen as the pretext used to legitimize the social and ritual activities which take place. In rural England a century ago, the weekly market and the periodic fair were social as much as economic meetings.

These remarks apply as much to egalitarian as to hierarchically structured societies. But when the behaviour of elites is considered, there are further aspects of travel to be considered. Travel involves contact with other, sometimes mysterious worlds. It is in the nature of things that only those that travel may return as bearers of exotic knowledge as well as exotic goods. They can achieve or enhance power thereby. Mary Helms (1988) has stressed how, in a wide range of societies, privileged access to 'outside things' can be used to enhance the prestige of an existing elite. As Shennan puts it (Beck & Shennan 1991, 138): 'the spatially distant, because of its strangeness, has great power'.

Part of the impact of these ideas has already been caught for archaeologists by the arguments of Flannery, Rathje, and Frankenstein and Rowlands, cited above, that exotic objects can be used to enhance the status of local elites, so that it is profitable for these elites to control the flow of exotic goods from outside. But the case argued by Helms is a much wider one, in which those goods are merely one small but tangible part of the wider reality. What gives power is knowledge, especially exotic and secret knowledge. The working of the power of an elite is itself something of a mystery. Power is mysterious, and power thrives on mystery. This is no doubt one of the reasons why religious cults, even purely local ones, are often controlled by dominant elites: in this way they control access to the forces of the 'other world'. But this process is analogous to and related to the way in which the elite can also control access to the sometimes equally mysterious but for the archaeologist much more tangible 'other world', the world beyond, in a spatial rather than a transcendental sense.

Reasons for travel

In the foregoing, communication has been stressed rather than commodity, and the symbolic (religious as well as social) rather than the material. But there is no need to set up a false opposition between the two. On the contrary, it is the conjunction of the two that is so powerful, and in the formation of that conjunction that concepts of value, and of the symbolic power of material goods are developed.

At this point it may be useful to broaden the discussion with a consideration of the reasons why people travel. Inevitably these questions are best posed at the level of the individual. I shall hope to argue below that to do so does not necessarily signal the retreat to subjectivity and relativism argued by some recent archaeological theorists.

QUESTIONS

Who travels? (Within a given society, what categories of person habitually travel, as defined in terms of age, status, profession, ethnic affiliation etc., and in what numbers?)

Where to? (Who in practice goes where, and how often?)

Why? (For what purposes do they leave, what determines their destination?)

What do they do there? (How long do they stay, what range of activities do they perform, and how many of them were envisaged before their initial departure?)

When and why do they return, if they do? (In this discussion it is implied that the travellers return: the discussion does not centre on one-way journeys, although a comparable, careful consideration of patterns of migration (in this sense) would undoubtedly be illuminating)

What are the material correlates of their travel? (What do they take with them, what do they bring back with them by way of goods? What do they do while away that has permanent effects? What do they do on their return that they would not otherwise have done?)

What are the consequences of their travel? (Are there implications in terms of gene flow, in terms of propagation of disease, or in terms of the flow of what Richard Dawkins would term 'memes' – i.e. ideas which they have learnt as a consequence of their travel and which they may now pass on to others?)

These questions are obvious enough. But they have rarely been made explicit. Yet they serve to set the notion of travel in a broader context, and in one where semiotic issues, relating to communication, may play a wider role than purely economic ones in terms of the flow of commodities.

WHY?

To answer these questions adequately for any society would be a complex task. But it may be appropriate to initiate it by reflecting on the range of answers which might be offered to the 'why' question. Just a few answers will be outlined, not in any particularly well-considered order.

(1)   To obtain goods – whether by direct collection, by gift exchange or in some more 'commercial' exchange transaction. This is the answer most often advanced (sometimes the only answer advanced) by archaeologists specializing in the study of trade.

(2)   To trade in (sell) produced goods (whether produced by oneself or at second hand). This is a more 'commercial' trading enterprise, where the welfare of the craft-specialist (whether whole or part-time) depends on some efficient distribution mechanism by which the product may be disposed of gainfully.

(3)   To participate in the larger social meetings whose scope of involvement goes beyond the boundaries of the local segmentary unit. These are the periodic meetings discussed at some length above.

(4)   To seek exotic information (experience, wisdom, knowledge) whose ownership or control will bring enhanced prestige for the returning traveller. This was the point (mentioned above), so effectively discussed by Mary Helms (1988).

(5) To visit a distant holy place, possibly at a special time: to go on a pilgrimage (see Renfrew 1985, 255). This may not differ altogether from (3), but here the specific place is crucial, as is the participation in religious rituals associated with it.

(6) To learn or to train. This is related to point (4). There is no assumption here, however, that the learning is of a restricted kind, associated with mysterious or exotic powers, but simply that the returning individual has acquired a useful skill.

(7) To find work and to earn wealth. To seek one's fortune.

(8) To serve as a mercenary – often as much for the experience of deeds of valour as for the financial good fortune which may follow.

(9) To find a spouse. One of the most basic reasons for travel in a wide range of human societies.

(10) To visit relatives and friends. There is the assumption here of a pre-existing relationship of friendship or of kinship.

(11) As a licensed carrier or emissary. Cases where the traveller has been sent overseas by some higher authority to which he or she is subordinate. Clearly this would only apply in a hierarchically structured society.

CONSEQUENCES

To raise such issues opens the way, I would argue, for the better understanding of systems of interaction, including on the one hand those which have hitherto been considered as 'trading systems', and on the other, those where the symbolic aspect has long been seen as predominant. At once, however, we impinge upon two further themes which should not be far removed from any consideration of travel: language and ethnicity.

Not once, I believe, during the course of the conference of which this volume of papers is the product, were questions of language or of language diversity raised. Yet if the concept of communication is implicit within the discussion, that of language can surely not be far away. The notion of 'symbolic language' (in contrast to verbal language) is further touched upon below.

Ethnicity remains one of the most intriguing and one of the least understood of the concepts used by archaeologists. Like value, it is a construct, something which takes its reality from what people believe. Although constrained by certain material realities, it is not entirely determined by them. Like value it is a concept which archaeologists have so far failed to consider in any coherent way. Yet even in the narrowest interpretation of trade, ethnicity is bound to have a powerful role, since preferential trading links will frequently be forged with ethnicity as a basic factor. One pioneer work in this direction has been the study of British Iron Age coinage undertaken by Haselgrove (1979; 1982; also Collis 1971). But it may not be unfair to say that the notion of tribal identity in those works was taken to

some extent as a given. In reality it is one of the most difficult and most frequently overlooked questions in the whole field of archaeological theory and discussion.

Some potential examples

Amber. The case of the amber trade has already been mentioned, and has been sympathetically considered by Shennan (Beck & Shennan 1991) in a pioneering study which raised a number of the above points. It is a good example to quote here, because it reflects eloquently the question of changing values. And of course the point is well made that a particular object may take on a whole series of different values and symbolic significances as it proceeds through a number of exchange systems. It is implicit in the concept of 'the social life of things' (Appadurai 1986) that individual objects have 'life histories', and that knowledge of the history of a particular object may influence both its value and meaning. The financial effect of a 'good' provenance of any antiquity in a London sale room, and the political sensitivity of the Stone of Scone are evident modern examples.

Shennan's series of three maps for the archaeologi-

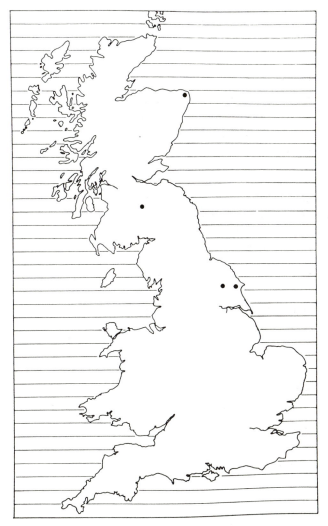

Figure 2.1. Neolithic amber finds in Britain (after Beck & Shennan 1991)

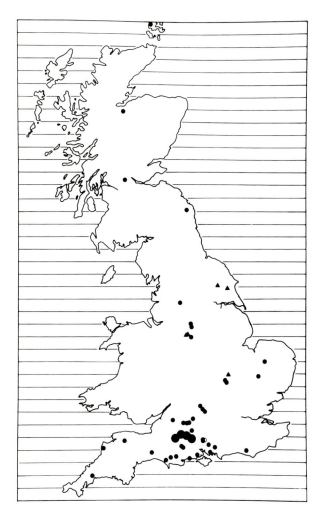

Figure 2.2. Early Bronze Age amber finds in Britain (after Beck & Shennan 1991)

Figure 2.3. Middle Bronze Age amber finds in Britain (after Beck & Shennan 1991)

cal finds of amber in Britain in the Neolithic, Early Bronze Age and Middle Bronze Age periods successively illustrates how much we have to learn (Figs 2.1–2.3). Amber must have been physically available in the Neolithic, but either it was not valued and used, or the objects which were used did not find their way into the archaeological record. The high prestige role of amber in the succeeding Wessex culture has long been known, and is well illustrated in the second map. The apparent decline in its importance is seen in the third map. This is all the more striking since it was at the time of the British Middle Bronze Age that the use of amber – a valued exotic import – seems to have reached its apogee in the Aegean. I suggest that if we avoid speaking of an amber 'trade' – with the implication that the supply of amber was the prime motivating force for the displacements involved, we shall be in a much better position to consider the evidence. As an adjunct to what categories of travel (in terms of the above) did the amber travel?

Henge monuments. My second example is the well-known case of the henge monuments and the grooved

ware of the British Isles. Convenient maps by Bradley and Chapman (1986, 128 & 133), prepared to illustrate their paper on peer-polity interaction, serve to emphasize the points made above (Figs 2.4 & 2.5). To explain the wide distribution of henge monuments in Britain during the later Neolithic, as well as that of grooved ware, it is necessary to consider what agencies of communication were operating here. The grooved ware may have been traded, or it may in most cases have been made locally. These are matters eminently suited to a systematic characterization study which has not yet been initiated on a sufficiently wide scale (although parts of the work have already been begun: see Williams 1979). What we urgently need now are specific models for the kinds of interactions which were involved. The concept of 'peer polity interaction' may be useful here in avoiding the too-ready assumption that a centre/periphery model must be applicable. But we need to think in terms more specific to individual societies, and to individual persons, whose travels, with a range of motivations, must have underlain the widespread symbolic unities involved at this time in Britain (and to some extent in Ireland) but not to any considerable

Figure 2.4. Late Neolithic core areas in Britain and Ireland, defined by henge monuments and related structures (solid lines) and major groups of passage graves (broken lines) (after Bradley & Chapman 1986)

Figure 2.5. Passage Grave art (crosses) and Grooved Ware (dots) in Britain and Ireland (after Bradley & Chapman 1986)

extent on the continent. There were of course comparable areas of symbolic unity there, but in this discussion the henges and grooved ware have been the focus of the example.

The role of the individual

The casual reader might at first suppose that the above discussion leads back to the sort of subjective consideration of the 'individual' advocated in some recent writings of the anti-processual school. It should at once be asserted that no philosophical or epistemological tendency can be allowed to claim exclusive rights to the human individual!

Within the processual tradition of archaeological reasoning (and this applies to the cognitive processual as much as to the earlier functional-processual emphasis), there is a continuing emphasis upon the need for generalization in explanation, and on the use of models. Explanation in archaeology is not seen as different in kind from explanation in the sciences, although a whole range of new concepts is needed when dealing with human societies. Some of these concepts refer to beliefs within the societies which cannot be directly observed today, but can only be considered through processes of inference. 'Value' is such a term, referring to a symbolic construct of the society in question. Like any 'meaning' in the past it is not fully knowable to us today, although the way it worked to shape behaviour in that society is indeed susceptible of study.

Models which seek to aid the investigation of past human behaviour often need to work at the individual level. This is not, in fact, any novelty to archaeology, since models of economic behaviour, at what is often termed the 'microeconomic level' have been a commonplace of processual archaeology (originally in what I have termed the functional-processual phase) for some considerable time (see Renfrew & Cooke 1979). Any consideration of decision-making is likely to consider the decision at the level of the individual, as well perhaps of the group (e.g. Keene 1979; Mithen 1990). It does not follow, however, that the decision is based upon maximizing or minimizing assumptions, where the only goals are the maximization of material gain and the minimization of risk. Other strategies may be in play. Game theory (von Neumann & Morgenstern 1947) often tends to assume entirely rational behaviour among the players, but there is no necessity for it to do so.

It is my belief that any approach to the cognitive aspects of society needs to give consideration to the cognitive processes of individuals and of ranges of individuals within society. That view was set out explicitly some years ago in what I termed the 'THINKS' model (Renfrew 1987; see Renfrew & Bahn 1991, 340). The approach has been identified by the philosopher James Bell as one of 'methodological individualism', and it is one which deliberately seeks to avoid the hermeneutic subjectivities advocated by some exponents of the anti-processual approach.

To set out to prepare models in terms of the individual in society does not, however, imply that we can hope very often to have a very clear vision of specific individuals. Yet even here the task is far from an impossible one (Hill & Gunn 1977).

The most obvious glimpse which the archaeologist sees of the past individual within his or her social context is offered to us by burial. It is of course increasingly realized that what we see in a burial assemblage is what the living put there, and it thus constitutes a rather special refraction of the material world of the deceased person. But in nearly every case that world is the starting point for the funerary deposition process. But there are other glimpses available, of which the most telling come from the category of sudden, involuntary, natural burial. Such burials are almost inevitably, from the standpoint of the individual, disasters, since in most cases they entail, virtually by definition, his or her sudden death. The most celebrated recent case is the Alpine Ice Man. But shipwrecks offer us a similar moment, frozen in time, of the individual or the group. Settlements destroyed rapidly by violent volcanic eruption offer comparable possibilities. These are rare cases, but they remind us that the individual is not always entirely beyond our archaeological grasp.

Back to the material

The above discussion has taken us some way from the finds of material goods which form the natural starting point for most studies of prehistoric trade and exchange. But it leads us to some conclusions necessary if we are to avoid the mistake of imagining that what we see in our distribution maps is in itself an adequate reconstruction of a system of exchange or interaction.

The first, perhaps obvious point is that the material remains recovered are the by-product, the drop-outs, from a composite series of systems of interaction. In those systems the material objects may have played a secondary or very minor role. The amber trade is surely a case in point. We do not need to posit early 'prospectors', for whom the motivation for travel would have been the establishment of exchange systems. There may have been such persons on occasion, but far more often the exchange system as we most immediately interpret it in terms of displaced goods is merely the material relic of patterns of interaction which had symbolic dimensions of a much wider kind. The material culture remains should thus often be seen merely as the by-product of the interaction and communication.

That being said, however, it is perhaps even more important to envisage a very different point, which might seem to contradict the first. In some cases the material objects actually *constitute* the communication. Exotic goods, their power deriving not only from the special and rare qualities of the material, but from the symbolic associations of the source (often with ritual overtones) and with their own specific life histories, can in themselves be objects of great power. They can carry with them messages which cannot be communicated effectively in any other way. In the British parliamentary system, for instance, the Mace is an object treated, almost unfailingly, with great veneration and respect. When it is brought into the House of Lords, in procession before the Lord Chancellor, it is customary for those present to bow the head as it passes. It is not however customary to do this to the Lord Chancellor himself. It would be easy to write at length about the Mace as a symbol of parliamentary government, but the point here is that there is no authoritative official written text to this effect. The Mace is a symbol, a signifier, whose significance is rarely made explicit, and one for which there is no single authoritative explanation. It has a function, and its 'meaning', not explicitly defined, is involved in the way it fulfils that function.

The central point of this paper, however, is not simply to point out that material goods often have a symbolic value which transcends any of the dimensions of their physical or material existence. It is to argue that we must seek to investigate more effectively the ascribed values and significances of such objects, and to do so in a more carefully structured way. Our models for human behaviour need to take account of individual valuations and aspirations, but they have then to relate back to the archaeological data in a coherent way. We need to develop analyses of travel and models for the displacement of goods which succeed in integrating the symbolic and the utilitarian aspects of transported goods, and which do so in relation to the specific exchange systems within which they are travelling. Characterization alone is not enough.

References

Appadurai, A., (ed.) 1986. *The Social Life of Things*. Cambridge: Cambridge University Press

Barbujani, G., & Sokal, R.R., 1990. Zones of sharp genetic change in Europe are also linguistic boundaries. *Proceedings of the National Academy of Sciences of the U.S.A.* 87, 1816–19

Beck, C., & Shennan, S., 1991. *Amber in Prehistoric Britain*. Oxbow Monograph 8. Oxford: Oxbow

Bradley, R., & Chapman, R., 1986. The nature and development of long-distance relations in Later Neolithic Britain and Ireland, in *Peer-Polity Interaction and Socio-political Change*, eds. C. Renfrew & J. Cherry. Cambridge: Cambridge University Press, 127–36

Bradley, R., & Edmonds, M., 1993. *Interpreting the Axe Trade*. Cambridge: Cambridge University Press

Cann, J.R., & Renfrew, C., 1964. The characterization of obsidian and its application to the Mediterranean region. *Proceedings of the Prehistoric Society* 30, 111–33

Childe, V.G., 1930. *The Bronze Age*. Cambridge: Cambridge University Press

Childe, V.G., 1936. *Man Makes Himself*. London: Watts

Childe, V.G., 1957. *The Dawn of European Civilization*. 6th ed. London: Routledge

Clark, J.G.D., 1952. *Prehistoric Europe: the Economic Basis*. London: Methuen

Clark, J.G.D., 1965. Traffic in stone axe and adze blades. *Economic History Review* 18, 1–28

Coles, J.M., & Harding, A.F., 1979. *The Bronze Age in Europe*. London: Methuen

Collis, J.R., 1971. A functional and theoretical interpretation of British coinage. *World Archaeology* 3, 71–84

Dalton, G., 1977, Aboriginal economies in stateless societies, in *Exchange Systems in Prehistory*, eds. T.K. Earle & J.E. Ericson. New York: Academic Press, 191–202

Ericson, J.E., 1982. Production for obsidian exchange in California, in *Contexts for Prehistoric Exchange*, eds J.E. Ericson & T.K. Earle. New York: Academic Press, 29–48

Flannery, K.V., 1968. The Olmec and the Valley of Oaxaca: a model for interregional interaction in Formative times, in *Dumbarton Oaks Conference on the Olmec*, ed. E. Benton. Washington D.C.: Dumbarton Oaks Library, 79–110

Frankenstein, S., & Rowlands, M.J., 1978. The Internal structure and regional context of Early Iron Age society in south-western Germany. *University of London Institute of Archaeology Bulletin* 15, 74–112

Haselgrove, C., 1979. The significance of coinage in pre-conquest Britain, in *Invasion and Response: the Case of Roman Britain*, eds B.C. Burnham & H. Johnston. Oxford: British Archaeological Reports, 197–209

Haselgrove, C., 1982. Wealth, prestige and power: the dynamics of Late Iron Age political centralisation in southeast England, in *Ranking, Resource and Exchange*, eds C. Renfrew & S. Shennan. Cambridge: Cambridge University Press, 79–91

Helms, M.W., 1988. *Ulysses' Sail. An Ethnographic Odyssey of Power, Knowledge, and Geographical Distance*. Princeton, N.J.: Princeton University Press

Hill, J.N., & Gunn, J., (eds) 1977. *The Individual in Prehistory*. New York: Academic Press

Hodder, I., 1982. *The Present Past*. London: Batsford

Hodder, I., & Orton, C., 1976. *Spatial analysis in archaeology*. Cambridge: Cambridge University Press

Junghans, S., Sangmeister, E., & Schröder, M., 1960. *Metallanalysen kupferzeitlicher und frühbronzezeitlicher Bodenfunde aus Europa*. Studien zu den Anfängen der Metallurgie 1. Berlin: Mann

Junghans, S., Sangmeister, E., & Schröder, M., 1968. *Kupfer und Bronze in der frühen Metallzeit Europas*. Studien zu den Anfängen der Metallurgie 2. Berlin: Mann

Keene, A.S., 1979. Economic opitimization models and the study of hunter-gatherer subsistence settlement systems, in *Transformations: Mathematical Approaches to Culture Change*, eds C. Renfrew & K.L. Cooke. New York: Academic Press, 369–404

Keiller, A., Piggott, S., & Wallis, F.S., 1941. First report of the sub-committee of the south-western group of museums and art galleries on the petrological examination of stone axes. *Proceedings of the Prehistoric Society* 7, 50–72

Kohl, P.L., 1987. The use and abuse of World Systems theory, in *Advances in Archaeological Method and Theory* 11, ed. M.B. Schiffer. New York: Academic Press, 1–36

McBryde, I., 1979. Petrology and prehistory: lithic evidence for exploitation of stone resources and exchange systems in Australia, in *Stone Axe Studies*, eds T.H.McK. Clough

& W.A. Cummins. London: Council for British Archaeology Research Report 23, 113–26

McBryde, I., 1984. Kulin greenstone quarries: the social contexts of production and distribution for the Mount Williams site. *World Archaeology* 16, 267–85

Malinowski, B., 1922. *Argonauts of the Western Pacific*. London: Routledge

Mauss, M., 1925. *The Gift*. London: Routledge

Mithen, S.J., 1990. *Thoughtful Foragers. A Study of Prehistoric Decision Making*. Cambridge: Cambridge University Press

Otto, H., & Witter, W., 1952. *Handbuch der ältesten vorgeschichtlichen Metallurgie in Mitteleuropa*. Leipzig

Pires Ferreira, J.W., 1976. Obsidian exchange in formative Mesoamerica, in *The Early Mesoamerican Village*, ed. K.V. Flannery. New York: Academic Press, 292–305

Pittioni, R., 1951. Prehistoric copper mining in Austria: problems and facts. *Annual Report of the Institute of Archaeology* 7, 16–43

Polyani, K., 1957. The economy as instituted process, *in Trade and Market in the Early Early Empires*, eds K. Polyani, C.M. Arensberg & H.W. Pearson. New York: Academic Press, 243–69

Rathje, W.L., 1973. Models for mobile Maya: a variety of constraints, in *The Explanation of Culture Change: Models in Prehistory*, ed. C. Renfrew. London: Duckworth, 731–60

Renfrew, C., 1972. *The Emergence of Civilization: the Cyclades and the Aegean in The Third Millennium B.C.* London: Methuen

Renfrew, C., 1974. Space, time and polity, in *The Evolution of Social Systems*, eds J. Friedman & M.J. Rowlands. London: Duckworth, 89–113

Renfrew, C., 1975. Trade as action at a distance, in *Ancient Civilization and Trade*, ed. C.C. Lamberg-Karlovsky. Albuquerque: University of New Mexico Press, 3–60

Renfrew, C., 1985. Epilogue, in *The Prehistory of Orkney*, ed. C. Renfrew. Edinburgh: Edinburgh University Press, 243–61

Renfrew, C., 1986. Varna and the emergence of wealth in prehistoric Europe, in *The Social Life of Things*, ed. A. Appadurai. Cambridge: Cambridge University Press, 141–8

Renfrew, C., 1987. Problems in the modelling of sociocultural systems. *European Journal of Operational Research* 30, 179–92

Renfrew, C., in press. Cognitive-processsual archaeology, in *The Ancient Mind*, eds C. Renfrew & E. Zubrow, Cambridge: Cambridge University Press

Renfrew, C., & Bahn, P., 1991. *Archaeology: Theories, Methods and Practice*. London: Thames & Hudson

Renfrew, C., & Cherry, J.F., (eds) 1986. *Peer-Polity Interaction and Socio-Political Change*, Cambridge: Cambridge University Press

Renfrew, C., & Cooke, K.L., (eds) 1979. *Transformations: Mathematical Approaches to Culture Change*. New York: Academic Press

Rowlands, M., Larsen, M., & Kristiansen, K., (eds) 1987. *Centre and Periphery in the Ancient World*. Cambridge: Cambridge University Press

Sahlins, M., 1972. *Stone Age Economics*. Chicago: Aldine

Service, E.R., 1962. *Primitive Social Organisation*. New York: Random House

Stone, J.F.S., & Thomas, L.C., 1956. The use and distribution of faience in the Ancient East and prehistoric Europe. *Proceedings of the Prehistoric Society* 23, 37–84

Stone, J.F.S., & Wallis, F.S., 1947. Second Report of the Sub-Committee of the South-western Group of Museums and Art Galleries on the petrological examination of stone axes. *Proceedings of the Prehistoric Society* 13, 47–55

Stukeley, W., 1740. *Stonehenge. A Temple Restored to the Druids*

Thomas, H.H., 1923. The source of the stones of Stonehenge. *Antiquaries Journal* 3, 239–60

Torrence, R., 1986. *Production and Exchange of Stone Tools: Prehistoric Obsidian in the Aegean*. Cambridge: Cambridge University Press

Veblen, T., 1925. *The Theory of the Leisure Class*. New York: Macmillan

von Neumann, J., & Morgenstern, O., 1947. *Theory of Games and Economic Behavior*. Princeton: Princeton University Press

Wallerstein, I., 1974 & 1980. *The Modern World System*. 2 vols. New York, Academic Press

Wells, P.S., 1980. *Culture Contact and Culture Change: Early Iron Age Central Europe and the Mediterranean World*. Cambridge: Cambridge University Press

Williams, D.F., 1979. Appendix D: Petrological Analysis of Pottery, in C. Renfrew *Investigations in Orkney*. Report of the Research Committee of the Society of Antiquaries of London 38. London: Thames & Hudson, 94–6

3

Trade and World Systems
in Early Bronze Age Western Asia

Christopher M. Edens & Philip L. Kohl

World systems analysis of the ancient world is increasingly popular, despite numerous reservations. One example of an ancient world system is western Asia during the Early Bronze Age. In this essay, the authors conceptualize ancient world systems by focusing on several basic factors that distinguish them from the modern world system. These factors include the organizational and ideological properties of political economies, the possibilities of dependency and the logistics of transportation, the technological differentation between centres and peripheries, violence as an alternative to trade, and the variability of economic and political conditions within and between regions. At the same time, ancient world systems present properties absent from other kinds of interregional relationships (e.g. Neolithic exchange networks, early state expansion) in ancient western Asia. Using the Iranian plateau and the Persian Gulf as example components, the essay defines the west Asian world system and examines its properties and historical dynamics.

L'analyse du monde antique dans la perspective des 'world systems' ('systèmes mondiaux') est aujourd'hui de plus en plus fréquente; bien qu'elle suscite encore de nombreuses réserves. A cet égard l'Asie occidentale du Bronze ancien constitue un bon exemple de ce système mondiale antique. Dans cet article, les auteurs formalisent les systèmes mondiaux de l'antiquité en mettant l'accent sur plusieurs caractéristiques essentielles qui les distinguent des systèmes mondiaux modernes. Celles-ci incluent les propriétés idéologiques et organisationnelles des économies politiques, les possibilités de dépendance et la logistique des communications, la différentiation technologique entre centres et périphéries, la violence en tant que substitut au commerce, et la variabilité des environnements politiques et économiques entre régions, ou à l'intérieur de l'une d'entre elles. D'autre part, les systèmes mondiaux antiques présentent des propriétés absentes des autres types d'échanges interrégionaux de l'Asie occidentale ancienne (comme par exemple les réseaux d'échanges néolithiques, ou les premiers expansions étatiques.) L'emprunt à des exemples du plateau iranien et du Golfe persique permet de définir le système mondial de l'Asie occidentale, d'examiner ses caractéristiques et sa dynamique historique.

Introduction

Despite the current popularity of the world-systems approach to interregional interaction in pre-capitalist settings, Wallerstein's analysis of the modern world system contains a number of basic features that seem inappropriate to the ancient world. This study addresses the interregional trade of Bronze Age western Asia as a suitable candidate for a world-systems analysis. In examining the west Asian case, the paper is concerned equally with conceptualizing pre-capitalist political economies, and with describing the historical properties of interregional interactions in western Asia itself. The paper also addresses a set of methodological issues concerning the nature and limitations of both archaeological and textual evidence for long-distance exchange, and the need for unified theoretical perspectives within which material and textual evidence may be combined in the analysis of archaic exchange systems.

Pre-capitalist 'world systems'

Wallerstein's work on the emerging modern world presents a fruitful model of centre-periphery relations. The Wallersteinian model coordinates aspects of geographical location and sociological contrast, implies transregional structures of economic, political and ideological inequality, and brings to the fore the location of economic forces with respect to institutional and ideo-logical patterns in the communities bound together by centre-periphery relations. Wallerstein's concept of world-economies has recently attracted attention in archaeological circles both in western Asia (Kohl 1978; 1987a; b; Algaze 1989) and elsewhere (e.g. Blanton & Feinman 1984; Whitecotton & Pailes 1986); some Assyriologists have also begun to view the ancient world in Wallersteinian terms (Larsen 1987). Even if, as argued here, qualitative differences distinguished ancient from modern world systems, the Wallersteinian terminology couches discussion in the more realistic framework of unequal relations between trading part-ners. The world-systems model contrasts with the often Pollyanna-ish (Polanyish) 'primitivist' and 'substantivist' literature, and with the uncritical archaeological mod-els of balanced reciprocity and redistribution that are unexploitative and essentially harmonious (e.g. Ren-frew & Bahn 1991, 334, 338); the latter usually employ functionalist and systems theoretical frameworks that misrepresent the contradictory and competing interests within and between human societies.

Leaving aside uneasy receptions in the historical and sociological literature of Wallerstein's account of the modern world system (e.g. Brenner 1977; Skocpol 1977; Chirot 1985; Giddens 1987), various critiques recognize that the model contains some fundamental incongruencies and conceptual lacunae when applied to pre-capitalist settings. Various assessments dispute Wallerstein's assertions of a single system-wide mode of production (e.g. Wolf 1982); the asymmetrical de-pendency of peripheries on centres (e.g. Mintz 1985) and the inability of peripheries to resist core attempts at domination; the irrelevance of trade in luxuries as a connective and generative force (e.g. Schneider 1977); and the marginality of culture and ethnicity to historical analysis (e.g. Ragin & Chirot 1984). Several basic features separate pre-capitalist from capitalist settings, including logistical restrictions on bulk transportation and transportation costs, technological similarities be-tween centres and peripheries, access by peripheries to multiple centres, and the instability of centres them-selves (Kohl 1987a; b). These factors limited the ability of centres to dominate peripheries, and nowhere in the ancient world may one properly speak of 'world' struc-tures of unequal exchange, of 'world' labour markets, or of economic dependence and underdevelopment in the same way that development theorists speak of them in the modern world. The ancient world was not articu-lated to the degree that justifies such language.

Another issue must also be raised. The Wallersteinian separation of 'economic' from 'political' forces does fundamental violence to the nature of complex socie-ties. Interregional trade occurred within a complex set of non-economic as well as economic relations which also channelled materials and labour between societies; the latter included warfare and tribute extraction, dip-lomatic gift exchange, elite marriage exchanges, and interregional ideological hegemony. Trade was often an aspect of diplomacy, was usually an alternative to force, and was in any case circumscribed by changing political relations. Moreover, local competition envel-oped trade as economic transaction, and the competi-tive activation of commodities effected the systemic political consequences of trade.

Appeals to Wallersteinian world systems in pre-capitalist settings fail precisely on this point: the in-separable combination of political and economic forces together determined the shape and consequences of interregional actions. Following Giddens' emphasis on sociopolitical over economic forces in class-divided societies, the political incentives to trade and the politi-cal benefits of wealth generated by trade often configured societies more deeply than the economic generation and use of that wealth. This language, of course, sets up a false opposition between 'sociopolitical' and 'economic' actions: aspects of each are always present, though in differing measures in different systems. Giddens (1987) forcefully makes this point with respect to the emer-gence of the modern world system itself, which was shaped jointly by political (the formation and actions of nation-states) and economic (interregional division of labour and capitalist markets) forces rather than by the latter alone. This argument is even stronger for antiq-uity.

One analytic implication of these revisions of Wallersteinian world systems is the conceptualization of trade. Exchange cannot be examined as an analytically isolated phenomenon (a 'subsystem'), but rather must be situated within the broader political economy. Following Marx, production, exchange and consumption form an indissoluble analytic unity. Analysis cannot limit itself to the unity's economic aspects in any reductionist fashion, but must also centrally address social institutions and cultural attitudes as basic to political economies. Thus production involves mobilization of labour, knowledge and skill, and materials within institutions, ascriptive groups, and other collectivities. These settings not only coordinate basic economic forces but also locate those forces in social relations, politics, and ideology. Simi-larly, consumption of goods reproduces the demands for which the commodities were produced. But consumption is equally a socially and politically conditioned act, enmeshed in cultural patterns of status display, authority and legitimation, and of mass acceptance of, or submis-sion to, hegemonic ideology. Consumption, in turn, provides the symbolic conditions for the reproduction of the relations of production. The consumption of luxu-ries, already mentioned as a basic component of pre-capitalist 'world systems', thus provides the rhetorical markers (Appadurai 1988) for the ideological structur-ing of political economies.

When analysis ignores the production and consump-tion aspects of a trading system, or separates them from exchange as 'subsystems', basic questions are left un-approachable: the terms of trade, the costs and benefits for each trading partner, the relative values of the materials exchanged, and the degree to which trade was balanced or unequal. The nature of the archaeological record usually obstructs a satisfactory exploration of these basic economic aspects of exchange networks. And the value-laden (ideological) character of consumption further complicates most archaeological reconstructions. Despite these real difficulties, comprehension of prehistoric trading systems will not advance by restricting analysis to the archaeologically more accessible spatial distribution of materials.

Methodological issues

The conceptual points at the end of the previous section may be made more concretely with a specific and appropriate example of Bronze Age trade: the flow of marine shell from the Indian Ocean to Mesopotamia as part of the Bronze Age maritime trade through the Arabian Gulf. This example serves to illustrate the fundamental inseparability of local consumption patterns from transregional exchange systems, and points out some important methodological implications and problems that arise from changing consumption patterns. The example also makes explicit the nature of the archaeological and textual evidence for the Bronze Age trade. This evidence is sparse, episodic and ambiguous, and is best suited to delimiting the spatial extent of exchange relations, but less directly informative of the scale, regularity, organization, and wider social mechanisms of exchange. Moreover, the two categories of evidence, textual and material, often lie in uneasy juxtaposition, sometimes complementary, at other times contradictory, and all too often silent on the same issue.

SHELL GAME: MESOPOTAMIA AND THE INDIAN OCEAN

Gastropod columellae (the central column to which the outer shell body whorls are attached) provided a common material for cylinder seals and for beads in late fourth and third millennium Mesopotamia. The size of these columellar segments implies use of the larger species found beyond the straits of Hormuz. These same species were also cut into shell lamps or cups, which had a comparable chronological duration in Mesopotamia (Aynard 1966; Genscheimer 1984; Kenoyer 1984). The popularity of these objects experienced significant changes throughout the third millennium. Examples of the shell lamps/cups come from well dated contexts as early as the Jemdet Nasr period (Delougaz *et al.* 1967) and as late as the Old Babylonian period (Woolley & Mallowan 1976, 198; Strommenger 1964, 37) (Table 3.1). The great majority of these objects, however, belong to Early Dynastic and Akkadian times (cf. Aynard 1966). Indeed, analysis of their presence in the more systematically controlled context of grave lots at Ur and Kish indicates a peak popularity during Early Dynastic (ED) II-III times (Edens 1992).

Table 3.1. The south Mesopotamian sequence is the most frequently cited in this paper; the following table provides the conventional dates (rounded off to the nearest half century) for its various periods.

'Ubaid	5500–3800 BC
Uruk	3800–3100 BC
Jemdet Nasr	3100–2900 BC
Early Dynastic I-II	2900–2600 BC
Early Dynastic III	2600–2350 BC
Akkadian	2350–2100 BC
Ur III	2100–2000 BC
Isin-Larsa	2000–1800 BC
Old Babylonian	1800–1600 BC

While other local sequences are mentioned, lack of space prohibits a detailed presentation, and the Mesopotamian chronology serves as the temporal baseline of this study.

The only published textual allusion to these objects (bur-pes-SAL.ANSE, 'bowl of "donkey mare's vulva" shell': Biggs 1974, 81) also belongs to this time. Shell cylinder seals express a similar history of popularity, with their peak popularity during ED III and Akkadian times and a sharp decline thereafter (cf. Edens 1992).

This shifting popularity occurred within the general trend of reduced use of shell products in southern Mesopotamia late in the third millennium BC and after. In the case of cylinder seals, the sharp reduction of shell coincided with a more general shift from softer to harder materials in Mesopotamian seal production; Gorelick and Gwinnet (1990), who trace this general trend through 5000 years of Mesopotamian history, see in it a reflection of changing systems of status display and of mobilization of skilled labour. A similar theory for the disappearance of shell lamps/cups might also be entertained. The two kinds of objects are produced from the same set of species, and the post-Akkadian decline in their popularity is linked in terms of their production (H. Wright, pers comm. 1991).

Contradictory evidence for exchange relations

The shell evidence indicates Mesopotamian relations with communities in the Gulf of Oman and the Indian Ocean from Jemdet Nasr to Akkadian times, but also indicates a decline in these relations during the Akkadian period, accelerating thereafter. The archaeological record of the Gulf itself reproduces this picture of Mesopotamian-Gulf relations: Mesopotamian pottery and other materials are relatively common throughout Early Dynastic times but become rare later in the third millennium (see Cleuziou & Tosi 1989; Potts 1990; Zarins 1989b for reviews of the archaeological evidence). In contrast to the archaeological evidence, the cuneiform textual evidence for the Gulf trade suggests a sharp intensification of relations only beginning in Akkadian times and developing during later centuries.

In the Bronze Age texts, the three principal partners in the Gulf trade were Dilmun, Magan and Meluhha. Dilmun is the area of Bahrain and the adjacent mainland, Magan most plausibly is southeast Arabia (the Oman peninsula) and perhaps also portions of Iran on the opposite shore of the Gulf, and Meluhha is probably the Indus region. The earliest written evidence contains only a few allusions to copper from Magan in Jemdet Nasr period texts (Englund 1983). The late ED III Lagash texts (Lambert 1953) list the transshipment of copper, presumably from Magan, through Dilmun. A Fara lexical text (Pettinato 1972, 91) may contain an oblique reference to Meluhha. The first direct allusion to Magan and to Meluhha appears with Sargon, and the most intensive direct connection with Magan belongs to the Ur III period; the most substantial traffic in copper and other goods occurred during Isin-Larsa times (Leemans 1960). The textual evidence thus suggests patterns of expanding scale and integration of trade through the Gulf during the third millennium, peaking during the Ur III and Isin-Larsa periods. In other words, the archaeological and textual evidence describe contradictory chronological patterns. Such contradictions could, of course, be resolved by facile proposals to combine evidence. The issues involved are, however, far more complicated and fundamental.

CONCEPTUALIZING POLITICAL ECONOMIES

The contradiction underscores the need to consider production, exchange and consumption as components of political economies. The changing volumes of imported shell and their changing variety of uses responded to a culturally contingent hierarchy of status markers. The systems of status markers reacted to the economic supply of appropriate imported materials, which established basic parameters of 'price formation' and valuation: scarce or controlled supplies made suitable a given exotic material as a status marker. These systems also responded to the changing conditions of internally generated 'demand formation'. Several basic forces combined to redefine status markers – the changing forms of social and political competition, the changing institutional control of labour and materials, and altered cultural practices that assigned objects a symbolic value with reference to a wider ideological field of meaning. In some respects, these forces were very closely tied to the economic aspects of supply and 'price formation'. Even so, the cultural investment in objects of symbolic value and specific meaning must be understood as largely arbitrary with respect to the economic conditions of social life, precisely because the specific meaning made reference to the wider ideological field. The economic/institutional and cultural contexts for the consumption of exotic goods thus formed semi-autonomous realms of social life, each of which provided sources of change in inter-regional relations.

NEGATIVE EVIDENCE: ARCHAEOLOGY

In considering patterns of consumption to be arbitrary responses, at least in part, to the availability of foreign commodities, the issue of negative evidence becomes critical. Negative evidence in fact has two potential but incompatible implications. The first of these is information about spatial and/or temporal breaks in interregional connections, thereby providing a basis for a history of exchange relations. The second is information about the changing contents of a trading system, where the appearance/disappearance of a good reflects shifts of value formation that are internal to a given political economy. A choice between these options can be achieved, if at all, only by attending to the broader contexts of the political economies within which economic exchanges existed.

The archaeological evidence for interregional trade is often very slender and usually ambiguous. The case of southeast Arabia provides an example: the number of reported Mesopotamian or Mesopotamian-derived objects from the third millennium is no more than several hundred, including pottery (Potts 1990). This evidence could again be taken literally to imply only very tenuous relations between opposite ends of the Persian Gulf, or interpreted more liberally as supplying a non-quantifiable and partial framework for considering these relations. Here, the more pervasive problem of 'invisible exports' presents a fundamental difficulty – the cereals, textiles, wool, unguents, oils, woods, dried fish, intoxicating beverages, slaves and other organic commodities so important to regional and interregional exchange systems of western Asia (Crawford 1973) are largely absent from the archaeological record. And even some durable commodities such as metals may be systematically underrepresented due to recycling: the Mesopotamian archaeological record contains far fewer metal objects than is implied in the cuneiform sources, and fewer objects compared to many peripheries where such wealth was regularly immobilized in tombs, votive deposits, and hoards.

Archaeological studies of trade are faced with a choice: to emphasize, in the traditional manner, the small list of goods thought to have been traded and present them as the proverbial tip of a much larger iceberg (e.g. Adams 1974, 247; Kohl 1978, 465); or to emphasize the smallness of that list as indicative of the fundamental marginality of trade, as is being increasingly done in some circles (e.g. Shaffer 1982). The first choice involves an extrapolation from a narrow known to a much wider unknown, and therefore is to an unassessed (and potentially unassessable) degree speculative; the second constitutes a strongly empiricist reading of the evidence which by its very refusal to extrapolate is equally speculative. The occasional spectacular discovery strongly argues for the first choice, an example being the cargo of the Kas shipwreck – copper and tin ingots; finished metal weapons, tools, jewelry, and other objects; elephant and hippopotamus tusks; wood, resins, and other perishables, etc. – the diversity of which suggests a coast-wise peddling trade as well as long-distance haulage (Bass 1986; Bass *et al.* 1989). The choice of interpretative strategy usually, however, comes down to personal predilection and intellectual tradition. That a choice must be made, even when only implicitly, reveals the uncertain status of many archaeological studies of trade in western Asia.

NEGATIVE EVIDENCE: TEXTS

Negative evidence is also an issue to textually-based approaches to ancient trade in western Asia. The Gulf trade again provides a useful illustration. The textual evidence for this trade comes from heterogeneous social contexts: religious texts, royal inscriptions, temple archives, state administrative accounts, and private correspondence of joint investment corporations. The cuneiform evidence for trade can properly be undertood only within these individual contexts, leaving unspecified gaps of articulation between contexts. Evidence with restricted and incompatible contextual ranges dominates discussions of individual periods – the Lagash palace texts for ED III; royal inscriptions for the Akkadian period; state bureaucratic operations for the Ur III period; temple tithe records for the earlier Isin-Larsa period; private correspondence for the later Isin-Larsa period – and a textually based account of the Gulf trade must also confront the issue of negative evidence.

Furthermore, since many of these sources are embedded in such specific circumstances, they generally refer to Mesopotamian ventures into the Gulf but not to foreign cargoes unloaded in Mesopotamian ports. The textual sources thus are fundamentally incomplete in scope, since they seriously underreport the regularity, scope and scale of the trade, and describe only selectively the mechanisms by which merchandise reached Mesopotamia. The situation of partial evidence casts into serious doubt Oppenheim's generally accepted picture of the Gulf trade as 'a process of gradual and slow restriction of the geographical horizon' of the trade, where first Meluhha and then Magan disappeared from the economic texts after the Akkadian period (Oppenheim 1954, 14). Interpretation of the cuneiform sources thus faces the same analytic dilemma as that presented by the archaeological sources, namely the choice between excessively empiricist and largely unconfirmable speculative accounts of the trade.

CONCLUSIONS

These problems introduce considerable uncertainty into any analysis of the Bronze Age trade of western Asia, including the present one; for the moment, no blanket solution is possible. At the same time, this irreducible uncertainty should not discourage analysis, for such pessimism would preclude virtually all reconstructions

of human history. The point is to reconceptualize basic procedure. Cuneiform texts and archaeological materials count as evidence and take meaning only within the framework of an interpretative model. Thus, as Finley (1986) reminded his classicist colleagues, the epistemological status of an archive is no different from that of the mute archaeological record; and conversely, the latter is no more privileged than the former, despite some claims to the contrary (e.g. Deagan 1982, 171). The issue, then, is the construction and defence of interpretative models. The modified world-systems model presented here makes explicit the conditions and implications of analysis, and more openly encourages discussion about the connections between ancient political economies, social change, and interregional relations.

Pre-Bronze Age 'trade' in western Asia

Interregional exchange networks have been a prominent feature of western Asia since the establishment of permanent farming communities some ten thousand years ago. These early exchange links encompassed obsidian, semi-precious stones, copper and other metals, marine shell, pottery and other goods. Some of these materials figured centrally in economic production, others were always luxuries, while still others initially were luxuries and later became means of production (e.g. copper). These exchange relations prefigured interregional circulation during the Bronze Age; examples of this continuity pertinent to this paper include movements of turquoise, lapis lazuli, copper, and Indian Ocean shells. Such continuities cannot disguise the basic differences between the early exchange networks and those of the Bronze Age. Having to do with organization and scale, the exchange differences reflect fundamental evolutionary trends, and the emergence of state level societies. Thus, one popular evolutionary perspective postulates that as social units expanded from largely autarkic and self-sufficient villages to state societies, interregional exchange transformed from 'down-the-line' linkages between adjacent communities into more centralized, specialized and heterogeneous systems involving direct contact among geographically (and socially) disparate societies (e.g. Beale 1973; Renfrew 1975).

Obsidian provides the best documented example of an early exchange system in western Asia. Beginning around 8000 BC and continuing throughout prehistoric times, obsidian from central and eastern Anatolia and from Transcaucasia appears in numerous archaeological sites of southern Anatolia, Syro-Palestine, Mesopotamia and the Persian Gulf (Renfrew & Dixon 1976). Movements of obsidian also formed more regionalized systems in Transcaucasia (Badaljan *et al.* n.d.) and around the southern Red Sea (Zarins 1989a). Some commentators ascribe the precocious 'urbanism' at Çatal Hüyük in central Anatolia to its control of an important obsidian source, which led in turn to a population agglomeration, regional specialization of activities, and wealth accumulation (e.g. Jacobs 1969; Kohl & Wright 1977). The most popular interpretation, however, has been that of Renfrew and his colleagues (Renfrew & Dixon 1976), who see an initial down-the-line indirect movement of materials evolving into regional networks of 'obsidian interaction zones', characterized by greater directionality, during Late Neolithic/Chalcolithic times, and the emergence of specialized centres with preferential access to obsidian sources.

Current research shows how incompletely we understand the exchange of this utilitarian material, and reveals its complicated history of circulation in western Asia. Recent analysis of eastern Anatolian and Transcaucasian obsidian reveals complex systems of exchange that responded not only to geographical distance but also to cultural/historical factors (see Badaljan *et al.* n.d). For example, Transcaucasian obsidian from a source in southeastern Armenia occurs on sites in southern Azerbaijan and northwestern Iran that also contain distinctive painted Chalcolithic pottery (Pisdeli ware). Other sites in adjacent regions of northeastern Iraq and western Iran, lacking this ceramic connection, obtained their obsidian elsewhere. Distributional evidence shows that the exchange of obsidian waxed and waned in a manner that defies simplistic evolutionary modelling. These fluctuations were probably associated with dimly perceived historical events, possibly involving the actual movements of peoples.

The work of the Soviet archaeological expedition to northern Iraq, for example, has revealed a fascinating pattern of obsidian utilization from Early Neolithic down to 'Ubaid times in a region 400 km from the closest obsidian sources (all figures cited here taken from Yoffee, forthcoming). Obsidian forms roughly three quarters of the chipped stone in the earliest aceramic levels of Tell Maghzaliyah. The material declines to less than half the chipped stone in later aceramic levels at the same site. Obsidian is practically non-existent in the subsequent pre-Hassuna levels at Tell Sotto, and contributes less than a quarter of the chipped stone at Yarim Tepe I during the Hassuna period. During Halaf times at Yarim Tepe II, the trend reversed and obsidian again provided three-quarters of the knapped stone.

The latter change suggests the extension and transformation of an exchange network. Many commentators view both the Halaf and the 'Ubaid phenomenon in terms of 'chiefdoms' and 'interaction spheres', with materials circulating across wide regions in response to shared ideologies of elite symbolic display. Halaf painted pottery, the obvious index of the interaction sphere, achieved an immense distribution across northern Mesopotamia, Syria, eastern Anatolia and into Transcaucasia. 'Ubaid pottery enjoyed an equally wide circulation, appearing as far north as Transcaucasia (Narimanov 1986). Chemical characterization studies of Halaf pottery suggest a very complex set of interactions that involved potteries whose products circulated over very long distances, and also supplied local communities subordinate to centres (Davidson & McKerrell 1976; 1980). Interaction spheres also involved control of obsidian exchange; here the location of Tilki tepe adjacent to the Vannic sources is often cited (Korfman 1982).

With Mesopotamian state formation, long-distance exchange assumed a different form, manifested in the 'Uruk expansion' of the mid-fourth millennium BC (Algaze 1989). The Uruk enclaves and trading posts to the north, the intensive interaction with more distant settlements, and the cultural (political?) absorption of Susiana, all mark an interregional interaction that differed qualitatively from the earlier pre-state exchange systems. A common interpretation finds in the Uruk expansion an attempt to control nodal trade routes, and to intensify or even direct production for exchange, largely though perhaps not exclusively as a state-administered enterprise (e.g. Algaze 1989; Lamberg-Karlovsky 1985; Sürenhagen 1986). The exotic wealth of Uruk cities reflects the success of these exchange relations, the range of which was enormous. The Uruk system was not unique among the early states of western Asia: Susa, the Indus and Egypt all established enclaves at their peripheries.

The Uruk expansion differed in basic ways from pre-state exchange networks. Exchange now occurred between societies at very different levels of complexity, between the Uruk state(s) on the one hand and surrounding communities on the other. Significantly different social complexity presents differences in the scale and organization of production, the size of labour pools also available for military application, the institutional organizations of economic and political affairs, and ideological constructions of consumption. Moreover, the Uruk state(s) could act as the pivotal node of interregional exchanges: by controlling transportation routes, the Uruk(s) state not only ensured reliable access to commodities for metropolitan consumption, but could also regulate exchanges between societies within the adjacent regions, and act as intermediary in exchanges between societies not otherwise connected (see Algaze 1993). The Uruk state(s) interjected an institutional political apparatus into the ordering of trade relations. Exemplified by written records and seals, these institutional contexts helped to 'rationalize' and encapsulate increasingly complicated economic activities. The Uruk expansion was a consciously directed process, involving tens of thousands of people in planned settlements along the Upper Euphrates. The very scale of this phenomenon distinguishes it qualitatively from earlier exchange patterns and probable movements of peoples. Moreover, the apparent political framework of the Uruk expansion invites inclusion of non-commercial modes of exchange: military operations and diplomatic prestation are means of acquiring wealth, and also help to secure advantageous terms of trade.

The 'World System' of third millennium western Asia

Numerous commentators have observed two synchronisms across much of western Asia (Dales 1977; Lamberg-Karlovsky 1985; Lamberg-Karlovsky & Tosi 1973; Weiss 1983; 1986). The first synchronism falls in the mid third millennium BC, when 'proto-urban' and urban developments marked a dramatic increase in regional social complexity. The second synchronism, at the end of the third and beginning of the second millennium BC, collates the collapse of these expressions of urban complex society. The urbanization-deurbanization cycles of regional cultural traditions are not precisely synchronous, however, and several different chronological patterns may be distinguished.

The Mesopotamian urban cycle began in the later fourth millennium, culminating in the hyperurban patterns of the Early Dynastic that Adams has so clearly presented (Adams 1981). Although the urban emphasis in Mesopotamia declined somewhat during the second half of the third millennium, major disruptions did not occur until the second quarter of the second millennium, especially in the south of Babylonia as the centre of political power permanently shifted to the area of Babylon.

A second chronological pattern appears outside the Mesopotamian core. In the Indus area, massive urban growth occurred around 2600/2500 BC, and a shift back to small towns and villages around 2000 BC or shortly thereafter (Possehl 1990). In Turkmenistan, urban settlement (e.g. Altyn Depe, Namazga Depe) developed during the Namazga V period, roughly c. 2600–2200 BC; subsequently, populations shifted and dispersed eastwards, establishing towns and villages on the lower Murghab river (ancient Margiana) and in southern Uzbekistan and central Afghanistan (ancient Bactria) (Biscione 1977). The Helmand-Seistan region of western Afghanistan and eastern Iran experienced a progressive urbanization that culminated in the second half of the third millennium BC, notably at Shahr-i Sokhta; this urban expression abruptly disappeared around 2000 BC. On the south Iranian plateau the settlement at Shahdad achieved a considerable size during the second half of the third millennium BC (Salvatore & Vidale 1982). To the north and west of Babylonia, urbanization of the social landscape began abruptly around 2600/2500 BC. The Khabur triangle held a number of massive sites by 2500 BC, the rapid growth of which is best understood at Tell Leilan (Weiss 1983; 1990). Elsewhere in the Jazirah and inland northern Syria, cities grew soon afterwards at places such as Tell Taya and Ebla/Tell Mardikh.

The third chronological pattern, evident in fewer places around Mesopotamia, marks a slightly later development, beginning in about 2200 BC. In the Fars area of southwestern Iran, following a sharp mid-third millennium depopulation, Tal-i Malyan (ancient Anshan) grew to cover over 100 ha during the Kaftari phase (2200–1600 BC), before once again declining in size, though not as dramatically as the other cases just considered (Sumner 1988). In the Persian Gulf, the urban expression of the Barbar culture (Dilmun) may be placed roughly between 2200 and 1700 BC (Potts 1990). In southeastern Arabia, sites of the Umm an-Nar period, together with evidence for copper production, became more frequent around 2200 BC, but never developed urban forms. The major expansion and subsequent contraction of settlement size in central Anatolia (e.g. the lower cities at Kultepe, Hattusha) falls in this same chronological pattern.

Discussions of the latter two patterns have focused on several kinds of factors and consequences. Urbanization is often seen as part of secondary state formation in regions connected by trade and other forces to Mesopotamia; recent arguments along these lines pertain to the Mature Harappan (Possehl 1986; 1990), and to the Khabur triangle (Weiss 1990). Similar accounts for Central Asia with respect to the Indus and Mesopotamia have also been proposed. Other factors may also be considered. Many commentators see Mesopotamian-Elamite political relations as providing a basic element in the changes on the Iranian plateau and in the development of the Gulf trade (e.g. Alden 1982). Another basic political force was Mesopotamian eastward imperialism during the final third of the third millennium, the consequences of which can be traced as far east as the Indo-Iranian borderlands (e.g. Cleuziou & Tosi 1989). Deurbanization is often considered with reference to the ecological degradation that is the frequent consequence of intensified production (e.g. Biscione 1977; Adams 1981; Nissen 1988). Flexible social strategies are also commonly invoked, especially the village and pastoralist alternatives to the demands of the centralized state (e.g. Marfoe 1979; Adams 1974). And disruptive population movements may also partly be held to account, whether in the west (e.g. the Amorites) or the east (e.g. Central Asians in southern Iran and Baluchistan: Lamberg-Karlovsky & Hiebert 1992).

The centre-periphery perspective allows integration of these observations and proposed causative factors within a single model of interregional political economic structure. The synchronisms of local developmental cycles reveal an emergent world system that took form around 2600 BC and endured into the second millennium BC. The local developmental cycles were connected to each other through transregional economic, political, and ideological forces that produced increasingly complex social formations. These forces are best imagined as intersecting regional networks characterized by spatially uneven concentrations of connections within and between networks. Individual societies were differentially caught up in the play of transregional forces according to their location in the uneven connective networks. The play of forces could be direct or mediated, could involve different mixes of political, military, economic and ideological actions, and promote different local responses. The archaeological evidence that defines the system as a loosely coherent whole is the wide distribution of materials, iconography, styles, and technologies, all within the context of broadly isomorphic and roughly synchronous social movements of increasing and decreasing complexity.

Although social complexity and the state appeared first in southern Mesopotamia, and although Mesopotamia concentrated the means both of production and of destruction on a scale perhaps not matched elsewhere, Mesopotamian history did not determine other regional histories. Southern Mesopotamia was not the only centre orchestrating developments throughout this vast interconnected area. Other centres, particularly those that could support dense populations, also became cores to neighbouring hinterlands in their own right; the Indus, Turkmenistan, southwestern Iran, and northern Syria provide cases in point.

Moreover, social forces did not act in the same mixes and with the same consequences throughout this vast region. Despite formal (evolutionary) similarity, the responses of societies in the Khabur plain and the Indus built on different existing sociocultural patterns, contrastive environmental potentials, and distinctive geographical location within the emerging world system. In addition, the urban-centred secondary states of the mid-third millennium responded to a very different set of forces than did later episodes of urbanization, at a time when the world system was already established, and new forces were at play. Thus urbanization at Kaftari phase Malyan (Sumner 1988) or Shimashki state formation were probable consequences of resistance to late third millennium Mesopotamian imperialism, while late third millennium urban developments in central Anatolia (e.g. at Kanesh) responded to intensified commercial exchange (with northern Syria, then Ashur). World-systems do not form and act as units of social evolution in any mechanical way; rather, they frame local and regional histories.

World-systems language implies the existence of both internal boundaries separating centres and peripheries, and external boundaries separating the system from the world outside. Neither kind of boundary was static or impermeable. The dynamic relationship between centres and peripheries fuels the histories of world systems, as peripheries change under the impact of centres and eventually redefine the conditions of interaction or even supplant the centres. Similarly, peripheries may drop out of the system or join it, according to changing historical circumstances. The external boundaries are even more difficult to establish, and formed along both social and geographical limits. The EBA II-III urban cycle in the southern Levant expresses a process of secondary state formation, this time connected to the Egyptian world and beginning slightly earlier than the cases mentioned above (Esse 1989). Some interaction between Palestine and regions to the north and east did occur, but the area

still remained subject to a different set of forces, belonging to a different 'world'. That there was contact in other directions also existed is evidenced by the occasional find of silk in Central Asian sites (e.g. at Sapalli-Tepe) or southeast Asian items in Syro-Mesopotamia (e.g. cloves at Terqa). Such discoveries demonstrate connections with regions far to the east, but they hardly warrant the inclusion of the latter regions in the west Asian 'world system'. The comparative social context is decisive: pronounced social complexity and the state were just appearing in north China at the end of the third millennium BC, and developed even later in southeast Asia. In Sherratt's useful phrase, these regions among others form the margins of the west Asian world system, perhaps in frequent interaction but not embedded in the structural whole.

This model of a west Asian Bronze Age 'world system' hinges on the several fundamental modifications of Wallerstein's conceptualization mentioned in the opening section of this paper. In particular, the present model grants politics a central role in the formation of interregional structures. Politics established a basic modality of interregional exchange and of accumulation, by state-sponsored trade, military violence, forcible and voluntary movements of people, tribute extraction, and more pacific diplomatic means. Politics also expressed the local consequences of interaction by providing the authoritative channels of political economies, the ideological construction of elite consumption, the location of the transformative effects of exchange, and organized resistance to external violence. The modified model also insists on the logistical limitations, basic technological uniformity, structural instability, and multiplicity of archaic world systems. These characteristics imply that peripheral dependency was weakly present at best, and 'the development of underdevelopment' in the modern sense only rarely, if ever, occurred.

Two relatively well known components of Mesopotamia's position in the west Asian 'world system' involve overland trade across the south Iranian plateau and maritime traffic through the Persian Gulf. These components provided alternative access to similar kinds of goods from similar sources, but they differed in relative transportation costs, probable scale and regularity of exchange, and application of military pressure. Despite their differences, the overland and maritime systems were similar in their organization and contexts of production, and in the consequences of exchange to political economies. The remainder of this study addresses these contrasts and similarities in the framework of the west Asian 'world system' during the later third and early second millennium BC.

Political economies
and commodity production

The first set of contrasts and similarities involves the organization, technology and scale of production for exchange. The following discussion considers carved chlorite vessels at Tepe Yahya (Iran), copper smelting at Maysar (Oman), and textiles in Mesopotamia. These examples differ in several basic ways: the relative complexity of the societies in which production occurred; the kinds of commodities being produced; and the nature of the evidence for production. They thus serve both to illustrate the contrasts between societies involved in the west Asian world system, and to work through some of the methodological problems reviewed above.

CHLORITES IN IRAN

Steatite, chlorite and other soft stone compounds provided a common material for production of various decorated vessels in Bronze Age west and central Asia. The 'intercultural style' vessels find a wide distribution, from Syria to Central Asia and the Indus. The focus of this distribution encompasses southern Mesopotamia, the western Persian Gulf, southwestern Iran, and southern Iran (Miroschedji 1973; Kohl 1978). Archaeological evidence for the production of these vessels is far more restricted, and is best available at Tepe Yahya.

The Tepe Yahya production belongs to Period IVB of that site. Here, waste by-products, roughly shaped vessels, finished vessels, and tools occur in three separate non-residential zones of the site. Furthermore, chlorite outcrops in the mountains near the site exhibit traces of working (Kohl 1978). The sum of this evidence permits a reasonable reconstruction of production techniques. After extraction, the raw material was transported to workshops at Tepe Yahya, where the blocks were flaked to create vessel rough-outs, which were then hand-scraped to final form. After smoothing, many vessels were decorated by the carving or cutting of elaborate designs, often in low relief.

The social context of production is more difficult to ascertain. Tepe Yahya is a very small site (about 4 ha), and during Period IVB is one of only a few sites in the Soghun Valley. Furthermore, the recovered Period IVB architecture is unimpressive, consisting of insubstantial walls and rooms. Despite the specialized craft production evident in the chlorite vessels themselves, this production may not have been a full-time pursuit, nor were these craft specialists necessarily permanent members of the community. While no accompanying cemetery has been discovered, the relevant levels of the site itself contained relatively few luxury objects or exotic materials such as turquoise, carnelian, or lapis, implying a comparatively low degree of wealth accumulation and, probably, of social differentiation. The available evidence thus indicates a small community characterized by a fairly low degree of social differentiation and organizational complexity.

This local setting of production contrasts with the implications of the Shahdad evidence, some 250 km to the northeast. Shahdad is much larger (50–80 ha), and

seems to have been spatially segregated into fairly discrete production zones, including one associated with metallurgy (Salvatore & Vidale 1982; Amiet 1986). The site includes very wealthy cemeteries that exhibit a considerable differentiation in grave goods and burial form, and reveal strong material connections both with Tepe Yahya and with Central Asia (Lamberg-Karlovsky & Hiebert 1992). Despite the distance between the two sites, the chlorite production at Yahya should be considered within this larger regional framework – direction of the chlorite production may have emanated from the regional centre rather than being locally based. Even so, the Yahya chlorite production must be assessed as relatively small in scale and simple in organization.

COPPER IN OMAN

Field research in recent years has greatly elucidated Bronze Age copper production in southeastern Arabia. Bronze Age smelting sites are now documented in at least half a dozen localities (Hauptmann 1985; Hauptmann *et al.* 1988). These sites contain up to 4000 tons of slag, and collectively represent two to four thousand tons of copper. The peak period of this production falls in the late third millennium BC (the late Umm an-Nar period), and is best documented at Maysar 1. This small settlement covers about one hectare on a wadi bank, and contains a small number of residential structures. Evidence for smelting comes from a limited area of the settlement (Weisgerber 1980; 1981), and includes ores, slags, pieces of matte, furnace fragments, crucibles and a hoard of ingots. Archaeometallurgical analysis reveals a fairly simple production process. Oxide and sulphidic ores from neighbouring sources were smelted (apparently without preliminary roasting) with iron oxide fluxes in furnaces that reached 1200°C for a limited time. The furnace fragments indicate small reaction vessels less than half a metre in diameter. The resulting metallic copper seems not to have been refined after the smelt, but was poured directly into small concave open moulds to form bun-shaped ingots.

The Bronze Age settlements of southeastern Arabia, particularly those of the interior, form small residential enclaves interspersed with circular towers and groups of repeatedly used tombs, all set on agricultural land with accessible water (wadi terraces and beds, piedmont outwash formations). This settlement form and distribution argues that agriculture rather than industrial production was the primary settlement determinant for the region. Moreover, the settlement pattern suggests that the regional social organization was founded in lineages or other corporate kinship groupings, each of which controlled one or more circular towers, a group of ancestral tombs, adjacent agricultural land and pasture, and, in the geologically appropriate places, copper production. The Akkadian reference to the 32 'cities' and 'kings' of Magan (Sollberger & Kupper 1971, IIA3b) reflects the resulting political division of the region into multiple and competing small polities, probably founded on hierarchically ranked kin groups.

The technological evidence at Maysar reveals fairly small scale production, indicated by the size both of tailings and slag heaps, and of furnaces; the smelting procedure itself was simple. The settlement context of production reinforces this impression – copper production and working confined to portions of small settlements whose inhabitants were principally engaged in subsistence activities. In other words, Maysar contained a community that produced copper for exchange as a part-time activity, one that for most residents was secondary to agricultural and pastoral pursuits.

TEXTILES IN MESOPOTAMIA

Jacobsen (1970) and Waetzoldt (1972) provide the classic studies of textile production in Mesopotamia at the end of the third millennium BC. Jacobsen's assessment of the Ur 'Wool Office' exposes a massive production system, all aspects of which were subject to bureaucratic control, from animal herding to disbursements of the final products. Several organizational and scalar aspects of these operations deserve emphasis in the present context. Jacobsen's commentary indicates that the office handled 6400 tons of wool in a single year. Using Waetzoldt's figures for average wool yields, Adams (1981, 148) equates this tonnage with herds totalling 2.3 million animals. The total labour force controlled by the 'Wool Office' was comparably large: the ration lists imply 12,000 or more weavers within the bureaucratic purview (Waetzoldt 1972, 106). While an integrated and centralized multi-level bureaucracy coordinated and controlled production, the labour force itself was decentralized and dispersed. Individual weaving establishments usually had work-crews of five to twelve individuals, but could encompass hundreds of workers (see Waetzoldt 1972; Gelb 1976, 199). Akkadian weaving establishments attained a similar size, while late ED III ration lists document only slightly smaller work teams (best seen at Lagash: Maekawa 1974). The labour force itself consisted principally of women, 'geme', a term that in these contexts is translated as 'helot' (Diakonoff), 'serf' (Gelb), and, more generally 'unfree' or 'dependent' female worker. The term thus expresses the authoritative nature of institutional production in Mesopotamia, and points to the political and legal, as well as customary, conditions of the Mesopotamian political economy.

Much of this institutionalized production was directed not to internal consumption, but to foreign exchange. Textiles figured prominently in the list of south Mesopotamian exports for all periods documented in the cuneiform sources. Although these textiles were often of low grade by local standards (cf. Waetzoldt 1972 for the Ur III situation), they nonetheless commanded high value outside the region. The equivalency lists from Ebla, for example, clearly reveal the high value attached to the highest quality textiles imported from southern Mesopotamia (Pettinato 1979). The 'Akkadian' textiles involved in the Assyrian Cappadocian trade, though of variable quality, also commanded high prices (Veenhof 1972, 158). Such esteem likely reflected not only the superior character of Sumerian textiles, but also local cultural preference and symbolic value.

COMPARISONS

These three examples of production for exchange provide concrete illustrations of some of the basic differences that distinguished centres from peripheries, as well as the similarities that they shared. The similarities between these cases pertain to the nature of productive technologies. Although the three cases concern different kinds of commodities, all three may be characterized as labour-intensive, with relatively simple technologies and low capital requirements, a characterization generally appropriate to most palaeotechnical commodity production. Moreover, specific productive techniques may be found over wide areas, as illustrated by that for stone vessels, stone beads, and metal production. An additional similarity among the cases is the predominance of luxuries that could be used as rhetorical markers of social standing and of ideological claims to authority. The copper ingots produced in Oman, a semi-finished rather than a finished commodity, provide only a partial exception to this generalization.

The differences concern the scale and organizational complexity of production, where Yahya and Maysar stand at the low end, and Mesopotamia at the high end, of a continuum. Elsewhere in western Asia, organization and scale of production were intermediate between these extremes. Shahr-i Sokhta, Hissar, Shahdad, Mohenjo-daro and Altyn Depe provide examples of craft quarters and probable coordination and direction of production in more urban settings. The examples also differ in the social location of production. In Mesopotamia, the large 'public' households (palace and temple) achieved the requisite concentration of materials, labour, skill and organization to produce commodities in large amounts. Private production, so little attested in the textual sources, was probably small scale, and destined for domestic consumption or a petty peddling trade. State-sponsored workshops thus dominated the production side of Mesopotamian involvement in interregional trade, with all the consequences of political and economic inequalities that such a productive system entails. Although caught up in wealth accumulation and unequal displays of prestige, commodity production at Yahya and Maysar was still ancillary to the business of food production; semi-specialized or part time craft production occurred within the context of communities whose sources of political and social power rested primarily in control over agricultural resources.

The differences in organizational complexity and specialization of production for exchange suggest that unequal relations and asymmetrical terms of trade characterized the interregional movements of goods throughout the Bronze Age west Asian 'world system'. While the specifics of these unbalanced relations remain elusive, Yahya and Maysar were not equal trading partners with the 'great institutions' of a Mesopotamian city-state or empire. Analytical evidence for the production of the carved chlorite vessels shows that Yahya was only one of several production centres (Kohl 1978). Bun ingots have a wide distribution in western Asia, a reflection as much of multiple production centres using similar techniques as of the wide circulation of Magan copper itself. The fact that multiple small workshops turned out identical commodities for a given urban market prevented monopolies of production in peripheral regions. The elites that coveted these goods could play off, economically and politically, the separate production workshops against each other. At the same time, shared iconography, style, and inventory of commodities across most of western Asia implies producers' awareness of the consumers' market, and even a common formal system of meaning (however much that meaning may have been subject to local interpretation). These commonalities and differences are basic structural features of the west Asian world system.

Political economies and consumption

Stronger divergences between southern Iran and the Arabian Gulf characterized the location and consequences of consumption. These differences related to variable rhetorical and material uses of imported goods, and contrastive potentials for economic dependency. The differences in turn reflected the geographical and logistical conditions, and the contingent suitability of social forces such as violence, that distinguished maritime from overland systems.

THE ARABIAN GULF AND MARITIME TRADE

Trade in the Gulf included a wide range of commodities that encompassed both raw materials and finished goods (see Leemans 1960; Pettinato 1972; Heimpel 1987). Despite the variety of goods, the fundamental exchanges of the trading system were Mesopotamian textiles and cereals on the one side, and Arabian (Magan) copper on the other. The cuneiform economic texts (and particularly those of the Ur III and Isin-Larsa periods) explicitly list far larger amounts of these materials than of the others. Whatever the relative economic value of the other materials, copper, textiles and cereals formed the bulk of cargoes, and in this sense provided the basic exchange structure within which the other goods flowed. A broader perspective on the social location of this trade reveals a fundamental shift through time of these basic commodities, but

not of the others. During the third millennium the Gulf trade grew considerably in scale, reflected in larger individual cargoes and, seemingly, more traffic in total. Initially, all the traded goods were luxuries, commodities whose value arose from ideological contexts of consumption, and whose uses were fundamentally rhetorical and political. This evaluation applied even to copper imported into Mesopotamia and to textiles and cereals imported into Gulf societies. By the end of the ED III period, however, these same commodities had more directly productive uses (Edens 1992).

In Mesopotamia, the redefinition of copper consumption involved fundamental socioeconomic transformations during the Akkadian period. Sargon's success in creating new power sources by non-traditional patterns of clientage, land tenure, and military organization (Glassner 1986; Diakonoff 1991) transformed the longer-term shifting balance between palace, temple and corporate lineage as the institutional containers of political and economic power (Gelb 1969; Diakonoff 1982; Zagarell 1986). In this historical context, the expanded uses of imported copper contributed to the broader sociopolitical configuration: accumulation and control of copper provided the means both of production and of destruction, and reinforced the new and politically driven patterns of land tenure.

The expanding scale of trade had divergent consequences for Gulf societies. In Dilmun, the greater availability of imported grain in the last three centuries of the third millennium BC corresponded to a shift from the coast and inshore islands of the Arabian coast to Bahrain as the focus of settlement, and at the same time to a growth of urban centres such as the Qala' on Bahrain. This temporal correlation reflects a common effect of a maritime carrying trade: the concentration of the growing and economically diversified populations in port cities, and intensified production in the agricultural hinterland of these port cities (Larsen 1983). At the same time, large grain deliveries provided a critical supplement to local production that helped to feed these port cities, a characteristic feature of the regional economy in the Gulf in more recent historical times.

Comparison of estimated population sizes with the scale of grain shipments implied by the cuneiform texts indicates that imported grain could have supported substantial proportions of local communities on the Gulf littoral (see Edens 1992 for this argument). Dilmun may have become dependent on imported Mesopotamian grain, and the urban character of its society was largely predicated on commercial exchange. In Magan, on the other hand, settlements were always small, widely dispersed, predominantly agricultural, and often at some distance across mountain passes from the coast; these inland settlements, including Maysar, were the principal sources of exported copper ingots. In view of the geographical setting, and of the political divisions mentioned above, communities of the Magan interior could not guarantee access to imported food in the bulk or frequency necessary to form any dependency on it, whether those imports came from Mesopotamia or the Indus.

THE IRANIAN PLATEAU AND OVERLAND TRADE

Evidence for trade on the Iranian plateau has a very different character from that for the Gulf. The textual evidence for trade is fundamentally deficient. In the general absence of economic records explicitly concerned with trade, literary texts provide the best evidence, most notably the much discussed myth 'Enmerkar and the Lord of Aratta'. The archaeological record, on the other hand, documents the circulation of various raw materials (metals, stones, shell) and finished goods (such as beads, stone vessels, seals) across the Iranian plateau. Some interculturally shared iconography also achieved a wide distribution, forming bonds of ideological expression between regions; stylistic elements of disparate origin often appeared together on prestige goods of local manufacture (for example in the Fullol, Quetta, and Ashkhabad hoards). In these cases, however, the common iconography may mask divergent meanings of the shared representation, inhibiting more detailed and nuanced interpretations.

These differences of evidence make difficult even qualitative comparisons between the Iranian plateau and the Gulf, but some broad conclusions are nonetheless possible. Possehl (1986) has remarked that many communities in southeastern Iran specialized in the production of a few commodities, the circulation of which formed an enclosed regional exchange network. This circulation pattern offered to lineage-organized farming communities increased flexibility and resilience through inter-community alliances, and underwrote much of the elite display evident in burial assemblages. Various historical forces complicate this picture, including social inequalities within and between communities, uneven levels of social complexity across regions, persistent interactions with surrounding centres, resistance to external imperialist pressures, and the changing importance of maritime routes. Nevertheless, the basic contrast with the Gulf littoral remains – the logistical constraints of overland traffic emphasize circulation of scarce high value commodities that have primarily rhetorical uses, and minimize the economic utility of bulk staples. Under these conditions, the social contexts of production, exchange, and consumption remained largely political, and local political change directed economic connections within the world system.

CONCLUSIONS

Maritime trade afforded littoral societies of the Arabian Gulf the opportunity both to profit by a carrying trade and to import staples in bulk. These circumstances

allowed the rhetorical and utilitarian uses of commodities to be combined in Dilmun, and initiated a dependency similar to that of peripheries in the modern world system. Overland traffic, by contrast, afforded Mesopotamian states little opportunity to establish a domination of the surrounding highland metalliferous regions, the communities of which did not readily become dependent on exchange relations with Mesopotamia. The weakness or absence of highland dependency reflects the economic constraints on overland traffic discussed in the next section of this paper and, just as importantly, the fundamentally rhetorical uses of traded goods.

Political economies and exchange

The political economy laid down other conditions for interregional exchange, offering alternatives to trade for acquiring foreign goods, and establishing some basic aspects of value formation. The politics of exchange were also instrumental to the existence and modalities of interregional dependencies, and to secondary state formation.

CULTURE AND EXCHANGE

Cultural attitudes toward the symbolic qualities of certain materials deeply conditioned economic transactions. Lapis lazuli provides an example pertinent to both overland and maritime exchange. Lapis reached Mesopotamia from the mines of Badakhshan in northeastern Afghanistan along several routes during the third millennium BC. The Hissar and Shahr-i Sokhta evidence indicates that production of lapis artefacts (mostly beads) was a prominent activity at these sites. Most commentators consider these sites as nodal intermediaries in transregional systems of production and overland exchange. At the same time, the cuneiform sources name Meluhha as a source of lapis along sea routes (cf. Heimpel 1987), and the similar inference of transshipped lapis through Meluhha is usually made. This interpretation encounters an empirical contradiction, namely that lapis rarely appears in the archaeological record of the Indus or of the Gulf littoral. The distribution patterns lead some commentators (e.g. Shaffer 1982), to see the Harappan settlement at Shortughai (Francfort 1989) in northeastern Afghanistan as a semi-sedentary nomadic installation, rather than a Harappan trading enclave.

The scarcity of Harappan lapis may however reflect culturally determined consumption patterns, such that the stone was not especially valued in the Indus region, even while lapis was transshipped through the region into the Gulf trade. In Mesopotamia, lapis enjoyed high value not only because of its economic scarcity and distant/mythologized origin, but just as fundamentally because of its symbolic reference to the ideological connections between divinity and political authority (see Cassin 1968, 114–19). The ideological content of substance and colour must have taken alternative forms in the Harappan setting, where sociopolitical structure and ideology appear to have been very different from those of the Mesopotamian city-states (Miller 1985; Jacobson 1986; Fairservis 1989). Thus the differences in political ideology and symbolic power may account for the distribution of lapis.

Divergent cultural attitudes toward exchange itself may also distinguish regions. The institutional and individual contexts of Mesopotamian trade are now seen as combining important aspects of entrepreneurial mercantilism and of profit-seeking (Adams 1974; Powell 1977; Foster 1977; Gledhill & Larsen 1982; Zagarell 1986), though still contained within the relatively inelastic structures of wealth accumulation and the constrained logistical capacities of transportation and communication characteristic of early agrarian civilizations. In particular, the ability of individuals acting on behalf of large institutions (palace, temple, private stock corporations) simultaneously to trade for personal gain is now widely recognized as a strong force of social and political change during Mesopotamian history, since these forms of private accumulation helped to create new forms of social power. On the Iranian plateau, the social and political situation of economic transactions ensured a different morality of exchange. Possehl (1986) suggests that contrastive goals and rules of exchange generated incompatible moral expectations, inhibiting trade between Mesopotamia and southern plateau societies. Possehl's analysis raises several important conceptual issues – the cultural contexts of interregional exchange, and the potential ramifications of these contexts – that the extant archaeological literature rarely considers.

The military option

In addition to the ideological aspects of interregional affairs that may promote or hinder, but certainly contour, transregional circulation of goods, military force also acted to transfer goods and people from place to place. Akkadian military operations provide an apt illustration of the problem. The goal of Akkadian campaigns outside southern Mesopotamia was less to secure formal territorial control and administration than to acquire loot and tribute. The scale of material transfers apparently was enormous: although the texts often do not allow quantitative assessment, one source lists nearly 15 kg of gold and two metric tonnes of copper as gifts to the temple of Enlil at Nippur (only a fraction of the total takings) after a campaign in Khuzistan, and another text mentions thousands of prisoners; individual objects are inscribed as booty from various places. Many commentators have remarked that Akkadian militarism focused on important resource zones (e.g. the Cedar Mountains, the Silver Mountains, etc.), and involved direct control over the

routes giving access to these resources (such as Susa to the east, or Tell Brak to the northwest). The common inference is an economic motive for Akkadian warfare (Bottero 1965, 107; Larsen 1979, 78–9; Glassner 1986, 23). Indeed, Glassner points out that Mesopotamian participation in interregional trade declined sharply at this time, so effective was regular military campaigning in satisfying Akkadian demand for raw materials and labour (see also Powell 1977). At issue here is not a simple espousal of this view of Akkadian militarism, but rather the claim that military force was in the ancient world a means of exchange and accumulation at least as potent as trade.

Peripheries were not passive objects of military exploitation. The series of coalitions that faced the Akkadians on the Iranian plateau were composed of widely distributed societies, including Anshan, Serihum, Marhasi, and Magan, that is to say, much of southern Iran and also southeastern Arabia. Marhasi is plausibly identified as the area of modern Kirman (Steinkeller 1982), and so provides a toponymic correlate for Shahdad and Tepe Yahya. The organizational requirements of resistance to military pressure worked to centralize authority, while the political coalitions themselves expanded regional channels of economic circulation, offering possibilities for increased centralization and intensification of craft production. The emerging social complexity in the Shahdad area thus must be seen as a response to combinations of military pressure and commercial activity.

Nor were peripheries in similar geographical and commercial relations to centres necessarily affected in comparable ways. For example, Dilmun and Magan differed profoundly in their political relations with Mesopotamia. Magan was involved, if only peripherally, in military coalitions that opposed eastward Akkadian imperialist pressures. Two Akkadian kings claim to have raided Magan, and several stone vessels inscribed as 'booty from Magan' appear in the Mesopotamian archaeological record. Dilmun, on the other hand, was neither involved in military coalitions nor the victim of raids. This discrepancy reflects the Akkadian use of warfare as a basic instrument of accumulation: whatever wealth Dilmun had amassed as the intermediary in the maritime trade, it produced few goods and contained no valuable raw materials, whereas Magan possessed copper and other desirable goods.

The efficiency of militarism in interregional circulation derived from the organizational properties of aggressive states; these organizational properties were not persistently available to centres and were usually available only in weaker forms to peripheries. Routine violence is not itself incompatible with continued trade: for logistical reasons, military force loses its effectiveness with distance, and the mix of violence and trade forms a spatial continuum. The economic rationale of violence demands that, over the long-term, rates of looting and tribute-taking be adjusted to allow continued accumulation of wealth in peripheries; seen in this way, violence by centres is an important factor in calculation of protection costs in peripheries, but does not overturn the rationale of trade until these protection costs become too high and the risks too great. The intensity of accumulation by violence thus further distinguished centres from peripheries, but always in unstable mixes of military and commercial acquisition: trade finds its conditions in histories of political economies.

The contrasts between the plateau and the Gulf seen in both the written and the archaeological evidence might be understood to reflect a more 'politicized' context of overland exchange and a more 'commercialized' context of maritime exchange. More precisely, the constellation of diplomatic, military, and commercial action offered great flexibility to the Mesopotamian acquisition of foreign goods. Campaigning, extortion, and diplomatic exchanges, together with trade, could bring these goods from regions to which expansionary pressures could regularly (if only periodically) be applied, without consideration of more routine commercial arrangements. But when imperial pressures could not regularly be applied, Mesopotamia could engage in routine commercial arrangements, as during periods when the organizational requirements of imperialism were lacking.

VIOLENCE AND COSTS

A common view holds that, prior to modern transportation technologies, overland costs far exceeded maritime or riverine costs, sharply inhibiting overland movements of goods (Finley 1985, 126–7). Recent challenges to this view (e.g. Hopkins 1979, 42–52) oblige a less extreme assessment, by showing that overland traffic was a regular feature of the classical economy. Indeed, in western Asia of the early 17th century AD, overland traffic was no more, and perhaps even less, expensive than maritime transportation, when considered in terms of cargo weight (Steensgard 1974, 40). However, relative transportation costs were always indisputably high for long-distance movements of such high bulk and low value materials as food staples. Examples from both the classical world (Ste. Croix 1981, 11–12) and 17th century Iran (Steensgard 1974, 39–40) indicate that transportation costs over several hundred miles equalled the original purchase price of cereals. Transportation by water thus provided the only economically effective way of moving these bulk staples.

Protection costs include the variety of official imposts, permit fees, customs excises and duties; irregular payments to government officials; extorted payments to brigands, pirates and pastoralists for safe passage; hired armed guards (often from these same extorting groups); and other payments that lowered risk of loss to human predators. In many historical examples of commercial traffic, the cost of protection greatly outweighed that of transportation (e.g. Steensgard 1974). The relationships between protection costs and the political circumstances of interregional trade are thus complex, involving the calculated violence of states and other predatory groups, the strength of regional political integration, the security conditions of a region, and the serial exaction of official and unofficial payments along a given route. Commodity price formation responded strongly to these kinds of political forces. At the same time, merchants' calculations of risk and acceptable profit margins constrained rates of state exaction and private predation, and enforced an acceptable degree of security, under the penalty of driving trade into alternate routes and consequent loss of state or private revenues. In many cases, maritime traffic potentially incurs lower protection costs than overland movement, since the opportunities for the various forms of revenue exaction are often lower. The high variability of tax policies, political uncertainty, and rapacity of local groups, however, leave this only a potential advantage.

The various political calculations and economic limitations expressed in the two kinds of costs result in two ideal types of centre-periphery relations within premodern world systems, only one of which may be characterized as 'dependency'. Water transport offers the possibility of bulk movement of staples; under conditions of relatively low and predictable protection costs, societies may come to rely on imported food stuffs and thereby be dependent on suppliers. The Mediterranean world provides ample illustration of this commonplace, as do ports around the Persian Gulf in more recent historical times. In Bronze Age western Asia, regional systems of bulk transfers characterized the riverine civilizations, even when divided into multiple states, as in Mesopotamia, but of the peripheries considered here, only Dilmun qualifies as dependent on centres.

The high relative transportation and protection costs of overland traffic promoted circulation of high value commodities, and limited bulk transfers. High value imported commodities were exactly those that figured as rhetorical markers in the ideological construction and reproduction of political power throughout the ancient 'world system'. Centres and peripheries were thus equally dependent on interregional exchange, and the conditions for dependency of peripheries on centres were, with few exceptions, absent. Several other factors reinforced this blockage of dependency. Political instability or brigandage easily disrupted overland traffic, producing fluctuating intensities and shifting routes of exchange. The existence of multiple centres afforded peripheries the opportunity to resist dependency on any one centre. The wide distribution of technologies left centres unable to monopolize commodity production in the way possible in the emerging modern world system; export of raw materials was not a mark of dependency.

Conclusions

This paper has argued for the utility of a modified

world-systems perspective on developments that occurred throughout much of western Asia during the Early Bronze Age. In order to justify such a model, one must demonstrate that the participating societies systemically articulated with one another such that political and economic developments in one region deeply conditioned local histories. The model requires connections between societies that were more basic, fundamental, and long-lived than other forms of contacts such as technological diffusion, simple exchange networks, or even movements of peoples.

World systems ideas cannot usefully be applied haphazardly to world history. Prior to the Early Bronze Age, communities in western Asia interacted across long distances without forming a world system, even during Halaf or 'Ubaid times. And the expansion of the Uruk and Proto-Elamite states does not fit comfortably in a world-systems model, since these episodes were relatively short-lived, involved colonial implantations, and asserted considerable direct control over peripheries.

The 'reading' of the archaeological record presented here finds systemic articulations that formed and intensified across most of western Asia during the middle of the third millennium BC. During this period 'secondary states' and 'proto-urban' centres appeared throughout the region, and the archaeological and textual records document an increasingly sophisticated movement of finished goods and raw materials into resource-deficient riverine plains. The action of an ancient world system is recorded in the largely synchronous rise and collapse of cities and political complexity in the participating societies, synchronous cycles that can only reflect a historically connected process.

As Wallerstein (1974) and others have long remarked, the world-system model raises explicitly the issue of the proper spatial units of analysis for interpreting developmental processes. Pre-modern 'world' systems did not encompass the globe, and so must be bounded as social as well as physiographic units. These boundaries were not fixed nor impermeable, but expanded and contracted over time as the world system changed in constituents or dynamics, allowing intercourse with the 'barbarian worlds' or with other world systems. The maximal boundaries of the Early Bronze Age world system of western Asia stretched from the eastern Mediterranean in the west to the Indus valley and Central Asia in the east. Some boundaries are clearer than others; among the clearest are the great Caucasus range or the Kara Kum and Kyzyl Kum deserts which provided barriers that separated the South Russian and Eurasian steppes from western Asia. Elsewhere, especially to the west, social boundaries distinguished less tangibly the Egyptian and eastern Mediterranean worlds from the west Asian world system.

Use of the world-systems model also explicitly raises thorny questions about conceptualization of the pre-modern world and interpretation of the recalcitrant archaeological and textual records. One cannot satisfactorily reconstruct a trading system without some control over its three basic components: production, distribution, and consumption. Shortage of evidence usually obscures the extent and terms of the trade, the degree to which exchange relations were unbalanced and asymmetrical, and the extent of dependencies among contrasting regions. Even in those atypical cases with relatively copious evidence, reconstructions must make assumptions that are ultimately speculative and untestable. And trade was not the only means by which commodities circulated within a world system: distribution patterns leave open the question of mechanisms. For these reasons, reconstruction of a west Asian Early Bronze Age world system represents only one 'reading' of an extremely complex and fragmentary archaeological and textual record.

The ancient Bronze Age world system which emerges from this analysis differs in fundamental respects from that modelled by dependency theorists for the modern world system. A number of basic features distinguish ancient from modern world systems: the existence of multiple centres; logistical constraints impeding movements of materials, especially staples, along overland routes; the omnipresent military option to raid rather than trade; and technologies common to both peripheries and centres. These differences suggest that dependencies in the modern sense only rarely characterized centre-periphery relations in the ancient world.

References

Adams, R. McC., 1974. Anthropological perspectives on ancient trade. *Current Anthropology* 15, 239–58

Adams, R. McC., 1981. *Heartland of Cities*. Chicago: University of Chicago Press

Alden, J., 1982. Trade and politics in Proto-Elamite Iran. *Current Anthropology* 23, 613–40

Algaze, G., 1989. The Uruk expansion: cross-cultural exchange in early Mesopotamian civilization. *Current Anthropology* 30, 571–608

Algaze, G., 1993. Expansionary dynamics of some early pristine states. *American Anthropologist* 95 (in press)

Amiet, P., 1986. *L'Age des Echanges Inter-Iraniens, 3500–1700 av. J.-C.* Paris: Editions de la Réunion des Musées Nationaux

Appadurai, A., 1988 Introduction: commodities and the politics of value, in *The Social Life of Things: Commodities in Cultural Perspective*, ed. A. Appadurai. Cambridge: Cambridge University Press, 3–63

Aynard, J.M., 1966. Coquillages mésopotamiens. *Syria* 43, 21–37

Badaljan, R.C., Blackman, M.J., Kikodze, Z., & Kohl, P.L., n.d. Neutron activation analyses of Caucasian obsidians: patterns of exchange and utilization. Unpublished manuscript

Bass, G., 1986. A Bronze Age shipwreck at Ulu Burun (Kas): 1984 campaign. *American Journal of Archaeology* 90, 269–96

Bass, G., Pulak, C., Collon, D., & Weinstein, J., 1989. The Bronze Age shipwreck at Ulu Burun: 1986 campaign. *American Journal of Archaeology* 93, 1–29

Beale, T., 1973. Early trade in highland Iran: a view from a source area. *World Archaeology* 5, 133–48

Biggs, R,D., 1974. *Inscriptions from Tell Abu Salabikh.* Oriental Institute Publications 94. Chicago: University of Chicago Press

Biscione, R., 1977. The crisis in Central Asian urbanization in II millennium BC and villages as an alternative system, in *Le Plateau Iranien des Origines à la Conquête Islamique*, ed. J. Deshayes. Colloques Internationaux du CNRS 67. Paris: CNRS

Blanton, R., & G. Feinman, 1984 The Mesoamerican world system: a comparative perspective. *American Anthropologist* 86, 673–82

Bottero, J., 1965. Das erste semitische Grossreich, in *Fischer Weltgeschichte 2: Die Altorientalischen Reiche I*, eds. E. Cassin, J. Bottero & J. Vercoutter. Frankfurt: Fischer, 91–128

Brenner, R., 1977. The origins of capitalist development: a critique of neo-Smithian Marxism. *New Left Review* 104, 25–92

Cassin, E., 1968. *La Splendeur Divine.* Paris: Mouton

Chirot, D., 1985. The rise of the west. *American Sociological Review* 50, 181–95

Cleuziou, S. and M. Tosi, 1989. The southeast frontier of the ancient Near East, in *South Asian Archaeology 1985*, eds. K. Frifelt & P. Sorensen. London: Curzon Press, 15–47

Crawford, H.E.W., 1973. Mesopotamia's invisible exports in the third millennium BC. *World Archaeology* 5, 232–41

Dales, G., 1977. Shifting trade patterns between the Iranian plateau and the Indus valley in the third millennium BC, in *Le Plateau Iranien et l'Asie Centrale des Origines à la Conquête Islamique*, ed. J. Deshayes. Colloques Internationaux du CNRS 67. Paris: CNRS

Davidson, T.E., & McKerrell, H., 1976. Pottery analysis and Halaf period trade in the Khabur headwaters region. *Iraq* 38, 45–56

Davidson, T.E., & McKerrell, H., 1980. The neutron activation analysis of Halaf and 'Ubaid pottery from Tell Arpachiyah and Tepe Gawra. *Iraq* 42, 155–67

Deagan, K., 1982. Avenues of inquiry in historical archaeology, in *Advances in Archaeological Method and Theory 5*. New York: Academic Press, 151–77

Delougaz, P., Hill, H., & Lloyd, S., 1967. *Private Houses and Graves in the Diyala Region.* Oriental Institute Publication 88. Chicago: University of Chicago Press

Diakonoff, I.M., 1982. The structure of Near Eastern society before the middle of the second millennium BC. *Oikumene* 3, 9–100

Diakonoff, I.M., 1991. *Early Antiquity.* Chicago: University of Chicago Press

Edens, C., 1992. Dynamics of trade in the ancient Mesopotamian 'world system'. *American Anthropologist* 94, 118–39

Englund, R., 1983. Dilmun in the archaic Uruk corpus, in *Dilmun: New Studies in the Archaeology and Early History of Bahrain*, ed. D. Potts. Berlin: Dietrich Reimer

Esse, D., 1989. Secondary state formation and collapse in Early Bronze Age Palestine, in *L'Urbanisation de la Palestine à l'Age du Bronze Ancien*, ed. P. de Miroschedji. BAR International Series 527. Oxford: British Archaeological Reports, 81–96

Fairservis, W., 1989. An epigenetic view of the Harappan culture, in *Archaeological Thought in America*, ed. C.C. Lamberg-Karlovsky. Cambridge: Cambridge University Press, 205–17

Finley, M.I., 1985. *The Ancient Economy.* (2nd ed.) Berkeley: University of California Press

Finley, M.I., 1986. *Ancient History: Evidence and Models.* New York: Viking

Francfort, H-P., 1989. *Fouilles de Shortughai: Recherches sur l'Asie Centrale Protohistorique.* Paris: Boccard

Foster, B., 1977. Commercial activity in Sargonic Mesopotamia. *Iraq* 39, 31–43

Gelb, I.J., 1969. On the alleged temple and state economies in ancient Mesopotamia, in *Studi in Onore di Edouardo Volterra 6*. Milan: A. Giuffre, 137–54

Gelb, I.J., 1976. Quantitative evaluation of slavery and serfdom, in *Kramer Anniversary Volume*, ed. B. Eichler. Alter Orient und Altes Testament 25, 195–207

Genscheimer, 1984. The role of shell in Mesopotamia: evidence for trade exchange with Oman and the Indus valley. *Paléorient* 10, 65–73

Giddens, A., 1987. *The Nation-State and Violence.* Berkeley: University of California Press

Glassner, 1986. *La Chute d'Akkade: L'Evènement et sa Mémoire.* Berlin: Dietrich Reimer

Gledhill, J., & Larsen, M., 1982. The Polanyi paradigm and a dynamic analysis of archaic states, in *Theory and Explanation in Archaeology*, eds A.C. Renfrew, M.J. Rowlands, & B. Segraves. New York: Academic Press, 197–229

Gorelick, L., & Gwinnet, A., 1990. The ancient Near Eastern cylinder seal as social emblem and status symbol. *Journal of Near Eastern Studies* 49, 45–56

Hauptmann, A., 1985. *5000 Jahre Kupfer in Oman, Bd.1: Die Entwicklung der Kupfermetallurgie vom 3.Jahrtausend bis zu Neuzeit.* Der Anschnitt Beiheft 4. Bochum: Bergbau Museum

Hauptmann, A., Weisgerber, G., & Bachmann, H., 1988. Early copper metallurgy in Oman, in *The Beginning of the Use of Metals and Alloys*, ed. R. Maddin. Cambridge: Massachusetts Institute of Technology, 34–51

Heimpel, W., 1987. Das untere Meer. *Zeitschrift für Assyriologie* 77, 22–91

Hopkins, K., 1979. Economic growth and towns in classical antiquity, in *Towns in Societies: Essays in Economic History and Historical Sociology*, eds P.Abrams & E. Wrigley. Cambridge: Cambridge University Press, 35–77

Jacobs, J., 1969. *The Economy of Cities.* New York: Vintage

Jacobson, J., 1986. The Harappan civilization: an early state, in *Studies in the Archaeology of India and Pakistan*, ed. J. Jacobson New Delhi: Oxford & IBH Publishing, 137–73

Jacobsen, T., 1970. On the textile industry at Ur under Ibbi-Sin, in *Towards the Image of Tammuz and Other Essays on Mesopotamian History and Culture*, ed. W.L. Moran. Cambridge: Harvard University Press, 216–29

Kenoyer, M., 1984. Shell working industries of the Indus civilization: a summary. *Paléorient* 10, 49–64

Kohl, P.L., 1978. The balance of trade in southwestern Asia in the mid-third millennium BC. *Current Anthropology* 19, 463–83

Kohl, P.L., 1987a. The use and abuse of world systems theory: the case of the 'pristine' west Asian state, in *Advances in Archaeological Method and Theory 11*. New York: Academic Press, 1–35

Kohl, P.L., 1987b. The ancient economy, transferable technologies northeastern frontier of the ancient Near East, in *Centre and Periphery in the Ancient World*, eds M. Rowlands, M. Larsen, & K. Kristiansen. Cambridge: Cambridge University Press, 13–24

Kohl, P.L. & Wright, R., 1977. Stateless cities: the differentiation of societies in the Near Eastern neolithic. *Dialectical Anthropology* 2, 271–83

Korfmann, M., 1982. *Tilkitepe: Die ersten Ansatze prähistorischer Forschung in der östlichen Turkei*. Istanbuler Mitteilungen 26. Tubingen: Wasmuth

Lamberg-Karlovsky, C.C., 1985. The longue durée of the ancient Near East, in *De l'Indus aux Balkans: Receuil à la mémoire de Jean Deshayes*, ed. J.-L. Huot, M. Yon, & Y. Calvet. Paris: Ed. Recherche sur les Civilisations, 55–72

Lamberg-Karlovsky, C.C. & Hiebert, F., 1992. Central Asia and the Indo-Iranian borderlands. *Iran* 30 (in press)

Lamberg-Karlovsky, C.C., & Tosi, M., 1973. Shahr-i Sokhta and Tepe Yahya: tracks on the earliest history of the Iranian plateau. *East and West* 23, 21–53

Lambert, M., 1953. Textes commerciaux de Lagash (époque présargonique). *Revue d'Assyriologie* 47, 57–69, 105–20

Larsen, C., 1983. *Life and Land Use on the Bahrain Islands*. Chicago: University of Chicago Press

Larsen, M.T., 1979. The tradition of empire in Mesopotamia., in *Power and Propoganda: A Symposium on Ancient Empires*, ed. M. Larsen. Copenhagen: Akademisk Forlag, 5–103

Larsen, M.T., 1987. Commercial networks in the ancient Near East, in *Centre and Periphery in the Ancient World*, eds M. Rowlands, M. Larsen & K. Kristiansen. Cambridge: Cambridge University Press, 47–56

Leemans, W.F., 1960. *Foreign Trade in the Old Babylonian Period*. Leiden: Brill

Marfoe, L., 1979. The integrative transformation: patterns of socioeconomic organization in southern Syria. *Bulletin of the American Schools of Oriental Research* 234, 1–42

Miller, D., 1985. Ideology and the Harappan civilization. *Journal of Anthropological Archaeology* 4, 34–71

Minz, S., 1985. *Sweetness and Power: The Place of Sugar in Modern History*. New York: Viking

Miroschedji, P. de, 1973. Vases et objets en steatite susiens du musée du Louvre. *Cahiers de la Délégation Archéologique Française en Iran* 3, 9–79

Narimanov, I.G., 1986. Obeidskiye plemena Mesopotamii v Azerbaidzhane. Abstracts of papers delivered at Vsesoyuznaya Arkheologicheskaya Konferentsiya Dostizheniya Sovetskoi Arkheologii v XI Pyatiletke. Baku, 271–2

Nissen, H., 1988. *The Early History of the Ancient Near East, 9000–2000 BC*. Chicago: University of Chicago Press

Oppenheim, A.L., 1954. The seafaring merchants of Ur. *Journal of the American Oriental Society* 74, 6–17

Pettinato, G., 1972. Il commercio con l'estero della Mesopotamia meridionale 3. millannio av. Cr. alle luce delle fonti litterati e lessicale. *Mesopotamia* 7, 43–166

Pettinato, G., 1979. *The Archives of Ebla: An Empire Inscribed in Clay*. New York: Doubleday

Possehl, G., 1986. *Kulli: An Exploration of an Ancient Civilization in South Asia*. Durham NC: Carolina Academic Press

Possehl, G., 1990. Revolution in the urban revolution: the emergence of Indus urbanization. *Annual Review of Anthropology* 19, 261–82

Potts, D., 1990. *The Arabian Gulf in Antiquity*. Oxford: Clarendon Press

Powell, M., 1977. Sumerian merchants and the problem of profit. *Iraq* 39, 23–9

Ragin, C., & Chirot, D., 1984. The world system of Immanuel Wallerstein: sociology and politics as history, in *Vision and Method in Historical Sociology*, ed. T. Skocpol. Cambridge: Cambridge University Press, 276–312

Renfrew, C., 1975. Trade as action at a distance: questions of integration and communication, in *Ancient Civilization and Trade*, eds J. Sabloff & C.C. Lamberg-Karlovsky. Albuquerque: University of New Mexico Press, 3–59

Renfrew, C., & Bahn, P., 1991 *Archaeology: Theories, Methods and Practice*. New York: Thames and Hudson

Renfrew, C., & Dixon, J.E., 1976. Obsidian in western Asia: a review, in *Problems in Economic and Social Archaeology*, eds. G. de G. Sieveking, I.H. Longworth & K.E. Wilson. London: Duckworth, 137–50

Ste. Croix, G.E.M. de, 1981. *The Class Struggle in the Ancient Greek World*. London: Duckworth

Salvatore, S., & M. Vidale, 1982 A brief surface survey of the protohistoric site of Shahdad (Kerman, Iran): preliminary report. *Rivista di Archeologia* 6, 5–10

Schneider, J., 1977. Was there a pre-capitalist world-system? *Peasant Studies* 6, 20–9

Shaffer, J., 1982. Harappan commerce: an alternative perspective, in *Anthropology in Pakistan*, eds S. Pastner & L. Flam. Cornell: Cornell University Press, 166–210

Skocpol, T., 1977. Wallerstein's world capitalist system: a theoretical and historical critique. *American Journal of Sociology* 82, 1075–90

Sollberger, E. & Kupper, J.R., 1971. *Inscriptions Royales Sumériennes et Akkadiennes*. Paris: Editions du Cerf

Steensgard, N., 1974. *The Asian Trade Revolution of the Seventeenth Century: The East India Companies and the Decline of the Caravan Trade*. Chicago: University of Chicago Press

Steinkeller, P., 1982. The question of Marhasi: a contribution to the historical geography of Iran in the third millennium BC. *Zeitschrift für Assyriologie* 72, 237–65

Strommenger, E., 1964. Die Kleinfunde aus dem Gebiet des Sinkasid-Palastes, in *20. vorläufige Bericht über die von dem Deutschen Archäologische Institut und den Deutschen Orient-Gesellschaft aus Mitteln der Deutschen Forschungsgemeinschaft unternommenen Ausgrabungen in Uruk-Warka*. Mitteilungen des Deutsches Archäologisches Institut, Abteilung Baghdad, 33–7

Sumner, W., 1988. Maljan, Tall-e (Ansan). *Reallexikon der Assyriologie* 7(3/4), 306–20

Sürenhagen, D., 1986. The dry farming belt: the Uruk period and subsequent developments, in *The Origins of Cities in Dry-Farming Syria and Mesopotamia in the Third Millennium BC*, ed. H. Weiss. Guilford CT: Four Quarters Publishing Co, 7–43

Veenhof, K., 1972. *Aspects of Old Assyrian Trade and its Terminology*. Leiden: Brill

Waetzoldt, H., 1972. *Untersuchungen zur neusumerischen Textilindustrie*. Rome: Centro por le Antichita e la Storia dell'Arte del Vicino Oriente

Wallerstein, I., 1974. *The Modern World-System: Capitalist Agriculture and the Origins of the European World-Economy in the Sixteenth Century*, vol. 1. New York: Academic Press

Weisgerber, G., 1980. . . und Kupfer in Oman. *Der Anschnitt* 32, 62–110

Weisgerber, G., 1981. Mehr als Kupfer in Oman. *Der Anschnitt* 33, 174–263

Weiss, H., 1983. Excavations at Tell Leilan and the origins of north Mesopotamian cities in the third millennium BC. *Paléorient* 9, 39–52

Weiss, H., 1986. The origins of Tell Leilan and the conquest of space in third-millennium Mesopotamia, in *The Origins of Cities in Dry-Farming Syria and Mesopotamia in the Third Millennium BC*, ed. H. Weiss. Guilford: Four Quarters, 71–108

Weiss, H., 1990. Tell Leilan 1989: new data for mid-third millennium urbanization and state formation. *Mitteilungen der Deutschen Orient-Gesellschaft* 122, 193–218

Westenholz, A., 1984. The Sargonic period, in *Circulation of Goods in Non-Palatial Contexts in the Ancient Near East*, ed. A. Archi. Istituto per gli Studi Micenei ed Egeo-Anatolici. Rome: Edizioni dell'Ateneo, 17–30

Whitecotton, J., & Pailes, R., 1986. New World precolumbian world systems, in *Ripples on the Chichimec Sea: New Considerations of Southwestern-Mesoamerican Interaction*, eds F. Mathien & R. McGuire. Carbondale: Southern Illinois University Press, 185–204

Wolf, E., 1982. *Europe and the People without History.*

Berkeley: University of California Press

Woolley, L., & Mallowan, M.E.L., 1976. *Ur Excavations VII: The Old Babylonian Period*. London: British Museum Publications Limited

Yoffee, N., forthcoming. *Early Stages in the Evolution of Mesopotamian Civilization: Soviet Excavations in the Sinjar Plain, Northern Iraq*. Tucson: University of Arizona

Zagarell, A., 1986. Trade, women, class, and society in ancient western Asia. *Current Anthropology* 27, 415–30

Zarins, J., 1989a. Ancient Egypt and the Red Sea trade: the case of obsidian in the Predynastic and Archaic periods, in *Essays in Ancient Civilization Presented to Helene J. Kantor*, eds A. Leonard & B. Williams. Chicago: Oriental Institute, 339–68

Zarins, J., 1989b. Eastern Saudi Arabia and external relations, selected ceramic, steatite and textual evidence: 3500–1900 BC, in *South Asian Archaeology 1985*, eds K. Frifelt & P. Sorensen. London: Curzon Press, 74–103

4

Exchange, Foraging and Local Hominid Networks

Clive Gamble

Following the work of Féblot-Augustins and Perlès (1991), the distance over which hunters and gathers move stone resources is investigated from both archaeological and ethnographic evidence. Attention is paid to Geneste's principle (1988) that irrespective either of age or hominid, distant raw materials are represented by the later stages of the reduction sequence. The distinction between so-called local and exotic resources is examined with reference to data from Australia. The importance of the social context is stressed, since social and spatial distance are not equivalent. Using a model of exclusive and inclusive social systems (Peterson 1986), the role of exchange acting as either a form of 'membership dues' or 'insurance premiums' is explored against the background of variation in resources. Finally, a common spatial structure of tool-assisted behaviour — here named the local hominid network — is proposed, and its evolutionary implications briefly examined.

A la suite du travail de Féblot-Augustins et de Perlès (1991), la question des distances sur lesquelles les chasseurs-cueilleurs transportent la matière première lithique est abordée par l'intermédiare de données à la fois archéologiques et ethnographiques. Le principe défini par Geneste (1988), et selon lequel les sources de matières premières éloignées sont représentées, indépendamment de la période ou de type humain, par les dernières phases de la séquence de réduction, est pris en compte. La distinction entre les matériaux dits 'locaux' ou 'exotiques' est envisagée à partir de données provenant d'Australie. L'importance du contexte social est souligné, étant donné que les distances sociales et spatiales ne sont pas équivalentes. En recourant à un modèle de systèmes sociaux de type inclusif ou exclusif (Peterson 1986), le rôle de l'acte d'échange en tant que 'droit d'entrée' or de 'prime d'assurance' est analysé en relation avec la variation des matières premières disponibles. Enfin, une structure spatiale commune de comportement par outil assisté — il s'agit ici du réseau local hominidé — est proposé et ses implications en termes d'évolution sont envisagées.

Introduction

How exotic is exotic? How local is local? What do such terms mean when applied to the distributions of stone, stone tools and other Palaeolithic materials? Moreover, do the activities of trade and exchange, which such terms measure, change dramatically with the appearance of food production in the Neolithic?

One reason for asking these questions is the growing interest in the distribution of raw material among prehistoric societies, believed to be highly mobile, in late Pleistocene and early Holocene Europe. This development is interesting since until recently European archaeologists (Clark 1965 excepted) did not expect hunters and gatherers to trade or exchange in a serious fashion, just as they were 'forbidden' to have polished axes, domestic animals and, with a few exceptions to the rule, settled communities. Now, as hunters look

increasingly like farmers (Thomas 1991) and farmers have been characterized as failed hunters (Binford 1983), the moccasin is on the other foot. All the more important therefore to understand the terms *local* and *exotic* which are frequently applied to Palaeolithic distribution maps. Not only to assist in understanding the exchange process, but also to examine if the exchange and transfer of goods and materials played any role in the evolution of other more complex, but not necessarily more complicated, societies. One way to achieve this goal is to broaden the base for comparisons and examine how these issues have been profitably examined in other regions, most notably Australia.

Studying the distribution of raw materials

Geneste (1988a & b) has provided an elegant analysis of raw material provisioning in a number of Middle Palaeolithic sites in southwest France. He found three distances over which materials were regularly transported and which influenced the composition of the stone assemblages (Table 4.1). I have labelled the extremes in his table as 'local' and 'exotic'. In this paper these distances of < 5 km and > 30 km from which lithic materials came will be used to discuss the terms.

Table 4.1,. Proportions of raw materials present and utilized on Middle Paleolithic sites in southwest France in relation to distance from source, after Geneste 1988a & b

Km radius from site	% of stone on site	% utilised, made into tools
'Local' = within 5 km	55–98	1–5
Region = 5–20 km	2–20	1–20
'Exotic' = 30–80 km	< 5	74–100

The characterisation of stone and other materials to source in the European Palaeolithic serves two functions. On the one hand such sourcing has been used to predict technological and typological variation in tool kits. One of Geneste's major findings is that exotic flints are always rare and more likely to be present as retouched tools (cores are never found), while local material dominates assemblages and is represented by all stages of manufacturing debitage (1988b, 488–90). This finding is confirmed by Kozłowski (1982) in a Middle Palaeolithic level at Bacho Kiro in Bulgaria. Flint is not found within a radius of 100 km from the cave. This exotic raw material makes up 13 per cent of the total stone in level 13. Yet 32 per cent of all the retouched artefacts, but only 11 per cent of unretouched flakes, were of this raw material. By contrast, local volcanic rocks make up 73 per cent of the total chipped stone, 29 per cent of tools and 79 per cent of flakes.

It is possible to make a general observation from Geneste's data (1988a & b) about the use of stone resources by foragers: *distant raw materials are represented by the later stages of the reduction sequence.* This rule crosses the major cultural divides for prehistoric foragers such as the Upper and Middle Palaeolithic (e.g. Tavoso 1984; Malina 1970; Perlès 1992) and Mesolithic (Perlès 1989). When exotic stone is found in assemblages it will generally be rare, heavily retouched and/or broken when compared with the larger quantities of unmodified debitage, complete flakes and implements with simple retouch, made from local materials (Rolland & Dibble 1990).

The observation can also be made for Neolithic sites, where Perlès, using Greek data, has concluded for stone tools that 'a general contrast [exists] between artefacts in exotic raw materials, which are dominant in number and are of good to superior workmanship, and artefacts in local raw materials, made more occasionally, and of inferior workmanship' (1989, 11).

The significant difference is that the proportions of exotic tools vary inversely with distance between the foragers and farmers (Fig. 4.1).

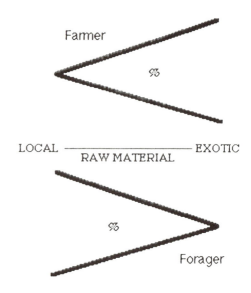

Figure 4.1. Expected proportions of local and exotic stone materials as finished artefacts in forager and farmer assemblages

The second aspect of characterizing raw materials to source in the Palaeolithic has concentrated upon objects of presumed social value rather than utilitarian function — shells, amber, ochre, ivory as well as those where value has been added, such as lumps of limestone carved into figurines. These can travel very great distances as Soffer (1985) has shown for amber and shell coming from the Black Sea into Ukrainian sites 15,000 years ago, while the compilation of sources by Roebroeks *et al.* (1988) shows how the increased distances for exchange in the Upper rather than the Middle Palaeolithic are due to the addition of these objects to the inventory. The ethnographic and archaeological exchange systems from the western Arctic during the Holocene confirm these large-scale patterns (Gerlach & Mason 1992, 67).

Féblot-Augustins and Perlès (1991) conclude, in a cross-cultural comparison of ethnographic records of exchange, that *only* the category of exchange goods they label BFV (*Biens Fortement Valorisés*), the geegaws of social life — such as beads, jewellry and ornaments — the embodiments of social position, transcend any charges of ethnocentrism when interpreted as items of value. In this case the extreme distances they travel do measure the importance of BFVs in the social and ritual rather than functional realm. They cite distances of between 600–3000 km in down-the-line trade for BFVs which have been recorded ethnographically. They also note the tautology in the equation of distance and value (1991, 13). By travelling far an exchange item is automatically transformed from being mundane to being special (Gould 1980, 142–3), as in the case of European glass beads in the exchange systems of Native North Americans.

But where does this transition in value occur, the passage from local to exotic, and why and how do the distances vary? This is not an easy question to answer; and certainly tabulating the distances items travel from either archaeological or ethnographic examples, plotting and comparing the shape of fall-off curves, will not identify the local-exotic threshold among mobile foragers. Consequently the mechanisms and significance of exchange will remain obscure until the Neolithic, agriculture and settled life.

Féblot-Augustins and Perlès (1991) argue that what need to be understood are the contexts which require the transformation in value. But can we predict in which social and ecological contexts this conversion from local to exotic occurs and the types of materials involved in the process?

Continental exchange in Australia

I will attempt such predictions by examining exchange in Australia, the continent of hunters and gatherers in prehistory. Exchange systems have been studied by McBryde (1978; 1986; 1988) in her seminal work on the Victorian greenstone axe quarries and Lake Eyre region and by Mulvaney in his paper on the chains of connection which criss-crossed the continent (1976). These chains are a material aspect of the songlines which linked Aborigines by partnerships and alliances across large distances (Moyle 1983). These relations were supported by the transfer of goods as well as ownership of songs, or parts of them, which were an essential means of recognizing and celebrating the tracks of the Dreamtime ancestors who called the world into being.

The first step in examining the contexts of exchange in Australia is to recognize the great social diversity within the continent — diversity stemming in part from ecology. While the Dreamtime was ubiquitous as a system of belief this should not imply similarity in societies or customs. Neither should the European

perspective of an apparent uniformity among some aspects of the material culture confuse the political reality of the continent. There existed at the level of social organization (including exchange) enormous diversity within the uniformity — probably best revealed in the proliferation of languages.

As proposed by Stanner (1965), and recently examined by Peterson (1986) in his work on territorial organization, much of the social variation can be interpreted as a systematic transformation of common principles. Stanner proposed the concepts of estate (the religious core of a local group of about 18–75 people) and range (the area from which supplies, including food, were obtained). It was Stanner's contention that the spatial relationship between estate and range varied with ecology. Where resources were plentiful then estate and range came together, where resources were poor (which usually means rainfall and the availability of permanent water) then ranges would increase and most importantly, overlap (Fig. 4.2).

It is instructive to consider these territorial relations in terms of the local-exotic threshold. In rich areas distances are highly constrained while in poor regions there is the opportunity for enormous differentiation in the distances from which items might be obtained and returned to the estate area. To the extent they were picked up by the members of the local estate while out foraging through their range, however, they remain local. This suggests that everything is in fact local unless the involvement of strangers can be demonstrated. This is a simple but important point — social and spatial distance are not the same thing.

How can this conclusion help to examine exchange? What is needed is an appreciation of how the systematic transformation of social and spatial relations results in the definition of strangers, outsiders to the concerns of the local group. Peterson provides the following assessment of how Aboriginal societies change along a resource gradient (Table 4.2).

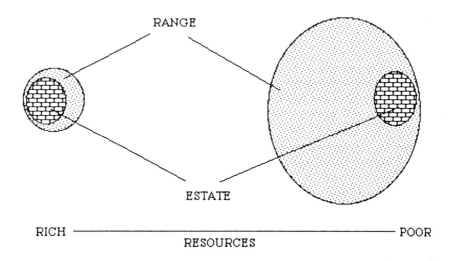

Figure 4.2. The variable relation between estate and range on an ecological gradient

Table 4.2. Resource quality, population density and social traits, after Peterson 1986, fig. 6:5

Resources	Persons per km²	Integration	Ties to land	Marriage	
Poor	1:200 (Pintupi)	generational moities	conception	monogamy	INCLUSIVE
Medium	1:86 (Walpiri, Pitjantjatjara)	patrilineal generational moities	section/ sub-section managers		
Rich	1:20 (Yolngu) 1:4 (Kurnai)	none	descent groups	polygany	EXCLUSIVE

The point to appreciate is that in those areas such as the deserts, where conditions stretched sociality to the limit, the emphasis was on inclusion of people within groups and networks (Cane 1984; 1990). The reverse obtained in areas such as Arnhem Land (Peterson 1986), coastal Queensland (Brayshaw 1990) where population densities could reach 1 person per km², the Murray River corridor (Pardoe 1988) and southeast Victoria (Lourandos 1977; Pardoe 1990). In many of these areas exclusion frequently formed the principle of organization between territorial groups (Pardoe 1990, 61).

How does the local-exotic distinction for raw materials operate along this resource gradient with its expected changes in inclusion and exclusion?

Exchange in areas with poor resources

The Pintupi live in a very harsh area of the western desert (Cane 1984; 1990) where population densities of around 1 person per 200 km² are found in the area of the Stansmore Ranges. Within his study area Cane found a tremendous overlap in foraging ranges and consequently no territoriality between different estate groups. Raw material sources are distributed throughout the area and no stone used in manufacturing artefacts is found more than 40–50 km away from its source. White chalcedony was the most prized raw material because of its flaking quality, but for all raw materials the proportion of debitage decreased in sites the further away they were from a major source. Large cores were found within 10 km of source, few were discarded between 10–17 km away, while more than 25 km away saw a substantial increase in the discard of small, worked out, cores (1984, 243–4, fig. 9.6a). The distribution of stone from the sources provided an exceptional correlation (1984, 252–3) with the movement of people between their dry and wet season campsites. The presence of visitors, sometimes from several hundred kilometres away, is possibly indicated by other, exotic, raw materials in sites at the northern and southern edges of the study area (1984, 255 & table 9.3).

Other arid areas, such as northern Queensland, produce very similar results although at less extreme

low population densities, probably ranging between 1 person per 50–80 km². In an archaeological study at Lawn Hill, Hiscock (1986) has demonstrated a *rationing* model for raw material use. He argues that as stone was carried from quarries so it was increasingly rationed to maximize use before a return to the quarry was necessary. Once again the distances for the discussion of local are informative. Hiscock has two source areas for cherts and greywackes 15–19 km apart (1986, 180). The difference in quality between the two raw materials is shown in Table 4.3.

Table 4.3. Working properties of chert and greywacke and their differential use, after Hiscock 1986

Chert	Greywacke
softer	brittle
no cortex	cortex
130 mm	300–400 mm nodule size
which leads to	
no preparation	preparation flakes
used for backed blades	not used for backed blades
used for tula adze flakes	used for unifacial and bifacial points due to size of material

The eight sites at Lawn Hill are no more than 17.6 km from one or other of the two source areas. Over such short distances Hiscock is able to show that proportions of raw materials, size of cores and flakes all decrease with distance, irrespective of raw material, while secondary retouch (i.e. the number of artefacts) increases with distance from source (Figs. 4.3–4.5). Assemblage variation is therefore adequately explained as the product of raw material rationing (1986, 188).

Elsewhere, in the semi-arid regions of Western New South Wales there is no naturally occurring stone in the landscape. Webb (in press) has found deliberate caching of material, beginning in the late Pleistocene. The landscape was stocked with silcrete and quartzite cobbles from sources a minimum of 40 km away and

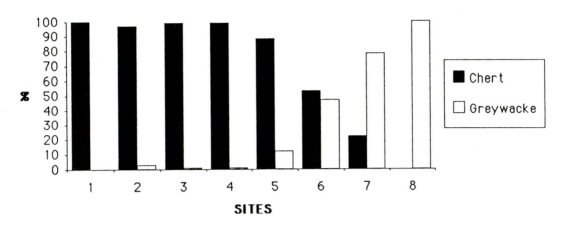

Figure 4.3. *The changing proportion of raw materials on sites at Lawn Hill, Northwest Queensland, as a function of distance from the respective sources, after Hiscock 1986*

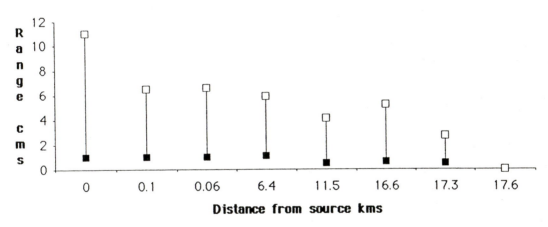

Figure 4.4. *The size-ranges of chert flakes from sites at Lawn Hill, Northwest Queensland, as a function of distance from source, after Hiscock 1986*

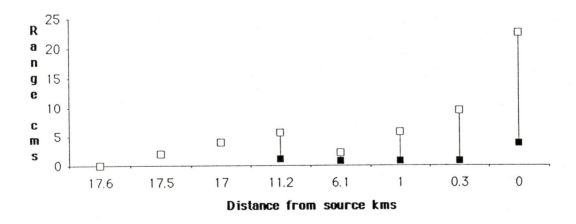

Figure 4.5. *The size-ranges of greywacke flakes from sites at Lawn Hill, Northwest Queensland, as a function of distance from source, after Hiscock 1986*

generally between 60–80 km distant. Rationing behaviour then proceeded from these caches.

These archaeological examples, from a range of resource-poor environments with low population densities, should fall toward the inclusive end of the spectrum of social relations which are systematically altered by the prevailing ecology (Table 4.2). The conclusion is that the distances reported here for the transport of stone, either as lumps or artefacts, and varying between 5 and 80 km, are all local in scale, as defined by the social context of inclusion. This includes the ethnographic example of the Pintupi.

A final example emphasizes the point about local scale. In an arid region west of Alice Springs in the territory of the Pitjantjatjara (Table 4.2), Gould excavated large numbers of adzes made on exotic stones (1980, 141–59). These exotics came from more than 40 km away and were inferior in quality to the local white chert. He explains these as 'righteous rocks' used in a trading network whose function was to ensure that resources were shared in an uncertain and risky environment. Davidson (1988) has questioned this interpretation by exposing the ethnocentric problem of value (referred to earlier) when deciding on local and exotic. He points out that Gould has ignored the key observation that his exotic rocks are worn-out adze slugs. They are neither items still with some use-life nor lumps of raw material waiting to be knapped. They are there because people visited the site and threw away worn-out tools, as expected in the Geneste principle outlined above. It is unlikely that spent flakes were traded down the line as a symbol of the principle of inter-group and inter-regional sharing. In this context it is also unlikely, as Davidson argues, that the visitors were also strangers; rather they formed part of the pervasive inclusive system of social relations in such ecologically harsh environments.

These 'righteous rocks' and the cobbles studied by Webb raise a general issue of whether the distributions of materials result from embedded systems of procurement or rather from exchange for raw materials. I believe at these local scales, and in the general site and landscape contexts where the materials are found, it will be difficult to distinguish the mechanism by which they were obtained. The unmodified cobbles cannot be interpreted in terms of inter-group exchange for raw materials. They could just as easily have been brought to lakes Menindee and Cawndilla as a result of foraging in the surrounding ranges. As such they would be a classic example of embedded procurement (Webb in press). The same would apply to finished artefacts unless, as Torrence reminds us (1986), the quarry had been identified and the range of knapping decisions unravelled. Féblot-Augustins and Perlès (1991) identify weapons — spear points — as likely candidates in their category of prestige goods, and hence items for exchange, among foragers. However, any archaeological interpretation of the spear points from the Ngilipitji

quarry in Arnhem Land, described by Donald Thomson (1949; Jones & White 1988) in his classic study of forager exchange, would be faced with similar problems of interpretation to Gould's 'righteous rocks', unless they were excavated at much greater distances from the quarry than any in these local systems.

Exchange in areas with rich resources

The same pattern of local rationing can be seen in areas with richer resources and higher population densities. For example, Byrne (1980) studied distributions from archaeological scatters on the Lower Murchison (Western Australia). He divided his analysis into the following distances, 0–2.5 km, 2.5–10 km and 10–27 km, in order to examine the distribution of material from source.

In a sub-tropical coastal survey in southeast Queensland, McNiven (1990; 1991; 1992) identified two sources of raw material at either end of the 50 km-long Cooloola beach and a third silcrete source 25 km inland. The stone assemblages from the coastal midden sites showed very strong rationing behaviour. Four major trends corresponded with increasing distance from any one of the sources of raw material:

— a decrease in the proportional use of stone from that source
— a decrease in the total number of stone artefacts discarded from that source
— a decrease in the size of the stone artefacts
— a decrease in the amounts of cortex (McNiven 1990, 338).

Stone artefact rationing thus played a major role in inter-site assemblage variation among the Cooloola sites. Over time the inland silcrete source became very rare in the coastal assemblages which, it is argued, reflects localized population growth following a restructuring of social relations in the Cooloola region (McNiven 1991, 24). This explanation is preferred to a model of intrinsic population increase throughout coastal Queensland in the late Holocene (Hall & Hiscock 1988). Higher population densities may well have changed the estate:range configurations in the region (Fig. 4.2). It appears, however, that at the level of stone procurement there are no clear indications of exclusivity other than some restriction of the spatial scales involved.

Exotic, prestige goods among foragers

Lithic analysis, using the observation that distant raw materials are represented by the later stages of the reduction sequence, can confer the description 'local' on archaeological collections, but not all rocks are local. This is shown by the second class of exchange goods, referred to by Féblot-Augustins and Perlès (1991) as BFVs, the ones which travel great distances.

Once again the key to unravelling the distinction between local and exotic must be specifying social contexts, rather than measuring distances. While the transport distances for some types of raw materials, whether fashioned into artefacts or not, may be impressive, it is always possible that the distributions are plotting the movement of individuals as they negotiated through their extended social networks. The correspondence between exotic item and the category of stranger or outsider still needs to be demonstrated.

One possibility is provided by Peterson's social gradient (Table 4.2) with the transformation of inclusive into exclusive (territorial, land holding) systems (Peterson 1986). Understanding this conversion rests, as we have seen, on the premise that the pattern of land ownership is largely conditioned by selective pressure from ecological processes on the organization of foraging (Stanner 1965). Elsewhere, such selection has been studied through technological organization and accounted for by risk-buffering behaviour (Torrence 1989). What I am proposing here is a social and spatial framework to investigate the tactical outcomes, such as the organization of technology, prior to making assumptions about what factors control behaviour.

Against this conceptual background I offer the following two general points. In exclusive systems the function of exotic items in the exchange networks is to pay *membership dues*. They provide a means of establishing insider status through negotiation outside the immediate group. Within the group women are an essential item of exchange, as indicated by the marriage rules (Table 4.2). A system, once described by Woodburn as 'farming the females' (1980), defines and perpetuates the land holding group. Moreover, in such exclusive systems higher population densities and the seasonal aggregation of population around lakes results in some degree of economic defendibility for critical seasonal resources (Dyson-Hudson & Smith 1978). Shifting political alliances between tightly packed clans, each in its own estate, are expected.

In terms of material culture it is not surprising that in exclusive systems there is an accent on death spears and weapons, including stone hatchets. The distances these artefacts travel are impressive. McBryde's reconstruction of the greenstone quarries in Victoria records some hatchets travelling 800 km from Mt William (1986, 79) while the average distance from the same quarry was 228 km (1978, table 1). McBryde favours an interpretation of small scale, individual and group transactions where the direction of exchange is determined by affiliation, and where social and ceremonial factors have as much significance as technological and economic elements (1986, 78).

McBryde has also shown how the movement of hatchets correlates very well with language groupings, in other words *within* the network of potential allies. The absence of axes among the Kurnai, whose country, in southeastern Victoria, abuts the Kulin where most of the greenstone quarries are located, is particularly striking.[1]

But how exclusive should we expect foraging systems in Victoria to be? The Kurnai had high population densities (Table 4.2; Lourandos 1977), but these were probably exceeded by the groups which lived along the fertile Murray River to the north. As described by Pardoe, 'the River Murray is a 2000 km [fertile] corridor that winds through a semi-arid to arid hinterland' (Pardoe 1990, 60). Moreover, citing Birdsell (1953) the population densities for tribes in this River Nile-like strip were 20 to 40 times greater than those of non-riverine populations in the same region (Pardoe 1990, 61). The Murray corridor has many cemeteries, interpreted by Pardoe (1988) as symbols of land-holding, and evidence for an exclusive system of tribal territories (Pardoe 1990, fig. 4).

The low population densities in the arid areas immediately to the north and south of the Murray form a marked contrast to the high population densities in southern Victoria, such as the Kulin and Kurnai where the axe quarries are found. It is interesting to observe the selective way axes from these greenstone quarries penetrated the exclusive systems along the Murray river (McBryde 1978, figs. 2–4) even though Mt William lies only 150 km south of the river and Mt Camel even closer.

The second general point refers to alternative ecological conditions. In the resource-poor areas it is not membership dues but rather *insurance premiums* that such exotic exchange supports. Gould (1980) was essentially correct but used the wrong data. Once again McBryde points the way with her work in Lake Eyre — a very harsh arid region. Here was one of the great exchange routes through Australia with quarries for grinding slabs, hatchets, ochre and areas where the narcotic pituri was grown and processed (Watson 1983; McBryde 1988, 260–1). Direct visits were made to the owners of the quarries and pituri fields. These involved regular, direct procurement of 400 to 650 km (McBryde 1988, 266, 271). While skills and ownership of such important resources may have been local, the social effects for an inclusive system were very widespread.

Local hominid networks

So what have we learnt in this brief excursion through some of the Australian data about hunter-gatherer exchange systems? How much closer are we to understanding something about the terms local and exotic on prehistoric timescales?

I hope I have shown that a consideration of local and exotic, while difficult to define for mobile foragers, leads us to interesting questions about social and spatial dimensions. Indeed, the interest in defining such terms lies not in fixing distances, from either ethnographic or archaeological data, but rather in identifying a common structure in foraging spatial behaviour, past and present.

I refer to this common structure as a *local hominid network*, based on the same observations between space, resources and mobility which underpinned site catchment analysis and the territorial analysis of prehistoric locational behaviour (Vita-Finzi & Higgs 1970). A local hominid network is a basic spatial unit encompassing subsistence and social behaviour. It contains other hominids, non-hominid competitors and resources. From an archaeological perspective it implies both a site and off-site focus to regional analysis. In terms of size the evidence from rationing behaviour and the distribution of stone resources points to a radius of 40 km, roughly equivalent to two days' walking, as a significant distance for a local hominid network. An upper limit of 80–100 km is also indicated. It is possible to understand variation in the size of local hominid networks due to ecological circumstances.

Furthermore, the archaeological evidence for the distribution of raw material points to local hominid networks as an adjunct to behaviour which is tool-assisted (Binford 1989), rather than culturally mediated. The evidence for rationing behaviour from the Middle and Upper Pleistocene (Dibble & Rolland 1992; Rolland & Dibble 1990; Geneste 1988a & b; Roebroeks *et al.* 1988; Turq 1992; Gamble 1986a), which involves 'archaic' *Homo sapiens*, follows the same principles of distance, abundance and quality of raw material as Hiscock and Cane discovered in Australia where only modern *Homo sapiens* is known. At these local distances we are recovering a basic aspect of behaviour as hominids, of whatever evolutionary grade, optimize an aspect of their provisioning strategies. For example, Henry (1992) has recently discussed the use of raw materials from two Middle Palaeolithic sites on the Jordanian Plateau. These are possibly 65,000 years old. At Tor Faraj up to 95 per cent of the raw material comes from 16–20 km away. Cortical flakes, cores and primary knapping debris are common. At Tor Sabiha the primary knapping was largely restricted to cherts obtained from no more than 2 km away (1992, 152). Henry expresses surprise at these results, since initial knapping debris is expected to decline away from the raw material source. While this same effect of distance decay was shown by both Hiscock (1986; see Figs. 4.3–4.5) and McNiven (1990) it was in the context of competing raw material outcrops. Moreover, Henry's distances fall well below Geneste's threshold for the absence of cores as a factor of distance (Geneste 1988b; see Table 4.1). I would prefer to interpret the Tor Faraj data as illustrating a local hominid network rather than use the data to measure humanness and planning depth, thereby inferring for its Middle Palaeolithic inhabitants a logistical strategy which would have demanded 'a mature "operational" (Piaget) cognitive level' (Henry 1992, 159). The Tor Faraj hominids were simply doing what comes naturally — participating in a local hominid network. Consequently, raw material rationing within such a network should not be taken to imply either curation or expedient use of raw material and any implications this might have for the comparison of archaic and modern *Homo sapiens*.

A useful distinction can be drawn between the *local hominid network*, where life routines, assisted by tools, are played out sequentially, and the construction of *social landscapes*, where local networks are linked together by negotiation. While all hominids share the organizational framework of a local network, only modern humans have elaborated and reticulated them into diverse social landscapes. The complexities of estate and range relations (Peterson 1986) are one such example. The sequencing of social and subsistence life are now played out in parallel. A major historical difference between the two systems of networks and landscapes was the activity of exchange which, I would argue, starts about 50,000 years ago and can be recognized by the appearance of the exotic BFVs.

Conclusion

What does this opposition of local hominid networks and social landscapes tell us about the construction and evolution of social life? Prior to the appearance of exotic exchange items I would argue that the principle of social life was always one of exclusion. Life was local. Now with the BFVs, which include for the first time stones from socially 'exotic' contexts (i.e. obtained from, or through negotiation with outsiders), there is the *possibility* for both inclusion and exclusion. The possibility of both systems does not however imply that they were always present. For example, some of the perceived differences between the Pleistocene and Holocene in Australian prehistory (White & O'Connell 1982) may be due to the weaker development of inclusive systems in the former period. The possibility of inclusive systems among modern humans is not sufficient reason for assuming their presence. They need to be demonstrated, as indicated in this paper.

Neither can we assume, as Table 4.2 implies, that inclusive to exclusive systems currently exist as a continuum. It is likely that the transition is abrupt rather than gradual. This has been commented upon many times in descriptions of contemporary hunters and gatherers (e.g. Steward 1936; Woodburn 1980; Keeley 1988). In prehistory the evolution from exclusive to exclusive *and* inclusive foraging societies was probably also punctuated; a bifurcation rather than a seamless progression. There is not space here to pursue this interesting point and its implications for modern human origins. It will however be pertinent to use the insight to examine the difference between exchange among foragers and farmers. The Australian evidence, especially the Lake Eyre systems, questions Perlès' model (1989) that the transition in exchange terms between the Mesolithic and Neolithic is that long distance exchange moves from the symbolic to large quantities of utilitarian objects. Australia managed this transition without requiring agriculture. Hatchets and grindstones, paint and drugs moved in considerable quantities. The only difference is demographic as suggested earlier (Perlès 1989, 11). The revolution which set us on the course for civilization was not Neolithic but came much earlier with the advent of modern behaviour (Gamble 1986b).

The choices for the later prehistory of so-called complex societies are plain. Either trade and exchange are unimportant (Binford 1983) to explain social change, or monuments such as Stonehenge with its amalgamation of local (sarsen) and exotic (bluestone), the equivalent of chipped stone scraper and polished greenstone hatchet, are the natural outcome of the foraging way of life as the local hominid network and social landscape were formalised with monuments.

Acknowledgements

Discussions and information supplied by Elaine Morris, Robin Torrence, Robert Whallon, Joanna Freslov, Cathie Webb, Ian McNiven, Isabel McBryde and the staff and students at the Department of Archaeology, LaTrobe University are all gratefully acknowledged. The comments and papers, published and unpublished of Catherine Perlès were extremely helpful and I take full responsibility for any misunderstandings. The research was supported by a grant from the British Academy and the Sir Robert Menzies Australian Studies Centre.

Note

1. There may, however, be another reason than ethnographically-recorded hostility for this distribution. The Kulin and Kurnai lie on either side of the major watershed which, as Peterson (1976) and others (Gamble 1986, 71) have noted, is the closest we get to a 'natural' unit of analysis among foragers.

References

Binford, L.R., 1983. *In Pursuit of the Past*. London: Thames & Hudson

Binford, L.R., 1989. Isolating the transition to cultural adaptations: an organizational approach, in *The Emergence of Modern Humans. Biocultural Adaptations in the Later Pleistocene*, ed. E. Trinkaus. Cambridge: Cambridge University Press, 18–41

Birdsell, J.B., 1953. Some environmental and cultural factors influencing the structuring of Australian Aboriginal populations. *The American Naturalist* 87, 171–207

Bordes, F., 1961. Mousterian cultures in France. *Science* 134, 803–10

Brayshaw, H., 1990. *Well Beaten Paths: Aborigines of the Herbert Rurdekin District, North Queensland. An Ethnographic and Archaeological Study*. Department of History, James Cook University of North Queensland

Byrne, D., 1980. Dynamics of dispersion: the place of silcrete in archaeological assemblages from the Lower Murchison, Western Australia. *Archaeology and Physical Anthropology in Oceania* 15, 110–19

Cane, S., 1984. *Desert Camps*. Canberra: Ph.D. Dissertation. Australian National University

Cane, S., 1990. Desert demography: a case study of pre-contact aboriginal densities in the western desert of Australia, in *Hunter-Gatherer Demography: Past and Present*, eds B. Meehan & N. White. Sydney: University of Sydney, Oceania Monographs, 149–59

Clark, J.G.D., 1965. Traffic in stone axe and adze blades. *Economic History Review*, 2nd series, 18, 1–28

Davidson, I., 1988. The naming of parts: ethnography and the interpretation of Australian prehistory, in *Archaeology with Ethnography: an Australian Perspective*, eds B. Meehan & R. Jones. Canberra: Research Center for Pacific Studies, 17–32

Dibble, H.L., & Rolland, N., 1992. On assemblage variability in the Middle Palaeolithic of western Europe: history, perspectives, and a new synthesis, in *The Middle Palaeolithic: Adaptation, Behavior, and Variability*, eds H.L. Dibble & P. Mellars. Philadelphia: University Museum, 1–28

Dyson-Hudson, R., & Smith, E.A., 1978. Human territoriality: an ecological reassessment. *American Anthropologist* 80, 21–41

Féblot-Augustins, J., & Perlès, C., 1991. Perspectives ethnoarchéologiques sur les échanges à longue distance. Unpublished manuscript. Colloques 'Ethnoarchéologie' Antibes

Gamble, C.S., 1986a. *The Palaeolithic Settlement of Europe*. Cambridge: Cambridge University Press

Gamble, C.S., 1986b. Hunter-gatherers and the origin of states, in *States in History*, ed. J. A. Hall. Oxford: Basil Blackwell, 22–47

Geneste, J-M., 1988a. Systèmes d'approvisionnement en matières premières au paléolithique moyen et au paléolithique supérieur en Aquitaine. *L'Homme de Néandertal* 8, 61–70

Geneste, J-M., 1988b. Les industries de la Grotte Vaufrey: technologie du débitage, économie et circulation de la matière première lithique, in *La Grotte Vaufrey à Cenac et Saint-Julien (Dordogne), Paléoenvironments, Chronologie et Activités humaines*, ed. J.-P. Rigaud. Mémoires de la Société Préhistorique Française 19, 441–518

Gerlach, C., & Mason, O.K., 1992. Calibrated radiocarbon dates and cultural interaction in the western Arctic. *Arctic Anthropology* 29, 54–81

Gould, R.A., 1980. *Living Archaeology*. Cambridge: Cambridge University Press

Henry, D.O., 1992. Transhumance during the late Levantine Mousterian, in *The Middle Palaeolithic: Adaptation, Behavior, and Variability*, eds H.L. Dibble & P. Mellars. Philadelphia: University Museum, 143–62

Hiscock, P., 1986. Raw material rationing as an explanation of assemblage differences: a case study of Lawn Hill, Northwest Queensland, in *Archaeology at Anzaas 1984*, ed. G. Ward. Canberra: Australian Institute of Aboriginal Studies, 178–90

Jones, R., & White, N., 1988. Point blank: stone tool manufacture at the Ngilipitji Quarry, Arnhem Land, 1981, in *Archaeology with Ethnography: an Australian Perspective*, eds. B. Meehan & R. Jones. Canberra: Research Center for Pacific Studies, 51–87

Keeley, L.H., 1988. Hunter-gatherer economic complexity and 'population pressure': a cross-cultural analysis. *Journal of Anthropological Archaeology* 7, 373–411

Kozłowski, J.K., (ed.) 1982. *Excavations in the Bacho-Kiro Cave, Bulgaria (Final Report)*. Warsaw: Paristwowe Wydarunictwo, Naukowe

Lourandos, H., 1977. Aboriginal spatial organization and population: south-western Victoria reconsidered. *Archaeology and Physical Anthropology in Oceania* 12, 202–25

Malina, J., 1970. Die jungpaläolithische steinindustrie aus Mähren, ihre Rohstoffe und ihre Patina. *Acta Praehistorica et Archaeologica* 1, 157–73

McBryde, I., 1978. Wil-im-ee Moor-ring: or, where do axes come from? *Mankind* 11, 354–82

McBryde, I., 1986. Artefacts, language and social interaction: a case study from south-eastern Australia. In, *Stone Age Prehistory*, eds G. Bailey & P. Callow. Cambridge: Cambridge University Press, 77–93

McBryde, I., 1988. Goods from another country: exchange networks and the people of the Lake Eyre basin. In *Archaeology to 1788*, eds J.Mulvaney & P.White. Sydney: Waddon Associates, 253–73

McNiven, I.J., 1990. Prehistoric aboriginal settlement and subsistence in the Cooloola region, coastal southeast Queensland. Ph.D. Thesis. University of Queensland

McNiven, I.J., 1991. Teewah beach: new evidence for Holocene coastal occupation in southeast Queensland. *Australian Archaeology* 33, 14–27

McNiven, I.J., 1992. Bevel-edged tools from coastal southeast Queensland. *Antiquity* 66, 701–9

Moyle, R., 1983. Songs, ceremonies and sites: the Agharringa case, in *Aborigines, Land and Land Rights*, eds N. Peterson & M. Langton. Canberra: Australian Institute of Aboriginal Studies, 66–93

Mulvaney, D.J., 1976. 'The chain of connection': the material evidence, in *Tribes and Boundaries in Australia*, ed. N. Peterson. Canberra: Australian Institute of Aboriginal Studies, 72–94

Pardoe, C., 1988. The cemetery as symbol. *Archaeology in Oceania* 23, 1–16

Pardoe, C., 1990. The demographic basis of human evolution in southeastern Australia, in *Hunter-Gatherer Demography: Past and Present*, eds B. Meehan & N. White. University of Sydney, Oceania Monographs, 59–70

Perlès, C., 1989. *From Stone Procurement to Neolithic Society in Greece*. David Skomp Distinguished Lectures in Anthropology. Department of Anthropology, Indiana University.

Perlès, C., 1992. In search of lithic strategies: a cognitive approach to prehistoric chipped stone assemblages, in *Representations in Archaeology*, eds J.-C. Gardin & C. Peebles. Bloomington & Indianapolis: Indiana University Press, 223–47

Peterson, N., 1986. *Australian Territorial Organisation*. University of Sydney, Oceania Monograph 30

Roebroeks, W., Kolen, J., & Rensink, E., 1988. Planning depth, anticipation and the organization of Middle Palaeolithic technology: the 'archaic natives' meet Eve's descendants. *Helinium* 28, 17–34

Rolland, N., & Dibble, H., 1990. A new synthesis of Middle Palaeolithic variability. *American Antiquity* 55, 480–99

Soffer, O., 1985. *The Upper Palaeolithic of the Central Russian Plain*. New York: Academic Press

Stanner, W.E.H., 1965. Aboriginal territorial organisation: estate, range, domain and regime. *Oceania* 36, 1–26

Steward, J.H., 1936. The economic and social basis of primitive bands, in *Essays in Anthropology Presented to A.L.Kroeber*, ed. R.H. Lowie. Berkeley: University of California Press, 331–50

Tavoso, A., 1984. Réflexions sur l'économie en matières premières au moustérien. *Bulletin de la Société Préhistorique Française* 81, 79–82

Thomas, J., 1991. *Rethinking the Neolithic*. Cambridge: Cambridge University Press

Thomson, D.F., 1949. *Economic Structure and the Ceremonial Exchange Cycle in Arnhem Land*. Melbourne: MacMillan

Torrence, R., 1986. *Production and Exchange of Stone Tools*. Cambridge: Cambridge University Press

Torrence, R., (ed.) 1989. *Time, Energy and Stone Tools*. Cambridge: Cambridge University Press

Turq, A., 1992. Raw material and technological studies of the Quina Mousterian in Périgord, in *The Middle Palaeolithic: Adaptation, Behavior, and Variability*, eds H.L. Dibble & P. Mellars. Philadelphia: University Museum, 75–86

Vita-Finzi, C., & Higgs, E.S., 1970. Prehistoric economy in the Mount Carmel area of Palestine, site catchment analysis. *Proceedings of the Prehistoric Society* 36, 1–37

Watson, P., 1983. *This Precious Foliage*. University of Sydney: Oceania Monographs 26

Webb, C., in press. The lithification of a sandy environment. *Archaeology in Oceania*

Woodburn, J., 1980. Hunters and gatherers today and reconstruction of the past, in *Soviet and Western Anthropology*, ed. E. Gellner. London: Duckworth, 95–117

5

Neolithic Quarries, the Exchange of Axes and Social Control in the Southern Vosges

Pierre Pétrequin, Françoise Jeudy & Christian Jeunesse

Following the recent discovery of Neolithic quarries for black stone in the south-eastern Vosges, we suggest a view of the production system for polished stone axes during the Neolithic. In Middle Neolithic II the distribution of extraction, roughout manufacturing and polishing sites shows a division of labour, in which certain strategic tasks (the flaking of large axes, the supply of implements into exchange networks) were the subject of clear competition and political control (high status burials with roughouts or large polished axes, hoards of roughouts and finished implements). We then define the relationship between the distribution networks for polished axes and the spatial organisation of the hierarchy of contemporary settlements, dominated by hilltop villages and fortified enclosures. The wider distribution of polished implements of black stone from the Vosges, especially from the quarries of Plancher-les-Mines between 4100 and 3700 BC, seems closely linked to the establishment and subsequent abandonment of large hilltop enclosures. Exchange between these central places across different stylistic provinces (Burgundian Middle Neolithic, Munzingen, Cortaillod, formative Pfyn) in effect perpetuated an older network, established at the end of the Rössen culture, when a certain stylistic unity prevailed along the eastern Burgundy-Lake Constance axis.

Après la récente découverte de carrières néolithiques de roches noires dans le sud-est des Vosges, on propose une présentation des chaînes opératoires de fabrication de lames de pierre polie pendant le Néolithique. La répartition des sites d'extraction, de préparation des ébauches et de polissage des lames montre, au Néolithique moyen II, une segmentation de la chaîne opératoire, où certaines tâches stratégiques (le débitage de grandes lames, l'alimentation des réseaux d'échange) font l'objet d'une compétition et d'un contrôle politique évidents (sépultures privilégiées avec ébauches ou grandes lames polies, dépôts d'ébauches et de lames). Les rapports sont ensuite précisés entre les réseaux de diffusion des lames polies et l'organisation spatiale des habitats hiérarchisés au profit de villages de hauteur et d'enceintes fortifiées. La plus grande diffusion des haches en roches noires vosgiennes, et en particulier à partir des carrières de Plancher-les-Mines entre 4100 et 3700 av. J.C., apparaît intimement liée à la mise en place puis à la désaffection des grandes enceintes de hauteur. Les échanges entre ces places centrales au travers de provinces stylistiques différentes (Néolithique Moyen Bourguignon, Munzingen, Cortaillod, période formative du Pfyn) auraient en fait prolongé dans le temps un réseau plus ancien, mis en place à la fin du Rössen, au moment d'une certaine unité stylistique selon l'axe Bourgogne orientale-lac de Constance.

Introduction

We intend to synthesise information on the manufacture of an essential tool, the polished stone axe which, technically, forms the basis of Neolithic social reproduction; on the distribution of these axes within exchange networks which were in the course of transformation during the Middle Neolithic; on the phenomena of social intensification and the concentration of population in enclosures which could be built only with a long collective investment of labour. We will, in other words, ask what were the relationships between the raw material sources, the exchange networks and the widespread construction of enclosures. We will thus address the question of cultural relations over an area extending from Lake Constance to Burgundy, along the preferred axis for the exchange of black stone axes from the Vosges in Middle Neolithic II (Fig. 5.1).

Notes: *'Axe' is used in this paper in a general sense, without prejudice as to whether the implements in question were hafted as axes or adzes. Chronology is expressed in calibrated radiocarbon years BC.*

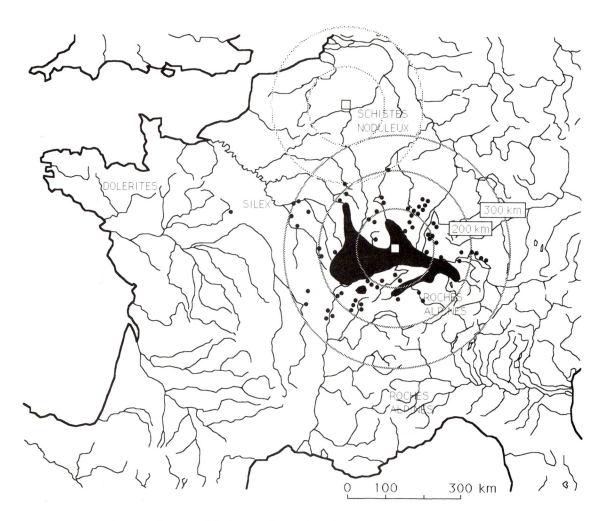

Figure 5.1. The overall distribution of polished axes of stone from the south-eastern Vosges (mudstones, volcanic tuffs and nodular schists from Plancher-les-Mines and Sondernach). In black: areas where black stone amounts to more than 50% of polished axes dating from Middle Neolithic II. The dots indicate sites where black stone is present but in lower percentages. The distribution of implements from the Vosges follows a rough east-west axis, with extensions into the valleys of the Marne, the Moselle, the Aar and the upper Rhine.

From an early stage, prehistorians applied the geologically incorrect term 'aphanite' to a group of fine-grained black rocks which took on a greyish to yellowish patina when exposed to the air. From the end of the nineteenth century onwards there are descriptions of polished stone axes made from aphanitic rocks likely to outcrop in the Devonian-Dinantian formations of the southern Vosges between the upper Moselle and the Belfort Gap, but not more precisely located (Piningre 1974).

In 1989 we succeeded in locating a large group of quarries at Plancher-les-Mines (Haute-Saône), in the upper valley of the Rahin (Fig. 5.2). The 'aphanites', in fact quartz mudstones (Diethelm 1989), were worked at quarry faces or in successive funnel-shaped pits in the upper and lower valley of a stream called the Marbranche; the workings have left thousands of cubic metres of waste on the valley sides and in the stream bed. After three years of survey and petrological identifications we think that Plancher-les-Mines provided most of the polished quartz mudstone axes that were

exported over distances of up to more than 200 km at the turn of the fifth and fourth millennia BC.

Chronology of techniques

The polished quartz mudstone axes of Plancher-les-Mines were made, with rare exceptions, on blanks which made it possible to orient the cutting edge perpendicular to the bedding planes of the stone. Over time, this technique led to a preference for long, flaked axes, the form best suited to the orientation in which the rock is used. In economic and technological terms this makes for the most efficient use of slabs and blocks of black stone, provided that it is accompanied by a high level of skill. There was a case for testing the validity of this general tendency, dictated by the mechanical properties of the stone. In other words, we needed to assess the role played by cultural factors which could counter or favour this general technological tendency, according to period, necessity and needs.

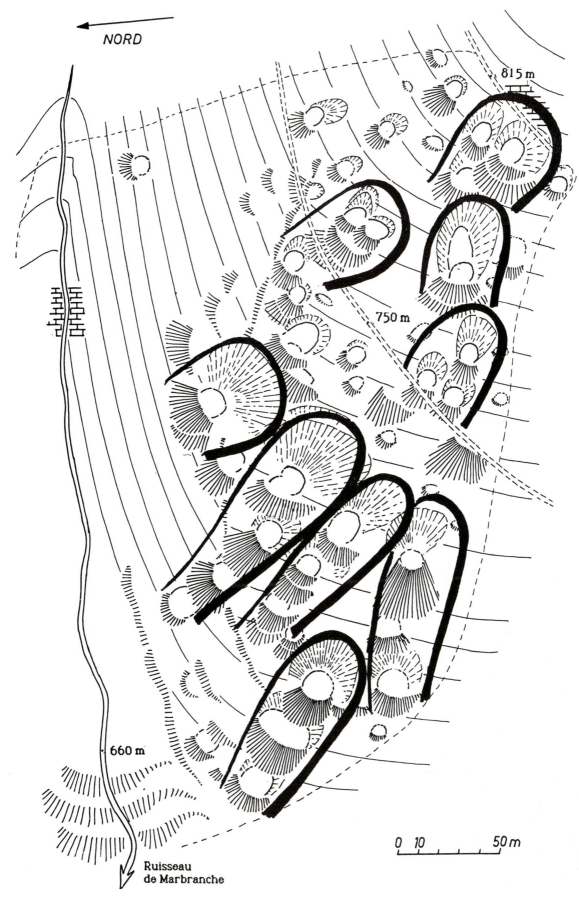

Figure 5.2. Plancher-les-Mines (Haute-Saône). Plan of the quarries on the upper part of the Marbranche stream. The pits in each group were worked successively and aligned on a particular band of raw material, in relation to the geological strata, which here run vertically.

Pierre Pétrequin, Françoise Jeudy & Christian Jeunesse

To determine the evolution of stone-working techniques we studied several thousand pieces of waste and several hundred polished implements from Haute-Alsace, Territoire de Belfort and Haute-Saône (Jeudy 1990). Most of the artefacts came from surface sites, which could have make it difficult to establish a fine chronology. In the event, the clear diagonal patterning of the results (Fig. 5.3) shows that most of these surface sites could represent short-lived axe-manufacturing villages, perhaps lasting for at most two to three generations, and that they could easily be placed in the chronological scheme.

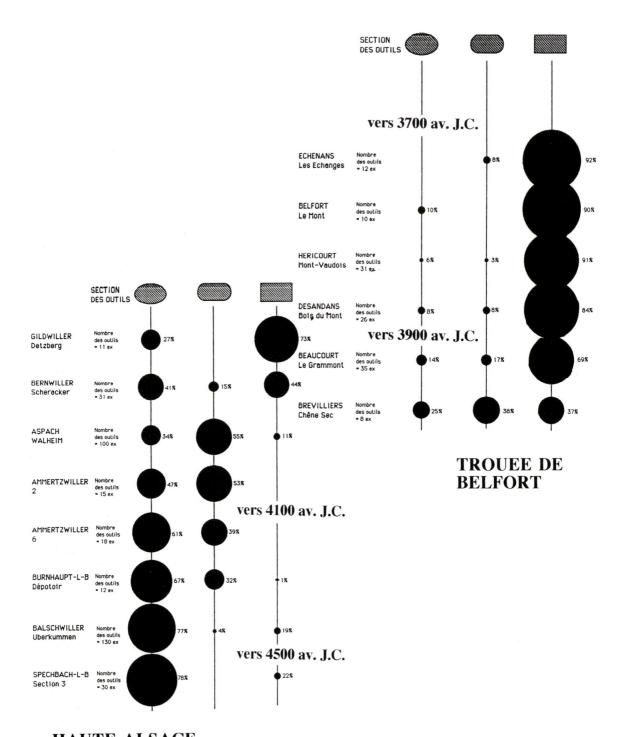

Figure 5.3. Chronological seriation of polished axes of black stone from the Vosges (principally mudstone) in the Altkirch and Belfort regions (left- and right-hand columns respectively). The seriation focuses on the transverse section of the implements in relation to the evolution of manufacturing techniques (Figs. 5.4–5).

In outline, it is possible to define three main groups of axes produced during the Middle Neolithic (Fig. 5.3):

1. Circular- or ovoid-sectioned, typologically later than the Grossgartach culture, at least in Alsace (Lichardus-Itten 1980), and probably current from Rössen times in the Belfort Gap (Pétrequin 1970).
2. Intermediate-sectioned, similar to Breton and Alpine greenstone forms (Giot *et al.* 1977; Cordier & Bocquet 1973). They are also similar to Glis type axes (Speck 1988; Jeunesse 1990), well known in the Rhine valley between Haute Alsace and Lake Constance at the end of the fifth millennium BC. This group of oval-sectioned axes reflects a supra-regional entity probably not unrelated to the emergence of the Chassean.
3. Quadrangular-sectioned, probably produced from the end of the Linearbandkeramik onwards. A fashion for these developed over a wide area *c.* 4000 BC; they derive from the large-scale exploitation of the Plancher-les-Mines quarries and coincide with the maximum geographical expansion of exchange networks.

These three groups of polished axes, identified here by their cross-sections, correspond to technological transformations which accompanied the transition from a production system which favoured pecking to a process where direct percussion was preferred. Beyond the inevitable constraints of the raw material, cultural choices played a large part. There is a clear opposition between:

1. An early phase when production, within the capability of everyone, consisted in imitating techniques applied elsewhere to greenstones or coarse-grained rocks, on which pecking is effective (Fig. 5.4).
2. A later phase, when specialised production called for a far higher level of skill (Fig. 5.5), for increased efficiency of production permitting the exchange of long axes beyond the simple regional circuit. It was also at this time that the practice of sawing the alpine rocks developed in Switzerland, in response to the need for exceptionally large symbol-tools (Pétrequin & Pétrequin 1990).

Marks of individuality and prestige

Whether production systems favoured a slow manufacturing method, easy and within the reach of everyone (like pecking), or whether they favoured a rapid method, certainly reserved for the better knappers (like the flaking of large axes), the makers of polished axes employed distinctive domestic tool-kits. In axe-manufacturing settlements flint tools were rare in the early phases (second half of the fifth millennium BC): where the black stone of the Vosges were worked, flakes and blades were of black quartz mudstone instead of flint. This replacement industry, which implies a certain difficulty in obtaining flint, includes scrapers and even sickle flints (Fig. 5.6).

Furthermore, these makers of polished axes used quartz mudstones to make chisels, normally made on longitudinally sawn longbones elsewhere. These chisels, most of them found in axe-manufacturing villages, increased in frequency as true axes gradually became more important and adzes less so, although adzes nonetheless remained in use in the region, at least until the end of the Middle Neolithic. Also characteristic of the production area are gently curved flakes of roughly triangular outline, only the cutting edge of which is generally polished. Their function is uncertain (scrapers? adzes?) but their geographical distribution clearly relates them to the makers of polished axes.

The distribution of large roughouts in the Belfort Gap and Haute Alsace shows two clear groups: one is centred on Mont Vaudois at Héricourt (Haute-Saône), a short day's walk from Plancher-les-Mines; the other is made up of exceptional pieces in the Sundgau region (Haute Alsace), two days' walk from the nearest extraction sites. In the first case, the prestige of these long roughouts belonged to the producers and in particular to the communities who flaked the stone rather than pecked it. Their level of technological knowledge is implicit in this display of competition between two communities. In the second case, the Sundgau region, the large roughouts reflect the presence of the communities who polished the roughouts produced at the foot of the Vosges (especially the flaked axes of Plancher-les-Mines) and who controlled a good part of the exchange towards the users in northern Switzerland.

Competition is even better evidenced by the longest polished axes, used or ready to be used. This control, and the retention within the region of at least some of the large axes, remained quite rare as long as the level of technological skill was within the reach of all (Fig. 5.7, top): large, ovoid-sectioned polished axes of the period between about 4500 and 4200 BC are found up to 80 km from the outcrops, almost as numerous as in the manufacturing communities. These implements, probably derived from burials like that of Breurey-les-Faverney (Haute-Saône), could distinguish high-ranking men, without any relation to control of a strategic moment in the manufacture of polished axes. On the other hand, with increased levels of production and specialisation at the quarries of Plancher-les-Mines (Fig. 5.7, centre and bottom), the large polished axe came to characterise communities responsible for polishing and communities at the head of exchange networks. Some isolated pieces from this zone could have come from burials, but a good number of them have been found in hoards, of which Bennwihr (Haut-Rhin) is the best-known example (Piningre 1974), alongside others which have long gone unnoted, like Flaxlanden and Willer (Glory 1942). It is even possible that

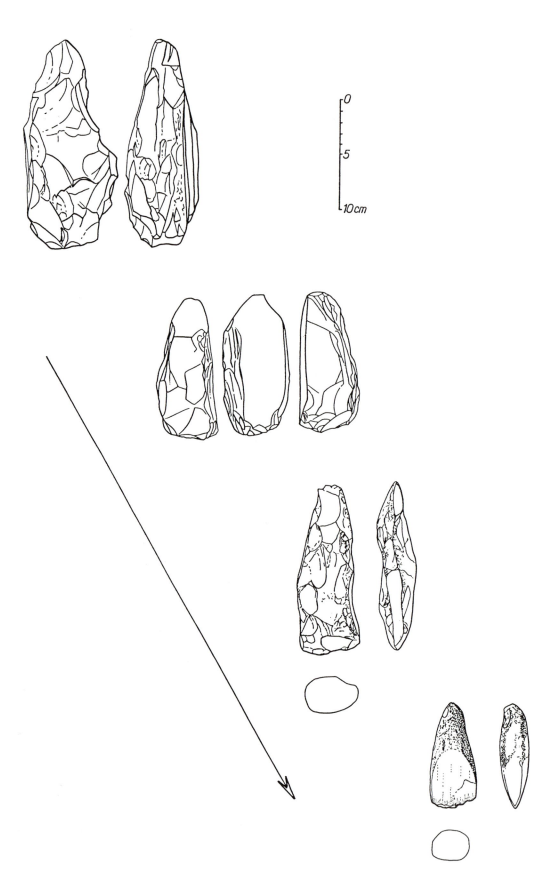

Figure 5.4. Altkirch region: the manufacture of a roughout from a fragment of mudstone by removing small flakes and by pecking. This time-consuming technique was that most frequently used during the early phases of exploitation of the extraction sites. It persisted more-or-less to the end of Middle Neolithic II in the Mulhouse-Altkirch region.

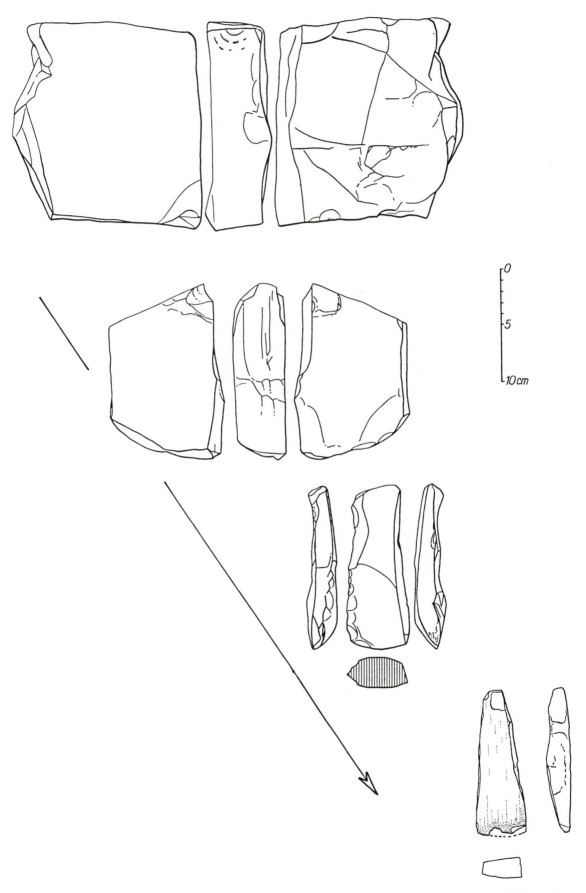

Figure 5.5. Plancher-les-Mines: the production of a quadrangular roughout by flaking a slab of mudstone. This technique, very effective for producing adze blades, was known from the earliest phases of exploitation; it came to be systematically applied as production intensified, especially at Plancher-les-Mines where the quartz mudstones have mechanical properties close to those of flint.

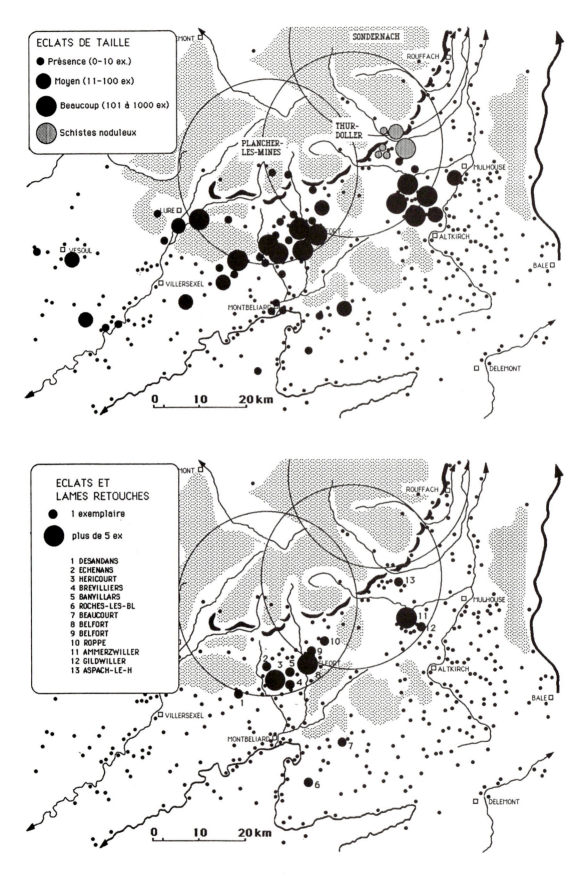

Figure 5.6. From the plateaux of Haute-Saône to Alsace: the distribution of unretouched flakes from roughout manufacture (above) and of retouched implements on flakes or blades (below). It is clear that only those who directly worked the Vosges quarries used flakes and blades of black stone for their domestic tool-kit: scrapers and sickle-flints. The smallest black dots represent all the Neolithic sites known in the region.

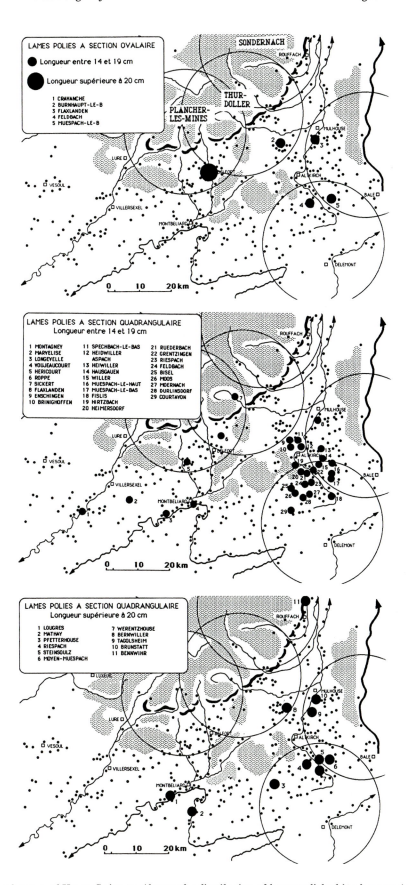

Figure 5.7. From the plateaux of Haute-Saône to Alsace: the distribution of large polished implements (axes and adzes) which could have some prestige value. There is a contrast between areas of roughout production (one day's walk from the quarries) and areas of polishing and outward distribution (two days' walk). In the same way, there is a contrast between the Sundgau region, where the largest polished implements are concentrated, and the west of the Belfort Gap where such pieces are far rarer. These distinctions are attributable to differing social and cultural configurations during MiddleNeolithic II.

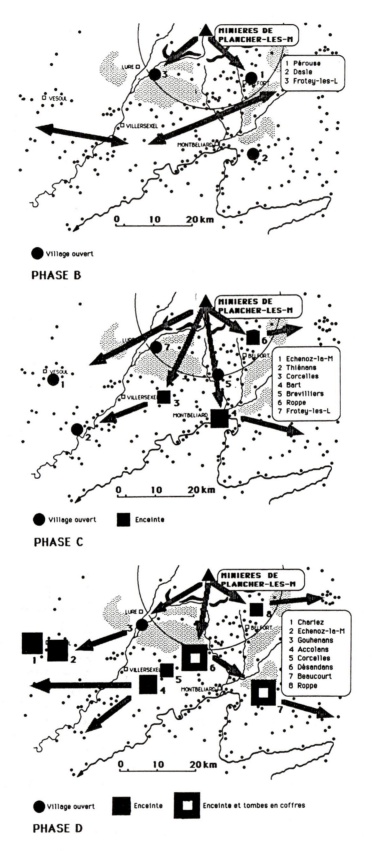

Figure 5.8. Neolithic colonisation and the development of a hierarchy among villages in the Belfort Gap. Phase B, probably around the middle of the fifth millennium BC: quarries exploited by open villages, lying less than a day's walk from the foot of the Vosges. Phase C, probably during the second half of the fifth millennium BC: the first hilltop settlements appear on the foothills of the Jura, while agricultural colonisation intensifies. Phase D, probably at the end of the fifth millennium: the villages in the valleys disappear, to be replaced by stronger communities based in enclosures on the edge of the plateau. The first barrow burials appear, linked to the largest enclosures and to control of the Plancher-les-Mines quarries.

polished implements found in other communes in the Sundgau region, at Franken, Ruederbach, Largitzen and elsewhere, could equally come from hoards and burials disturbed by the plough.

Enclosures and social intensification in the Belfort Gap

After this rapid overview of technological developments and of implements seen as social markers we will turn to the organisational dynamics of settlements in the Belfort Gap between 4500 and 3600 BC, in other words during the period when exploitation of the black stone quarries of the Vosges was at its peak. We will examine relations between the exploitation of the Plancher-les-Mines quarries and the development of enclosure construction in the Belfort Gap.

We know that the black stone of the Vosges was exploited from the Linearbandkeramik onwards, but, although a few polished implements are known from settlement contexts, no adze-manufacturing community has yet been found. This may be because, in this first phase of exploitation, which covers, as well as the Linearbandkeramik, the Grossgartach culture and the early and middle phases of the Rössen culture, the successive stages of production were not separated in space, basic thinning and roughing-out being performed at the extraction sites. This procedure is certainly adopted elsewhere by small groups of men going to make roughouts in hunting or high altitude territories removed from their permanent agricultural bases (Pétrequin & Pétrequin 1990).

The spatial separation of different stages of production began towards the middle of the 5th millennium. The black stone was roughly trimmed at the quarries; the preforms — thick fragments, blades, tested and thinned blocks — were brought to villages less than a day's walk away, on the old terraces of the streams flowing down from the Vosges (Fig. 5.8, top). The villages of Haute-Alsace, specialising in the production of stone axes, exemplify this period, when small blocks of stone from the superficial outcrops and morainic deposits of Plancher-les-Mines were collected in preference to quarrying deep beds and the slabs of the Marbranche stream. This first large scale exploitation occurred within the Rössen culture, especially its last stage, when the wider entity was splitting into regional groups (Jeunesse 1990). In this early phase, polished axes already reached as far as the southern fringes of Haute-Marne and the upper Rhine valley. This axis is in fact no more than the resumption of an exchange network established long before, in the Linearbandkeramik.

During the second phase (Fig. 5.8, centre) there were two new developments. On the one hand, villages involved in manufacturing polished axes become more numerous and now extended up to two days' walk from the quarries, as far as Vesoul to the west and a little

beyond. On the other hand, the first fortified villages were established on the foot-hills of the Jura and the Vosges, without this phenomenon of upland settlements becoming general, and without any possibility of understanding its role in the management of agricultural land and of the quarries. Surface finds indicate that some of these early enclosures could equally be attributed to the immediately post-Rössen phases (Pétrequin & Piningre 1974). In the north of the French Jura, this increase in population could be synchronous with the proliferation of settlements around the central Swiss lakes. Regrouping into larger communities could then have been a response to the social problems posed by population growth, under the influence of the phenomena of 'chalcolithisation' which were beginning to affect the whole of Europe.

Regrouping into upland settlements, most of them promontory forts, seems to have taken place during phase D (Fig. 5.8, bottom), which probably equates with the beginning of the wider distribution of polished implements originating from Plancher-les-Mines. We would place this episode roughly at the beginning of the Burgundian Middle Neolithic, probably about 4100 BC. The distances between the most important enclosures, in terms of the collective labour invested in their construction, still seem such that communities two days' walk away could, stage-by-stage, go and replenish their stocks of preforms and cores at Plancher-les-Mines. But the quality of knapping — or of technological skill — seems lower in these more distant communities than in the groups closest to the quarries. This may mark the acquisition of political control over the best raw materials, the slabs of the Marbranche stream at Plancher-les-Mines, the exploitation of which seems to have become more and more restricted to the knappers of the Belfort and Héricourt area, a day's walk away. At the same time, signs of social hierarchy appeared, with barrow burials close to or within the ramparts of the enclosures. These rare tombs, furnished sparsely if at all, would have been reserved for only some of the population.

With phase E, attributed to the early phase of the Burgundian Middle Neolithic, polished axes in black quartz mudstone from Plancher-les-Mines attained their widest distribution, along exchange networks still oriented east-west (Fig. 5.9). To the west they reached as far as the Yonne and the site of Noyen-sur-Seine (Seine-et-Marne) in the early phases of the Michelsberg culture; to the south-east they extended more-or-less to the Swiss lakes in the period 4000–3750 BC, during the early and classic Cortaillod culture (Willms 1980; Gross *et al.* 1987; Suter 1987); to the east, imports of implements from the Vosges reached as far as Lake Constance, at least around 4000–3900 BC (Schlichtherle 1990). The exchange networks were thus an unequivocally supra-cultural phenomenon which penetrated deeply into the Burgundian Middle Neolithic, Munzigen and Cortaillod cultures, and to a lesser degree, the

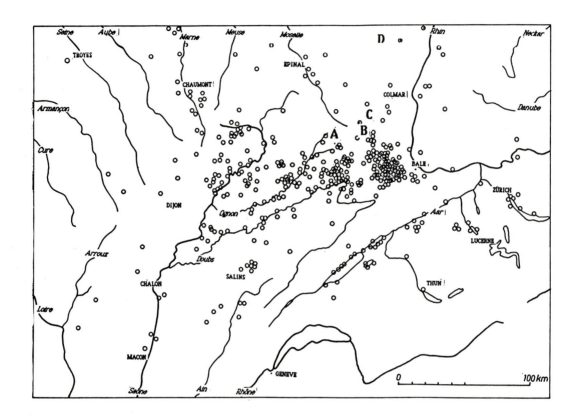

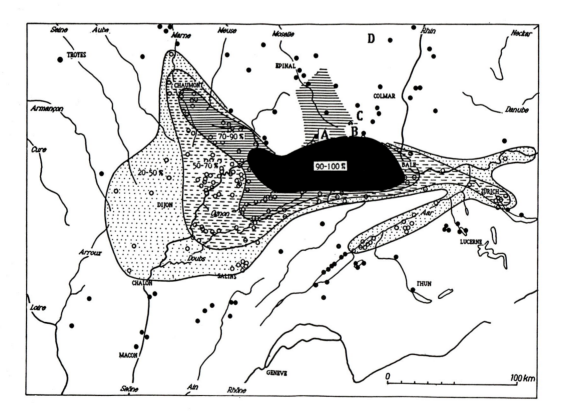

Figure 5.9. From Burgundy to the Rhine valley, the distribution of polished axes of black stone from the Vosges. Above: all the communes where black stone implements have been found. Below: implements of black stone from the Vosges as a percentage of all polished axes, at the peak of production from the quarries, at the beginning of the fourth millennium. A. Plancher-les-Mines quarries (Haute-Saône), quartz mudstones. B. Sondernach quarries (Haut-Rhin), nodular schists.

formative Pfyn and Noyen groups. In contrast to regional fragmentation of pottery styles, the middle distance exchange networks seem to have been a reunifying element at the technological level, which, interestingly, used the links established at the time of the expansion of the Rössen pottery styles some centuries before.

The hierarchisation of settlements in the Belfort Gap, now almost all fortified, seems to have reached its maximum, with a very large central enclosure, Mont-Vaudois at Héricourt (Haute-Saône), at the southern mouth of one of the valleys leading to Plancher-les-Mines. Large roughouts on fine quartz mudstone flaked blanks, made from the slabs of the Marbranche stream, show that some burials in the rampart of Mont-Vaudois were high-status; they could be interpreted as the tombs of specialists, according to the most classic hypothesis (Lichardus & Lichardus-Itten 1985). In our opinion, the state of the record does not permit this: they could equally have been the tombs of privileged men who controlled the political management of the quarries without themselves being specialists (Burton 1984).

By this time access to the source area was sufficiently restricted that communities more than a day's walk away could no longer exploit the quarries themselves. Preforms, prepared cores and roughouts circulated by exchange, to polishers then to users. The tight network of settlements had led to greater social control.

In the Belfort and Salins areas analysis of artefacts found in the fortified villages has revealed some peculiarities. Almost exclusive to these territories are implements of hyaline quartz (rock crystal) probably from the central Alps, perhaps from the Valais (Sainty *et al.* 1975). These tools (bladelets, scrapers, arrowheads) indicate privileged middle-distance relations for two territories both controlling rare mineral resources (polished implements and salt). It is a predictable outcome to see prestige or ritual objects (for a rock crystal arrowhead is no more and no less effective than one of flint or bone) centralised by the groups who controlled a quarry area or a salt source. What is more surprising, and tends to show the complexity of contemporary exchange, is that the hyaline quartz did not come from areas where polished axes of black stone from the Vosges were in everyday use. There must have been numerous intermediaries, reflecting the political organisation of fairly small territories.

On a smaller scale, thinking again in terms of Haute Alsace, Haute-Saône and the Territoire de Belfort (Fig. 5.10), the quarries seem to have been exploited initially and predominantly by groups living within one day's walk, Mont-Vaudois at Héricourt and Le Mont at Désandans being the keys to political control of Plancher-les-Mines. In the Belfort Gap in particular, the highest level of technological skill was linked to a type of stone which flaked well. Improvement of techniques coincided with the need to increase production to provide objects for exchange.

As in all areas of large-scale axe production, the knappers were rarely the polishers. The highest density of fragments of sandstone from the Vosges, imported and used for polishing within the fortified enclosures, occurs two days' walk form the mining area (Fig. 5.10). This is the way most communities absorb production surplus to the domestic needs of roughout manufacturers. Those who undertake the long and unprestigious work of polishing are at the head of exchange networks for the finished products, the polished axes. And it is polished axes that can reflect social competition most clearly (Pétrequin & Pétrequin 1990). It is not at all surprising that the largest polished implements are found precisely in hoards and burials within two days' walk of the quarries. The polygonal network of territories controlled by the enclosures was thus superimposed on concentric systems radiating from the foot of the Vosges, in which preforms, roughouts and axes acquired increased technological efficacity and symbolic value in proportion to their distance from the quarries (Fig. 5.10).

After 3700 BC the dispersal of axes of black stone from the Vosges became static then diminished rapidly (Willms 1980). In Switzerland, axes became rare in the Cortaillod culture and disappeared almost completely in the Pfyn. From the Cortaillod Port-Conty culture onwards greenstones from the moraines at the foot of the Alps were again exploited in place of stone acquired by exchange from the Vosges. This slowing-down of transfers and the abandonment of tree-felling implements as markers of status seem to accompany the end of Middle Neolithic II, the agricultural colonisation of the interfluves, the abandonment of enclosures and upland sites, and also the end of a cultural style, before the establishment of a new, Horgen, cultural cycle.

The quarries of Plancher-les-Mines and the southeastern Vosges continued to be exploited during the Late Neolithic. But the stone was by then only of regional interest, and exchanges scarcely reached beyond Gray to the west and Basle to the east. Burials (and hence probably settlements) moved away from the foot of the Vosges and the area within one day's walk of the mining area (Fig. 5.16, bottom) to realign themselves on an east-west axis which facilitated exchange between the upper Rhine and the Saône plain. Prestige passed from the large tree-felling axe to the dagger, the battle-axe and the arrowhead. Social control passed from the abandoned enclosures to chambered collective tombs.

For all this, there was no diminution in the level of technological skill at Plancher-les-Mines: during the late Neolithic those working the site continued to favour a complex technique for flaking large, regular axes which could be rapidly polished. The evidence indicates that the slackening of social control from the enclosures, seen as central places, had no effect whatever on the actual technology. What appeared, in Middle Neolithic II, to be a complex technique, the development of which was favoured by a hierarchical organisation of communities,

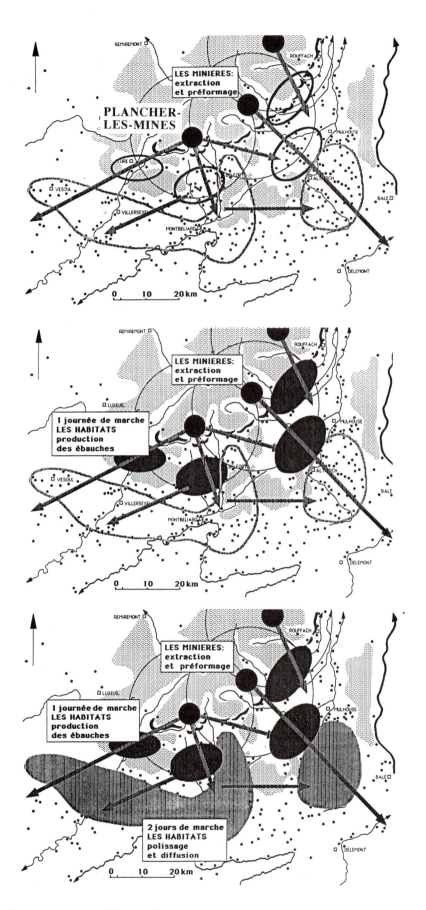

Figure 5.10. The spatial segmentation of the production system in Middle Neolithic II. Areas of extraction and preform production (top), roughout production (centre) and polishing (bottom) form concentric bands around the foot of the Vosges.

was in no way weakened. The notion of the specialist, favoured by the 'chalcolithisation' of Europe, is thus either a concept which is not applicable here, or a specifically cultural attribute, favoured by one society and rejected by another.

Conclusions

The overall picture could be seen as quite simple, conforming to the models proposed above and the results to be expected from them. On the evidence, the widespread construction of enclosures in the Belfort Gap coincides with the peak effectiveness of the exchange networks which, between 4100 and 3700 BC, transported polished axes as far as the Yonne-Seine confluence to the west and as far as Lake Constance to the east. With the progressive abandonment of the enclosures, then their total disuse, exploitation of the quarries was concerned only with strictly regional, short distance exchange. The two phenomena are thus clearly linked: mounting demographic pressure led to a phase of renewed colonisation, social reorganisation, intensified competition, and, by the same token, intensified exploitation of mineral resources. All these events, related to each other here, extended far beyond the limited framework provided by the stylistic provinces of Middle Neolithic II. In the sphere of polished implements, we still see the long range dissemination of large polished axes of Alpine rocks, with flat ovoid or lenticular sections, as a marker of the beginning of this cycle of intensification, probably coinciding with the expansive phase of the Chassean.

But it is time to introduce some nuances into the simplistic scenario. During the earliest phase of renewed agricultural colonisation towards the interfluves and the establishment of the enclosures, the ovoid-sectioned polished axe appears across France as a powerful item of exchange, on the same scale as the initial stylistic unity of the Chassean. But this situation, the use of a widely-valued prestige good, does not last. The flint mines in the sedimentary basins and the black stone quarries in the Vosges take over from these objects transported over very long distances. In eastern France we see the revival of an old cultural network, utilised for the transport of polished axes from the Vosges. As has already been shown (Jeunesse 1990), this network was established at a time of relative cultural unity, probably during the last stage of the Rössen culture, in other words at the time when the regrouping of large communities into enclosures was only just beginning. The distribution of polished axes from the south-eastern Vosges (Fig. 5.9) is particularly significant: it is coterminous, to the west and south, with that of Rössen or epi-Rössen material (Duhamel 1989; Gallay 1997). These networks related, when they were established, to common ideas and to the expression of a cultural identity through pottery styles, with their feeling of a common vocabulary. It was long after the disappearance of the

Rössen entity that they were re-used and intensified by polished axes from the Vosges, with the same eastern and western limits. The phenomenon of the concentration of settlements and the use of defended enclosures is thus rather remote in time from the establishment of these exchange networks, even if it later came to relate to them. Here we see again the classic pendulum swing of cultural cycles: early stylistic unity and long-distance exchange in contrast to later regionalisation and the predominance of medium-distance exchange.

In conclusion, we will return to the Belfort Gap and Haute Alsace towards the beginning of the fourth millennium. Here, the transport of polished axes outwards from the extraction sites shows two contrasting forms of political and social organisation. West of the Belfort Gap, farming communities are for the most part regrouped into upland villages and enclosures; axe hoards are absent, big polished axes uncommon, and single large roughouts are found in some of the rare burials; yet it is these people who are at the head of exchange networks which extend as far as eastern Burgundy and Haute-Marne. On the contrary, east of the Belfort Gap, at the head of exchange networks leading to Switzerland and the Rhine valley, there are no big enclosures at all, while large roughouts and large polished axes are strongly represented, whether they come from disturbed burials or from hoards. It is highly probable that these two different forms of organisation, by contemporary communities, are to be ascribed to cultural choice, relating to the Burgundian Middle Neolithic to the west and the Munzigen culture to the east — two disparate orientations and two different social expressions of the same fact: the control of the quarries of the south-eastern Vosges. In this case, the presence or absence of enclosures would be irrelevant; the exchange of polished axes would not be a determining criterion by which to explain the mechanisms of political control of communities which have chosen to surround themselves with a rampart. The limits reached by the dissemination of polished black stone axes would then be more explicable in terms of regional traditions in the form of the persistence or the revival, independently of the enclosures and of stylistic provinces, of the old Rössen exchange network between Burgundy and the upper Rhine plain. The true stimuli of the revival then the diminution of traditional east-west exchange through the Belfort Gap remain to be identified. The history of episodes of population growth followed by crises of equilibrium with the environment could be an interesting path to pursue, and one so far little explored.

References

Buret, C., & Ricq-de Bouard, M., 1982. L'industrie de la 'pierre polie' du Néolithique moyen d'Auvernier (Neuchâtel-Suisse): les relations entre matière première et les objets. *Centre de Recherches Archéologiques, CNRS, Notes Internes* 41

Burton, J., 1984. *Axe Makers of the Wahgi, Pre-colonial Industrialists of the Papua New Guinea Highlands*. Canberra: Ph.D. thesis, Australian National University

Cordier, G., & Bocquet, A., 1973. Le dépot de la Bégude-de-Mazenc (Drôme) et les dépots de haches néolithiques en France. *Etudes Préhistoriques* 6, 1–17

Diethelm, I., 1989. Aphanit — ein pseudowissenschaftliche Begriff? Eine mineralogisch-petrographische Bilanz. *Jahrbuch der Schweizerischen Gesellschaft für Ur- und Frühgeschichte* 72, 201–14

Dubouloz, J., 1989. Problématique de recherche sur les enceintes néolithiques de la vallée de l'Aisne: un ensemble représentatif du Bassin Parisien ?, in *Enceintes, Habitats Ceinturés, Sites Perchés du Néolithique au Bronze Ancien dans le sud de la France et les Régions Voisines*, eds. A. D'Anna & X. Gütherz. Montpellier: Mémoires de la Société Languedocienne de Préhistoire 2, 55–68

Duhamel, P., 1989. Passy, Richebourg, La Sablonnière, in *L'Yonne et son Passé, 30 Ans d'Archéologie*, catalogue d'exposition, eds J.P. Delor & C. Rolley. Comité Régional de la Recherche Archéologique de Bourgogne

Gallay, A., 1977. *le Néolithique Moyen du Jura et des Plaines de la Saône, Contribution à l'Etude des Relations Chassey-Cortaillod-Michelsberg = Antiqua* 6. Publications de la Société Suisse de Préhistoire et d'Archéologie. Frauenfeld: Verlag Huber

Glory, A., 1942. *La Civilisation du Néolithique en Haute-Alsace = Publications de l'Institut des Hautes Etudes Alsaciennes* 1. Strasbourg: Université de Strasbourg

Gross, E., Brombacher, C., Dick, M., Diggelmann, K., Hardmeyer, B., Jagher, R., Ritzmann, C., Ruckstuhl, B., Ruoff, U., Schibler, J., Vaughan, P.C. & Wyprächtiger, K., 1987. *Zürich 'Mozarstrasse', neolithische und bronzezeitliche Ufersiedlungen Band 1 = Berichte der Zürcher Denkmalpflege* Monographien 4. Zürich: Orell Füssli Verlag

Jeudy, F., 1990. *De la Roche à la Lame de Pierre Polie: les Minières de Plancher-les-Mines*. Besançon: mémoire de maîtrise, Préhistoire, Université de Franche-Comté

Jeunesse, C., 1990. Le Néolithique alsacien et ses relations avec les régions voisines, in *Die ersten Bauern, Pfahlbaufunde Europas* 2. Zürich: Schweizerisches Landesmuseums, 177–94

Lichardus-Itten, M., 1980. *Die Gräberfelder der Grosgartacher Gruppe im Elsass = Saarbrücker Beitrage zum Alterstumskunde* 25. Bonn: Rudolf Habelt Verlag

Lichardus, J., & Lichardus-Itten, M., 1985. *La Protohistoire de l'Europe. Le Néolithique et le Chalcolithique*, Nouvelle Clio. Paris: Presses Universitaires de France

Pétrequin, A.M., & Pétrequin, P., 1990. Haches de Yeleme, herminettes de Mumyeme, la répartition des lames de pierre polie en Irian Jaya central (Indonésie). *Journal de la Société des Océanistes* 91(2), 95–113

Pétrequin, P., 1970. *La Grotte de la Baume de Gonvillars*, Annales Littéraires de l'Université de Besançon. Paris: Les Belles Lettres

Pétrequin, P., & Gallay, A. (eds), 1984. *Le Néolithique Moyen Bourguignon = Archives Suisses d'Anthropologie Générale* 48 (2), numéro spécial, Actes du Colloque de Beffia (Jura, France)

Pétrequin, P., & Piningre, J.F., 1971. Elemente der Rössener Kultur in der nördlichen Franche-Comté. *Germania* 49(1–2), 187–91

Piningre, J.F., 1974. *Un Aspect de l'Economie Néolithique: le Problème de l'Aphanite en Franche-Comté et dans les Régions Limitrophes*, Annales Littéraires de l'Université de Besançon. Paris: Les Belles Lettres

Sainty, J., Claudel, J., & Loigerot, D., 1975. Utilisation du cristal de roche (quartz hyalin) et carte de répartition pour le nord de la Franche-Comté. *Revue Archéologique de l'Est* 26(3–4), 413–22

Schlichterle, H., 1990. *Siedlungsarchäologie im Alpenvorland 1. Die Sondagen 1973–1978 in der Ufersiedlungen Hornstaad-Hörnle 1 = Forschungen und Berichte zur Vor- und Frühgeschichte in Baden-Würtemburg* 36. Stuttgart: Konrad Theiss Verlag

Speck, J., 1988. Spitznackige Feuersteinbeile aus der Zentralschweiz. *Archéologie Suisse* 11, 53

Suter, P.J., 1987. *Zürich 'Kleiner Hafner', Tauchgrabungen 1981–1984 = Berichte der Zürcher Denkmalpflege* Monographien 3. Bern: Orell Füssli Verlag

Willms, C., 1980. Die felsgesteinartefakte der Cortaillod-Schichten, in *Die Neolithischen Ufersiedlungen von Twann (9)*, Bern: Staatlicher Lehrmittelverlag

6

Trade in Neolithic Jadeite Axes from the Alps: New Data

Monique Ricq-de Bouard

Most of the 'jadeite' axes found in western Europe can be attributed to west Alpine sources, on the evidence of their petrographic characteristics and their distribution, which is centred on this region. The predominance among the implements of fine-grained, little-altered rocks indicates that most of them were made on raw material collected from secondary deposits in which the finer-grained 'jadeites' have become concentrated because of their toughness, rather than from primary deposits in which coarse-grained forms are the most frequent. Secondary, detrital deposits containing fragments and pebbles of 'jadeite' have been identified in western Liguria, Piedmont and western Switzerland. Three main routes of dispersal from these raw material sources are inferred from the details of implement distribution.

La plupart des haches polies en 'jadéite' (éclogite et clinopyroxénites sodiques) trouvées en Europe de l'ouest proviennent des Alpes occidentales comme le démontrent leurs caractères pétrographiques et leur distribution, centrée sur cette région. Dans l'outillage, les roches à grains fins, peu altérées, prédominent. On en conclue que ce sont les dépôts secondaires, où ces roches se concentrent du fait de leur particulière résistance, qui ont été exploités plutôt que les affleurements primaires. Des formations détritiques contenant des blocs et des galets de 'jadéite' ont été repérées en Ligurie occidentale, dans le Piémont et en Suisse occidentale. Trois axes principaux de circulation des outils sont envisagés, à partir des ces sources de matières premières.

Introduction

The exchange of 'jadeite' axes is one of the best-known instances of the long-distance circulation of artefacts in the Neolithic period. Studied for many decades, it still gives rise to problems, particularly with regard to the origins of the 'jadeite'.

The purpose of this paper is to present new data concerning the origins and the main routes of diffusion of 'jadeite' axes. These data are based on the results of many field surveys in the Alps and also on the petrographic identification of more than 3,000 artefacts from the Mediterranean regions of France and from alpine and peri-alpine areas. About half of these artefacts are made of 'jadeite'.

Following Woolley *et al.* (1979, 90), the term 'jadeite' in quotation marks will be used in this paper to describe rocks formed by different sodic pyroxenes (jadeite, omphacite, chloromelanite, etc.), with or without garnet. This nomenclature differs from that used in recent papers, where specific problems of origin necessitated the distinction between jadeite in the strict mineralogical sense and other sodic pyroxenes

(Ricq-de Bouard *et al.* 1990, 131–2; Ricq-de Bouard & Fedele 1993).

The rocks of which Neolithic implements are made were identified mainly by optical microscopy in thin section. X-ray diffraction was used to verify and supplement analysis in thin section in cases of extremely fine-grained rocks, where minerals could not be distinguished by optical microscopy. The determination of specific gravity was useful in some cases because it is not a destructive method.

In this preliminary paper, small- to medium-sized functional implements and large ceremonial axes will not be distinguished, although these two groups probably followed different exchange routes. Chronology will not be taken into account, although it is an important factor for the analysis of exchange.

The distribution of 'jadeite' axes in western Europe

In the 1950s Piggott and Powell (1951) were among the first to recognise the importance of 'jadeite' axes in Britain, as evidence of the import of artefacts from continental Europe. This was the starting point of a wide programme of recording combined with typological and petrological analysis of jade finds from the British Isles (Campbell Smith 1963; 1965; 1972; Coles *et al.* 1974; Jones *et al.* 1977).[1] In one of these publications Campbell Smith also drew attention to the location of some of the jade implements found in continental Europe (1965, fig. 1).

In 1987 Schut, Kars and Wevers published a pre-liminary report on the distribution of jade implements in the Netherlands, with additional data from Belgium and north-western Germany supplied by de Boe and Hubrecht (unpublished), Brandt (1967) and Hoof (1970).

In Brittany and the neighbouring regions, many petrographic studies of stone axes have been conducted first by Giot & Cogné and subsequently by Le Roux & Cordier. In northern Brittany less than 10 per cent of polished implements are made of 'jadeite' (Le Roux &

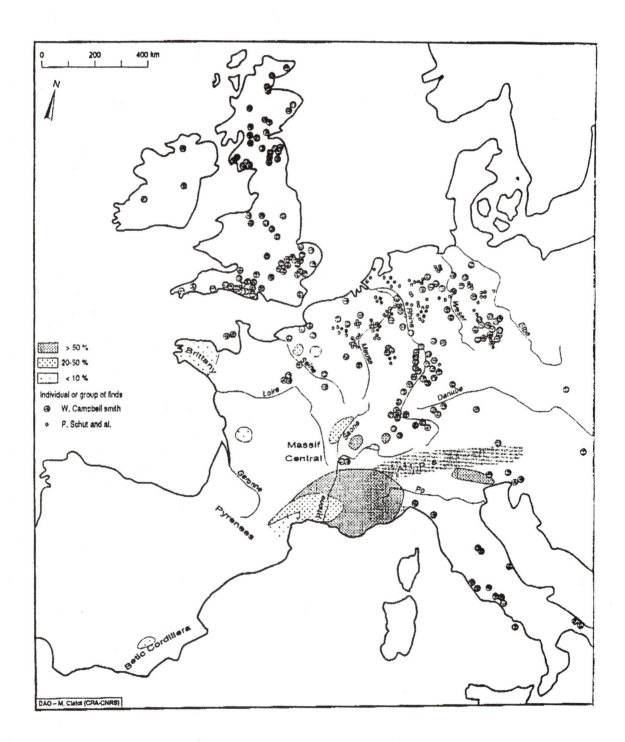

Fig. 6.1. The distribution of Neolithic 'jadeite' axes in western Europe

Lecerf 1980; 1981). In the middle Loire valley this percentage increases to nearly 20 per cent (Le Roux & Cordier 1974; Le Roux *et al.* 1980).

In Limousin (Massif Central), 'jadeite' makes up 10 per cent of the axes (Santallier *et al.* 1986, 17). At the sites of Chalain and Clairvaux (Jura), analysis of finds from the old excavations has shown that about 50 per cent of the implements are of 'jadeite' (Ricq-de Bouard 1985). 'Jadeite' axes can also be found in the Saône valley, where they represent nearly 25 per cent of the polished implements (Ricq-de Bouard & Compagnoni 1991, 278).

The highest frequencies of 'jadeite' axes occur in the alpine and peri-alpine zones of Italy and France. In western Liguria, western Piedmont, Provence and the middle Rhône valley, more than 50 per cent (often between 70 and 90 per cent) of implements are made of 'jadeite' (Ricq-de Bouard *et al.* 1990; Ricq-de Bouard & Fedele 1993). To the west, in the Mediterranean regions of France, 'jadeite' implements diminish in frequency but remain present as far as the Pyrenees.

In northern Catalonia, on the other side of the Pyrenees, no 'jadeite' finds have been reported, despite petrographic studies (Angel Bosch 1984). In southern Spain, near the Cordillera Bética, six 'jadeite' axes have been found among 66 stone implements from the Granada area (Carrion & Gomez 1983).

This broad distribution of 'jadeite' axes, from the south of Italy to Scotland and from Austria to Brittany (Fig. 6.1), is surprising when set against the relative scarcity of outcrops of 'jadeite'.

Sources of 'jadeite'

Possible sources of 'jadeite' in western Europe are the Bohemian Massif, the Alps, Brittany, the Massif Central and the Cordillera Bética. The rocks themselves may be roughly divided into two main groups, formed under different metamorphic conditions. These may be differentiated, for example, on the basis of the minor minerals associated with the sodic pyroxenes. The first group, formed at higher temperatures, contains climax minerals or retrogressive minerals such as kyanite, diopside + plagioclase, or hornblende + plagioclase intergrowth. The second group, formed at lower temperatures, never contains these minerals and may contain paragonite, glaucophane or actinolite + albite intergrowth.

'Jadeites' from the Bohemian Massif, found in Czechoslovakia, Poland and eastern Germany (O'Brien *et al.* 1990), from the Massif Central in France (Coffrant & Piboule 1971) and from the Cordillera Bética in Spain (Gomez-Pugnaire & Fernandez-Soler 1987) belong to the first group. Only a few alpine 'jadeites', found in the external crystalline massifs of the western Alps (Aiguilles Rouges, Argentera Massif) and in the eastern Alps (Switzerland, Austria) belong to this group (Magetti *et al.* 1987; Miller *et al.* 1988). In contrast, 'jadeite' from Brittany and from most of the western

Alps (i.e. the piedmont zone, the internal crystalline massifs and the Sezia zone) are similar to those of the second group.

'Jadeite' of the first type was little used for axe manufacture in the Neolithic. Archaeological finds of such 'jadeite' have been reported from the Massif Central (Santallier *et al.* 1986, 13) and from the area around Granada, not far from the Cordillera Bética (Carrion & Gomez 1983, 467–72). In both areas, they amount to less than 10 per cent of the polished implements. In striking contrast, the 'jadeite' used for all the axes I have studied, from Mediterranean settlements, from alpine and peri-alpine areas and from the Paris Basin, is similar to those of the second type. Artefacts from the British Isles, from the Netherlands and from Moravia are made from the same type of 'jadeite', on the evidence of the descriptions published by Campbell Smith (1963; 1965; 1972), Schut *et al.* (1987, 81–2), and Schmidt & Steel (1971, 143–4).

On petrological grounds alone, most of these 'jadeite' implements could come from Brittany or from the Alps. In Brittany, however, 'jadeite' axes amount to less than 10 per cent of the total, so that it is highly improbable that Brittany was a starting point for exchanges across the whole of western Europe. Therefore, not only is it certain that most Neolithic 'jadeite' axes came from the western Alps, but a more precise provenance may also be defined.

All the outcrops of 'jadeite' similar to the raw material of the majority of the artefacts studied occur in the metamorphic ophiolite belt of the internal piedmont zone, between the Mediterranean and the upper Rhône valley (Fig. 6.2; Ricq-de Bouard *et al.* 1990, 133). Theoretically, jadeite *sensu stricto* should also exist in the external piedmont zone, but despite careful survey neither outcrops nor secondary deposits of this rock have ever been found.

The southernmost outcrops of 'jadeite' occur in the Voltri Massif in Liguria (Cortesogno *et al.* 1977). Other widespread outcrops are situated in the Monviso valley, the Lanzo valley and the Val d'Aosta, up as far as the Zermatt area (Compagnoni *et al.* 1980).

Microscopic analysis of finds indicates that in the Neolithic 'jadeite' was collected not from primary outcrops but from secondary deposits, where it became concentrated because of its extraordinary hardness and resistance to weathering. The 'jadeites' of which axes are made are fine-grained and fresh, while in primary outcrops the coarse-grained forms prevail (Ricq-de Bouard *et al.* 1990, 133). At the same time, sodic pyroxenes (omphacite, chloromelanite, jadeite) without garnet are frequent among implements, but rarer in primary outcrops.

Between the southern extremity of the Alps and the Val d'Aosta, primary outcrops of 'jadeite' occur exclusively east of the Alpine divide (Fig. 6.2). 'Jadeite' clasts and pebbles can thus be found only on the Italian side of the Alps, in both the Tertiary and

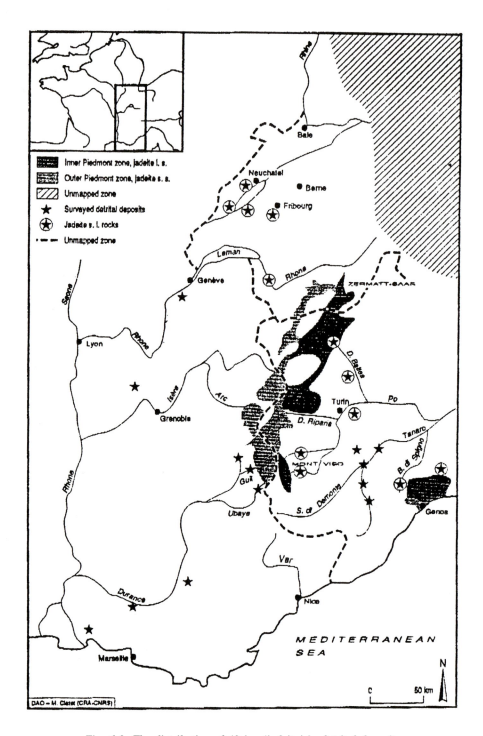

Fig. 6.2. The distribution of Alpine 'jadeite' in detrital deposits

Quaternary deposits of Piedmont and Liguria. Field-work has confirmed the presence of 'jadeite' pebbles, notably in the rivers Po, Torre Pellice and Bormida di Spigo (Fig. 6.2). Some of these pebbles are microscopically similar to the rocks used to make stone axes in the Neolithic.

North of the Val d'Aosta, the 'jadeite' outcrops of the piedmont zone are located on the northern side of the Alps; 'jadeite' pebbles are present in the deposits of the Rhône and especially in the Quaternary glacial deposits of western Switzerland. Preliminary surveys indicate that they are rare but present in the areas of Neuchatel and Fribourg (Fig. 6.2).

The main exchange routes from the Alps: preliminary data

In western Europe, the wide distribution of Neolithic 'jadeite' implements, coming as we have suggested from the western Alps, implies complex systems of exchange, which await further study. But we can already make some preliminary observations. Three main extraction and production areas and exchange routes have been identified.

The first, from Liguria, reached the Mediterranean regions of France and perhaps some of the middle Rhône valley (Fig. 6.3). This route is indicated by the abundance of stone axes between Genoa and the river Tanaro, in the hilly region of the Langhe. Petrographic analysis of a great number of these finds at the Genova-Pegli Museum shows that the majority of these imple-

ments are made of 'jadeite' (Ricq-de Bouard, unpublished). This abundance shows that the area was quite active in 'jadeite' implement production, and that it was probably a starting point for exchanges. Unfortunately, most of these axes are surface finds made at the beginning of the century and any manufacturing sites that may have existed are now covered by buildings. This southern flow is also suggested by the distribution of 'jadeite' axes, the density of which decreases regularly from Liguria to the Pyrenees (Fig. 6.3).

The second route starts from western (and maybe

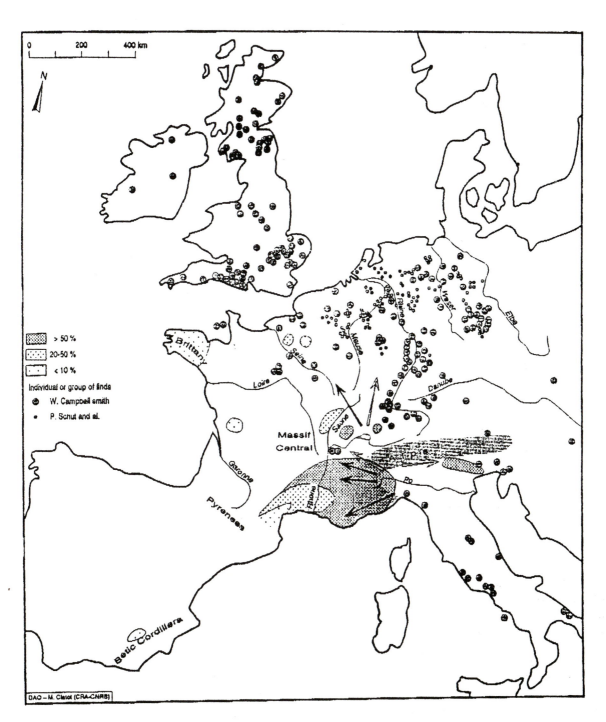

Fig. 6.3 The dispersal of Neolithic 'jadeite' axes from the Alps

southern) Piedmont and crosses the Alps through passes (Fig. 6.3). A large proportion (if not all) of the 'jadeite' implements found in the middle Rhône valley were probably transported along it. The frequency of polished 'jadeite' implements in the high alpine valleys of Guil and Ubaye seems to demonstrate this point (Ricq-de Bouard, unpublished). This flow may have reached the Massif Central and the countries of northern Europe, but this cannot be verified due to the lack of data.

The third area of departure for exchanges was western Switzerland. Exchange towards the west is demonstrated by the presence of 'jadeite' axes in the lakeside settlements of Chalain and Clairvaux in the Jura (Fig. 6.3; Ricq-de Bouard 1985).[2] These axes certainly came from Switzerland, on the evidence of the presence of chloritoïde in some thin sections (Ricq-de Bouard et al. 1990, 134). This circulation reached at least as far as the Paris Basin, on the evidence of the association, at the site of Bury-en-Vexin, of a 'jadeite' axe with a fragment of a shaft-hole axe in serpentine, certainly from Switzerland.

And now what about the northern routes by which 'jadeite' axes reached Belgium, Germany, the Netherlands and the British Isles? As stated above, most of these axes are likely to have come from the western Alps. The exchange routes probably started from western Switzerland, perhaps reaching northern Europe by way of the Rhine valley, as several authors have suggested. However, because of the relative scarcity of 'jadeite' pebbles in Swiss deposits, it seems that we have to consider other starting points, such as Piedmont, for the northern material.

At present, we do not have sufficient petrographic and geochemical data for either outcrops or implements, to link the northern finds to one origin or another. It may never be possible to achieve this by analysis. This is nevertheless the aim of our future work.

Acknowledgement

I would like top thank Roberto Compagnoni (University of Turin) for his important and continuing co-operation on petrographic matters.

Notes

1. Jade finds include predominantly 'jadeite' and a few nephrite implements.
2. In this paper it was suggested the these 'jadeites', coming from the primary outcrops of the Zermatt area, might be present in the Quaternary deposits of the Jura. Since then, surveys have demonstrated that 'jadeite' is absent from the Jura.

References

Angel Bosch, 1984. Les destrals polides del nord de Catalunya: tipologia i petrologia. *Fonaments* 4, 221–45

Brandt, K.H., 1967. *Studien über steinerne Äxte und Beile der Jüngeren Steinzeit und der Stein-Kupferzeit Nordwestdeutschlands*. Hildesheim

Campbell Smith, W., 1963. Jade axes from sites in the British Isles. *Proceedings of the Prehistoric Society* 29, 133–72

Campbell Smith, W., 1965. The distribution of jade axes from sites in Europe with a supplement to the catalogue of those from the British Isles. *Proceedings of the Prehistoric Society* 31, 25–33

Campbell Smith, W., 1972. Second supplement to the catalogue of jade axes from sites in the British Isles. *Proceedings of the Prehistoric Society* 38, 408–11

Carrion-Mendez, F., & Gomez-Pugnaire, M.T., 1983. Analisis petroarqueologico de los artefactos de piedra trabajada durante la prehistoria reciente en la provincia de Granada. *Cuadernos de Prehistoria de la Universidad de Granada* 8, 447–77

Coffrant, D., & Piboule, M., 1971. Les écologites et roches associées des massifs basiques de Saint-Joseph (monts du Lyonnais, Massif Central français). *Bulletin de la Société Géologique de France* 13(3–4), 283–91

Coles, J., Orme, B., Bishop, A.C., & Woolley, A.R., 1974. A jade axe from the Somerset Levels. *Antiquity* 48, 216–20

Compagnoni, R., Fiora, L., & Lombardo, B., 1980. The Monviso ophiolite complex, in *Proceedings of the International Ophiolite Symposium*, 332–40

Cortesogno, L., Ernst, W.G., & Galli, M., 1977. Chemical petrology of ecologitic lenses in serpentinite, gruppo di Voltri, Ligurian Alps. *Journal of Geology* 85(3), 255–77

Giot, P.-R., 1965. Le problème européen des haches d'apparat en jadéite et roches voisines, in *Actes du Vième Congrès International des Sciences Pré- et Protohistoriques, Florence*, 281–6

Gomez-Pugnaire, M.T., & Fernandez-Soler, J.M., 1987. High-pressure metamorphisn in metabasites from the betic Cordilleras (S-E Spain) and its evolution during the Alpine orogeny. *Contributions to Mineralogy and Petrology* 95, 23–44

Hoof, D., 1970. *Die Steinbeile und Steinäxte im gebiet des Niederrheins und der Maas*. Bonn: Antiquitas Reihe 2(9)

Jones, V., Bishop, A.C., & Woolley, A.R., 1977. Third supplement to the catalogue of jade axes from sites in the British Isles. *Proceedings of the Prehistoric Society* 43, 287–93

Le Roux, C.-T., & Cordier, G., 1974. Etude pétrographique des haches polies de Touraine. *Bulletin de la Société Préhistorique Française* 71, 335–54

Le Roux, C.-T., & Lecerf, Y., 1980. Les outils polis de l'arrondissement de Dinan. Eléments pour une préhistoire du nord-est de l'Armorique bretonne. Saint-Malo: *Dossiers du Centre Régional Archéoloique d'Alet* 8, 21–44

Le Roux, C.-T., & Lecerf, Y., 1981. Les haches polies du nord-est de la Bretagne: l'arrondissement de Saint-Malo. St-Malo: *Dossiers du Centre Régional Archéologique d'Alet* 9, 67–79

Le Roux, C.-T., Despriée, J., & Leymarios, C., 1980. Les haches polies du Loir-et-Cher: étude pétrographique et considérations sur leur diffusion dans les pays de la Loire moyenne et le sud-ouest du Bassin parisien, in *Etudes sur le Néolithique de la Région Centre. Actes du Colloque Interrégional tenu à Saint-Amand-Montrond (Cher) 28–30 Octobre 1977*. Saint-Amand: Association des Amis du Musée Saint-Vic, 49–66

Magetti, M., Galetti, G., & Stosch, H.G., 1987. Eclogites from the Silvretta nappe (Switzerland): geochemical constraints on the nature and geotechnic setting of their protoliths. *Geochemical Geology* 64, 319–34

Miller, C., Stosch, H-G, & Hoernes, S., 1988. Geochemistry and the origin of ecologites from the type locality Koralpe and Saualpe, eastern Alps, Austria. *Chemical Geology* 67, 103–18

O'Brien, P.J., Carswell, D.A. & Gebauer, D., 1990. Ecologite formation and distribution in the European Variscides, in *Ecologite Facies Rocks*. London & Glasgow: Blackie, 205–26

Piggott, S., & Powell, T.G.E., 1951. The excavation of three Neolithic chambered tombs in Galloway, 1949. *Proceedings of the Society of Antiquaries of Scotland* 83, 103–61

Ricq-de Bouard, M., 1985. Identification pétrographique et origine des outils en pierre polie des sites de Chalain et Clairvaux (matériel des Musées de Lons-le-Saunier et Dole), in *Présentation des Collections du Musée de Lons-le-Saunier Nº 1. Néolithque Chalain-Clairvaux Fouilles Anciennes*. Lons-le-Saunier: Musée Archéologique, 141–3

Ricq-de Bouard, M., Compagnoni, R., Desmons, J., & Fedele, F., 1990. Les roches alpines dans l'outillage polie Néolithique de la France méditeranéenne: classification, origine, circulation. *Gallia Préhistoire* 32, 125–49

Ricq-de Bouard, M., & Compagnoni, R., 1991. La circulation des outils polis en éclogite alpine au IVᵉ millénaire. Premières observations relatives au sud-est de la France et à quelques sites plus septentrionaux, in *Identité du Chasséen. Actes du Colloque de Nemours 1989*, eds A. Beeching, D. Binder, J.-C. Blanchet, C. Constantin, J. Dubouloz, R. Martin, D. Mordant, J.P. Thevenot & J. Vaquer. Nemours: Mémoires du Musée de Préhistoire d'Ile de France 4, 273–80

Ricq-de Bouard, M., & Fedele, F., 1993. Neolithic rock sources across the western Alps: circulation data and models. *Geoarchaeology* 8(1), 1–22

Santallier, D., Tardiveau, D., & Vuaillat, D., 1986. Les haches polies en roche dure du Limousin. Premières réflexions sur la base de leur étude pétrographique. *Revue Archéologique du Centre de la France* 25(1), 7–20

Schmidt, J., & Steel, J., 1971. Jadeites from Moravia Neolithic period. *Acta Universitatis Carolinae, Geologia* 1–2, 141–52

Schut, P., Kars, H., & Wevers, J.M.A.R., 1987. Jade axes in the Netherlands: a preliminary report. *Helinium* 27, 71–87

Woolley, A.R., Bishop, A.C., Harrison, R.J., & Kinnes, I.A., 1979. European Neolithic jade implements: a preliminary mineralogical and typological study, in *Stone Axe Studies*, eds T.H.McK. Clough & W.A. Cummins. London: Council for British Archaeology Research Report 23, 90–6

7

Towards a Context for Production and Exchange: the Polished Axe in Earlier Neolithic Britain

Mark Edmonds

A good prospector should not trust in appearances, because the rock, which seems dead, instead is full of deception; sometimes it changes its nature even while you're digging

(Primo Levi: The Periodic Table*)*

The production, circulation and consumption of polished stone and flint axes in early Neolithic Britain is viewed in the context of contemporary social organisation. The potentially multiple value of axes, symbolic and mnemonic as well as utilitarian, is examined. The social implications and repercussions of mining and quarrying are discussed. Changes over time in the character and organisation of production are linked to wider contemporary developments. The exploitation of often remote mines and quarries, and the exchange and consumption of their products, is related to cyclical gatherings at causewayed enclosures.

Cet article passe en revue la production, la circulation et la consommation des haches polies de roches dures et de silex en Grande Bretagne pendant le Néolithique ancien dans le cadre de l'organisation sociale contemporaine. On souligne la signification probablement multiple des haches, symboles et mnémoniques autant qu'objets utilitaires. On examine les implications et les conséquences sociales de l'exploitation des mines et des carrières. Les changements à travers le temps dans le caractère et l'organisation de la production sont liés à des développments contemporains plus étendus. L'exploitation des mines et des carrières, souvent lointaines, et la circulation et la consommation de leurs produits, sont reliées aux réunions communales périodiques qui avaient lieu dans les enceintes.

Introduction

For some time now, the character of the earlier Neolithic in Britain has been the subject of heated debate. Recent studies have begun to question many of the assumptions underlying the argument that the Neolithic can be defined as a simple economic entity, separated from the later Mesolithic on the basis of major changes in the selection and exploitation of resources. In fact, the picture that we have suggests a rather more complex pattern of both continuity and innovation between the two periods. This complexity is compounded by problems with our radiocarbon chronology, and by the fact that the 'transition' marks the meeting point between different analytical traditions (Kinnes 1988; Herne 1988; Thomas 1988). Nevertheless, the empirical sequence raises a series of important questions concerning the character of what has traditionally been seen as one of the major watersheds in British prehistory.

Although generalisations should be made with caution, there is little evidence to suggest that the beginning of the Neolithic witnessed a wholesale switch to sedentary agriculture. Rather, we see the more gradual emergence of suites of activities, in which small scale cultivation or horticulture served as an adjunct to the husbandry of animals and the exploitation of wild resources by dispersed and relatively mobile communities. This is not to play down the significance of

---

Note: Chronology is expressed in uncalibrated radiocarbon years bc.

domesticates for the ways in which human groups use and make sense of their environment and themselves. The shift to food production may create the potential for major changes in the manner in which social relations are mediated, in the perception of thresholds between culture and nature, and in conceptions of space and time. But given the gradual nature of subsistence change in Britain, we must ask why it is that we see the rather more rapid appearance of monuments, highly visible mortuary practices, and novel classes of material culture towards the end of the fourth millennium bc (Bradley 1984; Herne 1988).

Julian Thomas has argued that the Neolithic is best seen as a cultural rather than an economic package, an integrated system of ideas concerning the character of social relations and the links between society, the ancestors and the natural world, taken on board by largely indigenous communities. In his view, there is little to be gained from seeing the tombs and causewayed enclosures of the earlier Neolithic as secondary phenomena — as responses to new subsistence practices or as consequences of a process of 'settling down' (*contra* Case 1969). Rather, these sites, and the activities that they witnessed, were central to what he calls the idea of 'being Neolithic' — an idea which took the form of a transformation of the social relations of production (Thomas 1988).

There is little to be gained from going into this argument in any detail here beyond saying that the distinction that Thomas draws between the economy and this network of ideas is somewhat rigid. Perhaps because of this, there is a sense in which this concept of 'being Neolithic' appears to hang in the ether. In other words, it remains difficult to understand how relations within and between small scale, dispersed and probably lineage-based communities were actually grounded in day-to-day practice and reproduced over space and time. It is against this background that I would like to consider the evidence for the production and circulation of one of the artefacts that characterise (and occasionally stand for) the earlier Neolithic in Britain — the polished flint or stone axe.[1] In what follows, I shall try to give a sense of the broad conditions in which many of these items were produced, circulated and consumed. On this basis, we may be better placed to discuss the ways in which the creation and engagement of material culture may have contributed to the broader process of social reproduction.

Axe production and dispersal

To a large extent, our picture of axe production and dispersal owes its existence to the work of the Implement Petrology Committee of the Council for British Archaeology, and to the long history of research on early Neolithic flint mines and, rather more recently, stone axe quarries. In the former case, some sixty years of research have enabled us to build up a static picture of

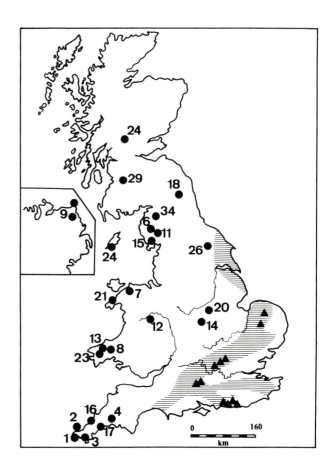

Fig. 7.1. Principal sources of non-flint stone identified through petrological analysis. The hatched area represents the main outcrops of flint. Triangles mark the position of Neolithic flint mines.

the distribution of non-flint stone axes away from a number of known sources (Fig. 7.1; Clough & Cummins 1988). In the latter, excavations at extraction sites have provided information on the character and chronology of production (Bradley & Edmonds 1988; Curwen & Curwen 1924; 1926; Pye 1968; Warren 1922). With the exception of a number of Mesolithic examples recovered from Wales and Ireland (see below), it seems that the production of polished stone axes was first undertaken in Britain towards the end of the fourth millennium bc. This seems to have been followed by an increase in the scale of dispersal patterns during the first half of the third millennium. Problems with the characterisation of flint have meant that we do not understand the distribution of flint mine products in anything like the same detail (Bush & Sieveking 1968; Craddock *et al.* 1983). However, it does seem that they may also have circulated over relatively broad areas from around the same time.

Traditionally, the interpretation of these broad patterns has been regarded as something of a secondary problem, and in certain cases as unproblematic. In keeping with our tendency to consider technology within a largely utilitarian framework, the appearance of polished axes at the beginning of the Neolithic has been understood as a function of the changing demands that

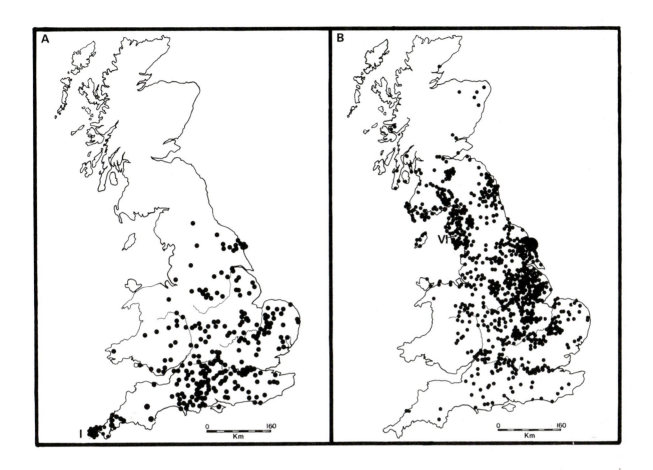

Fig. 7.2. Distribution of stone axes from Cornish (petrological group I) and Cumbrian (petrological group VI) sources.

accompanied a switch to sedentary agricultural prac-tices. As I have argued elsewhere, these same ideas have informed our understanding of the mechanisms responsible for the dispersal of axes (Edmonds 1990). Thus the literature abounds with references to 'bulk trade', 'factories' and entrepreneurial middlemen, with mines and quarries cast as evidence for '. . . the first of a series of European industrial revolutions' (Sieveking 1979, 6). More recent studies have highlighted an association between axes and causewayed enclosures, and have cast these sites as nodal points within large-scale trading monopolies (Mercer 1980). Others have drawn upon formal models of exchange to argue that our broad dispersal patterns reflect the bulk movement of certain groups of axes to secondary redistribution centres (Cummins 1979).[2] A full discussion of the legacy bequeathed by these earlier studies is beyond the scope of this short paper (but see Bradley & Edmonds 1993). Here it is perhaps sufficient to suggest that the scale of our analyses, and the language we have used to capture the character of axe production and dispersal have sustained a series of images of the Neolithic which should — at the very least — be open to question.

Now, it should be clear that the problems we en-counter in our attempts to understand these phenomena stem from a variety of sources. At one level, it easy to be misled by the overall scale of axe dispersal. In other words, we frequently grant our patterns a measure of coherence which may bear little or no relation to the varied conditions under which they were formed, or to the partial knowledge of the wider exchange 'system' held by participants situated in different local tradi-tions. This is a problem which is by no means confined to studies of the 'axe trade' (e.g. Kristiansen 1984). Equally, it is all too easy to take the scale of a number of the sources at face value, using this as the basis for inferring the existence of factories and industrially organised labour (Felder 1979). In fact, radiocarbon dates and simulation studies indicate that our distribu-tion maps reflect patterns of hand-to-hand circulation that unfolded over a number of generations (Smith 1979). Similarly, the evidence from mines and quarries suggests that the field monuments that we see today are the result of exploitation undertaken over several cen-turies. It is perhaps significant that we have never found it necessary to invoke an industrially organised labour force to explain the construction of contempo-rary ceremonial monuments.

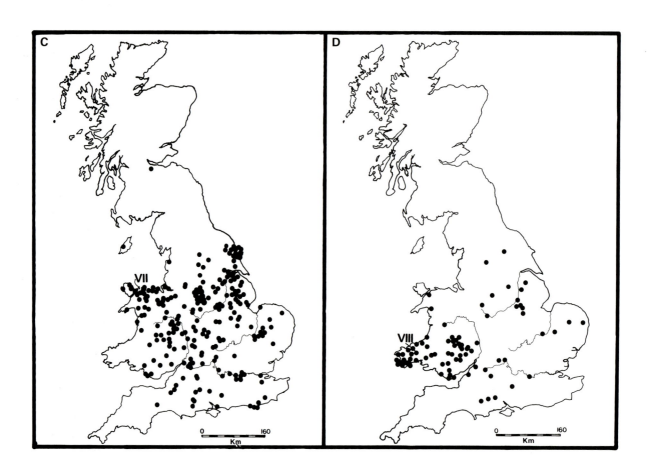

Fig. 7.3. Distribution of stone axes from sources in north (petrological group VII) and south (petrological group VIII) Wales.

To this confusion of scale can be added the problems of motivation and demand. If we accept that the earlier Neolithic did not witness a wholesale economic transformation, it becomes difficult to see the relatively sudden appearance of polished flint and stone axes as a simple reflection of new practical demands. Moreover, this general model does not really account for the manner in which certain axes were treated. More often than not, axes have been recovered as stray finds, and many show signs of having been used for practical tasks. With others, we get the impression that they may have been deposited with some formality: in pits, in enclosures and funerary contexts, in hoards, and even in rivers (Adkins & Jackson 1978; Chappell 1987). Similarly, clusters of exotic stone and mined flint axes may occur near to monuments, and large numbers are found in areas which are themselves rich in raw materials (Barrett *et al.* 1991; Bradley 1984; Clough & Cummins 1988; Woodward 1991). Many of the axes recovered from these more formal deposits may themselves have been used for practical tasks, and although some would have been of limited utility, these patterns call into question the rigid distinction that we have tended to draw between the functional and symbolic properties of material culture. They also require us to look again at the idea that the dispersal of axes can be simply understood as a reflection of utilitarian demand.

Beneath these issues lies a rather more basic problem of perception. Concepts derived from modern economics, notions of practical utility and formal models of exchange may be useful as tools with which to think about our data. But they may not in themselves provide a sufficient basis for understanding patterns of production, circulation and consumption in the past (cf. Hodder 1982). Over the last few years, we have begun to explore the rather more complex roles that objects may play in mediating people's understandings of themselves and their relations with others. In particular, attention has focused upon the sense in which the production and routine use of material culture may contribute to the reproduction or reworking of the categories that obtain in a particular society. Produced and used within specific fields of social practice, items may come to objectify particular sets of ideas and associations, and as such, may 'act back' upon or refer to aspects of those practices. In this way, their creation and engagement serves to sustain people's tacit understanding of themselves and of their world. They might refer to particular practices or divisions of labour, to persons or properties of persons, or to concepts of affiliation and obligation. Smoothed with service and patinated with history, artefacts may serve as metaphors or mnemonics — presencing a variety of concepts which are understood through practice, and in relation to context and audience.

At the same time, the ideas inculcated through the habitual use of material items may also be pulled into sharper focus at specific junctures. They may be referenced and reinterpreted in social discourse as people attempt to rework aspects of the conditions under which they live (Barrett 1988). In the small-scale societies with which we are likely to be dealing in the British Neolithic, distinctions and divisions are often drawn on the basis of age, gender and group affiliation. Moreover, tensions commonly arise in the reproduction of relations between age grades, the negotiation of marriage ties, and in competition within and between lineages for particular material and symbolic resources (Larick 1985; 1986; Meillassoux 1968; Strathern 1988). Indeed, it is often around these symbolic resources, rather than the means of production *per se*, that contradictions and conflicts of interest may arise.

It is this potential for objects to carry a constellation of ideas and associations which is often drawn upon in exchange, and here it is useful to consider the distinction that has been made between commodities and gifts (Gregory 1982). That distinction should not be drawn too firmly. Nor should it be reified so that it comes to stand respectively for the character of transactions in capitalist and non-capitalist societies. As Thomas has recently pointed out, there is a pressing need to question many of our tacit assumptions regarding the impersonal nature of commodity transfers and the 'faceless' qualities of barter (N. Thomas 1991). Even in contemporary western society, the creation, circulation and consumption of objects may be quite literally 'entangled' in a disparate and at times obscure web of social and political concerns (Bourdieu 1977; Miller 1987). Equally, there can be little justification for our tendency to romanticise non-capitalist societies, ignoring their '*calculative, impersonal and self-aggrandising features*' (Appadurai 1986, 11). Important though these caveats are, the distinction between commodities and gifts goes some way towards capturing the sense in which the circulation of objects in non-capitalist societies may play an intimate role in the classification of people. Although forms of gift exchange may differ in terms of the ways in which they reproduce social relations, the practice of *keeping while giving* is often an important medium through which webs of kinship, authority and obligation are negotiated and sustained (Rowlands 1987, 6–7; Strathern 1988; Weiner 1985). Put simply, exchange may play a central part in the creation of genealogies. Through its engagement, and its passage from one context to another, the exchanged object acquires a history which refers not only to the past and present condition of social relations, but also to future ties and obligations.

At the same time, it is important to recognise that whilst exchanged objects may possess cultural biographies, their significance is nevertheless dependent upon context. Their associations may be reworked through emulation, through changes in the conditions under which they are acquired and circulated, or through their deployment in different settings. For example, objects obtained as commodities may subsequently be deployed as gifts in different contexts (Godelier 1977). Equally, the significance accorded to gifts may be transformed as they move through different spheres and from one 'regime of value' to another (Appadurai 1986). In archaeological terms, then, we must acknowledge that the significance accorded to an object and the circumstances of its transfer may change though time and space (Edmonds 1990). At the very least this raises serious questions concerning the idea that we can reconstruct or excavate the plethora of meanings and associations ascribed to the objects that we recover (Hodder 1989). For that reason, we need to shift our focus — to consider relations between objects and their contexts, and the broader conditions in which their meanings would have been sustained or transformed.

These ideas are important for our understanding of axe production and exchange during the early Neolithic. It is not possible to draw a neat line between the practical functions of these artefacts and their symbolic qualities. Nor can we assume that the significance accorded to the products of specific mines or quarries remained unchanged as they circulated in contexts away from their source (Bradley & Edmonds 1993). The vast majority of axes were undoubtedly used for everyday tasks. But at the same time they may have possessed significance as markers of social identity, derived from their association with particular tasks and people, and thus with specific divisions of labour, age, gender and affiliation. On the basis of recent research in Brittany and the Channel Islands, there is some basis for suggesting that polished axes were associated with concepts of maleness and adulthood (Patton 1991; Thomas & Tilley in press). Indeed, Thomas and Tilley suggest that the axe may have been a particularly important symbol — linking networks of signification that extended across a variety of different contexts. Although imported jadeite axes have been recovered from Neolithic contexts, it is open to question how far their introduction involved a reworking of their significance. For that reason, we should exercise caution in applying these more specific inferences to the British evidence. However, this should not prevent us from asking how the production, use and circulation of these objects might have contributed to the broader process of social reproduction.

Source criticism

Turning to the evidence for axe production, it is perhaps important to stress that we are not dealing with black and white patterns, but with trends and differences of emphasis. Polished axes of both flint and stone were produced away from the major sources throughout the Neolithic, reflecting the exploitation of surface exposures of flint, coastal and riverine deposits, and glacially distributed material (Briggs 1976; Gardiner 1990). The same patterns of exploitation are indicated by the cores, debitage and other tools that characterise many earlier Neolithic assemblages (Gardiner 1984; Holgate 1989; Richards 1990; Woodward 1991). Like many tranchet forms, those Mesolithic polished axes that have been recognised in Wales and Ireland suggest that this pattern of surface exploitation had a history which extended far into the past (Care 1982; David 1989; Woodman 1978). What is important here is that the majority of these earlier polished axes are made from mudstones, schists, shales and pebbles. In other words, they do not reflect the development and use of the major axe sources prior to the Neolithic. In those few cases where a major Mesolithic raw material source has been investigated, there is no evidence to suggest that these sites witnessed any particular emphasis upon axe production. Put simply, it seems that the practice of selecting, developing and exploiting mines and quarries for the production of polished axes was itself an innovation — no less significant than the appearance of tombs and enclosures.

Information regarding the particular character of this innovation can be gained from the sources themselves. Despite certain obvious differences, the upland quarries and the chalkland mines of the earlier Neolithic have a number of characteristics in common. For example, it is clear than many of these sources were set apart form the main areas of contemporary settlement, even though adequate raw material could be found 'closer to home'. In the case of the Sussex flint mines, the physical distance involved may have been relatively small, and many of the upland sources such as Tievebulliagh, Graig Lwyd, or Great Langdale would have been visible from areas of settlement in the lowlands. This may also have applied to flint mines, where the white scars of shafts and dumps would have been in stark contrast to their heavily wooded environs. Nevertheless, it seems that these sites were physically marginal, a possibility supported by the lack of any evidence for settlement or domestic activity in their immediate environs.

Further links can be made in terms of the scheduling of source exploitation. Evidence from a number of sources suggests that the earlier use of these sites may have been episodic or 'event-like'. For example, palaeoenvironmental data from Great Langdale indicate that the immediate area of the source witnessed the development of grassland and pasture rather earlier than other parts of the Cumbrian uplands (Bradley & Edmonds 1988). Here at least, the evidence would accord with a model of episodic or even seasonal exploitation by small groups, embedded in broader cycles of movement associated with animal husbandry. In the case of the flint mine complexes, it is likely that only a small number of the shafts what we see today (Fig. 7.4) would have been exploited at any one time, again, probably by relatively small groups (Gardiner 1990; Holgate 1991; Pye 1968).

Connections can also be made in terms of the character and organisation of production. Whilst items such as mining tools, sickles, laurel leaves and arrowheads were also made at flint mines, the assemblages from all of these sources are dominated by evidence for axe production (Gardiner 1990). Indeed, at many of the upland sources, these are the only artefacts that were made in any numbers (Edmonds 1989; Warren 1922). Many sources also share similar characteristics in respect of the spatial organisation of production. For example, it is clear that the flaked or roughed-out axes produced at many sites were taken elsewhere for grinding and polishing. There is no reason to question the idea that this final stage of production generally took place within the lowland settlement zone. However, the presence of 'axe polishing grooves' at West Kennet (Piggott 1962), and of polissoirs at enclosures such as the Trundle and Etton, indicates that the final form of axes may occasionally have been realised in rather more specialised contexts (see below).

At a more detailed level, the character of a number of sources offers clues as to the choreography of activities on the site. In the case of Great Langdale, recent research suggests that the earliest phases of exploitation saw small groups procuring raw material along the outcrop of volcanic tuff and undertaking initial reduction at the point of extraction. This seems to have been followed by the movement of angular blocks and large flakes of tuff to a series of temporary campsites which have been recognised on the major access routes away from the source. Similar patterns have also been noted at Graig Lwyd (Warren 1922). The majority of these camps lie within 0.75 km of the outcrop itself, and all are close to upland water sources. Here, these blocks were further reduced to create crude roughouts which possessed symmetry in plan if not in section. The debitage found at these locations also suggests that the sequences of action followed during roughout production were varied and relatively unstructured. Little concern appears to have been given to the anticipation and avoidance of errors during flaking, or to the final form of the axes themselves. These roughouts were then taken down to the lowlands for grinding and polishing (Bunch & Fell 1949; Bradley & Edmonds 1993; Manby 1965).

Due to their physical characteristics, the chalkland flint mines offer a rather different set of potentials for our understanding of the manner in which activities were structured. On the basis of evidence from sites such as Harrow Hill, it is possible that the digging of the main shafts may have taken place alongside the small-scale open-cast working of the flint seams

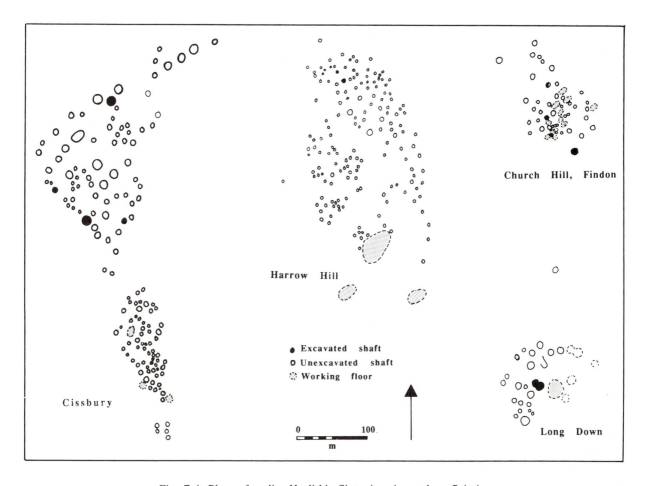

Fig. 7.4. Plans of earlier Neolithic flint mines in southern Britain.

outcropping on or near the surface. Variation in extractive techniques is also attested at some of the upland stone axe quarries, and in one case at least may be related to changes in the social context of production through time. We shall return to this point below, but first we must move into the mine shafts themselves.

There can be little doubt that the practice of winning flint in this manner was one fraught with risks and uncertainties. On the basis of excavations at Cissbury, Blackpatch, Harrow Hill and Church Hill, it seems likely that the process of actually sinking the shafts would have been a group effort — requiring co-operation between a number of individuals. This may also have applied to the backfilling of shafts, which often appears to have taken place after an interval of only a few days (Gardiner 1990; Park-Harrison 1878). However, once the shaft had been dug to the required level, often below higher seams of flint that would have been adequate for axe production, it is possible to detect changes in the physical character of working. The radial galleries that run off from the majority of excavated shafts are generally quite narrow, although variations do exist in terms of the distance that they travel (Fig. 7.5). As such, it would have been impractical for more than one person to work in a gallery at any one

time. Indeed, abrasions and smoothing on the gallery walls at Harrow Hill give a vivid sense of the physical constraints within which individuals would have worked (Curwen & Curwen 1926, 114).

In certain cases, notably at Harrow Hill and Cissbury, links between galleries, and even with backfilled shafts, were established during the course of working. However, the majority of excavations suggest that the entrances to individual galleries were maintained as discrete features. This is particularly clear in the case of one of the shafts at Blackpatch, where a wall of chalk blocks and debris was constructed to separate the entrances to two galleries (Fig. 7.5; Curwen *et al.* 1924, 70). Small 'nests' of debitage and broken roughouts have been located in the shafts and gallery entrances at a number of sites, indicating that a limited amount of axe production was conducted at the point of extraction. However, the bulk of the flint located during the sinking of the shaft and the working of the galleries was taken up to the surface in relatively unmodified state. It was at working areas on the surface that the creation of roughout axes was generally undertaken.

For the most part, discussions of flint mines have emphasised the practical constraints imposed by the local geology and topography. Thus shafts are seen as

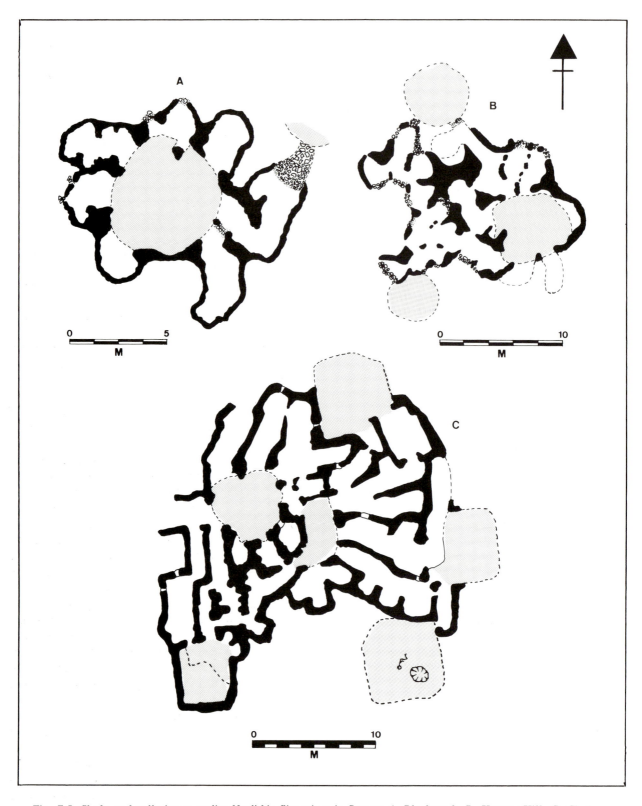

Fig. 7.5. Shafts and galleries at earlier Neolithic flint mines in Sussex: A. Blackpatch, B. Harrow Hill, C. Cissbury.

the only practicable method of reaching buried flint seams, whilst narrow, curving galleries represent the safest and most efficient strategy for maximising returns and minimising risks. Similarly, the fact that higher seams of flint have often been cut through in pursuit of lower deposits is usually taken to indicate that the miners were after flint of the highest quality. It is not my intention to challenge all of these arguments here. What can be questioned is our tendency to take these characteristics, together with the overall scale of mine complexes, as evidence that mining was an 'industry' in the hands of specialists (e.g. Bush & Sieveking

1986; see Gardiner 1990 for further criticisms of this view).

As we have already seen, there is little evidence to indicate that working was conducted on the scale suggested by these industrial models. It is also worth noting that, whilst the highest 'quality' stone in the lower seams may have been difficult to extract, it would also have been the easiest to work. If we accept the existence of distinct and highly skilled groups of specialists as implied by these models, then we must also accept that these individuals would have been quite capable of working much of the flint derived from higher seams. In fact, it may be just as important that the flint from the lower seams is often highly distinctive and thus easily recognisable. Equally, I would not wish to question the idea that many of the features of these sites may be understood as attempts to cope with the dangers that accompanied the sinking of shafts and the cutting of galleries. The point to emphasise here is that these features would also have provided a 'frame' that structured the arrangement and movement of people (Moore 1985). As such, they would have provided a series of cues for peoples' understandings of their social as well as their physical relationship with others.

Perhaps the most obvious case to be made concerns the shafts themselves. It remains to be seen how far flint might also have been obtained through more extensive open-cast mining on certain sites. What is important here is that the shafts that characterise so many flint mines are distinct and bounded entities. They demarcate the areas within which work could be undertaken, and allow distinctions to be drawn between people in terms of who might participate. Once established, the sinking of shafts would have involved close physical contact and co-operation between a small number of individuals. In this sense, the demarcation and sinking of shafts would have been both a product of group endeavour and a medium through with the identity of that group was reaffirmed. In other words, the choreography of activities at flint mines may have been implicated in the reproduction of relations ordered on the basis of kinship and/or group affiliation (Burton 1984). Indeed, if the use of mines involved a measure of temporary separation from the wider community, this would have provided the conditions in which distinctions could be made in terms of who was allowed to travel to the source. For this reason, it is possible that these arrangements may have served to sustain age and gender distinctions.

Given their limited size, the galleries that emanate from the base of many shafts may have provided the potential for distinctions to be drawn between individuals, and for links to be made between people and raw materials. This may also have been the case where individuals produced axes within the shaft itself, adjacent to the galleries from which the raw material had been obtained. However, the task of removing the bulk of the flint from the shaft and the process of backfilling

and restoring the ground would again have required close co-operation. With the move from the shaft to the surface working areas, further potentials would have existed for the creation of links between individuals and the artefacts that they produced. This may also have applied at the camps established on the margins of several upland sources. Contrary to recent arguments, there is no technological or spatial evidence to support a model of a 'production line' approach to stoneworking at these sites (Claris & Quartermaine 1989). Working in close proximity, people would have been able to observe the creation of axes by others and would themselves have been observed. Carried away from the source and back to the world of day-to-day activity, these artefacts would, in their turn, have carried associations with specific people, and with the circumstances in which they were produced. The depressions and scars that remained on the hillside would have served as tangible reminders of the activities that had been undertaken there. These would have been encountered on subsequent trips to the source, and in certain cases may even have been visible from a distance. For people returning to flint mines after an interval of time, and particularly for later generations, these traces would have influenced the orientation of new episodes of activity, and may have served to reaffirm the traditional associations and historical significance of their actions. For a variety of reasons, then, it may be helpful to consider mines and quarries as monuments.[3]

The removal of flaked axes from the flint mines and upland sources returns us to the broader context within which their exploitation was situated. Once we accept that working may have been both small-scale and episodic, there is no need to invoke notions of full-time specialists or factories. Rather, it seems more likely that these sources served as discrete contexts within which it was appropriate to produce objects that marked aspects of a person's social identity. This spatial and temporal disjuncture may have been one of the media through which the links between axes and social identity were sustained. Not only that, the techniques and gestures learnt at a source may have played their own small part in marking the social identity of people once they had returned to their settlements. At the same time, the organisation of journeys to and from the source, and the character of activities in and around particular shafts, would have served as a frame for the classification of people. Embedded in routines of movement through the landscape, the character and tempo of activities at the sources may also have been keyed into broader conceptual schemes concerning patterns and cycles in the lives of the individual and the community.

Axes and enclosures

These same themes are important when we consider another category of context with which axes appear to have been closely associated during the earlier Neolithic

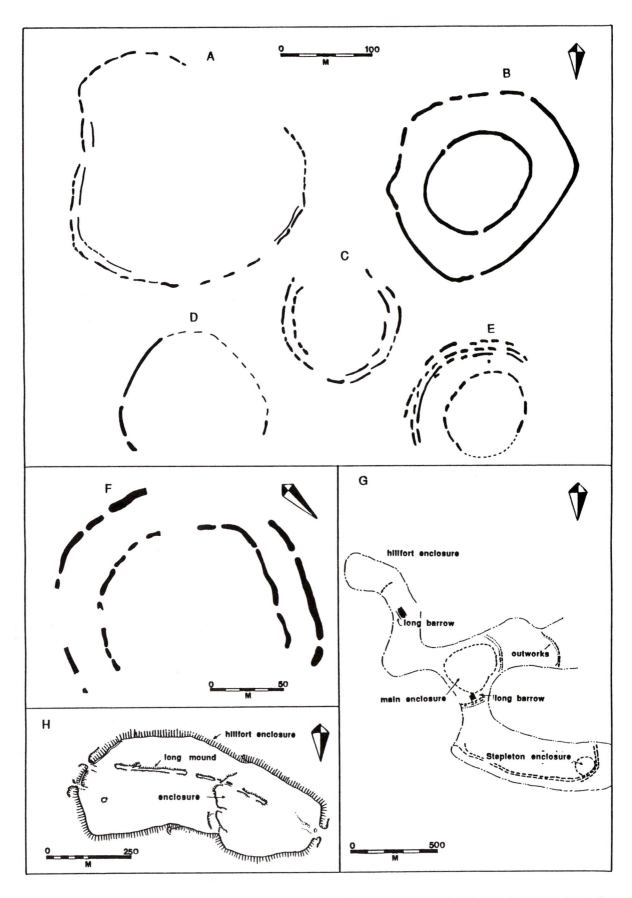

Fig. 7.6. Outline plans of selected causewayed enclosures: A. Haddenham, Cambridgeshire; B. Robin Hood's Ball, Wiltshire; C. Great Wilbraham, Cambridgeshire; D. Etton, Cambridgeshire; E. Orsett, Essex; F. Staines, Surrey; G. the Hambledon Hill complex, Dorset; H. Maiden Castle, Dorset.

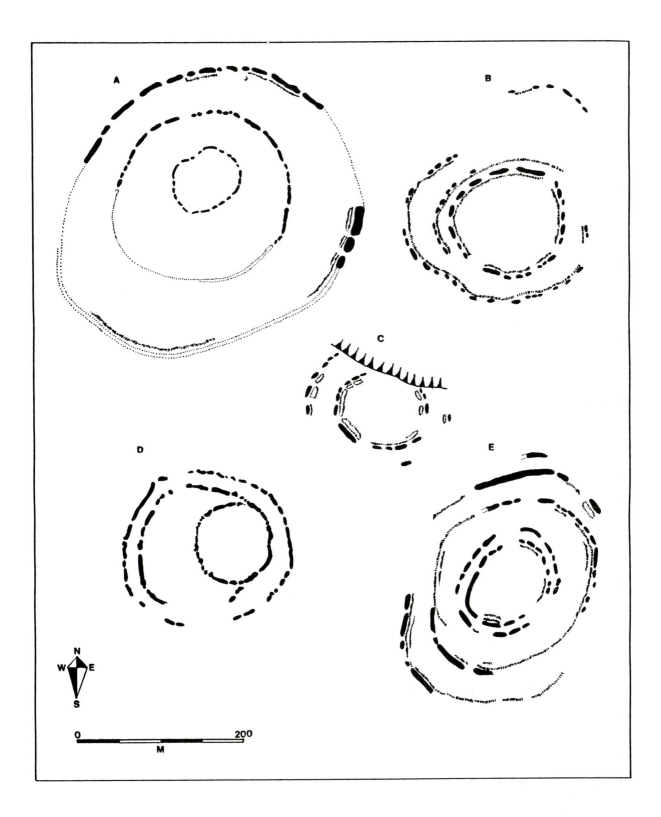

Fig. 7.7. Outline plans of selected causewayed enclosures: A. Windmill Hill, Wiltshire; B. the Trundle, Sussex; C. Coombe Hill, Sussex; D. Briar Hill, Northamptonshire; E. Whitehawk, Sussex.

(Figs. 7.6–7.7). Like the majority of the sources, many causewayed enclosures were themselves situated in locations which were peripheral to the main areas of contemporary settlement. Indeed, a number are situated on or near to sources of raw material (Care 1980; Healey & Robertson-Mackay 1983). The vast majority were also used on an episodic basis: constructed, abandoned, reused and reconstructed over considerable periods of time. Unlike their continental counterparts, very few contain evidence for permanent settlement, and in those cases where this is apparent, it is generally associated with the final phases of their use (e.g. Dixon 1988). Other sites may only have witnessed one or two brief episodes of activity before permanent abandonment.[4]

It would take another paper to discuss the particular character and changing significance of causewayed enclosures, and we should be wary of treating them as a unitary category with common functions and common sequences. The passage of time saw major changes in the physical character of particular sites, and their location within the social landscape (Edmonds in press; Whittle 1988). But it does seem that, in the context of cycles of movement around the landscape, different groups may have come together at these locales (Smith 1965). Indeed, like the activities that were undertaken within their bounds, the episodic construction and reconstitution of enclosures would have required communal effort, and may itself have provided a medium for the evocation of ties between dispersed and fragmented communities (Evans 1988).

In general terms, the assemblages recovered from many enclosures appear to reflect an emphasis upon specific episodes of consumption. The ditches which demarcate the perimeter of these sites may contain a variety of formal deposits of pottery, lithic debitage, stone and flint axes, animal bone and other food remains. Pits may also contain deliberate deposits of a similar character. Indeed, it is deposits such as these which have been used to argue that enclosures were elite centres controlling large-scale trading networks (Bradley 1984; Mercer 1980). The faunal assemblages recovered from a number of sites are dominated by elements of the cattle skeleton which may reflect feasting, and there is evidence that many witnessed activities associated with the treatment of the dead. Fragmentary human remains are found in a variety of contexts, and complete skeletons have been recognised at a number of sites (Mercer 1980; Thorpe 1984; Robertson-Mackay 1987; Whittle 1988). As I have argued elsewhere, this emphasis on episodes of consumption is significant, because such activities often occur in the context of a variety of rites of passage — events which attend and animate important junctures in the life of the individual and the community (Edmonds in press). Such events are often divided into stages: an initial phase of separation giving way to one of liminality, in turn followed by one of reincorporation (Turner 1961; Van Gennep 1960).

These ideas have been explored in a number of studies of earlier Neolithic funerary traditions, where it is possible to detect an emphasis upon the creation and veneration of ancestors and a denial of the substantive individual in death (Bradley 1984). Recent work has highlighted subtle variations on this theme (J. Thomas 1991; Thomas & Whittle 1986), but it is at the liminal stage that the transformation of individual identity generally occurs, often through the removal of flesh. In these circumstances, one of the purposes that many enclosures may have served was the provision of a demarcated context in which such activities could be undertaken, their liminal nature being emphasised by their peripheral location. The conditions established at enclosures would have provided a context within which the dead could be moved closer to tombs and to incorporation with the ancestors. They may also have provided a frame within which to contain or transform the properties of those who were generally excluded from tombs, and here the frequency of young children at enclosures may be significant (Thorpe 1984; Woodward 1991). Indeed these conditions would have made it possible to synchronise the chance event of death itself with established routines or cycles of movement and social practice (Barrett pers. comm.).

It is against this backdrop that we need to consider the evidence for flint and stone axes being consumed at enclosures: burnt, smashed, and placed in formal deposits (Bradley 1984; J. Thomas 1991). Rather than invoke notions of monopolies, or of nodal points in large-scale trading networks, it is useful to relate these episodes of deposition to other practices conducted at a number of sites. If objects such as axes signified certain ideas about personal identity, then their deployment in different contexts would have effectively 'presenced' those ideas — conditioning the ways in which particular activities or phenomena were to be understood. Given this potential, the destruction or deposition of axes may have been undertaken in the context of funerary rituals which were concerned with the transformation of the social individual in death. This can be seen at Hambledon Hill, where pits containing stone axes may also have been linked to the defleshing of bodies (Mercer 1980). In other words, the consumption of axes may have been one of the means by which the category of the person could be reworked. Moreover, because of their connotations, deposits containing axes, fragmentary human remains and other cultural material may have served to reaffirm the links between particular sites and specific social groups.

The concept of rites of passage has further implications for this discussion, because death is just one of the thresholds at which conceptions of the social order may be brought into sharp relief. As we have seen, many enclosures are situated on or near to sources of raw material, and a number contain evidence for the production of tools such as axes and laurel leaves and for the manufacture and working of cores (Bradley 1982).

At Maiden Castle, for example, which is located on an outcrop of flint, recent work has shown that the production of axes took place within the enclosure and not outside (Sharples 1992; Woodward 1991). It is unlikely that this contrast is quite as dramatic as it seems. Nevertheless, there is a basis for arguing that objects such as axes may have been produced and obtained in the context of other events at these sites. It is tempting to see this association as further evidence that the procurement of markers of social identity was bound by convention and embedded within other important social practices. This process of demarcation is often crucial in contexts where identity and social position are expressed in terms of the possession and use of things. This may well have been the case, although evidence for the production of axes away from these specialised contexts reminds us that these traditions were by no means rigid or inflexible. It is equally unlikely that this idea captures the broader purposes that may have been served by the circulation and consumption of axes at these locales.

Because of their associations with particular practices and perhaps with specific categories of person, axes would also have provided an appropriate medium for exchanges which were implicated in the reproduction of relations within and between communities. In these circumstances, the location of enclosures, their association with rites of passage, and the episodic character of their use may all have contributed to their suitability as contexts within which different groups might come together, and in which a variety of exchanges could be conducted. As we have seen, the capacity for exchanged objects to carry histories and project social relations into the future is often enhanced by traditional conventions regarding the times and places at which appropriate responses can be made and obligations discharged or reworked. Furthermore, the circulation of objects within local regimes of value may require a transformation or reworking of their associations when they are introduced from outside (Appadurai 1986). More often than not, these transitions are effected not only in demarcated places, but also at specific times. In both these cases, then, the episodic use of many enclosures is potentially significant. Undertaken within a demarcated spatial and temporal context which was itself linked to broader routines of movement and economic activity, the circulation of artefacts, livestock and people would have served to create or reaffirm relations of authority and obligation within and between fragmented social groups. Such events would also have served to sustain the significance of objects such as the axe as important tokens of value.

Given that a number of sites witnessed sequences of use, re-use and remodelling that spanned centuries, it is difficult to determine precisely when non-local stone axes began to play a part in the use of enclosures. This development does appear, however, to be broadly contemporary with an apparent expansion in the scale of stone axe dispersal patterns in the second quarter of the third millennium bc, and with the end of activity at many of the early flint mines (Gardiner 1990; Smith 1979). In addition, recent work at Great Langdale suggests that the character and perhaps the social context of stone axe production may also have changed at around the same time (Bradley & Edmonds 1993). It would be simplistic to assume that the demise of earlier Neolithic flint mines can be 'explained' as a direct result of the expansion in stone axe dispersal patterns. Nevertheless, the particular character of these changes may contribute to our broader understanding of the ways in which relations within and between communities may also have been changing at this time.

In the case of Great Langdale, it is again important to stress that we are not dealing with simple dichotomies, but with changes of emphasis. Radiocarbon dates indicate that small groups may have continued to exploit the source and work the raw material along similar lines to those followed by earlier generations of producers. But it is at this juncture that we see the creation and maintenance of formal quarries, often placed in highly inaccessible locations. Mechanical tests indicate that the use of these locations had little to do with the physical quality of the stone itself. Raw material with precisely the same properties was available at other locations which presented far fewer problems of access.

Further changes can be detected in the spatial organisation of working, with a far greater emphasis placed upon the execution of all stages in roughout production at the point of extraction. In other words, the passage of time appears to witness an increasing concern with the demarcation of areas in which it was appropriate for working to be undertaken, perhaps by different groups. In addition, technological analyses indicate radical changes in the actual process of working around a piece of raw material. The debitage from many of these later sites reflects a greater concern with the anticipation and avoidance of errors, and with the maintenance of recurrent routines during flaking. Put simply, the massive waste assemblages found on these sites suggest an increasing concern with the careful realisation of the final form of the axe during flaking. The roughouts that were carried away from these sites would have required relatively little grinding and polishing before their final form was achieved.

The sequence identified at Great Langdale finds echoes in the data from the southern flint mines, where there is also evidence for the use of different extractive techniques and often different forms of spatial organisation. Axes produced at mines may well have served as media for exchange, but in the absence of similar studies at these sites and a clearer understanding of dispersal patterns, direct parallels should be made with caution. The changes in Cumbria appear to reflect a greater emphasis upon local production for exchange with groups outside of the region. But as before, there is no need to assume that they can be captured by industrial metaphors, or that they involved the development of monopolies or bulk trade. Nor should we see them simply as a reflection of increases in the *scale* of demand. Rather it seems that the *character* of that demand, and particularly the nature of exchange, may have changed towards the close of the earlier Neolithic.

Of particular importance here is the idea that the end of the earlier Neolithic in Britain is marked by changes in a number of different fields of social practice. These appear to include a greater concern with the substantive individual in death, changes in the extent to which particular groups may have exercised control over the activities conducted at certain enclosures and tombs, and the gradual emergence of a series of distinctive regional systems (Bradley 1984; Darvill 1987; Kinnes 1985; J. Thomas 1991). These changes are paralleled by increases in inter-assemblage variability, and in the proliferation of artefact forms (Bradley 1982). This suggests that different categories of material culture were increasingly drawn upon in a more explicit and considered manner to signal a wider range of attributes of personal identity (Edmonds & Thomas 1987). One feature of these trends is the increased importance that appears to have been attached to exotica — objects, motifs, and even ideas about monuments and practices that were drawn from distant sources. With the passage of time, it is possible that stone axes may also have been deployed in exchanges that established networks of contact and communication extending beyond the horizons of local lineage systems. They may have continued to circulate within particular regimes of value as one of the media through which distinctions drawn on the basis of age, gender and affiliation were negotiated. But their exotic origins may have provided a rather different set of potentials for the signification of broader ties between people, and perhaps a measure of control over patterns of circulation (Helms 1988). In effect, their movement may also have contributed to the reworking and reproduction of relations of dominance and subordination between different lineages.[5]

In certain respects, the sequences of change identified at sources such as Great Langdale invite models which work at a relatively general level. Thus it is tempting to combine these sequences with evidence for the demise of flint mines, and to argue that some of the more remote western sources developed in the way they did precisely because they were more distant. In other words, we might argue that the scale of the deposits at these sites reflects the considerable lengths of time over which the exclusivity of their products was maintained as they circulated in different regions and in different social contexts. By the same token, the end of activity at earlier Neolithic flint mines could be seen as a reflection of the difficulties that may have been encountered in controlling access to the raw materials that were used to produce important markers of social identity. Given that the end of the earlier Neolithic

witnessed changes in a variety of fields of social practice, including the character of exchange, the differences between these different categories of source may reflect a greater concern with controlling access to objects through established exchange networks, rather than control over production *per se*. However, whilst the argument remains at this level, it is difficult to understand the consequences that these broader changes would have had within specific local contexts.

No doubt the relationship was far from direct. But these broader changes in the spheres in which axes and other exotica circulated, and in the purposes that their passage served, would have had important consequences in their areas of origin. In the case of certain upland sources, the long established practice of axe production may have become a field within which specific groups might have come to exercise a greater degree of control and influence. In other words, the changes at Great Langdale may reflect the emergence of distinctions between local communities, in terms of their relationship with the source and with the broader social networks which carried the products beyond the regional horizon. Although our understanding of the Neolithic sequence in Cumbria is rather limited, it can be argued that these distinctions may themselves have become an important medium for the renegotiation of local regimes of authority and obligation (Bradley & Edmonds 1993).

Conclusion

The quotation with which this paper began may have been drawn from a very different context, but it nonetheless captures some of the problems that we encounter in our attempts to 'make sense' of the axe trade. Throughout this discussion, I have tried to show how the use of industrial metaphors and utilitarian models may not provide us with a sufficient basis for understanding the broader context of Neolithic axe production. Mines and quarries may be associated with an unequivocal economic activity; but at the same time the character of their use may have served to sustain or rework some of the categories of the social world. Similarly, I have tried to show how the analysis of broad dispersal patterns must begin with an acknowledgement that the significance accorded to particular objects, and the conditions under which they moved from one context to another, would have been far from constant. Given the properties of material culture, it is more than likely that the circulation and consumption of axes in earlier Neolithic Britain may have served a much wider range of purposes than those that I have touched upon here. Evidence from the Thames suggests that the conspicuous disposal of axes — the giving of 'gifts to the gods' may have served as a field in which relations to power and authority could be created and reaffirmed (Adkins & Jackson 1980). Objects such as axes may also have been handed down, linking individuals with previous generations and with established practices and lines of inheritance.

It should also be clear that this discussion has sacrificed a significant degree of detail in favour of a more general argument. For example, there may be little justification for the uncritical application of these ideas to all of the major sources that were exploited during the course of the period. Although the sinking of shafts may have ceased, certain mines continued to provide a focus for the surface procurement of flint, whilst others were established in association with settlements and with new forms of monument (Gardiner 1990; Stone 1931). Dispersal patterns demonstrate that, whilst stone axes from certain sources travelled considerable distances (Figs. 7.2–7.3), the products of others are found only 'close to home' (Clough & Cummins 1988; Darvill 1989). Similarly, radiocarbon dates suggest that at least one small axe source — Creag na Caillich in Scotland — was not exploited until the second half of the third millennium bc (Edmonds *et al*. in press). As work at the later Neolithic mines at Grime's Graves has shown, these patterns reflect important synchronic variations and changes through time in both the character and the broader context of stone tool production at particular locales (Healy 1991; Mercer 1981). Similar arguments may also apply to the evidence from Beer Head in Devon and from Flamborough Head in Yorkshire (Tingle pers. comm.; Manby 1988).

Inevitably, the explicit discussion of the ways in which objects may serve to sustain people's understanding of their world, and their place within it, almost contradicts the tacit and unconsidered manner in which this is often achieved. In the case of this paper I have tried to build upon the idea that the beginning of the Neolithic in Britain took the form of a transformation of the social relations of production. The construction and use of a variety of funerary and other ceremonial monuments undoubtedly played a central role in facilitating and sustaining that transformation. But on a day-to-day basis, specific ideas concerning relations between the individual, society and nature may also have been sustained and reworked through the production and routine use of material culture.

Because of their intimate association with particular practices and divisions of labour, and thus with specific categories of person, objects such as axes would also have provided an appropriate medium for exchange. The manner in which the procurement of these items was choreographed, and the conditions under which they were circulated, may thus have been crucial to the creation and protection of a variety of distinctions and divisions in society. But at the same time, these broad conditions would also have served to sustain the interpretation of objects such as axes as appropriate markers of identity and tokens of value. Put simply, the periodic procurement and exchange of axes in specified contexts may have had important consequences for the significance accorded to those that were made and used more

widely. With the passage of time, those properties may have been drawn upon in different ways as new concerns and conflicts of interest arose within and between contexts. Just as these concerns may have drawn axes into new social contexts and into new realms of significance, so they also draw this discussion to an end.

Notes

1. Whilst it is important to differentiate between flaked and polished axes, no distinction is drawn between grinding and polishing in this paper.

2. Attempts to apply formal exchange models to stone axe dispersal patterns have been made on a number of occasions, most recently in a study which combines distributional data with information on the morphology of axes from different contexts (Chappell 1987). Information of this nature is clearly of great importance. For example, the existence of different 'regimes of value' may be reflected in the manner and range of uses to which different raw materials are put (Bradley & Edmonds 1993). Nevertheless, formal models have yet to deal with the problem that, just as different forms of exchange may exist in a given context, so there may be no one-to-one correlation between distributional pattern and exchange process. Moreover, as Hodder has argued, we say very little when we note that a particular archaeological pattern 'fits' or deviates from a regression line (Hodder 1982). Formal models retain their greatest value where they are used as heuristic devices — as tools with which to explore different aspects of our empirical record. They may not in themselves provide a basis for substantive inferences or predictions.

3. The association of these traces with specific groups may also have been strengthened in those cases where burials were placed within shafts. This is apparent at Cissbury, where the remains of a small number of individuals have been recovered (Park-Harrison 1978; Pye 1968). Given the circumstances of the excavations, little can be said regarding the character of these deposits. But, unlike the disarticulated remains generally found within contemporary tombs, the burials at Cissbury were of articulated bodies. In other words, these burials were of substantive individuals drawn from communities of the living. They were categorically different from the bundles of disarticulated tomb deposits that may have been more closely associated with the realm of the ancestors (Bradley 1984).

4. Here it is useful to consider Evans' notion of 'monuments as projects', initiated, reworked and abandoned, but never finished (Evans 1988).

5. It is also clear that the onset of the later Neolithic in Britain sees an increased emphasis upon the local production of artefacts from distinctive raw materials and in different styles. These patterns appear to reflect an increasing use of easily recognisable portable artefacts to signify a wider range of ideas concerning the social identity of individuals. There is little to be gained from subsuming all of these patterns within a generalised model of prestige goods. nor are they simply reflections of 'peer polity interaction', a term which implies a conception of communities as rigidly bounded entities. Rather, it may be more useful to consider them in relation to changes in

other fields of social practice, as reflections of an increased concern with the drawing of distinctions amongst the living, and with the explicit reproduction of lines of genealogy, descent and inheritance.

References

Adkins, R., & Jackson, R., 1978. *Neolithic Stone and Flint Axes from the River Thames*. London: British Museum Occasional Paper 1

Appadurai, A., (ed.) 1986. *The Social Life of Things. Commodities in Social Perspective*. Cambridge: Cambridge University Press, 3–63

Barrett, J.C., 1988. Fields of discourse: reconstituting a social archaeology. *Critique of Anthropology* 9, 313–39

Barrett, J.C., Bradley, R., & Green, M., 1991. *Landscape, Monuments and Society. The Prehistory of Cranborne Chase*. Cambridge: Cambridge University Press

Bourdieu, P., 1977. *Outline of a Theory of Practice*. Cambridge: Cambridge University Press.

Bradley, R., 1982. Position and possession: assemblage variation in the British Neolithic. *Oxford Journal of Archaeology* 1(1), 27–38

Bradley, R., 1984. *The Social Foundations of Prehistoric Britain: Themes and Variations in the Archaeology of Power*. London & New York: Longman

Bradley, R., & Edmonds, M., 1988. Fieldwork at Great Langdale, Cumbria, 1985–1987: preliminary report. *Antiquaries Journal* 68(2), 181–209

Bradley, R., & Edmonds, M., 1993. *Interpreting the Axe Trade*. Cambridge: Cambridge University Press

Briggs, S., 1976. Notes on the distribution of some raw materials in later prehistoric Britain, in *Settlement and Economy in the Third and Second Millennia B.C.*, eds. C. Burgess & R. Miket. Oxford: British Archaeological Reports, British Series 33, 267–82

Bunch, B., & Fell, C., 1949. A stone axe factory at Pike of Stickle, Great Langdale. *Proceedings of the Prehistoric Society* 15, 1–20

Burton, J., 1984. Quarrying in a tribal society. *World Archaeology* 16, 234–47

Bush, P., & Sieveking, G. de G., 1986. Geochemistry and the provenance of flint axes, in *The Scientific Study of Flint and Chert*, eds G. Sieveking & M. Hart. Cambridge: Cambridge University Press, 133–40

Care, V., 1982. The collection and distribution of lithic materials during the Mesolithic and Neolithic periods in southern England. *Oxford Journal of Archaeology* 1(3), 269–285

Case, H., 1969. Neolithic explanations. *Antiquity* 43, 176–86

Chappell, S., 1987. *Stone Axe Morphology and Distribution in Neolithic Britain*. Oxford: British Archaeological Reports, British Series 177

Claris, P., & Quartermaine, J., 1989. The Neolithic quarries and axe factory sites of Great Langdale and Scafell Pike: a new survey. *Proceedings of the Prehistoric Society* 55, 1–25

Clough, T. H. McK., & Cummins, W.A., (eds), 1988. *Stone Axe Studies Volume 2*. London: Council for British Archaeology Research Report 67

Craddock, P.T., Cowell, M.R., Leese, M.N., & Hughes, M.J., 1983. The trace element composition of polished flint axes as an indicator of source. *Archaeometry* 25, 135–163

Cummins, W. A., 1979. Neolithic stone axes: distribution and trade, in *Stone Axe Studies*, eds T. K. McK. Clough & W.A. Cummins. London: Council for British Archaeology Research Report 23, 5–12

Curwen, E., & Curwen, E.C., 1926. Harrow Hill (Sussex) flint mine excavation, 1924–1925. *Sussex Archaeological Collections* 67, 103–38

Curwen, E., Curwen, E.C., Frost, M., & Goodman, C., 1924. Blackpatch flint mine excavation 1922. *Sussex Archaeological Collections* 65, 69–111

Darvill, T., 1987. *Prehistoric Britain*. London: Batsford

Darvill, T., 1989. The circulation of Neolithic stone and flint axes: a case study from Wales and the mid-west of England. *Proceedings of the Prehistoric Society* 55, 27–43

David, A., 1989. Some aspects of the human presence in west Wales during the Mesolithic, in *The Mesolithic in Europe. Papers Presented at the Third International Symposium Edinburgh 1985*, ed. C. Bonsall. Edinburgh: John Donald, 241–53

Dixon, P., 1988. The Neolithic settlements on Crickley Hill, in *Enclosures and Defences in the Neolithic of Western Europe*, eds C. Burgess, P. Topping, C. Mordant & M. Maddison. Oxford: British Archaeological Reports, International Series S403, 75–88

Edmonds, M., 1990. Description, understanding and the chaîne opératoire. *Archaeological Review from Cambridge* 9(1), 55–71

Edmonds, M., in press. Interpreting causewayed enclosures in the present and the past, in *Interpretative Archaeology*, ed. C. Tilley. London & New York: Berg

Edmonds, M., Sheridan, A., & Tipping, R., in press. Survey and excavation at Creag na Caillich, Perthshire. *Proceedings of the Society of Antiquaries of Scotland*

Edmonds, M., & Thomas, J., 1987. The archers: an everyday story of country folk, in *Lithic Analysis and Later British Prehistory*, eds A.G. Brown & M.R. Edmonds. Oxford: British Archaeological Reports, British Series 162, 187–99

Evans, C., 1988. Acts of enclosure: a consideration of concentrically organised causewayed enclosures, in *The Archaeology of Context in the Neolithic and Bronze Age, Recent Trends*, eds J.C. Barrett & I.A. Kinnes. Sheffield: Department of Archaeology and Prehistory, 85–97

Felder, P.J., 1979. Prehistoric flint mining at Ricjkholt-St Gertruid and Grime's Graves, *Staringia* 6, 57–62

Gardiner, J., 1984. Lithic distributions and Neolithic settlement patterns in central southern England, in *Neolithic Studies: a Review of Some Current Research*, eds R. Bradley & J. Gardiner. Oxford: British Archaeological Reports, British Series 133, 15–40

Gardiner, J., 1990. Flint procurement and Neolithic axe production on the South Downs: a reassessment. *Oxford Journal of Archaeology* 9(2), 119–40

Godelier, M., 1977. *Perspectives in Marxist Anthropology*. Cambridge & New York: Cambridge University Press

Gregory, C.A., 1980. Gifts to men and gifts to god: gift exchange and capital accumulation in contemporary Papua. *Man* 15, 628–52

Gregory, C.A., 1982. *Gifts and Commodities*. Cambridge & London: Cambridge University Press

Healey, E., & Robertson-Mackay, R., 1983. The lithic industries from Staines causewayed enclosure and their relationship to other earlier Neolithic industries in southern Britain. *Lithics* 4, 1–27

Healy, F., 1991. The hunting of the floorstone, in *Interpret-*

ing Artefact Scatters: Contributions to Ploughzone Archaeology, ed. A.J. Schofield. Oxford: Oxbow Monograph 4, 29–37

Helms, M.W., 1988. *Ulysses' Sail. An Ethnographic Odyssey of Power, Knowledge, and Geographical Distance.* Princeton, N.J.: Princeton University Press

Herne, A., 1988. A time and a place for the Grimston bowl, in *The Archaeology of Context in the Neolithic and Bronze Age, Recent Trends*, eds J.C. Barrett & I.A. Kinnes. Sheffield: Department of Archaeology and Prehistory, 9–29

Hodder, I., 1982. Towards a contextual approach to prehistoric exchange, in *Contexts for Prehistoric Exchange*, eds J.E. Ericson & T.K. Earle. New York: Academic Press

Hodder, I., 1989. This is not an article about material culture as text. *Journal of Anthropological Archaeology* 8, 250–69

Holgate, R., 1988. *Neolithic Settlement of the Thames Basin.* Oxford: British Archaeological Reports, British Series 194

Holgate, R., 1991. *Prehistoric Flint Mines*. Princes Risborough: Shire

Kinnes, I.A., 1985. Circumstance not context: the Neolithic of Scotland as seen from outside. *Proceedings of the Society of Antiquaries of Scotland* 115, 15–57

Kinnes, I.A., 1988. The cattleship Potemkin: the first Neolithic in Britain, in *The Archaeology of Context in the Neolithic and Bronze Age, Recent Trends*, eds. J.C. Barrett & I.A. Kinnes. Sheffield: Department of Archaeology and Prehistory, 2–9

Kristiansen, K., 1984. Ideology and material culture: an archaeological perspective, in *Marxist Perspectives in Archaeology*, ed. M. Spriggs. Cambridge: Cambridge University Press, 72–100

Larick, R., 1985. Spears, style and time among Maa-speaking pastoralists. *Journal of Anthropological Archaeology* 4, 206–220

Larick, R., 1986. Age grading and ethnicity in Loikop (Samburu) spears. *Journal of Anthropological Archaeology* 4, 269–83

Manby, T.G., 1965. The distribution of rough-out Cumbrian and related axes of Lake District origin in northern England. *Transactions of the Cumberland and Westmorland Archaeological Society* 65, 1–37

Manby, T.G., 1988. The Neolithic in eastern Yorkshire, in *Archaeology in Eastern Yorkshire*, ed. T.G. Manby. Sheffield: Department of Archaeology and Prehistory, 35–88

Mellassoux, C., 1968. Ostentation, destruction, reproduction. *Economie et Société* 2, 760–72

Mercer, R.J., 1980. *Hambledon Hill a Neolithic Landscape.* Edinburgh: Edinburgh University Press

Mercer, R.J., 1981. *Grimes Graves, Norfolk, Excavations 1971-72: Volume I.* London: Department of the Environment Archaeological Report 11

Miller, D., 1987. *Material Culture and Mass Consumption.* Oxford: Blackwells

Moore, H., 1985. *Space, Text and Gender.* Cambridge: Cambridge University Press

Park-Harrison, J., 1878. Further discoveries at Cissbury. *Journal of the Royal Anthropological Institute* 7, 412

Patton, M. A., 1991. Axes, men and women: symbolic dimensions of Neolithic exchange in Armorica (northwest France), in *Sacred and Profane. Proceedings of a Conference on Archaeology, Ritual and Religion. Oxford 1989*, eds. P. Garwood, D. Jennings, R. Skeates & J.

Toms. Oxford: Oxford University Committee for Archaeology, 65–79

Piggott, S., 1962. *The West Kennet Long Barrow, Excavations 1955-56.* London: Ministry of Works Archaeological Reports 4

Pye, E.M., 1968. *The Flint Mines at Blackpatch, Church Hill and Cissbury, Sussex. a Report on the Late J.H. Pull's Excavations 1922-55.* Edinburgh: unpublished M.A. dissertation, University of Edinburgh

Richards, J., 1990. *The Stonehenge Environs Project.* London: English Heritage Archaeology Report 16

Rowlands, M., 1987. Core and periphery: a review of a concept, in *Centre and Periphery in the Ancient World*, eds M. Rowlands, K. Kristiansen & M. Larsen. Cambridge: Cambridge University Press

Sharples, N., 1991. *Maiden Castle: Excavations and Field Survey, 1985-6.* London: English Heritage Archaeological Report 19

Sieveking, G. de G., 1979. Grime's Graves and prehistoric European flint mining, in *Subterranean Britain. Aspects of Underground Archaeology*, ed. H. Crawford. London: John Baker, 1–43

Smith, I.F., 1965. *Windmill Hill and Avebury.* Oxford: Clarendon Press

Smith, I.F., 1979. The chronology of British stone implements, in *Stone Axe Studies*, eds T.H.McK. Clough & W.A. Cummins. London: Council for British Archaeology Research Report 23, 13–22

Strathern, M., 1988. *The Gender of the Gift.* Cambridge: Cambridge University Press

Stone, J.F.S., 1931. Easton Down, Winterslow, Wilts. Flint mine excavation 1930. *Wiltshire Archaeological and Natural History Magazine* 45, 350–65

Thomas, J., 1988. Neolithic explanations revisited: the Mesolithic-Neolithic transition in Britain and southern Scandinavia. *Proceedings of the Prehistoric Society* 54, 59–67

Thomas, J., 1991. *Rethinking the Neolithic.* Cambridge: Cambridge University Press

Thomas, J., & Tilley, C., in press. The axe and the torso, in *Interpretative Archaeology*, ed. C. Tilley. London & New York: Berg

Thomas, J., & Whittle, A.W.R., 1986. Anatomy of a tomb: West Kennet revisited. *Oxford Journal of Archaeology* 5, 129–56

Thomas, N., 1991. *Entangled Objects: Exchange, Material Culture and Colonialism in the Pacific* Cambridge (Mass.) & London: Harvard University Press

Thorpe, I.J., 1984. Ritual, power and ideology: a reconstruction of earlier Neolithic rituals in Wessex, in *Neolithic Studies: a Review of Some Current Research*, eds R. Bradley & J. Gardiner. Oxford: British Archaeological Reports, British Series 133, 41–60

Turner, V.W., 1961. *The Ritual Process: Structure and Anti-Structure.* New York: Cornell

Van Gennep, A., 1960 (1909). *The Rites of Passage.* London: RKP

Warren, S.H., 1922. The Neolithic stone axes of Graig Lwyd, Penmaenmawr. *Archaeologia Cambrensis* 77, 1–35

Weiner, A., 1985. Inalienable wealth. *American Ethnologist* 12(2), 210–27

Whittle, A.W.R., 1988. Contexts, activities, events — aspects of Neolithic and Copper Age enclosures in central and western Europe, in *Enclosures and Defences in the*

Neolithic of Western Europe, eds C. Burgess, P. Topping, C. Mordant & M. Maddison. Oxford: British Archaeological Reports, International Series S403, 1–20

Woodman, P., 1978. *The Mesolithic in Ireland*. Oxford: British Archaeological Reports, British Series 58

Woodward, P.J., 1991. *The South Dorset Ridgeway, Survey and Excavations 1977–84*. Dorchester: Dorset Archaeological and Natural History Society Monograph 8

8

Megalithic Tombs and Megalithic Art in Atlantic Europe

Elizabeth Shee Twohig

This paper reviews briefly some of the main trends in the past thirty years of study of megalithic tombs in Atlantic Europe. Binford's 1971 paper, together with the work of Renfrew and Fleming, was seminal to the discussions which have followed. In Atlantic Europe, tombs can now be dated to the fifth millennium cal. BC in both western France and Iberia. Megalithic art appears in France at this time on stelae as well as in tombs; this art has a distinct repertoire of motifs, many of which are identifiable. During the fourth millennium, art appears in Iberia and Ireland in addition to France, with broad similarities between the regions in this period.

Cette communication introduit une brève critique des tendances principales de l'étude des monuments mégalithiques de l'Europe atlantique, depuis ces trente dernières années. L'article de Binford paru en 1971, ainsi que les travaux de Renfrew et Fleming, constituent le fondement des discussions développées par la suite. Dans l'Europe atlantique, les monuments mégalithiques peuvent désormais être datées du cinquième millénaire av. J.C. en datation calibrée, à la fois dans l'ouest de la France et dans la péninsule Ibérique. C'est à ce moment qu'apparaît l'art mégalithique en France, à la fois sur les stèles et dans les tombes. Cet art présente un répertoire exclusif de motifs, dont plusieurs sont identifiables. Durant le quatrième millénaire, l'art apparaît dans la péninsule Ibérique et en Irlande, en plus qu'en France, avec des grandes similarités entre ces trois régions.

Introduction

The invitation to present a short paper under this title poses an interesting challenge which I shall try to meet by summarizing some of the current views on megalithic tombs: this will be followed by a review of what appear to be the more important results of recent research in three main geographical areas (north west Iberia, western France and Ireland) and a consideration of contacts between the areas. The intention is to condense, but hopefully not oversimplify, a topic which tends, on occasion, to be dealt with in terms more likely to confuse than to clarify.

Mortuary studies 1971–1992

Studies of mortuary ritual were greatly stimulated by Binford's 1971 paper 'Approaches to the social dimensions of mortuary practices', and this has acted as a catalyst for much subsequent discussion of prehistoric mortuary practices. It re-opened the possibility of using controlled information from ethnography which was at the time somewhat in disrepute, particularly in the wake of Ucko's famous 1969 lecture to the Prehistoric Society where he showed that 'ethnographic parallels' could be used to support nearly any particular interpretation of archaeological evidence that one wished to have supported (Ucko 1969).

Among the main topics examined by Binford was the comparison between four socio-cultural systems in regard to distinctions in burial practice. The four groups were hunter-gatherers, shifting agriculturalists, pastoralists and settled agriculturalists. He found that the last group had a greater number of dimensional distinctions in mortuary practices than any of the others. Another interesting aspect examined by Binford was that of symboling, which he defined as the 'arbitrary assigning of meaning to form'. Nothing intrinsic in the form of a symbol limits it to any particular referent. Thus in any one area or society river burial could be reserved for chiefs, or for the drowned, or it could be the norm. From this followed the important principle that the use of common symbols does not imply a common cultural influence as was formerly believed by the diffusionists.

From studying a variety of ethnographic situations

Binford found that differential treatments do, however, follow a pattern. One correlation is between age at death and the location of the burial. Another relates sodalities to orientation either within a cemetery or from cemetery to cemetery. Here orientation of the grave refers to topographic features or solar reference points commonly significant in the origin mythology of the sodality; for instance, graves might face the particular direction from which the group was believed to have come. Sex and status were mainly distinguished by differences in grave furniture but could also be reflected in the location and preparation of the body.

Binford suggested that the attention and energy given to an individual in death is commensurate with his importance in life. His paper thus marked a new departure in studies of mortuary rituals, not only for megalithic tombs but also for later periods in prehistory and sometimes for historic sites also. The collection of papers entitled *The Archaeology of Death*, edited by Chapman, Kinnes and Randsborg (1981), contained a number of important papers, many of which were influenced by Binford. One was a summary of late Mesolithic burials by Chapman, who considered whether special cemetery treatment of bodies could be identified in the period before the development of megalithic tombs. Chapman drew attention to the appearance of 'formal disposal areas' in Mesolithic societies and claimed that they occurred where there was a settled economy with access to important food resources such as estuarine fish stocks. The principal examples are Mesolithic communities of the north east coast of Zealand (late Ertebølle), those around the Gulf of Morbihan, and those along the Portuguese coast, though others can also be found (Kayser 1990). Chapman suggested that the development of formal burials marked a stage of imbalance between society and critical resources and that both the cemeteries of the Linear Pottery culture and the elaborate Mesolithic burials represent new mechanisms to regulate access to these resources. Later writers, however, have questioned the assertion of high population density in western Europe (e.g. Hodder 1984) and also whether there is any real evidence for stress or competition for resources (Whittle 1988).

Other explanations for the development of megalithic tombs have mostly included some aspect of territoriality. This mode of argument became particularly common in the 1970s following Renfrew and others who argued that it was a critical factor in explaining the function of megalithic tombs. Renfrew maintained that 'the initial step is to see in these monuments an expression of territorial behaviour in small scale segmentary societies.' These societies were defined by Renfrew as consisting of cellular and modular autonomous units lacking the centralized, hierarchical structure of a chiefdom or state. The second step is to suggest that such forms of territorial behaviour may be particularly frequent in small-scale segmentary societies of this kind in circumstances of population stress. Renfrew claimed that the

numbers of megalithic tombs found along the North Sea coast and the Atlantic seaboard related to the increased stress caused by settlers arriving at the limits of the area which could be settled. The tombs marked the territory as being owned by a particular group. Scandinavian archaeologists also urged the territorial aspect. Madsen, for example, suggested that the tombs marked critical resources and the most desirable land and were placed on or close to them (Madsen 1982).

Fleming (1972; 1973; 1975) saw the monuments serving as foci for the territory of a particular group, adding that by containing the bones of former leaders they were a reminder of the importance of living leaders, and thus served to validate their status.

Hodder (1984) believed that tombs evoked houses and acted as territorial markers for restricted resources. In his paper 'Burials, houses, women and men in the European Neolithic' he claimed that women as labour force were the most valuable commodity in the Early Neolithic but that competition for control over them gradually gave way to competition for control of land. The tombs served as territorial markers for the land. He explained the development of large scale monumental tombs in north central Europe by the change-over from the long houses of the Linear Pottery culture to wooden chambered long barrows.

Shanks & Tilley (1982) and Tilley (1984) put forward an interpretation of megalithic tombs based on the study of the grouping of bones in five tombs, three English long barrows and two Swedish megalithic tombs. They claimed that the way the disarticulated bones were regrouped in the tombs showed an attempt to re-create basic body symmetries such as body/limbs, upper/lower, left/right. This, in their view, indicated an assertion of the collective and a denial of the individual and of differences between individuals. Furthermore, they held that the principles in placing the bones stressed relations of power in society. The boundedness they demonstrated served to create an 'us and them' distinction, and opposition between different social groups using individual tombs as shown by the grouping of the bones and the use of bounded forms for funerary ceramics.

In summary, it is clear that archaeologists have moved away from the notion of megalithic religion and the idea that the use of megalithic tombs may have been spread by missionaries or colonists. They have also moved from the idea that tombs were built because the adoption of agriculture had made life so easy that there was suddenly spare time to enable people to indulge in elaborate tomb-building activities. In contrast, most writers now see the farming option as a potential source of stress and many believe the construction of tombs is a response to this stress, the tombs acting either

(i) as a marker of owning territory

(ii) as a unifying force for a community, to reinforce the power of the leaders by bringing the group together to construct the monument and as an ongoing reminder of the structure of society by containing the bones of the ancestors, or

(iii) as a complex statement of the conflicts in society, as envisaged by Tilley from the deposition of the bones.

Other questions have also been raised, such as when is a monument a burial site and when a site with burials, and what is the relationship between mortuary practice and social practice as a whole? Ongoing rituals are also now recognized as an aspect of considerable interest. It was not only the construction and primary burials which were important but also the secondary burials, the final closing of the tomb, and the enduring significance of the site in the landscape.

Recent research in the field

1. WESTERN IBERIA (*for location of sites see Fig. 8.1*)

There is now growing confirmation from radiocarbon dating and finds in tombs that the earliest Iberian megalithic monuments were small chambers without formal passages, as had already been suggested (e.g. Shee Twohig 1981, 21–22). On the Serra de Aboboreira, Baião, in north Portugal, thirty-three of the thirty-seven known monuments have been excavated in recent years, the majority (twenty-six) being small chambers or pits under a mound without any passage (Oliveira Jorge 1991, 93–107). Many date to the late fifth to early fourth millennium (using calibrated chronology, see Fig. 8.2). The only passage tomb proper, Cha de Parada 1 (Fig. 8.3) is somewhat later (4610±45 BP). A summary of the dates for northern Portugal is given by da Cruz (1988) and the smaller number of Galician dates are given in the same volume by Fabregas Valcarce (1988). Figure 8.2 here is based on this information with the addition of dates from central Portugal and two thermoluminescence dates from sites in southern Portugal. In another recent paper, Criado Boado and Fabregas Valcarce have summarized the chronological phases or 'regularities' in the north west in graphical form. The initial phase is characterized by small chambers containing axes, adzes, geometric microliths and flint blades. In the second phase, with passage tombs, which follows in the fourth millennium, there is a steady process of enrichment 'with evidence of contacts with the Millaran and south Portugal chalcolithic circles' (Criado Boado & Fabregas Valcarce 1989).

The dating I had suggested for the beginning of megalithic art in Iberia, at around 5000 BP (Shee Twohig 1981, 22), still seems valid. Researchers in Iberia have been able to add many new sites to the corpus published at that time, but a list of the forty or so painted sites now known (Devignes 1992) shows that the range of motifs is much the same as that I had identified in 1981, with a major emphasis on serpentiform and zigzag panels. Among the more important newly discovered paintings are those of Dombate in Coruña, revealed during excavations by Bello Dieguez

(Fabregas Valcarce 1988, note 40) but not yet fully published. No complete list of the newly discovered carvings in Iberia is available but special mention must be made of those at Mota Grande, Castro Laboreiro in the Parque Nacional da Peneda-Gerès (Martinho Baptista 1990) and at Afife, Viano do Castelo (Lopes da Silva

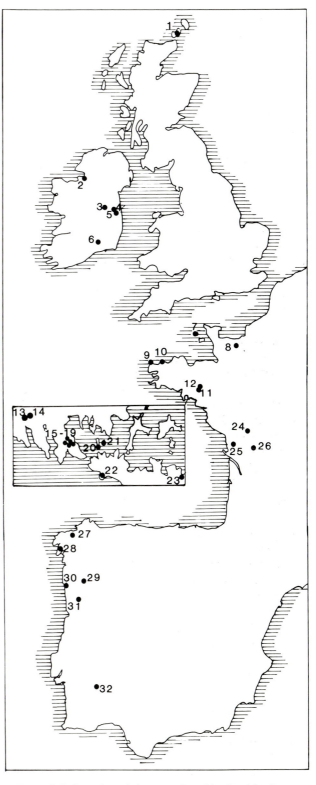

Figure 8.1. Location of sites mentioned in the this chapter

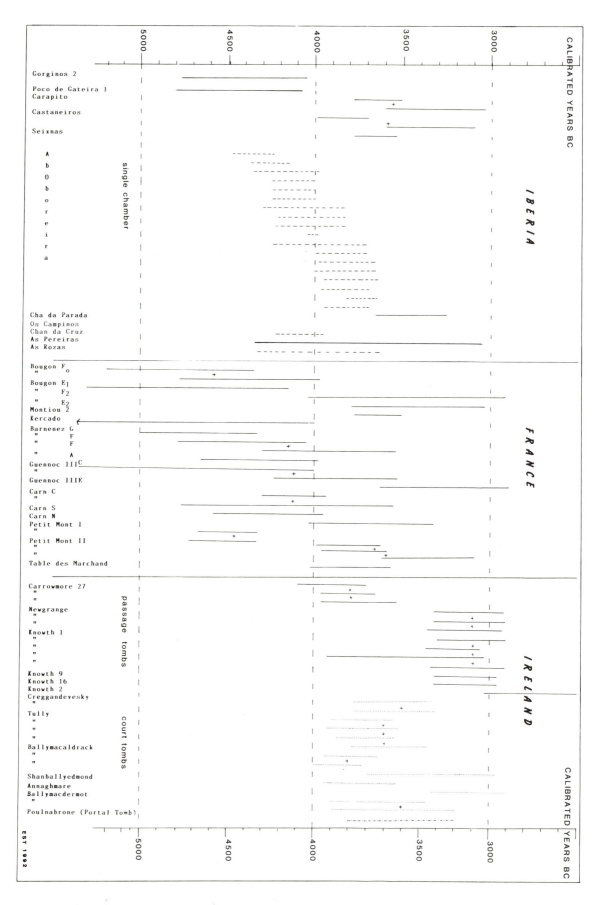

Figure 8.2. Chronological chart of radiocarbon dates relating to megalithic tombs (calibrated to two standard deviations after Pearson et al. 1986)

Figure 8.3. Cha de Parada 1
(author's photo)

Figure 8.4. Anthropomorphic carving at
Afife, Viana do Castelo (author's photo)

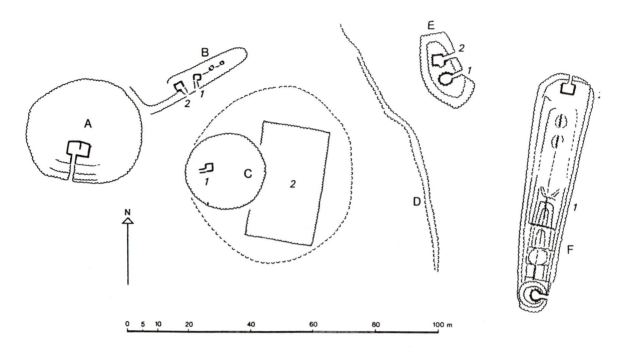

Figure 8.5. Bougon, Deux Sèvres (after Mohen 1990)

1988). The latter, a late type of undifferentiated tomb on the coastal plain of northern Portugal, has an anthropomorphic carving on an orthostat near the entrance (Fig 8.4). The Galician art was published by Rodríguez Casal (1992), while the whole of the peninsula is discussed by Bueno Ramírez and de Balbin Behrmann (1992).

Excavations in north west Iberia have revealed more about the general structure of monuments and details of ritual aspects such as the presence of anthropomorphic idols or stelae in front of tombs, for example at Parxubeira, La Coruña (Rodriguez Casal 1988; 1990).

2. WESTERN FRANCE

Moving northwards we find tombs with early dates in the centre-west of France, notably at Bougon, Deux Sèvres, where the small round chambered passage tombs E and F0 date to the fifth millennium cal. BC and the more developed Angoumoisin type with square chambers (tombs A, B1 and B2) date to the fourth millennium (Fig. 8.5). In this area also there are smaller chambers of probably early date such as the cists in Bougon B associated with impressed ware in a long mound (Mohen 1990). The small corbelled passage tombs in western France have been labelled the 'Atlantic' type. A good example is the site of Colpo at Larcuste in Brittany which seems very similar to Bougon E. (L'Helgouach & Lecornec 1976).

On the north coast of Brittany are the passage tombs with trapezoidal or rectangular cairns such as Barnenez (Giot 1970) with early dates for G in the primary cairn and for A and F in the secondary cairn. Normandy too has early Atlantic type tombs (e.g. La Hoguette,

Fontenay le Marmion, though in an oval cairn). In some areas there are long barrows. Les Fouaillages on Guernsey has early dates (Kinnes 1982) and Le Manio near Carnac in southern Brittany may also be of this period. In the Carnac region there are elaborate burial rituals in the late Mesolithic period at Hoëdic and Téviec and the long mounded burials are only a little later. Important excavations at Petit Mont (Fig. 8.6) on the east side of the Gulf of Morbihan have shown that the first monument was a low oval earthen mound, then a trapezoidal cairn dated to the mid fifth millennium with the passage tombs built later, the first (S3 on the plan) in the fourth millennium (Lecornec 1987).

In western France therefore we find both long barrows with small chambers and others with passage tombs proper. Are we to see here the 'dual tradition', to use a term employed many years ago by Daniel — the long barrow element from northern or central Europe, the passage tombs a separate Atlantic invention, whether in one or, as Renfrew (1976) proposed, in several different regions independently? Sherratt (1990) has proposed a scenario where the long barrow idea reached this area from north-central Europe via the Paris Basin and the passage tomb form developed as a response by the indigenous population, influenced by their tradition of building circular rather than long houses. This suggestion, however, does not explain the appearance of passage tombs in Iberia where no long barrow influence is known. There the indigenous tradition must have been paramount.

Spectacular recent discoveries in Brittany have centred on Locmariaquer on the western side of the Gulf of Morbihan. Here excavations have been carried out by L'Helgouach and Le Roux at La Table des Marchands

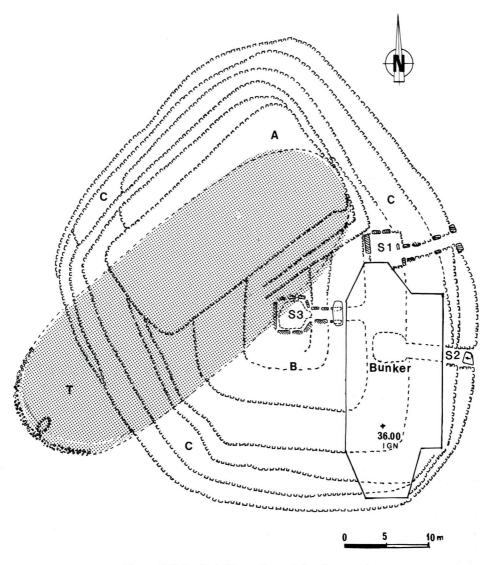

Figure 8.6. Le Petit Mont, Arzon (after Lecornec)

and the Er Grah long cairn respectively. Near the former, considerable evidence of pre-tomb occupation and ritual activities have been found including a line of at least sixteen standing stones leading to the fallen Grand Menhir nearby (L'Helgouach, pers. comm., and site leaflet). The elaborately carved backstone of the Table des Marchand is believed to have been erected in this phase also and only later incorporated into the tomb.

The practice of incorporating complete or partial menhirs or stelae into tombs was recognized by L'Helgouach some years ago (L'Helgouach 1983) Dramatic confirmation came from Le Roux's excavations at Gavrinis where it was found that part of a 14 m high menhir had been used as the chamber capstone. Another part of this menhir formed the capstone of the chamber at La Table des Marchands and a third part may have been used in the chamber of the Er Grah long cairn (Le Roux 1984; 1985). The carvings on it included two very clear representations of oxen with long curving horns, adding reinforcement to Le Roux's claim (1984; 1985; forthcoming) that a southern, Medi-

terranean bull cult reached this area in the Neolithic. L'Helgouach (forthcoming) suggests that the bull cult represents a male element, the idoliforms a female cult. Petit Mont S3 also had several stelae incorporated into its construction (Lecornec 1987; 1990).

It now seems clear that in the Morbihan, if not elsewhere in Brittany, megalithic art appeared in the mid to late fifth millennium on menhirs and stelae, many of which were later broken up and incorporated into passage tombs. The tombs built with these re-used slabs are invariably square in plan, implying a later date than the classic early passage tombs with circular chambers. The repertoire of motifs (Fig. 8.7) consists of the idoliform (known also as the buckler); the crook (in French 'le crosse'); the cross ('le croix'); the oxen and its possible derivatives the crescent, U and 'yoke' motifs; the bow; and finally the axe in its various forms, hafted or unhafted, in a sleeve, or the axe/ plough ('hache/charrue'). The last-mentioned is an important motif on many menhirs and slabs although its real significance is not clear.

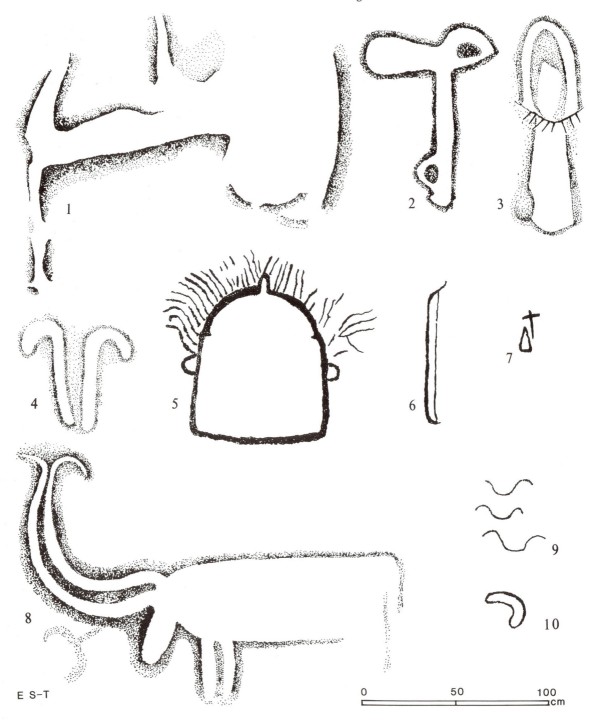

Figure 8.7. Early Breton megalithic art: 1. Axe/plough (hache/charrue) from the Grand Menhir Brisé; 2. Hafted axe from La Table des Marchands; 3. Axe in sleeve (hache en gaine) from Gavrinis (after Le Roux 1982); 4. Crook (crosse) from Kermarquer; 5. Idoliform/buckler (bouclier) from Ile Longue; 6. Bow from Gavrinis; 7. Axe blade and cross (croix), from Barnenez (after Giot); 8. Ox from Gavrinis (after Le Roux 1984); 9. Horns?/yoke (jugiformes) from Ile Guennoc IIC; 10. Horns? from La Table des Marchands

The idoliform may also occur in three-dimensional form, as it were, in the passage tombs of Ile Guennoc (Fig. 8.8) and Barnenez G and as an orthostat in the chamber at Kercado, recognized over twenty years ago by Giot (1971). Decorated menhirs still extant (i.e. not incorporated into tombs) include those of Kermaillard at Sarzeau (Lecornec 1990, fig. 5), Kermarquer at Moustoirac (L'Helgouach & Lecornec 1969), and the Grand Menhir at Locmariaquer with its 1.75 m long axe/plough (Shee Twohig 1981, fig. 171). It is now evident that the technique of false relief carving belongs to the early phase of megalithic art as well as to the much later gallery graves. The crook motif occurs in the centre west of France in relief, for example at Ardillères and La Boixe A and B (Shee Twohig 1981, figs. 198, 202 & 203). It appears also in southern Portugal on menhirs,

Figure 8.8. Idol/stela from Ile Guennoc III, Finistère (author's photo)

for instance at Bulhòa (Shee Twohig 1981, fig. 75) and on several others more recently discovered (Gomes 1989). These are thought to date to the Late Neolithic, but could perhaps be earlier.

The distinctive early art of fifth millennium Brittany is succeeded in the fourth millennium mainly by serpentiforms, zigzags, irregular linear patterns and radial lines, as well as retaining some of the earlier motifs, notably the idoliforms which appear in distinctive form on the angled passage tombs of the Morbihan area in the late fourth millennium and on the gallery graves a little later. The fourth millennium art finds some parallels in Iberian tombs of the same period, especially the occurrence of serpentiforms. In Ireland also the art seems to develop in the second half of the fourth millennium.

Bradley (1989) has suggested a possible interpretation of megalithic art in terms of entoptic images, associated with altered states of consciousness as Lewis Williams and Dowson (1988) showed for south African and perhaps Upper Palaeolithic art. The more developed fourth millennium art shows the closest correspondence with the entoptic images and Lewis-Williams and Dowson (1993, 61) have pointed out that those motifs which are shared over Atlantic Europe are 'principally entoptic in form and that non-entoptic motifs tend to be more restricted in their distribution'. The more developed fourth millennium art shows the closest correspondence with the entoptic images.

3. IRELAND

In Ireland the question of chronology is still unresolved. There are a few 'fixed points', notably the dating of the Boyne Valley sites to the later fourth millennium. At Knowth it is clear that the large tomb, Site 1, is later than the small tombs, nos. 13 and 16 (Eogan 1986, fig. 9). We would expect other small passage tombs to be earlier but as yet there are no dates except the controversial ones from Carrowmore (Burenhult 1984). I have included only those from the cruciform tomb (no. 27) on Fig. 8.2, as those from nos. 4 and 7 appear to relate to pre-tomb activities. Court tombs have been included on Fig. 8.2 to show they are broadly contemporary with Carrowmore 27 and with the putative earlier stages of Irish passage tomb building. For a general discussion of Irish megalithic tombs see Shee Twohig (1990).

The spectacular nature of the Boyne Valley tombs has been well documented over the years by the excavators of Newgrange (O'Kelly 1982) and Knowth (Eogan 1986) where a fourth decade of excavation has just begun. The excavations at Knowth in particular are crucial to the problem of outside contacts as they have produced some exotic material which finds parallels along the Atlantic seaboard. The magnificently decorated flint macehead from the entrance to the right hand chamber of Knowth 1 east (Eogan & Richardson 1982) resembles the British series of maceheads, though taking its symbols from megalithic art. The sandstone phalliform object (Fig. 8.9) from near the entrance to the western tomb at Knowth is closely paralleled in southern Portugal by the limestone pieces from Fohla das Barradas and Casainhos (Eogan 1990, figs. 7 & 8). Decorated bone and antler pins from Irish passage tombs also resemble those of southern Portugal (Eogan 1990, figs. 9 & 10). Eogan (1990) suggests a number of other parallels between Irish and Iberian passage tombs, under the headings of grave goods, tomb morphology and megalithic art.

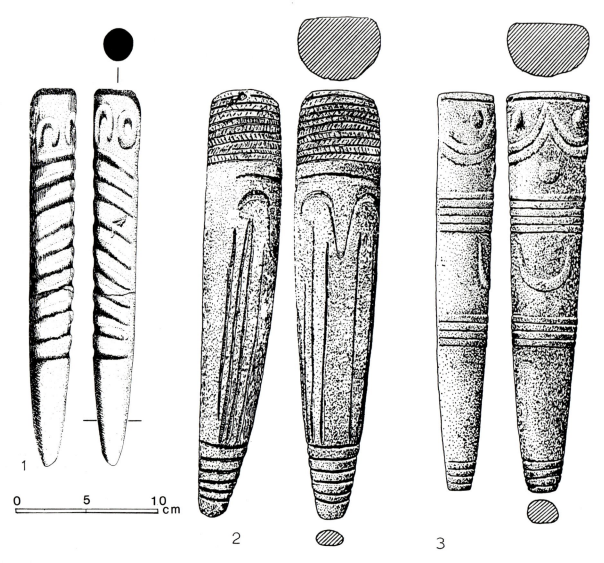

Figure 8.9. Phalliform cylinders: 1. Knowth (after Eogan); 2. Fohla das Barradas (after Almagro Gorbea); 3. Casainhos (after Almagro Gorbea)

A Breton influence must also now be acknowledged at Knowth where Eogan's 'rectilinear style' of art reflects the carvings of the contemporary angled passage tombs in Brittany (Shee Twohig 1981, fig. 7). At Knowth this art is found in the inner parts of Site 1 west (Eogan 1986, fig. 84) and of Site 1 east (Eogan 1986, fig. 83) as well as on the kerbstones at the entrances to both tombs at Site 1. The Irish art tends more towards the setting of arcs one inside the other than does the art of the angled passage tombs, but these multi-arcs are of course characteristic of phase 2 at Gavrinis and have also been found now at Petit Mont (Lecornec 1987, fig. 16). Another Irish site with carvings similar to Gavrinis has recently been identified at Knockroe, Co Kilkenny (Fig. 8.10), well to the south of the recorded occurrences of passage tombs with art (O'Sullivan 1987) and excavations in progress should help date the site. The curious resemblance between the elaborately decorated basin stone in Knowth 1 east (right hand chamber) and

the decoration of Breton Kerugou ware has already been noted (Shee Twohig 1981, 120) and this pottery is also contemporary with the Boyne Valley tombs.

In general the motifs of Irish passage tomb art may be found over a wide area, though the regional styles are still distinctive. In Britain both the carvings and the mobiliary pieces from the habitation site of Skara Brae reflect the angular art of the Boyne tombs (Shee Twohig 1981; forthcoming) and these motifs occur in the Late Neolithic throughout Britain, for example on grooved ware, and often in ritual contexts. This widespread use of similar symbols was noted by Bradley and Chapman (1984).

In Ireland we are beginning to appreciate that these monuments were part of a ritual landscape rather than merely places for burial. At a conference in Cork in February 1992 Richard Bradley observed that 'A monument is firstly an experience and secondly a type', and the elaborate Irish passage tombs certainly bear this

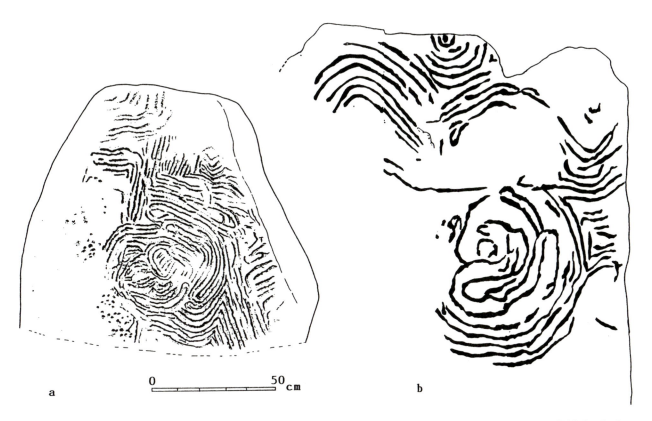

Figure 8.10.a. Knockroe, Co Kilkenny, orthostat 8 (after O'Sullivan); b. Gavrinis, Morbihan, orthostat R11 (author)

out. Carvings were not only inside the tombs, where access may have been restricted, but were often also on kerbstones and visible to all. Quartz facings at the larger sites also emphasized their importance. Circular settings in front of the tomb entrances at Knowth, Newgrange and Loughcrew cairn T show that rituals took place in front of the tombs (evidence for the latter is based on photographic records in the Office of Public Works). It is certain that Newgrange was deliberately orientated on midwinter sunrise (Patrick 1974; Ray 1989) and it surely cannot have been unique in this respect. Further observations will have to be made at Knowth to check on Brennan's (1983) claim that sunlight enters the eastern tomb at sunrise and the western tomb at sunset at the equinoxes. O'Brien *et al.* (1987) have corroborated Brennan's observations of sunlight entering cairn T at Loughcrew at sunrise on the equinoxes and the effect of the successive illumination of parts of the tomb, including several carved radial line patterns, is very dramatic

Conclusions

1. It appears that the early art (fifth millennium BC) in Brittany, much of it on menhirs and stelae, stands apart from the art of other areas in terms of context, content and chronology.
2. Following this precocious art there are broad similarities between the three regions considered in terms of tomb architecture and megalithic art throughout the fourth millennium, with serpentiform and zigzag motifs particularly significant, and with some continuity in Brittany from the earlier phase and much re-use there of older pieces incorporated into new tombs.
3. In the late fourth millennium, the time of angled passage tombs in Brittany and the elaborate Boyne Valley tombs in Ireland, there is a period when symbols are shared over a wide area from the Orkney Islands through Ireland and down to Iberia. This may well have been a symbolism for the elite, being found especially on prestige pieces and in elaborate burial/ritual monuments, on pottery at ritual sites and on special habitation sites.
4. At the same time, and a little later, the French *allées couvertes*, rock-cut tombs and a widely dispersed series of statue-menhirs also share an iconography concerned mainly with the human (or divine) figure and also incorporating elements from the earlier Breton passage tomb series.

Acknowledgements

Sincere thanks to all the colleagues who have shown me their sites and sent offprints, some over many years, in particular George Eogan, Muiris O'Sullivan, Joel Lecornec, Charles-Tanguy Le Roux, Jean L'Helgouach, Vitor Oliveira Jorge, Antonio Rodriguez Casal and Eduardo Lopes da Silva.

References

Binford, L., 1971. Mortuary practices: their study and potential, in *Approaches to the Social Dimensions of Mortuary Practices*, ed. J.A. Brown. Memoirs of the Society for American Archaeology 25, 1–29

Bello Dieguez, J.M., 1988. Debate. *Trabalhos de Antropologia e Etnologia* 28, 54

Bello Dieguez, J.M., 1989. Monumento Megalitico de Dombate (Cabana, a Coruña). *Arqueoloxia. Informes I, Campaña 1987*, 24–30

Bradley, R., 1989. Deaths and entrances: a contextual analysis of megalithic art. *Current Anthropology* 30, 69–75

Bradley, R., & Chapman, R., 1984. Passage graves in the European Neolithic — a theory of converging evolution, in *The Archaeology of Carrowmore, Co Sligo*. Theses and Papers in North European Archaeology 14. Stockholm: Institute of Archaeology, 348–56

Brennan, M., 1983. *The Stars and the Stones*. London: Thames & Hudson

Bueno Ramírez, P., & de Balbin Behrmann, R., 1992. L'art mégalithique dans la péninsule Iberique: une vue d'ensemble. *L'Anthropologie* 96, 499–572

Burenhult, G., 1984. *The Archaeology of Carrowmore, Co Sligo*. Theses and Papers in North European Archaeology 14. Stockholm: Institute of Archaeology

Chapman, R., 1981. The emergence of formal disposal areas and the problem of megalithic tombs in prehistoric Europe, in *The Archaeology of Death*, eds R. Chapman, I. Kinnes, & K. Randsborg. Cambridge: Cambridge University Press, 71–82

Chapman, R., Kinnes, I., & Randsborg, K., (eds) 1981. *The Archaeology of Death*. Cambridge: Cambridge University Press

Criado Boado, F., & Fabregas Valcarce, R., 1989. The megalithic phenomenon of northwest Spain: main trends. *Antiquity* 63, 682–96

Cruz, D.J. da, 1988. O megalitismo do norte de Portugal. *Trabalhos de Antropologia e Etnologia* 28, 15–49

Devignes, M., 1992. Analyse du phénomène des dolmens peints ibériques. *Trabalhos de Antropologia e Etnologia* 32, 113–40

Eogan, G. 1986. *Knowth and the Passage Tombs of Ireland*. London: Thames & Hudson

Eogan, G., 1990. Irish megalithic tombs and Iberia. Comparisons and contrasts. *Probleme der Megalithgräberforschung*. Berlin: de Gruyter, 113–38

Eogan, G., & Aboud, J., 1990. Diffuse picking in megalithic art, in *La Bretagne et l'Europe Préhistoriques*. Revue Archéologique de l'Ouest, Supplément no. 2, 121–40

Eogan, G., & Richardson, H., 1982. Two maceheads from Knowth, Co Meath. *Journal of the Royal Society of Antiquaries of Ireland* 112, 123–38

Fabregas Valcarce, R., 1988. Megalitismo de Galicia. *Trabalhos de Antropologia e Etnologia* 28, 57–77

Fleming, A., 1972. Vision and design: approaches to the study of ceremonial monument typology. *Man* 7, 57–73

Fleming, A., 1973. Tombs for the living. *Man* 8, 177–93

Fleming, A., 1975. Analytical approaches to the study of monument typology, in *Les Réligions de la Préhistoire*. Valcamonica: Centro Camuno di Studi Preistorica, 191–5

Giot, P.-R., 1970. *Barnenez*. Rennes: Direction des Antiquités Préhistoriques de la Bretagne

Giot, P.-R., 1971. Circonscription de la Bretagne. *Gallia Préhistoire* 14, 339–61

Gomes, M.V., 1989. Arte rupestre e contexto arqueologico. Coloquio Internacional de Arte Prehistorica. *Revista de Cultura* 7, 225–69

Hodder, I., 1984. Burials, houses, women and men in the European Neolithic, in *Ideology, Power and Prehistory*, eds D. Miller & C. Tilley. Cambridge: Cambridge University Press, 51–68

Kayser, O., 1990. Sur les rites funéraires des chasseurs-collecteurs de l'Europe de l'ouest et du nord-ouest à la fin du mésolithique, in *La Bretagne et l'Europe Préhistoriques*. Revue Archéologique de l'Ouest, Supplément no. 2, 75–80

Kinnes, I., 1982. Les Fouaillages and megalithic origins. *Antiquity* 56, 24–30

Lecornec, J., 1987. Le complexe mégalithique du Petit Mont (Arzon, Morbihan). *Revue Archéologique de l'Ouest* 4, 37–56

Lecornec, J., 1990. L'ornementation du Petit Mont dans le contexte mégalithique morbihannais, in *La Bretagne et l'Europe Préhistoriques*. Revue Archéologique de l'Ouest, Supplément no. 2, 141–52

L'Helgouach, J., 1983. Les idoles qu'on abat. *Bulletin de la Société Polymathique du Morbihan* 110, 57–68

L'Helgouach, J., forthcoming. Déesses et figurations cornues du néolithique. *Proceedings of the Colloque du Monte Bégo, Tende*, 1991

L'Helgouach, J., & Lecornec, J., 1969. Le menhir de Kermarquer à Moustoirac (Morbihan). *Bulletin de la Société Polymathique du Morbihan* 93, 107–15

L'Helgouach, J., & Lecornec, J., 1976. Le site mégalithique 'Min Goh Ru' près de Larcuste à Colpo, Morbihan. *Bulletin de la Société Préhistorique Française* 73, 370–97

Le Roux, C.-T., 1982. Nouvelles gravures à Gavrinis, Larmor-Baden (Morbihan). *Bulletin de la Société Préhistorique Française* 79, 89–96

Le Roux, C.-T., 1984. A propos des fouilles de Gavrinis (Morbihan): nouvelles données sur l'art mégalithique armoricain. *Bulletin de la Société Préhistorique Française* 81, 240–5

Le Roux, C.-T., 1985. New excavations at Gavrinis. *Antiquity* 59, 183–7

Le Roux, C.-T., 1992. Cornes de pierre. *Actes du 17ème Colloque Interrégional sur le Néolithique*. Revue Archéologique de l'Ouest, Supplément no. 5, 237–44

Lewis-Williams, J.D., & Dowson, T.A., 1988. The signs of all times: entoptic phenomena in Upper Paleolithic art. *Current Anthropology* 29, 201–45

Lewis-Williams, J.D., & Dowson, T.A., 1993. On vision and power in the Neolithic: evidence from the decorated monuments. *Current Anthropology* 34, 55–56

Lopes da Silva, E.J., 1988. A mamoa de Afife: breve sintese de 3 campanhas de escavaco. *Trabalhos de Antropologia e Etnologia* 28, 127–35

Martinho Baptista, A., 1990. Actividades do Departamento de Arqueologia do PNPG. *Juriz, Boletim Trimestral* 6–7, 40

Madsen, T., 1982. Settlement systems of early agricultural societies of East Jutland, Denmark; a regional study of change. *Journal of Anthropological Archaeology* 1, 197–236

Mohen, J.-P. 1990. Le site mégalithique de Bougon (Deux-Sèvres): Les aspects symboliques et sacrés de la nécropole, in *Probleme der Megalithgräberforschung*. Berlin: de Gruyter, 73–82

O'Brien, T., *et al.* 1987. The equinox cycle as recorded at cairn T, Loughcrew. *Riocht na Midhe* 8, 3–1

O'Kelly, M.J., 1982. *Newgrange: Archaeology, Art and Legend*. London: Thames & Hudson

Oliveira Jorge, V., 1991. Arqueologia social dos sepulcros megaliticos atlanticos: conhecimentos e perspectivas actuais, in *Incursãoes na Prehistoria*. Porto, 59–151

O'Sullivan, M., 1987. The art of the passage tomb at Knockroe, County Kilkenny. *Journal of the Royal Society of Antiquaries of Ireland* 117, 84–95

Patrick, J., 1974. Midwinter sunrise at Newgrange, Co Meath. *Nature* 249, 517–19

Pearson, G.W., Pilcher, J.R., Baillie, M.G.L., Corbett, D.M., & Qua, F., 1986. High-precision ^{14}C measurements of Irish oaks to show the natural ^{14}C variations from AD 1840–5210 BC. *Radiocarbon* 28 (2B), 911–34

Ray, T.P., 1989. The winter solstice phenomenon at Newgrange: accident or design? *Nature* 337, 343

Renfrew, C., 1976. Megaliths, territories and populations, in *Acculturation and Continuity in Atlantic Europe*, ed. S.J. de Laet. Brugge: De Tempel, 198–220

Rodriguez Casal, A., 1988. *La Necropolis Mégalitica de Parxubeira, a Coruña*. La Coruña: Monografias do Museu no. 4

Rodriguez Casal, A., 1990. Die Megalithkultur in Galicien, in *Probleme der Megalithgräberforschung*. Berlin: de Gruyter, 53–72

Rodriguez Casal, A., 1992. Elements symbolicaux funéraires dans le mégalithisme Galicien. *Actes du 17ème Colloque Interrégionale sur le Néolithique*. Revue Archéologique de l'Ouest, Supplement no. 5, 213–2

Shee Twohig, E., 1981. *The Megalithic Art of Western Europe*. Oxford: Clarendon Press

Shee Twohig, E., 1990. *Irish Megalithic Tombs*. Aylesbury: Shire

Shee Twohig, E., forthcoming. Engravings at the Neolithic habitation site of Skara Brae, Orkney Islands, Scotland. *Proceedings of the Colloque du Mont Bégo, Tende*, 1991

Shanks, M., & Tilley, C., 1982. Ideology, symbolic power and ritual communication: a reinterpretation of Neolithic mortuary practices, in *Symbolic and Structural Archaeology*, ed. I. Hodder. Cambridge: Cambridge University Press, 129–54

Sherratt, A., 1990. The genesis of megaliths: monumentality, ethnicity and social complexity in Neolithic North-West Europe. *World Archaeology* 22, 147–67

Tilley, C., 1984. Ideology and the legitimation of power in the middle neolithic of southern Sweden, in *Ideology, Power and Prehistory*, eds D. Miller & C. Tilley. Cambridge: Cambridge University Press, 111–46

Ucko, P.J., 1969. Ethnography and archaeological interpretation of funerary remains. *World Archaeology* 1, 262–80

Whittle, A., 1988. *Problems in Neolithic Archaeology*. Cambridge: Cambridge University Press

9

New Evidence on the Exchange of Obsidian in Italy

Albert J. Ammerman & Christopher Polglase

This article presents new evidence on the exchange of obsidian in Italy. Arene Candide, a cave site on the coast of Liguria with a good stratigraphic sequence for the Neolithic period, is the main focus of the study. The comprehensive sourcing of obsidian reveals marked changes in the material reaching the site over time. In the Early Neolithic period, obsidian comes only from Sardinia and Palmarola. By the Late Neolithic period most of the obsidian at Arene Candide is from the more distant source of Lipari. In terms of methodology, the study shows the gains to be made by moving towards a more comprehensive approach to the sourcing of obsidian at a site. The situation at Arene Candide is placed in a wider context by comparing it to what is observed among the Neolithic sites at Acconia in Calabria. The suggestion is made that it is now time to develop a new generation of models for the exchange of obsidian.

Dans cet article sont présentés de nouveaux témoinages de la circulation de l'obsidienne en Italie. L'étude est centrée sur la grotte d'Arene Candide, sur la côte de Ligurie, qui fournit une bonne séquence stratigraphique pour le Néolithique. La détermination détaillée des zones d'origine de l'obsidienne révèle des changements importants dans l'approvisionnement lithique du site au cours du temps. Au Néolithique ancien, l'obsidienne provient exclusivement de Sardaigne et de Palmarola. Au Néolithique final, en revanche, la plupart de l'obsidienne d'Arene Candide est importée du gisement plus lointain de Lipari. Du point de vue méthodologique, l'étude souligne l'intérêt qui peut être tiré d'une analyse fine des sources d'approvisionnenemt en obsidienne. Le cas d'Arene Candide est replacé dans un contexte plus large, et confronté aux observations réunies sur les gisements néolithiques d'Acconia, en Calabre. On suggère qu'il est temps désormais de développer une nouvelle génération de modèles relatifs à l'échange de l'obsidienne.

Introduction

There are three things that we would like to do in this paper. The first is to give a preliminary report on the sourcing of obsidian from three phases of occupation at the site of Arene Candide in northern Italy.[1] As we shall see below, marked changes in patterns of exchange are observed over time. In the Early Neolithic period, obsidian from only two island sources, Sardinia and Palmarola, reached Arene Candide. A third source was to make its appearance in the Middle Neolithic period; one third of the obsidian now came from Lipari. By the Late Neolithic, the island of Lipari had become the chief source and all of the obsidian at the site occurs in the form of finished blades. These diachronic changes at Arene Candide are linked with the high quality of the obsidian from Lipari and it circulation, especially in later Neolithic times, as a prestige item.

The second aim is to illustrate the recent shift in approach to the characterization of the obsidian recovered at prehistoric sites in the Mediterranean area. In terms of methodology, there is now a change in emphasis from the selective sourcing of a few samples from a given site to what may be called the comprehensive sourcing of the obsidian found at a site. There is a tendency to think that basic work on the characterization of obsidian has already been done with regard to obsidian and that it is now time for interpretation or general commentary on the results of previous studies. In fact, it is time for a new round of empirical work to begin: one in which a much closer look is taken at individual sites such as Arene Candide.

The third purpose of the paper is to note the need for a new generation of models for the exchange of obsidian and to point out briefly some of the new directions that we may want to explore. Most of our previous studies on obsidian have been concerned with Neolithic sites in Calabria, the region in the toe of southern Italy (for an overview of this work, see Ammerman 1985b). Almost all of the obsidian comes from the nearby island of Lipari. In this case, we are dealing with sites near the 'head' of an exchange network. In contrast, in turning to Arene Candide, we are examining the situation in what, as far as obsidian is concerned, amounts to the 'tail' of an exchange network. In previous models, the working assumption was often made that practices with regard to the production and consumption of obsidian were much the same at different points in the exchange network (e.g. Renfrew 1977; Ammerman *et al.* 1978). When we start to compare the situation in Calabria with that at Arene Candide, however, it becomes clear that this simplifying assumption is no longer a sound one. In short, what is happening in the 'tail' of an exchange network may be quite different from what is happening at or near its 'head'. The implication is that we have to allow for variation in such things as reduction techniques, the use-life of tools, and the prestige value of obsidian with increasing distance from source. Obviously, the task of modelling the exchange of obsidian is not made any easier by this realization; the challenge now becomes that of trying to formulate the changing character over space of that which is happening in different parts of the exchange network (Read 1989).

Comprehensive sourcing

In west Mediterranean prehistory, one of the more successful chapters in the sourcing of a raw material is that of obsidian, a volcanic glass used for making stone tools. In previous studies (Hallam *et al.* 1976; Williams Thorpe *et al.* 1979; 1984), it was common practice to select only one or a few pieces of obsidian from a given site and to have them characterized to source by means of techniques such as optical emission spectrometry or neutron activation analysis. This was done for many different Neolithic sites in a region with the aim of

developing a distribution map. The goal was thus to make an assessment of trade routes and exchange models on the basis of the patterns recognized on such maps. One of the limitations of selective sourcing, however, was that it often did not document the full range of sources represented at a site. For example, in previous work at Arene Candide (Williams Thorpe *et al.* 1979), only two pieces of obsidian from the Early Neolithic levels were analyzed and both turned out to come from Sardinia (compare Table 9.1). In addition, it was not possible, on the basis of a selective approach to sourcing, to obtain information on the relative proportion of obsidian from different sources within a given assemblage. Nor was it possible to trace the changes in such relative proportions over time at a given site.

We began to move toward a more comprehensive approach to sourcing (that is, an attempt to attribute to source all of the pieces found at a site) in a study of the obsidian from Gaione, an open air settlement of Middle Neolithic age located on the Po Plain (Ammerman *et al.* 1990). This study revealed a clear association between island source and lithic morphology: obsidian from Lipari occurs at Gaione predominantly in the form of blades, the target product of the reduction technology, while that from Sardinia consists mainly of cores and the by-products of the reduction of obsidian. In short, obsidian from Lipari appears to have reached the site in finished form whereas that from Sardinia was worked locally at Gaione. It will be recalled that the main motivation for many previous obsidian studies in the Mediterranean area was to identify the mechanism of exchange (e.g. Torrence 1986). The results from Gaione imply a more complex situation; with respect to even a given site, more than one kind of mechanism of circulation may have been in operation at the same time.

Here, using Arene Candide as a case study, we want to show how comprehensive sourcing can yield a new and more dynamic view of obsidian exchange. Located on the Ligurian coast, Arene Candide is a cave site that is well known for its stratigraphy and its chronological sequence. Excavated by Bernabò Brea (1946; 1956)

Table 9.1. Obsidian from the Early Neolithic levels at Arene Candide: two-way classification by source and class of lithic reduction

Class	Sard A	Sard B	Sard C	Palmarola	Lipari	Totals
Blade	-	9	-	8	-	17
Flake	-	-	-	-	-	-
Core trim	-	2	1	-	-	3
Trim	1	-	1	2	-	4
Core	1	-	-	1	-	2
Totals	2	11	2	11	-	26

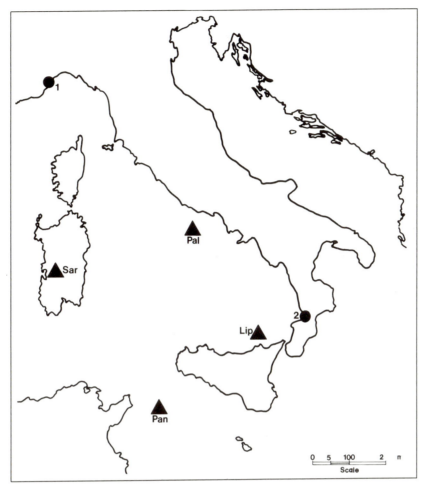

Figure 9.1 Map of Italy. Neolithic sites (solid dots): 1. Arene Candide, 2. Piana di Curinga.
Island sources of obsidian (solid triangles): Pantellaria, Lipari, Palmarola and Sardinia

and more recently by Tinè, the site is well suited to lithic studies since sieving was employed during the course of the excavations. In addition, the site has available a good series of radiocarbon dates for its Neolithic levels (Bagolini & Biagi 1990). In the present study, three phases of Neolithic occupation at the site will be considered: (1) the impressed ware pottery levels (*c.* 5800–5300 BC, Early Neolithic); (2) the square mouth pottery levels (*c.* 4900–4300 BC, Middle Neolithic); and (3) the Chassey pottery levels (*c.* 4000–3500 BC, Late Neolithic). It has been known for some time that four islands in the western Mediterranean possess sources of obsidian of workable quality (Buchner 1949). In the case of Arene Candide, the closest island source, Sardinia, is located at a distance of approximately 450 kilometres. As shown in Figure 9.1, Palmarola and Lipari are at distances of 500 km and 800 km respectively. The distances cited here are as the crow flies; obviously, given the limited means of transport available in Neolithic times, the actual distances involved in the circulation of obsidian from these island sources would have been greater. No obsidian from Pantellaria is attested at Arene Candide.

The characterization method chosen was neutron acti-

vation analysis, which gives good discrimination between the four island sources. Analysis was carried out in Milan on a total of 54 obsidian artifacts from Arene Candide. The sample size is three times that of any other Neolithic site previously studied in the region. Measurements were made on three major elements (Na, K and Fe) and ten minor and rare earth elements. In particular, lanthanum, scandium and cesium give good discrimination between the island sources (Figure 9.2). In the case of Sardinia, one can distinguish chemically three kinds of obsidian among various individual sources all associated with Monte Arce (Michels *et al.* 1984).[2] The emphasis in this study is on characterization to island source and not to the individual sources on a given island. Each of the pieces analysed can be securely attributed to its island source.

Obsidian comprises 5.4 per cent of the chipped stone assemblage from the Early Neolithic levels at Arene Candide. The relationship between source and class of lithic morphology is given in Table 9.1. Just over one-half of the obsidian comes from Sardinia; type B obsidian is the most common but all three of the chemical types on Sardinia are represented at the site. Blades constitute a full 60 per cent of the material from Sardinia. While two fragments of cores and several other

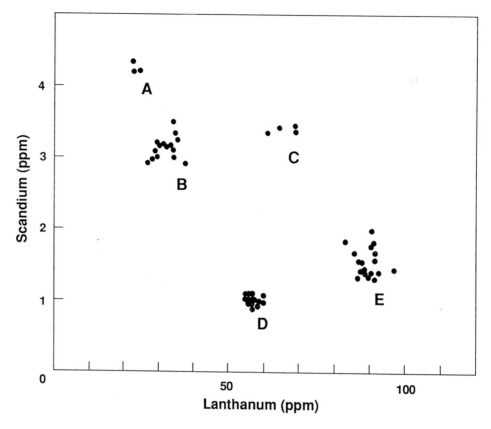

Figure 9.2. Neutron activation analysis of obsidian from Arene Candide: values for lanthanum and scandium. A. Sardinia (A), B. Sardinia (B), C. Sardinia (C), D. Lipari and E. Palmarola

by-products of the reduction of obsidian are also present, the evidence for the actual working of obsidian at the site is modest in comparison with the number of blades recovered (for the quantitative relationship between blades and the by-products of reduction when a core is worked, see Ammerman & Andrefsky 1982). At the same time, both of the core fragments from the Early Neolithic levels at Arene Candide indicate the use of a bipolar reduction technique (that is, the working of the core against an anvil), which permits the full reduction of a core even when it reaches a small size. The inference to be drawn is that the limited amount of obsidian reduction that was done at Arene Candide (or in the vicinity of the site) tried to make the most of what was to hand. In contrast, as we shall see below, no evidence for the use of the bipolar technique is found at Neolithic sites in the Acconia area of Calabria. In other words, one observes a more intensive approach to obsidian reduction in the case of Arene Candide. The rest of the obsidian in the Early Neolithic levels at the site comes from Palmarola. Again, the obsidian from this island source, like that from Sardinia, occurs largely in the form of blades. It is worth adding that many of the blades from both Sardinia and Palmarola show evidence

Table 9.2 Obsidian from the Early Neolithic levels at Arene Candide: selected aspects of lithic technology and use-wear

Class	Intentional retouch	Definite use-wear	Possible use-wear	Bipolar technique
Blade	5	9	3	1
Core trim	1	1	2	-
Trim	-	-	-	-
Core	1	-	1	2

See Table 9.1 for the number of pieces that belong to each class of lithic reduction

for either intentional retouch along their lateral edges or well developed signs of use-wear (Table 9.2).[3] The indication, then, is that most of the blades, in one way or another, were actively utilized as tools.

Obsidian from the Island of Lipari first makes its appearance in the square mouth pottery levels at Arene Candide. Table 9.3 gives a summary of the changes observed at the site between the Early Neolithic and the Late Neolithic In the Middle Neolithic, there is a decline in the percentage of obsidian from both Sardinia and Palmarola; obsidian from Lipari, notwithstanding its much greater distance from the site, now comprises one-third of the material. As in the Early Neolithic levels, blades still constitute almost two-thirds of the pieces of obsidian recovered. But obsidian cores are no longer present in the levels with square mouth pottery at Arene Candide. And again the blades from the Middle Neolithic period, as well as those dating to the Late Neolithic, show good signs of use-wear at Arene Candide. When we turn to the Late Neolithic, only blades are observed; for obsidian, no other class of lithic morphology is attested at the site during this period. The implication is that, by this time, the reduction of obsidian had completely stopped at the site. In other words, only blades in finished form – that is, blades produced elsewhere – were now reaching Arene Candide. What is perhaps even more striking, as shown in Table 9.3, is that 87.5 per cent of the Late Neolithic obsidian is from Lipari. Thus, at Arene Candide, over the course of the Neolithic as a whole, we see a progressive increase in the relative proportion of obsidian from Lipari. Despite the much shorter distances to Sardinia and Palmarola, Lipari over time comes to supplant the two other island sources of obsidian. By the Late Neolithic period, distance, as a factor conditioning the exchange of obsidian to Liguria, is apparently no longer king.

It is evident that comprehensive sourcing, as exemplified by the present case study, gives us a rather different picture of obsidian exchange than the one offered by selective sourcing (compare the results for Arene Candide as given in Williams Thorpe *et al.*

1979). In effect, this means that we have to undertake a new cycle of empirical work.[4] It is clearly not the time to sit back and to attempt merely to reinterpret the results of earlier work. Building on the earlier generation of characterization studies, much closer attention will now have to be paid to individual sites. In the new work, it will be important to combine comprehensive sourcing (that is, an attempt to attribute to source all of the pieces of obsidian recovered from a site) with detailed studies on both reduction technology and traces of use-wear for the full assemblage of obsidian pieces from a site or from a sub-unit of a site such as a household (Ammerman *et al.* 1988; Ammerman 1988–89). As shown by the new results from Arene Candide, the greater effort called for would seem to be well worthwhile. Over time, as more Neolithic sites in northern Italy are examined in this way, we can expect to obtain significant advances in our understanding of the circulation and exchange of obsidian.

Models for obsidian exchange

The results from Arene Candide also raise fundamental questions with regard to some of our previous ideas about models for the exchange of obsidian. As mentioned earlier, we need to consider Arene Candide in terms of its place in the 'tail' of an exchange network. If we compare the situation in the levels with impressed ware Neolithic pottery at Arene Candide with that of a coeval site near the 'head' of a network such as Piana di Curinga in Calabria, we find several major differences. Obsidian comprises 90 per cent or more of the chipped stone assemblage at Piana di Curinga and other Neolithic sites in the Acconia area (Ammerman 1979; Ammerman 1985a). This is in contrast with the low percentages observed at Arene Candide. At the Acconia sites, there are abundant by-products (core rejuvenation flakes, core trim flakes and shatter) from the reduction of cores but no evidence is found for the use of the bipolar technique. While this technique of production is well represented at Arene Candide, evidence for the actual working of cores at the site is quite

Table 9.3. Obsidian at Arene Candide. Three phases of occupation. Percentage of island sources and percentage of reduction technology

Neolithic Period	Island Source			Reduction Technology		
	Sardinia	Palmarola	Lipari	Blade	Flake	Core
Late	12.5	0.0	87.5	100.0	0.0	0.0
Middle	33.3	33.3	33.3	64.3	35.7	0.0
Early	57.7	42.3	0.0	65.4	26.9	7.7

modest. Again, with regard to tool use, as seen in terms of traces of microwear on the edges of blades, the obsidian from Piana di Curinga shows some evidence for use-wear but it appears to be much lighter, in general, than what is observed at Arene Candide. It will be recalled, for example, that half of the blades recovered from household H at Piana di Curinga present no indication of even possible microwear (Ammerman *et al.* 1988; Ammerman 1988–89). In short, such a comparison reveals that there is a tendency toward the intensification of production (the greater yield of blades or cutting edges per unit mass of obsidian; see for example Sidrys 1979) and also of consumption (the fuller use of blades suggesting that they probably had longer use-lives) in the 'tail' of an exchange network.

In the formulation of an earlier generation of exchange models, the working assumption was often made that much the same kinds of things with regard to production and consumption were happening at different places in a down-the-line exchange network (Renfrew 1977; Ammerman *et al.* 1978). As we have just seen, there is now good reason to think that things are more complex. What is called for is a new generation of exchange models in which the treatment of rates of production and consumption is more flexible; allowance has to be made for practices of reduction and use to vary between different positions in an exchange network. For example, it may be more appropriate to treat the discard rate of tools (originally called the 'dropping rate' in Ammerman *et al.* 1978) as decreasing, in general, with distance from an obsidian source. In formal terms, this will mean the formulation of much more complicated models.

Finally, more attention will have to be paid to the question of the quality of the raw material. Obsidian from different sources was treated in earlier studies as if it were all the same. We now realize that quality matters. The best quality obsidian from Lipari is much clearer and more glass-like than that from Sardinia and Palmarola. As seen in the Gaione study (Ammerman *et al.* 1990), there was a preference in northern Italy for clear blades of Lipari obsidian as a prestige item already in the later part of the Middle Neolithic period. One way to explain the diachronic changes observed at Arene Candide is by the demand for blades in high quality obsidian from Lipari – one which led over time to a more controlled and perhaps even more efficient organization of the long-distance exchange of this prestige item. At Arene Candide, there may be a direct reflection of the move toward greater control and efficiency as seen in the reduced sizes of blades in Lipari obsidian (particularly in blade thickness) between the Middle and Late Neolithic periods. But whatever interpretation we may wish to advance for the new results from Arene Candide, greater emphasis will now have to be placed on the dynamics of change over the Neolithic period as a whole in the circulation and exchange of obsidian.

Notes

1. We would like to thank P. Biagi, R. Maggi and E. Starnini for their help in the study of the obsidian from Arene Candide. A more detailed report on the obsidian from the site will appear in a forthcoming Festschrift in honour of L. Bernabò Brea.

2. New work on the identification of the obsidian sources associated with Monte Arce and the characterization of obsidian pieces found at prehistoric sites in Sardinia is currently being undertaken by Tykot (1992).

3. For a contemporary approach to the study of use-wear on flaked stone tools and bibliography see Vaughan (1985). While striations and other forms of edge damage can be observed along the edges of obsidian tools used in experiments, polishes of the kind found on flint and chert tools are not consistently observed on obsidian. Recent claims by Hurcombe that polishes can be observed on pieces of Sardinian obsidian may not hold for obsidian from other sources (this may be due to the specific character of the surface of much of the obsidian from Sardinia). This is an unresolved issue that calls for further study.

4. When the obsidian assemblage is particularly large, it may not be possible to process all or most of the pieces from a given site. Analytical strategies that involve first the visual screening of pieces (by a well experienced analyst) and then blind tests on a sample of the material, using techniques such as neutron activation analysis, in order to evaluate the degree of success of visual attributions, may have to be implemented. All of the pieces from the Early Neolithic levels at Arene Candide have been examined directly by means of neutron activation analysis. This also applies to the material from the Chassey or Late Neolithic levels at the site. In the case of the Neolithic sites in the Acconia area of Calabria, characterization studies (Crummett & Warren 1985; Ammerman *et al.* 1990) and extensive visual screening (e.g. Ammerman 1979) indicate that all but a very small number of obsidian pieces come from the nearby island of Lipari. Sourcing is not a major issue in this case. Comprehensive sourcing of the kind recommended here will be most useful in areas such as northern Italy where obsidian from several different island sources is likely to occur at a given site.

References

Ammerman, A.J., 1979. A study of obsidian exchange networks in Calabria. *World Archaeology* 11, 95–110

Ammerman, A.J., 1985a. *The Acconia Survey: Neolithic Settlement and the Obsidian Trade*. London: Institute of Archaeology, University of London. Occasional Publication no. 10

Ammerman, A.J., 1985b. Anthropology and the study of Neolithic exchange systems in Calabria. *Dialoghi di Archeologia* 3, 25–33

Ammerman, A.J., 1988–89. Toward the study of Neolithic households. *Origini* 14, 73–82

Ammerman, A.J. & Andrefsky, W., 1982. Reduction sequences and the exchange of obsidian in Neolithic Calabria, in *Contexts for Prehistoric Exchange*, eds J.E. Ericson & T.K. Earle. New York: Academic Press, 149–72

Ammerman, A.J., Cesana, A., Polglase, C. & Terrani, M., 1990. Neutron activation analysis of obsidian from two Neolithic sites in Italy. *Journal of Archaeological Science* 17, 209–20

Ammerman, A.J., Matessi, C., & Cavalli-Sforza, L.L., 1978. Some new approaches to the study of the obsidian trade in the Mediterranean and adjacent areas, in *The Spatial Organisation of Culture*, ed. I. Hodder. London: Duckworth, 179–96

Ammerman, A.J., Shaffer, G.D., & Hartmann, N., 1988. A Neolithic household at Piana di Curinga, Italy. *Journal of Field Archaeology* 15, 121–40

Bagolini, B. & Biagi, P., 1990. The radiocarbon chronology of the Neolithic and Copper Age of Northern Italy. *Oxford Journal of Archaeology* 9, 1–23

Bernabò Brea, L., 1946. *Gli scavi nella caverna delle Arene Candide. Parte I, gli strati con ceramiche, vol. l.* Bordighera, Liguria: Istituto di Studi Liguri.

Bernabò Brea, L., 1956. *Gli Scavi nella Caverna delle Arene Candide. Parte I, Gli Strati con Ceramiche, vol. 2.* Bordighera, Liguria: Istituto di Studi Liguri

Buchner, G., 1949. Ricerche sui giacimenti e sulle industrie di ossidiana in Italia. *Rivista di Scienze Preistoriche* 4, 162–86

Crummett, J.G., & Warren, S.E., 1985. Appendix I. Chemical analysis of Calabrian obsidian, in *The Acconia Survey: Neolithic Settlement and the Obsidian Trade*, ed. A.J. Ammerman. London: Institute of Archaeology, University of London. Occasional Publication no. 10, 107–14

Hallam, B.R., Warren, S.E., & Renfrew, C., 1976. Obsidian in the western Mediterranean: characterisation by neutron activation analysis and optical emission spectroscopy. *Proceedings of the Prehistoric Society* 42, 85–110

Michels, J.W., Atzeni, E., Tsong, I.S.T., & Smith, G.A., 1984. Obsidian hydration dating in Sardinia, in *Studies in Sardinian Archaeology*, eds M.S. Balmuth & R.J. Rowland. Ann Arbor: University of Michigan Press, 83–113

Read, D.W., 1989. Statistical methods and reasoning in archaeological research: a review of praxis and promise. *Journal of Quantitative Anthropology* 1, 5–78

Renfrew, C., 1977. Alternative models for exchange and spatial distribution, in *Exchange Systems in Prehistory*, eds T.K. Earle & J.E. Ericson. New York: Academic Press, 71–90

Sidrys, R., 1979. Supply and demand among the classic Maya. *Current Anthropology* 20, 594–97

Torrence, R., 1986. *Production and Exchange of Stone Tools*. Cambridge: Cambridge University Press

Tykot, R., 1992. Regional interaction in the prehistoric central Mediterranean: chronological variation as evidenced by obsidian exchange. Paper delivered at the Symposium on Social Dynamics of the Prehistoric Central Mediterranean, 57th Annual Meeting of the Society for American Archaeology, Pittsburgh, April 1992

Vaughan, P., 1985. *Use-wear Analysis of Flaked Stone Tools*. Tucson: University of Arizona Press

Williams Thorpe, O., Warren, S.E. & Barfield, L.H., 1979. The source and distributions of archaeological obsidian in Northern Italy. *Preistoria Alpina* 15, 73–92

Williams Thorpe, O., Warren, S.E., & Courtin, J., 1984. The distribution and sources of archaeolgoical obsidian from southern France. *Journal of Archaeological Science* 11, 135–46

10

Neolithic Exchange in Central and Southern Italy

Robin Skeates

The first half of this paper is concerned with describing the repertoire of mechanisms and commodities of exchange that might have existed in different social and spatial contexts in central and southern Italy during the Neolithic. The importance of alliance and ceremonial behaviour in the functioning of production and exchange networks is emphasised, as is the limited archaeological visibility of most kinds of Neolithic commodity and exchange. The second half of the paper then goes on to describe and explain, particularly from a socially deterministic perspective, the general changes that took place in production and exchange in the east-central Italian Abruzzo-Marche region. The constantly peripheral position of Neolithic communities in this region is emphasised, particularly in relation to developing inter-regional exchange networks in the central Mediterranean.

La première partie de cet article décrit la gamme de méchanismes et de commodités d'échange qui auraient pu exister dans des contextes sociaux et spatiaux différents en Italie méridionale pendant le Néolithique. On souligne l'importance des alliances et des cérémonies dans le fonctionnement des réseaux de production et d'échange, ainsi que la visibilité archéologique limitée de la majorité des formes de commodités et d'échanges Néolithiques. La deuxième partie de l'article décrit et explique, surtout du point de vue du déterminisme sociale, les changements géneraux qui eurent lieu dans la production et les échanges dans la région Abruzzo-Marche de l'Italie Est-centrale. La position toujours périphérique des communités Néolithiques de cette région est soulignée, surtout en rapport avec les réseaux d'échange inter-régionaux qui se développaient alors en Méditerranée centrale.

Introduction

In 1985 Ammerman ended his paper 'Anthropology and the study of Neolithic exchange systems in Calabria' with the statement that, 'there is a need to develop a new and more complex generation of models of Neolithic exchange' (Ammerman 1985, 31). With this statement in mind, I have prepared what might be described as a somewhat theoretically oriented paper. Throughout it I shall be considering different commodities and mechanisms of exchange, including variations in the types, functions, symbolism and values attributed to them in different contexts (Hodder 1982; Appadurai 1986). (I am using the word 'commodity' broadly, following Appadurai (1986), to mean any class of thing intended for exchange.) I shall also be drawing upon the work of Marxist economic anthropologists, such as Friedman & Rowlands (1977) and Bender (1979, 1981, 1985), which I find particularly relevant and useful, although I do recognize that other approaches are also valid for the

study of Neolithic exchange. From a more archaeological perspective, I have three main points to make: the first is the limited archaeological visibility of most kinds of Neolithic commodity and exchange; the second is the importance of alliance and ceremonial behaviour in the functioning of production and exchange networks during the Neolithic in central and southern Italy; and the third is the constantly peripheral position of Neolithic communities in the east-central Italian Abruzzo-Marche region in relation to inter-regional exchange networks in the central Mediterranean.

Possible mechanisms and commodities of exchange in different socio-spatial contexts

To begin with, I want to describe the repertoire of possible mechanisms and commodities of exchange that might have existed in different social and spatial contexts in central and southern Italy during the Neolithic.

At one end of the spectrum, exchanges were carried

out at an intra-community level. Here, the community, comprising one or more closely situated small hamlets, would have provided the spatial, social and economic context for exchange; and the household, comprising one or more houses and their occupants, might have formed the focus of labour and production. Sahlins (1972) has described this as the 'domestic mode of production'. Incidentally, an agriculture-based subsistence economy, comprising crop-cultivation, stock-keeping and varying degrees of gathering, hunting and fishing, appears to have been practised at most sites in central and southern Italy during the Neolithic (Barker 1975; Whitehouse 1968). At this intra-community level, at sites such as Piana di Curinga in south-west Italy (Ammerman 1983), exchange is likely have taken place within the context of everyday interaction and face-to-face contact between members of different households. The dominant modes of exchange involved at this level probably included 'generalized reciprocity' and 'redistribution'. Examples of these include mutual assistance between households, in which there was a moral obligation to share, but only a vaguely defined duty to reciprocate, and the redistribution of the results of co-operative food production.

The main types of commodity exchanged at this level can be categorized as 'primary commodities'. These would have been relatively common, but necessary things, with a high use-value in relation to the production and reproduction of immediate life. Staple foodstuffs, such as cereals, were probably the most important of these, considering the high probability of crop-failure at the level of the individual household. However, the most archaeologically visible types of primary commodity found at residential sites in Neolithic Italy are artefacts used in the production of food, shelter and clothing. These include pottery vessels, large ground stone work axes, flint and bone tools and grindstones. Labour would have comprised a less archaeologically visible type of primary commodity.

Turning to the other end of the spectrum, other kinds of exchange were carried out at an inter-community level. Here, the spatial context for exchange was provided by a pattern of communities distributed within fairly restricted and separated habitats, which stretched along and across much of the Italian peninsula. The lowland Tavoliere plain is a good example of a fairly discrete Neolithic settlement zone (Jones 1987, fig. 7). The social and economic context for exchanges between communities located within and in different settlement zones might have been provided by a large-scale alliance and ceremonial system (Friedman & Rowlands 1977; Bender 1981). In this, compacts of peace, friendship, marriage and kinship, or of revenge and war, would have been made between communities and their representatives.

The main types of commodity exchanged at this level can be categorized as 'valuables', as opposed to 'primary commodities'. Valuables can be defined as those commodities to which a high symbolic value would have been ascribed, due to their ability to carry and display culturally constructed meanings and messages (Appadurai 1986; Renfrew 1986). They would also have been ascribed a fairly high exchange value, as exotic goods which were exchanged over long distances. Access to them would have been restricted, not only as a result of their real scarcity but perhaps also by social and cultural sanctions. Good material examples of valuables from the Abruzzo region include painted fineware vessels, decorated in inter-regionally recognizable styles (Figs 10.1–2), a triton-shell trumpet, and a red coral ornament (Malone 1985; Skeates 1991b). Marriage partners, possibly accompanied by dowries, may also have been exchanged as valuables, if individuals were obliged to obtain marriage partners from other communities, as is common in lineage systems of social organization. Other possible examples of valuables exchanged at this level include sea shell ornaments, decorated textiles, cattle, non-staple foodstuffs (including meat, fortuitous crop surpluses, dried fish, wild fruits and nuts), special drinks, drugs, medicines, military assistance and special knowledge.

The presence of special archaeological deposits, containing relatively high proportions of valuable artefacts as well as evidence of ceremonial or ritual behaviour, provides some indication of the kinds of place where the inter-community exchange of valuables might have occurred. Such places appear to have included some of the major lowland open sites in central and southern Italy and a few caves. A good example, dating to the later Neolithic, is provided by Grotta dei Piccioni in the Abruzzo region (Cremonesi 1976; Skeates 1991a). Here, valuable artefacts, including inter-regional style painted pottery and relatively large quantities of sea shell ornaments, including a rare and exotic red-painted triton shell trumpet, were found in and around a special deposit, which has been called the 'Level of the Circles'. The deposit comprised a great quantity of animal bones, artefacts and ashes, structured spatially in relation to a line of circles of stone and the remains of children. Meat parts predominated amongst the animal bones, which suggests food if not feasting. Intentional pottery smashing appears to have taken place in the northern half of the deposit, and a group of five intact fineware vessels (one covered by a lid) were placed at the other end of the deposit, significantly close to a pair of child skulls. Some unusual pottery vessel forms, bird-bone artefacts and clay weights were also found there. I suggest that these deposits indicate, however indirectly, that this cave was used as an arena for the ceremonial exchange and deposition of valuables, and that cultural meanings and symbolic uses were ascribed to the valuables displayed within this context.

Stretching this point even further, I suggest that the open sites and caves where such special deposits are found might also be regarded as regional *foci* for aggregation and ceremonial activities. Inter-community alliances could have been formed within such arenas, accompanied by ceremonial exchanges of valuable gifts, public feasts and entertainments. These might also have coincided with other major ceremonies, such as initiations, marriages, funerals and cults of the ancestors. Such meetings would have been occasional during the Neolithic, considering the limitations of human labour in producing any considerable food surplus over and above its maintenance costs, which would have been necessary for the sustenance of the participants.

As a final speculation, I suggest that the origin of such meetings might lie the late Upper Palaeolithic, in the form of winter aggregations in and around the decorated cave sites located along the coasts of southern Italy and Sicily. A good example is Grotta dell'Addàura in Sicily, where some sort of ceremonial activity appears to have been depicted on one of the cave walls (Graziosi 1956). Turning to the middle of the spectrum of exchange, other types of commodity and exchange can be placed between the intra- and inter-community levels that I have de-

scribed so far. The commodities exchanged at this level are characterised by a high use value, and comprise useful raw materials and tools, most of which were used for special tasks in subsistence activities. Archaeologically recognizable examples found regularly at residential sites include obsidian (in the form of easily worked cores and sharp bladelets), long blades of high quality flint, greenstone axes for delicate woodworking, pieces of pumice, the earliest copper artefacts in central and southern Italy (including a small blade and an awl), and seeds and breeding stock.

Commodities of this group also had a high exchange value, which ensured their indirect transport over distances of at least 40 kilometres from production sources to distant communities, via neighbouring territories and groups. This point has been well established in the central Mediterranean by, for example, characterization studies of obsidian (e.g. Hallam *et al.* 1976; Ammerman *et al.* 1990). In addition, such commodities sometimes also gained symbolic value, especially towards the per-

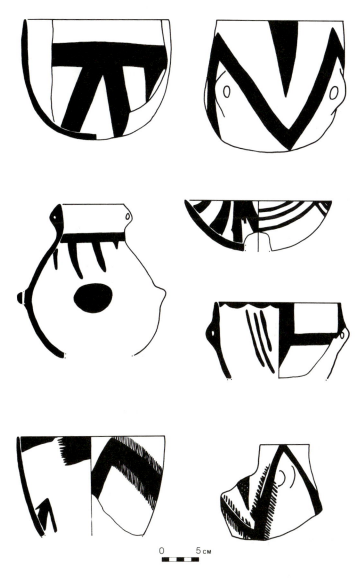

0   5 CM

Figure 10.1. Middle Neolithic red painted pottery from Catignano, after Pitti & Tozzi (1976) and Tozzi (1978)

iphery of their distribution networks, at the greatest distances from their sources. In southern Italy, for example, miniature polished axes of greenstone were occasionally placed in graves or converted into amulets; and at Gaione, in northern Italy, obsidian blades have recently been found in a grave along with south Italian Serra d'Alto style pottery (A. Ammerman pers. comm.).

I suggest that exchanges at this middle level may have been more commercial in nature than those involving primary commodities and valuables, although they probably still functioned under the general principle of reciprocity. They may, for instance, have involved some bargaining, but are unlikely to have involved entrepreneurial barter. During the early Neolithic, for example, any commercial element involved in the spread of novel agricultural commodities did not go so far as to hinder the exchange of information relating to their use and production. Such exchanges were probably made, most commonly, between relatives, allies, or exchange partners belonging to different communities, rather than between complete strangers. This applies both to overland and to maritime exchanges, for only short island-hopping or coast-hugging voyages are likely to have been made during the Neolithic. Occasional inter-community aggregations in caves and at large lowland open sites, where ceremonial exchanges of valuable gifts might have formed a focus of attention, may also have provided the main context for these less spectacular, but equally important, middle-level exchanges. This might explain the high proportions of obsidian blades and bladelets found in a few inland caves and lowland residential sites in central and northern Italy, and also the high frequency of small greenstone axes found in caves in southern Italy (Malone 1986; Leighton 1989; O'Hare 1990).

Changes in production and exchange during the Neolithic

The second part of this paper is concerned with describ-

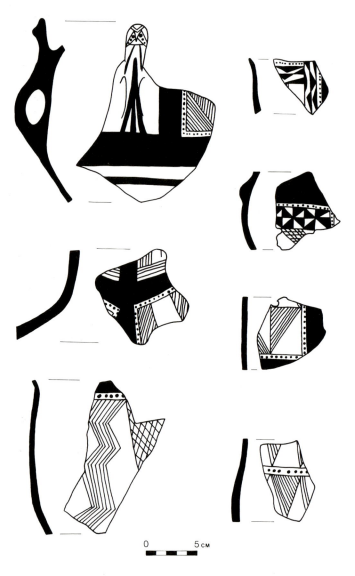

Figure 10.2. Late Neolithic red and brown painted pottery from Ripoli, cavity 12 (drawn from the originals in Atri museum, by kind permission of Dott. V. D'Ercole)

ing and explaining, particularly from a socially deterministic perspective, the general changes that took place in production and exchange in the somewhat peripheral Abruzzo-Marche region during the Neolithic. The bulky archaeological data from which these patterns are drawn are presented in my D. Phil. thesis (Skeates 1992).

For one reason or another indigenous Mesolithic groups in the Abruzzo-Marche region entered an expanding southern Adriatic inter-regional alliance and exchange network during the late 6th millennium cal. BC. As a result, they adopted not only a Neolithic agricultural package, but also, I would suggest, strong social obligations to participate in that alliance and exchange network from then on. These obligations of reciprocity may, in turn, have activated local institutional and individual strategies of desire and demand for commodities.

Within communities, demands might have been made upon subsistence production in order to realize potential food surpluses. Such demands are likely to have been made by individuals in authority, such as a family council of elders or temporarily elected community representatives, employing a combination of personal exhortation and ritual symbolism (cf. Whitehouse 1990). When large surpluses of crops or stock were produced, either as a result of these demands or fortuitously, they are likely to have been used to provision socially and ritually important inter-community alliance and ceremonial gatherings. Furthermore, and without wishing to over-politicize Neolithic Italy, I would suggest that such occasions, and particularly the exchanges of gifts that took place during them, might have been exploited by the participants for political and material gain. Superficially, the formation or strengthening of alliances on such occasions would have encouraged the growth of inter-community solidarity. But, more subtly, such occasions and the exchanges involved in them could have been exploited, particularly by the hosts, to transform relations of power between the participating communities. This could have been achieved through what Mauss (1967) and Bourdieu (1977) describe as 'games of sociability or hospitality'. The goals of such games were, politically, to enhance community prestige, authority and status through the creation of debt and dependency via reciprocal gift-exchange, and, materially, to accumulate middle-level and valuable commodities.

By the end of the early Neolithic, that is by the end of the 6th millennium cal. BC, participation in this inter-community system of alliance and exchange had led to the successful emergence of a few open sites as nodes of production and exchange and as regional aggregation centres for settlement and ceremonial. Such sites, including late Neolithic Ripoli (Rellini 1934; Cremonesi 1965), stand out in the archaeological record. Relatively high proportions and quantities of imported commodities were deposited at them, for example. Such sites also stand out for their large size and the presence of special mortuary deposits within them. This social and economic differentiation of lowland communities can in part be explained by geographical factors, such as access to good arable and grazing land or to major exchange routes, but it surely also relates to the active political strategies of community leaders. These leaders, through encouraging the production of surpluses, hosting feasts and giving gifts, could have attracted in return exotic commodities and dependent people, and could have elevated their own status, perhaps especially as members of dominant lineages. Strategies of social closure may also have been used increasingly in this process (Rowlands 1985), with, for example, distinctive styles of painted pottery being produced at dominant sites, such as Catignano (Tozzi 1978), not only as a commodity for exchange but also for local consumption in order to enhance feelings of community identity (Figs. 10.1–2).

On a central Mediterranean scale, however, even the most successful later Neolithic communities in the Abruzzo-Marche region remained sluggish and peripheral with respect to significantly diverting the long-distance flow of commodities from sources such as Lipari. Quantities of obsidian imported into the region, for example, remained fairly small throughout the 5th millennium cal. BC. In addition, communities remained, for the most part, tied to traditional patterns of exchange, which linked Abruzzo-Marche to south-east and west-central Italy, and established only weak or short-lived relations with groups to the north and east. Ultimately, communities in the Abruzzo-Marche region appear to have had little of outstanding inter-regional economic value to offer at this time. They lacked, for example, abundant supplies of special raw materials, large surpluses of crops or stock, or major technological innovations, and they therefore received little in return.

The final Neolithic, however, which dates to between the end of the 5th and the end of the 4th millennia cal. BC, saw a major expansion in production and exchange in the Abruzzo-Marche region. This can be measured both locally and on an inter-regional scale. Ripoli's pre-eminence as an economic node and as a social centre continued, but more sites now also emerged as nodes of production and exchange throughout the region. Flint quarries were established in the Apennine mountains, at sites such as Torre Beregna (Pigorini & Gnoli 1888), and significant quantities of relatively high quality pink flint appear to have been exported from them to lowland residential sites. The quantity and range of exotic commodities flowing into the region also increased notably, and included Lipari obsidian, early copper artefacts, south Italian Serra d'Alto and Diana-Bellavista style pottery, and north Italian Lagozza style pottery.

Internally, this expansion in exchange can be explained as the result of the major developments in production which started to take place towards the end of the late Neolithic in response to escalating socio-economic demands and pressures on lowland production. Growing social demands for food surpluses and greater ecological pressure on old arable and grazing land, led to the development of a more diversified subsistence economy. There was a significant increase in the consumption of wild foods throughout the region; early attempts may have been made to exploit sheep and cattle for their secondary products at certain sites in the lowlands; and settlement expanded significantly into the forested interior of the region. These developments in production might have directly fuelled further exchanges of hospitality and gifts between increasingly competitive lowland communities, but would also, as Sherratt (1984) first explained, have encouraged more extensive exchanges between divergent communities settled extensively throughout the region.

From a broader perspective, however, this final Neolithic expansion in exchange and production was not unique to the Abruzzo-Marche region; neither did it originate there. Most regions in southern Europe exhibited similar symptoms at this time, and in the central Mediterranean they spread via an inter-regional exchange network which had reached a peak of stability and extent. Communities in the Abruzzo-Marche region had little control over this process; they were simply fortunate enough, finally, to find themselves swept by a tide of change via their more influential neighbours. When this tide receded, during the Copper Age, communities in the Abruzzo-Marche region found themselves even more isolated than before.

References

Ammerman, A. J., 1983. Early Italian pottery. *Expedition* 25:2, 15–25

Ammerman, A.J., Cesana, A., Polglase, C. & Terrani, M., 1990. Neutron activation analysis of obsidian from two Neolithic sites in Italy. *Journal of Archaeological Science* 17, 209–20

Appadurai, A., 1986. Introduction: commodities and the politics of value, in *The Social Life of Things. Commodities in Social Perspective*, ed. A. Appadurai. Cambridge: Cambridge University Press, 3–63

Bender, B., 1979. Gatherer-hunter to farmer: a social perspective. *World Archaeology* 10, 204–22

Bender, B., 1981. Gatherer-hunter intensification, in *Economic Archaeology. Towards an Integration of Ecological and Social Approaches*, eds A. Sheridan & G. Bailey. Oxford: British Archaeological Reports, Inter. Series 96, 149–57

Bender, B., 1985. Emergent tribal formations in the American midcontinent. *American Antiquity* 50, 52–62

Bourdieu, P., 1977. *Outline of a Theory of Practice*. Cambridge: Cambridge University Press.

Cremonesi, G., 1965. Il villagio di Ripoli alla luce dei recenti scavi. *Rivista di Scienze Preistoriche* 20, 85–155

Friedman, J. & Rowlands, M., 1977. Notes towards an epigenetic model of the evolution of 'civilisation', in *The Evolution of Social Systems*, eds J. Friedman & M. Rowlands. London: Duckworth, 201–76

Graziosi, P., 1956. Qualche osservazione sui graffiti rupestri della Grota dell'Addàura presso Palermo. *Bullettino di Paleontologia Italiana* 65, 285–95

Hallam, B.R., Warren, S.E. & Renfrew, C., 1976. Obsidian in the western Mediterranean: characterization by neutron activation analysis and optical emission spectroscopy. *Proceedings of the Prehistoric Society* 42, 85–110

Hodder, I., 1982. *Symbols in Action. Ethnoarchaeological Studies of Material Culture*. Cambridge: Cambridge University Press

Jones, G.D.B. (ed.), 1987. *Apulia 1: the Neolithic Settlement in the Tavoliere*. London: Report of the Research Committee of the Society of Antiquaries 44

Leighton, R., 1989. Ground stone tools from Serra Orlando (Morgantina) and stone axe studies in Sicily and southern Italy. *Proceedings of the Prehistoric Society* 55, 135–59

Malone, C., 1985. Pots, prestige and ritual in Neolithic southern Italy, in *Papers in Italian Archaeology IV. The Cambridge Conference. Part ii. Prehistory*, eds C. Malone & S. Stoddart. Oxford: British Archaeological Reports, International Series 244, 118–51

Malone, C.A., 1986. *Exchange Systems and Style in the Central Mediterranean 4500–1700 BC*. Unpublished Ph.D. dissertation, University of Cambridge

Mauss, M., 1967. *The Gift: Forms and Functions of Exchange in Archaic Societies*. London: Norton

O'Hare, G., 1990. A preliminary study of polished stone artefacts in prehistoric southern Italy. *Proceedings of the Prehistoric Society* 56, 123–52

Pigorini, L., & Gnoli, G., 1888. Stazioni dell'Età della Pietra nel circondario di Camerino. *Bullettino di Paleontologia Italiana* 14, 41–6

Pitti, C. & Tozzi, C., 1976. Gli scavi nel villaggio neolitico di Catignano (Pescara). Nota preliminare. *Rivista di Scienze Preistoriche* 31, 87–107

Rellini, U., 1934. *La Più Antica Ceramica Dipinta in Italia*. Roma: Meridonale

Renfrew, C., 1986. Varna and the emergence of wealth in prehistoric Europe, in *The Social Life of Things. Commodities in Social Perspective*, ed. A. Appadurai. Cambridge: Cambridge University Press, 141–68

Rowlands, M., 1985. Exclusionary tactics in the logic of collective dynamics. *Critique of Anthropology* 5:2, 47–69

Sahlins, M., 1972. *Stone Age Economics*. London: Routledge

Sherratt, A., 1984. Social evolution: Europe in the later Neolithic and Copper Ages, in *European Social Evolution. Archaeological Perspectives*, ed. J. Bintliff. West Chiltington: Chanctonbury Press, 123–34

Skeates, R., 1991a. Caves, cult and children in Neolithic Abruzzo, central Italy, in *Sacred and Profane. Proceedings of a Conference on Archaeology, Ritual and Religion. Oxford, 1989*, eds P. Garwood, D. Jennings, R. Skeates & J. Toms. Oxford: Oxford University Committee for Archaeology, 122–34

Skeates, R., 1991b. Triton's trumpet: a Neolithic symbol in Italy. *Oxford Journal of Archaeology* 10, 17–31

Skeates, R., 1992. *The Neolithic and Copper Age of the Abruzzo-Marche region, central Italy*. Unpublished D.Phil. dissertation, University of Oxford

Tozzi, C., 1978. Un aspetto della corrente culturale della ceramica dipinta in Abruzzo: il villaggio di Catignano (Pescara). *Quaderni de la Ricerca Scientifica* 100, 95–111

Whitehouse, R.D., 1968. Settlement and economy in southern Italy in the Neothermal period. *Proceedings of the Prehistoric Society* 34, 332–66

Whitehouse, R.D., 1990. Caves and cult in Neolithic southern Italy. *The Accordia Research Papers* 1, 19–38

11

The Origin of Metal Used for Making Weapons in Early and Middle Minoan Crete

Zofia Stos-Gale

In the third millennium BC, Crete was a centre of production of the earliest European copper weapons. The origin of the metal is a puzzle, because copper minerals on Crete are scarce and they seem never to have been exploited in any quantity. On the other hand, the metallurgy of copper was well developed by that time in the Near East, Cyprus, and Egypt. Many imported artefacts excavated on Crete leave no doubt that the Minoans at that time had frequent trading contacts with all these areas. Was copper also one of the imports? The results of lead isotope analyses of a number of Early Minoan weapons indicate that in the third millennium BC there was a well organised production of copper metal in the Aegean. The composition of the majority of the analysed artefacts is consistent with their origin from minerals smelted on the Cycladic islands.

Au troisième millénaire av. J.C. la Crète était un des centres de production d'armes en cuivre les plus anciennnes d'Europe. L'origine de ce métal est incertaine, puisque les minerais de cuivre sont rares en Crète et ne semblent jamais avoir été exploités en quantité. D'autre part, la métallurgie de cuivre était alors déjà bien développée au Proche Orient, en Chypre, et en Egypte. De nombreuses importations retrouvées en Crète ne laissent pas douter que les minoens avaient des contacts commerciaux fréquents avec toutes ces régions. Le cuivre faisait-il partie de ces importations? Les résultats des analyses des isotopes de plomb des armes du Minoen ancien montrent qu'au troisième millénaire avant J.C. il existait en Egée une production bien organisée du cuivre. La composition de la majorité des objets analysés s'accorde avec une origine dans des minerais fondus aux Cyclades.

Introduction

Early Minoan metal objects provide the earliest example in the Aegean of sophisticated and highly developed copper, silver and gold metallurgy. Branigan (1974) demonstrated that Crete played a leading role in the development of the Aegean Bronze Age metal industry which culminated in the middle of the second millennium BC in the exquisite silver, gold and bronze objects deposited in the Shaft Graves in Mycenae. The variety and individuality of Minoan metalwork are unequalled in Europe during the Aegean Bronze Age period. It seems that all the major developments in Minoan copper metalworking took place in the Early Minoan II and Early Minoan III periods. Branigan sees the speed of development of Minoan metallurgy as due both to Minoan inventiveness and to influences from beyond Crete. He sees the impetus coming ultimately from Syria-Cilicia, but in Early Minoan I also from the Cyclades. The Minoan inventiveness referred to so far

was in metalsmithing, which consists of devising shapes, casting, and working copper-based alloys, silver and gold. There is no conclusive evidence for Bronze Age mining and smelting of copper on Crete. Indeed copper ores on Crete are scarce (Wheeler *et al.* 1975; Gale & Stos-Gale 1986). The metallurgical workshops of Mallia and Knossos probably represent the debris of smiths making objects from metal, not the production of metal from the mineral, and the quantity of slag is small. There is no doubt, however, that the quantity of metal and the quality and innovative character of the objects must represent an economic situation where metal was in plentiful and continuous supply to the Minoan metalsmiths throughout the Bronze Age.

Where did this metal originate, if not from indigenous sources? Minoan trade with various parts of the eastern Mediterranean and beyond is well documented by many exotic objects excavated from archaeological sites throughout Crete: there are Babylonian seals, Egyptian stone vessels and scarabs, and elephant tusks as well as Aegean, Cypriot and Anatolian pottery. Minoan pottery has been found on most of the islands of the Aegean, in mainland Greece, Cyprus and Anatolia (Catling 1979). There is no doubt that pottery was made on Crete from local clay, but the same certainty cannot be extended to the metal objects that are typical of the local Minoan workshops. Copper, lead, silver and gold can travel long distances in the form of ingots or artefacts which can then easily be melted down and made into new objects.

In the past decade a scientific method has been developed for tracing the origin of single metal objects (Gale & Stos-Gale 1982). The method is based on the mass spectrometric analysis of the isotopes of lead present in metals and ores. This method seems an ideal tool for trying to decipher the origin of copper metal used by the Minoans.

The principles of lead isotope provenance studies

1. LEAD ISOTOPES: THEIR ORIGIN AND VARIATION

The element lead consists of four isotopes, that is four types of chemically identical atoms built of the same numbers of protons and electrons, but different numbers of neutrons, which result in different atomic masses. The atomic masses of the four isotopes of lead are 204, 206, 207 and 208 atomic mass units. The last three of those isotopes are formed as the products of radioactive decay of uranium and thorium, whilst the isotope ^{204}Pb is the original, 'primeval' lead isotope. Radioactive decay is a nuclear process which progresses at a constant rate dependent only on the nuclear structure of the isotope and independently of chemical and physical conditions like temperature, pressure, humidity and elemental composition. The rate of decay can be measured and used to calculate the time since the beginning of the process. The half-lives of the relevant radioactive Uranium and Thorium isotopes are very long: an original amount of ^{235}U is reduced by half, due its decay to ^{207}Pb, in 704 million years, whilst ^{238}U decays to ^{206}Pb with a half life of 4,468 million years. The half life of ^{232}Th decaying to ^{208}Pb is 14,010 million years. Such long half lives are suitable for reconstructing the history of the earth and for dating geological events measured on scales of millions of years. Scientists have proposed several quantitative models for the isotopic evolution of lead in the earth from which the age of the earth and the age of common lead minerals can be determined.

In practice the lead of most ore deposits will have had a complicated history involving, for example, residence in the earth's mantle followed by a period of crustal residence accompanied possibly by metamorphism, erosion and sedimentation, until the lead was finally extracted during a volcanic cycle or by the action of hot brines and concentrated in an ore deposit.

Because of all these events and the differences in the contents of uranium and of thorium in the initial stage of the ore formation, the lead isotope compositions of mineral deposits from different geographical regions but of the same geological age are usually not quite identical. These local lead isotope compositions can be measured and used as a lead isotope 'fingerprint' of a given ore deposit.

The principle of lead isotope 'fingerprinting' was used for the first time by Brill *et al.* (1965), and independently by Houtermans and his colleagues (Grogler *et al.* 1966), to identify the origin of some ancient lead objects. In the last twenty years lead isotope provenance studies have broadened to include glass (Brill 1970), silver coins (Gale *et al.* 1980), copper (Gale and Stos-Gale 1982), iron (Gale *et al.* 1988), painter's pigments (Keisch 1970) and other materials such as lead in bones (Molleson *et al.* 1986). The method used for provenance studies is based chiefly on experimental data, whereby measurements of the lead isotope compositions of minerals collected in specific locations provide unique 'fingerprints' characteristic for given ore deposits. In one ore body all elements have basically the same geochemical origin from the time of the ore formation. Some secondary minerals are formed due to the erosion and/or weathering of the ore body, processes which do not alter the lead isotope composition. Therefore primary galena and secondary lead carbonate (cerussite) will contain lead of the same isotopic composition. Likewise all the lead disseminated in the ore body and its gossan, and also present in various chemical forms in other minerals, will be the same lead with the same isotopic composition. Numerous measurements of different minerals from the same ore deposit prove that there is no isotope fractionation during the weathering and oxidation processes (Gulson 1986).

Also vital for archaeometallurgical studies is the fact that the lead isotope composition does not change during metallurgical processes — therefore the ore, slag and metal produced from a given ore deposit all have the same unchanged lead isotope fingerprint. Results of laboratory experiments proving this point were published by Barnes *et al.* (1978). Since then many analyses at Oxford of ore, slag and metal from archaeologically dated smelting sites on Cyprus (unpublished data), Kythnos (Stos-Gale 1989) and other sites, have confirmed and strengthened this conclusion. Lead isotope 'fingerprints' are so far the only measurable characteristics of the ore-slag-metal chain which are not altered during the metallurgical processes. Furthermore remelting and mixing metal smelted from ores from the same deposit does not influence the fingerprint. In the case of mixing of metals characterised by different isotope 'fingerprints' the resulting lead isotope composition either remains within the range of one of them or falls between the original compositions. Statistical methods can provide numerical probabilities for the consistency of the origin of each single object from a given ore deposit.

2. ANALYTICAL METHODS AND THE RANGE OF LEAD ISOTOPE COMPOSITIONS IN ONE ORE DEPOSIT

The most accurate method of measurement of lead isotope ratios is by means of thermal ionisation mass spectrometry; the instruments used are often called solid source mass spectrometers. A mass spectrometer is an instrument designed to separate ions of different masses, by accelerating them in a curved trajectory in an electromagnetic field (Duckworth *et al.* 1990).

For thermal ionisation of lead the sample is deposited in the form of lead nitrate on a metal (rhenium) filament, which is mounted in the source of the machine. Most modern mass spectrometers can take a number of filaments (the Oxford instrument has a turret with 16 filament positions). A filament is heated by an electric current and the lead from the sample is thermally ionised in a vacuum. When the ion beam enters the magnetic field generated by an electromagnet, the magnetic field deflects the ions into circular paths whose radii are proportional to the masses of the isotopes (the heavier ions are deflected less than the lighter ones). The ions of each isotope are then simultaneously electronically counted on the collectors. One run (set of measurements obtained from the same sample in a continuous manner) consists usually of 60 to 100 separate measurements. The final lead isotope ratios are calculated as mean values of each set of ratios. One lead isotope composition run on our multicollector VG mass spectrometer at Oxford takes less than half an hour.

Modern, properly conducted measurements of lead isotope ratios are highly accurate (usually the overall 95% error for an isotopic ratio is less than 0.03%). In all laboratories thermal ionisation mass spectrometers are calibrated for each element using a set of internationally accepted standards with extremely well defined isotope ratios (for lead the standards used are NBS SRM 981 and 982 issued by the United States National Institute of Standardisation), and all measured data is normalised taking into account repeated measurements of standards. This procedure makes it possible to cross-compare lead isotope data published by different groups. An inter-laboratory comparison of lead isotope data on bronze objects from Troy analysed in Mainz and Oxford has been discussed by Gale (1989, 474–75); very good agreement was demonstrated between the two laboratories.

Provenancing metals using lead isotope analyses is very simple in principle: it is enough to make comparative measurements of lead isotope compositions of artefacts and ore deposits and then search for matching compositions. One of the greatest strengths of lead isotope provenance studies lies in the geochronological nature of the range of values of lead isotope ratios in one ore formation. To a major degree the lead isotope composition of the ore is related directly to the age of the mineral formation, and as such can include only a very limited range of different lead isotope composi-tions, correlated to the geological history of the formation. This fact makes it possible on the one hand to predict the approximate age of the ore from which metal was produced to make a particular artefact, and on the other hand to exclude, on geological and/or lead isotope bases, ore deposits of quite different age as possible sources of this metal.

Each lead isotope measurement gives the parameters of a point in three-dimensional space. A set of lead isotope ratios measured for a series of minerals from one ore deposit forms a three dimensional 'globule' of a strictly limited size, which forms the lead isotope 'fingerprint' of this ore source.

To obtain a properly representative lead isotope characterisation of an ore deposit it is necessary to analyze a number of ore samples collected from various parts and depths and from different minerals. For some Aegean ore deposits, like those of Lavrion in Greece or of Cyprus, we have at present more than one hundred data points. These measurements demonstrate clearly that the size of each lead isotope 'fingerprint' is strictly limited by the isotope geochemistry of the ore formation. In most ore deposits of a relatively simple geological history the range of lead isotope ratios is usually less than 0.5%. Twenty measurements of well selected samples from a single ore deposit are usually sufficient to outline the size of the three-dimensional 'globule' of lead isotope compositions. Some mineral deposits are more complicated and may consist of minerals formed at different times, but since the provenance method is based on direct comparison, the correct interpretation depends on the correct isotope characterisation of each ore deposit used for comparison.

Our database at Oxford consists of a large number of such lead isotope 'fingerprints' of various metal deposits from Europe and the Near East (Gale & Stos-Gale 1991). The lead isotope compositions of ancient artefacts measured in our laboratory are directly trans-ferred into a database and can be compared with the 'fingerprints' of ore deposits using our own graphics programme (Picture). Statistical probabilities of the origin can be calculated by another direct transfer of the data into the BMDP statistical software. Particu-larly useful for interpretation of lead isotope data is stepwise discriminant analysis (Manly 1986). In prac-tice however, the two dimensional lead isotope ratio diagrams are most often quite sufficient to eliminate most of the ore deposits as the source of metal for the artefact. This allows the statistical evaluation to be used only to discriminate between the most closely related isotope 'fingerprints' of two or three deposits. There is no record, as yet, of two distant ore sources having exactly the same range of isotopic composi-tions, but some deposits overlap in their lead isotope 'fingerprints' to a certain degree. A typical plot of a group of such clusters of ore deposits is presented in Figure 11.1. Stepwise discriminant analysis is used to separate the overlapping data (Stos-Gale 1991).

COPPER ORES IN THE AEGEAN ANATOLIA AND SINAI

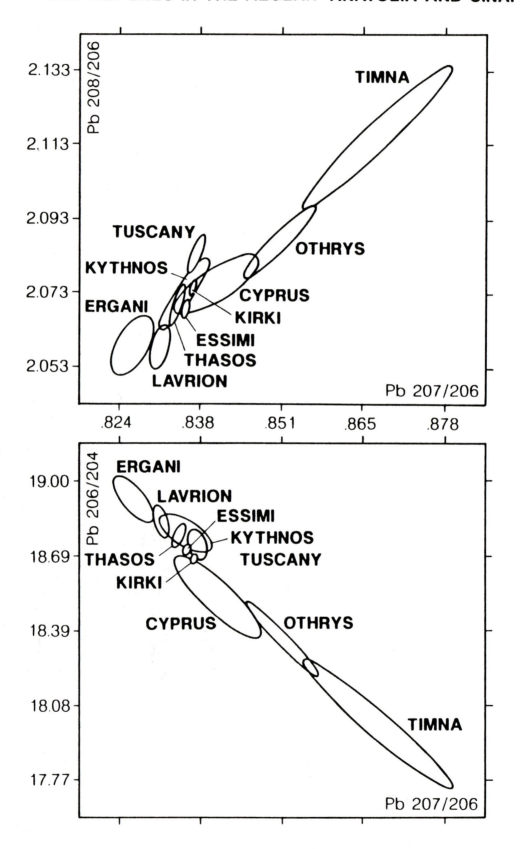

Figure 11.1. Typical lead isotope fingerprints of ore deposits in the eastern Mediterranean. The ellipses were calculated with 95% confidence level around groups of more than 15 (for Cyprus and Lavrion more than 100) lead isotope ratios from a range of mineral samples.

The origin of the metal used to make Minoan weapons

1. WEAPONS IN EARLY BRONZE AGE CRETE

In his seminal work on the beginnings of the Aegean civilisation Renfrew (1972, 319–20) wrote

> One of the problems concerning the development of Aegean metallurgy is to understand why it underwent its tremendous expansion in the Early Bronze Age 2 period . . . the appearance of the dagger perhaps presents a clue. For while the Aegean smiths of the final Neolithic could make flat axes and awls . . . daggers are not seen . . . anywhere in Europe until the inception of the Aegean Early Bronze 2 period. In Europe and the Near East, daggers and intensive bronze metallurgy are almost coterminous . . . the correlation is an extremely striking one.

The Minoan culture is often presented in the archaeological literature as a peaceful, 'flower-loving' civilisation, where art and religion were of great importance and defenceless palaces housed a sophisticated aristocracy together with stores full of grain, olives, oil, ivory and large copper ingots of great value. However, already in Early Minoan times (third millennium BC) copper-based weapons, and particularly daggers, are prominent amongst the archaeological metal finds. Some of these stylistically Minoan weapons have been found also in other parts of the Aegean and on Cyprus. If the Minoan daggers heralded the beginning of extensive copper metallurgy on Crete, then these weapons must represent the result of the first plentiful and reliable supply of copper. There is no doubt, it seems, that the daggers were made on Crete. Perhaps the Cretans found, and learned to smelt, copper ores on their island? Or maybe the copper was imported from the Near East or Anatolia, where copper metallurgy was already in full swing at the beginning of the third millennium BC? Finding the answer to the question of the origin of this metal would be an important contribution to our knowledge of Early Minoan history.

2. COPPER DEPOSITS IN THE EASTERN MEDITERRANEAN AND THEIR POSSIBLE ANCIENT EXPLOITATION

The development of metallurgy in the third millennium BC eastern Aegean has sometimes been considered as a result of the exploitation of the local ore deposits (Renfrew 1969; Branigan 1971), but arguments suggesting the import of metals are also strong. There is little evidence for the extensive production of copper on Cyprus before the Late Bronze Age, but the possibility of some import of Cypriot copper to Early Minoan Crete cannot easily be rejected. The Anatolian plateau is very rich in multimetallic deposits and the Ergani Maden copper mines in eastern Turkey have often been suggested as a source of this metal for the Bronze Age Aegean. More recently archaeometallurgical fieldwork and lead isotope analyses have indicated that copper metal from Cyprus and Ergani Maden is not very common in Bronze Age Greece (Stos-Gale & Macdonald 1991). On the other hand, some of the Greek copper deposits, like Lavrion and the small copper occurrence on the Cycladic island of Kythnos, seem to have been used in the Bronze Age.

There are several other copper deposits in the Aegean which should perhaps also be considered as possible sources of copper for Early Minoan weapons. For example there are copper occurrences in the Othrys Mountains in Central Greece, and lead/silver and copper mines in the areas of Chalkidiki, Kirki and Essimi in northern Greece. Other large multimetallic deposits (including gold) are to be found in present day Bulgaria. The earliest examples of flourishing European copper metallurgy are known from fifth millennium BC sites in this region (Chernykh 1978) and in Yugoslavia (Jovanovic 1980), and the possibility of copper metal coming to the Aegean from these directions cannot be ignored. The most important modern copper deposit in Greece is that of Ermioni in the eastern Peloponnese. At present there is no evidence that the Ermioni mines were active in antiquity. Copper deposits in Ermioni are very deep and it is possible that their depth prevented their earlier exploitation, though there are some surface expressions. On the other hand, copper, lead and silver from the Troad peninsula were exploited from the Early Bronze Age (Stos-Gale 1992) and it is not inconceivable that this metal might have been included in the Minoan trade network.

And what about copper minerals on Crete? Our own field survey shows that the copper occurrences on Crete are meagre (Gale & Stos-Gale 1986, 96). Muhly and Rapp conducted a survey in 1974 which discounted many of the alleged copper deposits reported by Faure (Wheeler *et al.* 1975). They concluded that Crete should probably not be called a major producer of copper in the Bronze Age. Becker (1976) in the course of extensive field work on Crete, conducted primarily to establish soft stone sources, demonstrated also that many alleged copper sources on Crete have been incorrectly identified. There are, however, several mineral occurrences (predominantly iron) with some copper mineralisation in west Crete and on the south coast. Perhaps the best known copper mineralisation is on the edge of the Mesara plain, where at a place called Chrysostomos some malachite and azurite are still visible in the limonite rock in a large open pit. It is difficult to assess how much copper mineral might have been there some four thousand years ago. From the geochemical point of view it is rather unlikely that the mineralisation has ever been very extensive, but some oxidised copper ores from Chrysostomos might have been used in antiquity. In west Crete some copper was mined about 40 years ago in a place called Sklavopoulou; again the mineralisation there is not very extensive but should not be overlooked. Both deposits seem to have copper mineralisation near the surface and some open-cast exploitation of these ores in antiquity is quite possible, therefore the lead isotope 'fingerprints' of the Cretan ores should also be compared with early copper artefacts.

3. LEAD ISOTOPE ANALYSES OF EARLY AND MIDDLE MINOAN COPPER-BASED WEAPONS

The Early Minoan Cretan weapons analysed for their lead isotope composition are listed in Table 11.1. The metal of the Early and Middle Minoan objects can be classified as arsenical copper with only a small amount of lead (in most cases below 1%); only very few of them contain tin (Junghans *et al.* 1968). Alloys of such composition are common in the earlier periods of the Bronze Age. Apart from tin, all other elements of the alloy are the result of the smelting of multimetallic ores, rather than the deliberate alloying of different metals (Merkel 1990 & 1992 and references therein). The small amount of lead in such metal also comes from the mineral used in copper smelting.

The lead isotope composition of these Early Minoan weapons from Crete was compared with 36 Cycladic and 42 Cypriot daggers and axes. Figure 11.2 represents the bivariate plot of lead isotope analyses of all Early Minoan weapons analysed for their lead isotope composition. For comparison there are also included on this diagram ellipses showing the extent of the lead isotope fingerprints of copper ore deposits falling in this region of the lead isotope diagram. The ellipses have been calculated from a number of ore samples analysed in our laboratory. A number of copper ore deposits mentioned above can be instantly rejected as inconsistent with the lead isotope fingerprints of these weapons — notably the Balkans and northern Greece, Sklavopoulou, Ermioni and Ergani Maden. It is also clear that the probability of some of these weapons being made from Cypriot copper is very low.

The large range of the lead isotope ratios measured for the Early Minoan weapons indicates that the artefacts do not originate from a single ore deposit. There is at present reliable evidence that in the Mediterranean the range of lead isotope compositions of ores in one geological formation usually can be expected not to exceed 0.5%. The Cypriot lead isotope fingerprint, which on Figure 11.2 covers a wider range, represents a cluster of several different fingerprints of ores from various copper deposits on Cyprus (Gale & Stos-Gale 1992). The lead isotope composition of the majority of the Early Minoan weapons is concentrated around the lead isotope ratios of 2.0754, 0.84 and 18.7. These lead isotope ratios fall on the edges of three isotopic fingerprints of ores: Kythnos High, Chrysostomos and Cyprus. On the upper (208/206 versus 207/206) diagram of Figure 11.2 it seems equally likely that the metal used for those weapons originated from any of these three copper deposits. However, the second plot (206/204 versus 207/206) shows the majority of the artefacts

now falling above the Chrysostomos and Cypriot fields. Apart from this major central group of weapons two other isotopic groups of objects can be distinguished on this diagram: two axes from Ayia Photia (4660 and 4667), a bronze adze (1533) and a triangular dagger (1265) from Ayia Triadha plus an undated dagger from Mochlos (1556) form a group which seems to be consistent with the fingerprint of the Lavrion ores, whilst two triangular daggers (1280 and 1285) and a long dagger (1295) from Ayia Triadha plot far away in the much higher 208/206 region of the diagram.

Sorting the lead isotope data in order of magnitude, one can see that the data in the large central group divide into three smaller groups (marked EMW2, EMW3 and EMW4). The next step is the comparison of the isotope groups formed by these Early Minoan weapons with the relevant groups of lead isotope compositions for the ore deposits. Group 1 seems consistent with the ores from Lavrion, groups 2 and 3 correspond best to the two Kythnian isotope fields and group 4 might be consistent with the ores from Chrysostomos or Cyprus (though the latter with very low probabilities). The nearest lead isotope ratios of copper ore deposits corresponding to Group 5 are found amongst the copper ores from the Turkish Black Sea coast at Kure and the ores of the Othrys mountains. The next stage of the data interpretation is the stepwise discriminant analysis of the lead isotope data of the weapons and of the relevant ores to calculate the probabilities of each object originating from the matching ore deposit.

4. THE ORIGIN OF METAL USED FOR THE WEAPONS AND COPPER PRODUCTION IN THE EARLY BRONZE AGE AEGEAN

In the first isotopic group of the Early Minoan weapons three have high probabilities (over 90%) of originating from the Lavrion minerals. They are a tin bronze double adze from Ayia Triadha No. 1533 (50% probability), a dagger from Mochlos No. 1556 (80%) this object might be in fact of a later date — and an axe-adze from Ayia Photia No. 4660 (22%). The other two weapons from this group, a triangular dagger from Ayia Triadha No. 1265 and a small axe-adze from Ayia Photia No. 4667, show higher probabilities (16% and 22% respectively) of belonging to the group of ores and slags designated Kythnos Low than to Lavrion (2.4% and 1.9%). The origin of copper metal from the Lavrion deposit in Attica does not come as a surprise. This source of metal seems to have been of importance to the Aegean world throughout antiquity. Silver, lead and copper were smelted there in different periods of prehistory in varying quantities. What *is* surprising though is the great rarity of this metal amongst the Early Minoan weapons (in fact the dagger from Mochlos is made of tin bronze, as is the double adze from Ayia Triadha; both are quite probably of late Bronze Age date). The small axe-adze from Ayia Photia has lead isotope compositions falling between the Lavrion and

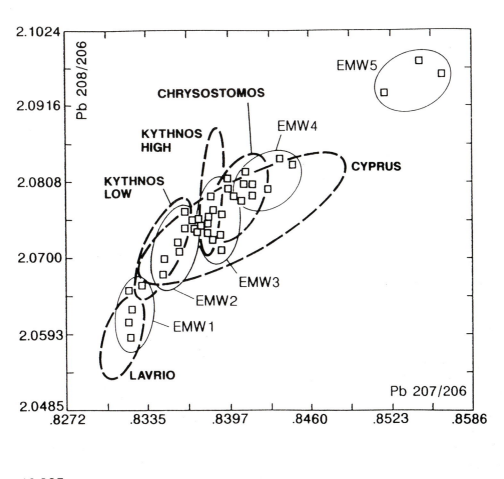

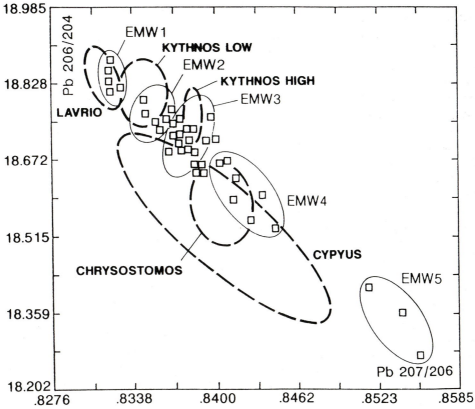

Figure 11.2. Lead isotope compositions of Early and Middle Minoan weapons compared with the lead isotope 'fingerprints' of ore deposits.

Table 11.1. Early and Middle Minoan weapons

Object number	Chronology	Site	Description	208Pb/206Pb	207Pb/206Pb	206Pb/204Pb	Isotope group	Origin
9405 HM 9943	EMI-LM	Ayios Onufrios	Dagger, unidentified type Brag	2.07555	.83737	18.758	EMW3	Kythnos High
4657	EM II	Ayia Photia	Axe/adze	2.07446	.83637	18.759	EMW2	Kythnos Low
4658	EM II	Ayia Photia	Dagger with cloth	2.07122	.83899	18.661	EMW3	Kythnos/Cyprus?
4660	EM II	Ayia Photia	Axe/adze	2.06278	.83217	18.878	EMW1	Kythnos Low
4667	EM II	Ayia Photia	Axe/adze, small	2.06624	.83295	18.822	EMW1	Kythnos Low
4670	EM II	Ayia Photia	Dagger	2.06771	.83464	18.799	EMW2	Kythnos Low
4672	EM II	Ayia Photia	Dagger, killed	2.07368	.83695	18.755	EMW3	Kythnos High
4675	EM II	Ayia Photia	Axe/adze	2.07242	.83570	18.749	EMW2	Kythnos Low
1258	EMI-MMIa	Ayia Triada	Triangular dagger	2.07899	.84137	18.634	EMW4	Chrysostomos
1263	EMI-MMIa	Ayia Triada	Triangular dagger	2.07801	.84046	18.671	EMW4	Chrysostomos
1264	EMI-MMIa	Ayia Triada	Triangular dagger	2.08216	.84084	18.675	EMW4	Chrysostomos
1265	EMI-MMIa	Ayia Triada	Triangular dagger	2.06600	.83203	18.857	EMW1	Kythnos Low
1271	EMI-MMIa	Ayia Triada	Triangular dagger	2.07387	.83811	18.709	EMW3	Kythnos High
1272	EMI-MMIa	Ayia Triada	Triangular dagger	2.08066	.84098	18.676	EMW4	Chrysostomos
1278	EMI-MMIa	Ayia Triada	Triangular dagger	2.07543	.83679	18.778	EMW3	Kythnos High
1280	EMI-MMIa	Ayia Triada	Triangular dagger	2.09368	.85170	18.411	EMW5	Kure/Othrys?
1281	EMI-MMIa	Ayia Triada	Triangular dagger	2.07912	.83825	18.737	EMW3	Kythnos High
1285	EMI-MMIa	Ayia Triada	Triangular dagger	2.09631	.85595	18.268	EMW5	Kure/Othrys?
1292	EMI-MMIa	Ayia Triada	Long dagger	2.08410	.84347	18.599	EMW4	Chrysostomos
1295	EMI-MMIa	Ayia Triada	Long dagger	2.09794	.85431	18.359	EMW5	Kure/Othrys?
1532	EMI-MMIa	Ayia Triada	Double axe	2.07866	.83997	18.720	EMW3	Kythnos High
1533	EMI-MMIa	Ayia Triada	Bronze double adze	2.06096	.83205	18.836	EMW1	Lavrion

Table 11.1. *Early and Middle Minoan weapons (Cont.)*

Object number	Chronology	Site	Description	208Pb/206Pb	207Pb/206Pb	206Pb/204Pb	Isotope group	Origin
727	EMI-MMIa	Ayia Triada	Dagger	2.07127	.83592	18.735	EMW2	Kythnos Low
9406 HM 1269	EMI-MMIa	Ayia Triada	Triangular dagger, type III	2.07463	.83762	18.695	EMW3	Kythnos High
9412 HM 1277	EMI-MMIa	Ayia Triada	Triangular dagger, type II	2.08043	.84097	18.512	EMW4	Chrysostomos/Cyprus
9413 HM 1291	EMI-MMIa	Ayia Triada	Triangular dagger, type IV	2.07541	.83732	18.725	EMW3	Kythnos High
9415 HM 1268	EMI-MMIa	Ayia Triada	Triangular dagger, type I	2.07487	.83786	18.693	EMW3	Kythnos High
9440 HM 1495	EMI-MMIa	Kalathiana	Triangular dagger type I	2.07510	.83730	18.707	EMW3	Kythnos High
9422 HM 1181	EMIIa-MMIa	Koumasa	Long dagger, type IIIa	2.08064	.84143	18.593	EMW4	Chrysostomos
9423 ??	EMIIa-MMIa	Koumasa	Dagger	2.07006	.83476	18.767	EMW2	Kythnos Low
9430 HM M16	EMIIa-MMIa	Malia	Dagger	2.07305	.83858	18.664	EMW3	Kythnos/Cyprus?
9433 HM 2006	EMII-MMIa	Marathokephalo	Triangular dagger type III	2.07684	.83843	18.689	EMW3	Kythnos High
9435 HM 2008	EMII-MMIa	Marathokephalo	Triangular dagger type III	2.08369	.84473	18.537	EMW4	Chrysostomos
9437 HM 2011	EMII-MMIa	Marathokephalo	Spearhead with tang	2.07622	.83919	18.648	EMW3	Kythnos High
9375 HM 1556	EM/LM	Mochlos	Dagger	2.05892	.83206	18.812	EMW1	Lavrion
1359	EM/LM	Palaikastro	Long dagger	2.07993	.84257	18.550	EMW4	Chrysostomos/Cyprus
9382 HM 1931	EMII-MMI	Platanos	Long dagger, type IV (Lap 313.31)	2.07587	.83806	18.736	EMW3	Kythnos High
9384 HM 1881	EMII-MMI	Platanos	Dagger	2.07983	.83946	18.713	EMW3	Kythnos High
9385 HM 1842	EMII-MMI	Platanos	Triangular dagger, type II	2.08128	.83965	18.764	EMW3	Kythnos High
9392 HM 1876	EMII-MMI	Platanos	Long dagger, type IV (Lap 313.31)	2.07383	.83682	18.725	EMW3	Kythnos High
9393 HM 1877	EMII-MMI	Platanos	Long dagger, type IVa	2.09342	.84203	18.743	EMW4	Chrysostomos?
9397 HM 1860	EMII-MMI	Platanos	Long dagger, Brag Type 5a, 4 rivets	2.07517	.83740	18.714	EMW3	Kythnos High
9402 HM 1934	EMII-MMI	Platanos	Dagger	2.07337	.83886	18.646	EMW3	Kythnos/Cyprus?
9390 HM 1871	EMIII-MMII	Platanos	Dagger	2.07495	.83317	18.920	Kythnos?	Kythnos/Cyprus?
1927.1260	EM	Psychro Cave	Votive axe/adze	2.07658	.83631	18.691	EMW2	Kythnos Low

Kythnos Low field, so in fact might not be from Lavrion, but from Kythnos; this possibility seems strengthened by the fact that all the other objects from Ayia Photia are consistent with the Kythnian fields.

The second and third isotopic groups plot side by side and the objects falling on the contiguous edges of the two groups are obviously 'borderline cases' which can belong to either of the groups. In fact both reference groups, Kythnos Low and Kythnos High, were constructed largely from the lead isotope data obtained from the same third millennium copper slag heap called Skouries on the Cycladic island of Kythnos (Stos-Gale 1989). However, all copper ores from the occurrences on the island of Kythnos plot only in the Kythnos Low field. The only ores which are consistent with the Kythnos High field (as outlined by a group of copper slags from Skouries) are samples of minerals from Siphnos (Gale & Stos-Gale 1981). On the other hand several samples of copper slags from two undated ancient copper slag heaps on the island of Seriphos fall squarely into the Kythnos Low field. While the island of Siphnos is mostly known for its silver and lead production in the Early Bronze Age (Gale & Stos-Gale 1981; Wagner *et al.* 1988), some copper ores have also been found there (Pernicka 1988, 61, table 13). Pernicka also comments on a piece of a copper slag found near the mines of Ayios Sostis on Siphnos (1988, 68) '. . . a contemporary smelting of copper and silver containing lead is possible . . . but since the copper slag is relatively rare, the copper smelting must have played a small role only in comparison with smelting of lead and silver.' It seems that copper slag of an Early Bronze Age date and consistent with the lead isotope composition of the Siphnian ores is very common on the next Cycladic island Kythnos. The island of Seriphos does not have any large copper occurrences, but we found small amounts of copper minerals there during our geological field survey in 1982. The galena occurrences on Seriphos are of quite different geological formation, at quite different part of the island and their lead isotope composition (Gale & Stos-Gale 1981) is quite different from any of the Kythnian and Siphnian ores and slags. The large ancient copper slag heaps at Kephala and Avyssalos on Seriphos were quite a surprise to the Institute of Geological and Mineralogical Exploitation geologists, who thought it impossible that enough copper ore was ever found on Seriphos itself to support this extensive copper production (Dr. S. Papastavrou, pers. comm.). Some amount of copper slag was also found by Greek archaeologists on the island of Kea (Caskey *et al.* 1988). Only much more thorough field and analytical work on these islands can provide more reliable information.

Additional interesting preliminary lead isotope data have been obtained from a thin scatter of slag from the site of Chrysokamino in the Mirabello Bay in north-west Crete. In the introduction I have stated that there is no scientific evidence for copper smelting on Crete.

In fact there is a small slag heap in Chrysokamino, discovered by Hadziddakis, which was described more than eighty years ago by Mosso (1910) as the Minoan copper smelting site. Early and Middle Minoan sherds and a cave which was thought to be a mine are said to have been found there. No other archaeologists ever found any additional proof of the Bronze Age date of this metallurgical debris. Branigan (1968) even suggested that the site was the scene of metallurgical operations carried out by a minority group of metalsmiths of the fourteenth century AD called the Chalkiades. The curiosity of the slag in Chrysokamino is highlighted by the fact that in this part of Crete there are no metal ores of any kind. Together with Noel Gale, I visited this site several years ago and we were rather disappointed by the small amount of slag visible there, with no obvious hints of a Bronze Age date: no datable pottery or other artefacts, which were so obvious amongst the Kythnian slags at Skouries. We saw the curious pieces of what looked like furnace lining, but with small circular holes described by Mosso (1910). Brief examination of the slag fragments at Oxford proved it to be a primitive copper slag. Some pieces are full of copper prills. The copper also contains up to several percent of arsenic. We were not able to find any pieces of charcoal in the slag which would allow ^{14}C dating, but the composition of the copper prills is not inconsistent with the arsenical copper used in the Early Bronze Age. Far more work is necessary to prove or disprove the Minoan origin of this slag. At present it constitutes only the faint possibility of a small Early Bronze Age copper smelting operation on the northeast cost of Crete, far away from any known copper occurrences.

It is already clear though that in the Early Bronze Age, certainly on Kythnos, and perhaps on Seriphos, there was quite a considerable production of copper metal. Kythnos might have had more suitable copper minerals than Seriphos, but the lead isotope compositions of the slags indicate that the remote copper smelting site of Skouries might have been used for smelting copper minerals brought there from other Cycladic islands. One must remember that smelting of copper metal from its ores is a highly skilled operation. Any large operation must have been carried out by a specialised group of metallurgists who were prospecting for suitable ore sources and then smelting the metal. Smelting of the ore requires specific conditions: good supplies of wood, strong winds or the means of producing forced draughts, and finally the minerals used as ores and fluxes — the essential ingredients of metal smelting. The site of Skouries on Kythnos is famous for its winds! Water and flux are easily available on both Kythnos and Seriphos. At present most of the Cycladic islands have very few trees, but it is not impossible that the conditions in the third millennium BC were different in this respect — metallurgy may even have contributed to the deforestation of these islands. One can imagine that once a good smelting site was found it might have been more convenient to ship ore in some quantity to the same place where the smelting was conducted (this approach is known from the past century in many smelters in Greece). The remoteness of the Kythnos slag heap — it is situated on a high cliff, the nearest landing bay (Ayios Yoannis) is an hour's walk away — might have been an advantage if the operation was to be kept secret and safe.

Another question which comes to mind is how unique are the lead isotope compositions of Chrysostomos and 'Kythnos'? Our quite comprehensive eastern Mediterranean lead isotope database does not show any significant overlap of other copper ores with the Kythnian fields. There are, however, several copper deposits in north-west Turkey which seem to have lead isotope composition falling at least partly in this region of the lead isotope diagram (Seeliger *et al.* 1985). Particularly the copper and lead minerals numbered TG133, TG142, TG143, TG156 and TG192 fall in the area consistent with the isotope field described as Kythnos Low. Without more lead isotope measurements of the copper ores from these Turkish deposits it is very difficult to assess the degree of the overlap between them and the Cycladic copper slag from Kythnos. However, at present one has to keep in mind the possibility that the signature described in this study as Kythnos Low might overlap to an unknown degree with the signatures of some of the copper ores from the north-west Turkey. Two samples published as TG188 from the mines of Ikiztepe near the Turkish/Bulgarian border fall near the ores from Chrysostomos and Cyprus. None of the published lead isotope data overlaps with the greatest concentration of the lead isotope compositions of the weapons (lower part of the Kythnos High field). In the light of archaeological and ^{14}C dating of the copper slags on Kythnos, which agree well and prove Early Bronze Age copper smelting on the site of Skouries (Stos-Gale 1989), it seems quite reasonable to accept at present that the two isotope groups of Minoan weapons described in this study (groups 2 and 3) are the result of Cycladic metal production. It seems certain that in due course there will be more published lead isotope analyses of copper ores from Turkey (two archaeological/archaeometallurgical groups are at present working there) and then the data should be again reassessed.

The calculated probabilities of group EMW2 belonging to Kythnos Low and EMW3 to Kythnos High are very high. It is however clear that there is a considerable affinity amongst all four groups. The division of the Kythnos field into two groups is rather tentative, and it must be remembered that this lead isotope fingerprint is based to a large extent on the analyses of Bronze Age copper slags, not minerals from a specific geological formation. If all the lead isotope data are taken together, then the 'Kythnos' field has a larger range of lead isotope ratios then usual for a single ore deposit. Such a situation is only to be expected if we accept that the ore from several islands was smelted on one or two of them and then exported to Crete. There must have been a certain amount of mixing of the metal from different deposits. On the other hand the scatter of data is not so great as to suggest that there was much mixing of metal from distant and isotopically different sources.

The two remaining lead isotope groups (EMW4 and EMW5) are quite distinct and not very numerous. Group EMW4 includes 10 weapons from different sites. Their lead isotope composition is to a certain degree consistent with the few lead isotope analyses of the copper ores from Chrysostomos copper mineralisation in southern Crete. They also plot on the edge of the Cypriot ore field, but on the whole the statistical probability of any of those objects being made from Cypriot copper is very low. This conclusion is not really greatly surprising because the production of copper on Cyprus did not start in earnest until the middle part of the Aegean late Bronze Age (thirteenth to twelfth century BC). The production of some copper from the meagre mineralisation of central-southern Crete is not impossible. As has been discussed earlier, there is no proven evidence of Bronze Age copper smelting on Crete. However, Diallinas mentioned to me that some 'slag' was found on the beach at Lebena, some 20 kilometres east from Chrysostomos. Our search for slag along the southern Cretan beaches did not bring any finds of copper slag, but it must be said that copper carbonates are still visible in Chrysostomos, and the mineralisation is surrounded by Early Minoan sites. If any copper metal was produced there in the Early Bronze Age, then it seems that the production was very limited. Perhaps this is not surprising, because market forces would certainly make Cycladic copper, where the metal production was very professionally carried out on a large scale, a more competitive source of metal.

There is an alternative origin for those objects which fall into the Chrysostomos lead isotope field: such lead isotope compositions might result from the melting together of metal from, for example, Kure and the Cyclades. If indeed there was a certain amount of northern Anatolian metal in circulation in the Aegean, depending on the lead content of such scrap, it might or might not show in the lead isotope composition. Any further discussion of the origin of these objects must be based on chemical analyses of various ores and objects, as well as many more lead isotope data from Turkish ore deposits.

The three daggers from Ayia Triadha forming the EMW5 lead isotope group are at present of rather mysterious origin. The isotopically closest ore deposits of Kure, on the Turkish coast of the Black Sea, and Othrys, in mainland Greece 200 km north of Athens, do not show very high statistical probabilities as the source of metal. In this particular case the metal from the

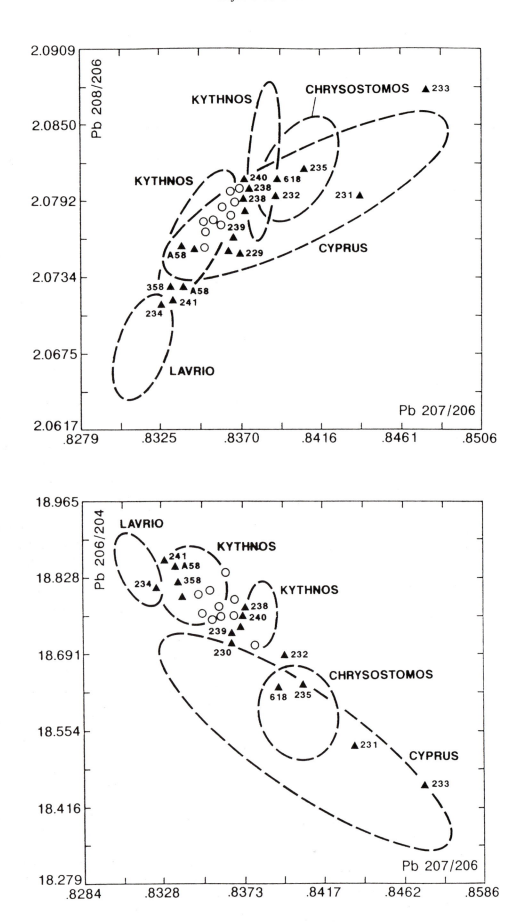

Figure 11.3. Lead isotope compositions of Early Bronze Age Cycladic weapons compared with the same ore deposits as in Figure 11.2.

Black Sea coast seems a more probable solution. I have records of many other Bronze Age objects from Greece which fall into the same region of the lead isotope diagram, and correspond more convincingly to the Turkish ores. This problem will soon be discussed in another publication, with further more ore data for comparison from Mainz and the Smithsonian. Even now, however, it seems that a certain amount of copper metal was coming to the Aegean in the Early Bronze Age from the direction of the Black Sea (Stos-Gale 1992). Our survey of copper ore occurrences in the Othrys mountains indicated that the exploitation of this resource might have been quite important in the later periods. We collected some charcoal from copper slags which was dated in the Oxford Radiocarbon Accelerator Unit to the ninth to fourth century BC. So far there is no definite evidence of any earlier metal production in this area. However, only much more extensive study of the Othrys slag heaps combined with archaeological excavations can provide a more definite answer.

5. THE ORIGIN OF WEAPONS FROM THE CYCLADIC ISLANDS FROM THE PERIOD CONTEMPORARY WITH EARLY AND MIDDLE MINOAN TIMES

The lead isotope analyses show that the majority of the Early Minoan weapons was probably made from copper imported to Crete from the Cycladic smelters. If the Cycladic islands indeed held a sort of monopoly of copper production then the weapons made and found on these islands should certainly reflect the local copper smelting industry. Some time ago we analysed a number of Cycladic daggers, axes and spearheads from the collections of the Ashmolean Museum and the British Museum (Gale & Stos-Gale 1989). Figure 11.3 shows their lead isotope data plotted in exactly the same layout as the Early Minoan weapons. It is quite clear that the pattern of the lead isotope compositions of those two groups is remarkably similar: the majority of lead isotope ratios falls into the Kythnian fields, some objects seem to be consistent with the Cyprus/ Chrysostomos lead isotope region. Two spearheads from the Ashmolean (ERE 231 and ERE 233) stand out from the main group and might be made of metal originating either in Cyprus or, more probably, in north-western Anatolia.

Conclusions

During the Third Thera Conference Malcolm Wiener examined the proposition that at the time of the Thera eruption sites in the Cyclades, The Dodecanese and along the coast of Asia Minor constituted complementary parts of a Minoan empire. Lead isotope analyses of the pre-late Minoan I weapons from Crete and the Cyclades show that the great majority of the copper metal is consistent with the lead isotope 'fingerprint' of the Early Bronze Age copper slags from the Cycladic

island of Kythnos, with copper slags from Seriphos and with ores from Kythnos and Siphnos. Some metal seems also consistent with an origin from the copper occurrence of Chrysostomos near the Mesara Plain, and three objects are made from metal possibly imported from northern Turkey. Copper from Lavrion is practically absent amongst the Early and Middle Minoan weapons.

Copper occurrences on the Cycladic islands are quite small and their presence was confirmed only on a few of them (Kythnos, Seriphos and Siphnos). At present there is nothing known with certainty about the origin and date of the copper slags found on Kea, Seriphos and at Chrysokamino on Crete. However, a possibility exists that, in spite of comparative scarcity of copper ore in the Cyclades, the Minoan state provided the right environment for Early Bronze Age skilled metallurgists to carry on an efficient and ample copper production on Cycladic islands. We still know very little about the organisation of metallurgical operations in the Mediterranean in the initial phase of the age of metals. It was not unusual though, in historical times, to bring ores to a well sited and equipped smelter, rather than to smelt metal near the mines. Even in rich mineral deposits like Lavrion in the fourth century BC silver was smelted only on a few sites (Panormos, Pefkos) and the ores were brought there from many different mines. This process of establishing smelters and bringing the ore to them from several sources might have started much earlier.

These results seem to agree very well with the evidence accumulated by Wiener and also support strongly Warren's conclusion that 'At the very least we can postulate ... a strong degree of linkage, economic and perhaps populational, between the Cyclades and northern Crete in full EB1 or transitional EB 1/2.' (Warren 1984, 60). It is not impossible that this period was the beginning of a Cycladic-Minoan metallurgical co-operation, so that the availability of copper for the Minoan smiths was organised in close proximity to Crete and not left to occasional imports from various sources. By the end of the Early Bronze Age a quite extensive metal smelting industry seems to have been organised amongst the Cycladic islands with possible state protection and assured demand from the Minoans. More lead isotope analyses of Early Bronze Age metal from the eastern Aegean can provide evidence of the geographical range of export of the copper from Cyclades. In the early part of the Bronze Age some of it might have found its way as far north as Lesbos (Stos-Gale 1992). Our unpublished lead isotope analyses of daggers from Early Bronze Age Cyprus show that a small amount of this Minoan/Cycladic copper may also have been reaching this island. It seems likely that the Minoans organised a quite extensive metal industry at the end of the Early Bronze Age. The comparative lack of metal resources perhaps did not matter too much at this early phase of metal use, but the development of craft specialisation and state protection might have been decisive factors in establishing metal production on the Cyclades. There is also evidence for production of lead and silver in the Cyclades and its use on Crete (Gale & Stos-Gale 1981).

Much more lead isotope and geological fieldwork on the Cycladic islands is still needed to solve the puzzle of copper slags and ores on these islands and to confirm the hypothesis of the origin of the Early Minoan and Cycladic copper artefacts, but at least lead isotope analysis provides the means of objective scientific characterisation of ores, metal and slag for such a study.

Acknowledgements

This work was carried out within the British Academy project on Bronze Age trade in the Mediterranean. Samples of Early Bronze Age artefacts from Crete were kindly provided by Dr H. Schichler of the Stuttgart Museum; those from Aghia Photia were sampled with the kind permission of Dr C. Davaras and the Greek Ministry of Culture.

References

Barnes, I.L., Gramlich, J.W., Diaz, M.G., & Brill, R.H., 1978. The possible change of lead isotope ratios in the manufacture of pigments; a fractionation experiment. *Archaeological Chemistry* II, 16–22

Becker, M., 1976. Soft stone sources in Crete. *Journal of Field Archaeology* 3, 361–74

Branigan, K., 1971. An Early Bronze Age metal source in Crete. *Studi Micenei ed Egeo-Anatolici* 13, 10–24.

Branigan, K., 1974. *Aegean Metalwork of the Early and Middle Bronze Age*. Oxford: Oxford University Press

Brill, R.H., & Wampler, J.M., 1965. Isotope studies of ancient lead. *American Journal of Archaeology* 69, 165–6

Brill, R.H., 1988. The examination of some Egyptian glass objects, in *The Egyptian Mining Temple at Timna*, ed. B. Rothenberg. London, Institute for Archaeometallurgical Studies, 217–23

Caskey, M., Mendoni, L., Papastamataki, A., & Beloyannis, N., 1988. Metals in Keos: a first approach, in *The Engineering Geology of Ancient Works, Monuments and Historical Sites*, eds. P.G. Marinoos & G.C. Koukis. Rotterdam: Balkema, 1739–45

Catling, H.W., 1979. Copper in Cyprus, bronze in Crete: some economic problems. *Acts of the International Archaeological Symposium The Relations Between Cyprus and Crete, 2000–500 BC*. Nicosia, 69–75

Chernykh, E.N., 1978. *Gornoe delo i Metallurgia v Drevneishei Boulgarii*. Sofia

Cumming, G.L., & Richards, J.R., 1975. Ore lead isotope ratios in a continuously changing earth. *Earth and Planetary Science Letters* 28, 155–71

Duckworth, H.E., Barber, R.C., & Venkatasubramanian, V.S., 1990. *Mass Spectroscopy*. Cambridge: Cambridge University Press

Faure, G., 1986. *Principles of Isotope Geology*, Second Edition. New York: Wiley & Sons

Faure, P., 1966. Les minerais de la Crète antique. *Revue Archéologique* 1, 45–78

Gale, N.H., Gentner, W., & Wagner, G.A., 1980. The mineralogical and geographical silver sources for Archaic Greek coinage, in *Metallurgy in Numismatics I*, ed. M. Metcalf. London: British Museum, 3–50.

Gale, N.H. and Stos-Gale, Z.A., 1982. Bronze Age copper sources in the Mediterranean: a new approach. *Science* 216, 11–19

Gale, N.H., Bachmann, H.G., Rothenberg, B., Stos-Gale, Z.A., & Tylecote, R.F., 1988. The adventitious production of iron in the smelting of copper in Timna, in *Ancient Metallurgy in Timna, W. Arabah*, ed. B. Rothenberg. London: Thames and Hudson, 182–91

Gale, N.H., 1989. Lead isotope analyses applied to provenance studies — a brief review, in *Archaeometry — Proceedings of the 25th International Symposium, Athens 1986*, ed. Y. Maniatis. Amsterdam: Elsevier, 469–502

Gale, N.H., & Stos-Gale, Z.A., 1981. Cycladic lead and silver metallurgy. *Annual of the British School of Archaeology at Athens* 76, 169–224

Gale, N.H., & Stos-Gale, Z.A., 1989. Some aspects of early Cycladic Metallurgy in *Proceedings of the Colloquium Mineria y Metalurgia en las Antiguas Civilizaciones Mediterraneas y Europeas*, eds C. Domergue & J.M. Blazquez Martinez. Madrid: Ministerio de Cultura, 21–38

Gale, N.H., & Stos-Gale, Z.A., 1991. Lead isotope studies in the Aegean, in *Advances in Science-Based Archaeology*, ed. M. Pollard. London: Royal Society/British Academy Special Publication, 63–108

Gale, N.H., & Stos-Gale, Z.A., 1992. Evaluating lead isotope data: comments on E.V. Sayre, K.A. Yener, E.C. Joel and L.I. Barnes, 'Statistical evaluation of the presently accumulated lead isotope data from Anatolia and surrounding regions'. *Archaeometry* 34 (2), 311–17

Grogler, N., Geiss, J., Grunenfelder, M., & Houtermans, F.G., 1966. Isotopenuntersuchungen zur Bestimmung der Herkunft romischer Blieirohre und Bleibarren. *Zeitschrift zur Naturforschungen* 21, 1167–72

Gulson, B.L., 1986. *Lead Isotopes in Mineral Exploration*. Amsterdam: Elsevier

Jovanovic, B., 1980. The Origins of Copper Mining in Europe. *Scientific American* 242 (5), 152–67

Junghans, S., Sangmeister, E., & Schroder, M., 1968. *Kupfer und Bronze in der frühen Metallzeit Europas, Studien zu den Anfangen der Metallurgie II*. Berlin: Verlag Gebr. Mann.

Keisch, B., 1970. On the use of isotope mass spectrometry in the identification of artist's pigments. *Studies in Conservation* 15, 1–11

Manly, B.F.J., 1986. *Multivariate Statistical Methods*. London: Chapman and Hall

Merkel, J., 1990. Experimental reconstruction of Bronze Age copper smelting based on archaeological evidence from Timna, in *The Ancient Metallurgy of Copper*, ed. B. Rothenberg. London: Institute for Archaeometallurgical Studies, 78–122

Merkel, J.F., Shimada, I., Swann, C.P., & Doonan, R., 1992. Investigation of prehistoric copper production at Batan Grande, Peru: interpretation of the analytical data for ore samples. *Proceedings of the 28th International Symposium on Archaeometry, Los Angeles*

Molleson, T.I., Eldridge & Gale, N.H., 1986. Identification of lead sources by stable isotope ratios in bones and lead from Poundbury Camp, Dorset. *Oxford Journal of Archaeology* 5:2, 249–53

Mosso, A., 1910. *The Dawn of Mediterranean Civilisation*. London: Fisher Unwin, 289–93

Pernicka, E., Seeliger, T.C., Wagner, G.A., Begemann, F., Schmitt-Strecker, S., Eibner, C., Oztunali, O., & Baranyi, I., 1984. Archeometallurgische Untersuchungen in Nordwestanatolien. *Jahrbuch des Romisch-Germanischen Zentralmuseums* 31, 533–99

Pernicka, E., 1988. Erzlagerstatten in der Agais und ihre Ausbedeutung in Altertum: Geochemische Untersuchungen zur Herkunftsbestimmung archaometallurgische Metallobjekte. *Jahrbuch des Romisch-Germanischen Zentralmuseums* 35, 1–108

Renfrew, C., 1969. The autonomy of the SE European Copper Age. *Proceedings of the Prehistoric Society* 35, 12–34

Renfrew, C., 1972. *The Emergence of Civilisation*. London: Methuen

Stos-Gale, Z.A., 1989. Cycladic copper metallurgy, in *Old World Archaeometallurgy. Der Anschnitt, Beiheft 7*, eds A. Hauptman, E. Pernicka & G.A. Wagner. Bochum: Deutschen Bergbau Museums, 279–92

Stos-Gale, Z.A., Gale, N.H., & Zwicker, U., 1986. The copper trade in the south-west Mediterranean region. Preliminary scientific evidence. Nicosia: *Report of the Department of Antiquities*, 122–44

Stos-Gale, Z.A., & Macdonald, C.F., 1991. Sources of metals and trade in the Bronze Age Aegean, in *Trade in the Bronze Age Mediterranean*, ed. N.H. Gale. Studies in Mediterranean Archaeology 90, 248–80

Stos-Gale, Z.A., 1991. Lead isotope studies in archaeometallurgy. *Proceedings of the Summer School of Archaeometallurgy, Siena*. Florence: Edizioni Allinsegna del Giglio

Stos-Gale, Z.A., 1992. The origin of metal objects from the Early Bronze Age site of Thermi on the island of Lesbos. *Oxford Journal of Archaeology* 11 (2), 155–78

Wagner, G.A., & Weisgerber, G., (eds.), 1985. *Silber, Blei und Gold auf Sifnos. Der Anschnitt, Beiheft 3*. Bochum: Deutschen Bergbau Museums

Wagner, G.A., Oztunali, O. & Eibner, C. 1989. Early copper in Anatolia. Archaeometallurgical field evidence, in *Old World Archaeometallurgy. Der Anschnitt, Beiheft 7*, eds A. Hauptman, E. Pernicka & G.A. Wagner. Bochum: Deutschen Bergbau Museums, 299–306

Wagner, G.A., Pernicka, E., Vavelidis, M. Baranyi, I., & Bassiakos, Y., 1986. Archaeometallurgische Untersuchungen auf Chalkidiki. *Der Anschnitt, Beiheft 5*, 166–86

Warren, P., 1984. Early Cycladic — Early Minoan chronological correlations, in *The Prehistoric Cyclades*, eds J.A. MacGillivray & R.L.N. Barber. Edinburgh: Department of Classical Archaeology, 55–61

Wheeler, T.S., Maddin, R., & Muhly, J.D., 1975. Ingots and the Bronze Age copper trade in the Mediterranean. *Expedition* 17 (4), 31–39

Wiener, M.H., 1990. The isles of Crete? The Minoan thalassocracy revisited, in *Thera and the Aegean World III*, ed. D.A. Hardy. London: the Thera Foundation, 128–61

12

The Circulation of Amber in Prehistoric Europe

Colette du Gardin

Amber is a variety of fossil resin found primarily around the Baltic sea but with a natural distribution extending across the whole of northern Europe. Analyses undertaken over the last three decades have shown that it is distinguished from other fossil resins by a particular infrared spectrum, but also that it was used preferentially for the manufacture of prehistoric ornaments. The usefulness of these analyses is limited to distinguishing between amber and other fossil resins. It is the study of typology, combined with the study of manufacturing techniques and modes of exploitation, which makes it possible not only to determine the form in which amber circulated in prehistoric Europe but also to deduce the existence of amber-working centres outside the natural distribution of the raw material.

L'ambre est une variété de résine fossile récoltée essentiellement sur le pourtour de la mer Baltique mais dont l'aire de diffusion naturelle s'étend sur tout le nord de l'Europe. Les analyses entreprises ces trois dernières décennies ont montré qu'il se distinguait des autres résines fossiles par un spectre infra-rouge particulier, mais aussi qu'il avait été de préférence utilisé pour la confection des parures préhistoriques. Le secours des analyses se limitant à une distinction ambre/résine fossile, c'est l'étude typologique doublée d'une étude des techniques de fabrication et des modes d'exploitation qui permettent non seulement de déterminer la forme sous laquelle l'ambre circulait dans l'Europe préhistorique mais également de définir l'existence d'ateliers de production en dehors de la zone de distribution naturelle de la matière première.

Introduction

To avoid any confusion, it is necessary briefly to spell out what is now meant by 'amber'. This term, synonymous with succinite, is used today to denote only that variety of fossil resin found most frequently around the Baltic but with a natural distribution in fact extending from the Ukraine to the Baltic States, covering all of northern Europe and running out on the east coast of England (Savkevich 1981). This vast distribution represents the secondary deposits from an 'amber forest' centred on present day Finland, dispersed all over northern Europe by the action of glaciers and rivers. Amber is distinguished by a specific infrared spectrum, represented by a curve in which a near-horizontal 'shoulder' is followed by a peak of absorption between 1150 and 1250 cm^{-1}. This spectrum has not so far been recognised in any other European fossil resin (Beck 1986). 'Fossil resin' is used to denote all the other varieties of resin which are not amber.

Physical and chemical analyses carried out over the last three decades have established that in most cases it was amber rather than other fossil resins which was used for the manufacture of ornaments in prehistoric Europe. These results thus make it possible to look to northern Europe for the origin of the raw material in most cases. But the usefulness of the analyses stops there. The infrared spectrum is the same for amber found in the Ukraine, in Poland and on the east coast of England, since it all comes from the same primary forest. To determine where amber artefacts were made it is necessary to rely on the classic use of typology, combined with study of the manufacturing techniques. These two approaches help to define zones of production, to infer the form in which amber circulated in prehistoric Europe, and to deduce the existence of amber working sites outside the traditional Baltic area.

Chronological overview

For the Neolithic, when the distribution of amber artefacts was essentially limited to the lands bordering the Baltic, it has been possible to recognise several consistent features of the treatment and circulation of the material, whether in Denmark, in Poland or in the Baltic States:

— The existence of a certain number of amber working sites within permanent or seasonal settlements specialising in this activity only. The best examples are the sites of Wybicko and Niedźwiedziówka in the Gdańsk area, where a vast depression, inundated in winter, was visited regularly by amber workers who came to collect the nodules deposited by the retreating waters and to work them there. The existence of these amber working sites was linked to the presence of easily accessible amber in the immediate vicinity (Mazurowski 1985, 86).

— The transport of the raw material to other regions, such as Lake Lubānas in Latvia where, in the middle and late Neolithic, the occupants of a group of settlements located around the lake edge imported raw amber from the Baltic coast some 200 km away and worked it (Loze 1979).

— The distribution, from these same Latvian centres of production, of finished ornaments to sites in the Volga basin (Loze 1975). The removal of finished products to other areas is further evidenced by their absence from the production sites (Mazurowski 1985).

From the very beginning of the Bronze Age the use of amber, previously more-or-less confined to northern Europe, expanded into the centre, west and south of the continent. At the same time, in the areas which had traditionally worked and used amber in the Neolithic, not only did amber working sites disappear but amber ornaments declined in frequency in both settlements and burials, where they did not disappear completely.

The forms of ornament used in the Neolithic were very stereotyped, of predetermined form and sometimes produced in almost industrial quantities, as in the case of tubular beads and V-perforated buttons. The Bronze Age picture contrasts with this in that, alongside the production of fairly standardised objects, there was a proliferation of original or idiosyncratic forms, some of which give the impression of having been produced as 'one-offs', at the behest and inspiration of their inventors. An example is the abundant assemblage of amber ornaments from the Grotte des Duffaits at La Rochette in Charente (Gomez 1973), which includes a whole series of beads of forms unknown elsewhere as well as objects such as small plaques with multiple perforations the clumsy execution of which evokes not so much the carefully-made spacer-plates of the Tumulus culture as the casual, unskilled imitation of forms seen elsewhere.

In some cases careful examination of groups of artefacts can identify a technological homogeneity, a particular style of manufacture, which makes it possible to attribute them to one or another culture or cultural complex, even to see the hand of a single skilled worker. It has been possible to do this for ornaments from Wessex culture, Únětice and Tumulus culture burials. Such observations are unfortunately made only with difficulty on isolated ornaments.

These observations, together with the diversification of forms and the differentiation of technological peculiarities across time and space, suggest that amber circulated in Bronze Age Europe as unworked nodules or partly worked artefacts. Having reached their recipient, or an amber-working centre, they were reduced by workers who were skilled in both flaking amber and making it into ornaments. Two levels of skill can be distinguished in Bronze Age ornaments in Europe:

— work executed with little or no care, even clumsily, such as can be seen in numerous beads of irregular outline and doubtful finish, probably produced by non-specialists.

— work of the very highest quality, as in Wessex culture ornaments, implying knowledge and familiarity with the material on the part of the manufacturer.

Unfortunately no Bronze Age amber-working site has yet been found in Europe, whether in areas of exploitation or of use. The disappearance of these working sites in areas where amber occurs naturally could support the view that in this period amber was transported in the form of unworked nodules. However, the total lack of working sites in groups which used a great deal of amber, like the Tumulus culture, makes it impossible to verify. The proposition that amber circulated in the form of unworked nodules or unfinished objects is thus advanced as an hypothesis, based on the technological examination of amber ornaments.

Amber working

Amber in some ways has the same characteristics as flint, since it can be flaked. Having, however, a low index of hardness (2–3 on Mohs' scale), it can equally well be cut with a string and is easily polished. There are furthermore different varieties of amber: transparent, cloudy, bastard and osseous or blended, each of which contains a smaller or larger number of air bubbles. The transparency and the solidity of the amber depend on the frequency and size of these bubbles.

The observations of Mazurowski (1985) at the amber working sites of Wybicko and Niedźwiedziówka in Poland have shown that the blended variety, that is the one with the most bubbles, was rejected for ornament manufacture. There was further selection based on the form of the nodule, the size of the ornament to be made, and the way in which it was to be perforated. The cloudy and especially the transparent varieties, were the most solid and of the highest quality and were preferred for the manufacture of objects with long perforations. The bastard and osseous varieties were adequate for smaller pieces, like V-perforated buttons.

In the natural state a nodule of amber is covered with a thick, altered crust. Only those truly familiar with the material could recognise the variety of amber of which the nodule consisted at a glance or after lightly testing it. The evidence from different working sites in northern Europe has shown that internal impurities or flaws could lead to breakage of the object in the course of manufacture, as could accidents of manufacture itself, especially during perforation, which is the most delicate stage in the production of an amber ornament. From the Bronze Age onwards, this risk was probably reduced by the use of heated metal awls, since these entail applying less pressure (du Gardin 1986). However skilful the worker, breakages due to internal flaws could still not have been avoided.

Examination of the amber from Bronze Age sites in the museums of western and central Europe, combined with descriptions given in the literature, shows that it was essentially transparent amber which was chosen for the manufacture of ornaments. This assumes, of course, that the progressive alteration of the succinite since manufacture has not affected its internal composition. The amber which we see, when its surface condition is sufficiently good, is most often a transparent dark red. This indicates that the material originally selected was yellow-coloured, the reddening of the amber corresponding to the natural process of oxidation. It thus appears that it was essentially the transparent yellow variety of amber, in other words the variety with the best technological qualities, with was selected and destined for transport to other areas.

Drawing on technological observations made on Middle and Late Neolithic amber working sites, it is possible to envisage the different practices of the Bronze Age. The peoples living around the Baltic, who were familiar with the material, would have collected nodules of amber as they were thrown up by the sea or turned up in the soil in the course of cultivation, and would then have selected the transparent variety. Collection was perhaps accompanied by superficial decortication intended to reveal latent flaws.

The nodules were then passed to others who redistributed them to working sites or to individuals who made them into finished artefacts in accordance with local taste and fashion. The lack, in the present state of research, of amber working areas on Bronze Age sites in central and western Europe unfortunately makes it impossible to confirm this hypothesis. It must nonetheless be emphasised that waste fragments, flakes and unfinished products, which would characterise an amber-working area, could, if they were not made into other ornaments, have been used as incense, as a means of lighting, or even as a rare and valued medicine. These uses for fossil resins are recorded from as recently as the beginning of this century in the ethnographic literature.

References

Beck, C.W. 1986. Spectroscopic investigations of amber. *Applied Spectroscopy Reviews* 22 (1), 57–110

du Gardin, C., 1986. La parure d'ambre à l'âge du Bronze en France. *Bulletin de la Société Préhistorique Française* 83 (11–12), 546–80

Gomez, J., 1973. La grotte sépulcrale des Duffaits (La Rochette, Charente). Etude archéologique. *Bulletin de la Société Préhistorique Française* 70, 401–44

Loze, I., 1975. Neolithic amber ornaments in the eastern part of Latvia. *Przegląd Archeologiczny* 23, 49–82

Loze, I., 1979. *Pozdnij neolit i rannyaya bronza Lubanskoj ravniny.* Riga

Mazurowski, R., 1983. Bursztyn w epoce kamienia na ziemiach Polskich. *Materiał y Starożytne* 5, 7–134

Mazurowski, R., 1985. Amber treatment workshops of the Rzucewo culture in Żuławy. *Przegląd Archeologiczny* 32, 5–60

Savkevich, S.S., 1981. Physical methods used to determine the geological origin of amber and other fossil resins: some critical remarks. *Physics and Chemistry of Minerals* 7, 1–4

13

Social Evolution and Horse Domestication

Marsha A. Levine

From its beginnings in the Late Neolithic or Eneolithic the domestication of the horse would have had a profound impact upon human life. The horse would have provided its keepers with hitherto unattainable mobility and power. Until very recently, few attempts have been made to consider the relationship between social change and horse domestication. In this paper, ethnological, historical and archaeological data will be used to reassess our knowledge of some of the relevant issues: horse domestication and the development of social ranking; the recognition of domestication and its relation to horse usage; and the context of early horse domestication.

Depuis ses origines à la fin du Néolithique ou durant la période énéolithique, la domestication du cheval a dû profondément modifier la vie des hommes. La possession d'un cheval devait fournir une mobilité et une puissance jusqu'alors inégalée. Jusqu'à très récemment, très peu d'études ont envisagé les relations entre les changements sociaux et la domestication du cheval. Dans cet article, les données fournies par l'ethnologie, l'histoire et l'archéologie sont mobilisées, pour faire le point des connaissances relatives à certains problèmes cruciaux, tels ceux de la domestication du cheval et du développement des formes de hiérarchie sociale, de la mise en évidence de la domestication du cheval en relation avec son utilisation, et enfin du contexte de cette domestication précoce.

Introduction

With the domestication of the horse, human life was transformed. The mobility provided by the horse would have allowed people to move further, faster and to take more with them than ever before. They could inhabit previously inhospitable ecological zones. Moreover, other things being equal, a man on foot would be no match for a man on horseback. In 1990 Gilman wrote

> It seems unreasonable to suggest . . . that possession of metal weapons would provide rulers with control of the 'means of destruction' . . . A mob of peasants armed with slingshots could overcome the best equipped Bronze Age hero, provided that they were organized to resist.
> (Gilman 1990, 158)

A bronze arrowhead might be no more lethal than one made of flint, but a man on horseback is another matter altogether.

From the start, the horse would have provided its masters with a potent weapon with which to intimidate, to do injury or to win patronage. The earliest historical records of the impact of the horse date from around 1800 BC and recount invasions rather vaguely described as from the 'north' (Edwards *et al.* 1980; Mann 1986). Michael Mann writes

> The Aryans conquered north India in successive waves sometime between about 1800 and 1200 BC . . .; the Hittites had established an identifiable kingdom in Asia Minor by 1640 BC; the Mitanni were established in Syria by 1450 BC; the Kassites overran most of Mesopotamia by about 1500 BC; the Hyksos conquered Egypt about 1650 BC. All were charioteers by the time they reached our records; all were aristocratic federations rather than single-state-centered peoples; and most knew greater private-property differentiation than had been prevalent among the indigenous peoples of the Near East.
> (Mann 1986, 181)

The Chinese of the Sung Dynasty (AD 960–1279) understood the situation perfectly. A high official wrote

> The reason why our enemies to the north and west are able to withstand China is precisely because they have many horses and their men are adept at riding; this is their strength. China has few horses, and its men are not accustomed to riding; this is China's weakness . . . The

court constantly tries, with our weakness, to oppose our enemies' strength, so that we lose every battle . . . without horses, we can never create an effective military force. (quoted in Sinor 1972, 173–4)

Significantly, the political systems of all of these various equestrians and charioteers are usually described as 'feudal': 'the extraction of surplus labor through ground rent by a class of landlords from a dependent peasantry' (Mann 1986, 375). In order to make the best military use of the horse, human society was transformed. In his study of the military history of the Eurasian Steppe David Sneath observed that

> [a] 'feudal' type of society dates back to the Hsiung-nu of 200 BC. . . The Chinese records describe the way in which the Hsiung-nu ruler had 24 lords beneath him, each of 10,000 men, and each one responsible for a specific area in which these subjects nomadized. . . . The lords of the steppe, then, controlled the means of destruction – the large numbers of horses required to equip an army, and the people needed to ride them . . . As long as the horse remained the vital military asset, feudalism – or something very much like it – dominated the parts of Eurasia that could raise horses.
> (Sneath 1991)

This kind of political organization was necessary in order to ensure that both horses and pasturage would be available when needed and it persisted until the horse was superseded by firearms as the main instrument of destruction in warfare, that is, until around AD 1500.

The introduction of the horse into North America had similarly profound affects upon the culture of the North American aboriginal peoples (Ewers 1955). Ewers has documented that by the end of the Buffalo Period, only about 150 years after the horse had first been obtained by them, it had permeated almost every aspect of Blackfoot life: political, economic, social, religious. Ewers wrote

> During the Pedestrian Culture Period, when men literally stood on an equal footing, class distinctions must have been less marked than in historic times. The cooperative hunt was an organization of near equals in which the kill was equally divided among participating families. Limited transportation facilities inhibited the accumulation of property and militated against social stratification based upon wealth. . . . After the introduction of horses permitted the accumulation of property, social status came to depend less upon a man's physical and mental qualities and more upon the number and quality of his possessions. A class system began to develop in which there were rich, middle-class, and poor families, distinguished primarily on the basis of their relative wealth or poverty in horses . . . Yet under the conditions of life prevailing in buffalo days the Blackfoot class system did not become crystallized. Hazards beyond their control prevented members of the wealthy class from becoming permanently entrenched. Enemy horse raiders, winter storms, or disease might wipe out the rich man's herd quickly and without warning.
> (Ewers 1955, 314–5)

Social evolution and the horse

It is impossible to believe that the spread of horse husbandry, almost from its earliest appearance in Eurasia, would not have resulted in important social changes, as was the case amongst the North American indigenous peoples when the horse was introduced to them. To date, however, prehistorians have rarely addressed the relevant issues and, even when they have, progress has been impeded by inattention to the archaeozoological data. The salient points will be discussed below under the following headings: horse domestication and the development of social ranking; the recognition of domestication and its relation to horse usage; and the context of early horse domestication.

HORSE DOMESTICATION AND THE DEVELOPMENT OF SOCIAL RANKING

The tremendous impact which the development of horse husbandry must have had on human society during the Metal Ages has scarcely been considered by English speaking prehistorians, Anthony (1985) and Gimbutas (1988) being two notable exceptions. For example, in spite of the fact that *Ranking, Resources and Exchange* (eds Renfrew & Shennan 1982) covers the period when the economic and military potential of the horse was being developed, a glance at the index shows that the word 'horse' is mentioned only six times in the volume. Further investigation shows that even there it is mentioned only in passing.

Champion's article on 'Fortification, ranking and subsistence' is a case in point. Discussing the Rhine-Main basin between 1500 and 500 BC, he only mentions the word 'horse' in the context of eighth century horse-gear in the 'richest burials' (Champion 1982). Does not the presence of horse-gear in these graves say something about the value of horses to these people? After all, by the end of this period the Eurasian Steppe from the Carpathians to China was under the control of steppe nomads (Marchenko & Vinogradov 1989; Rudenko 1970). In fact, all the changes he describes as taking place during this period could well have been in some way related to an increase in the importance of the role of the horse — for example, climatic deterioration, an increase in the importance of pastoral activities and meat products, a deterioration in agricultural land and the expansion of the amount of land under the control of individual communities, the burial of horse-gear and other manifestations of 'enhanced social ranking'.

Harding, discussing the transition from the Copper Age to the Bronze Age, similarly underplays the significance of the horse:

> Of crucial importance is the question of land division and control. Agricultural technology, important though it is, does not — in my view — show marked differences in the Bronze Age from the Neolithic . . . What changes is the

relationship of labourer and land. Here the great bulk of our evidence comes from the British Isles.
(Harding 1984, 142)

The evidence, he suggests, points to

the existence of a peasant class, perhaps toiling on land formally annexed by someone else in return for a share in the produce . . . the familiar syndrome of serfdom being near at hand in any landbased labour-dependent hierarchy.

The several lines of approach followed here provide abundant evidence that elites existed in the Bronze Age. It remains to ask how they achieved that elite status. . . . I have already hinted at what I believe to be the crucial importance of economic factors in this development, but one cannot ignore the role of political factors. The means by which elites achieve their dominance . . . are essentially unknowable to the prehistorian . . . the problem of the missing link, namely how control of people was initially achieved.
(Harding 1984, 143)

These comments are particularly poignant because the Copper Age appears to be the period when horse husbandry began to develop. This is not to say that feudalism was already in place by the beginning of the Early Bronze Age, but the example of the Blackfoot indicates that social changes resulting from the domestication of the horse should not have taken long to appear (Ewers 1955).

In spite of the inadequacies of the work on the subject, it is quite clear that by the Bronze Age, the horse was rapidly spreading throughout Europe (Gimbutas 1970; Wijngaarden-Bakker 1975; Sherratt, 1983; Petrenko 1984; Dergachev 1989; Anthony 1991). Nowhere in his paper does Harding mention the horse at all. That is, however, quite commonplace in such syntheses.

THE RECOGNITION OF DOMESTICATION AND ITS
RELATION TO HORSE USAGE

Unfortunately, the few scholars who do discuss the development of horse husbandry and pastoral nomadism almost invariably quote from sources that are either obsolete or based upon methodologically or theoretically weak studies.

For example, in spite of the fact that the criteria used in the past by Bökönyi (1974a; 1974b; 1978; 1984), Nobis (1971), Bibikova (1969; 1970) and others for deciding whether horses were domesticated or not are largely obsolete, the results of their work are still quoted unquestioningly. Anthony and Brown comment rather ambiguously that

The Sredni Stog culture was the first Copper Age culture of the Ukrainian grasslands to exploit horses intensively as a food source. This rise in horse usage is thought to

correlate with the domestication of the horse in the grasslands of the Ukraine and the North Caspian lowlands during the Copper Age, *c.* 4500–3500 BC.
(Anthony & Brown 1991, 32)

The references they use include the present writer's 1990 *Antiquity* paper, a 1974 book by Bökönyi, a 1971 book by Nobis and a 1970 paper by Bibikova. In fact, my interpretation of the material from the site in question, Dereivka (Fig. 13.1), is diametrically opposed to that of the other authors. Whilst they claim that all the horses from Dereivka had been domesticated and that most had been raised for meat, I believe that the fact that most had been killed between the ages of 5 and 8 years strongly suggests that the vast majority had been wild (Fig. 13.2). Note that all the references except mine date from the 1960s and 1970s.

Since I have already discussed this site in detail elsewhere (Levine 1990), only a few of the salient points need be reiterated here. In 1978 Bökönyi wrote

Essentially, the presence of complete skeletons, the absence of old animals, and an overwhelming majority of mares are indications of a domesticated population. The absence of vertebrae and breastbones, the occurrence of old animals, and an equal proportion of stallions and mares point to a wild population . . . More recent methods of determining early horse domestication include the osteological analysis of individual variations in enamel patterns and body size and the detailed investigation of artifacts connected with horse-keeping.
(Bökönyi 1978)

These criteria are all unsatisfactory. Indeed, some are better indications of hunting than herding. Although these are the criteria that workers say they use, in fact the principal, though more or less unacknowledged, criterion is the increase in the quantity of horse bones found at a particular site or sites (for example see Anthony & Brown, 1991, as quoted above; Bibikova 1969; Bökönyi,1984; Petrenko 1984; Mallory 1989; Matyushin 1986; Dergachev 1989; Telegin 1986; Gimbutas 1988).

High percentages of horse bones are taken as strong evidence of domestication. Moreover, at sites where there are both wild and domesticated species, if horses are present they are automatically categorized as domesticated. If the resulting proportion of domesticated taxa is higher than that of wild taxa, this is taken as further evidence that the horses at the site in question were domesticated.

Dereivka is a case in point (Telegin 1986). Sixty-one per cent of the identifiable mammal bones and teeth (28 per cent according to the MNI) belong to horse (Table 13.1). If they were counted as domesticated, then the percentage of domesticated mammals at the site would be 83 per cent (55 per cent according to the MNI). That is, most of the animals from the site could be regarded as domesticated. If, however, the horses were regarded as wild, the percentage of wild taxa would be 78 per

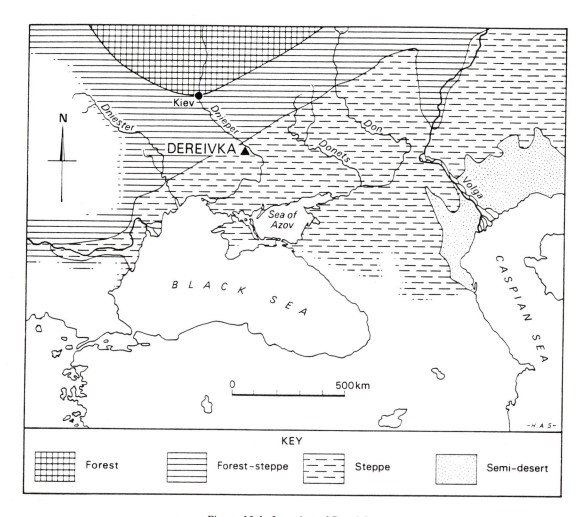

Figure 13.1. Location of Dereivka

cent (74 per cent according to the MNI), in which case the majority would be wild. This kind of reasoning is, of course, absurd. The overall percentage of wild and domesticated taxa at the site is no indication of the status of the Eneolithic horse.

Although an increase in the quantity of horse bones might well indicate a change in the relationship between people and horses, domestication is not the only answer. For example, climatic effects or a change in hunting techniques could also account for an increased number of horse bones at archaeological sites. The population structure of the horses from Dereivka strongly suggests that the vast majority were hunted (Fig. 13.2; Levine 1990), while the bit-wear study of Anthony and Brown (1991) strongly suggests that at least one horse, either tamed or domesticated, was ridden. Perhaps the increase in the number of horses arose when people discovered that their pets would make effective hunting tools.

THE CONTEXT OF EARLY HORSE DOMESTICATION

In fact, mixed fishing/hunting/small-scale stock raising economies have been characteristic of large parts of Eastern Europe as well as Central and Inner Asia, in

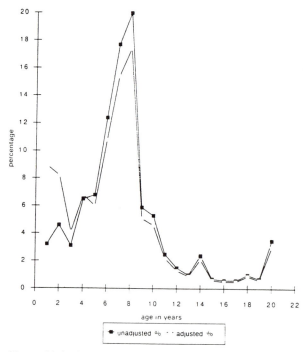

Figure 13.2. Age structure: loose teeth + teeth in bone –
Dereivka

Table 13.1. Dereivka taxon list according to Bibikova (adapted from Telegin 1986)

Taxon	Number of bones	Minimum number of individuals
Horse *(Equus caballus)*	2412	52
Cattle, domesticated *(Bos taurus)*	618	18
Sheep/goat *(Ovis aries/Capra hircus)*	88	16
Pig *(Sus scrofa)*	114	9
Dog *(Canis familiaris)*	33	5
Red deer *(Cervus elaphus)*	394	18
Roe deer *(Capreolus capreolus)*	99	12
Wild boar *(Sus scrofa)*	50	11
Elk *(Alces alces)*	12	3
Badger *(Meles meles)*	9	4
Bear *(Ursus arctos)*	5	2
Otter *(Lutra lutra)*	2	2
Wolf *(Canis lupus)*	4	2
Fox *(Vulpes vulpes)*	26	7
Beaver *(Castor fiber)*	50	15
Hare *(Lepus sp.)*	22	7
Total – mammals	**3938**	**183**
Mallard *(Anas platyrhynchos)*	14	4
Pintail *(Anas acuta)*	3	2
Duck *(Anas sp.)*	3	2
Goose *(Anser anser)*	1	1
Teal *(Querquedula querquedula)*	1	1
Coot *(Fulica atra)*	3	2
Total – birds	**25**	**12**
Silurus *(Silurus glanis)*	94	21
Perch *(Lucioperca lucioperca)*	20	5
Roach *(Rutilus rutilus)*	11	5
Red-eye *(Scardinus erythrophtalmus)*	2	1
Carp *(Cyprinus carpio)*	3	2
Carp *(Asdpius aspius)*	1	1
Pike *(Esox lucius)*	5	2
Total – fish	**136**	**37**
Tortoise *(Emys onbicularis)*	177	32
Total – all taxa	**4276**	**264**

some cases, up to recent times (Zvelebil & Zvelebil 1990; Dolukhanov 1986a; 1986b; Matyushin 1989; Petrenko 1984; Vainshtein 1980; Anthony 1991; Ellis 1984). The conventional Near Eastern scenario in which hunting plunges in importance following the domestication of sheep, goat, pig and cattle is not valid in this part of the world. This leads us to another point. If the horse was domesticated in this region around the fourth or fifth millennium BC, then its domestication did not necessarily arise in a context of settled agriculture.

It has been widely assumed that pastoralism could only have arisen out of a settled agricultural background and that pastoralists are dependent upon settled agriculturalists for their existence. It may well be the case that nomadic pastoralists have always in some degree been dependent upon agricultural products, but that is in itself not evidence of dependence upon settled agriculturalists.

Again, archaeologists' notion of what pastoral nomadism is all about seems to be limited to Near Eastern desert-based, camel-driven, nomadic pastoralism. Bedouin may indeed be dependent for their survival on

their relationships (trade or raid) with settled peoples. The steppe, however, is a very different environment from the desert. Generalizations valid for the latter are unlikely to be valid for the former.

The Tuvans of South Siberia are a case in point. Amongst these people hunting and farming, as well as pastoralism, were all important activities. In *The Nomads of South Siberia* Vainshtein (1980) describes the agricultural practices of the Tuvans during the nineteenth and early twentieth centuries:

> [The] Tuvinian nomadic pastoralists usually cultivated areas, as far as possible, which were close to their spring and autumn camps. Sometimes, however, there might be as much as 30 or 40 km between them. Then only the men would ride out to their fields, leaving the women behind in the settlements to do the housework and tend the animals. This was rare, however, since most households had their cultivated land less than 5 km from the spring and autumn camps. In fact, only about 15 per cent of all the households had to travel more than 5 km to attend to their farming . . . Similar agricultural practices were maintained by the Kirghiz, the Mongols, and other Central Asian pastoral peoples.
> (Vainshtein 1980, 148)

According to Vainshtein, a 1931 survey shows that only 29 per cent of a total of 15080 households did not have arable land. The principal crops were millet, barley, and to a lesser extent, soft wheat and oats. This excludes collectivized land, which covered less than 5 per cent of the total area sown. He observes, and Caroline Humphrey (1980) confirms, that 'There is a constantly growing body of facts which suggest that agricultural activity is a feature of the mountain-steppe type of nomadic pastoralism in the temperate zone of Eurasia' (Vainshtein 1980, 164).

Conclusion

So far, the only concrete evidence we have for the beginnings of horse domestication is the single premolar from Dereivka, identified by Anthony and Brown (1991) as having bit-wear. On the other hand, we also know that, whether wild or domesticated, large numbers of horse bones and teeth have been recovered from Eneolithic sites from the Ukraine to north Kazakhstan. By the Early Bronze Age, evidence for horses was becoming increasingly widespread, particularly to the west of their apparently original distribution.

It seems most likely that the horse was domesticated or at least tamed by the late Neolithic or Eneolithic. It is very clear that the implications for human society were immense, but almost nothing is known about where, when and how this took place and how human social behaviour changed as horse husbandry developed and spread. Both the archaeological data on this subject and the models recently used to interpret that data are largely obsolete. New and important sites have recently been excavated in Central Eurasia (for example, in the

Urals and South Siberia: Koryakova pers. comm.; in northern Kazakhstan: Zdanovich & Zaibert, 1989; Zaibert pers. comm.; in the Volga region: Matyushin 1986; and in the northern Caucasus: Korenevsky 1991 & pers. comm.). Recent political changes now make it possible for westerners to obtain access to much of this new data. Moreover, it is now also possible to carry out ethnoarchaeological research on the Steppe. Such work is in progress and will be used for the development of new models of human-horse interaction.

That being said, it must be admitted that we are unlikely ever to be able to understand the evolution of horse husbandry without reference to the actual bones and teeth from archaeological deposits. Furthermore, without a thorough understanding of this material it will never really be possible to understand human social evolution. The same is true for all the animals of economic importance to human beings.

The attitude of most archaeologists towards archaeozoology – that it is only of peripheral interest to our understanding of human social evolution and change – has had some rather unfortunate consequences. The first is the inadequacy of funding for faunal analysis. Since it is regarded neither as mainstream archaeology nor as scientific archaeology it tends to fall between these two main categories of funding. Moreover, because bones are not generally regarded as important, unqualified people are very often put in charge of the analysis of faunal collections. Their frequently inadequate studies do nothing to convince other archaeologists that faunal analysis can yield important and interesting information about a site. The problem of the origins of horse domestication is a case in point and shows how conventional attitudes to archaeozoology have worked to the detriment of our understanding of the past.

Acknowledgements

I would like to thank N. Postgate (Faculty of Oriental Studies, Cambridge), D. Sneath and N. di Cosmo (Mongolian and Inner Asian Studies Unit, Cambridge), S.N. Korenevsky (Institute of Archaeology, Moscow) and L. N. Koryakova (Academy of Sciences, Ekaterinburg) for discussions related to topics referred to in this paper. I am extremely grateful to D.Y. Telegin (Institute of Archaeology, Kiev) and V.F. Zaibert (Pedagogical Institute, Petropavlovsk) both for discussions and for allowing me to study the data from Dereivka and Botai, and to C. Scarre (McDonald Institute, Cambridge) and M. K. Jones (Department of Archaeology, Cambridge) for reading and commenting upon this paper.

This research has been supported by the British Academy, The Leakey Foundation, The Wenner-Gren Foundation and the McDonald Institute for Archaeological Research.

References

Anthony, D.W., 1991a. The domestication of the horse, in *Equids in the Ancient World*, Vol. II, eds R.H. Meadow & H.-P. Uerpmann. Wiesbaden: Reichert Verlag, 250–77

Anthony, D.W., & Brown, D.R., 1991. The origins of horseback riding. *Antiquity* 65, 22–38

Bibikova, V.I., 1969. On the history of horse domestication in south-east Europe, reprinted in *Dereivka, A Settlement and Cemetery of Copper Age Horse Keepers on the Middle Dnieper*, by D.Y. Telegin (1986). Oxford: British Archaeological Reports International Series S287, 163–82

Bibikova, V.I. 1970. A study of the earliest domestic horses of Eastern Europe, parts 1 and 2, reprinted in *Dereivka, A Settlement and Cemetery of Copper Age Horse Keepers on the Middle Dnieper*, by D.Y. Telegin (1986). Oxford: British Archaeological Reports International Series S287, 135–62

Bökönyi, S., 1974a. *History of Domestic Mammals in Central and Eastern Europe*. Budapest: Akademiai Kiado

Bökönyi, S., 1974b. *The Prezevalsky Horse*. London: Souvenir Press

Bökönyi, S., 1978. The earliest waves of domestic horses in East Europe. *Journal of Indo-European Studies* 6, 17–73

Bökönyi, S., 1984. Horse, in *Evolution of Domesticated Animals*, ed. I. L. Mason. London: Longman, 162–73

Champion, T., 1982. Fortification, ranking and subsistence in *Ranking, Resources and Exchange*, eds C. Renfrew & S. Shennan. Cambridge: Cambridge University Press, 61–72

Dergachev, V., 1989. Neolithic and Bronze Age cultural communities of the steppe zone of the USSR. *Antiquity* 63, 793–802

Dolukhanov, P.M., 1989a. The Late Mesolithic and the transition to food production in Eastern Europe, in *Hunters in Transition*, ed. M. Zvelebil. Cambridge: Cambridge University Press, 109–19

Dolukhanov, P.M., 1989b. Foragers and farmers in west-Central Asia, in *Hunters in Transition*, ed. M. Zvelebil. Cambridge: Cambridge University Press, 121–32

Edwards, I.E.S., Gadd, C.J., Hammond, N.G.L., & Sollberger, E., (eds) 1980. *The Cambridge Ancient History, vol. II, part 1. The Middle East and the Aegean Region c.1800–1380 BC*. Cambridge: Cambridge University Press

Ellis, L., 1984. *The Cucuteni-Tripolye Culture: a Study in Technology and the Origins of Complex Society*. Oxford: British Archaeological Reports International Series S217

Ewers, J.C., 1955. *The Horse in Blackfoot Indian Culture*. Washington DC: Smithsonian Institution Press

Gilman, A., 1990. The Mafia Hypothesis, in *When Worlds Collide: the Indo-Europeans and the Pre-Indo-Europeans*, eds T.L. Markey & J.A.C. Greppin. Ann Arbor, Michigan: Karoma, 151–69

Gimbutas, M., 1970. Proto-Indo-European culture: the Kurgan culture during the fifth, fourth and third millennia BC, in *Indo-European and Indo-Europeans*, eds. B. Cordona, H.M. Koenigswald & A. Senn. Philadelphia: University of Pennsylvania Press, 155–97

Gimbutas, M., 1988. Review of Archaeology and Language by C. Renfrew. *Current Anthropology* 29, 453–6

Harding, A., 1984. Aspects of social evolution in the Bronze Age, in *European Social Evolution, Archaeological Perspectives*, ed. J. Bintliff. Bradford: University of Bradford, 135–45

Humphrey, C., 1980. Editor's introduction, in *Nomads of South Siberia, the Pastoral Economies of Tuva*, by S. Vainshtein. Cambridge: Cambridge University Press, 1–36

Korenevsky, S.N., 1991. Questions concerning the Maikop Culture in the Middle Terek Basin [K voprosu o maikope na srednem Tereke], in *The Maikop Phenomenon in the Ancient History of the Caucasus and Eastern Europe [Maikopskii Fenomen v Drevnei Istorii Kavkaza i Vostochnoi Evropy]*, ed. V.A. Trifonov. Proceedings of an International Symposium, Novosibirsk 1991, 38–42

Levine, M.A., 1990. Dereivka and the problem of horse domestication. *Antiquity* 64, 727–40

Mallory, J.P., 1989. *In Search of the Indo-Europeans*. London: Thames & Hudson

Mann, M., 1986. *The Sources of Social Power, 1: A History of Power from the Beginning to AD 1760*. Cambridge: Cambridge University Press

Marchenko, K., & Vinogradov, Y., 1989. The Scythian period in the northern Black Sea region (750–250 BC). *Antiquity* 63, 803–13

Matyushin, G., 1986. The Mesolithic and Neolithic in the southern Urals and Central Asia, in *Hunters in Transition* ed. M. Zvelebil. Cambridge: Cambridge University Press, 133–50

Nobis, G., 1971. *Vom Wildpferd zum Hauspferd*. Cologne & Vienna: Böhlau Verlag

Nobis, G., 1974. The origin, domestication and early history of domestic horses. *Veterinary Medical Review* 3, 211–25

Petrenko, A.G., 1984. *Ancient and Medieval Animal Husbandry in the Volga and Ural regions. [Drevnee i Spednevekoboe Zhivotnobodstvo Srednevo Povolzh"ia i Predural"ia]*. Moscow: Academy of Sciences

Renfrew, C., 1987. *Archaeology and Language. The Puzzle of Indo-European Origins*. London: Jonathan Cape

Renfrew, C., & Shennan, S., (eds) 1982. *Ranking, Resources and Exchange*. Cambridge: Cambridge University Press

Rudenko, S.I., 1970. *The Frozen Tombs of Siberia*. London: Dent

Sherratt, A., 1981. Plough and pastoralism: aspects of the secondary products revolution, in *Patterns of the Past*, eds N. Hammond & I. Hodder. Cambridge: Cambridge University Press, 261–305

Sherratt, A., 1983. The secondary exploitation of animals in the Old World. *World Archaeology*, 15, 90–104

Sinor, D., 1972. Horse and pasture in Inner Asian history. *Oriens Extremus* 19, 171–83

Sneath, D., 1991. Military Development and the History of the Eurasian Steppe. Unpublished paper

Telegin, D.Y., 1986. *Dereivka, A Settlement and Cemetery of Copper Age Horse Keepers on the Middle Dnieper*. Oxford: British Archaeological Reports International Series S287

Vainshtein, S., 1980. *Nomads of South Siberia. The Pastoral Economies of Tuva*. Cambridge: Cambridge University Press

Wijngaarden-Bakker, L.H. van, 1975. Horses in the Dutch Neolithic, in *Archaeozoological Studies*, ed. A.T. Clason. Amsterdam: North-Holland Publishing Company, 341–4

Zdanovich, G.B., & Zaibert, V.F., 1989. Basic regularities in the development of food producing economies in the Ural-Kazakh steppe [Osnovnye zakonomernosti stanovleniia khoziaistva proizvodiashchevo tipa v Uralo-Kazakhstaniskikh stepiakh], in *The Coming into Being and Development of Producing Economies in the Urals [Stanovlenie i Vazvitie Prooizvodiashchevo Khoziaistva na Urale]*, ed. V.S. Korshunov. Sverdlovsk: Academy of Sciences of the USSR, 70–83

Zvelebil, M., (ed.) 1986. *Hunters in Transition*. Cambridge: Cambridge University Press

Zvelebil, M., & Zvelebil, K.V., 1990. Agricultural transition, 'Indo-European origins' and the spread of farming, in *When Worlds Collide: the Indo-Europeans and the Pre-Indo-Europeans*, eds T.L. Markey & J.A.C. Greppin. Ann Arbor, Michigan: Karoma, 237–66

14

From Villanova to Seddin. The Reconstruction of an Elite Exchange Network during the Eighth Century BC

Kristian Kristiansen

The distribution of certain metalwork types, combined with a shared iconography, is interpreted as evidence for a long-distance exchange network extending from central Italy to the Elbe and beyond. The emergence and the shape of this network are linked to the decline of Hungarian centres of metalworking and the rise of Italian ones, the existence of chiefly centres in northern Europe, the emergence of a strongly-defined Lausitz cultural area, and Cimmerian expansion along the Danube. Its implications for the extent of chiefly control and for a supralocal level of political and social organisation are considerable.

La répartition de certains types métalliques, associées à une iconographie commune, est interprétée comme témoinage d'un réseau d'échange qui s'étendait d'Italie centrale jusqu'en Europe septentrionle. Le développement et la forme de ce réseau sont liés au déclin des ateliers hongrois et à l'émergence de ceux d'Italie, à la présence des centres princiers en Europe septentrionale, au développement d'une région culturelle lusatienne fortement définie, et à l'expansion cimmérienne le long du Danube. Ce réseau témoigne d'un niveau élevé de contrôle princier et d'une organisation politique et sociale dépassant le plan local.

The emergence of the Villanova-Seddin link

Looking at distribution maps of selected types of metalwork enables the archaeologist to discover both regional traditions and international connections and regularities that were unknown to prehistoric people, although they might have been aware of larger parts of such networks from combined personal experience and myth (Helms 1985). Their knowledge would thus be contextualized and localized within a social and ritual framework at a specific point in space within the network. Although the abstraction of the distribution map summarizes large-scale geographical interrelations, it may also make us forget to ask the most relevant questions, such as how far did people travel when they married, when they traded, etc., and how far did their knowledge about the world around them reach? What context do the finds come from — burials, hoards, etc. — and what social groups did they belong to? In a world of rapid and widespread international communication of ideas and objects everybody meets everybody, in principle, in a chain of exchanges. To enable such rapid exchanges as are evidenced, networks cannot have passed from one settlement to the next, although for some objects they clearly did. In the

Bronze Age there was already a well-organized hierarchy allowing exchange to be carried out over longer intervals, thereby speeding up the pace of change and the spread of new information (Jockenhövel 1991; Larsson 1984). To explore the nature of such long-distance exchange, the length of journeys, and the nature of local distribution and exchange, let us first examine some distribution maps and their evidence for a regular long-distance network from Italy to northern Germany and Denmark during the eighth century BC. This will be followed by an analysis of the internal context and structure of a selected chiefly centre along the route, Seddin on the Elbe.

By the eighth century BC the production of elite metalwork had passed from Hungary to central and northern Italy. Italian products were distributed northwards and eastwards to establish long-distance trade relations with, among others, the Nordic region. Here amber was one of the commodities in demand, as Italy was also beginning to manufacture and distribute amber, for example to Jugoslavia, where we find amber used in increasing quantities on fibulae, as at Glasinac and Vergina, as well as in Italy itself. The rise to dominance of the so-called Pfahlbau route to northern Germany and southern Scandinavia (Sprockhoff 1951)

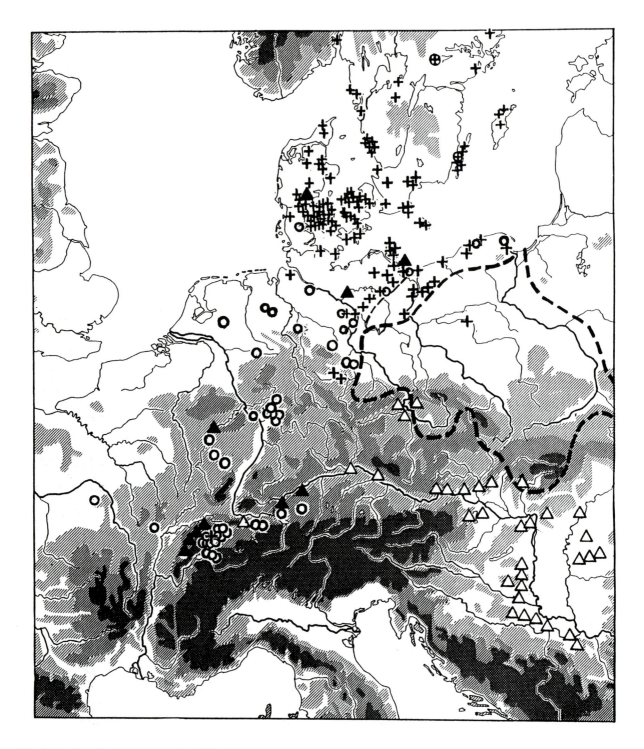

Fig. 14.1. The distribution of period 5/Ha B3 lanceheads of Pfahlbau type (open circle) and Nordic type (cross), after Thrane (1975, fig. 30), and the distribution of 'Cimmerian' bits (open triangle, filled triangle the western type) after Kossack (1954, Kart 5). The distribution of the Lausitz culture in its latest phase is shown by a heavy broken line, after Bukowski (1974, Abb. 1); the lighter broken line indicates the area of Nordic settlement and influence, after Fogel (1988, map IX).

should be seen as resulting from these changed condi- tions. But they are in turn to be understood within the framework of a general westward shift of metal pro- duction and an upsurge in the volume and quality of products. An overall impression of the exchange net- works of the period is given in Figs 14.1–2. These define the major characteristics: clusters in the Phahlbau

region in Switzerland, south of the 'knee' of the Elbe — an old centre, and from here further on to the Oder, where there is one line of exchange towards Pomerania and the Vistula and another to the Danish Islands. A third line went up the Elbe to Jutland through at least some of the period.

We note two characteristics of the distribution maps:

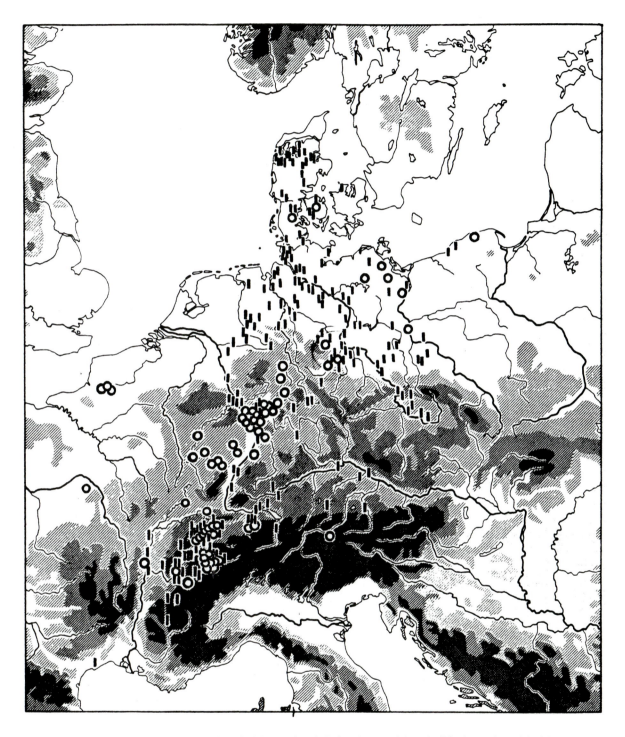

*Fig. 14.2. The distribution of period 5 vase-headed pins (rectangle) and ribbed armrings (circle),
after Thrane (1975, fig. 103).*

firstly, prestige goods, such as swords and spears, are directional: they move along well-defined lines with marked clusters of destination along the line. As other types, such as pins, fill in the empty spaces between the clusters, we can assume that the clusters represent political centres that were able to control both the exchange and the consumption of certain types of pres-

tige good. The clusters thus represent distribution to local chiefs or vassals. Müller-Karpe's regional sword types, especially type Weltenburg (Fig.14.3), give a good indication of the chiefly centres (Müller-Karpe 1961, Tafeln 98–101). This implies that chiefly centres were able to organize trade expeditions over distances of sometimes several hundred kilometres. As we shall see

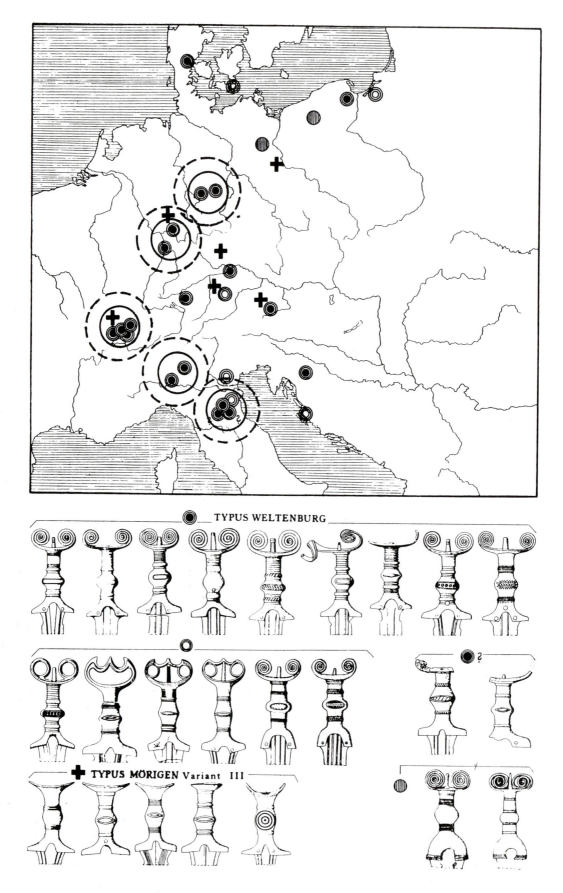

Fig. 14.3. The distribution of variants of the period 5 swords of types Weltenburg and Möringen, after Müller-Karpe (1961, Tafel 98), with suggested political catchment areas circled. The swords are only one element in a group of prestige objects that all cluster in the same areas, representing well-known cultural groups (Golasecca, Pfahlbau, etc.).

later, the average distance was generally less. Blurrings of the pattern occur, and can be explained by alternating lines of exchange and/or local redistribution of prestige goods. Fig. 14.1, which shows the distribution of Pfahlbau and Nordic spears, is illuminating in demonstrating not only the directional nature of exchange, but also the rapid change of style coinciding with the beginning of the Nordic zone at the Elbe. It further suggests that exchange took place over longer distances in the Urnfield culture than in the Nordic culture.

The second characteristic of the distribution maps is avoidance of the Lausitz region with its strong fortified settlements. If one compares a map of the Lausitz culture with the exchange system just outlined, the complementarity of the two distributions is clear (Fig. 14.1). That this represented a well-considered strategy is apparent from the considerable detour necessary to reach Pomerania by way of the Elbe and the Oder. Instead of continuing directly through Lausitz territory from Saxony (the 'knee' of the Elbe), the route ran northwards to the Oder, then turned eastwards. The journey thus remained within the territory of the Nordic/North German culture, which must have been decisive. We may conclude from this that the rich Pomeranian amber sources had now begun to be exploited and that the amber trade was in the hands of Nordic traders, competing with and avoiding the Lausitz region. The reasons for this could be many, but it suggests that polities above the local level were realities in Late Bronze Age Europe, supporting the picture we have drawn of the highly organised nature of trade and exchange, not to mention local populations. In the following section I shall substantiate these propositions by considering the local contexts of princely burials and elite exchange in two particular case studies.

Princely burials and the context of elite exchange

Anyone travelling from Villanova to Seddin or the opposite way during the eighth century BC, as some adventurous persons at the time may even have done, would have met with familiar social and cultural practices, at least if he or she happened to belong to the elite that was able to travel. To illuminate this, let us take as our point of departure an amphora from a rich warrior burial at Veii in central Italy and examine the history of its production and distribution, including related centres of metalworking (Jockenhövel 1974). Originating from one of the specialist centres of metalworking that developed in Italy under Hungarian/ Urnfield influence, it belonged to the aristocratic lifestyle of chiefly dining/drinking. The symbol of the 'Sonnenbarkenvogel' (sunship bird), which appears from Italy to Scandinavia and from France to the Carpathians, signifies the ritual *koine* of the Urnfield culture (Fig. 14.4), as well as stressing the ritualized nature of social conduct and legitimization. When we consider the dis-

Fig. 14.4. *The common Urnfield sunship bird motif from a selection of objects with repoussé decoration, (after Jockenhövel 1974, Abb. 7–8).*

tribution and social context of these amphorae, nearly all of them are found in aristocratic burials, as at Veii.

In an analysis of the whole group of amphorae and buckets, Albrecht Jockenhövel made a number of important observations (Jockenhövel 1974, 32 sqq., Abb. 6), allowing us to distinguish between south and north Alpine traditions. One metalworking centre was located in southern Etruria, while it is more difficult precisely to locate the central European ones, apart from Hungary. Among the amphorae there is a parallel to the Veii example in an aristocratic burial from Gevlinghausen in north-west Germany (Fig. 14.5), demonstrating once again how close contacts were at the chiefly level. It is interesting, however, that Jockenhövel, on the basis of technological details, suggests that the Gevlinghausen amphora was made north of the Alps, in imitation of pieces like the Veii one, perhaps by 'imported' craftsmen travelling between chiefly courts. It has long been recognised that during the eighth century BC there emerged in northern

Fig. 14.5. Bronze amphorae from Veii and Gevlinghausen, after Jockenhövel (1974, Abb. 2 & 4).

Germany a group of repoussé metal cups in 'Punkt-Buckel' (point-buckle) style which were locally made (Sprockhoff 1956). As the Nordic tradition employed only casting techniques, this suggests that specialists were imported from central Europe or Italy to chiefly centres in northern Europe. Another, plainer amphora was found in the 'royal' burial at Seddin on the Elbe. It is paralleled by an amphora from northern Jutland in Denmark; both were probably made within a north European chiefly context (Jockenhövel 1974, Tafel 6). The recent find of 14 repoussé Herzsprung shields in a bog in Sweden may support such an hypothesis (Hagberg 1988). It offers a rare glimpse of a highly developed system of production and distribution, beyond that of traditional gift exchange but in accordance with an organized system of elite exchange and trade. So too does the hoard of nine bronze corselets from Marmesse in France (Mohen 1987).

These elite burials with amphorae and buckets demonstrate an astonishing similarity in burial ritual, ranging from small details, such as wrapping the burnt bones up in linen — also described by Homer (*Illiad* 23, 252) — to the Dionysian drinking rituals and the employment of standardized symbolic motifs and figures on the amphorae. Elite burials during the eighth century BC from Italy to Denmark and from France to the Balkans and Greece thus share

– drinking and dining habits linked to common social and ritual traditions
– the exchange of prestigious drinking services (amphorae, buckets and cups), and sometimes also of specialist craftsmen (Kytlicova 1985)
– the employment of costly four-wheeled wagons for social and ritual purposes, sometimes evidenced by metal miniature wagons taking part in ritual processions, found in Italy, Iberia and central Europe (Pare 1985)

– the employment of metal horse equipment: harness, phalerae, etc. (Thrane 1975, ch. 5)
– the exchange of prestige weapons and metal body armour, sometimes in large quantities (Schauer 1975; Goetze 1984)
– the use of monumental barrows, confined, however, to northern Europe, Italy and south-eastern Europe.

Let us now consider in more detail an example of the internal context of such elite burials, in order to establish the level of social organisation of the group.

Seddin

Along the Elbe there emerged during this period several chiefly centres, regularly spaced 80–100 km from each other (Fig. 14.6). Chief amongst them is the Seddin area, with a remarkable concentration of rich graves, culminating in the royal burial in one of the largest barrows of northern Europe, 80 m in diameter and 11 m high, containing a stone-built chamber with a corbelled roof. An analysis of all the Seddin burials and hoards by Wüstemann (1974) has made it possible to outline the structure of the metal depositions as well as the burial ritual. The region is defined by clusters of barrows and urnfields, in an area north of the Elbe just above its southward bend, extending approximately 60 km from east to west and from north to south.

Wüstemann's analysis of the richest burials, mainly from barrows, has revealed differentiation within this stratum of interments. Some of it may be chronological, one group of grave goods being later than another (Wüstemann 1974, Abb. 7). A perhaps more important ritual differentiation is seen in the use of either barrows or cemeteries. Urnfield burials are generally poor, only 17 per cent containing grave goods. To this may be added a spatial separation between the two contempo-

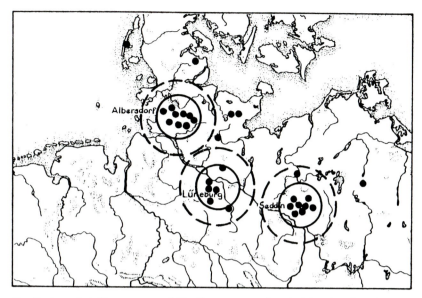

Fig. 14.6. The distribution of richly ornamented Nordic tweezers of period 5, after Sprockhoff (1956, fig. 21b). These represent chiefly elites along the Elbe, with their political catchment areas circled.

rary rites, suggesting that people buried in barrows wanted to distinguish themselves from the commoners by taking up the archaic tradition of barrow burial, as well as furnishing their graves with sometimes extraordinary riches. In accordance with this interpretation of the ritual expression of social differentiation, there is a total of 320 burials in 240 barrows against 1000 burials in urnfields. The latter represent traditional village communities with village chiefs above whom a ruling elite had established themselves.

The barrows, however, also showed diversification and internal ranking: a larger group of cairns (built of stone), with rather sparse grave goods, stands out against a smaller group of sometimes rather large barrows (built of turf and earth), with stone packing around a cist. Nearly half of the cairns and barrows contained burials with metal grave goods, often of high quality. Among them a few burials stand out as extraordinary, in terms of both the nature of the grave goods and the size and construction of the mound and the burial chamber, especially a group of large, richly-furnished 'royal' barrows in Seddin. The most famous of these was 11 m high and 80 m in diameter. The burial chamber was constructed with a corbelled roof, parallels for which have been sought in Bulgaria and the Balkans (Wüstemann 1974, Abb. 5; Sprockhoff 1957). The stones were specially selected or imported. In some cases special treatments are evidenced — in the royal chamber at Seddin the walls were covered with plaster decorated with beautiful red-white-black paintings (paralleled on the house walls of another chiefly centre at Voldtofte on Funen).

The Seddin paramount chief was buried with two women, also accompanied by grave goods and thus most probably wives. His bones were put in the amphora, and were accompanied by weapons (swords), metal vessels, and Nordic razors and tweezers, as well

as by a miniature lance and a decorated knife, both Nordic, and by several unique pottery types. In general, these burials often contained unique objects specially produced for the paramount chiefs. Other chiefly graves display variations around the ritual of the royal burial; a few of them belong to the paramount group, and they all include the Nordic paraphernalia of chieftainship: razors/tweezers, knives and pins.

The Seddin region thus evidences the expansion of Nordic trade and the concomitant rise of new paramount elites in nodal points of exchange, employing barrows to impress and to demonstrate their new position as regional chiefs above the level of traditional chieftains. These were reduced to the status of vassal chiefs within the local network of political control and redistribution; and at the lowest level we find village heads in the urnfields. This new three-level structure was probably approaching archaic state formation. However, despite differentiation and separation in grave goods and ritual, both village heads and paramount chiefs employed metalwork in the same, mostly Nordic, tradition, but with qualitative differentiation. It appears as if there still existed a continuum of kinship relations between top and bottom, as they appear in the burial record, but separation and potential class distinctions were probably not far away.

The rise of the Seddin region during the period V/ Ha B3 can be explained only by its strategic position as the point of entry to the Nordic and North German region, controlling trade westwards alone the Elbe and towards Jutland, further northwards to the Danish islands, and eastwards toward the Oder and beyond to Pommerania. This position emerges from the distribution maps of all prestige goods. We can thus link control of long-distance trade in prestige goods to the emergence of centres of wealth accumulation and the formation of social and political hierarchies approach-

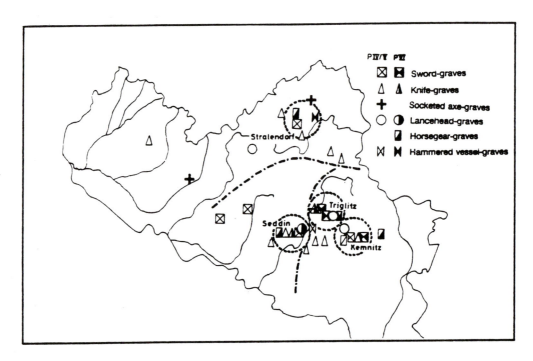

Fig. 14.7. The distribution of rich burials in the Seddin area, with suggested political centres and their boundaries in broken lines, after Wüstemann (1974, Abb. 9).

ing archaic state formation. It is characterized by paramount chiefs controlling tributary vassal chiefs by the redistribution of prestige goods. I thus prefer to interpret the evidence presented by Wüstemann as representing a single hierarchical structure, perhaps with some spatial shifts of paramount centres, rather than as several autonomous tribal territories each with its own paramount chief (Fig. 14.6). Although this is a possibility, especially if the autonomous territories formed a confederation, it does not seem compatible with the kind of control of long-distance trade that is evidenced. The Seddin region was able for several generations to maintain a central position in the north-south trade network, preventing competing centres from arising in its vicinity, until the monopoly was finally broken in period VI by the takeover of long-distance trade from Pommerania and eastern Scandinavia to northern Italy and the eastern Alps by the Billendorf culture and other Lausitz groups, then experiencing a last *floruit*. This disruption is marked by a break in the use of cemeteries and barrows (Wüstemann 1974, Abb. 10). Whether or not Seddin declined peacefully is yet to be demonstrated.

The Seddin centre was no unique phenomenon in the north, although rare. A similar centre, Voldtofte, has been documented on south-west Funen in eastern Denmark, exhibiting the same basic characteristics (Thrane 1984). Both belong to a group of north European chiefly centres of late Period V/Ha B3 (Höckmann 1987; Thrane in press). The development and maintenance of common religious and social value systems from Italy to southern Scandinavia during the Late Bronze Age was due to the operation of long-distance exchange networks operating

through chiefly centres, in a complicated process of acceptance, recontextualization and rejection of new influences (Sørensen 1987).

The basic operator in keeping the system together was the gift — between royal families maintaining dynastic links and alliances, from royals to vassals, and as gifts to the gods offered by the chiefs or kings in votive offerings. In all cases social bonds of loyalty were established. The gift was the principal form of exchange in archaic society. 'There was hardly any area in the life of archaic man that was not coded through an appropriate exchange of gifts: for making friends, for marriage, funeral, initiation, etc. Since the king's behaviour was ritualized to the highest degree, it is precisely in relations between rulers that this feature of the archaic customary law can be expected to be best reflected' (Marazov 1989, 91). This was true in Thrace, described by Marazov, as well as in northern Europe, as we have seen. In Thrace the archaeological evidence is reinforced by historical sources which describe gift-giving between the Thracian kings and their neighbours the Greeks. The archaeological reconstruction of the connections between Villanova and Seddin, however, entails all the basic elements of heroic or Archaic Greek society, which were also common to Italy and the North. Shared norms of social and ritual conduct from Greece to Denmark were the basis for maintaining these royal and chiefly networks of elite exchange and trade. We may therefore assume that they operated according to the archaic traditions of gift giving as known from Homer, Hesiod, Thucydides, etc. Prestige and wealth (political and social profit) were the operators of the system that channelled both people and valued goods, sometimes in rather large quantities, between Scandinavia, central Europe and Italy.

Seddin and Voldtofte reflect the opening-up and the take-over of a western trade network along the Elbe, in opposition to an earlier Ha B1 network from Zealand across the Baltic to the Oder and further south (Kristiansen 1981, figs. 18.6, 18.7). New political and economic conditions in the Lausitz culture and beyond had closed this route, or reduced its importance, giving way to the Elbe-Pfahlbau-Villanova network. To this we may add the effect of a Cimmerian expansion along the Danube, leading to social transformations which for a period may have prohibited north-south trade (Fig. 14.1). Did the Lausitz culture block Nordic trade or were the Cimmerian expansion and the decline of specialist workshops in Hungary the decisive factors? And can we really suppose such controlled actions at a supralocal level of political intervention, calling for a knowledge of conditions hundreds of kilometres away? Having penetrated the Italian-Nordic network and made interpretative visits to their archaeological remains at Seddin, the answer is in the affirmative.

References

Bukowski, Z.,1974. Characteristik der sogenannten skytischen Funde aus Polen. *Zeitschrift für Archaeologie* 8, 45–66

Fogel, J., 1988. *'Import' Nordyjski na Ziemiach Polskich u Schykku Epoku Brazu* [Nordlicher 'Import' in die polnischen Länder in der Spätbronzezeit]. Poznan: Uniwersytet im. Adama Mickiewicza w Poznaniu, Seria Archeologia 30

Goetze, B.-R., 1984. Die frühesten europäischen Schutzwaffen. Anmerkungen sum zusammenhang einer Fundgattung. *Bayerische Vorgeschichtsblätter* 49, 25–53

Helms, M.W., 1988. *Ulysses' Sail. An Ethnographic Odyssey of Power, Knowledge, and Geographical Distance*. Princeton, N.J.: Princeton University Press

Hagberg, U., 1988. The Bronze Age shields from Fröslunda. near Lake Va'hern, west Sweden, in *Trade and Exchange in Prehistory: Studies in Honour of Berta Stjernquist*, eds B. Hårdh, L. Larsson, D. Olausson & R. Petré. Lund: Acta Archaeologica Lundensia (8° series) 16

Höckmann, O., 1987. Beiträge zur Datierung des Brandgrabes mit gegossenem Bronzebecken von Winzlar, Kr. Nienburg. *Jahrbuch des Römisch-Germanischen Zentralmuseums, Mainz* 34(1), 235–59

Jockenhövel, A., 1974. Eine Bronzeamphore des 8. Jaharhunderts v. Chr. von Gevlinghausen, Kr. Meschede (Sauerland), mit Beiträgen von Hans Beck, Hans-Jürgen Hundt und Günter Lange. *Germania* 52(1), 16–53

Jockenhövel, A., 1991. Räumliche Mobilität von Personen in der mittleren Bronzezeit des westlichen Mitteleuropa. *Germania* 69(1), 49–62

Kossack, G.,1954. Pferdegeschirr aus Gräbern der älteren Hallstattzeit Bayerns. *Jahrbuch des Römisch-Germanischen Zentralmuseums, Mainz* 1, 111–78

Kristiansen, K., 1981. Economic models for Bronze Age Scandinavia — towards an integrated approach, in *Economic Archaeology*, eds A. Sheridan & G. Bailey. Oxford: British Archaeological Reports International Series S96, 239–62

Kytlicova, O., 1988. K sociálni struckture kultury popelnicových polí [zur sozialen Struktur der Urnenfelderzeit]. *Pamatky Archeologicke* 79, 342–89

Larsson, T., 1984. Multi-level exchange and cultural interaction in the Late Scandinavian Bronze Age, in *Settlement and Economy in Later Scandinavian Prehistory*, ed. K. Kristiansen. Oxford: British Archaeological Reports International Series S211, 63–83

Marazov, I., 1989. The gifts of the Odrysian kings, in *The Rogozen Treasure*, ed. A. Fol. Sofia: Publishing House of the Bulgarian Academy of Sciences

Mohen, J.-P., 1987. Marmesse, in *Trésors des Princes Celtes*, Galéries Nationales du Grand Palais 20 Octobre 1987–15 Février 1988. Paris: Edition de la Réunion des Musées Nationaux

Müller-Karpe, H., 1961. *Die Vollgriffschwerter der Urnenfelderzeit aus Bayern*, Münchner Beiträge zur Vor- und Frühgeschichte 6. Munich: Beck

Pare, C. F. E., 1987. Der Zeremonialwagen der Bronze- und Urnenfelderzeit — seine Entstehung, Form und Verbreitung, in *Vierrädige Wagen der Hallstattzeit. Untersuchungen zu Geschichte und Technik*. Mainz: Monographien des Römisch-Germanischen Zentralmuseums, 12, 189–248

Schauer, P., 1975. Die Bewaffnung des 'Adelskrieger' während der späten Bronze- und frühe Eisenzeit. *Ausgrabungen in Deutschland 1950–1975*. Mainz: Monographien des Römisch-Germanischen Zentralmuseums 1

Sørensen, M.-L., 1987. Material order and cultural classification: the role of bronze objects in the transition from Bronze Age to Iron Age in Scandinavia, in *The Archaeology of Contextual Meaning*, ed. I. Hodder. Cambridge: Cambridge University Press, 90–101

Sprockhoff, E., 1951. Pfahlbaubronzen in der Südzone des Nordischen Kreises während der jüngeren Bronzezeit. *Archaeologia Geographia, Beiträge zur vergleichenden geographisch-kartographischen Methode in der Urgeschichtsforschung* 2 (3/4), 120–8

Sprockhoff, E., 1956. *Jungbronzezeitliche Hortfunde der Südzone des Nordlichen Kreises (Periode V)*. Mainz: Römisch-Germanischen Zentralmuseum Katalog 16

Sprockhoff, E.,1957. Seddin-Serajewo. *Vjesnik za Arheologiju i Historiju Dalmatinsku* 56-9, 16–44

Thrane, H., 1984. *Europæiske Forbindelser*. Bidrag til studiet af fremmede forbindelser i Danmarks yngre broncelader (periode IV-V). Copenhagen: Nationalmuseet

Thrane, H., 1984. *Lusehoj ved Voldtofte — en sydvestfynsk storhøj fra yngre Broncealder*. Odense: Fynske Studier 13

Thrane, H., in press. Centres of wealth in northern Europe, in *Europe in the 1st Millennium BC*, eds J. Jensen & K. Kristiansen. Sheffield: University of Sheffield Department of Archaeology and Prehistory

Wüstemann, H., 1974. Zur Sozialstruktur im Seddiner Kulturgebiet. *Zeitschrft für Archäologie* 8, 67–107

15

Europe and the Mediterranean in the Bronze Age: Cores and Peripheries

Anthony Harding

The application of core-periphery models to prehistory has been fashionable for some years, but principally in periods no earlier than the Iron Age. In a Bronze Age context, Aegean-barbarian relations might seem to be a good test-bed for the appropriateness of such models. The study of links between north and south assumes that the relationship was one of inequality, with the southern states sucking in large quantities of raw materials and finished products from distant, undeveloped, peoples. An iron find of Middle Bronze Age date from Serbia is presented and discussed as an example of potential importation from the south-east. Weaponry in general serves as a good indicator of the degree of dependence or otherwise in such situations, and demonstrates a number of suggestive features. The discussion concludes that the study of regional economies is more likely to be useful and possible in the immediate future than an abstracted dependency model.

L'application à la préhistoire des modèles de type centre-périphérie a connu un grand succès pendant plusieurs années, mais n'a guère concerné que des périodes contemporaines ou postérieures à l'Age du Fer. Dans un contexte de l'Age du Bronze, les relations entre égéens et barbares paraissent constituer un bon test de référence pour évaluer la validité de tels modèles. L'étude des relations entre le nord et le sud du secteur considéré montre que ces échanges étaient déséquilibrés, les états du sud important de grandes quantités de matières premières et de produits finis des peuples éloignés et peu développés. Une trouvaille de fer datant de l'Age du Bronze Moyen, découvert en Serbie, est présentée et sa valeur comme témoinage d'importation originaire du sud-est est discutée. Dans de telles situations, l'armement constitue en général un bon indicateur des relations de dépendance ou autres, et révèle un certain nombre de caractéristiques signifiantes. Pour conclure, l'étude des économies régionales semble, pour l'avenir immédiat, plus fructueuse que l'emploi des modèles de dépendance abstraits.

Introduction

The use of core-periphery models has enjoyed a considerable vogue in recent years as a means of providing explanatory power for processes of culture change and societal development (Rowlands *et al.* 1987; Champion 1989), in spite of scepticism on the part of some authorities (Kohl 1987). Instead of relying on vague and unspecified assumptions of diffusion, it spells out clearly what processes are at work and how the interaction of communities at different levels of technological and social development produced particular effects that are reflected in the archaeological record. Many such studies have been concerned with societies at an iron-using stage, and typically involve the relations between states or proto-states on the one hand and less

developed groupings, such as tribal units, on the other, but more recently several authors have attempted to apply the model to earlier, Bronze Age, societies (e.g. Kristiansen 1987). Yet a classic case to which such models might be applied is the whole question of Aegean-barbarian interaction in the Bronze Age, which has assumed so large a role in the writings of many Bronze Age scholars over the years. In this short contribution I will look at a specific example of potential importation and consider its implications for a general model of core-periphery interaction in the Balkans in the Bronze Age.

The interaction between the Mediterranean, especially the East Mediterranean, and the world of Bronze Age Europe has been discussed so often that a consensus should surely prevail (Harding 1984; Bouzek 1985).

153

This well-worn topic has tended to revolve around the identification of the movement of goods from one area to another; the name of the game has been to spot the foreign goods. By this means a whole chapter of European prehistory has been written, going back to the early years of this century, and treated by many authorities. There is a considerable body of material, and an even greater literature surrounding these matters; but conceptually the discussion has remained firmly within a framework of economic inequalities: rich southern 'states' trading (*sic*) with poor northern ones, fed by the necessity for advanced societies with large consumer needs to suck in raw materials to satisfy the needs of their culturally sophisticated elites. So materials such as copper, gold and amber were brought in from afar to keep the craftsmen of the Mediterranean palace civilizations busy, and their patrons satisfied. It is not hard to see where this model came from, propounded as it was in the context of industrialized twentieth-century states.

By this means a study of 'links' and 'contacts' has been built up, though students of the matter have been extremely coy about what they mean by such terms. Henrik Thrane (1990) has rightly referred to the 'Mycenaean fascination' which lends the peoples of Bronze Age Greece such an appeal, and makes the finding of Mycenaean material — or Near Eastern material generally — desirable; one can see the excitement generated by the finding of East Mediterranean material in successive countries to the north and west of Greece — Albania (Andrea 1972), Sardinia (Ferrarese Ceruti 1979), and now Spain (Martín de la Cruz 1990; Podzuweit 1990). Such developments, brought about by the chances of excavation, are unpredictable, and involve no new conceptualization of the economic and social situation. For that one must turn to those few scholars who have given a lead on such matters in recent years, such as Colin Renfrew (1975) and Kristian Kristiansen (1987).

It is true that advances in dating brought about by dendrochronology mean that certainty is now possible about the timespan of many of the periods of the Bronze Age in the 'barbarian' world, so that it should be possible to see whether particular examples of interaction were actually feasible (Becker *et al.* 1985); but at the same time, the chronology of the East Mediterranean has been thrown into confusion by the controversy over the date of the Theran eruption and the relationship of the period in question to Egyptian chronology (Thera 1990). The change in attitudes that has become evident in recent years, with the widespread acceptance of the validity of radiocarbon dating even by those who used to express their doubts in the strongest terms, is remarkable, and is already leading to a gratifying degree of agreement between former adversaries about which links and synchronisms are possible, and which impossible. But in fact most archaeologists today would probably agree that questions of chronology are really secondary, and what is important is the modelling of the mechanism and effect of the interaction on the communities of the Bronze Age world.

Those who favour core-periphery models in the context of north-south trade in the Bronze Age would see European communities as peripheral to, which implies dependent on, a Greek or East Mediterranean core, though in fact published statements on this matter are more flexible than this, and Kristiansen, for instance, has allowed the possibility of regional exchange models. Such models have benefits in understanding the local situation in terms of social complexity, and in suggesting mechanisms by which goods assumed roles that differentiated and supported distinctions, for instance between different ages, sexes, social groupings and other affiliations. While this may be helpful in particular circumstances, it can hardly be the whole story, which must have been as varied as Europe itself is varied. The situation in Italy, for instance, must have been different from that in continental Europe: Italy was demonstrably in contact with Greece in the Bronze Age, and probably on the receiving end of regular voyages from the East Mediterranean, as work on metal ingots, pottery and other material shows. Such a situation is clearly quite different from that north of the Alps, or in the Balkans. There are strong grounds for seeing a special connection between Greece and south Italy/Sicily, where it is perhaps reasonable to take the view that core-periphery interactions were involved. All the indications in Sicily are that the local economy and society were strongly influenced from the east, as seen in burial form, the use of imported goods in tombs, and possibly even in settlement form. By contrast, the situation in central and northern Italy was very different; imported material is much thinner on the ground, and is not found in burials. A spin-off from the search for metals may be what determined the quantity and eventual location of imported goods in these areas.

In continental Europe and the north, too little can be said for any clear view to be formed, as far as contact with the south is concerned, since the available sources are too scanty for any systematic picture to be built up. But there is one area that should, if anywhere, represent a laboratory for such models to be tested, since it lies geographically close to Greece, and is accessible overland: the Balkan peninsula, and particularly those territories immediately adjacent to Greece: Albania, Macedonia, Bulgaria and the countries adjoining them. Imported goods in this area are in fact surprisingly scarce, consisting mainly of bronzes, some of them not canonical in Greek terms; pottery is by contrast infrequently found, which makes the extent and nature of the contact difficult to monitor and assess. There are, however, certain finds of unusual importance which illustrate well the problems we face in specifying the nature of the relationship between south and north in this period, and it is to these that I now turn.

The sword from Duškovci and its position in the Bronze Age cultures of the Balkans

The sword from Duškovci (Figs. 15.1a & 15.2) was found in a grave consisting of a stone slab construction under a tumulus in the hilly country north of Požega in western Serbia (Zotović 1985, 43, pl. 11, 1). No other objects accompanied it, according to the available indications. The sword belongs to a small group, attributable to the Middle Bronze Age (MD II in Hänsel's (1968) chronology), and found in northern Jugoslavia, Hungary and the north Alpine zone. In Croatia this type is exemplified by a piece from Vukovar (Vinski-Gasparini 1973, 31, 221, pl. 6, 9). The oval pommel-plate of the Duškovci sword, decorated with concentric arcs and dashed band, is seen not only on the piece from neighbouring Arilje (Fig. 15.1b; Zotović 1985, pl. 11, 3), but on the similar swords from Letkés grave 37,

Budapest-Zuglo and Neckenmarkt (Kemenczei 1988, pls 4 no. 41, 6 no. 61; Schauer 1971, pl. 3 no. 27a), as well as on the pommels of Au swords (Holste 1953, 9 ff., pl. 3). What really marks it off as unusual, however, is the spike attaching the pommel end to the pommel proper: this is of iron, and thus joins a highly select group of objects in continental Europe made of this material from such an early date: the dagger from Gánovce (Vlček & Hajek 1963), traces on a bronze bowl from Vel'ká Lomnica, also in Slovakia (Novotná 1963), and an iron awl from a trackway in Holland (Fig. 15.3; Casparie 1984; Charles 1984). It is certainly much earlier than other central Balkan finds (László 1977; Čović 1980). These early finds have been discussed many times (Vladár 1973, 293; Bouzek 1978; Pleiner 1980; Pleiner 1981; Furmánek 1988; Bukowski 1989), and the general opinion has been that an origin in Anatolia is to be sought. A recent discus-

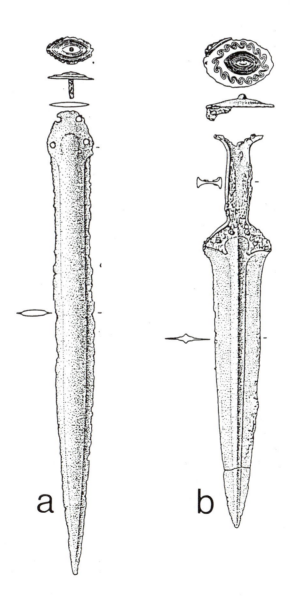

a   b

Figure 15.1. a. Sword and pommel from Duškovci, Serbia. The spike of the pommel is of iron.
b. Sword and pommel from Arilje, Serbia. Scale: 1:3

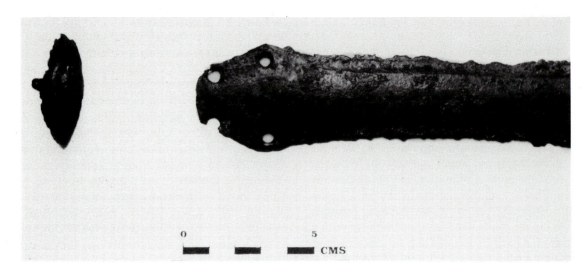

Figure 15.2. Sword and pommel from Duškovci

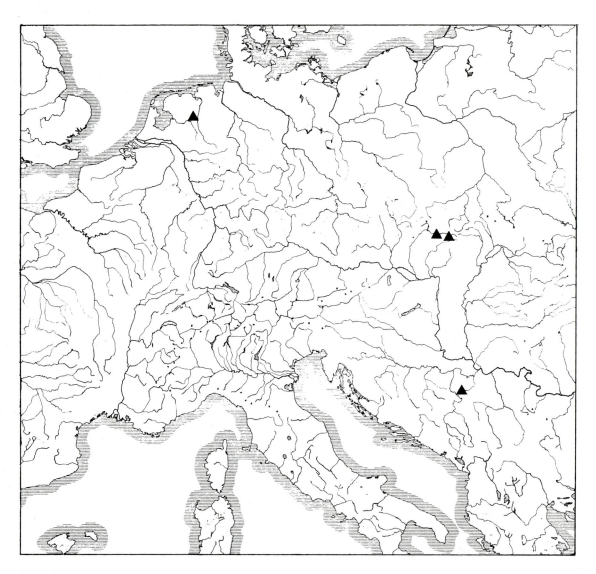

Figure 15.3. Iron finds of the Early and Middle Bronze Age in continental Europe

sion by Timothy Taylor (1989) follows the original publication in suggesting that the so-called dagger from Gánovce is in fact a knife handle, and that the iron was hardly intended to be seen, in fact used as a makeweight to make up the bronze with a cheap by-product — though how 'cheap' iron might have been at this early stage is of course open to question.

This is not the place to consider the entire question of the origins of the earliest iron-working in Europe. There is currently no reliable means of determining the real origin of the Gánovce object, either analytically or typologically. The debate turns partly on whether the technology and materials involved in these small iron objects require input from outside the area, and partly on whether one thinks that central and south-eastern Europe were dependent on the south for those elements in it that we do not properly understand. The first half of this question is not likely to be resolved quickly. Many authorities still believe that iron at such an early stage of the Bronze Age must have come from Anatolia (Waldbaum 1980 for a convenient survey of the Near Eastern evidence), although as is now well-known an attribution of a monopoly of iron-working to the Hittites is misplaced. It is perhaps time for a complete review of the technological reasons why such importation of skills and materials is really necessary; certainly many archaeologists find the notion of an Anatolian derivation for early European iron implausible. In the absence of such a discussion, we can only assign the Duškovci piece to the small but growing number of such objects for which no specific explanation can currently be found.

The importance of weaponry

The only category of material of Greek type which is regularly found north of the Greek border is that of weaponry, principally swords (see Harding 1984, ch. 6 for discussion). Such a situation has obvious implications for the role of artefacts in warrior-dominated societies. A number of interrelated factors may be discerned in this general pattern (cf. Harding 1992). There are a number of instances of southern types going north, notably in Albania, Macedonia, Kosovo and Bulgaria, with mutations on the basic form being common, apparently evidence of local imitation of southern models. Equally, in the Late Bronze Age northern types go south (Catling 1956). What is very striking, however, is that in this collection of material from the Aegean area most types found in the Balkans do *not* occur in the south; those that are found are on the whole much closer to Italian types than Balkan. Solid-hilted swords (*Vollgriffschwerter*), for example, do not penetrate further south than the Danube-Sava corridor, save for one or two doubtful exceptions (such as the piece alleged to come from Pella: Hachmann 1957, 216 no. 596, pl. 60, 2). Coupled with this one may note the great variability in time and space in

weapon deposition – and therefore presumably production — in the whole Balkan area. There is a huge concentration on the Sava-Danube area, and a dominance of finds of the early Urnfield period, equivalent to Hallstatt A1. But of course the same can be said for metal finds generally, especially hoards, so that one cannot necessarily read into this any special significance for weaponry. What is clearly important is the context of deposition, which where hoards are involved may be far from the context of creation and use. Without this information our attempts at understanding the significance of 'foreign' objects are likely to fail.

If the study of long-distance trade depends on the satisfactory identification and characterization of the materials and artefacts involved, and is not yet developed as fully as we need in order to make the sort of statements about the past that we would like, the study of short-distance movement of goods is in many cases much easier to spot. An interesting study by Albrecht Jockenhövel (1991) documented the occurrence of ornament types in female graves between Lower Saxony and Alsace in the Middle Bronze Age, producing convincing arguments to suggest that each type has a 'core area', with a 'periphery' to which it could also penetrate; the peripheral areas overlap with their neighbours, and the phenomenon is interpreted as representing the movement of women in marriage between neighbouring cultural groups. The idea has been extended to encompass also the movement of male goods, but here the underlying conceptualization has not so far been explored (Wels-Weyrauch 1989). The movement of goods, notably bronze goods, is not in doubt; what is needed is a robust methodology for explaining such movements in social and economic terms.

Cores and peripheries

The debate over the significance of the movement of goods is a well-known one, and takes us back to the whole question of the relationship between parts of so-called barbarian Europe and the developed civilizations of the east Mediterranean and the Near East in the Bronze Age. There is still a big divergence of opinion between those who see the main technological developments in the north as being inspired by the south, and those who are sceptical or pessimistic about such possibilities and seek independent confirmation of external origin before accepting other than a local, or relatively local, derivation for particular groups of objects. In their extreme form, such views can lead to a damaging polarization. The main classes of evidence that affect the argument are well-known and will not be reviewed here. For the central and northern Balkans there is no certain evidence of importation from the Aegean area: the most northerly claimed Aegean sherds are those from Debelo Brdo near Sarajevo (Sakellarakis & Marić 1975), while the bronze rapiers of Romania, whether or not they reflect the traditions of Aegean swordsmithing, are certainly not Aegean productions (but for new evidence see Wanczek 1991). The evidence of faience beads, though at first glance seductive, was long ago shown to reflect the adoption of specific technologies rather than actual importation of objects. The most enduring material that is taken as evidence of Aegean influence is that involving decorative motifs, principally spiral-based. Some of these objects do, of course, seem in their syntax very close to Aegean designs, and despite all current uncertainties about Aegean chronology cannot be very far apart in time. The usual explanation for these objects signally fails, however, to provide any kind of convincing context for the transfer of such artistic ideas.

In the traditional model used to describe and explain the central and northern Balkans in the Bronze Age, the influence of the civilized south has been seen as percolating down to more distant regions through some kind of contact, probably commercial. Especially in the case of the faience beads, a distribution of trade goods down some kind of exchange line has often been assumed, the nature and directness of that line varying with the scholar making the assumption. The diffusion of goods was perhaps accompanied by a diffusion of technologies, but the important conceptual point was that the starting-point for both was the advanced, civilized world of the south. Little attention was paid to the effects of such influence or importation on the societies who received them. Indeed, little attention was focused on social reconstruction in the barbarian world at all. The whole argument was seen in terms of economic advantage, in the assumption that 'economizing' behaviour occupied a paramount place then as now.

The core-periphery model which has become fashionable implies that the peripheral region is dependent on the core, and that from this a model of social and economic relations can be constructed. While this may well be a satisfactory way of representing intergroup relationships in many arenas of world history, there is no particular reason why it should be imposed on all situations regardless of the actual configuration of evidence on the ground. The original development of World Systems Theory by Wallerstein was done in the context of the early modern world, specifically to understand the origins and present-day dominance of the modern capitalist state. Some have suggested that the ideas involved could profitably be applied to earlier situations, going as far back as the pre-Roman Iron Age; the rapid development of society and economy in that period could plausibly be related to the growing dominance of Rome as a major economic influence, though already in this Iron Age context there are some signs that the dependency model does not always fit as naturally as one might like. When one goes still further back in time, to the Bronze Age, much will depend on the area where one is working. In the rich cultures of the Near East, where economic life was highly visible and large volumes of material

were exchanged on a local or not-so-local basis, the possibilities of applying dependency theory are perhaps considerable, though Kohl (1987) is just one author who has expressed reservations about this. But when one moves to *terra incognita* in the form of 'barbarian' Europe, the scope for doing more than speculate is extremely limited.

What *is* possible is to show that there were centres — cores, if you prefer — that served as major production and distribution zones for the industrial products of the Bronze Age world, and that around these centres were areas — peripheries — that for the most part drew on the centres for their industrial needs. But were they dependent on them? Were they politically involved with them? Of the many types of evidence that do not survive, the lack of subsistence goods is crucial in this respect. Although palaeobotany has made great strides forward in understanding the processes and choices of the later prehistoric farmer, it is not yet possible to demonstrate convincingly that foodstuffs were moved from one area to another. My own instinct would be to doubt that such movement was likely, even if it was possible, except on a strictly limited scale and over limited distances, to enable specialized communities to fulfil their function effectively within a tribally organized landscape. It is to be hoped that new methods of provenience testing will be able to help with such problems.

On such an analysis, Bronze Age Europe would have consisted of a series of core zones, the extent and nature of which would have varied, and about which we need to accumulate a lot more information. Areas such as the Hungarian plain, or Denmark — both of them notable for the extent and excellence of their metal production — were clearly capable of acquiring significant amounts of raw metal from outside their immediate vicinity, and of supplying relatively distant regions with finished high-quality artefacts. As discussed above, it is hard on the available evidence to see that such local centres were dependent on still richer cores around Mediterranean shores.

Rather than put all our eggs in the core-periphery basket, we might equally well develop the study of regional systems, for instance of local settlement patterns and local economies. Already there are parts of Europe where such patterns are starting to emerge with great clarity. This is the case in Switzerland, for example, or in areas dominated by tells, where we may note for instance the pioneering excavations of Hänsel at Feudvar in the Vojvodina (Hänsel 1991). With the range of techniques now available to the field and laboratory archaeologist, the tasks at hand are enormous, and the opportunities for understanding Bronze Age lifeways exciting. Since rich Bronze Age sites in most parts of Europe have not yet benefited from a full treatment using modern techniques, there seems to be ample scope for extending our knowledge of these regional systems.

References

Andrea, Zh., 1972. Kultura e timave të pellgut të Korcës dhe vendi i saj në Ballkanin juglindor. *Studime Historike* 26 (4), 81–105

Becker, B., Billamboz, A., Egger, H., Gassmann, P., Orcel, A., Orcel, Chr. & Ruoff, U., 1985. *Dendrochronologie in der Ur- und Frühgeschichte. Die absolute Datierung von Pfahlbausiedlungen nördlich der Alpen im Jahrringkalender Mitteleuropas*. Basel: Verlag Schweizerische Gesellschaft für Ur- und Frühgeschichte

Bouzek, J., 1978. Die Anfänge der Eisenzeit in Mitteleuropa. *Zeitschift für Archäologie* 12, 9–14

Bouzek, J., 1985. *The Aegean, Anatolia and Europe: Cultural Interrelations in the Second Millennium BC*. Prague: Academia/Göteborg: Åström

Bukowski, Z., 1989. Bemerkungen zur Problematik des frühen Eisens in Mittel- und Nordeuropa (Inga Serning in Memoriam). *Kungl. Vitterhets Historie och Antikvitets Akademiens Konferenser* 22, 115–41

Casparie, W.A., 1984. The three Bronze Age footpaths XVI (Bou), XVII (Bou) and XVIII (Bou) in the raised bog of Southeast Drenthe (the Netherlands). *Palaeohistoria* 26, 41–94

Catling, H.W., 1956. Bronze cut-and-thrust swords in the East Mediterranean. *Proceedings of the Prehistoric Society* 22, 1–26

Champion, T.C. (ed.), 1989. *Centre and Periphery: Comparative Studies in Archaeology*. London: Unwin Hyman

Charles, J.A., 1984. The Middle Bronze Age iron punch of Southeast Drenthe. *Palaeohistoria* 26, 95–9

Čović, 1980. Počeci metalurgije željeza na sjeverozapadnom Balkanu. *Godisnjak (Sarajevo)* 18, 63–79

Ferrarese Ceruti, M.L., 1979. Ceramica micenea in Sardegna (notizia preliminare). *Rivista di Scienze Preistoriche* 34, 243–53

Furmánek, V., 1988. Eisen während der Bronzezeit in der Slowakei. *Zeitschift für Archäologie* 23, 183–9

Hachmann, R., 1957. *Die frühe Bronzezeit im westlichen Ostseegebiet und ihre mittel- und südosteuropäischen Beziehungen*. Beihefte zum Atlas der Urgeschichte, Band 6. Hamburg: Kartographisches Institut, Flemmings Verlag

Hänsel, B., 1968. *Beiträge zur Chronologie der mittleren Bronzezeit im Karpatenbecken*. Bonn: Habelt

Hänsel, B. & Medović, P., 1991. Vorbericht über die jugoslawisch-deutschen Ausgrabungen in der Siedlung von Feudvar bei Mošorin (Gem. Titel, Vojvodina) von 1986–1990. *Bericht der Römisch-Germanischen Kommission* 72, 45–204

Harding, A.F., 1984. *The Mycenaeans and Europe*. London: Academic Press

Harding, A.F., 1992. Late Bronze Age swords between Alps and Aegean. in *Festschrift zum 50 jährigen Bestehen des Institutes für Ur- und Frühgeschichte der Leopold-Franzens-Universität Innsbruck* (Universitätsforschungen zur prähistorischen Archäologie, Band 8). Bonn: Habelt, 207–14

Holste, F., 1953. *Die bronzezeitlichen Vollgriffschwerter Bayerns*. Munich: Beck

Jockenhövel, A., 1991. Räumliche Mobilität von Personen in der mittleren Bronzezeit des westlichen Mitteleuropa. *Germania* 69, 49–62

Kemenczei, T., 1988. *Die Schwerter in Ungarn, I (Griffplatten-, Griffangel- und Griffzungenschwerter)*. Prähistorische Bronzefunde, Abt. IV, 6. Munich: Beck

Kohl, P.L., 1987. The Use and Abuse of World Systems Theory: The Case of the Pristine West Asian State. *Advances in Archaeological Method and Theory* 11, 1–35

Kristiansen, K., 1987. Center and periphery in Bronze Age Scandinavia, in *Centre and Periphery in the Ancient World*, eds M. Rowlands, M. Larsen & K. Kristiansen. Cambridge: Cambridge University Press, 74–86

László, A., 1977. Anfänge der Benützung und der Bearbeitung des Eisens auf dem Gebiete Rumäniens. *Acta Archaeologica Academiae Scientiarum Hungaricae* 29, 53–75

Martín de la Cruz, J.C., 1990. Die erste mykenische Keramik von der iberischen Halbinsel. *Prähistorische Zeitschrift* 65, 49–52

Novotná, M., 1963. Nález najstarší bronzovej nádoby na Slovensku. *Sborník Ceskoslovenské Spolecnosti Archeologické* 3, 137–40

Pleiner, R., 1980. Early iron metallurgy in Europe, in *The Coming of the Age of Iron*, eds T.A. Wertime & J.D. Muhly. New Haven & London: Yale University Press, 375–416

Pleiner, R., 1981. Die Wege des Eisens nach Europa, in *Frühes Eisen in Europa. Festschrift Walter Ulrich Guyan zu seinem 70. Geburtstag*, ed. R. Pleiner. Schaffhausen: Verlag Peter Meili, 115–28

Podzuweit, Chr., 1990. Bemerkungen zur mykenischen Keramik von Llanete de los Moros, Montoro, Prov. Córdoba. *Prähistorische Zeitschrift* 65, 53–8

Renfrew, C., 1975. Trade as action at a distance: questions of integration and communication, in *Ancient Civilization and Trade*, eds J.A. Sabloff & C.C. Lamberg-Karlovsky. Albuquerque: University of New Mexico Press, 1–60

Rowlands, M., Larsen, M. & Kristiansen, K., eds. 1987. *Centre and Periphery in the Ancient World*. Cambridge: Cambridge University Press

Sakellarakis, J.A. & Marić, Z., 1975. Zwei Fragmente mykenischer Keramik von Debelo Brdo in Sarajevo. *Germania* 53, 153–6

Schauer, P., 1971. *Die Schwerter in Süddeutschland, Österreich und der Schweiz I. Griffplatten-, Griffangel- und Griffzungenschwerter*. Prähistorische Bronzefunde, Abt. VI, 2. Munich: Beck

Taylor, T., 1989. Iron and Iron Age in the Carpatho-Balkan region: aspects of social and technological change 1700–1400 BC, in *The Bronze Age-Iron Age Transition in Europe. Aspects of Continuity and Change in European Societies c. 1200 to 500 BC*, eds M.L. Stig Sørensen & R. Thomas. Oxford: British Archaeological Reports, International Series S483 (i), 68–92

Thera 1990. *Thera and the Aegean World, III: Chronology. Proceedings of the Third International Congress, Santorini, Greece, 3–9 September 1989*, ed. D.A. Hardy with A.C. Renfrew. London: Thera Foundation

Thrane, H., 1990. The Mycenaean fascination: a northerner's view, in *Orientalisch-Ägäische Einflüsse in der europäischen Bronzezeit. Ergebnisse eines Kolloquiums* (Römisch-Germanisches Zentralmuseum, Monographien Band 15). Bonn: Habelt, 165–79

Vinski-Gasparini, K., 1973. *Kultura polja sa žarama u sjevernoj Hrvatskoj*. Zadar: Filozofski Fakultet (University of Zadar)

Vladár, J., 1973. Osteuropäische und mediterrane Einflüsse im Gebiet der Slowakei während der Bronzezeit. *Slovenská Archeológia* 21, 253–357

Vlček, E. & Hajek, L., 1963. A ritual well and the find of an Early Bronze Age iron dagger at Gánovce near Poprad

(Czechoslovakia), in Genovés, S. (ed.) *Estudios a Pedro Bosch-Gimpera*. Mexico City: Instituto Nacional de Antropología e Historia, 427–42

Waldbaum, J.C., 1980. The first archaeological appearance of iron and the transition to the Iron Age, in *The Coming of the Age of Iron*, eds T.A. Wertime & J.D. Muhly. New Haven & London: Yale University Press, 69–98

Wanczek, B., 1991. Ein Gussmodel für einen Dolch mykenischen Typs von der unteren Donau. *Zeitschrift für Archäologie* 25, 1–28

Wels-Weyrauch, U., 1989. 'Fremder Mann'. *Germania* 67, 162–7

Zotović, M., 1985. *Arheološki i etnički problemi bronzanog i gvozdenog doba zapadne Srbije*. Dissertationes et Monographiae, XXVI. Belgrade: Savez Arheološki Društava Jugoslavije

Displacement and Exchange in Archaeological Methodology

Stuart Needham

This paper advocates a new, archaeologically specific methodology for interpreting exchange and other forms of material movement. It is suggested that when working with purely archaeological evidence any observed spatial effects be referred to collectively as displacement; *exchange will only account for some of these displacements. Other 'effects' of exchange are briefly discussed – temporal distance and social distance – only the former being discernible in archaeological data at a primary level. It is argued that the integration of exchange systems and social institutions means that they do not give independent support, one for the interpretation of the other. There are many individual expressions of these social sub-complexes and their interpretation needs to be drawn out in parallel. The pitfalls of dealing with distribution plots are restated and it is suggested that these be considered as* maps of recovery *to give adequate justice to the effects of underlying taphonomic processes. It is further argued that views on the life-cycles of objects and thereby the materials value systems of social groups need to be built up as a basis for interpretation. Only then might simulation studies, ethnographic analogues or hypothetical exchange systems be usefully invoked to explain the given patterning.*

Cet article recommande une méthodologie nouvelle et spécifique à l'archéologie pour l'interprétation des échanges et d'autres formes de transportation des materiels. L'auteur propose que, lorsque l'on a à faire à des données purement archéologiques, tout effet spatial soit dit collectivement déplacement; *il n'y a que quelques-uns de ces effets qui seront dus aux échanges. D'autres 'effets' des échanges sont considérés brièvement – la distance temporelle et la distance sociale, dont on ne distingue que la première dans les données archéologiques à un niveau primaire. L'auteur soutient que les systèmes d'échange et les institutions sociales sont trop intégrées pour que les uns puissent renforcer indépendamment l'interprétation des autres. Les expressions individuelles de ces sous-complexes sociaux sont multiples et il faut les interpréter en parallèle. Les problèmes qui attendent l'interprétation des cartes de répartition sont réitérés, et l'on propose qu'elles soient considérées comme* cartes de récupération *pour faire ressortir les effets des processus taphonomiques qui les ont produites. On soutient aussi qu'il faut développer nos idées sur les cycles d'utilisation des objets et par là sur les systèmes de valeur des matériaux des groupes sociaux. Ce n'est qu'alors qu'il serait utile d'invoquer les études de simulation, les analogues ethnographiques ou les systèmes d'échange hypothétiques pour expliquer une telle conformation de trouvailles.*

Introduction

Of all the major lines of enquiry into the behaviour of humankind, the issue of trade and exchange is superficially one of the most easy to describe, but in reality one of the most difficult to comprehend. In archaeology actions have to be inferred from their resultant residues – a fundamental limitation felt especially acutely for societies lacking written records. There is, however, a variable distance, seen both spatially and temporally, between any activity which might be of interest to us and the discard or loss which leads to archaeological residues. For many aspects of behaviour this distance may be relatively limited. This is particularly true, for example, in the spheres of production and construction, where the resultant residues may enter the archaeological record almost instantaneously. It is even true, somewhat surprisingly, of much in the realm of spiritual beliefs, where particular decisions or acts of veneration led to new monumental components or the

burial of special offerings. This does not of course
mean that it is any easier to infer the nature of the
beliefs held, but at least what we document archaeologically bears close spatial and temporal testimony to
some of the actions of interest. For exchange between
human groups (overlooking for present purposes exchange with the spiritual world) there is rarely any
proximity between the action and archaeological
residues, because exchange is, self-evidently, something that takes place wholly in the sphere of circulation, or the 'use life-cycle' of objects (Fig. 16.3; Earle
& Ericson 1977, 10). Exceptions will tend to be losses
in transit, which will often be close in time, though not
necessarily close in space, to an act of exchange. To
identify losses in transit is effectively impossible except
in the case of certain particular contexts such as shipwrecks, whose cargoes would be 'close' to an exchange
transaction.

With careful study the relevant material residues can
tell us much about the *occurrence* of exchange or, at
least, of transmission. But this is virtually a universal
phenomenon amongst human groups and merely to
chart it is of limited interest. It is the nature and
conduct of the actions responsible which really add
colour to our characterisation of past societies (Plog
1977, 133). We wish to know the perceived reasons for
exchange: *inter alia* its frequency and direction, its
social status, the benefits accrued, the bonds made or
the antagonisms created. To add this colour requires
considerable speculation and at the very least depends
on careful reading of an always distorted archaeological record.

To put the concerns of this paper into context it is
helpful to list the main themes that pervade the wealth
of existing literature on trade and exchange.

1) *Recognition and sourcing*: The isolation of intrusive goods and the identification of areas of origin,
   using morphological or physical characterisation.
   In many cases only the first stage is achieved, i.e.
   the recognition that objects or materials are locally
   anomalous in form or unavailable in material.
2) *The remit*: Consideration of what actions should be
   considered under the 'trade and exchange' heading
   (e.g. war and conflict, tribute, barter, gift exchange, itinerant craftspeople, population movements, dowries). These are component actions
   which may or may not be readily defined in isolation from the composite system (see 5).
3) *Modelling distribution*: Using mathematical means
   to model the dispersal of material from a source or
   sources given certain underlying premises (which
   aim to simulate certain mechanisms and constraints).
   These are notionally concerned with distribution
   within the systemic sphere.
4) *Taphonomy*: Assessing the combined formation
   processes affecting the assemblage at different stages
   – at burial or discard, preservation in the ground

and recovery from it. Strictly speaking 'recovery'
lies outside the definition of 'taphonomy'. However, they are treated together here as part of a
continuum of potential change from the living
assemblage through to the observable assemblage.
These equate to steps 1–4 in Clarke's hierarchy of
archaeological theory (1973, 16). Through appropriate analysis we are able to discern potential bias
in the representation of assemblages.
5) *Social context*: Consideration of the range of possible social contexts for exchange, both theoretical
   and archaeologically inferred. This may lead to
   classifications of exchange systems in relation to
   socio-economic structures in general. This theme
   builds on theme 2 by investigating how the different categories of exchange and movement were
   embodied in the particular system.

Theme 1, recognition and sourcing, underpins the
whole subject and will be taken for granted for the
purposes of this paper.

Something needs to be said about theme 2, the remit,
although it is well covered in previous literature (e.g.
Olausson 1988). Working from archaeological evidence, as opposed to historical or ethnographic evidence, we have little choice but to cast a wide net in our
consideration of this subject. Exchange, in the broad
sense of any transfer of material goods or people
between human groups or individuals, can only be
inferred from archaeological data. The indispensable
evidence for interpreting exchange in any purely archaeological approach has to be the recognition of
intrusive goods or influences. However, we know full
well that goods and people may change location for a
wide variety of reasons (e.g. those cited above and
others) some of which do not involve the goods changing hands. It is clear then that archaeology needs a
catch-all term relating directly to the evidence that we
are capable of documenting, evidence that will be
susceptible to a variety of explanations. What we may
observe archaeologically is the *displacement* of goods
in either a spatial or temporal dimension. The term
displacement should be understood to lack any precon-
ception of the *means* of transmission from one locus to
another, or one time-bracket to another, allowing us
simply to state the case that gross movement is detectable and definable. This is an important neutral stance
in a discipline which should be concerned at base level
with empirical approaches. *Displacement* thus admits
all possible means of transmission and will serve as a
base-level interpretation in cases where inadequate
evidence exists to encourage more specific interpretations. As more evidence is garnered, it could in this
way become a matter of unfettered debate as to how we
might best explain a particular series of displacements.

'Exchange' on the other hand is best regarded as
accounting for only a subset of the total occurrence of
displacement. It should be recognised at this point that

exchange, as an actual process in society, will not necessarily be identifiable as displacement (i.e. as an archaeologically detectable phenomenon; cf. Stjernquist 1967; Welinder 1988, 42). This does then mean that the totality of changed circumstances resulting from exchange transactions is not 'displacement' *per se*; instead a variable proportion will come to be manifest in the archaeological record and form part of the accumulated record of displaced material (Fig. 16.1). The transfer of goods between different persons is described as an *exchange transaction*, while the changed circumstances of any kind resulting from such transactions might collectively be termed *exchange effects*. When, therefore, discussion is proceeding in an interpretative or hypothetical mode (i.e. dealing with the systemic sphere), we can attempt to evaluate the relative balance between different exchange effects within the given system.

Exchange effects refer to any change of circumstances of an exchanged object considered to be important for understanding a system. At a very basic level there is a change of ownership, custody or responsibility. Beyond that we are interested in whether that change accompanies a shift in social status or the crossing of an ethnic divide. Such differences may create a *social distance* between stages of an object's life-cycle. It is now fairly well understood in archaeological thinking that the passage of exchanged goods through different social groups may often be accompanied by changing perceptions of them. Different societies frequently attach very different symbolic and functional values to the same objects, a point amply attested in ethnography. Differences will have resulted from such things as aesthetic taste, rarity, perceived foreign-ness, the exchange hierarchy involved, and religious connotations, not to mention locally specific functional requirements. In time the exchange transaction, or transactions, might result in dislocation in space and we might attempt to measure the aggregate *spatial distance* of remove. Although spatial distance is the exchange effect most readily seen in archaeological evidence, its significance is not necessarily straightforward, as was pointed out by Ericson (1977, 110, 118–20). Time itself is, of course, another important parameter which, in a given situation, exerts some limitations over the range of other effects. But we can also view this the other way round and see *temporal distance* as another effect of the trajectory experienced by objects in the given social system. While temporal distance can on occasion be discerned from the appearance of material in contexts dated later than accepted currency, little attention has been paid to this as a phenomenon. Current interpretations are prone to be heavily dependent on the duration of the deduced time interval. This relationship deserves future scrutiny.

The main value of theme 3, modelling distribution, is to show how different kinds of density distributions through space would result from different preconditions. Whether the mathematical preconditions set in such studies can be transplanted closely into real social situations, and whether taphonomic factors (theme 4) can ever be sufficiently countered to inspire confidence in any pattern matching is extremely doubtful at anything other than a rather general level (e.g. recognition, without further qualification, of a 'fall-off' pattern). Others have expressed doubts about the practical application of such models (e.g. Welinder 1988, 41–2). Simulation is an exercise which should be used to illustrate possibilities and will only exceptionally be capable of providing explanation for specific archaeological observations.

Theme 4, taphonomy, is as fundamental as theme 1 and although it has been paid much attention in the literature, serious attempts to demonstrate that archaeological data is representative or alternatively to identify distortion factors are still far too infrequent in archaeological practice. Some theoretical aspects of the taphonomic processes involved are dealt with below.

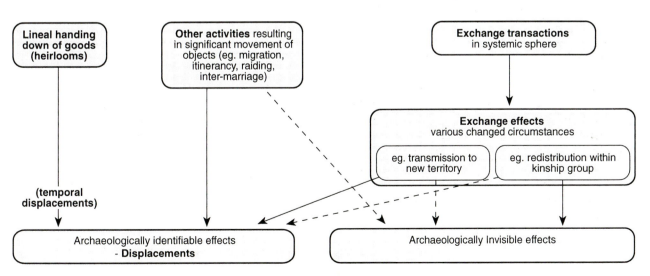

Figure 16.1. The relationship between exchange and displacement.

The importance of theme 5, social context, lies in the now generally acknowledged 'embeddedness' of exchange mechanisms within social fabric (e.g. Renfrew 1975, 6). Inevitably it draws extensively on ethnographic analogy – both historical and contemporary – to illustrate the full diversity, and it is thus laden with the implicit dangers of such analogy. What does consistently emerge from consideration of this relationship, however, is that decisions regarding exchange are often irrational (in our terms) and highly dependent on local social conditions (e.g. Callmer 1977, 178; Mauss 1970; Earle & Ericson 1977).

The embeddedness of exchange actually presents a potential problem – a vicious circle in interpretation. On the one hand, we acknowledge that exchange systems are fundamental to our reconstruction of social structure and this can encourage the situation where the interpretation of the latter is strongly influenced by that of the former. In turn, however, on the basis of a particular social interpretation there is often a tendency to assert a particular model of exchange. Such circular argument exposes the fallacy of treating the two aspects of social reconstruction discretely, indeed it can be read as confirmation of current thinking regarding the integration of production/distribution systems and social structure. To say that these two aspects are integrated, or even to a degree interdependent, does not mean that the state of one can be read off through knowledge of the other. We are interested in the workings of specific cultural systems, both exchange mechanisms and social structure being essential to definition of the composite whole. This does not mean to say, however, that only a few particular combinations are possible in the real world of social relations, even if it be acknowledged that some combinations would be incompatible because of the absence of essential institutions. It is suggested, then, that we should avoid using social structure as an independent justification for the mechanics of exchange, and *vice versa*. It is necessary that both are grounded in detailed consideration of the primary data (archaeological contexts) and they should ideally converge towards a unified interpretation of the socio-economic system.

Maps of recovery, traps and lacunae

To recognise the most appropriate approach in principle does not necessarily pave an easy path. Archaeology provides few basic aspects for categorization when dealing with individual finds: the geographical location of findspots, their topographic situations, their direct and indirect associations – both artefactual and structural. Distribution maps have always been a focus of attention for studies of exchange, but their utility has been increasingly questioned (e.g. Olausson 1988). To illustrate the danger of misinterpretation consider those situations where concentrations of widely disseminated materials occur at some remove from the source area.

These can all too readily be accepted as the end products of a planned set of movements (e.g. directed trade), or as evidence for central places. To help explore alternative explanations for such concentrations it may be useful to conceptualise them as *traps*. These are traps which hold material through both the systemic network and the archaeological formation process. They result from the conjunction of three basic conditions:

1) the ability and wish of a society to draw displaced goods inward,
2) a more restricted re-distribution outward leaving a net surplus, and
3) circumstances that led to deposition in contexts that are well preserved and liable to modern detection.

It follows from these conditions that many societies or regions successful in procuring transmitted items will nevertheless not be represented by traps, whilst on the other hand many traps are likely to represent exaggerated representations of any original imbalance in wealth or power.

Traps of variable strength are effectively what we focus on when we consider the geographical plots that we have come to call 'distribution maps'. This has always been an unfortunate term since 'distribution' has a dynamic dimension and implies process, whereas the maps we so earnestly study are representations of accreted static information with any time dimension variably conflated. We have actually drawn the particular usage of distribution from geographical studies on the spatial ranges of plants, animals, natural or manmade features in the landscape. Given the preconditions outlined above, we would do better to think of this manner of presenting archaeological information in a more explicitly objective way. They are in fact *maps of recovery*, 'recovery' here in the sense of recovery into the realm of archaeological documentation (rather than just the initial retrieval of an object from the soil).

Taking this further, the geographical patterning of the given finds should no longer be described as a distribution pattern. Although there may be virtual ignorance of the extent of spatial displacement of the individuals making up the data-set, it is still acceptable to refer to a *displacement pattern* since collectively the locations of those individuals are almost inevitably the product of a series of displacements. 'Distribution' can then be introduced in discussion of the way that displacement took place in the given social setting.

Taking the conditions set out above, we can draw up hypothetical situations to illustrate contrasting social strategies regarding circulation and deposition, and their effects on the archaeological record, both that present in the ground and that recovered from it. Fig. 16.2 takes the simple case where two social groups actually procure a foreign material at a similar rate which is, furthermore, retained in local circulation to a comparable

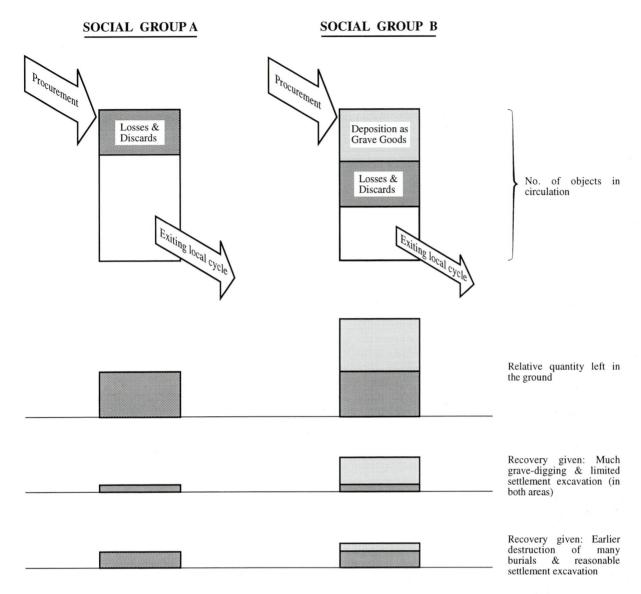

Figure 16.2. Hypothetical example of the effects of different materials value systems and different recovery factors on representation in the map of recovery.

degree. However, very different deposition strategies are assumed: in the one case (social group B) less than half of the objects in the given material are selected for deposition as grave goods, in the other no deliberate permanent deposition takes place. Losses and discards from the local system have been set at a similar, modest rate for the two groups. This means that a much higher proportion of the material was ultimately exiting group A than group B, either being transmitted on to other societies or being recycled locally to the point where its origin was obscured. From this construction it is quickly evident that there is already a marked imbalance in the quantity of identifiable finds in the ground. Furthermore, the potential for retrieval is very different so that in the event of a concerted grave-digging campaign finds from group B would come into prominence. On the other hand, if early agriculture had resulted in the destruction of burial deposits, there would be less likelihood of

preferential retrieval. Where good preservation allowed the in-ground disparity to be maintained through to modern times, then systematic fieldwork might well help redress imbalances to some extent by locating losses and discards in areas of high human activity (notably settlement). This process would itself depend on the extent to which the foreign type in question was still recognisable as such. For example, fragmentation and abrasion might prevent recognition of many examples. The main point, however, is that, even with equal survival and equal rates of retrieval of deposited material, group A will be in danger of appearing as a subsidiary 'distribution' when compared to a high-consuming society such as group B. This emphasises Stjernquist's point that blank areas do not necessarily mean that the given objects did not occur there (1967, 17).

Obviously many variant specifications could be set in this exercise and in reality they would often be more

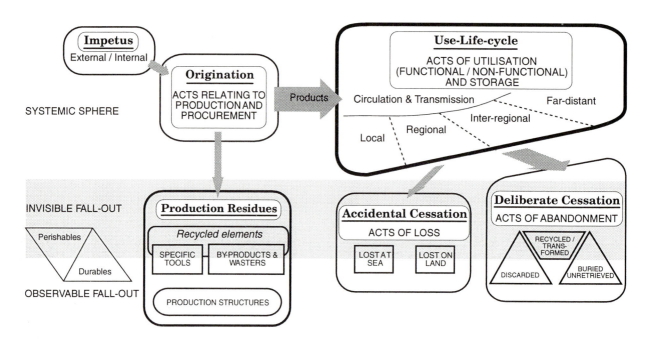

Figure 16.3. Main elements in the life-cycle of objects and the character of 'fall-out' into archaeological contexts, both observable and invisible. (NB There may be stages of exchange/transmission between raw material procurement and artefact production; for simplicity this distinction is not shown here).

complicated. This only goes to emphasise that density differences apparent in *maps of recovery* could result from a wide range of factors without necessarily equating with different quantities in circulation in antiquity, which is what is most often assumed.

It is clear from the foregoing that we need more often to question the lacunae in *maps of recovery*. Generally speaking lacunae will result from one of four situations, the first three relating to the systemic sphere, the fourth, to recovery factors:

a) The non-availability of a type in the territory concerned, all examples having been effectively 'consumed' (deposition, loss, recycling) before reaching it.

b) A genuine cultural 'resistance' to a type circulating in neighbouring territories; this may be of particular relevance when functionally complementary types are involved.

c) The type came to circulate in the territory, but was subject to a life-cycle that did not result in its entering the archaeological record.

d) The type not only circulated in the given territory, but also, in part, passed out into archaeological contexts; problems relating to survival in the ground and retrieval from it militate preferentially against representation in the map of recovery.

Life-cycles and materials value systems

The difficulties outlined above derive directly from the fact that life-cycles of objects are effectively hidden from our view. A life-cycle takes place between the

acts of production (or extraction) and deposition (Fig. 16.3); these two points, or 'nodes', alone being capable of archaeological definition, account for the set of data in a 'map of recovery'. Yet it is life-cycles that are the key to the definition of exchange and other forms of transmission, in order to get beyond mere recognition of displacement.

Few workers have acknowledged the importance of the histories of individual objects before they were consigned to the earth. These invisible stages of use and circulation contain, of course, the very acts of exchange which absorb us in social reconstruction. This invisibility even applies to the initial transfer to new hands, since we do not know and can only deduce at what distance (spatially, temporally, socially) that transfer occurs from the production locus.

There are various other ways in which exchange may be rendered invisible archaeologically, or left severely under-represented: the problem of perishables (i.e. many organics, including foods and people) is the most obvious one, and has received attention recently from Olausson (1988). She also reminds us that in some systems spatial dislocation can be negated in the course of multiple exchanges (Olausson 1988,19), so that the number of clearly displaced items might understate the amount of exchange activity. Less attention has been focused on recyclability, which is a vital issue with regard to certain materials, notably metals, where total conversion can take place, but also lithics where periodic reduction to maximise utility from a scarce resource can proceed to a point where original forms become difficult or impossible to reconstruct. In either case, of course, material composition may help to a degree in isolating intrusions into the local system, but may still leave obscure the character and extent of the intrusion.

Notwithstanding these invisible elements, there is a complex of pathways by which objects found their way ultimately into archaeological contexts. When an object had a life-cycle involving a number of exchanges, its passage would rarely have been pre-ordained; neither, however, was it completely haphazard in the sense that its pathway would have been intermittently restructured by the social relations it encountered down the line. In such situations and assuming some geographical distancing took place, people at the end of the chain of exchanges would have had at best a hazy, folklore-ish notion of the original source, based on transmitted and doubtless distorted oral information. It may also have been possible for certain information to be conveyed in symbolic form (Wright & Zeder 1977, 234), though with a clear danger of misinterpretation. Renfrew (1975, 53) has addressed the importance of information flow accompanying exchange. At the very least this is crucial when it comes to assessing the acquisition of know-how in a new region, since know-how cannot be transmitted by simple exchange of artefacts, nor in the course of passing acquaintanceship (Larsson 1988, 30).

If the greater part of any life-cycle is elusive, to obtain any small inkling of what was happening to material during this period we need to 'read' backwards from abandonment contexts and forwards from production loci. We may find some useful clues in study of the condition of deposited objects, but this will need to be considered in conjunction with context and geography. Important aspects of condition will be wear and damage, evidence for re-use or disuse; those of contexts are quantity and spread of the associated group, content range, functional connotations, etc.

Such basic aspects are not numerous and are individually susceptible to various interpretations. Even taken together they will not necessarily be unambiguous. Another point of concern in interpreting a find in isolation (whether single object or group) is that any information on condition and context will only refer to late stages of a life-cycle. Regional studies are therefore essential to allow sight of any broader spectrum of patterns which might bear on different stages of basically similar life-cycles, or the co-existence of varied life-cycles for the given type. The purpose of such studies should be to generate hypotheses regarding material circulation, or the *materials value system* of the given society. The intention is to encompass not simply the record of physical displacement in relation to general material fall-out into the archaeological record, but also the uses to which material was put and, implicitly therefore, a judgement on value to the particular society. Without doubt this stage is highly interpretative and fraught with problems. Alternative hypotheses may, however, be reduced by broadening the scale of detailed studies; a multiplicity of comparisons

between neighbouring territories, successive periods and co-existent cycles of circulation (of different types/ materials). How one society treated a given material, for instance, could well have a crucial effect on its availability to neighbouring groups.

The foregoing shows just how tenuous is the interpretation of exchange and circulation. Contrast this with the ease of cataloguing displacement.

Considerable help in forming a view on life-cycles would come from the discovery of exceptional contexts recording a 'moment in time' whilst in transit or everyday use; these represent a stage which would otherwise be lost to us in the hidden life-cycle. A case in point is the equipped and clothed human body now known as Otze, from the Italian/Austrian border, assuming we are right to think of him as an unwitting victim of a mishap which interrupted his regular pursuits. He is perhaps the closest we will ever get to witnessing objects in the course of displacement on dry land – this is a unique circumstance as yet which will be hard, one imagines, to replicate. As an isolated example of this context type many aspects of the evidence will doubtless remain ambiguous. I am not claiming that this individual was engaged in the transportation of goods intended for exchange; on the contrary it seems more likely that the finds about his person were his personal set of kit. If so, this might offer some kind of yardstick for the question of exchange, perhaps not directly, but indirectly through, for example, comparisons with contemporary grave goods.

As already noted, cargoes are a more familiar type of time-capsule; these can offer a disproportionate amount of information. The contrasts which they can present when compared with dry-land assemblages can be extremely illuminating, (e.g. Needham & Dean 1987).

This approach, centred on consideration of object life-histories, might be criticised on the grounds that the individuals merely constitute elements of the whole system (indeed this criticism was voiced at the Bristol Conference). However, this assumes a holistic approach to interpretation, whereas, as archaeologists, it is our duty to seek diversity where it exists or otherwise demonstrate homogeneity. In other words, we must be wary of predetermining the geographical scale at which we seek patterns relatable to materials value systems.

Conclusions

Undeniably archaeology needs to refer to classification schemes for exchange in order to help define different operational modes as part of social systems. Finding an appropriate scheme is, however, a problem. On a general level we can extrapolate backwards from ethnographically observed circumstance. Polanyi's definitions for 'exchange', 'reciprocity' and 'redistribution', for example (1957, 250–6), can be easily understood to embrace most circumstances possible for goods passing between hands (although one might add 'theft', and again 'lineal descent' to allow cases with greater time depth). The problem, however, lies in their application to archaeological evidence, firstly how to differentiate adequately these broad modes and, thereafter, how to refine them, as we should inevitably wish to do.

The same problems apply to theoretically-derived classifications such as that by Renfrew (1975, 41–46 and this volume). This scheme successfully raises a wide range of possible modes of transmission by exchange, but where documentary sources fail it lacks the machinery for a concordance with archaeological data. Plog lists instead a range of nine critical variables for the characterisation of exchange networks such as content, diversity, temporal duration, complexity (1977, 128–9). He regards these as fundamental if we wish to understand the organisation of exchange and its relationship to other organisational phenomena. It is important to recognise, however, that virtually all of his variables are second-order archaeological data, being based on the interpretation of the primary evidence in the light of the taphonomic problems highlighted above.

These problems of concordance are essentially intractable. The proposition here is not to disregard externally-generated schemes, but to be clear that matching these to archaeological patterns is by default extremely tenuous. In the meantime, we can use archaeological material in its own right to construct 'views' of the materials value systems for the given societies. These themselves will be interpretative, prone to ambiguity and complex to derive. But they will have the virtue of treating the archaeological data with due respect. It would be the materials value systems, not a 'distribution pattern' as derived from a 'distribution map', that might find explanation in one or another hypothetical model of exchange.

The main danger of not taking this approach lies probably in the tendency to give each occurrence across a map of recovery a common value, or common significance. This is turn spawns universal schemes relating to exchange mechanisms, even 'world systems'. This is not to deny the possibility of wide-scale systems in European prehistory; however, these need to be demonstrated through the construction of alike value systems, rather than asserted or assumed. In European later prehistory we are dealing with generally small-scale polities which are likely to have been receptive or rejective of objects for a range of, to us, idiosyncratic reasons. Taking these two factors together I would posit that the chances of a uniform system over wide areas are slender. This emphasises the importance of regarding distribution maps as maps of recovery – that is, just another format for cataloguing known occurrences.

There is then something of a polarisation in preferred interpretations which can be a matter of personal faith in a particular doctrine. In a sense the opposition of views here mirrors the *oikos* debate about the evolution of economies (summarised by Pearson 1957); it concerns contrasting beliefs in a 'primitive' structure (in our context, small-scale systems and low degree of organisation) and a 'modern' structure (common organising principles prevailing over large areas).

A full understanding of trade and exchange will not come from empirical study of this as a discrete topic. It may often be possible to recognise the existence of displaced objects by such methods, but rarely would it be possible to postulate the *means* of transmission or the *significance* attached to received goods by the recipients. For these aspects the necessary backdrop is an insight into the attitudes of human groups to material culture at large: practices of consumption (ritual or otherwise), modes and control of production, receptiveness or not to stylistic or technological influences, and level of exploitation of local resources – in short, the materials value systems of social groups. Interpretation will also need to take into account wider issues such as relations with immediate neighbours, subsistence economy, and demographic patterns. Only in this way will we characterise the social institution that is exchange.

Acknowledgements

The construction of this paper has been helped enormously by criticism from John Barrett, Sheridan Bowman and Ian Kinnes, although they would not necessarily concur with all herein. Thanks also go to Judy Cash for her forbearance with re-drafting.

References

Callmer, J., 1977. *Trade Beads and Bead Trade in Scandinavia, ca. 800–1000 AD.* Lund: Acta Archaeologica Lundensia (Qto. series) 11

Clarke, D.L., 1973. Archaeology: the loss of innocence. *Antiquity*, 47, 6–18

Earle, T.K. & Ericson, J.E. 1977. Exchange systems in archaeological perspective, in *Exchange Systems in Prehistory*, eds T.K. Earle & J.E. Ericson. New York: Academic Press, 3–12

Ericson, J.E., 1977. Egalitarian exchange systems in California: a preliminary view, in *Exchange Systems in Prehistory*, eds T.K. Earle & J.E. Ericson. New York: Academic Press, 109–26

Larsson, L., 1988. Aspects of exchange in Mesolithic societies, in *Trade and Exchange in Prehistory: Studies in Honour of Berta Stjernquist*, eds B. Hårdh, L. Larsson, D. Olausson & R. Petré. Lund: Acta Archaeologica Lundensia (8° series) 16, 25–32

Mauss, M., 1970. *The Gift.* London: Routledge

Needham, S. P., & Dean, M., 1987. La cargaison de Langdon Bay, Douvres (Grande Bretagne): la signification pour les échanges à travers la Manche, in *Les Relations entre le Continent et les Iles Britanniques à l'Age du Bronze: Actes du Colloque de Bronze de Lille, 1984*, ed. J.-C. Blanchet. Paris: Société Préhistorique Française, 119–24

Olausson, D., 1988. Dots on a map – thoughts about the way archaeologists study prehistoric trade and exchange, in *Trade and Exchange in Prehistory: Studies in Honour of*

Berta Stjernquist, eds. B. Hårdh, L. Larsson, D. Olausson & R. Petré. Lund: Acta Archaeologica Lundensia (8° series) 16, 15–24

Pearson, H.W., 1957. The secular debate on economic primitivism, in *Trade and Market in the Early Empires: Economies in History and Theory*, eds. K. Polanyi, C.M. Arensberg & H.W. Pearson. Glencoe, Illinois: The Free Press, 3–11

Plog, F., 1977. Modelling economic exchange, in *Exchange Systems in Prehistory*, eds. T.K. Earle & J.E. Ericsson. New York: Academic Press, 127–40

Polanyi, K., 1957. The economy as instituted process, in *Trade and Market in the Early Empires: Economies in History and Theory*, eds. K. Polanyi, C.M. Arensberg & H.W. Pearson. Glencoe, Illinois: The Free Press, 243–70

Polyani, K., Arensberg, C.M., and Pearson, H.W., (eds) 1957. *Trade and Market in the Early Empires: Economies in History and Theory*. Glencoe, Illinois: The Free Press

Renfrew, C., 1975. Trade as action at a distance : questions of integration and communication, in *Ancient Civilization and Trade*, eds. J.A. Sabloff & C.C. Lamberg-Karlovsky. Albuquerque: University of New Mexico Press, 3–59

Stjernquist, B., 1967. *Models of Commercial Diffusion in Prehistoric Times*. Lund: Scripta Minora Regiae Societatis Humaniorum Litterarum Lundensis 1965–66:2

Welinder, S., 1988. Exchange of axes in the Early Neolithic farming society of Middle Sweden, in *Trade and Exchange in Prehistory: Studies in Honour of Berta Stjernquist*, eds B. Hårdh, L. Larsson, D. Olausson & R. Petré. Lund: Acta Archaeologica Lundensia (8° series) 16, 41–8

Wright, H., & Zeder, M., 1977. The simulation of a linear exchange system under equilibrium conditions, in *Exchange Systems in Prehistory*, eds. T.K. Earle & J.E. Ericson. New York: Academic Press, 233–54

17

East-West Relations in the Paris Basin during the Late Bronze Age

Patrice Brun

During the Late Bronze Age the Paris Basin was a zone of contact between two separate cultural complexes. A quantitative analysis of the archaeological data from the frontier region shows the formation of a buffer zone with specific organizational features. These may be explained, we believe, by growing social competition which seems to have generated a strong demand for bronze. Thus the frontier elites were placed in a favourable position. They could procure both tin and copper at low transport cost from various raw material sources on both sides of the frontier. They could also supply two different markets. In this situation, it was advantageous to develop local production. Increased production meant savings at all levels, and therefore reinforcement of an individual's position in the exchange system. The development of major production centres with diversified activities increased the possibility of benefiting from external economies. These social formations nevertheless remained fragile because they were based on control of exotic goods rather than on control of subsistence products and their surplus.

Au Bronze final, deux complexes culturels sont en contact dans le bassin parisien. Une analyse quantitative des données archéologiques situées le long de leur frontière montre la formation d'une zone-tampon possédant des caractéristiques d'organisation spécifiques. Nous proposons de les expliquer par la compétition sociale croissante qui semble avoir engendré une forte demande de bronze. Les élites frontalières se sont alors trouvées dans une position favorable. Elles pouvaient se procurer les deux composants de l'alliage depuis différentes sources de matières premières, d'un côté comme de l'autre. Elles pouvaient aussi approvisionner deux marchés différents. Dès lors, il devenait avantageux de développer une production locale. Une forte production permettait de bénéficier d'économies d'échelle, donc de renforcer sa position dans le système d'échange. Le développement de gros centres de production aux activités diversifiées permettaient de surcroît de bénéficier d'économies externes. Ces formations sociales demeuraient cependant fragiles car fondées sur le contrôle de biens exotiques et non sur le contrôle des produits primaires de la terre et leurs surplus.

Introduction

For the Bronze Age specialist, east-west relations in northern France refer to all forms of relationship between the neighbouring north-Alpine and Atlantic cultural complexes. In archaeological terms, relations can be identified through changing artefact distributions. Exchange of goods implies non-material exchange, both prior to transaction, when an agreement has to be made, and subsequently, since the object itself conveys technical and symbolic information. Additional dimensions of exchange contribute to the formation of cultural entities.

After describing the culture-historical framework of the study, I will attempt to show, firstly, that exchange is the key to the formation and development of collective identities; secondly, that types of exchange generate communication networks of varying size; and lastly, that in zones of stylistic discontinuity exchange can generate specific forms of site distribution.

The chronological and cultural framework

North-Alpine Late Bronze Age chronology has been considerably modified in recent years. A new sequence has been proposed and is now widely accepted (Brun & Mordant 1988). By analyzing associations of bronze types (Brun 1988; 1991) reliable correlations can be

Brun	Hatt	Müller-Karpe	Briard/Burgess
Stage 1	Bronze final I Bronze final IIa	Bronze D Hallstatt A1	Horizon de Rosnoën/Penard
Stage 2	Bronze final IIb Bronze final IIIb	Hallstatt A2 Hallstatt B1	Horizon de St-Brieuc-des Iffs/Wilburton
Stage 3	Bronze final IIIb Hallstatt ancien	Hallstatt B2-3 Hallstatt C	Horizon de l'épée en langue de carpe/Ewart Park

Figure 17.1. Chronological table

established with the Breton hoard chronology (Fig. 17.1; Briard 1965). The three clearly defined stages constitute an indispensable basis for studying changing relationships between the north-Alpine complex and its Atlantic neighbour.

Recognition of these two cultural identities is not a new development. Until recently, however, the distinction was largely intuitive and based on virtual superimposition of distribution maps of arbitrarily chosen artefact types. Maps can now be drawn grouping all types of material for which specialists agree on cultural origins (Brun 1988, figs. 3 & 4). In this way the two cultural complexes can be differentiated quite clearly. Sub-groups are of course visible within each complex. Formalization has been attempted for the north-Alpine (Brun 1988) and Atlantic complexes (Brun 1991).

Identity through exchange

A cultural complex is obviously not a state and thus cannot be an actor in exchange. A cultural complex is a zone of relative stylistic uniformity, made up of nested sub-sets. In the current state of research we can distinguish within a complex groups of cultures, cultures and cultural groups. In later prehistory, entities larger than cultures cannot have constituted a centralized and autonomous political unit. If the factor behind uniformity is not political in nature, it can only have been based on exchange. In fact, when exchange of marriage partners or goods occurs, symbolic representations are also transferred between the participants and this leads to unification of world views. Stylistic homogeneity thus emerges spontaneously from interaction between communicators (Brun 1991). This process is amplified by the number, duration and form of individual and collective interactions. This situation prevails in alliance relationships, although these can be conflictual and thus may result in reciprocal exclusion. In this case, differences are deliberately marked, or even reinforced on frontiers, where identity is displayed more forcefully than elsewhere (Hodder 1982).

The two attendant principles of homogenization/heterogenization underlie all processes of identity formation. Individual or collective identity is formed both by mimetic appropriation of community models and also by differentiation. In other words, there has to be

a model to imitate and another model against which one can be distinguished, in particular the model of the indispensable foreigner. The formation and maintenance of cultural entities, which are social networks on a vast scale without centralized control, can be explained in this way (Brun 1991).

The means of transport available in the Late Bronze Age considerably limited the distance for widening homogenization, since this is based on repetitive face-to-face communication. The spatial dimension of a social network is therefore conditioned by this constraint on the flow of information.

Spheres of exchange

Marriage exchange cannot be detected in this Late Bronze Age evidence. Well-excavated burials are still rare, particularly for the Atlantic complex. Furthermore, cremation leads to the destruction or disappearance of elements of dress, the main collective expression of identity (through the type and position of ornaments). Such exchange must however have existed at the local level. A standard community occupying a territory of about 7 km radius (Brun & Pion, in press) must have belonged to a genetic pool of 200 to 400 people (Hassan 1981), representing a zone of preferential exchange including several small contiguous territories. Such local networks, bound by family relationships, expressed a stylistic uniformity reinforced by the fact that it was probably women who made and decorated the pottery and wove the clothing.

It seems likely that marriage links were maintained by elites to secure the alliance networks essential for procuring the prestige goods necessary for their social reproduction. This type of network was looser but still partially based on family relations. Exchange of exotic goods was probably controlled by these elites, operating on the principles of a gift economy (Mauss 1923–24). Thus two leaders met and in the course of a ceremony one offered the other valuable goods. This ostentatious gift called for reciprocity, in other words a counter-gift of equivalent value. If the recipient was unable to do this, he found himself in a position of inferiority. This form of goods transfer thus also represented a principle of distribution of social statuses. The flow of prestige goods and the capacity to monopolize these produced a hierarchy of community leaders. During the Bronze Age, alliance networks also tended to be organized in a centralized or hierarchichal manner, as in Wessex (Renfrew 1973) or Saxo-Thuringia (Otto 1955). The average distance of about sixty kilometres between rich burials of Stage 1 in the Yonne (Mordant 1992) also suggests the existence of a supra-local level of political integration.

The stylistic groups which we can define are generally larger, with a diameter of about 100 km. Territories of this size do not appear to have formed politically autonomous territories before the Hallstatt D period. In the Late Bronze Age these groups thus represented preferential goods-exchange networks, composed of several supra-local entities. Here we can suppose that equivalent chiefs were involved in reciprocal exchange of equivalent gifts, in other words transactions of balanced reciprocity, as opposed to the internal procedure for each supra-local entity where exchange had developed into redistribution (Polanyi 1944). The immediacy required by balanced reciprocity led to face to face relationships between chiefs. It was through these meetings that the elites stylistic norms must have been fixed and diffused. The new forms of stylistic expression then filtered down into the respective communities.

At this time, the goods whose movement was sufficiently distant and abundant to stimulate a gift economy were most probably bronze objects. The majority were prestige goods: ornaments, weapons, horse riding equipment or vessels. Distribution maps of numerous types of object indicate the considerable distances involved in exchange. In certain cases detailed study has shown the points of departure and arrival of objects. For instance single examples of a form of pin present in quantity in the Villethierry hoard have been discovered, with the same manufacturing defect, at Fort Harrouard and Agris, respectively at 150 and 350 km distance (Mordant 1989). Thus we note that goods were exchanged from hand to hand and that these operations tended to render vast areas uniform.

In certain places, however, uniformity came to a halt in front of a very different stylistic sphere, representing another set of exchange and alliance networks. The principle of distinction explains why such differences formed, but does not explain their precise location. Since bronze represented a crucial element in the reproduction of social organization, in the context of a gift economy, we can presume that the space occupied by spheres of preferential exchange was a function of possibilities for supply, in other words the location of extraction sites and the means of transport of copper and tin. Thus north-west France lies in the orbit of the Armorican massif while north-east France lies in the orbit of the Swiss Alps and the Sarre. But, with the exception of the Limousin, the nearest tin sources for the Rhine-Swiss-France culture, the westernmost of the north-Alpine complex, were rather in the Atlantic zone.

At the same time, there is some evidence for the export of north-Alpine raw materials towards the British Isles (Northover 1982). Several median-winged axes, virtually absent in England, were found in the Dover wreck cargo (Coombs 1975), extending a diffusion gradient centred on the Jura. The implication is that they were melted down on arrival as it was the raw material alone that counted. This means that, on both sides of the cultural frontier, the two supply sources were used when necessary — a logical attitude in a system where bronze was of overwhelming importance for the maintenance of social structure but where its flow was very irregular and subject to multiple uncontrollable factors.

Exchange of finished products between members of the two complexes involved different functional categories: this included the axes already mentioned, but mainly involved swords. In contrast to the axes, swords appear to have circulated well outside their original cultural sphere without losing their initial functional and social value. At the end of what was sometimes a long journey, these swords seem to have met the same fate as local swords in river finds. Exchange of objects was inevitably accompanied by exchange of information, including direct transmission of technical procedures which are unfortunately difficult to detect from the archaeological evidence, and indirect transmission by imitation of acquired objects. By this latter means we can detect a kind of technological transfer: the creators of the Atlantic leaf-shaped sword, for example, very quickly adopted the handle type of the first north-Alpine swords with a complete hilt which provided a much more effective grip.

The examination of frontiers between cultural complexes shows that they are neither rigid lines nor completely porous zones of mutual interpenetration. In certain situations, and especially during the Late Bronze Age, the contact zone apparently developed specific organizational features (Fig. 17.2). This hypothesis can be tested with data available in north-west France.

Case study: north-west France

Let us now examine the nature and development of relations between two cultural complexes in the central part of northern France where they are in contact. Administratively, this zone corresponds to the Nord-Pas de Calais, Picardy, Champagne-Ardennes (excluding the Haute-Marne département) and Ile-de-France. Rather than including the whole of the two regions of Normandy, where research has for some time progressed only slowly, the Eure-et-Loire département is added for reasons that will become clear.

For the zone studied here, the 'Rhin-Suisse-France orientale' culture (RSFO) in its two successive stages (pottery with shallow grooves then carinated pottery with incised comb decoration) faces the Manche culture (Brun 1991) with its successive Saint-Just-en-Chaussée/ Choisy-le-Roi and Caix/Boutigny II stages. The map of

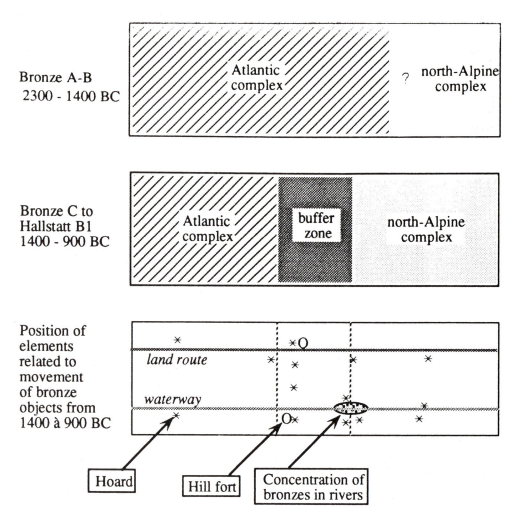

Figure 17.2. Schematic presentation of the research problem

Atlantic and north Alpine products during Stage 1 shows the opposition between these two cultures; one in the south-east, the other in the north-west (Fig. 17.3). The dividing line is a curved diagonal passing upstream of Paris. The map for Stage 2, established on the same principle, also reveals a south-east/north-west division, but the dividing line lies downstream of Paris and follows the Oise valley (Fig. 17.4). I have interpreted this shift as a widening of north Alpine cultural influence due to the arrival of colonists from the east.

By re-examining the situation at a regional scale with recently published data, we may now try to clarify the modes of exchange between the two cultural complexes. Where we might have expected to find either two competing entities reinforcing their differences along the frontier, or two complementary entities blending along a contact zone, we find instead a buffer zone which develops its own characteristics.

In Stage 1 north Alpine stylistic traits are in fact already present downstream of Paris. There are not only bronze objects (of significant quantity but in a minority), but also pottery on the settlement sites of Fort-Harrouard (Mohen & Bailloud 1987), dominating the Eure valley, and Chevrières in the Oise valley

(Blanchet *et al.* 1989). During Stage 2 the north Alpine types become more abundant in the Aisne and Oise valleys, but Atlantic types remain in the majority in the two major concentrations of bronze material from rivers; the Seine upstream of Paris and the Essonne. In fact we are not dealing here with a frontier, but with a buffer zone about 60 km wide. It is a zone of cultural uncertainty within which particular economic and political phenomena occur. These are reflected by isolated bronze artefacts, hoards and hillforts.

Isolated finds

The vast majority of Late Bronze Age stray finds come from river beds and especially from particular stretches of river. For the study zone these are, in order of importance:

— the Essonne near the Seine confluence
— the Seine just upstream of Paris
— the Oise near Compiègne
— the Somme near Amiens and Abbeville

The most prolific stretches are thus in Ile-de-France and Picardy, two regions where Bronze Age evidence

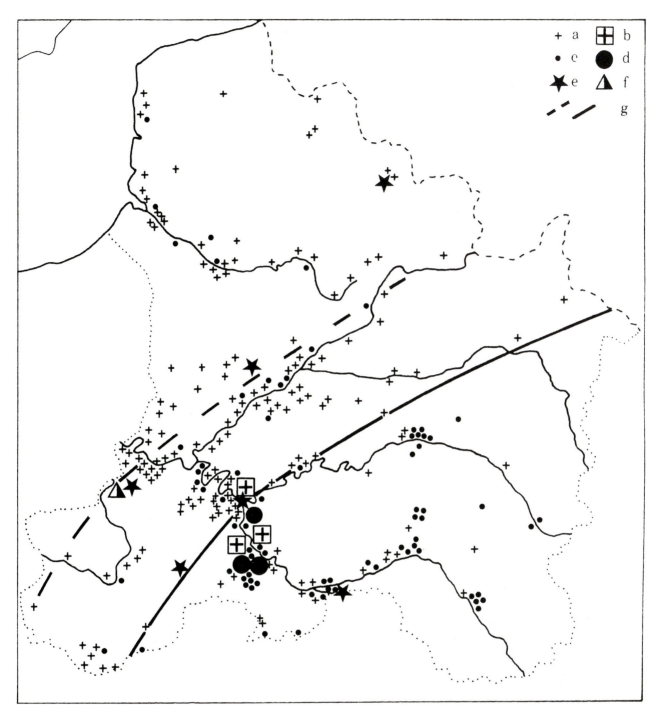

Figure 17.3. Distribution of north Alpine and Atlantic types in the study zone during Stage 1: a) Atlantic type; b) concentration of more than 40 Atlantic bronzes; c) north Alpine type; d) concentration of more than 15 north Alpine bronzes; e) hoard; f) hillfort (with Atlantic and north Alpine types); g) buffer zone

has been well recorded (Mohen 1977; Blanchet 1984). On this basis a quantitative analysis can be attempted.

The results shown in Fig. 17.5 were obtained through counting objects by functional category and by period. The total number of objects remains constant between Stages 1 and 2 but then slightly increases. Weapons always account for over 60 per cent of the finds, but reach 81 per cent in Stage 2. They are followed, some way behind, in decreasing order, by ornaments, axes and tools. This confirms that the isolated bronze objects

result from specific practices involving weapons and frontier zones.

Hoards

Of the six hoards in the study zone dated to Stage 1, four are located within or in immediate proximity to the buffer zone (66 per cent). In Stage 2, out of seventeen hoards, eleven are similarly located (64.7 per cent). While two out of three hoards are closely associated

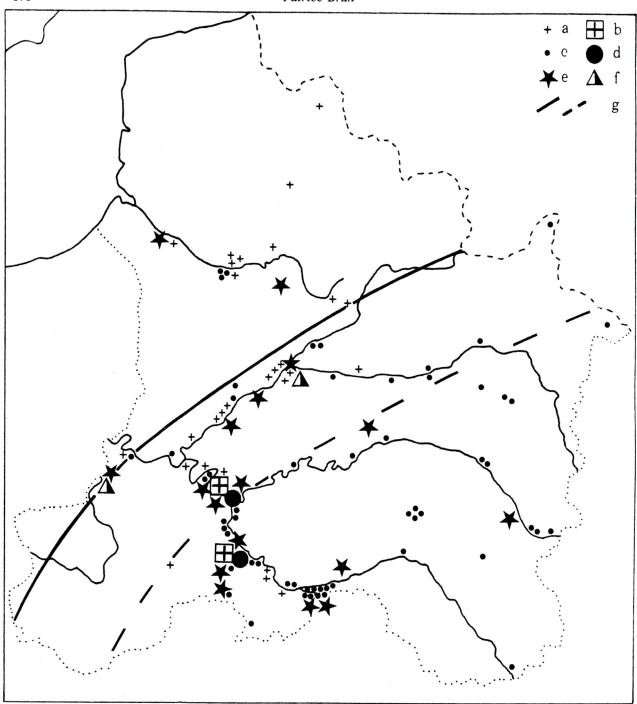

Figure 17.4. Distribution of north Alpine and Atlantic types in the study zone during Stage 2: a) Atlantic type; b) concentration of more than 30 Atlantic bronzes; c) north Alpine type; d) concentration of more than 10 north Alpine bronzes; e) hoard; f) hillfort (with Atlantic and north Alpine types); g) buffer zone

with the buffer zone in these two stages, only nine hoards out of 20 (45 per cent) are spatially linked to this zone during Stage 3. Furthermore, the count of objects by functional category and by period differs considerably from the isolated finds (Fig. 17.6).

The predominance of weapons only appears in Stage 2 where they constitute a mere 38.6 per cent of the objects. Ornaments dominate in Stage 1. These are also abundant in Stage 3, but axes are even more so. Most of the hoards in the study zone are stocks of bronze gathered for recasting. Their composition varies considerably from one hoard to another. The objects are

often broken into pieces suitable for a crucible. Small badly deteriorated fragments are common. We can suppose therefore that these hoards are broadly representative of the artefacts in use in a given period.

If the hoards contain stocks of material for recasting, we can trace the quantitative development of this practice through the Late Bronze Age (Fig. 17.7). From Stage 1 to 2, the number of objects increases at about the same rate as the number of hoards (Stage 1: 14 objects per hoard; Stage 2: 18 objects per hoard). In Stage 3, the number of objects per hoard (35) increases more than the number of hoards.

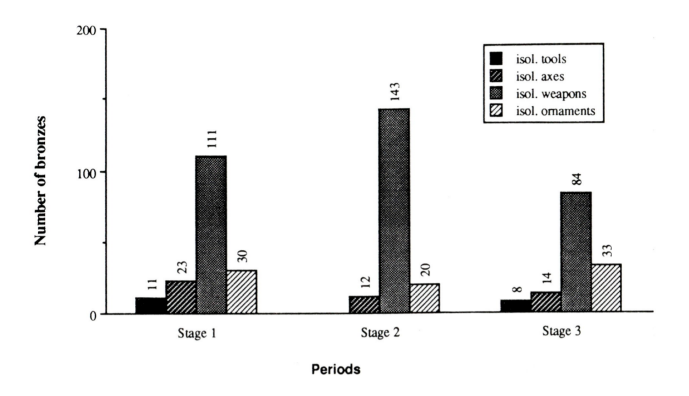

Figure 17.5. Frequency of objects by functional category (isolated finds)

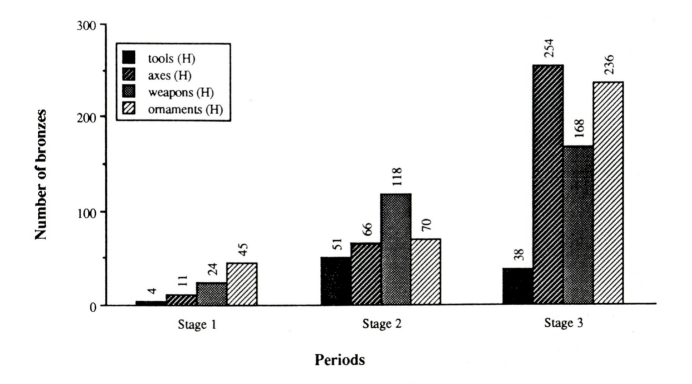

Figure 17.6. Frequency of objects by functional category (hoards)

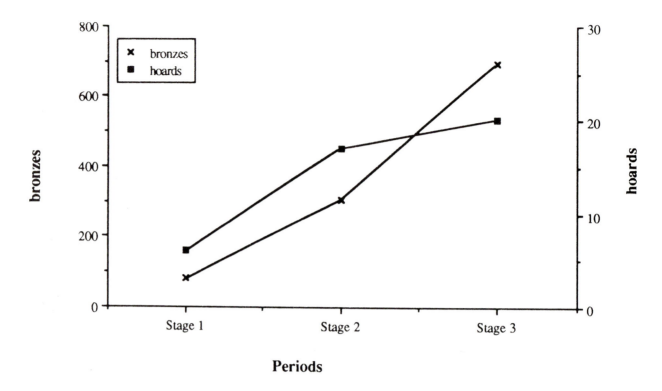

Figure 17.7. Comparative frequency of hoards and bronze objects in hoards

To summarize these observations, hoards seem linked to the buffer zone during Stages 1 and 2. Prestige artefacts such as weapons (spears and swords) and ornaments are particularly abundant in these hoards, especially in Stage 2. The trend breaks down in Stage 3. Hoards become more randomly distributed and in any case are not related to the buffer zone. Although they hardly increase in number, their content rises impressively and the weapons that were previously in majority have now fallen to third position (24 per cent), behind axes (36.5 per cent) and ornaments (34 per cent). This implies a greater dynamism for the buffer zone between 1400 and 900 BC, based mainly on control of prestige goods, then a decline of this zone, with a more even distribution of hoards. In other words, distribution and composition became more related to local needs after 900 BC.

Hillforts

During the first two stages, the only fortified sites in the study area lie in the buffer zone: Fort-Harrouard at Sorel-Mousel (Stages 1 and 2), and Saint-Pierre-en-Chastre (Vieux-Moulin) and the Camp de César at Catenoy (Stage 2). These settlements have yielded large numbers of bronze objects, as well as evidence for metalworking. For the first two sites, extensively excavated, interesting data are available (Fig. 17.8; Mohen & Bailloud 1987; Blanchet 1984).

Despite considerable quantitative variation due to different excavation conditions at the two sites, it is

striking that the relative numbers of functional categories of bronze artefacts are quite comparable. Ornaments dominate. Tools are important. Weapons account for 10 to 18 per cent of objects. Finally, axes are curiously infrequent, despite their production at these sites. At Fort Harrouard, the number of moulds seems to indicate production mainly orientated towards weapons for export (Fig. 17.9). Weapons are found in 22 per cent of the sectors, but 39 sword moulds were found, compared to only 29 swords. With the other categories, however, the relative quantities indicate production for local use, with the possible exception of ornaments, the moulds for which seem over-abundant in relation to finished products (as with the weapons).

The buffer zone thus contains a notable concentration of fortified settlements closely linked to the circulation and production of bronze objects, mainly involving prestige goods. In addition, north Alpine and Atlantic types coexist on these sites. Besides a predominately Atlantic metallurgy, especially for types produced on the sites, there is north-Alpine style pottery. This clearly reflects the cultural uncertainty and stylistic mixture which characterizes the buffer zone. The mixture was perhaps especially marked within a social elite probably occupying the hillforts. The relatively high number of weapons has been underlined. It is also worth pointing to other artefact types which may have been linked to an elite: beads and a block of amber, a double meat hook, antler cheek-pieces from Sorel-Mousel; a possible fragment of *cnémid* and an antler horse-bit from Vieux-Moulin.

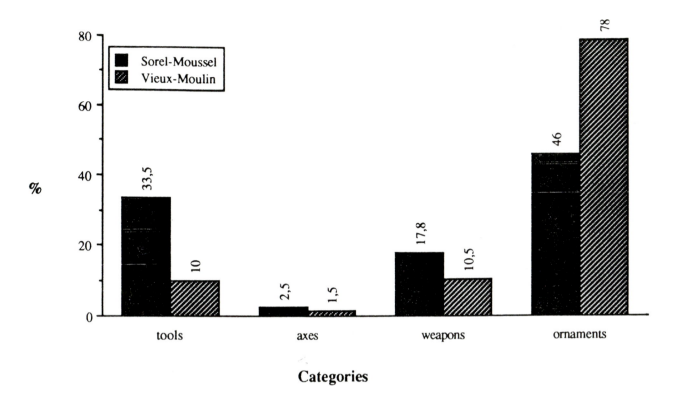

Figure 17.8. Percentages of functional categories at Fort Harrouard (Sorel-Mousel) and Saint-Pierre-en-Chastre (Vieux-Moulin)

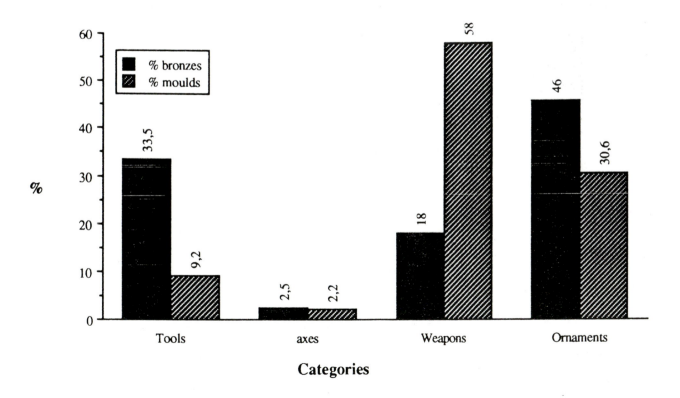

Figure 17.9. Percentages of bronze objets and moulds by functional categories at Fort Harrouard (Sorel-Mousel)

If we now compare the quantity of bronze objects by functional category with the three types of context (Fig. 17.10), we can see that these two fortified sites alone have produced slightly more bronze than all the Late Bronze Age hoards in the regions studied and over twice the number of bronze objects from isolated finds. This indicates the exceptional wealth of the fortified sites, as well as their specific function. These are clearly centres of intensive production, mainly of prestige goods. The tools, especially chisels and awls, are the equipment of craftsmen attached to a well armed and richly ornamented elite. There are very few tools directly related to subsistence activities, such as axes and sickles.

The three fortified sites continue into Stage 3, but their wealth declines. The number of fortified sites rises; so far eleven have been discovered. Significantly, none have produced a comparable wealth of bronze to the earlier sites.

Interpretation

In short, there is a good correlation between the frontier zone, about 60 km wide, and the high density of several elements:

— a concentration of bronze objects along certain stretches of river, with a clear predominance of weapons
— a concentration of hoards of more diverse composition, but mainly containing weapons and ornaments, especially in Stage 2
— a concentration of fortified sites, important centres of bronze production, especially for weapons and ornaments.

The phenomenon intensifies from Stage 1 to Stage 2.

The correlation disappears in Stage 3. Concentration of bronze artefacts in rivers decreases, except near Paris. Even here, however, the relative proportions change: 78 per cent of weapons in Stage 2 drops to 44 per cent in Stage 3. Hoards, containing a much greater quantity of material, become more evenly distributed throughout the study zone and include more axes and tools. Hillforts become more common and are more evenly distributed, but no longer produce evidence for massive bronze production.

It therefore appears that during Stages 1 and 2 the frontier zone was a particularly intensive transit area for bronze artefacts circulating in both directions. We may suggest that the exchange of bronze objects was controlled by community leaders and was based on the principle of gift exchange. Weapons are clearly over-represented in river finds and this must indicate selection. They were deliberately thrown into the river, perhaps during potlatchs between chiefs controlling extremely large quantities of metal goods and seeking to outbid each other, or perhaps more simply in the course of exchange along a frontier, not as part of large-scale destruction, but where a fine object had to be sacrificed to a divinity (Bradley 1990).

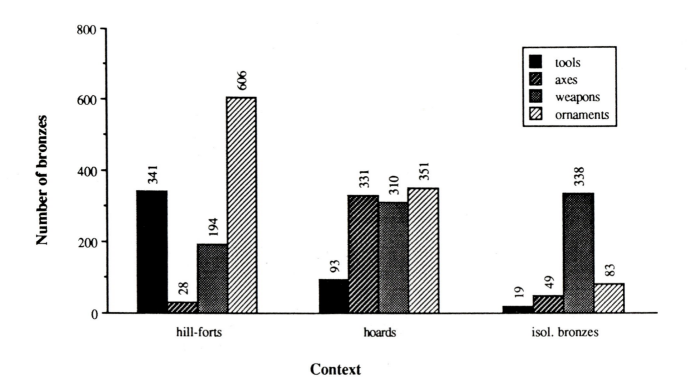

Figure 17.10. Number of bronze objects by functional category and context

In either case, the large quantity of bronze in circulation within the buffer zone resulted in more artefacts being deposited in rivers here than in rivers elsewhere.

Well-established chiefs, with a greater capacity for handing out gifts, could acquire greater power, which in the logic of the system means power over larger numbers of debtors. Controlling supra-local networks, these chiefs perhaps lived in the hillforts. With large quantities of bronze at hand they could reinforce local power and win broad alliance networks. It would also have been in their economic and political interest to develop their own production despite the distance to raw material sources. The evidence from Fort-Harrouard is eloquent here, in particular the recognition of local Parisian variants of Atlantic sword and spearhead types (Mohen 1977).

The relative importance of weapons from all kinds of site, though varying in degree, highlights the competitive nature of exchange. Strong competition is not surprising since because of their uneven geographical distribution raw materials were not uniformly accessi-

ble. The spatial inequality of this critical resource thus created social inequality. In addition, a gift economy with balanced reciprocity encouraged competition and the creation of a maximum number of debtors. We can thus use Alfred Weber's model to identify the most advantageous position for competitive elites (Weber 1909 [1971]). The best position is one where the costs of supply in raw materials and energy, as well as costs of dispatching finished products, are minimized. It is located within the triangle formed by the raw material source, the energy source and the market, as a function of the cost of transport (Fig. 17.11). During the Late Bronze Age in the study zone, energy necessary for bronze production was available everywhere, as relatively little fuel or manpower was required. Copper and tin, complementary but distant raw materials, came from diametrically opposed twin sources; copper from two sources in the east, tin from two or three sources in the west. The market was relatively dispersed, despite control by leaders of socio-political kinship networks.

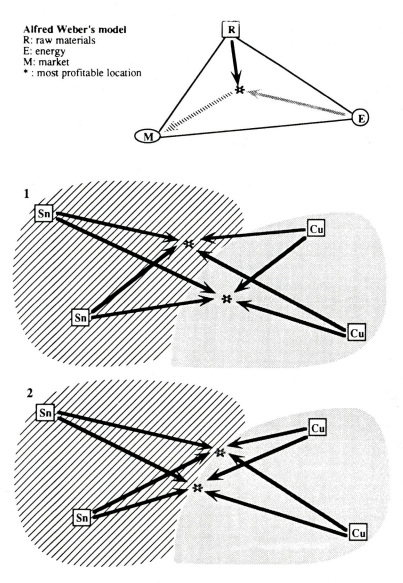

Alfred Weber's model
R: raw materials
E: energy
M: market
* : most profitable location

Figure 17.11. Application of Weber's locational model

Under these conditions, the most advantageous location for the residence of a community leader was one which controlled an important natural communication route and was situated on the centres of gravity of both the raw material supplies and the networks of the cultural complex, the latter representing a vast network of preferential exchange. In the study zone, the centre of gravity for the Atlantic complex was located in the lower Somme valley and for the north-Alpine complex at the Yonne-Seine confluence. The overall centre of gravity was the Paris area, precisely where the two complexes were in contact. Thus growing competition stimulated demand and placed the frontier elites in an extremely favourable position. They could procure both tin and bronze at low transport cost from various raw material sources to both sides of the frontier. They could also supply two different markets. In this situation, it was of course advantageous to develop local production. Increased production meant savings at all levels, and therefore reinforcement of ones position in the exchange system. The development of major production centres with diversified activities (different products, different materials, different techniques) increased the possibility of benefiting from external economies. This cumulative effect could explain the particular importance of sites like Fort-Harrouard or Saint-Pierre-en-Chastre.

The variety of evidence analyzed here shows that important changes took place in Stage 3; in particular the rapid decline of the two sites that have just been mentioned. These changes probably result from major problems with the supply of bronze. The fall in quality of alloys, the increase in the number and dispersion of large founder's hoards and the regular presence of iron products, some of which are quite elaborate, are well known in the north-Alpine complex. Beyond the economic difficulties which explain the beginning of the partial replacement of bronze by iron, it is obvious that the whole social organization must have been shaken. It looks as if communities tried to develop their autonomy in order to be less dependant on uncertain supplies. Local fortified centres increase in number and stylistic uniformity breaks down. The buffer zone becomes blurred. Atlantic bronze objects dominate again, so that the mixed character of the zone disappears. All that remains is a concentration of bronze objects in rivers and hoards in the Paris region, an ultimate survival of a rich past and the last hours of east-west complementarity as the quite different characteristics of the Iron Age begin to emerge.

References

Blanchet, J.-C., 1976. *Les Premiers Métallurgistes en Picardie et dans le Nord de la France. Mémoires de la Société Préhistorique Française, 17.* Paris: Société Préhistorique Française

Blanchet, J.-C., Brun, P., & Talon, M., 1989. Le Bronze moyen en Picardie et dans le Nord Pas-de-Calais, in *Dynamique du Bronze Moyen en Europe Occidentale,* *Actes du 113ᵉ Congrès National des Sociétés Savantes, Strasbourg-Haguenau 1988.* Paris: C.T.H.S., 491–500

Bradley, R., 1990. *The Passage of Arms: An Archaeological Analysis of Prehistoric Hoards.* Cambridge: Cambridge University Press

Briard, J., 1965. *Les Dépôts Bretons de l'Age du Bronze Atlantique.* Rennes: Travaux du Laboratoire d'Anthropologie de la Faculté des Sciences de Rennes

Brun, P., 1988. L'entité 'Rhin-Suisse-France orientale': nature et évolution, in Le Groupe Rhin-Suisse-France Orientale et la Notion de Civilisation des Champs d'Urnes, eds P. Brun & C. Mordant. *Actes du Colloque International de Nemours (1986).* Nemours: Mémoires du Musée de Préhistoire d'Ile-de-France 1, 599–618

Brun, P., & Mordant, C., (eds) 1988. Le Groupe Rhin-Suisse-France Orientale et la Notion de Civilisation des Champs d'Urnes. *Actes du Colloque International de Nemours (1986).* Nemours: Mémoires du Musée de Préhistoire d'Ile-de-France 1

Brun, P., & Pion, P., in press. L'organisation de l'espace dans la vallée de l'Aisne pendant l'Age du Bronze, in *Actes du Colloque sur l'Age du Bronze de Lons-le-Saunier (1990)*

Brun, P., 1991. Le Bronze atlantique et ses subdivisions culturelles: essai de définition, in *L'Age du Bronze Atlantique: Ses Faciès de l'Ecosse à l'Andalousie et leurs Relations avec le Bronze Continental et la Méditerranée,* eds C. Chevillot & A. Coffyn. Actes du 1ᵉʳ Colloque du Parc Archéologique de Beynac (1990), 11–24

Coombs, D.G., 1975. The Dover Harbour bronze find – a Bronze Age wreck? *Archaeologica Atlantica* 1, 193–5

Hassan, F.A., 1981. *Demographic Archaeology.* New York: Academic Press

Hodder, I., 1982. *Symbols in Action. Ethnoarchaeological Studies of Material Culture.* Cambridge: Cambridge University Press

Mauss, M., 1923. Essai sur le don, forme et raison de l'échange dans les sociétés archaïques. *L'Année Sociologique* 1, 30–186

Mohen, J.-P., 1977. *L'Age du Bronze dans la Région de Paris.* Paris: Musées Nationaux

Mohen, J.-P., & Bailloud, G., 1987. *La Vie Quotidienne: Les Fouilles du Fort Harrouard.* Paris: Picard

Mordant, C., 1989. L'Age du Bronze, in *L'Yonne et son Passé, 30 Ans d'Archéologie,* eds J.-P. Delor & C. Rolley. Auxerre: Comité Départemental de la Recherche Archéologique de l'Yonne, 71–98

Mordant, C., 1992. Les nécropoles du Bronze final de l'Yonne dans leur contexte régional. *Cahiers Archéologiques de Bourgogne* 3, 10–13

Northover, J.P., 1982. The exploration of long-distance movement of bronze in Bronze and Early Iron Age Europe. *University of London Institute of Archaeology Bulletin* 19, 45–72

Otto, K.H., 1955. *Die sozialökonomischen Verhältnisse bei den Stämmen der Leubinger Kultur in Mitteldeutschland. Ethnographische-archäologische Forschungen 3:1.* Berlin

Polanyi, K., 1944. *The Great Transformation.* New York: Rinehart

Renfrew, C., 1973. Monuments, mobilization and social organization in Neolithic Wessex, in *The Explanation of Culture Change: Models in Prehistory,* ed. C. Renfrew. London: Duckworth, 539–58

Weber, A., 1971. *Theory of the Location of Industries.* (First publ. 1909) New York: Russell & Russell

18

Relations between Brittany and Great Britain during the Bronze Age

Jacques Briard

Early studies of relations between Brittany and Great Britain initiated the concept of a homogeneous Armorico-Wessex complex, based on the similarity of daggers decorated with small gold pins, the use of gold and the arrowheads. Newer studies by Taylor and Eluère have shown that these are the products of different workshops. The Beaker complex of Brittany is not as important as that of Wessex, where it is represented by rich Beaker graves. Some Breton swords, of a type unknown in Wessex, have parallels in the Iberian Early Bronze Age. Study of urns has revealed their early origins. British vessels have been found in Armorica and some Breton vessels have been discovered in southern England. Trade in metal objects remained important during the Middle Bronze Age (Bignan armrings, palstaves, Irish goldwork). The Late Bronze Age communities are clearly related to each other (Rosnoën/Penard, Saint-Brieuc-des-Iffs/Wilburton). Contact in the Atlantic Bronze Age reached its peak with the Carp's Tongue Sword complex, and ended with the movement of Armorican currency axes.

Les premières études des relations Bretagne-Grande Bretagne ont été axées sur un complexe armoricano-Wessex, basé sur la parenté des poignards décorés de clous en or, la présence d'or et de pointes de flèches. Les travaux sur l'or de Taylor et Eluère montrent l'existence d'ateliers différents. Le phénomène campaniforme, réduit en Armorique, conduit en Grande-Bretagne a l'éclosion d'élites dirigeantes précédant celles du Wessex. L'étude des urnes conclut à leur ancienneté et à la présence en Armorique de poteries britanniques. Inversement, les céramiques armoricaines sont imitées Outre-Manche. Par la suite, les productions métalliques seront régulièrement échangées (bracelets de Bignan, haches à talon, bijoux irlandais). Les communautés du Bronze final sont parentes (Rosnoën/Penard, Saint-Brieuc-des-Iffs/Wilburton). L'apogée du Bronze atlantique se situe avec le complexe de l'épée en langue de carpe et son épilogue avec les haches armoricaines prémonétaires.

Introduction

Relations between Brittany and Great Britain have been the subject of several studies since the beginning of this century when Martin underlined the kinship of the Breton tumulus burials containing arrowheads with those of England, notably with the Bush Barrow (Martin 1904). The closeness of Armorican-Wessex relations was documented first by Piggott (1938) and then by Giot & Cogné (1951) in a diffusionist perspective which envisaged the disembarkation of new Bronze Age populations on both sides of the Channel as if they had been forerunners of the north European Vikings. The idea of a close Armorican-Wessex correlation was taken further by typological studies of weapons such as that by Gerloff (1975) on the daggers of the Wessex culture (Camerton-Snowshill type). This attempt at classifica-

tion remains more credible to the present writer than the more recent study by Gallay (1988), which creates a new range of types from series of daggers which are most often corroded and barely able to support such a fine typology, which must be regarded as largely imaginary.

In another domain, that of gold, studies by Joan Taylor (1980) and Christiane Eluère (1985) have shown that in their details the ornaments such as lunulae or the small gold pins which decorated dagger handles are the work of different workshops on each side of the Channel. Major exhibitions, such as those at Tournai and Edinburgh in 1984 and 1985 respectively, have allowed the British and continental material to be reviewed together.

The Beaker question

It is clear that the Beaker cultures often lay at the origin of Early Bronze Age developments. The evolution of certain Beaker artefact types such as flint arrowheads with central tang and lateral barbs was the source of the Armorican Early Bronze Age types and their variants.

In this domain, however, there is one notable difference between Great Britain and Brittany. The British Isles have yielded a whole series of Beaker graves with rich assemblages including items which can be termed 'symbols of power' (Clarke, Cowie & Foxon 1985). The burial at Radley in Oxfordshire, for example, contained a Beaker, three flint arrowheads and two beautiful gold earrings of the type known as basket earrings. Several graves have archer's wristguards decorated with gold studs. At Barnack in Cambridgeshire a male skeleton was furnished with a copper dagger and a Beaker. At Kelly Thorpe near Driffield in Yorkshire two amber beads accompanied a Beaker, wristguard and copper dagger. The grave group at Culduthel in Inverness is interesting for its Beaker, its wristguard with gold studs, its cylindrical grooved bone pendant, and its amber bead, but also for its eight flint arrowheads with central tang and serrated barbs (MacSween & Burgess 1984, 73). The relative abundance of arrowheads already foreshadows those associated with the Early Bronze Age barrows. Gold in the form of a small disc with solar motif appears in a Beaker context at Mere in Wiltshire, and this ornament recalls the gold discs from Kirk Andrews on the Isle of Man, or from Castle Treasure at Cork in Ireland.

In Brittany a number of small gold objects are associated with Beakers but only in re-used megalithic monuments. Examples are known from mixed contexts at Kerlagat and Grah Trimen at Carnac, and from a well-known closed context in the angled passage grave of Goërem at Gâvres (Morbihan), where four gold plaques accompanied the Beaker vessel (L'Helgouach 1970).

Arrowheads are rare in Beaker contexts. Chambers C and D at Barnenez yielded a single fine chalcolithic arrowhead accompanied by a copper dagger and Beaker sherds. The discovery at the Moulin de la Motte at Pornic is more exceptional since in addition to Beaker material there was found a necklace of nine tubular gold beads and an arrowhead of Breton type. This is however an old excavation in which it is difficult to distinguish the Beaker assemblage from a later re-use during the Bronze Age.

Recent excavations have demonstrated the existence of individual Beaker graves. They are very poorly furnished, with only a broken vessel or a few sherds. Examples are the small cist burials of La Guette at Paimpont (Ille-et-Vilaine), or of Roh Du at La Chapelle Blanche (Morbihan; Briard 1989, 68–9). To these we could add the small tombs near the Tressé allée couverte (Ille-et-Vilaine), or the cist beneath the burial mound of Kerbernard at Pluguffan (Finistère). Numerous Early Bronze Age tumuli had Beaker sherds within the body of the mound: for example Kersandy at Plouhinec (Finistère), or Priziac (Morbihan; Briard 1984, 171).

The link between the Breton Beaker and Early Bronze Age assemblages is clear from this discussion, but in contrast to Great Britain there is no evidence of a Beaker elite prefiguring the aristocratic societies of the Early Bronze Age.

In the Breton context we must however note one exception: the settlement site of Saint-Nicolas-du-Pelem in the Côtes d'Armor. This was patiently field-walked by Le Provost for many years and yielded traces of extensive Beaker and Early Bronze Age settlement (Le Provost & Giot 1972). The Beaker element is predominant here, ranging in pottery terms from early pan-European styles to developed Beakers with impressed decoration, triangles and chevrons. The material is very fragmentary but betrays influence both from south French Beakers and from English Beakers. This site, where recent excavations have revealed the foundations of dwelling structures, has yielded two exceptional prestige objects: a segmented faience bead and a fragment of gold pendant (Fig. 18.1). The gold fragment is decorated on its edges in the pointillé technique that is also found on certain basket earrings, such as those of Orbliston in Morayshire or Boltby Scar in Yorkshire (Taylor 1980, pl. 3). This edge decoration is also found however on the gold lunulae from the Kerivoa hoard at Bourbriac in the Côtes d'Armor (Eluère 1982, 60). The relative richness of Saint-Nicolas-du-Pelem remains difficult to explain. We can only underline the proximity of the dolerite workings at Plussulien, still in operation up to 1800 BC, and of the large Early Bronze Age tumuli of Bourbriac and Saint-Adrien some 20 km to the north.

The Armorican-Wessex complex

The relationship between the Armorican tumuli and those of Wessex has long been noted, and is shown by shared features such as daggers with six rivets, a central omega-shaped mark and a wooden haft decorated with gold pins. There was certainly a common basis, but both daggers and associated material show that there were also regional differences between the two groups. Daggers of Camerton type are unknown in Brittany; conversely, long swords of Carnoët type (Briard & Mohen 1974) are not found in England, although they have affinities with Iberian blades (e.g. Quinta da Agua Branca, Portugal: Fortes 1906), and with the blades of the North German Oder-Elbe group like those from Gau-Bickelheim (Hundt 1971).

The gold decoration of the wooden handles, practised on both sides of the Channel, was once considered the work of a single workshop. Study of the detail of the small gold pins by Christiane Eluère has however shown considerable typological variability which allows them to be classified into eight different categories (Eluère 1985, 66). The study has also shown that the gold which was used came from a number of sources. The levels of impurities in the gold from Bush Barrow

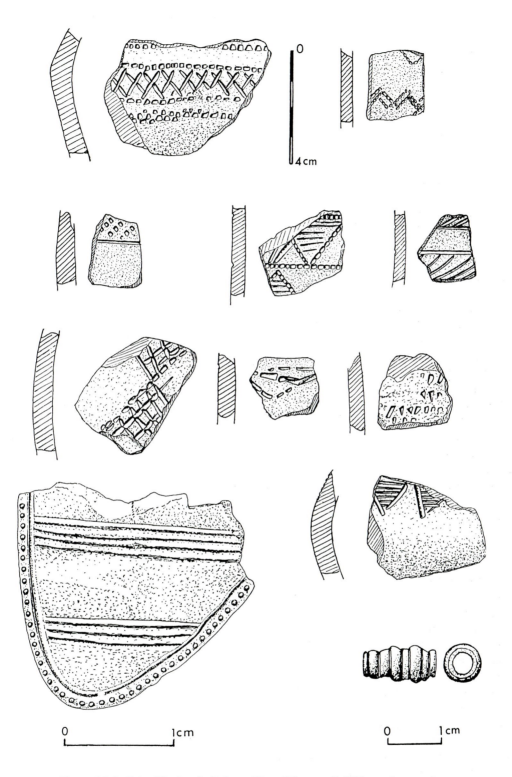

Figure 18.1. Saint-Nicolas-du-Pelem, Côtes d'Armor: Collédic settlement site.
Beaker pottery, fragment of gold ornament, segmented faience bead.

and that from Cruguel are relatively close (gold with 10 per cent silver and presence of copper and tin), but Corfield's analysis of the Wessex gold and the spectrographic analyses carried out by Hartmann show evidence of several different workshops.

The wide-bodied flanged axes from the Breton tumuli, with their relatively low flanges (Briard 1984, 80), also

differ from those of Wessex such as the Bush Barrow example, which tend to be more elongated (Annable & Simpson 1964, 99).

There are also differences in Early Bronze Age lithics. The perforated battle-axes known from several Beaker or Early Bronze Age assemblages in England (such as Wilsford and Manton) are paralleled in Brit-

tany only by the axe-hammer from the tumulus of
Creac'h Morvan at Saint-Thégonnec (Finistère; Briard
1984, fig. 65).

The Breton arrowheads also betray regional distinctions. The very large ogival arrowheads of the type
found at Saint-Vougay and Saint-Thégonnec in Finistère
are unknown in British contexts. Well-made triangular
arrowheads such as those from Breach Farm at
Llanblethian (Glamorgan; Savory 1980) are similar to
those found in Normandy at Beaumont Hague (Manche),
or in occasional Breton assemblages such as Lambader

and Keruzoret at Plouvorn (Finistère), and Cruguel at
Guidel (Morbihan).

To complete this survey of regional differentiation
we can also cite the architecture of tombs and tumuli.
It is clear that the megalithic tradition played a much
greater part in Brittany than in Wessex.

In conclusion, while we can say that there is an
undeniable relationship between Wessex and Brittany,
study of the detail of the burials reveals the care taken
on both sides of the Channel to preserve regional
identity.

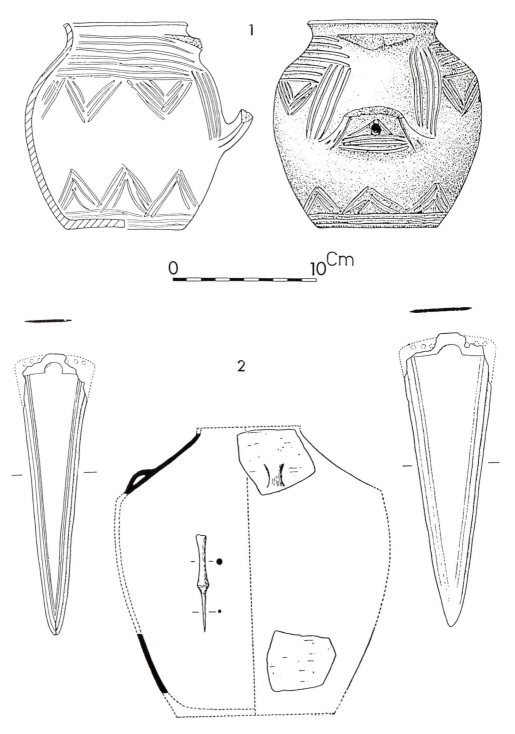

*Figure 18.2. 1. Pottery from Newbarn Down, Isle of Wight (after Tomalin). 2. Four-handled pottery vessel and daggers
from Winterbourne Stoke (after Annable & Simpson)*

Pottery

As we have seen, the presence of vessels of Breton style or inspiration on the other side of the Channel has long been recognized, notably the Biconical Urns from Doddington in Northumberland and from Winterbourne Stoke in Wessex (Annable & Simpson 1964, 105). It should be noted that the latter vessel was associated with two daggers of archaic type, having six rivets and central omega (Fig. 18.2.2), whereas in Brittany these are never associated with pottery in graves. To this series of early Breton material from Britain can be added the small vessel from Spitall Hill near Simondside in Northumberland (Briard 1987a) and more particularly that from the Newbarn Down barrow on the Isle of Wight (Basford 1980). This seems to be a local imitation from its globular form, its wide decorative incisions and espe-cially its curious red slip which gives it a somewhat metallic appearance. The recent discovery of another four-handled vessel of Breton type, as yet unpublished, in southern England (Kinnes, pers. comm.) confirms the cross-Channel influence of the Breton workshops.

Other pottery types such as urns allow us to identify material travelling in the opposite direction, from Great Britain to Brittany. Urns with horseshoe handles are found in contexts of the initial Early Bronze Age at the Le Moulin alignments at Saint-Just (Ille-et-Vilaine; Fig. 18.3.1), just as at Amesbury barrow G71 (Fig. 18.3.2; Moore & Rowlands 1972, pl. V). The latter vessel appears to be a secondary insertion accompanied by a small socketed razor which would make this of later date than the Saint-Just example. This is however from an old excavation and the depth of the horseshoe handle is very similar to that from Saint-Just.

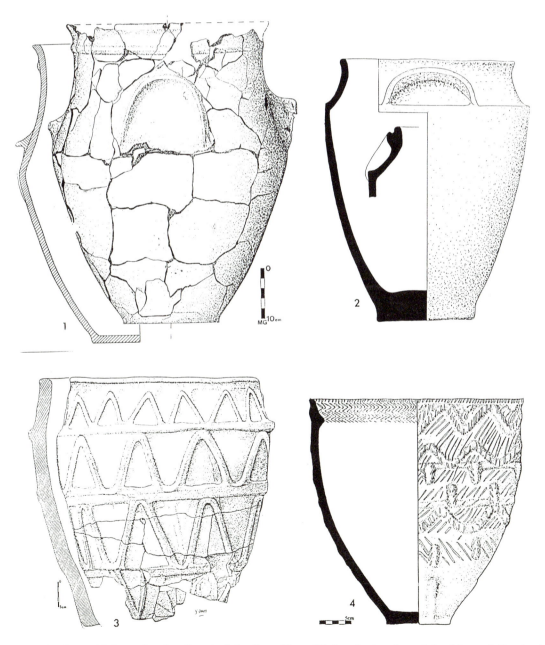

Figure 18.3. Urns with horseshoe handles: 1. Saint-Just, Ille-et-Vilaine; 2. Amesbury (after Moore & Rowlands).
Encrusted urns: 3. Le Quiou, Côtes d'Armor; 4. Shanahoe, Ireland (after Kavanagh)

Collared Urns of classic British type are unknown in Brittany, but they were evidently the basis of a derivative series of Breton types. These are characterized by a cordon below the rim which is attached to the rim by a progressive thickening of the rim itself. The first vessel of this type to be reported came from the beach of Tourony at Trégastel in the Côtes d'Armor (Briard 1965, fig. 110). Other urns of this type, with thickened rims, have been found by Le Bihan at Ergué-Armel, Quimper, in Finistère.

Many other comparisons could be drawn between urns with lugs or cordons known both in south-west Britain and in Brittany. The most striking ceramic connection is furnished by an urn recently discovered near the Château du Hac at Le Quiou in the Côtes d'Armor. This large vessel has both horizontal cordons and others arranged in arcs (Fig. 18.3.3). It is difficult to avoid comparison with the Encrusted Urns which are so well known in Ireland, such as that from Shanahoe in County Laois (Fig. 18.3.4; Kavanagh 1972). Other variants, possible intermediaries, are known in Great Britain, especially in Wales, such as Pendine at Merthyr Mawr Warren (Savory 1980, 208). All recent discoveries in Brittany show that urn burials assumed great importance from the end of the Middle Bronze Age. Some of them come from burials with surrounding ditches such as the urn from the Chapelle de l'Iff at Languenan in the Côtes d'Armor.

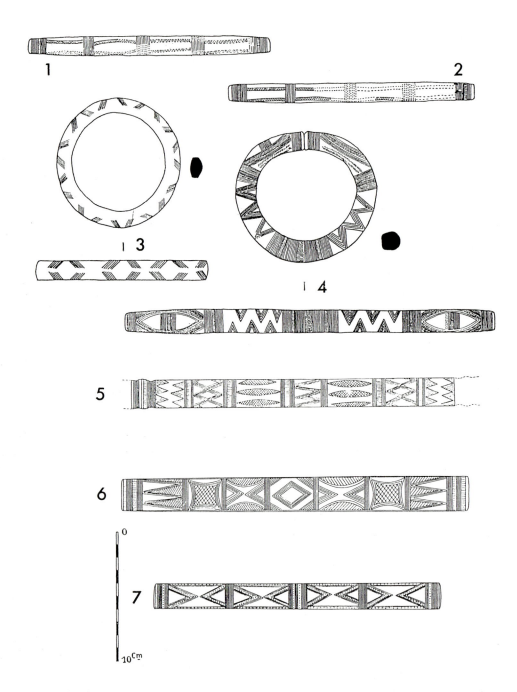

Figure 18.4. Middle Bronze Age decorated armrings: 1. & 2. Kent; 3. Ebbesbourne Wake; 4. Liss (after Rowlands); 5. Drouges, Ille-et-Vilaine; 6. Teillay, Ille-et-Vilaine; 7. Janzé, Ille-et-Vilaine

Metal products

It is out of the question here to undertake a complete review of the relations between Brittany and the British Isles suggested by Middle and Late Bronze Age metalwork. These have been discussed on several occasions, often from the perspective of the Channel Islands as staging-points. Regional variants are evidence of relations with the Tréboul group. In the case of palstaves, recent studies by Verney have allowed increasingly detailed analysis of the methods of production and of trade across the Channel. The most distinctive type was the heavy bronze armring with geometric decoration, known in Brittany as the Bignan type (Briard 1965, 123). The inventory of material by Rowlands (1971) included half a dozen hoards with armrings of this type in southern and south-eastern England: Liss in Hampshire, Grimstone in Dorset, Ebbesbourne Wake in Wiltshire. One armring came from the Thames in the London area. The close stylistic resemblance between these armrings and the Breton series is very clear (Fig. 18.4), especially (as Rowlands remarks) in the examples from the Thames and from Grimstone.

Gold was also the subject of frequent exchanges. Torcs of the Tara-Yeovil type from the transition between Middle and Late Bronze Age have been found in Brittany, for example at Cesson-Sévigné (Ille-et-Vilaine). A revised typology for these pieces and detailed distribution maps were published on the occasion of the restoration of the torc from Saint Helier in Jersey (Northover 1989). For Brittany, the only new development is the 'rediscovery' of a beautiful twisted torc, 110 mm long and weighing 1200 g. It came from the area of Daoulas (Finistère), and was for many years held in a private collection before being displayed in the Daoulas exhibition on the Bronze Age in 1988 (Le Goffic 1988, 92, no. 10–02–93).

At the beginning of the Late Bronze Age, rapiers of the Breton Rosnoën group, with either notches or four rivets, were exported to England. The mechanism of these exchanges has recently become clearer with the identification of wreck sites on the British coast at Moor Sand near Plymouth and Langdon Bay near Dover. The large cargo from the latter site shows a mixture of elements unusual for the Rosnoën group: swords together with median winged axes. As for the Moor Sand discovery, this has yielded a Breton-style palstave in association with an eastern-style sword of Pepinville type with umbrella-shaped hilt. This shows that the cargoes contained mixtures of bronzes of Atlantic and Continental type.

The Saint-Brieuc-des-Iffs group of Late Bronze II date has long been placed alongside the British Wilburton group. For new information about their interrelation we must again turn to the Channel Islands. In May 1976 a hoard of 115 bronze fragments was found at Le Clos de la Blanche Pierre at Saint Lawrence on Jersey (Finlaison & Coombs 1981). The material was charac-

teristic of Late Bronze II, with leaf-shaped swords, looped palstaves, and spear shaft ferrules. Special mention must be made of a beautiful looped phalera, similar to those in the Saint-Brieuc-des-Iffs hoard itself, but harness attachments are also found in England in the Wilburton and Isleham hoards. A spearhead with crescent-shaped perforations in the Blanche Pierre hoard is of typically British kind. This Jersey hoard appears then as a perfect intermediary between the Saint-Brieuc-des-Iffs and Wilburton groups. Recent metal analyses (Coombs 1988) have shown the progressive admixture of lead, as in both these groups.

Established Anglo-Breton relations continue with the Carp's Tongue complex, with no striking new discoveries to modify earlier accounts. The final stage in Bronze Age relations – already encroaching on the Iron Age – is marked by the export of Breton socketed axes, which recent studies have shown to have been a kind of palaeomoney or primitive currency (Briard 1987b).

References

Abercromby, J., 1912. *A Study of the Bronze Age Pottery of Great Britain and Ireland*. Oxford: Clarendon Press

Annable, F.K., & Simpson, D.D.A., 1964. *Guide Catalogue of the Neolithic Collections in Devizes Museum*. Devizes: Wiltshire Archaeological and Natural History Society

Basford, H.V., 1980. *The Vectis Report. A Survey of Isle of Wight Archaeology*. Isle of Wight Archaeological Committee

Briard, J., 1965. *Les Dépôts Bretons de l'Age du Bronze Atlantique*. Rennes: Travaux du Laboratoire d'Anthropologie Préhistorique de la Faculté des Sciences de Rennes

Briard, J., 1984. *Les Tumulus d'Armorique*. Paris: Picard

Briard, J., 1987a. Wessex et Armorique, une revision, in *Les Relations entre le Continent et les Iles Britanniques à l'Age du Bronze*. Supplément à la Revue Archéologique de Picardie, 77–87

Briard, J., 1987b. Systèmes prémonétaires en Europe préhistorique: fiction ou réalité? in *Rythmes de la Production Monétaire de l'Antiquité à nos Jours*. Louvain: Seminaire de Numismatique Marcel Hoc 731–43

Briard, J., (ed.) 1989. *Mégalithes de la Haute-Bretagne. Les Monuments de la Fort de Brocéliande et du Ploërmelais*. Paris: Documents d'Archéologie Française

Briard, J., & Mohen, J.-P., 1974. Le tumulus de la forêt de Carnoët à Quimperlé, Finistère. *Antiquités Nationales* 6, 46–60

Clarke, D.V., Cowie, T.G., & Foxon, A., 1985. *Symbols of Power at the Time of Stonehenge*. Edinburgh: H.M.S.O.

Coombs, D.G., 1988. The Late Bronze Age hoard from Clos de la Blanche Pierre, Saint Lawrence, Jersey, Channel Islands. *Oxford Journal of Archaeology* 7, 313–42

Eluère, C., 1982. *Les Ors Préhistoriques*. Paris: Picard

Eluère, C., 1985. Clous d'incrustation en or des tumulus armoricains. *Paléométallurgie de la France Atlantique 2*. Rennes: Travaux du Laboratoire d'Anthropologie, Université de Rennes I, 55–70

Finlaison, M., & Coombs, D., 1981. Bronze Age hoard. *Bulletin Annuel de la Société Jersiaise* 23, 124–42

Fortes, J., 1906. La sépulture de Quinta da Agua Branca, Porto, Portugal. *Revue Préhistorique* 5, 169–77

Gallay, G., 1988. Die mittel- und spätbronze- sowie älter-eisenzeitlichen bronze Dolchen in Frankreich und auf den Britischen Kanalinseln. Munich: Beck

Gerloff, S., 1975. *The Early Bronze Age Daggers in Great Britain and a Reconsideration of the Wessex Culture.* Munich: Beck

Giot, P.-R., & Cogné, J., 1951. L'âge du bronze ancien en Bretagne. *L'Anthropologie* 53, 425–44

Hundt, H.J., 1971. Der Dolchhort von Gau-Bickelheim in Rheinhessen. *Jahrbuch der Römisch-Germanisches Zentralmuseums Mainz* 18, 1–50

Kavanagh, R.D., 1973. The incrusted urns in Ireland. *Proceedings of the Royal Irish Academy* 73, 507–618

Le Goffic, M., 1988. *Avant les Celtes. L'Europe à l'Age du Bronze 2500–800 av. J.C.*. Daoulas: Association Abbaye de Daoulas

Le Provost, F., Giot, P.-R., & Onne, Y., 1972. Prospections sur les collines de Saint-Nicolas-du-Pelem, du chalco-lithique à la protohistoire. *Annales de Bretagne* 79, 39–48

L'Helgouach, J., 1970. La sépulture du Goërem à Gâvres. *Gallia Préhistoire* 13, 217–61

MacSween, A., & Burgess, C., (eds.) 1984. *Au Temps de Stonehenge.* Tournai

Martin, A., 1904. Les sépultures armoricaines à belles pointes de flèches en silex. *L'Anthropologie* 11, 159–78

Moore, C.N., & Rowlands, M., 1972. *Bronze Age Metalwork in Salisbury Museum.* Salisbury: Salisbury & South Wiltshire Museum

Northover, J.P., 1989. The gold torc from Saint Helier, Jersey. *Bulletin Annuel de la Société Jersiaise* 25, 112–37

Piggott, S., 1938. The Early Bronze Age in Wessex. *Proceedings of the Prehistoric Society* 4, 52–106

Rowlands, M.J., 1971. A group of incised decorated armrings and their significance for the Middle Bronze Age of southern Britain, in *Prehistoric and Roman Studies*, ed. G. de G. Sieveking. London: British Museum, 183–99

Savory, H.N., 1980. *Guide Catalogue of the Bronze Age Collections.* Cardiff: National Museum of Wales

Taylor, J.J., 1980. *Bronze Age Goldwork of the British Isles.* Cambridge: Cambridge University Press

19

Cooking for the Elite:
Feasting Equipment in the Late Bronze Age

José Gomez de Soto

During the Late Bronze Age, throughout the whole of Europe, ostentatious elite consumption of food and drink was an opportunity to affirm and consolidate social position. It became necessary to produce special feasting equipment: bronze buckets, cauldrons and other types of vessels, flesh-hooks and spits. The sumptuousness of these products anticipates the extraordinary furnishings used at the end of the Hallstatt period and during the La Tène period. The decoration of symbolic animal images, such as deer and birds, indicates that this consumption was closely associated with religious practices.

Pendant l'Age du Bronze final, dans toute l'Europe, les pratiques de consommation ostentatoire de nourriture et boisson par les élites, propices à l'affirmation et au renforcement du rang social, ont entraîné la production d'un instrumentum *spécifique: vaisselles variées, crochets à viande et broches à rôtir. La richesse de cette production anticipe sur les mobiliers somptueux qui seront utilisés plus tard à la fin du Premier Age du Fer et pendant la période de La Tène. L'ornementation d'images d'animaux symboliques (cerfs, oiseaux) indique que cette consommation était indissociable des pratiques réligieuses.*

The consumption of food and drink, particularly on rare or special occasions, as Sherratt reminds us (1991, 229), furnishes a communication system ideal for the expression of social competition.

This process must have begun at a very early period, perhaps during the Palaeolithic in the context of the division of game among members of individual human groups (Testart 1982, 212). Despite the commonly held view, social inequalities may have emerged before the adoption of food production in conjunction with the development of storage systems by certain hunter-gatherer societies; we certainly see it in operation in many hunter-gatherer societies of the present day. Feasting can become 'the occasion par excellence for the affirmation of rank and the consolidation of social position'; it provides the opportunity to display stored wealth, 'to demonstrate it by extravagant distribution, and to draw from it loyalty and prestige' (Testart 1982, 58). It may indeed become the real stimulus for the accumulation of wealth. The holding of feasts was sometimes linked to specific seasonal conditions (Mauss 1906).

The development of food production certainly led to a reduction in the risk of scarcity, but also facilitated the accumulation of surplus. The increase in numbers of herd animals could now take centre-stage in social competition, especially if the herds were essentially concentrated in the hands of the leaders. The present-day example of pig-rearing in the New Guinea Highlands illustrates this phenomenon (Pétrequin & Pétrequin 1988, 92). Wealth in the form of food could be put to good use by its distribution within the group or to an invited group through the medium of sumptuous and ostentatious feasts and banquets designed to increase the prestige of the person holding them, or of the group to which he belonged or whose identity he represented (Testart 1982). We may speculate that the batteries of pits full of heat-cracked stones and charcoal – pit-hearths often referred to as 'Polynesian ovens' – known in various parts of Europe are in at least some cases the remains of such a practice. This is especially likely in the case of the enormous aggregations of pit-hearths at sites such as Villeneuve-Tolosane, Haute-Garonne (France), which date to the Middle Neolithic (Clottes *et al.* 1979).[1]

In addition to feasts involving a large number of participants there may also have been events attended by a smaller number of guests, including ritual offerings and sacrifices in which only a few people participated. These are difficult to document in the Neolithic owing to scantiness of the material traces, but sacrifices in particular become much more evident in the metal ages. The Homeric poems provide evidence relating to a long period of time, in particular to the eleventh and tenth centuries BC. They give numerous examples of sacrifice and of the 'cuisine' which went with them, ending with a division of the fare between gods and mortals on principles which are already in essence those of the Classical age (Vernant & Detienne 1983). In barbarian Europe during the Middle and Late Bronze Age similar practices are suggested by the accumulations of animal bones at the *Brandopferplätzen* of the Alpine region (Fig. 19.1), one of the best examples being the site of Langacker in Bavaria (Chlingensperg 1904; Krämer 1966). The scale of accumulation at certain *Brandopferplätzen* is impressive: at Langacker, the debris covered an area 32 m in diameter and reached a height of 4 m. Study of the typology of the 700 vessels recovered indicates several centuries of use, and some authorities have estimated that 10 to 20 animals must have been sacrificed each year. In reality we do not know whether the sacrifices were spread fairly evenly over a long period, or were the result of only a few large-scale events, but the cult places were visible from a distance and the fires burning during the ceremonies would have made an impressive sight. It is unclear whether the mass of the population were given access to these vast cult places, and if so on what basis. If we assume that sacrifices were frequent, with only one or a few victims on each occasion, the common people may simply have been passive spectators, and participation in the sacrificial meal may have been reserved for a small number of chosen people.

By the time the *Brandopferplätzen* were in use society had long experienced the growing power of the elites, aided in particular by the control of trade networks in metals and in luxury goods such as amber or glass. From the Hallstatt A period a number of burials are characterized by especially rich grave goods which sometimes included a waggon or waggon parts.[2] The grave at Hart-an-der-Alz (Bavaria) contained several metal vessels: bronze bucket, cup and sieve (Fig. 19.2). A little later, in Hallstatt B2, the burial in the tumulus of Saint-Romain-de-Jalionas, Isère (France) included a bronze plate, bucket and dipper (Verger & Guillaumet 1988). Here feasting equipment takes its place alongside classic markers of social rank such as weapons or objects of precious metal. The principal elements are connected with drinking, which could have had several aspects: ostentatious consumption, liturgical function (in the context of libations) or sacred intoxication, a state attested in the Classical world (Dionysiac intoxication), and induced by different methods in other societies (e.g. peyotl). In the latter case, what we would be seeing here would be a marker of priestly function, one of the characteristics of the Indo-European ruler (Dumezil 1973, 358; Dubuisson 1978). What we are also seeing, however, are the beginnings of a funerary practice which becomes much more strongly manifest in Hallstatt D waggon burials of the late sixth and early fifth centuries BC, where the inclusion of a Greek or Etruscan bronze vessel adds yet further to the luxury of the feasting equipment. It is clear that there is no need to look for a new Mediterranean influence on the barbarian world at that period; what we recognize instead is the continuation of a practice already six centuries old.

Figure 19.1. The Brandopferplatz of Oberaudorf, Kr. Rosenheim, Bavaria, from the south. (From Krämer 1966)

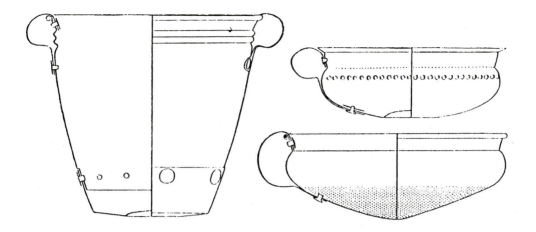

Figure 19.2. The drinking service from the waggon grave of Hart-an-der-Alz, Bavaria. (After Müller-Karpe)

The expansion in use of bronze tableware and cooking equipment begins from the start of the Late Bronze Age (Reinecke Bronze D). The value of the equipment, drawing on the skills of specialists who had mastered the complicated techniques of sheet metalworking and casting, limited its use to social elites who, as we have seen, were able to take the metal vessels with them into the afterlife. Communal ceremonies may also be envisaged in which some of these luxury goods belonged to the community as a whole.

The bronze vessels are very varied and have been the subject of numerous studies.[3] Suffice it to note here that two series can be distinguished: one central and east European, which includes carinated cups and flasks and penetrates no further west than eastern France; and an Atlantic equivalent which parallels the central and east European forms. The cauldron with cruciform handle attachments (Merhart 1952, map 1), for example, is to some degree equivalent to the cauldron made of riveted bands with ring handles found from the British Isles to the Iberian peninsula (Briggs 1984, 162 & 164). In contrast, despite regional variations introduced by different centres of production, the Kurd-type bucket seems to be widespread from the Atlantic to the Danube and Italy (Merhart 1952, map 5; Briggs 1984; Chaume & Feugère 1990, 41). The story of these vessel types continues after the Late Bronze Age: buckets of Kurd type and cauldrons with cruciform handle attachments are present for example in the Early Iron Age cemetery of Poiseul-la-Ville in the Côte-d'Or (France) (Chaume & Feugère 1990). Cauldrons with cruciform handle attachments only went out of use in the Hallstatt D period, or at the beginning of La Tène A (Deffressigne 1992).

As regards cooking implements, the principal elements are meat hooks and spits. Their typological aspects have already been adequately covered in previous studies.[4]

Meat hooks must have served to handle the meat in the cauldrons and lift it out when ready. They are based on a trans-European model consisting of a simple bent rod which was used throughout the Late Bronze Age. Elaborations of this model may be divided into two groups: a curved rod springing from a socket in the Atlantic zone (Fig. 19.3), and varieties in which the

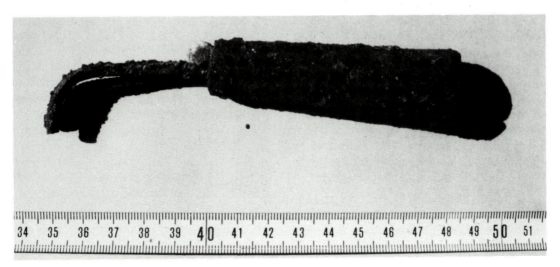

Figure 19.3. Meat hook (unpublished) from Bois du Roc at Vilhonneur, Charente, France. (Photo: J. Gomez de Soto)

hook is placed at right angles to the socket in the Continental and Italian zones (Fig. 19.4). By the end of the Late Bronze Age and the beginning of the Iron Age elaborate examples had come into use in the Atlantic zone, consisting of several separate elements either mounted on a wooden pole or hooked together. Good examples are the meat hooks from the Isle of Ely in Cambridgeshire (England), from Dunaverny in Co. Antrim (Ireland), from Coulon in Deux-Sèvres (France), and from Nostra Senhora da Guia (Portugal).

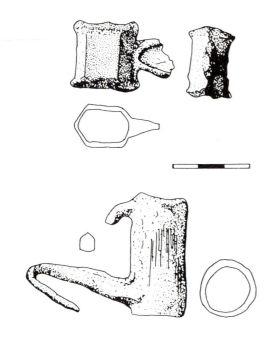

Figure 19.4. Meat hooks of central European type from the hoard of Cannes-Ecluse, Seine-et-Marne, France. (After Gaucher & Robert)

In the Atlantic zone, examples of rigid spits without clearly marked handle are known from the Iberian peninsula. In the course of the eleventh or tenth centuries BC articulated spits make their appearance in the Wilburton/Saint-Brieuc-des-Iffs horizon, as for example in the Isleham hoard. They are found from southern England to Portugal, those in France and the Iberian peninsula dating to the Hallstatt B phase. We know that spits of this type reached – or may even have been produced in – the Mediterranean region, where examples have been found at Amathonte on Cyprus, and on Sardinia at Monte Sa Idda and probably Pirozu Sa Benatzu (Lo Schiavo 1991, 223). The spit from Amathonte has been the source of controversy over the direction of relations between the East and West Mediterranean (Gomez de Soto 1991), a question which need not be elaborated in the present discussion. At the same period in central Europe we find non-articulated spits in Switzerland, Württemberg and Austria, and in Italy such as that from grave 277 at Este. These, like the articulated Atlantic examples, have a handle ending in a ring. From the Orientalizing period onwards these spits form part of

the equipment placed in warrior graves on the Tuscan coast of Italy. They figure at the same period in Hallstatt grave assemblages north of the Alps.

The context of deposition of these precious cooking implements and metal vessels varies greatly from region to region. In central Europe, eastern France and the Mediterranean the vessels are found in graves, as at Hart-an-der-Alz and Saint-Romain-de-Jalionas, examples belonging respectively near the beginning and end of the Late Bronze Age. They became standard equipment in all rich tombs. By contrast, in the Atlantic region these vessels are found either in dismantled and fragmentary state in bronze hoards – such as Prairie de Mauves and Vénat in western France – or they are the container vessel for the hoard itself, as for example at Notre Dame d'Or (France). In Ireland, many of them were thrown into marshes or bogs. Meat hooks and spits also figure in fragmentary form in hoards at Monte Sa Idda, Isleham, Notre Dame d'Or and Vénat. Others were thrown into wet contexts: marshes at Coulon and Dunaverny, or a river at Port-Sainte-Foy, Dordogne (France). Only in the Mediterranean region are they found in graves, as at Este and Amathonte, and only later do they become common in rich graves north of the Alps, as for example the meat hook in the Early Iron Age burial at Court-Saint-Etienne in Belgium, or the spits at Hallstatt. Finally, it should be mentioned that spits and meat hooks are also sometimes found at settlement sites, for example at Bois du Roc at Vilhonneur, Charente (France), or Cachouça at Idanha-a-Nova (Portugal).

The treatment experienced by this luxury cooking and drinking equipment was therefore very varied. Leaving aside possible cases of accidental loss – notably those pieces from settlement contexts – we can distinguish two categories:

— deposit in tombs or wet contexts, in the same way as for other luxury items such as waggons or waggon elements and prestige weapons. These are cases of abandonment in locations considered of great significance by the living who associated them with the dead and the gods. A piece as fragile as the meat hook from Coulon can have been made only for deposition in the marsh. We may recall that spits often figured in temple hoards in Greece, as for example at the Argive Heraeum.
— inclusion with other metal destined for recasting. In this case the process was the same for luxury goods as for objects of everyday usage (Verger 1990, 61).

In fact, the contradiction between these two modes of abandonment may be more apparent than real. On the one hand, the true significance of hoards, even of those which seem to consist of founder's material, is perhaps not always as trivial as it appears. On the other hand, a luxury object which is too damaged to be of further

Figure 19.5. Bird images on bronze vessels, spits and meat hooks. Bird-shaped handle terminals: 1. Richigen bei Worb, Bern, Switzerland (Early Iron Age). Relief (repoussé) decoration: 2. Siem, Denmark. Representation in the round: 3. Alpenquai and 4. Grosser Hafner, Zürich, Switzerland; 5. Dunaverny, Co. Antrim, Ireland. (1 & 2 after Merhart; 3 & 4 after Mohen; 5 after Jockenhövel) (Scales various)

use, such as a broken sword, may lose its power. Finally, procedures of deconsecration exist which in certain conditions allow goods dedicated for use in cult or as sacred offerings to be recycled (de Cazanove 1991, 208).

In the Late Bronze Age, therefore, metal equipment appears to have been inseparable from the ostentatious consumption of food and drink, probably on occasions associated with cultic practices. The frequency of symbolic forms and ornamentation brings them clearly into the religious sphere (Merhart 1952; Kossack 1954). The most widespread is bird symbolism. This had first been used at the end of the Early Bronze Age, around 1500 BC, and is found during the Late Bronze Age in

Atlantic Europe on both spits (at Port-Sainte-Foy, Compiègne, and elsewhere) and meat hooks (at Dunaverny). These find parallels on metal vessels in central and northern Europe and Italy. In the latter regions, birds often appear in the form of a double protome surrounding a disk, an image which may represent the solar barque. The power of this symbol was so great that it was able to traverse the centuries; during the early La Tène period it was still reproduced on torcs. It also seems that in vessels without figured decoration on the body, the bird protome is hidden in the decorative curves and counter-curves of the handle-ends (Fig. 19.5,1). Less common are representations of red deer, a symbol of fertility and resurrection associated with myths of springtime. They are represented by a deer head on the spit from Challans in the Vendée (France), or by a body – accidentally decapitated – at

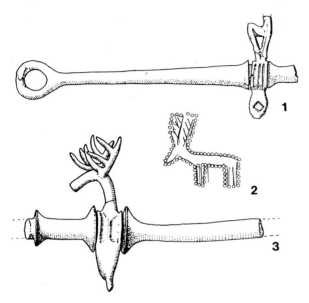

Figure 19.6. Deer images on bronze spits: 1. Notre Dame d'Or, Vienne, France; 3. Challans, Vendée, France. 2. Engraved and relief (repoussé) deer on gold cup from Zürich-Altstetten, Switzerland. (1 after Gomez de Soto; 2 after Nagy; 3 after Mohen) (Scales various)

Notre Dame d'Or, Monte Sa Idda and Cachouça. The deer symbol is rare in the north Alpine area, but is present on the gold cup from Zürich, which may date from the Late Bronze Age (Fig. 19.6).

This discussion leads us to conclude that behind the technological differences evident in the products of bronze-workers and cauldron-makers, and behind the apparent contrast between the Atlantic complex on the one hand and the central/north European and Italian complex on the other lay a common world of ceremonial ostentation and religious symbolism, and a deeply-rooted unity of mental universe. This was, in some measure, an archaic form of European integration.

Notes

1. Structures with heated stones of the 'Polynesian oven' variety are known from the Middle Neolithic to the Later Iron Age. Sometimes single, though occasionally arranged in groups (but never on the scale of Villeneuve-Tolosane), they probably had a simple domestic function.
2. For references see Gomez 1984. Another waggon burial has recently been found in southern Germany (Winghart 1991), and examples are also known from Switzerland.
3. See especially Merhart 1952. Later references are given in Briggs 1987, Chaume & Feugère 1990, and Thévenot 1991. See also the various volumes in the series *Prähistorische Bronzefunde*.
4. See especially Hundt 1953, Jockenhövel 1974, Almagro Gorbea 1974 and Mohen 1977. Later references are given in two recent articles: Gomez de Soto & Pautreau 1988

(meat hooks) and Gomez de Soto 1991 (spits), to which the reader is directed for examples discovered since the earlier publications. Since the 1988 article, details of a new meat hook from the Bois du Roc at Vilhonneur (Charente) have become available (Fig. 19.3 and Gomez de Soto forthcoming).

References

Almagro Gorbea, M., 1974. Los asadores de bronce del Suroeste peninsular. *Revista de Archivos, Bibliotecas y Museos* 77, 351–95

Briggs, C.S., 1984. Buckets and cauldrons in the Late Bronze Age of north-west Europe: a review, in *Les Relations entre le Continent et les Iles Britanniques à l'Age du Bronze*. Supplément à la Revue Archéologique de Picardie, 161–87

Cazanove, O. de, 1991. Ex-votos de l'Italie républicaine: sur quelques aspects de leur mise au rebut, in *Les Sanctuaires Celtiques et le Monde Méditerranéen*. Paris: Errance, 203–15

Chaume, B., & Feugère, M., 1990. *Les Sépultures Tumulaires Aristocratiques du Hallstatt Ancien de Poiseul-la-Ville (Côte-d'Or)*. Revue Archéologique du Centre, Supplément 10

Chlingensperg auf Ber, M. von, 1904. Der Knochenhügel am Langacker und die vorgeschichtliche Herdstelle am Eisenbichl bei Reichenhall in Oberbayern. *Mitteilungen der Anthropologisches Gesellschaft in Wien* 34, 53–70

Clottes, J., Giraud, J.-P., Rouzaud, F., & Vaquer, J., 1979. Le village chasséen de Villeneuve-Tolosane (Haute-Garonne). *Congrès Préhistorique de France* 21(1), 116–28

Deffressigne, S., 1992. Présentation de la tombe à char d'Estissac à 'La Côte d'Ervaux' (Aube). *Bulletin de l'Association Française pour l'Etude de l'Age du Fer* 10, 23–4

Dubuisson, R., 1978. Le roi indo-européen et la synthèse des trois fonctions. *Annales Economie, Sociétés, Civilisations* 1978, 21–34

Dumézil, G., 1973. *Mythe et Epopée, vol. II*. Paris: Gallimard

Gomez, J., 1984. Chars funéraires, chars rituels our chars de combat? in *Elements de Pré- et Protohistoire Européenne. Hommage à J.-P. Millotte*. Paris: Belles Lettres, 605–15

Gomez de Soto, J., 1991. Le fondeur, le trafiquant et les cuisiniers. La broche d'Amathonte de Chypre et la chronologie absolue du bronze final atlantique, in *L'Age du Bronze Atlantique. Actes du Premier Colloque de Beynac*. Beynac: Association des Musées du Sarladais, 369–73

Gomez de Soto, J., & Pautreau, J.-P., 1988. Le crochet protohistorique en bronze de Thorigné à Coulon (Deux-Sèvres). *Archäologisches Korrespondenzblatt* 18, 31–42

Hundt, H-J., 1953. Uber Tüllenhaken und galben. *Germania* 31, 145–55

Jockenhövel, A., 1974. Fleischhaken von der britischen Inseln. *Archäologisches Korrespondenzblatt* 4, 329–38

Kossack, G., 1954. *Studien zum Symbolgut der Urnenfelder- und Hallstattzeit Mitteleuropas*. Berlin: Römisch-Germanisches Forschungen 20

Krämer, W., 1966. Prähistorische Brandopferplätzen. *Helvetia Antiqua* 1966, 111–22

Lo Schiavo, F., 1991. La Sardaigne et ses relations avec le bronze final atlantique, in *L'Age du Bronze Atlantique. Actes du Premier Colloque de Beynac*. Beynac: Association des Musées du Sarladais, 213–26

Mauss, M., 1906. Essai sur les variations saisonnières des sociétés esquimos: étude de morphologie sociale. *L'Année Sociologique* 9, 39–132

Merhart, G. von, 1952. Studien über einige Gattungen von Bronzegefässen. *Festschrift des Römisch-Germanisches Zentralmuseum Mainz*, 1–71

Mohen, J.-P., 1977. Broches à rôtir articulées de l'age du bronze. *Antiquités Nationales* 9, 34–9

Pétrequin, A.-M., & Pétrequin, P., 1988. *Le Néolithique des Lacs*. Paris: Errance

Sherratt, A., 1991. Paleoethnobotany: from crops to cuisine, in *Paleoecologia e Arqueologia II*, eds F. Queiroga & A.P. Dinis. Vila Nova de Famalicao: Centro de Estudos Arqueologicos Famalicenses, 221–36

Testart, A., 1982. *Les Chasseurs-Cueilleurs ou L'Origine des Inégalités*. Paris: Société d'Ethnographie

Thévenot, J.-P., 1991. *L'Age du Bronze en Bourgogne. Le Dépôt de Blanot (Côte-d'Or)*. Revue Archéologique de l'Est, Supplément 10

Verger, S., 1990. Du dépôt métallique à la tombe fastueuse, in *Les Premiers Princes Celtes*. Grenoble: Musée Dauphinois, 53–71

Verger, S., & Guillaumet, J.-P., 1988. Le tumulus de Saint-Romain-de-Jalionas. Premières observations, in *Les Princes Celtes et la Méditerranée*. Paris: Documentation Française, 130–40

Vernant, J.-P., & Detienne, R., (eds) 1983. *La Cuisine du Sacrifice en Grèce*. Paris: Gallimard

Winghart, S., 1991. Ein Wagengrab der späten Bronzezeit. *Archäologie in Deutschland* 1991, 6–11

20

Prehistoric Seafaring in the Channel

Seán McGrail

Keith Muckelroy's 1981 paper is the starting point for a study of the seafaring aspects of prehistoric trade between the continent and Britain. Likely cross-Channel routes are identified and the difficulties of the Atlantic coastal route from the Mediterranean to North-West Europe are discussed. The qualities needed by cross-Channel vessels are defined and the evidence from known prehistoric boats compared with them. The earliest indisputable evidence for seagoing plank boats or ships is from the late Iron Age: before that time, hide boats were probably used, although so far no example has been excavated. Early cross-Channel vessels were operated from informal landing-places within natural harbours, and environmental, rather than instrumental, navigational techniques were used on voyages out of sight of land.

L'article publié en 1981 de Keith Muckelroy constitue la base d'étude du commerce maritime préhistorique entre le continent et la Grande-Bretagne. Il identifie les itinéraires probablément empruntés à travers la Manche, et montre les difficultés liées à la navigation côtière dans l'Atlantique, depuis la Méditerranée jusqu'à l'Europe du nord-ouest. Les performances requises par les navires effectuant la traversée de la Manche sont définies, et sont mises en regard avec les caractéristiques des bateaux préhistoriques connus. Les premiers témoignages incontestables d'embarcations ou de bateaux à bordé de planches, capables d'affronter la haute mer, remontent à la fin de l'Age du Fer. Auparavant, des bateaux à coque de peau cousue ont dû être utilisés, bien que on n'en ait encore découvert aucun en contexte archéologique. Les premiers vaisseaux traversant la Manche mettaient à profit des débarcadères improvisés à l'intérieur de ports naturels, et lorsque la côte était hors de vue, des techniques de navigation environnementales, plutôt qu'instrumentales, étaient utilisées.

Introduction

In a paper entitled 'Middle Bronze Age trade between Britain and Europe: a maritime perspective', Keith Muckelroy (1981) described some of the evidence for prehistoric voyages across the Channel, including his own underwater excavations of the Bronze Age sites of *c.* 1000 BC off Moor Sands, east of the Salcombe estuary in Devon, and in Langdon Bay, east of Dover harbour. In this present article, I aim to build on Muckelroy's pioneering work, which was brought to a premature end by his death in 1980 at the early age of 29. In particular I shall consider the routes, the boats, the landing-places and the navigational techniques used in this cross-Channel traffic.

Maritime Archaeology is thought by some to be at the margin or periphery of the discipline rather than at the core; nevertheless the middle phase of many an ancient artefact's 'life' (production-distribution-consumption) included an overseas voyage and thus the problems raised here relate to an important element in prehistoric economic and social life, not without interest to the most landlubberly of archaeologists, especially those from the archipelago of islands off the north-west coast of Europe.

Oversea trade routes

There are no excavated examples of vessels wrecked whilst actually crossing the Channel in prehistoric times, although the Langdon Bay underwater finds may have come from such a wreck.[1] The evidence for early voyages must therefore come indirectly, and after appropriate source criticism, from the distribution patterns of artefacts and of those ideas which are archaeologically visible as 'monuments', as 'ritual' and as technological innovations. Although early prehistoric distribution patterns do not indicate clearly which overseas routes were used, distribution patterns from later prehistory (O'Connor 1980; Bradley 1984; 1990; Northover 1982; Tomalin 1984; 1988) suggest that the predominant routes used then were where, on nautical grounds, one would expect them to be:

— mid-Channel routes linking the Normandy/Brittany region of France and the River Seine catchment area with the Wessex region of central southern England, via the Solent and the rivers at Christchurch and Poole
— eastern routes connecting the Rhine region to the Thames region, each of these rivers having enormous catchment areas.

In the protohistoric period, from the first century BC onwards, there is literary confirmation of cross-Channel voyages in the writings of late Classical authors

such as Caesar (*B.G.* III 8; IV 21-36; V 2.23), Pliny (*N.H.* IV 101 (xv); 102 (xvi)); Strabo (*Geog.* 4.1.14; 4.2.1; 4.3.3-4; 4.4.1; 4.5.1-2) and Diodorus Siculus (V 21-3; 22.2-4; 38.5). This documentary evidence, when combined with contemporary distribution patterns (Cunliffe 1982, 42-51; 1983; 1987; 1988a, 98-104, 145-9; 1991; Fitzpatrick 1985; McGrail 1983, 319-34) suggests that there were then four principal sea routes between the Continent and Britain, with associated coastal passages (Fig. 20.1):

— the Rhine to the Thames
— in the region of the Strait, at the shortest crossing
— mid-Channel routes
— from western Brittany to south-west Britain and to south-east Ireland, for vessels coming from the Loire and Garonne estuaries.

These Channel crossings linked the maritime trading networks of the Continental Atlantic coast and rivers to

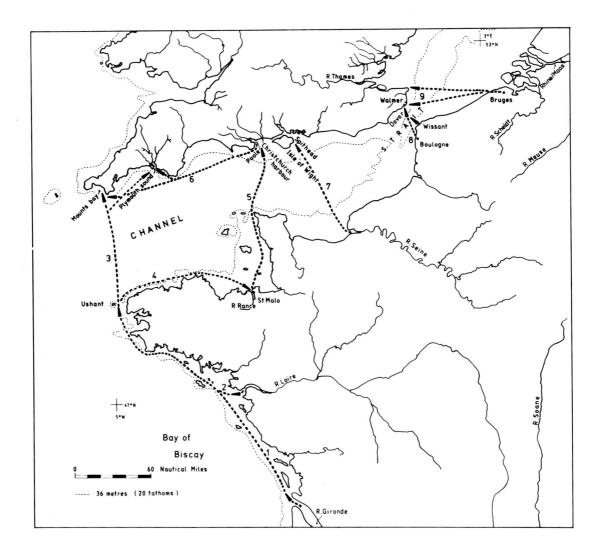

Figure 20.1. Cross-channel routes. 5, 7, 9 probably used from the 2nd millennium BC. 3, 5, 7, 8, 9 and associated coastal routes used in the late 1st millennium BC. Drawing: National Maritime Museum, Greenwich

the indigenous networks in British and Irish waters. Portages between the upper reaches of French rivers (Cunliffe 1988b; 1991) linked maritime north-west Europe to the maritime networks of the central and eastern Mediterranean, whilst the Iberian coastal maritime route linked north-west Europe to the western Mediterranean (Fig. 20.2). This Iberian coastal route would not have been an easy one, especially when northward-bound, as the summer winds would have been generally from the north, whilst the current would have set southerly. In addition, there were several prominent headlands to be rounded, for example Cape St Vincent to the south-west of the Algarve, which could involve a delay of several days whilst awaiting a favourable combination of wind and tidal stream. On such coastal passages it would have been necessary to work the tides, possibly involving anchoring or lying hove-to during foul winds and streams. It would probably also have been necessary to anchor during non-moonlit nights, and much use may have had to be made

of evening or early morning land breezes to work away from lee shores. The passage westwards from the Mediterranean to the Atlantic through the Strait at Gibraltar would also have been arduous, owing to the strong eastward-flowing currents in the Strait.

That this Atlantic coastal route was indeed used is suggested by extracts from a *Periplus* of the sixth century BC incorporated by Avienus in the fourth century AD into his *Ora Maritima* (Hawkes 1977, 19; Murphy 1977; McGrail 1990, 36) which describes what was evidently an established trade route along the western coast of Atlantic Europe and then along the northern shores of the Mediterranean to Massilia (Marseille).

This route is described in stages: from Ireland/ Britain to western Brittany; from western Brittany to Tartessus (a harbour in the Gulf of Cadiz); and from Tartessus through the Pillars of Hercules (Strait of Gibraltar) to Massilia, with a subsidiary route to Carthage. The text seems to suggest that Mediterranean

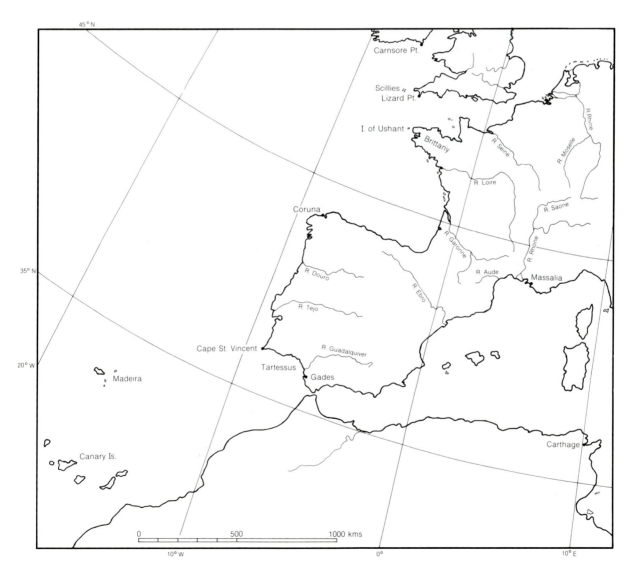

Figure 20.2. The Atlantic coast of Europe and NW Africa. Drawing: Institute of Archaeology, Oxford

merchants sailed to and from western Brittany, whilst the cross-Channel sections of these voyages were undertaken by the 'hardy and industrious peoples of the islands and coasts around Ushant' (Murphy 1977, lines 94-116). Pytheas also appears to have used this route in his late fourth century BC voyage of scientific and commercial exploration of the northern seas (Hawkes 1977; 1984). The fact that a lighthouse was built at La Coruña in north-west Spain during the Roman period (Hague 1973) further supports these arguments for early use of this difficult coastal route.

One of Columbus' major achievements five hundred years ago was to connect European maritime trade networks to the indigenous American networks (McGrail 1992). A little later, in 1497-9, Vasco da Gama sailed around southern Africa and re-connected European networks to those of the Indian Ocean (they had formerly been connected via a canal or by an overland portage from the River Nile to the Red Sea). These Indian Ocean networks were already connected to the networks of south-east Asia. Maritime connections were completed worldwide and the world encompassed by trade routes in 1519 to 1522 when Ferdinand Magellan and Sebastian del Cano, during their voyage of world circumnavigation, connected the American maritime trade networks to those of south-east Asia: this is probably the earliest examples of a commercial 'world system'. The establishment of individual European maritime trading networks in the earlier prehistoric period and their interconnection during the later prehistoric period may thus be seen as the first steps in a process which led to the European domination of world trade routes in the sixteenth to eighteenth centuries AD.

Boats used on the cross-Channel routes

Nowadays, in favourable conditions, people swim the Channel, and the Atlantic Ocean has been crossed by adventurers in the most unlikely vessels. Perhaps in prehistoric times there were similar adventurers with a 'Guinness Book of Records' attitude to the sea, and perhaps the Channel was crossed on occasions in what, by any standards, would be considered unseaworthy craft. Nevertheless, in an evaluation of early nautical possibilities it is essential to identify those types of vessel which, without special preparations, could carry a reasonable load and have a good chance of making return crossings of the Channel in the conditions then prevailing. This is not to claim that prehistoric humans had a modern attitude to reliability and timekeeping, nor our twentieth century expectations of low-risk, minimum-delay sea travel — on the contrary, in earlier times, when there was unseasonal weather, voyages were postponed until conditions improved, although doubtless there were occasional bad-weather crossings. The vessels regularly used on prehistoric cross-Channel voyages must have had certain qualities which made them reliable and seaworthy in Channel conditions, and

suitable to undertake the functions required of them, which may have included sea fishing as well as cross-Channel passages.

The principal desirable qualities required in a boat are listed in Table 20.1 under the headings of Safety and Performance. All these desirable characteristics, however, cannot be maximized in one boat: for high speed, for example, a boat should be long in proportion to its breadth and have the minimum wetted hull surface area. Such dimensional parameters impose constrictions on cargo capacity, transverse stability and seakindliness and thus these attributes cannot be maximized at the same time as speed. Every boat is thus a compromise: if some characteristics are maximized, less than optimum performance has to be accepted in other qualities.

Table 20.1. Desirable qualities in a seagoing vessel

SAFETY
    Seaworthiness — buoyancy
                        — strength and durability
    Stability

PERFORMANCE
    Cargo capacity
    Speed
    Manoeuvrability and controllability
    Closeness to the wind and minimum leeway (if sail)
    Sea-kindliness and dryness

The most important qualities for an early sea-going boat which could be used as a ferry and for fishing are probably the safety attributes of seaworthiness and stability — without these the boat would capsize, be swamped, or otherwise founder. High ratings would also be desirable in the performance attributes of closeness to the wind (otherwise the crossings could prove to be inordinately long and, on occasions, impossible) and seakindliness (without this quality the hull and rigging could be overstrained and the crew excessively seasick). The potential speed, manoeuvrability and cargo capacity of such a vessel would be residual attributes constrained by the necessity to achieve the qualities with higher priority, although without a reasonable (undefined) capacity for cargo, passengers and/or fishing catch there would be little point in going to sea.

The use of sail. The identification of the attribute 'closeness to the wind' as an important one implies that the ideal prehistoric cross-Channel ferry/fishing boat should be sailed. The earliest direct evidence for the indigenous use of sail in Atlantic Europe is from the first century BC: Caesar's description (*B.G.* III 13) of the leather sails of the boats of the Veneti of south-western Brittany; and the small gold model from

Broighter (Fig. 20.3) near Limavady in the north of Ireland (Farrell & Penny 1975) which has a mast stepped near amidships. There is, however, indirect evidence for earlier use in the sixth century BC Massiliote *Periplus* incorporated into Avienus' *Ora Maritima* (Hawkes 1977; Murphy 1977) which refers to voyages between western Brittany and Ireland which take two days. The speed of *c.* 5 knots which this implies and the long distance involved means that sail was almost certainly used. Sail was used in Egypt before 3000 BC and in the eastern Mediterranean from around 2000 BC (Casson 1971, fig. 6; figs 34-36). As sail, like the wheel, is its own advertisement, there is thus a possibility that sail was used in the seas off north-west Europe before the mid-first millennium BC, but probably not earlier than, say, the mid-second millennium.

As a working hypothesis it may be suggested therefore that, in Neolithic times, cross-Channel voyages were undertaken in paddled or oared vessels, which were possibly restricted to the shortest crossing in the

Strait. By the Iron Age, however, although some oared craft may have continued to be used across the Strait, the majority of voyages were under sail, but with oar power available for use in contrary or light wind conditions and when manoeuvring in inshore waters, i.e. a galley type of vessel. This use of sail would not only result in speedier and less arduous passages and higher cargo/crew ratios, but would also make the longer sea crossings in the western Channel a more practicable proposition.

Nowadays the predominant winds in the Channel region are between south-west and north-west. They have probably been from that sector from 1000 BC and possibly much earlier (a summary of the environmental evidence for early sea levels, coastlines, tidal regimes and weather patterns may be found in McGrail 1983, 303-7; 1987, 258-60). In the open sea, the wind would thus be more or less on the port beam of a vessel on a northward passage and on the starboard beam of a southbound vessel, i.e. at 80° to 100° to the intended track. This is as close as one would expect prehistoric

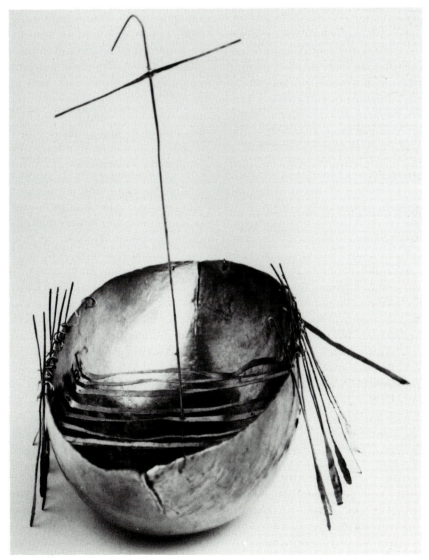

Figure 20.3. Small gold model boat of the 1st century BC from Broighter, Co. Derry, Ireland.
Photo: National Museum of Ireland

sailing craft to achieve, bearing in mind that it has been estimated that Classical Mediterranean and north European Viking age vessels with a single square sail could achieve only *c*. 75° to 80° (McGrail 1987, 260-2); and that the best which Columbus, with a three-masted vessel, appears to have achieved on his Atlantic voyage was *c*. 70° to 75° (McGrail 1992). A wind at right angles to the intended track is nowadays known as a 'soldier's wind' because the passage both ways can be made without tacking, and thus little nautical skill is needed. Indeed, for two-way voyages over relatively short distances such a beam wind is the best possible wind to have.

Logboats. In the lands bordering the Channel a dozen or so logboats ('dugout canoes') have been dated to pre-Roman times (Booth 1984; Bahn 1992). The dimensions of a simple basic logboat are however limited by the size of its parent log and thus its inherent stability, which is proportional to the cube of the waterline beam measurement, and its freeboard (height of the sides above the waterline) are generally insufficient to match the seaworthiness and stability criteria identified above as necessary attributes in a seagoing vessel. Furthermore, a basic logboat has insufficient stability to allow it to use sail other than in a light breeze from the stern sector.

On the other hand, there are many ethnographic examples, worldwide, of simple logboats which have been modified so that they gain the extra stability and freeboard they need to make them seaworthy. The hollowed parent log may be expanded in breadth after specialized treatment; a simple logboat may be fitted with stabilizing timbers along the sides at the waterline; or two such logboats may be paired side-by-side: such alternatives increase the waterline beam measurement and thereby enhance transverse stability (McGrail 1987, 66-73) which may then be sufficient to permit sail to be used. The freeboard (a measure of reserve buoyancy and thus of safety) of such stability-enhanced logboats may be increased by adding one or more strakes of planking to the sides.

There is, however, no indisputable evidence for such alterations and additions in the prehistoric logboats so far excavated in north-western France and southern Britain. Thus, on present evidence, logboats are unlikely to have been used on cross-Channel voyages.

Plank boats. Apart from the Hjortspring boat of the mid-fourth century BC from the Baltic island of Als, all prehistoric plank boats known to date come from Britain: three, or possibly four, from the northern shore of the Humber estuary at North Ferriby (Wright 1990) dated to *c*. 1300 cal. BC (Switsur & Wright 1989); the so-called Brigg 'raft' — actually a flat-bottomed, plank boat of *c*. 800 cal. BC (Switsur & Wright 1989) from the River Ancholme, a tributary of the Humber (McGrail 1981b; 1985b); and a plank fragment (Fig. 20.4) dated to the period 1594-1454 cal. BC recently excavated

from a waterlogged site near the River Nedern, a tributary of the Severn, at Caldicot Castle, Gwent (Parry & McGrail 1991). These boats were all built from oak planks fastened together by yew (*Taxus* sp.) lashings (Caldicot and Ferriby) or a by a continuous willow (*Salix* sp.) 'stitching' (Brigg).[2]

The Caldicot, Ferriby and Brigg boats were all narrow, relatively long, and flat-bottomed (Fig. 20.5), without stems or significant keels. The Brigg boat, having a rectangular transverse section and squared ends, would have been used mainly for upstream work; the Caldicot and Ferriby boats probably carried goods and people along and across the tidal estuaries and associated rivers — it is unlikely that they were seagoing except on very rare occasions. This is not because they were sewn boats — there are several examples of seagoing sewn plank boats, worldwide, from the twentieth century and the recent past (McGrail 1981a, 29-30, 47-8, 51, 54-5, 58, 63-4, 69, 80-1) — but because their shape and structure did not allow them to meet the stability and seakindliness criteria postulated above. Moreover, there is no evidence that they had mast and sail, although this has recently been suggested (Wright 1990, 110-3), or even oars: they were, in all probability, propelled by paddle and by poles in shallow water.

There is however a hint in the British archaeological record that there may have been an early tradition of planked boats with keel and stems which may have been more seaworthy than the boats of the Caldicot/Ferriby/Brigg tradition. One of the Bronze Age logboat-shaped coffins from Loose Howe, North Yorkshire, has a pseudo-keel and a pseudo-stem (Elgee & Elgee 1949; McGrail 1978); and the Iron Age logboat from Poole has a stem similarly worked in the solid (McGrail 1978). These features are unnecessary and non-functional in a logboat and may well have been copied from a plank boat: such a boat, however, has not yet been found.

By the late Iron Age, there is definite evidence for sea-going plank boats: the sail-propelled Channel trading vessels of the Veneti described by Caesar (*B.G.* 3.13) and by Strabo (*Geog.* 4.4.1); and cargo ships depicted on two first century AD bronze coins (Fig. 20.6) of Cunobelin (Muckelroy *et al.* 1978; McGrail 1990, 43-4). These first century BC/first century AD descriptions and depictions may be forerunners of the second/third century AD seagoing ships of the Romano-Celtic tradition excavated from Blackfriars, London (Marsden 1990), and from St Peter Port Harbour, Guernsey (Rule 1990): these two finds are the earliest remains of north-west European sailing ships which were indisputably seagoing.

Hide boats. Classical authors refer to the indigenous use of hide boats on inland waters and at sea off northwest Europe (Caesar *B.G.* 1.54; Pliny *N.H.* 7.206; Lucan *Pharsalia* 4, 130-8; Solinus *Polyhistor* 23). Pliny (4.104) quotes Timaeus' statement that the British used hide boats in the overseas tin trade during the

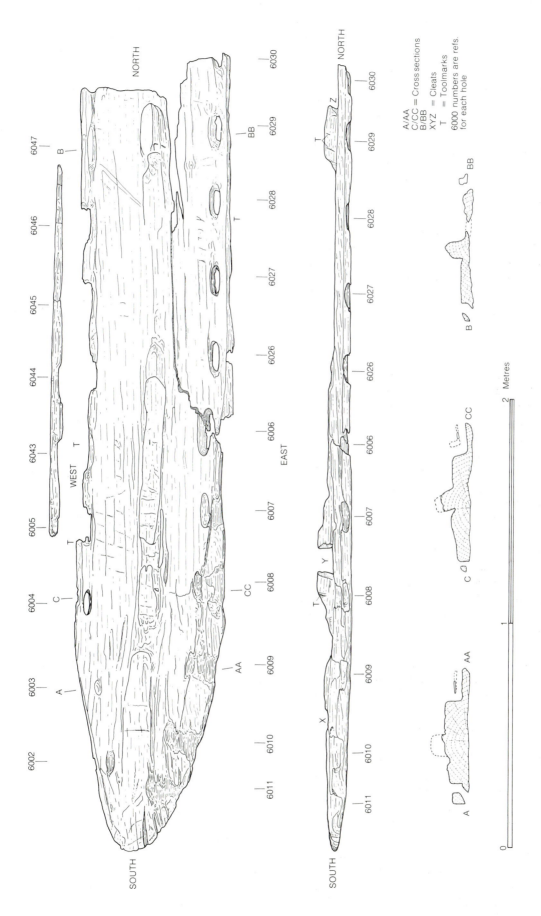

Figure 20.4. Plank fragment from Caldicot Castle, Gwent. Drawing: Institute of Archaeology, Oxford (based on G.G.A.T. drawings)

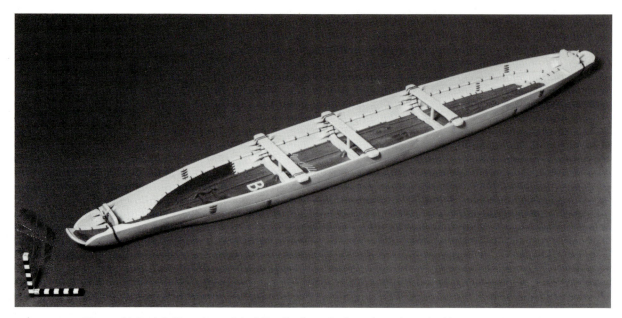

Figure 20.5. A 1:10 scale model of Ferriby boat 1: the parts coloured white are conjectural.
Photo: National Maritime Museum, Greenwich

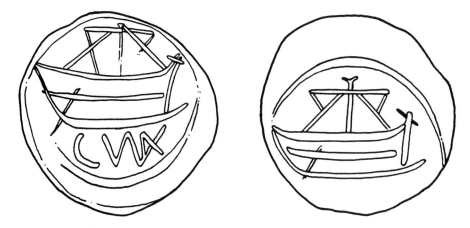

Figure 20.6. Drawing of 1st century AD Cunobelin bronze coins from Canterbury (left) and Sheepen near Colchester
(right). Drawing: Institute of Archaeology, Oxford (based on C.A.T. photographs)

third century BC; whilst the *Ora Maritima* of the fourth century AD is believed to include evidence for similar use in the sixth century BC. It seems very likely that the first century BC gold model from Broighter (Fig. 20.3) represents such as sail-powered, sea-going hide boat (McGrail 1987, 186-7).

Complex hide boats suitable for use at sea were technologically possible from Mesolithic times (McGrail 1990, 34). Hide boats are quickly built and readily repaired; they fit well into a crofter-style economy and can be operated from most types of shore using informal landing places, and they are excellent boats in a surf. Their resilient structure is lightweight, giving good freeboard even when loaded. In general, they are more seaworthy and seakindly and have more transverse stability than the equivalent plank boat. Their principal disadvantage is that, although they can be sailed in difficult conditions, their relatively light draft and good

freeboard mean that they are more susceptible to leeway (drift downwind) than a keeled plank boat (McGrail 1987, 184-5). Apart from this drawback, the hide boat, up to 12m or so in length, appears to match the specification for a cross-Channel vessel outlined above and it may be that it was so used in the Bronze Age. Hide boats were certainly used later, that is in the Iron Age; and possibly they were used earlier, in the Neolithic.

The foregoing argument is based almost entirely on theoretical considerations: the case for a Bronze Age seagoing hide boat can only be taken further if and when one is excavated.

Landing places

Harbours with breakwaters, waterfronts and other man-made facilities were used in the Mediterranean from the early first millennium BC (Casson 1971, 361-70) and probably earlier, although away from the main commercial and naval ports, informal landing places, such as we find described in the *Odyssey*, continued to be used. Apart from a few important commercial sites of the Roman period, as for example London, informal landing places with few if any man-made facilities were the rule in north-west Europe until the eighth or ninth century AD when formal harbours began to be built in selected places (McGrail 1981c; 1985a).

Cross-Channel boats were beached at such informal landing places on a falling (ebb) tide, or they were anchored off the beach and their goods unloaded into smaller boats (logboats?) or horse drawn carts (Ellmers 1985, 25-30); or these goods were carried ashore by people wading. When there was a firm beach there need be no fixed structures (Fig. 20.7). On soft, muddy beaches where a beached boat might have difficulty in floating off as the tide rose, or where people and horses would find movement difficult, hards of gravel (as found at Hengistbury Head within Christchurch Harbour: Cunliffe 1990) or of light timbers or hurdles (as found near the boat site at North Ferriby on the Humber foreshore: Wright 1990), would have been prepared. Similarly constructed causeways (colloquially labelled 'trackways', especially with reference to the Somerset Levels) may have connected such hards to firmer ground beyond High Water mark. Such sites may be difficult to locate precisely, but there would be certain characteristic features which may help to identify them (McGrail 1983b, 34-41).

Navigational techniques

In good weather, on the shortest Channel route across the Strait, either the Continental or British coast would have been visible all the time. In these circumstances visual pilotage techniques can be used — the seaman proceeds from one position, known by reference to landmarks (mountain peaks, cliffs, headlands, menhir, tumuli) and seamarks (shoals, reefs, races, etc.) to another position known by reference to similar features in the region of the destination (McGrail 1983a, 314-5).

Figure 20.7. The coasting ketch Charlotte, *of c. 90 tons capacity, being unloaded into horse and cart on the beach at St. Ives, Cornwall c. 1908. Photo: Gillis Collection*

On the mid-Channel routes land would be out of sight for between two and eight hours except in rare meteorological conditions of unusual refraction when land may be seen beyond the natural horizon. On the west Channel route from the vicinity of Ushant to a landfall at the Lizard there would have been a minimum of ten hours out of sight of land, even in midsummer. For such open sea voyages, deep sea navigational techniques were necessary, in addition to the skills of coastal pilotage (McGrail 1983a, 315-9).

The sounding lead can be used not only to measure depths of water and thus get warning of shoal water and hence the proximity of land, but also to sample the sea bed, which can give some indication of position. Sounding leads have been found with Egyptian model boats of the second millennium BC, and Herodotus (2.5.2) was familiar with their use in the sixth century BC on board ships approaching the River Nile. Leads (Fig. 20.8) have been recovered from Mediterranean wreck sites of the late centuries BC (Casson 1971, 246), but

early ones have not yet been recognized in northern waters.

Apart from the use of the sounding lead, non-instrumental techniques were used for open-sea navigation throughout the world until the twelfth or thirteenth century AD. Some indication of what these methods were can be found in such diverse sources as Homer, Caesar and the lives of early medieval sailor-saints such as St Brendan. Further light may be shed on the matter by a consideration of the non-instrumental methods used by recent navigators in the Pacific and the North Sea (McGrail 1983a).

Prehistoric navigators of the Channel probably used dead reckoning methods based on estimates of courses steered and speeds achieved, using every available clue from their environment (directions from the wind and the swell; signs indicating a change in the weather, and so on), and from the heavens (Polaris, the sun, and some constellations for directions; time from the sun's change in azimuth and from the relative position of

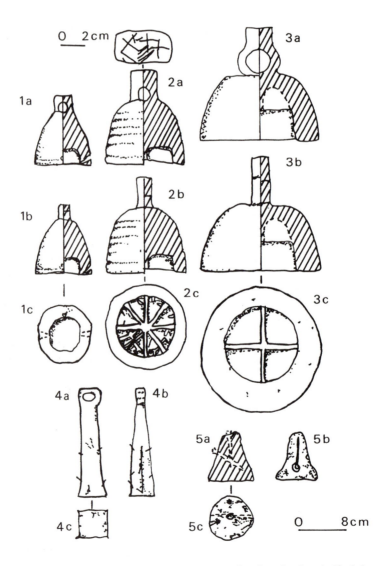

Figure 20.8. Sounding leads from the French Mediterranean coast, dated to the first half of the second century BC (nos. 4 & 5) and to the middle of the first century AD (nos. 1 & 2). Drawing after Fiori & Joncheray (1973)

circumpolar constellations); and a knowledge, based on inherited wisdom and long experience, of speeds achieved and leeway (drift downwind) experienced by their boat in a wide range of conditions. Apart from the use of the magnetic compass and the chart, these dead reckoning techniques were the ones used by Columbus when he first crossed the Atlantic in 1492 (McGrail 1992).

Notes

1. The arguments for and against the Langdon Bay site being that of a wreck are to be published by Keith Muckelroy's successors in this Dover Harbour research project. When the distribution of bronzes is published it may become clear whether a boat was wrecked or whether the bronzes were dumped overboard by a crew seeking to keep their vessel afloat. It is understood that these bronzes weigh around 60 kg and thus could have been suitable ballast (possibly saleable ballast: McGrail 1989, 357) for a small boat. The actual traded gods on this voyage would then have been of lower density/higher stowage factor materials, such as wool, pottery, corn, or even people (McGrail 1989, table 1).
2. During Autumn 1992 there were further finds of early sewn plank boats in Britain: two fragments of planking at Goldcliff, Gwent, on the northern foreshore of the Severn estuary; and substantial remains of a boat at Dover, Kent.

References

Bahn, P.G., 1992. Paris in the Neolithic. *Newswarp* 11, 21

Booth, B., 1984. Handlist of maritime radiocarbon dates. *International Journal of Nautical Archaeology* 13, 189-204

Bradley, R., 1984. *The Social Foundations of Prehistoric Britain: Themes and Variations in the Archaeology of Power*. London & New York: Longman

Bradley, R., 1990. *The Passage of Arms*. Cambridge: Cambridge University Press

Casson, L., 1971. *Ships and Seamanship in the Ancient World*. Princeton: Princeton University Press. (2nd ed., 1988)

Cunliffe, B., 1982. Britain, the Veneti and beyond. *Oxford Journal of Archaeology* 1, 39-68

Cunliffe, B., 1983. Ictis: is it here? *Oxford Journal of Archaeology* 2, 123-6

Cunliffe, B., 1987. *Hengistbury Head, Dorset, 1*. Oxford: Oxford University Committee for Archaeology, Monograph 13

Cunliffe, B., 1988a. *Mount Batten, Plymouth*. Oxford: Oxford University Committee for Archaeology, Monograph 26

Cunliffe, B., 1988b. *Greeks, Romans and Barbarians*. London: Batsford

Cunliffe, B., 1990. Hegistbury Head: a late prehistoric haven, in *Maritime Celts, Frisians and Saxons*, ed. S. McGrail. London: Council for British Archaeology Research Report 71, 27-31

Cunliffe, B., 1991. *Iron Age Communities in Britain*. 3rd ed. London: Routledge

Elgee, H.W., & Elgee, F., 1949. An Early Bronze Age burial in a boat-shaped wooden coffin from north east Yorkshire. *Proceedings of the Prehistoric Society* 15, 87-106

Ellmers, D., 1985. Loading and unloading ships using a horse and cart standing in the water: the archaeological evidence, in *Conference on Waterfront Archaeology in North European Towns*, ed. A.E. Herteig. Bergen: Historisk Museum, 25-30

Fiori, P., & Joncheray, J.-P., 1973. Mobilier métallique provenant de fouilles sous marines. *Cahiers d'Archéologie Subaquatique* 2, 86-9

Fitzpatrick, A.P., 1985. The distribution of Dressel 1 amphorae in north-west Europe. *Oxford Journal of Archaeology* 4 (3), 305-40

Farrell, A.W., & Penny, S., 1975. Broighter boat: a reassessment. *Irish Archaeological Research Forum* 2 (2), 15-26

Hawkes, C.F.C., 1977. *Pytheas: Europe and the Greek Explorers*. Eighth J.N.L. Myres Memorial Lecture. Oxford

Hawkes, C.F.C., 1984. Ictis disentangled and the British tin trade. *Oxford Journal of Archaeology* 3, 211-33

Hague, D.B., 1973. Lighthouses, in *Marine Archaeology* ed. D.J. Blackman. London: Butterworth, 293-314

McGrail, S., 1978. *Logboats of England and Wales*. Oxford: British Archaeological Reports British Series 51

McGrail, S., 1981a. *Rafts, Boats and Ships*. London: H.M.S.O.

McGrail, S., 1981b. *The Brigg 'Raft' and her Prehistoric Environment*. Oxford: British Archaeological Reports British Series 89

McGrail, S., 1981c. Medieval boats, ships and landing places, in *Waterfront Archaeology in Britain and Northern Europe*, eds G. Milne & B. Hobley. London: Council for British Archaeology Research Report 41, 17-23

McGrail, S., 1983a. Cross-Channel seamanship and navigation in the late 1st millennium BC. *Oxford Journal of Archaeology* 2, 299-337

McGrail, S., 1983b. Interpretation of archaeological evidence for maritime structures, in *Sea Studies*, ed. P. Annis. Greenwich: National Maritime Museum

McGrail, S., 1985a. Early landing places, in *Conference on Waterfront Archaeology in North European Towns*, ed. A.E. Herteig. Bergen: Historisk Museum, 12-18

McGrail, S., 1985b. Brigg 'raft': problems in reconstruction and in the assessment of performance, in *Sewn Plank Boats*, eds. S. McGrail & E. Kentley. Oxford: British Archaeological Reports International Series S276, 165-94

McGrail, S., 1987. *Ancient Boats in North West Europe*. London: Longman

McGrail, S., 1989. The shipment of traded goods and of ballast in antiquity. *Oxford Journal of Archaeology* 8, 353-8

McGrail, S., 1990. Boats and boatmanship in the late prehistoric southern North Sea and Channel region, in *Maritime Celts, Frisians and Saxons*, ed. S. McGrail. London: Council for British Archaeology Research Report 71, 32-48

McGrail, S., 1992. Ships, seamanship and navigation in the time of Columbus. *Medieval History* 2 & 3, 76-92

Marsden, P., 1990. A re-assessment of Blackfriars 1, in *Maritime Celts, Frisians and Saxons*, ed. S. McGrail. London: Council for British Archaeology Research Report 71, 66-74

Muckelroy, K., 1981. Middle Bronze Age trade between Britain and Europe: a maritime perspective. *Proceedings of the Prehistoric Society* 47, 275-97

Muckelroy, K., Haselgrove, C., & Nash, D., 1978. A pre-Roman coin from Canterbury and the ship represented on it. *Proceedings of the Prehistoric Society* 44, 439-44

Murphy, J.P., 1977. *Rufus Festus Avienus' Ora Maritima*. Chicago: Chicago University Press

Northover, P., 1982. Metallurgy of the Wilburton hoards. *Oxford Journal of Archaeology* 1, 68-109

O'Connor, B., 1980. *Cross-Channel Relations in the Later Bronze Age*. Oxford: British Archaeological Reports Internatioal Series S91

Parry, S., & McGrail, S., 1991. Prehistoric plank boat fragment and a hard from Caldicot Castle Lake, Gwent, Wales. *International Journal of Nautical Archaeology* 20, 321-4

Rule, M., 1990. Romano-Celtic ship excavated at St Peter Port, Guernsey, in *Maritime Celts, Frisians and Saxons*, ed. S. McGrail. London: Council for British Archaeology Research Report 71, 49-56

Switsur, V.R., & Wright, E.V., 1989. Radiocarbon dates and calibrated dates for the boats from North Ferriby, Humberside a reappraisal. *Archaeological Journal* 146, 58-67

Tomalin, D.J., 1984. The pottery: its character and implication for sea transport, in E. Greenfield, Excavations of the three round barrows at Pucknowle, Dorset, 1959. *Proceedings of the Dorset Natural History & Archaeological Society* 106, 63-76

Tomalin, D.J., 1988. Armorican vases à anses and their occurrence in southern Britain. *Proceedings of the Prehistoric Society* 54, 203-11

Wright, E.V., 1976. *North Ferriby Boats*. Greenwich: National Maritime Museum

Wright, E.V., 1990. *The Ferriby Boats*. London: Routledge

21

The Social Significance of Trade in Late Iron Age Europe

Greg Woolf

The late Iron Age in Europe is often represented, by British and American scholars, as a period in which trade contacts with the Mediterranean world resulted in the growth of new kinds of society north of the Alps. The first part of this paper considers the evidence for urbanism, state formation, state coinages and literacy in La Tène Europe and proposes an alternative description of Iron Age Europe, stressing the social and political fragmentation of the continent and the diversity of the ways in which expanding Iron Age societies made use of a common stock of cultural and technological resources. The second part considers the role of Mediterranean imports, arguing that their distribution does not correlate with any other social developments, but that they should be seen as simply a part of the late La Tène cultural repertoire that local societies might use in various ways or reject at will.

Plusieurs savants anglo-saxons ont récemment proposé que les sociétés européenes de l'âge du fer furent transformées, à la veille de la conquête romaine, par un commerce important avec le monde méditerranéen. Cependant, les habitats urbanisés, les états, les systèmes monétaires et les alphabétisations ne sont pas toujours aussi évidents dans les données archéologiques que dans les Commentaires *de César, texte difficile à lire et plus polémique qu'ethnologique. On imagine mieux l'Europe protohistorique comme une mosaïque de sociétés très localisées, partageants quelques technologies et traits culturels, mais sans aucune organisation politique analogue à celle de la cité antique. Parmi ces traits culturels il faut installer les importations méditerranéennes, des objets rares, bien sûr, mais dont l'emploi était varié et facultatif. En tout cas, la répartition de ces 'exotiques' - pour la plupart des amphores vinaires - ne correspond à aucune indice de la prétendue révolution sociale de La Tène finale.*

Trade and social change in Iron Age Europe

Trade plays a powerful explanatory role in many accounts of European prehistory. The Iron Age is no exception, to the extent that some recent accounts take it for granted that fluctuations in trade contacts between Europe and the Mediterranean world explain first the rise and fall of the Hallstatt princes, and then the rise of the *civilisation des oppida* in the late La Tène period (Collis 1984a; Cunliffe 1988). Others argue from the opposite premise, that endogenous factors are *a priori* more likely to provide explanations of social and cultural change than exogenous ones (e.g. Bintliff 1984).

But the significance of trade need not be a matter of faith. This paper starts from the premise that trade may have a socially transformative role, but that, in each case, the significance of trade needs to be argued not assumed. Ethnographic and historical analogies can be marshalled to demonstrate that trade may be exploita-tive, or a matter of mutual gratification; it may be part of an acculturative process, or it may take place with little exchange of information; it may deal in necessities or simply in things that are desired. It is important not to prejudge the issue, for example by treating all imports as prestige-goods or by assuming that trading centres are ports-of-trade designed to contain exchange, rather than centres designed to attract it. Our ignorance is such that it is not only impossible to establish local elites' attitudes to exchange, it is also far from easy to be sure what 'elite' might mean in an Iron Age context. Admitting these uncertainties does not help us construct broad schematic models of European social evolution, whether of the processual or the world-systems variety, but I hope to show that it allows the evidence for trade to contribute to a new, more nuanced picture of the late Iron Age.

The Iron Age societies that occupied temperate Europe in the last century BC are among the best documented in European prehistory. A very large number of sites of the period are known, most famously the enormous hillforts known as *oppida*, many of which have been extensively excavated since the late nineteenth century. As a result, the material culture of the period may be characterised in some detail (Collis 1984b). Considerable regional variations existed but more often at the level of style than of technology. For instance, coins were produced in many regions, but designs and even weight standards varied greatly. Similarly, decorated pottery is known from a number of areas, but the use of the wheel was generalised and finewares everywhere show a high level of control over both raw materials and firing. But what really distinguishes the late Iron Age from earlier periods is its proximity to the Roman world. As a result, the late La Tène has a chronology which, if still unclear on many points, is far more precise than that of any earlier periods, and in addition, classical texts preserve some eyewitness accounts of Iron Age societies in action.

Despite this wealth of material, little sophisticated social analysis of late La Tène society was carried out until the seventies. The models produced in that decade combined conventional wisdom about the *oppida* and close readings of classical writers, especially Caesar, with models drawn from a variety of traditions in social and cultural anthropology, especially social evolutionary theory and structural marxism (Crumley 1974; Nash 1976; 1978a & 1978b). These interpretations were very influential (e.g. Haselgrove 1982; Roymans 1983) and until recently dominated general accounts of late Iron Age society (e.g. Bradley 1984; Champion *et al.* 1984; Cunliffe 1988). Growing doubts have been voiced about a number of components of the picture they present (e.g. Champion 1987; Haselgrove 1988; Ralston 1988; Fitzpatrick 1989; Woolf 1993). Nevertheless, no new synthesis has emerged, and, at least on the continent, this paradigm remains extremely influential (e.g. Roymans 1990; Hedeager 1992).

On the eve of Roman conquest, it was argued, late Iron Age society underwent a period of widespread and fundamental changes which together comprised a social revolution. Nash's account of the late Iron Age societies of central France, for example, brought together urbanisation, state formation and the appearance of a market economy. The *oppida* were seen as towns at the head of developed settlement hierarchies, centres not only of production and exchange, but also of government. Politically, the area was conceived of as a series of archaic states with republican constitutions that issued state coinages and ruled over clearly defined territories. The economies of these societies were disembedded, that is exchange was no longer constricted by social relationships but was articulated through a monetarised market (Nash 1978a, 1978b and 1981). It was also argued, although not by Nash, that the appearance of literacy, connected both with commerce and bureaucracy, was also a feature of this social

revolution (Jacobi 1974; Champion *et al.* 1984, 318). The cumulative impact of these transformations was summarised by Champion *et al.* (1984, 297) as follows: 'Thus, even before the Roman conquest, large parts of "barbarian" Europe were occupied by literate societies with a high degree of social, economic and political development'.

What accounted for the late La Tène social revolution? A major role was attributed, in most accounts, to intensified commercial contacts with the Mediterranean world, although the emphasis varied between those who saw trade as the prime mover (e.g. Nash 1978a; Cunliffe 1988), those who saw it as one among a number of factors (e.g. Champion *et al.* 1984) and those who preferred to see late La Tène society as the culmination of local developments (e.g. Bintliff 1984). But most have followed Nash in seeing these changes as most pronounced in an area of central France adjacent to the Roman province of Gallia Narbonensis, and in seeing proximity to the Roman world as the main variable determining the relative social complexities of Iron Age societies. Less consensus existed about the exact means by which trade with the Mediterranean was supposed to have contributed to social change in Iron Age Europe. The social processes invoked ranged from secondary state formation to acculturation to the expansion of a world economy, much depending on the relative importance accorded by each analyst to particular components of the late La Tène social revolution. But it is possible, heuristically, to separate out two main strands of argument, although some accounts combine both mechanisms (e.g. Cunliffe 1988). One view sees the significance of trade as residing in its power to transform local economies by forcing them to produce commodities exchangeable for Mediterranean products. The commodities most often cited in this connection are metals, furs, agricultural produce, slaves and mercenary labour (e.g. Nash 1987b). The other view sees trade as important as the means by which emergent elites procured 'prestige goods', rare valuables the control of which allowed them to entrench their power vis-à-vis their social opponents. Both arguments are plausible in themselves and may be supported with ethnographic analogies. But although the two views are not strictly incompatible, the fact that they are in practice rarely distinguished and often combined, suggests that the transformative power of trade is regarded as unproblematic and uncontroversial. In fact, a careful re-consideration of the archaeological evidence both for a social revolution and for Roman goods in Iron Age contexts, suggests that the significance of Mediterranean trade with late La Tène societies was both less significant and more complex than it has often been presented.

Iron Age Europe without towns or states

It would be easy to criticise this picture of the late La Tène as theoretically outmoded. The 'Great Divides' that late Iron Age society was supposed to have crossed — non-urban to urban, embedded economy to market exchange, tribe to state and oral to literate — now look crude and overschematic. Economic anthropologists now see the relationship between gift exchange and commodity exchange as much more complex, with both activities present in most societies (e.g. Appadurai 1986; Morris 1986). Writing is no longer seen as the catalyst of new styles of thought and social organisation, but rather as a technology, the uses and significance of which are largely determined by its social context (Street 1984). More generally Great Divide type approaches may be seen as contributing to ethnocentric attempts to distinguish modernity from 'primitive' or 'traditional' societies, while even gradualist social evolutionary approaches reduce social analysis to social taxonomy by assimilating individual societies to types in such a way that their unique and unfamiliar features are ignored. It would be unfair to criticise archaeologists in the seventies for using state of the art social theory in modelling the late Iron Age. Nevertheless the emphasis on Great Divides and on social evolution did allow debates about the nature of late Iron Age societies to become framed in terms of deciding which great evolutionary steps had been taken before the Roman conquest and which after. The passage quoted above illustrates how easily this might become a contest between prehistorians and Romanists for the first 'European' towns, states, market economies or literacies. As a result, the social archaeology of the late La Tène needs more than simply a fresh coat of theoretical paint (Hill 1989).

But more seriously, these models of late Iron Age society are subject to empirical criticisms, not all which arise from new data. In brief, a critical re-assessment suggests that the evidence for settlement hierarchies and territoriality is very slight; that the *oppida* were not urban in the sense in which the term is usually understood; and that late Iron Age coinages were neither state issues nor designed for market exchange. Most importantly, the chronological and geographical distribution of these phenomena show that they did not originate together and never constituted a cultural package.

The idea that states might be identified in those parts of late La Tène Europe that were closest to the Roman empire was argued independently by Crumley (1974) and Nash (1978a). Both analyses depend largely on close readings of Caesar's *Gallic War*, used by Crumley to generate hypotheses that might be tested in the archaeological record, and by Nash in conjunction with a range of other types of evidence, numismatic and toponymic as well as archaeological. Arguably hypotheses may be only be falsified, not confirmed, by confrontation with additional data, and Crumley's analysis was thus aimed at showing that late La Tène settlement patterns, which she saw as reflecting urban hierarchies, were not in conflict with her reading of Caesar. Nash's argument about settlement was very similar. But inter-

estingly, although both saw settlement patterns as reflecting society as described by Caesar, their interpretations of Caesar were very different (Haselgrove 1987, 108–9; 1988, 77). Their accounts differed largely on the role of artisans and traders, which Crumley saw as forming an emergent middle-class (cf. Duval 1983), while Nash saw Gallic society, more conventionally, as composed of nobles and tribesmen, united by various forms of patronage. Perhaps the most important point to emerge from this debate is the ambiguity of Caesar's brief account, which in any case went into detail only in the case of one group, the Aedui, and on occasion shows clear signs of distortion for political ends, as has recently been shown in his use of the term *urbs* to describe settlements (Buchsenschutz & Ralston 1986). On the whole, it seems safer to leave aside the classical texts and assess the case on its archaeological merits.

Iron Age states, it is argued, are visible in settlement hierarchies, in territorial boundaries and in state coinages. But none of these can be identified with any certainty in the region in which both Crumley and Nash located them, central France. It is in any case difficult to establish that late Iron Age settlements were ranked in terms of the number of higher order functions they performed, as opposed to differentiated in a complementary manner, for example into summer settlements and winter ones. The *oppida*, treated by Nash as political centres, have produced little evidence for either central place functions or elite residence (Woolf 1993). When ranked in terms of size, the settlement patterns of central France show marked variations from region to region, and it is not possible to isolate criteria that distinguish these settlement patterns from those of areas further north, beyond Nash's 'archaic states band' (Ralston 1988). Nash (1978b) also argued that the boundaries of archaic Gallic states can be reconstructed from pre-revolutionary diocesan boundaries combined with Celtic and Latin toponyms referring to boundaries, and to the distribution of 'state' coinages. It is broadly correct that dioceses did originate in the territories of late Roman *civitates*, although these did not correspond exactly to those of early imperial Gaul, and there were presumably later changes too (Goudineau *et al.* 1980). But it is only an hypothesis that early Roman boundaries reflected Iron Age territories faithfully. Toponyms do not help, since Celtic place names continued to be generated by Celtic speaking locals after the conquest (Rivet 1980). In fact, some changes at least took place on conquest, with smaller units amalgamated into larger ones. More seriously, it is very unclear whether the notion of control of territory, as opposed to control of people, characterised Iron Age societies.

The most original component of Nash's account of late Iron Age society was her attempt to relate variation in the coinages of Iron Age Gaul to variations in political systems (Nash 1978a; 1981; 1987a, 51–5). To simplify a complex argument, Nash argued that phase

3 coinages differed from earlier issues in that they consisted of linked series of both precious metal and bronze coins; in that they were more distinct from neighbouring coinages than in earlier periods, reflecting a new sense of political identity; and in that their distributions corresponded to political territories. The difficulties in reconstructing Iron Age territories makes this last point difficult to assess, and in any case, some of the phase 3 coinages are distributed very widely beyond the proposed state territories, while other putative states are attributed more than one coinage. Moreover, a recent detailed critique of Nash's arguments, challenges the view that the introduction of a bronze coinage implies political centralisation (Haselgrove 1988, 75–8, 81–5). The conclusion seems inevitable that the case for state formation in Iron Age France is a weak one.

What of the other components of the late La Tène social revolution? The evidence for literacy is extremely slight, confined to less than a hundred graffiti of one or two words at most, many of them probably post-conquest, some very late coin legends, two passages of Caesar and some writing equipment from excavated contexts, which might or might not have been used by indigenous literates as opposed to Mediterranean visitors like the resident traders on the Magdalensberg in Austria (Moberg 1987; Goudineau 1989; Woolf forthcoming). It seems clear that writing was used in parts of La Tène Europe, but the paucity of the evidence, its late date and general theoretical considerations combine to suggest that we are not justified in arguing from that fact to the appearance of bureaucracy or dramatically enhanced levels of social or economic organisation. Arguments for an extension of the market economy derive entirely from the appearance of fractional and base metal coinages. That development was very late and in some regions was probably a consequence of the removal of bullion during the Gallic wars (Haselgrove 1988). Certainly it is conceivable that these coins enabled or responded to an increased commoditisation of goods and services, but it is not at all clear either that commodity exchange was new or that bronze coins did not circulate as gifts between leaders or from leaders to followers. But as neither literacy nor commodity exchange are now regarded as signs of a particular level of social complexity, the importance of the issue is greatly reduced.

Finally, did the late Iron Age see the first towns in temperate Europe? The issue is complex, and one I have treated elsewhere (Woolf 1993), so I shall do no more here than summarise my conclusions. The sites conventionally grouped together as *oppida* are in fact very diverse both in size and morphology and appear in different parts of Europe at different periods. Products of a long tradition of architecture in wood and earth, the fortified settlements of the late La Tène are distinctive chiefly in terms of the very large amounts of energy and materials invested in them. Settlement patterns vary enormously between regions, but in very few instances can hierarchies be demonstrated within which sites may be ranked in terms of the number of functions they perform. The level of intra-site differentiation is low, there are rarely recognisable elite residences, public spaces or structures or artisanal quarters. The most common structures are compounds which closely resemble the farms that had characterised the open settlement that *oppida* in many areas replaced. Virtually all these sites seem to represent the concentration of activities previously dispersed more widely in the landscape, rather than the major sites of differentiated, hierarchical, settlement systems of the sort usually implied by the term urbanism.

What can be concluded about Iron Age society in the light of this reassessment? One approach would be to revise estimates of social complexity downwards. But, whether or not the notion of social complexity is conceived of from an evolutionary standpoint (and it need not be), it has the analytical disadvantage that it only expresses one dimension of variability, making it difficult to describe differences between societies considered to be of equivalent complexity. Ideally, we should be able to say more interesting things about late Iron Age society than simply which taxonomic category it falls into. One approach is to focus on diversity within late Iron Age Europe so as to identify the limits of variation of each component of late La Tène societies. Chronology provides one easy way of doing this. It is increasingly clear not only that not all components of the late La Tène social revolution appear simultaneously, but also that they appear in different orders and with different prominences in different parts of Europe. The degree of variation and variations in chronology are clearest from settlements (Collis 1984b; Woolf forthcoming a). The large sites known as *oppida* appear from La Tène C in Bohemia and Bavaria, from various points in La Tène D in Switzerland and France and even later in Britain. These sites differ considerably in plan, in the design of ramparts and entrances, and there are contrasts between areas with large numbers of medium-sized settlements and others with a few very big ones. But what these settlements have in common is the technology used to construct them, and the immense amount of energy and resources invested in them.

Other kinds of variation are less easy to date, but contribute to the deconstruction of a uniform late La Tène cultural complex. It is difficult to plot literacy, but graffiti and coin legends allow an attempt to be made (Woolf forthcoming). The first Celtic graffiti appear in the south of France in the third century BC. Less than one hundred are known from temperate Europe and none can be dated much before the middle of the last century BC. Fifty-odd are known from Burgundy, a dozen from Colchester, probably rather later, and two from Manching in Bavaria. Allen's and Nash's (1980, 108) map of the distribution of coins with legends on them, shows not only a huge diversity of scripts, but also large areas where no epigraphic coinage was produced. Similar patterns of variation may be illustrated in the distribution of areas using decorated pottery or in the regional nature of particular mortuary rituals.

Cultural variations within late Iron Age Europe have long been known. It is important to note that these variations cannot be explained in terms of relative distance from Mediterranean civilisations: the cultural geography of late Iron Age Europe was much more complex, displaying regional variations in almost every level of material culture, and east-west differentiation as well as the north-south patterning so often evoked in world-systems analyses. This cultural variation seem often to be the product of local choices made from a broad common repertoire of technologies and symbols, shared by societies from the Atlantic to the Black Sea. What united Iron Age Europe was not a common cultural or social system, but common access to this repertoire and also to a high level of social power. Throughout Europe, the number of iron implements known increases, not just in deposits but also on settlement sites and, in the form of nails, within ramparts; agricultural expansion is attested from a number of regions; and the scale of linear ditches, monuments and boundary ditches as well as hillforts dwarfs those of earlier periods. The conclusion seems inescapable that late La Tène societies had more energy and resources at their disposal than had ever before been available in Europe (Champion *et al.* 1984, 304–9). If there was a social revolution, it was this growth in social power, but that process can be traced back well into the middle La Tène, if not earlier, and was not confined to regions bordering the Roman empire.

Late La Tène Europe, then, was socially and politically fragmented but culturally unified. The combination of high levels of social power and low levels of social organisation contrasts markedly with contemporary societies in the Mediterranean basin, where common cultural codes, high levels of urbanism and developed states and empires had been developed largely in an environment that has always been scarce in agricultural and other resources. That contrast cannot be expressed simply in terms of different levels of social complexity, but it is fundamental to understanding the nature of relations between Europe and the Mediterranean world in the last millennium BC and the first millennium AD.

Mediterranean goods in Iron Age Europe

Much has been written, and continues to be written, on the subject of Mediterranean trade with Iron Age Europe (e.g. Tchernia 1983; Roman 1983; Williams 1989). Virtually all the evidence for this trade consists of Dressel 1 amphorae, most of them manufactured in central and western Italy, virtually all of them apparently originally containing wine (Tchernia 1986; Hesnard

1990). The distribution of these amphorae is concentrated in southern and central France, but finds occur in Iron Age contexts throughout northern and western France, in Switzerland, the Rhineland and at some sites in southern and eastern Britain and southern Germany. A series of research projects have produced increasingly sophisticated understandings of their distribution in many, although not all, regions (e.g. Nash 1978a; Galliou 1984; Fitzpatrick 1985; Peacock 1984). Despite our increased understanding of this distribution, its social significance remains a matter of debate (Cunliffe 1988, 80–105; Fitzpatrick 1989, 31–4; Laubenheimer 1990, 39–75). Much of it takes for granted the kind of Iron Age Europe, characterised by urbanisation, state-formation and commercial expansion, that I have discussed and rejected above.

The connection made by Nash (1976; 1987a), and others following her, between trade and social change takes us back to the issues with which we began. Did prehistoric trade act as the midwife of social change, was it an irrelevance compared with endogenous factors, or was it of variable importance in different cases? In the case of the late La Tène, several objections can be made to any simple equation between Mediterranean imports and social revolution. Once the differences between central France and the rest of La Tène Europe have been exposed as illusory (Ralston 1988), one major counter-argument is that amphorae do not appear uniformly across La Tène Europe, and do not even reach those areas where the *oppida* phenomenon is held to have begun (Panella 1981; Collis 1984b, 142). Nash was quite right to point out the unusual density of amphorae in central and southern France, but that density does not correlate with any other archaeological traces of archaic states or towns, and Caesar's account of the Gauls is too general to contribute much to her picture of inter-regional differences. It has also been pointed out that the imports do not show any clear chronological correlation with elements of the supposed social revolution, and especially not with the Roman conquest of southern France in 125 BC, which Nash saw as providing the initial context for a commercial explosion (Fitzpatrick 1989, 33–4). In short, the distribution of Dressel amphorae in time and space is difficult to correlate with any social changes in central France.

More generally, social change has been linked to exchange between Europe and the Mediterranean through analyses in terms of centre-periphery relations. That approach can be challenged at a theoretical level: world systems analyses of this period have on the whole failed adequately to customise the model for pre-capitalist conditions (Woolf 1990). But in this instance, the approach is also susceptible to empirical falsification. World systems analyses have made much of the supposed 'layer cake' structure of European society, with east-west bands of societies at different levels of complexity, states in the Mediterranean basin, archaic states further north, and tribal societies in northern Europe. That layer cake structure has been related to the distribution of Mediterranean imports, conceived of as a gradual falling off northwards characteristic of a distance decay function. Amphorae, in short, have been thought to exemplify the gradually diminishing impact of a southern core over increasingly distant societies.

In fact, just as the layer cake structure dissolves on closer examination, so too the distribution of Dressel 1 amphorae turns out to be a good deal less simple when looked at in detail. Many of the problems inherent in the distribution map of Dressel 1 amphorae have been recently pointed out by Andrew Fitzpatrick (1987), in particular the problems that arise from different intensities of research in different areas (cf. Tchernia 1983). Nevertheless, it is possible to note some general patterns relevant to any assessment of the significance of trade, but which are concealed by a standard distribution map.

Each point plotted on the map hides two other important variables: the number of amphorae recorded at that site and proportion of contemporaneous sites which produce amphorae. It is well known that some sites have produced the remains of very large numbers of discarded amphorae. Chalon-sur-Saône, Essalois and Mont Beuvray in eastern France and Toulouse, Vieille-Toulouse and Bordeaux in the south-west are the best attested, and it is reasonable to estimate that each of these sites contains tens or even hundreds of thousands of amphorae (Tchernia 1983; Laubenheimer 1990, 44–52). At the other extreme, the majority of find spots in Brittany, the Paris Basin and southern England have produced only one or two examples each. Fitzpatrick (1987, 93–5) rightly points out that intensive campaigns of excavation can upwardly revise some figures dramatically, but in areas where amphorae are scarce even large excavations have produced very few examples: only thirty odd are known from Hengistbury Head (Williams 1989, 144) and only 120 or so sherds from the very extensive excavation at Manching (Stöckli 1979, 112–90; Will 1987), while the largest Czech sites have produced only one or two examples each (Fitzpatrick 1985, 330). By contrast, the stamped amphorae alone from the late nineteenth century excavations of Mont Beuvray numbered at least 195, more than 300 fragments are known, and some deposits contained up to forty amphorae. Nevertheless, the majority were discarded or used to back-fill the excavations (Laubenheimer 1991). Some sites can be identified which fall between these extremes, producing some 100 or more: Basel-Gasfabrik, the Titelberg in Luxemburg and the largest sites of the Aisne valley come into this category, although it is difficult to compare totals deriving from excavations and surface surveys of very different intensities and extents (Fitzpatrick 1985).

It is much more difficult to estimate the proportion of known sites in each region which have produced amphorae. Amphorae are clearly absent from virtually all sites in some areas - Britain north of Worcester (Peacock 1984), for example, or parts of Belgium, the Netherlands and north west Germany (Fitzpatrick 1987, 90). In other areas, like southern Britain, they are present only on some sites. Although it is very difficult to establish for certain, it also seems clear that amphorae maybe expected on virtually every site of the period in parts of southern and central France, especially the Aude and along the lower Saône (Roman 1983; Tchernia 1983). It seems clear that the very prolific sites are located in zones where most sites have produced some amphorae, while in areas where only a proportion of the sites have produced amphorae, the absolute numbers found tend to be low.

Unfortunately, the boundaries of these broad zones are very hard to draw, largely because many intermediate areas, like the Dordogne, are imperfectly known. It is also difficult to know whether or not sharp divisions existed, between areas where amphorae were plentiful and areas where they were rare. But several features suggest that we should not be too ready to accept a gradual distance-decay model of amphora distribution. First, just as amphorae appear in eastern England they become rarer in Brittany and central southern England (Fitzpatrick 1985, 313–5). Second, amphorae are absent from much of present-day Belgium and the Netherlands, although they reached both the Moselle valley and military posts on the lower Rhine (Fitzpatrick 1985, 314). It seems likely, then, that although distance from sources of supply was obviously an important factor in determining the distribution of amphorae in temperate Europe, it cannot account for the entire range of variation between regions.

It is important to be clear what these regional differences represent. It is often argued that the very prolific sites were transhipment points, centres where wine was removed from amphorae either to be sent on the next leg of a trade route in other containers, barrels or skins for instance, or in order to be redistributed locally (e.g. Roman 1983; Cunliffe 1988; Laubenheimer 1990, 48). But Chalon-sur-Saône is the only prolific site suitably sited to function in this way. No one would have transported full amphorae to the top of either Essalois or Mont Beuvray, only to have the wine brought down again in lighter containers, and Vieille-Toulouse is at the headwaters of the Garonne, not the Aude, so that the amphorae that reached it had already been transported overland. Nor is it plausible to see these sites as redistributive centres, since they are largely located in areas where amphorae are common on most sites. Finally, amphora sherds are scattered liberally across these sites rather than piled up in dumps as at Monte Testaccio in Rome. The conclusion must be that these are sites at which wine was consumed in very large quantities, and probably by locals (Tchernia 1983), rather than by soldiers as suggested by Middleton (1983). This pattern of consumption contrasts markedly with that in eastern England where full amphorae were included as grave goods in rich burials (Stead 1967), or with areas like Belgium where they seem not to have been consumed at all.

The existence of regional styles of consumption contributes to the picture I have already outlined of the social fragmentation of the late La Tène. Each regional society selected and combined elements of a common technological and cultural repertoire in its own particular way: wine was used in much the same way as techniques of rampart construction. Subject to availability, Iron Age elites might distribute wine at enormous feasts, they might restrict it to noble banquets, they might have themselves buried with it or even depict amphorae on their coins (Laubenheimer 1990, 71–5). Or they might ban it (Caesar, *Gallic War* 4.2). As a result, the wine trade had no single social significance in temperate Europe.

But while it is difficult to relate the wine trade to other changes in the archaeological record, it should perhaps not be dismissed altogether. Mediterranean wine was one component of the late La Tène technological and cultural repertoire, albeit one with a restricted distribution within Europe. No other item of Mediterranean manufacture appears in such quantities on La Tène sites, and at least one Roman governor thought the trade profitable enough to impose duties on (Cicero, *In Defence of Fonteius*). But it does not follow that Iron Age societies were either exploited by or dependent on Mediterranean traders. The difference in regimes of value between the parties would have enabled the trade to be a case of mutual gratification, and even if some Iron Age elites used wine to express their power, there is no reason to believe that they relied on it to maintain their position. Nor did the wine trade mark the first stages of acculturation: for Diodorus (5.26) the Gauls' love of wine and the Italians' love of profit were complementary, but distinguishing, vices.

Acknowledgements

I should like to take this opportunity to thank Andrew Fitzpatrick, Colin Haselgrove, J.D.Hill, Sander van der Leeuw and Ian Ralston for continual encouragement and constructive criticism while I have been developing my ideas about late La Tène societies in Europe.

References

Allen, D.F., & Nash, D., 1980. *The Coins of the Ancient Celts*. Edinburgh: Edinburgh University Press

Appadurai, A., (ed.) 1986. *The Social Life of Things. Commodities in cultural perspective*. Cambridge: Cambridge University Press

Bintliff, J., 1984. Iron Age Europe in the context of social evolution from the Bronze age through to historic times, in *European Social Evolution: Archaeological Perspectives*, ed. J. Bintliff. Bradford: Bradford University Press, 157–225

Bradley, R., 1984. *The Social Foundations of Britain*. London: Longman

Buchsenschutz, O., & Ralston, I.B.M., 1986. En relisant la Guerre des Gaules. *Aquitania*, supplément 1, 383–7

Champion, T.C., Gamble, C., Shennan, S., & Whittle, A., 1984. *Prehistoric Europe*. London: Academic Press

Champion, T.C., 1987. The European Iron Age: assessing the state of the art. *Scottish Archaeological Review* 4, 98–107

Collis, J.R., 1984a. *The European Iron Age*. London: Batsford

Collis, J.R., 1984b. *Oppida. Earliest Towns North of the Alps*. Sheffield: Department of Prehistory and Archaeology

Crumley, C.L., 1974. *Celtic Social Structure: the Generation of Archaeologically Testable Hypotheses from Literary Data*. Ann Arbor: Museum of Anthropology Papers 54

Cunliffe, B.W., 1988. *Greeks, Romans and Barbarians. Spheres of Interaction*. London: Batsford

Duval, A. 1983. Autour de Vercingétorix, de l'archéologie à l'histoire économique et sociale, in *Le Deuxième Age du Fer en Auvergne et en Forez et ses Relations avec les Régions Voisines*, eds J.R. Collis, A. Duval & R. Périchon. Sheffield: Department of Archaeology and Prehistory, 298–335

Fitzpatrick, A.P., 1985. The distribution of Dressel 1 amphorae in north-west Europe. *Oxford Journal of Archaeology* 4, 305–40

Fitzpatrick, A.P., 1987. The structure of a distribution map: problems of sample bias and quantitative studies. *Acta Rei Cretariae Romanae Fautorum* 25/26, 79–112

Fitzpatrick, A.P., 1989. The uses of Roman imperialism by the Celtic barbarians in the later Republic, in, *Barbarians and Romans in North-West Europe from the later Republic to late Antiquity*, eds. J.C. Barrett, A.P. Fitzpatrick & L. Macinnes. Oxford: British Archaeological Reports International Series S471, 27–54

Galliou, P., 1984. Days of wine and roses? Early Armorica and the Atlantic wine trade, in *Cross Channel Trade between Britain and Gaul in the pre-Roman Iron Age*, eds. S. Macready & F.H. Thompson. London: Society of Antiquaries Occasional Papers 4, 24–36

Goudineau, C., Février, P.A. & Fixot, M., 1980. Le réseau urbain, in *Histoire de la France Urbaine. I La ville Antique*, ed. G. Duby. Paris: Editions du Seuil, 71–137

Goudineau, C., 1989. L'apparition de l'écriture en Gaule, in *Le Temps de la Préhistoire 1*, ed. J.-P. Mohen. Paris: Société Préhistorique Française, 236–8

Haselgrove, C.C., 1982. Wealth, prestige and power; the dynamics of late Iron Age political centralisation in south-East England, in *Ranking, Resources and Exchange*, eds A.C. Renfrew & S. Shennan. Cambridge: Cambridge University Press, 79–88

Haselgrove, C.C., 1987. Culture process on the periphery: Belgic Gaul and Rome during the late Republic and early empire, in *Centre and Periphery in the Ancient World*, eds. M. Rowlands, M. Larsen & K. Kristiansen. Cambridge: Cambridge University Press, 104–24

Haselgrove, C.C., 1988. Coinage and complexity: archaeological analysis of socio-political change in Britain and non-Mediterranean Gaul during the later Iron Age, in *Tribe and Polity in late Prehistoric Europe*, eds D.B. Gibson & M.N. Geselowitz. New York: Plenum, 69–96

Hedeager, L., 1992. *Iron Age Societies. From Tribe to State in Northern Europe. c. 500 BC–AD 700*. Oxford: Basil Blackwell

Hesnard, A., 1990. Les amphores, in *Gaule Interne et Gaule Méditerranéene aux IIᵉ et Iᵉʳ siècles avant J.-C. Confron-

tations Chronologiques, eds. A. Duval, J.-P. Morel & Y. Roman, = *Revue Archéologique de Narbonnaise*, supplément 21. Paris: Editions du CNRS, 47–54

Hill, J.D., 1989. Rethinking the Iron Age, *Scottish Archaeological Review* 6, 16–24

Jacobi, G., 1974. Zum Schriftgebrauch in keltischen Oppida nördlich der Alpen. *Hamburger Beiträge zur Archäologie* 4, 171–81

Laubenheimer, F., 1990. *Le Temps des Amphores en Gaule. Vins, Huiles et Sauces*. Paris: Editions Errance

Laubenheimer, F., 1991. *Les Amphores de Bibracte. Le Matériel des Fouilles Anciennes. DAF* 29. Paris: Editions de la Maison des Sciences de l'Homme

Middleton, P., 1983. The Roman army and long distance trade, in *Trade and Famine in Classical Antiquity* eds P. Garnsey & C.R. Whittaker. Cambridge: Philological Society, 75–83

Moberg, C.-A., 1987. Quand l'archéologie rencontre les rencontres d'alphabets (quelques reflexions sur des monnaies épigraphes celtiques), in *Mélanges Offerts au Docteur J.-B. Colbert de Beaulieu*. Paris: Léopard d'Or, 639–49

Morris, I., 1986. Gift and commodity in archaic Greece. *Man* 21, 1–17

Nash, D., 1976. The growth of urban society in France, in *Oppida: the Beginnings of Urbanisation in Barbarian Europe*, eds B.W. Cunliffe & T. Rowley. Oxford: British Archaeological Reports International Series S 11, 95–133

Nash, D., 1978a. *Settlement and Coinage in Central Gaul c.200–1 BC*. Oxford: British Archaeological Reports International Series S39

Nash, D., 1978b. Territory and state formation in central Gaul, in *Social Organisation and Settlement*, eds. D. Green, C. Haselgrove & M. Spriggs. Oxford: British Archaeological Reports International Series S 47, 455–75

Nash, D., 1981. Coinage and state development in central Gaul, in *Coinage and Society in Britain and Gaul: some Current Problems*, ed. B.W. Cunliffe. London: Council for British Archaeology Research Reports 38, 10–17

Nash, D., 1987a. *Coinage in the Celtic World*. London: Seaby

Nash, D., 1987b. Imperial expansion under the Roman Republic, in *Centre and Periphery in the Ancient World*, eds M. Rowlands, M. Larsen & K. Kristiansen. Cambridge: Cambridge University Press, 87–103

Panella, C., 1981. La distribuzione e i mercati, in *Società Romana e Produzione Schiavistica IIa*, eds A. Giardina & A. Schiavione. Rome: Editori Laterza, 55–80

Peacock, D.P.S., 1984. Amphorae in Iron Age Britain: a reassessment, in *Cross Channel Trade between Britain and Gaul in the pre-Roman Iron Age*, eds S. Macready & F.H.Thompson. London: Society of Antiquaries Occasional Papers 4, 37–42

Ralston, I.B.M., 1988. Central Gaul at the Roman conquest: conceptions and misconceptions. *Antiquity* 62, 786–94

Rivet, A.L.F., 1980. Celtic names and Roman places, *Britannia* 11, 1–19

Roman, Y., 1983. *De Narbonne à Bordeaux, une Axe Economique au 1er Siècle Avant J.-C.*. Lyon: Presses Universitaires de Lyon

Roymans, R., 1983. The north Belgic tribes in the first century BC: a historical-anthropological perspective, in *Roman and Native in the Low Countries. Spheres of Interaction.* eds R. Brandt & J. Slofstra. Oxford: British Archaeological Reports, International Series S184, 43–69

Roymans, R., 1990. *Tribal Societies in Northern Gaul. An Anthropological Perspective*. Amsterdam: Universiteit van Amsterdam

Stead, I.M. 1967. A La Tène III burial at Welwyn Garden City. *Archaeologia* 101, 1–62

Stöckli, W.E., 1979. *Die Groß- und Importkeramik von Manching*. Wiesbaden: Die Ausgrabungen in Manching 8

Street, B.V., 1984. *Literacy in Theory and Practice*. Cambridge: Cambridge University Press

Tchernia, A., 1983. Italian wine in Gaul, in *Trade in the Ancient Economy*, eds P. Garnsey, K. Hopkins & C.R. Whittaker. London: Chatto & Windus, 87–104

Tchernia, A., 1986. *Le Vin d'Italie Romaine. Essai d'Histoire Economique d'après les Amphores*. Rome: Ecole Française de Rome

Will, E.L., 1987. The Roman amphoras from Manching: a reappraisal. *Bayerische Vorgeschichtsblätter* 52, 21–36

Williams, D. F., 1989. The impact of the Roman amphora trade on pre-Roman Britain, in *Centre and Periphery. Comparative studies in Archaeology*, ed. T.C.Champion = *One World Archaeology* 11. London: Unwin Hyman, 142–50

Woolf, G.D., 1990. World systems analysis and the Roman empire. *Journal of Roman Archaeology* 3, 44–58

Woolf, G.D., 1993. Rethinking the Oppida. *Oxford Journal of Archaeology* 12(2), 223–34

Woolf, G.D. forthcoming. Power and the spread of writing in the west, in *Literacy and Power in the Ancient World*, eds A.K. Bowman & G.D. Woolf. Cambridge: Cambridge University Press

22

Cheshire Cats, Mickey Mice,
the New Europe and Ancient Celtic Art

J. V. S Megaw & M. Ruth Megaw

This paper has its roots in the authors' current major research, the preparation of a supplement to Paul Jacobsthal's Early Celtic Art, *and is set against a background of the present debate in the United Kingdom as to the very existence of a pre-Roman 'Celtic' culture, let alone ancient Celts. The nature of the art of the La Tène Iron Age is examined in relation to various models of trade and exchange between the contemporary Mediterranean and non-Mediterranean worlds. Art as commodity and art objects as material evidence of belief systems are examined in the context of the transmission of concepts of cultural identity and a postulated early European Community of ideas and beliefs.*

Cet article a pour origine la recherche principale actuelle des auteurs, la préparation d'un supplément a l'ouvrage de Paul Jacobsthal, Early Celtic Art, *et se situe dans le contexte du débat qui se poursuit au Royaume-Uni au sujet de l'existence même d'une culture 'celtique' protohistorique, sans parler des Celtes anciens. La nature de l'art de l'Age du Fer de la Tène est examinée en rapport avec les divers modèles de commerce et d'échanges entre le monde méditerranéen et non-méditerranéen contemporain. L'art en tant que commodité et les objets d'art comme témoignage matériel des systèmes de croyance sont examinés dans le contexte de la transmission des concepts d'identité culturelle et selon le principe d'une première Communauté européene d'idées et de croyances.*

Introduction

At the outset, some explanation of the title of this collection of illustrated variations on a conference theme may be in order. An alternative if prosaic description might be 'Verbal Jottings for a Commissioned Supplement to Paul Jacobsthal's *Early Celtic Art*', a project which is our current major concern. In 1969 when one of us last spoke on an Iron Age topic in Bristol, a city long associated with trade and exchange, a paper entitled 'Cheshire Cat and Mickey Mouse: problems in the analysis of the art of the European Iron Age' was presented and later published (Megaw 1970b). In it was developed the idea, borrowed from Sir Ernst Gombrich (1977; 1979), that much of this art contained visually encoded representations of the human head. It was suggested that, in addition to the ambiguous heads described by Jacobsthal as 'Cheshire [Cat] style' (1944, 19), there were some which were perhaps better described as close to the products of the modern film cartoonist's skills (Figs. 22.1a, 22.1b). At the time the hapless author was much taken to task by some respected and senior mentors for what was seen as an improper lack of serious intent displayed in a learned

journal. Almost a quarter of a century later, however, when the best known ancient Gaul remains Astérix and the greatest publicity for France in 1992 was devoted to the launch of EuroDisney, the time would seem ripe for a return to the questions of the nature of Iron Age art, its meaning and modes of transmission.

In 1992 there could be few topics worthier of consideration by prehistorians living in the New Europe than the art of the pre-Roman La Tène Iron Age, often conventionally regarded as synonymous with ancient Celtic culture. Much of the writing on the evolution of La Tène Iron Age art has examined the importation and transformation of motifs from the Greek, Etruscan and Roman world (e.g. Castriota 1981; Frey 1976; Jacobsthal 1944; Kruta 1982a; b). Another preoccupation has been the possible influences from the east, from Scythians, Thracians, Dacians and others of the named actors on the stage of Iron Age Europe (Fischer 1983; 1988; Luschey 1983; Megaw 1975; Megaw & Megaw 1990a; Powell 1971; Sandars 1971; 1976). In search of the routes taken by such influences, archaeologists have concentrated, as they have to, on the material remains of non-Celtic cultures or geographical areas found in the territory defined as being that of 'Celtic' material culture.

Figure 22.1a. Mickey Mouse. Detail from a television advertisement, c.1958. © Walt Disney Productions

Figure 22.1b. ?Sardinia. Gold finger-ring. Diameter 25 mm. Victoria and Albert Museum, London. Photo: Crown copyright reserved.

Iron Age trade and exchange

Many recent attempts to explain the structure of Early Iron Age society have started from the remains of external trade and seen this, perhaps exaggeratedly, as the central engine of the society. Production has been viewed as driven by external trade, and the whole process of trade has been regarded as central rather than peripheral in La Tène society, while the society itself has been viewed as a peripheral part of a world system dominated by a Mediterranean core driven in turn by trade expansion and moving towards surplus value appropriation and state organisation on some one-way escalator of cultural evolution. The first major assertion of a prestige gifts model was Fischer's 1973 paper on 'Kemelia' or Iron Age gift exchange on a heroic Homeric pattern. This over-simplifies by its failure to recognise luxury objects as themselves commodities, but has been widely cited in Germany and central Europe.

Another prestige gifts model was first mooted by Frankenstein and Rowlands in 1978 in a paper which must have earned — maybe not entirely now to its authors' liking — something of a Guinness Book of Records status with regard to its citation frequency by anglophones. Frankenstein and Rowlands present the early Iron Age as reflecting a pattern of society similar to that of the Portuguese-influenced Kongo of west central Africa in the fifteenth century, where power is seen as resting upon the controlled movement of socially important items, often imported. Amongst the Kongo the major important import was guns, a form of superior weaponry which quite obviously caused disruption of previous patterns of social control. In our opinion and that of several others, the importation of pottery and metal vessels is unlikely to produce the same effect. Rowlands recently vigorously restated his position, though in our view he has not proved his assumption that the search for universalism validates the use of models imported, holus-bolus and often outdated, from other disciplines and other historical

contexts which has been the bane of archaeology for decades. This approach has been attacked by, among others, Gosden and Bradley for ignoring actual evidence in its attempt to build a neat and tidy model (Rowlands *et al.* 1987). Certainly when one looks at the original article, it is impossible not to be struck by the constant stream of assumptions paraded, and frequent assertions, without proof, that this that or the other is clearly upheld by the evidence are alarming. Equally, the use of a model of social debt is asserted, not demonstrated, for the Hallstatt Iron Age (Gosden 1989). We are interested to detect in several papers in this volume a more cautious approach to the Lego-like modelling of the past[1].

As archaeologists we are indeed in search of universalisms in understanding human societies, but we should not accept over-simplistic and reductionist models as a result. Theoretical archaeologists have sometimes sneered at descriptions of sites or societies or classes of object; certainly such descriptions may contain unconscious models of how societies function, but it is also naive in the extreme to assume that assigning an ethnographic or sociological label means understanding a society's structure and mode of operation. Theoretical models are good servants, but bad masters; their indiscriminate application can lead to the Procrustean ignoring or distortion of evidence. Throughout much of the theoretical writings of the last twenty years and more there is the constant assertion that we are dealing with dependent societies and economies, a Wallersteinian 'world system model' (1974) which once again owes its origins to the study of the period of modern European economic and territorial expansion, and should not be exported too easily to prehistoric times.

Gosden's own (1985) model of La Tène society prefers to draw on very much later Irish literature, that obscured window on the Iron Age (Jackson 1964), an approach which Rowlands has dismissed as Eurocentric for assuming that there might be traits recognisable as 'European' as opposed to universal (Rowlands, Bradley

& Gosden 1987); Rowlands has also attacked the Celts as 'barbarians' in a fashion which seems to pay little attention to the origin of the term itself, and seems to assume that Roman rule was always disinterestedly benevolent and non-violent. As, respectively, a prehistorian with art historical training and a political and cultural historian, our own worries would rather be chronological, in that such sources as the Taín are over a millennium later and may not reflect the society of a much earlier group in a different place as well as time. Gosden's own model of production and exchange is based on a detailed study of the first wheel-turned pottery production in the less agriculturally favoured regions of early La Tène north-west Bohemia (Gosden 1983; 1990). It favours local production rather than external trade and exchange as a determinant of social position. This viewpoint receives support from the recent work of Nataša Venclová and her colleagues in central Bohemia, where the third and second century BC production and distribution of iron objects and sapropelite ornaments are considered as contributing significantly to the subsequent development of late Iron Age *oppida* society (Venclová 1993). Wells (1980) on entrepreneurism and Nicholson (1989) on a Wallersteinian, not to say cultural evolutionary, study of the pottery of the Hunsrück-Eifel-Kultur, are also studies which apply modern theory to a past era in a further attempt to make the Late Iron Age the start of the modern capitalist era. One may observe in passing that evocation of Vere Gordon Childe is noticeably absent from almost all of this.

Rowlands has recently returned to the theoretical battlefield with a paper serendipitously entitled 'From the gift to market economies: The ideology and politics of European Iron Age studies' (forthcoming) which is concerned almost exclusively with interpreting the nature of the Late Iron Age, or *oppida* period, in contrast to that of the later Bronze Age. Rowlands challenges its interpretation 'as a pivotal period in terms of social and economic change because new kinds of linkage develop between trade and profit, profit and production'. He continues by querying a picture of 'the freeing of accumulation of wealth from a dominant principle of reciprocity into a more autonomous economic logic' in the light of 'the massive evidence of conspicuous consumption associated with the recruitment of retinues and small armies of clients on which political/military power depended'. In terms of continuity from the late Bronze Age and on into feudal societies, warfare is regarded as the cultural means of defining status and recruiting dependents. Here is more than a touch of Peschel's (1984) view of evolving and expanding Iron Age society driven by armed bands who come to plunder and remain to settle.

By and large all of these are so many Swiftian skirmishes between theoretical Big-endians and Little-endians who think that to label a society is to explain it. Greg Woolf's suggestion elsewhere in this volume

of a 'late La Tène Europe . . . socially and politically fragmented but culturally unified' is an eminently sensible statement of what should have long since been archaeologically obvious.

Finally in this opening gambit, we must observe that much of the continuing debate is too exclusively materialist in its failure to acknowledge, as Renfrew did many years ago, that nothing in trading networks is so potent as the invisible trade in and exchange of ideas (Renfrew 1972, esp. 474–5). Much more attention has been paid to the material products of past exchange than to the mechanisms of the transfer of ideas and beliefs within La Tène society, to the meaning of visual symbolism, or to whether the surviving relics of a visual language can or should be considered in isolation from other material remains of Iron Age society. Few European prehistorians, let alone art historians, seem comfortable with the study of this visual symbolic material. Instead, to a large extent in England there has been recently a particularly sterile debate developing which is at pains to deny the existence of any such thing as pre-Roman 'Celtic' culture let alone Celts, a point of view which, to some degree, reflects England's insular, 'outsider' approach to the concept of a united Europe and a positively racist approach to the definition of British.

There has also been some discussion of the concept of Europe in prehistory, a debate which is strongly informed by modern ideas of ethnic and national identity (Hobsbawm 1992; Megaw & Megaw 1992; Verdery 1992). Ideas which are drawn from the modern nation-state are certainly anachronistic in the prehistoric period. Modern nationality is largely defined by shared language and tradition, but there is only scant evidence for a prehistoric, or even early La Tène, use of Celtic language; until 20 years ago only half of the inhabitants of Italy spoke Italian as their cradle tongue. Since it is in fact the art which is the tangible evidence for a continuity of cultural tradition in later prehistoric Europe, then, as one of us once stated in the panic of extempore seminar delivery, the 'Celts' were indeed those who produced 'Celtic' or 'La Tène' art[2]. This is not to deny the obviously historically limited use of the (Greek) term 'Keltoi' or the regional variations detectable in the archaeological record. Nevertheless, if art styles are accepted as evidence of self-image or cultural identity, then the term 'Celtic' is as valid as 'European' or, for that matter, 'Aboriginal (Australian)'. Try informing an urban-based and conventional art school-trained Aboriginal artist — Gordon Bennett from Brisbane or Trevor Nickolls from Adelaide for example — that he has no true claim to being Aboriginal, because from a point of view of genetic descent he is as much or more white Australian as black, he speaks the English language, and his referential (post-modernist ?) style borrows from other cultures than his own. Nationality may be legally defined, but identity is a territory of the mind[3].

Ian Hodder has talked of 'the consumerised instant

Figure 22.2a. Weiskirchen, Kr. Merzig-Wadern, Germany, barrow 1. Bronze beltplate with coral inlay.
Width 75 mm. Rheinishes Landesmuseum, Trier. Photo: Univers des Formes

Figure 22.2b. San Polo d'Enza, Reggio Emilia, Italy. Openwork bronze belthook. Length 34 mm.
Museo Civico 'G. Chierici', Reggio Emilia

thrill of a post-modern heritage' (1990), in the seemingly unending appetite for the recreation and public display of the past, though it is often the 'past as wished for' of which Stuart Piggott wrote many years ago (1975, esp. 11). The high-tech past of 'Celtworld' at Tramore, Co. Waterford, where visitors are ferried, Jorvik style, through recreations of Celtic myths and legends, of Parc Astérix currently being offered as a chance to explore our common European heritage rather than further deify US theme park culture in the shape of nearest big neighbour EuroDisney, or the more archaeologically 'acceptable' 'Village gaulois au temps d'Astérix' (Musée en Herbe 1985) all prompt debate of the trade and exchange and the changes which take place in concepts of cultural ethnicity and nationhood (Megaw & Megaw 1992).

A case study: art as commodity

Permeability of societies to imported ideas is by no means uniform. The openness of La Tène artisans from the fifth century BC onwards to incorporation of some imported elements in their products as compared with that of their immediate Hallstatt predecessors is striking, yet there was an apparent reduction during the fifth to fourth century of manufactured imports of metal or pottery from the Mediterranean area in contrast to the Hallstatt C/D phase — Shefton considers that no imports from Etruria are later than about 450 BC (pers. comm.; see also Shefton 1988, esp. 118, and Megaw & Megaw 1990a, 36) — though an apparent increase of coral importation.

So far as the incorporation of exotic art motifs is concerned, one can continue to assert that only those elements of style which suited the Celtic visual grammatical syntax were used; elements which were non-narrative were welcomed. There are some exceptions (Fig. 22.2a), such as the ultimately oriental and orientalising 'Master (or Mistress) of the Beasts' — ingeniously but unconvincingly considered by Kruta (1986) to form part of a Mediterranean-sourced holy trinity of which the other two parts are the vine and coral. Its use is clearly symbolic rather than narrative, and with rare exceptions is largely confined to one class of object, the open-work so-called Ticino belthooks (Fig. 22.2b; Frey 1991; Megaw & Megaw 1990b). Mostly, however, it remains a truism that early La Tène art exhibits a restricted range of animals and very few entire humans, as opposed to human heads.

Importation of pattern elements such as palmettes or lotus flowers is merely a part of a long transmission, since they had been part of Egyptian, Greek, Phoenician, and Etruscan art. Ancient Celts, those first post-modernists, do not lose their claim to an identity through a borrowing of stylistic elements. There seems no doubt that the means of transmission of visual ideas was the trade in material objects with Mediterranean areas (see most recently Pare 1991). The Etruscan beaked metal flagon was adapted north of the Alps in both pottery and metal. The profiles were varied and spouts substituted for the pouring lip; ornate decoration and an often seemingly perverse technical complexity demanding the marshalling of several skills and access to a range of rare materials underline their importance as symbols of wealth and status. The value applied to the Etruscan *Schnabelkanne* is nowhere more clearly demonstrated than in the pastiche represented by that from the second Weiskirchen grave, assembled from three original imports and subsequently engraved locally (Haffner 1985). Most flagons were also to do with alcohol, especially wine, which, whatever the prior evidence for Danish or Hungarian vines (Facsar & Jerem 1985; Rausing 1990), in this period must reflect another important southern import. Thus there may well have been some importation of customs associated with the feast as well as of art styles and trade objects, customs which seem to extend north of the Alps back into the later Bronze Age (Piggott 1959). In other words art is not something 'extra' but something intrinsic to social custom and, with the burying of imported or local flagons and wine-strainers in the grave, with belief structures — a point made, with some variations, successively by de Navarro (1928), Piggott (1959) and Frey (1985).

As far as the famous flagons from Basse-Yutz are concerned, they are an eclectic product, best understood as the result of a co-operative effort by a number of specialised craftworkers from different regions (Megaw & Megaw 1990a). There is certainly no need to posit direct oriental or Greek influences. But should one follow one of our critics and interpret the unique association of a pair of local flagons (the only pair known) and an (unmatching) pair of imported Etruscan *stamnoi* as evidence not of a grave but as a cult offering following the Attic customs of Dionysos (Echt 1992)?

Should we assume, however, that the meanings of such symbols were also imported? Lotus flowers and palm fronds probably meant little other than decoration to Greeks and Etruscans in any case, whatever they had meant to the Egyptians, and the narrative scenes of human activities observed on Greek pottery were not copied. To adapt an analogy of Jacobsthal's (1944, 142), it seems more probable that what we are seeing is a process similar to the tea trade with eighteenth-century China, which was archaeologically invisible but left behind evidence in the form of imported and local tea services, while not importing the beliefs or social system of the Chinese. In the Iron Age, imports of metal goods were more probably devoted to serving the belief systems of the Celts, just as only carefully selected imported elements were incorporated into their art.

The geographic area of this early style Celtic art has also been dramatically extended in the last decade. Conventionally this has been regarded as centred in the Hunsrück-Eifel area of Germany, the Champagne area of France, and in Bohemia. Recent excavations have extended this area well beyond the rich graves of the

Figure 22.3a. Ossarn, Herzogenburg, Niederösterreich, grave 17. Bronze fibula. Length 34 mm.
Photo: Studio Fasching, St Pölten

saltminers of the Dürrnberg in western Austria, to whole cemeteries in eastern Austria close to the Hungarian border (Fig. 22.3a) and in western Slovakia (Megaw *et al.* 1989; Neugebauer 1992).

In Slovakia one can now add to the Stupava flat graves with their hints of a new western population element (Fig. 22.3b) those from the Bučany cemetery (Bujna & Romsauer 1983), both around 400 BC, with somewhat later material from Dubník (Bujna 1989). Yet again we are faced with explaining the appearance of this art; by the movement of people, by trade in objects, or by similarities in belief systems and ideas. In the past we have been inclined to see the appearance in Slovakia of early style material as exclusively evidencing importation of goods or the movement of owners (e.g. Megaw 1970a, no. 64), but the phenomenon seems now wide-

Figure 22.3b. Stupava, Okr. Bratislava-vidiek, Slovakia. Bronze beltplate. 66 x 33 mm.
Slovenské Narodne Múzeum, Bratislava. Photo: W. & B. Forman (courtesy of Artia, Prague)

spread enough to suggest local manufacture by a population which shared symbolic beliefs with peoples far to the west, and expressed those beliefs through a similar iconography executed with the same technology on similar objects.

Similarities between eastern and western areas of Early Style art have been explained by Kruta (e.g. 1982a, b) as radiating fan-like from northern Italy, while Bouloumié (1982, 184) suggests an alternative route for some Mediterranean and other imports not directly from Italy but via Bohemia from the Rhineland. Pauli (1974) suggested the valleys of the Salzach and Inn rivers as the possibly waterborne section of a route by which wine was imported from Italy and salt sent from the Dürrnberg and Hallstatt both north to Bohemia and southwards, and by which small groups were also able to make seasonal journeys, perhaps for the purposes of transhumance. Other, more localised distributions have been demonstrated for pottery in eastern central Europe: in early La Tène B kilns at Sopron-Krautacker seem to have supplied pots to areas in eastern Austria, including Mannersdorf (Jerem 1984). In contrast, Gosden (1983) has indicated that in north-western Bohemia, outside the the areas of the chieftains' graves, but on the putative route between those graves and the Rhineland, there is little sign of outside contacts and that with the introduction of the potter's wheel there is evidence that pottery production became more localised. The routes by which influences reached the lower Traisental are thus difficult to determine, but connections with western Europe (by way of an east-west route to Bohemia), southwards to Italy (via the Dürrnburg or even Hallstatt) and with western Hungary seem all to be candidates.

In 1980 Tim Champion, in the course of a valuable essay on the evidence for mass migration in later prehistoric Europe, while indicating the comparative rarity of such events, also noted the obvious availability of advanced transport technology — wheeled vehicles — and complex exchange networks assisting general geographical knowledge. Thus we may postulate an early European Community of ideas and beliefs, albeit with regional variations. It is difficult to achieve this without a reasonably free exchange of goods, and, for technological changes, people.

Invisible exports and art objects as belief systems

The concept of early La Tène art which we have advanced based on a system of ideas and beliefs, basically religious in nature, is applicable to the obviously human as well as monstrous imagery of, for example, the ornate neck- and arm-rings and the *Maskenfibeln* of the fifth to fourth century BC. Pauli has considered such objects with a range of amulets as products of an 'age of uncertainty' and has further written of '"Celts" . . . an idea endowed with a socio-psychic background [which] is firmly established in a real historical situation' (Pauli 1985, 29). An essential feature of such art is also — and here comes the smile of the Cheshire Cat first cited by Jacobsthal fifty years ago — the semi-concealed imagery of the late fourth century 'vegetai style', widely diffused throughout Europe from Bulgaria to Brittany (Figs. 22.4a-b). Surely this must represent more than the following of mere decorative fashion.

We may ask similar questions of the later fourth/ second century 'inter-Celtic currency' of the 'dragon-pairs' (Fig. 22.5b; de Navarro 1972, esp. 65–99;

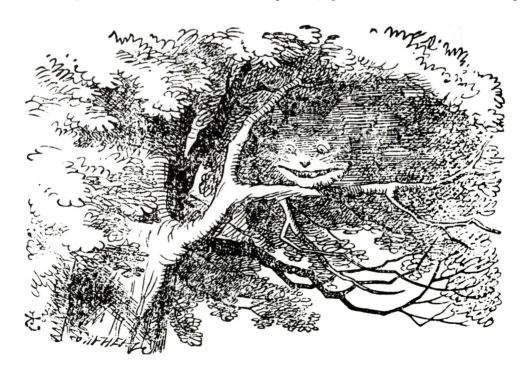

Figure 22.4a. The Cheshire Cat. Drawing by John Tenniel (first published 1865)

Figure 22.4b. Filottrano, San Paolino, Italy, grave 22. Iron-backed bronze scabbard fragment.
Length of detail c. *750 mm. Museo Nazionale delle Marche, Ancona. Photo: Univers des Formes*

Megaw & Megaw 1990b; Stead 1984; Szabó 1989). Whatever they represent they are certainly not dragons, but they remain a major symbol of the warrior over two centuries. The 'vegetal style' decorated sword scabbards and the scattering of splendid helmets from France and Italy (Figs. 22.4b, 22.5a; Megaw & Megaw 1989, ills 149–50, 153–4, pls X-XI; Moscati 1991, 292–3; Vitali 1988) offer a link across local cultural groups which are otherwise barely recognisable as 'Celtic', let alone La Tène. Take away such pieces from the material culture of, for example, those who dwelt on the often most inhospitable heights of Monte Bibele above Bologna and are identified unequivocally by contemporary classical sources as Celtic, and there is nothing to distinguish them from other indigenous groups in the region. Are we looking at the material evidence of belief patterns or merely the vagaries of local fashion? The distribution of the helmets ranges again as far west as Brittany and the fascinating but poorly recorded site of St Jean Trolimon (Duval 1990) and as far east as the cache of helmets, swords, spearheads and suspension chains alleged to have been found at the Förker Laas Riegal, in the Gailtal in Carinthia (Schaaff 1990; Neugebauer 1992, 84–6, Abb. 32). This period also shows us the very weak power of the archaeological record to display what written sources tell us were major displacements of peoples and considerable changes in the political and ethnic map of fourth-century Italy and indeed of Europe.

The Gailtal find, apparently a hoard of 'sets' of military equipment rather than grave goods, recalls the debate over the nature of the first century BC Snettisham finds, revived by the recent spectacular additions to the original 1948 discovery (Stead 1991b). With a pattern of pits within an enclosure — of admittedly later date — containing a wealth of neck-rings, coins and scrap one may suggest either a treasury or part of what Andrew Fitzpatrick (1984; 1992) and others (e.g. Bradley 1990) regard as a broader pattern of formal and structured deposition on the part of an Iron Age society without a sharp distinction between the sacred and the profane — another point of comparison with Aboriginal Australia. Such explanations are not in fact mutually exclusive as one is reminded by the blurring in Old Irish myths between this world and the Otherworld. Again, this raises interesting issues concerned with the disposal of wealth, burial customs, the possible purposes served by the selection and patterns of the dispersal of grave goods as well as trade and exchange reaching beyond the grave which we cannot pursue here.

Continuity of some of the imagery is also apparent. The 'Master (or Mistress) of the beasts' of the early fourth-century Ticino belt-hooks (Fig. 22.2b) may well be ancestral to the earliest or Type II dragon-pair scabbards (Fig. 22.5b; Frey 1991; Megaw 1971; Megaw & Megaw 1990b). This imagery seems almost interchangeable with the so-called tree of life, which one may trace through to late La Tène and pieces as far separated in space as the wooden figures from Fellbach-Schmiden (Fig. 22.6a) securely dated to the end of the second century BC and the more or less contemporary stamp on the 'Korisios' sword from Port, Kt. Bern (Fig. 22.6b), or the inlaid sword blade from Mihovo in Slovenia (Fig. 22.6c), not to mention the crested birds' heads on material from Britain and Ireland, down to the dragonesque brooches of the second century AD (Megaw & Megaw 1989, ills 252–3, 240, 254–5, 330, 332, 335–6, 404, 406, pls XII-XIII). The Mediterranean sources of the imagery are clear, even the transmission of such imagery is not beyond reconstruction, and it seems highly probable that its meaning could have been shared across a wide area of temperate Iron Age Europe. But here we

*Figure 22.5a. Agris, Charente, France. Bronze-covered iron helmet covered with gold and inlaid with coral.
Height 214 mm. Musée Municipale, Angoulême. Photo: Römisch-Germanisches Zentralmuseum, Mainz*

sail dangerously close to the stylistic siren songs emanating from such enticing mysteries as the Gundestrup cauldron, found one hundred years ago on the surface of a Danish peat-bog and portraying 'Celts' in a style definitely un-Celtic and variously claimed for several different parts of Europe and groups as diverse as Gauls, Thracians and, most recently, Gypsies (Allen 1971; Bémont 1979; Bergquist & Taylor 1987; Kaul 1991a, b; Kaul *et al.* 1991; Klindt-Jensen 1949, 1959; Megaw 1970a, nos. 209, 214, pl. VI; Olmstedt 1976; Powell 1971; Taylor 1992).

In sum, as the Champions have expressed it (1986, 64):

… it is a teasing question as to whether all the [Celtic] groups accepted the new symbols, rituals and art style because they already felt part of a larger ethnic group, or whether in accepting the symbols and styles, unable to reject their potency, they recognised themselves as a 'people' for the first time.

Conclusion — there are no easy answers

Clearly, like the other contributors to this volume, we have covered only a fragmentary part of our chosen topic. We conclude that art styles may be invisible exports or imports of the Iron Age, but they do need to be transmitted through the medium of people, even as

  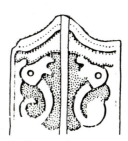

*Figure 22.5b. Type II dragon-pair scabbards from Italy. Left: Monte Bibele, grave 54. Centre: Monte Bibele, grave 6.
Right: Ameglia, grave 22. Widths c. 50 mm. Drawings after Vitali and Durante*

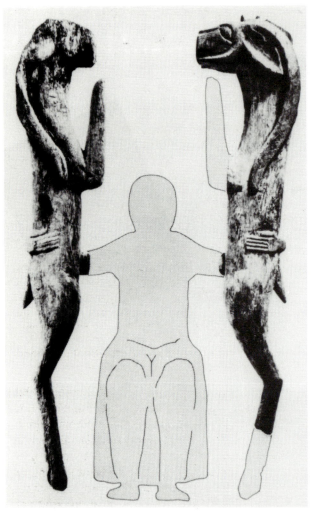

Figure 22.6a. Fellbach-Schmiden, Kr. Rems-Murr, Germany. Reconstruction of scene with seated figure and carved wooden ?goats. Height 870 mm. Würtembergisches Landesmuseum, Stuttgart. Illustration: Landesdenkmalamt Baden-Württemberg

Figure 22.6b. Port, Kt. Bern, Switzerland. Stamp on iron sword showing tree of life and in Greek the name Korisios. Length of stamp 27 mm. Bernisches Historisches Museum

from time to time some aspects of new technologies — such as the use of the potter's wheel, lost-wax casting and the striking of coins.

As an insular coda to our theme with variations we may point out what we have argued more fully elsewhere (Megaw & Megaw 1993). The occurrence in Britain and Ireland by at least some time in the early third century BC of a new art style is undeniable. In the Arras culture of eastern Yorkshire, this art is on objects recently found in inhumation graves, several of which contain two-wheeled vehicles, such as are found on the continent (Fig. 22.7a; Dent 1990; Stead 1991a). In Ireland no such graves have been found and the scabbards from Lisnacrogher and the river Bann (Fig. 22.7b) are supposedly ritual deposits in water and of a different type from the Yorkshire scabbards, though we detect more than a little insularity in recent claims for the exclusively Irish 'Irishness' of such material (e.g. Raftery 1991a, b). The art styles must, we believe, be

related to each other and, more distantly, both are related to those of continental Europe. Yet they are indubitably disposed of in different manners. If the appearance of the art is associated with the introduction of a new belief system, it seems strange that in northern Ireland the swords are not buried. Are these the material signs of changed beliefs among incoming sword-bearers abandoning their arms, or of the defeat of new ideas (and newcomers?) by a local population?

While the 30–year-long reaction amongst British archaeologists against change or innovation necessarily being equated with major population movements or 'invasions' undoubtedly has some merit, in each and every case the introduction of a new art style requires something more than just a random handful of imports. Rather one must assume a physical transportation (and acceptance) of external stylistic elements whether or not by isolated groups of dominant warriors and their attendant craftsmen or, certainly much more plausible,

Figure 22.6c. Mihovo, Slovenia. Bronze plate for iron scabbard. Width 50 mm. Naturhistorisches Museum, Vienna

native communities with links to the continent adopting through the agency of a few craftworkers a 'new' range of symbols of power [4].

What follows this still tantalisingly unclear early developmental phase is what we have called the 'mature' stage of insular Iron Age art as represented by the Witham shield and the Llyn Cerrig Bach mount (Megaw & Megaw 1989, ills 337–8). Such material is, on the whole, even more clearly differentiated from contemporary continental material of the middle or late La Tène. However, it too basically follows a stylistic continuum extending back at least to the fourth century BC.

In a lecture given at the Institute of Field Archaeolo-

Figure 22.7a. Wetwang Slack, N. Humberside, England, grave 2. Bronze 'bean-can'. Diameter 90 mm. Photo: courtesy of the Trustees of the British Museum

gists' annual conference in 1991 Richard Morrice (1992) cited with approval Podro's attempt 'to define what in art historical research is distinctive from the archaeological'. Podro sees the task of the art historian as being a consideration of 'how the products of art sustain purposes and interests which are both irreducible to the conditions of their emergence as well as inextricable from them' (Podro 1982, xviii). We are all too seized of the difficulty of the task before any student of past life styles and surviving visual modes of expression; we also happen to believe in the contemporary relevance of such studies. Ten years ago in a lecture to the Collège de France entitled 'Pourquoi "nos ancêtres les gaulois"?', the doyen of early Celtic art studies in France, Paul-Marie Duval, offered the following conclusion to an examination of the relevance of the study of the ancient Gauls to contemporary France (1989, 217):

Arrivés à ce point de rencontre, nous sommes moins loins que jamais des Gaulois de l'Age du Fer car nous constatons que le contenu de l'epithète 'gaulois' coincide avec ce que nous savons essentiel sur les Celtes anciens . . .

Latins? Gaulois? Latins par notre Midi, Latins d'adoption par notre histoire et notre langue, nous avons tout de même à coeur de découvrir ce qui nous rapproche, à travers les siècles, de ces frères ainés, aussi doués et réceptifs que joyeux compagnons de notre continuité: les gaulois . . . nos ancêtres.

From Waldalgesheim to Wetwang Slack, from Basse-Yutz to Brno-Maloměřice, from Cheshire Cat to Mickey Mouse and on to Astérix le gaulois, ancient Celtic art has something to say to the new Europe. Despite those who have taken us to task for being too close to

Figure 22.7b. River Bann at Toome, Co. Antrim, Northern Ireland. Bronze scabbard front plate: detail. Width 36 mm.
National Museum of Ireland, Dublin

supposedly out-dated approaches to Celtic art (e.g. Taylor 1991), we find it hard to improve on Jacobsthal's conclusion on early Celtic art, that ' . . . it is a real style, the first great contribution by the barbarians to European arts, the first great chapter in the everlasting mutual stock-taking of Southern, Northern, and Eastern forces in the life of Europe' (Jacobsthal 1944, 163). Like the society from which it evolved, it was open to foreign goods and ideas, yet its creators were individual enough to choose, from outside, those elements which reinforced its uniqueness.

Acknowledgements

We are grateful to the following colleagues who, despite, we are sure, disagreeing in part or whole with what we have argued here, have nonetheless been generous in the supply of material which at the time of writing was unpublished or in press: Rudolf Echt, Barry Raftery, Mike Rowlands, Ian Stead and Tim Taylor.

Notes

1. For the most recent critique of interpretations of the interaction between the Mediterranean and that of Hallstatt D/La Tène A Europe see Pare (1991).
2. Much the same suggestion has been made by Tim Champion (1987, 105): '. . . perhaps it was not so much a question of using Celtic art because you were a Celt, but being a Celt because you used Celtic art'.
3. The most recent and most even-handed contribution to the current fashionable deconstruction (?destruction) of the concept of ancient Celtic culture comes not from an archaeologist but an anthropologist (Chapman 1992).
4. The most vigorous recent claims for the long-term coherence of the 'Celticness' of Celtic art — more vigorous, we confess, than that which we make here — are to be found in Martyn Jope's 1987 Sir John Rhŷs Memorial Lecture (Jope 1987).

References

Allen, D.F., 1971. The Sark hoard. *Archaeologia* 103, 1–31

Bergquist, A.K., & Taylor, T.F., 1987. The origins of the Gundestrup cauldron. *Antiquity* 61, 10–24

Bémont, C., 1979. Le bassin de Gundestrup: remarques sur les décors végétaux. *Etudes Celtiques* 16, 69–99

Bouloumié, B., 1982. Remarques sur la diffusion d'objets grecs et étrusques en Europe centrale et nord-occidentale. *Savaria* 16 = *Nemzetközi Kollokvium 1982 Boszok-Szombathely* (1983), 181–92

Bradley, R., 1990. *The Passage of Arms: an Archaeological Analysis of Prehistoric Hoards and Votive Deposits*. Cambridge: Cambridge University Press

Bujna, J., 1989. Das latènezeitliche Gräberfeld bei Dubník I. *Slovenská Archeologia* 37, 245–354

Bujna, J., & Romsauer, P., 1983. Späthallstatt- und frühlatènezeitliches Gräberfeld in Bučany. *Slovenská Archeologia* 31, 277–324

Castriota, D.R., 1981. Continuity and Innovation in Celtic and Mediterranean Ornament: a Grammatical-Syntactical Analysis of the Process of Reception and Transformation in the

Decorative Arts of Antiquity. Ph.D. thesis, Columbia University 1981/ Ann Arbor: University Microfilms International 1982

Champion, T.C., 1987. The European Iron Age: assessing the state of the art. *Scottish Archaeological Review* 4(2), 98–107

Champion, T.C., & Champion, S., 1986. Peer polity interaction in the European Iron Age, in *Peer Polity Interaction and Socio-political Change*, eds A.C. Renfrew & J.F. Cherry. Cambridge: Cambridge University Press, 59–68

Chapman, M., 1992. *The Celts: the Construction of a Myth.* Basingstoke/New York: Macmillan/St Martin's Press

de Navarro, J.M., 1928. Massilia and early Celtic culture. *Antiquity* 2, 423–42

de Navarro, J.M., 1972. *The Finds from the Site of La Tène, Scabbards and the Swords Found in them.* London: Oxford University Press for the British Academy

Dent, J., 1990. Changes in the later Iron Age of eastern Yorkshire, in *Les Gaulois d'Armorique: Actes du XIIe Colloque de l'Association Française de l'Etude de l'Age du Fer*, eds A. Duval, J.-P. LeBihan & Y. Menez = *Revue Archéologique de l'Ouest* Supplément 3, 223–31

Duval, A., 1990. Quelques aspects du mobilier métallique en fer anciennement recueili à Tronöen, en Saint-Jean-Trolimon (Finistère), in *Les Gaulois d'Armorique: Actes du XIIe Colloque de l'Association Française de l'Etude de l'Age du Fer*, eds A. Duval, J.-P. LeBihan & Y. Menez = *Revue Archéologique de l'Ouest* Supplément 3, 23–45

Duval, P.-M., 1989. Pourquoi 'nos ancêtres les gaulois'?, in *Travaux sur la Gaule (1946–1986): Textes Revus et Mis à Jour*, ed. P.-M. Duval = *Collection de l'Ecole Française de Rome* 116(i), 119–217

Echt, R., 1992. Review of 'The Basse-Yutz Find: Masterpieces of Celtic Art' eds J.V.S. & M.R. Megaw, *Germania* 69, 452–5

Facsar, G., & Jerem, E., 1985. Zum urgeschichtlichen Weinbau in Mitteleuropa: Rebkernfunde von Vitis Vinifera L. aus der urnenfelder- hallstatt- und latènezeitlichen Siedlung Sopron-Krautacker. *Wissenschaftliche Arbeiten aus dem Burgenland* 71, 121–44

Fischer, F. 1973. KEIMHΛIA: Bemerkungen zur kulturgeschichtlichen Interpretation des sogenannten Südimports in der späten Hallstatt- und frühen Latène-Kultur des westlichen Mitteleurpa. *Germania* 51, 436–59

Fischer, F., 1983. Thrakien als Vermittler iranischer Metallkunst an die frühen Kelten, in *Beiträge zur Altertumskunde Kleinasiens: Festschrift für Kurt Bittel*, eds R.M. Boehmer & H. Hauptmann. Mainz: Philipp von Zabern, 191–202

Fischer, F., 1988. Celtes et Achéménides, in *Les Princes Celtes et la Méditerranée*, eds A. Duval *et al.* Paris: La Documentation Française, 21–31

Fitzpatrick, A.P., 1984. The deposition of La Tène Iron Age metalwork in watery contexts in southern England, in *Aspects of the Iron Age in Central Southern Britain*, eds B. Cunliffe & D. Miles. Oxford: Oxford University Committee for Archaeology Monograph 2, 178–90

Fitzpatrick, A.P., 1992. The Snettisham, Norfolk, hoards of Iron Age torques: sacred or profane? *Antiquity* 66, 395–8

Frankenstein, S., & Rowlands, M.J., 1978. The internal structure and regional context of early Iron Age society in south-western Germany. *University of London Institute of Archaeology Bulletin* 15, 74–112

Frey, O.-H., 1976. Du Premier style au style de Waldalgesheim: remarques sur l'évolution l'art celtique ancien, in *Celtic Art in Ancient Europe: Five Protohistoric Centuries*, eds P.-M.

Duval & C.F.C. Hawkes. London/New York: Seminar Press, 141–63

Frey, O.-H., 1985. Zum Handel und Verkehr während der Fruhlatènezeit in Mitteleuropa, in *Untersuchungen zu Handel und Verkehr der vor- und frühgeschichtlichen Zeit in Mittel- und Nordeuropa I*, eds K. Düwel *et al.*, = *Abhandlungen der Akademie der Wissenschaften, Göttingen* Phil.-Hist. Kl. 3 Folge, 143, 231– 57

Frey, O.-H., 1991. Einige Bermerkungen zu den durchbrochenen Frühlatènegürtelhaken, in S*tudien zur Eisenzeit im Hunsrück-Nahe-Raum: Symposium Birkenfeld 1987*, eds A. Haffner & A. Miron, = *Trierer Zeitschrift* Beiheft 13, 101–11

Gombrich, E.H., 1977. *Art and Illusion* (5th ed.). London: Phaidon

Gombrich, E.H., 1979. *The Sense of Order: A Study in the Philosophy of Decorative Art.* London: Phaidon

Gosden, C.H. 1983. *Iron Age Pottery Trade in Central Europe.* Unpublished Ph.D. thesis, University of Sheffield

Gosden, C., 1985. Gifts and kin in early Iron Age Europe. *Man* 20, 475–93

Gosden, C., 1989. Debt, production and prehistory. *Journal of Anthropological Archaeology* 8, 355–87

Gosden, C., 1990. Ethnoarchaeological case studies in Kenya and Europe. *Archeologické Rozhledy* 42, 73–90

Haffner, A., 1985. L' œnochoé de Weiskirchen I: étude technique. *Les Ages de Fer dans la Vallée de la Saône*, eds L. Bonnamour, A. Duval & J.-P. Guillaumet = *Revue Archéologique de l'Est et du Centre-Est*, sixième supplément, 279–82

Hobsbawm, E.J., 1992. Ethnicity and nationalism in Europe today. *Anthropology Today* 8, 3–7

Jackson, K.H., 1964. *The Oldest Irish Tradition: a Window on the Iron Age.* Cambridge: Cambridge University Press

Jacobsthal, P., 1944. *Early Celtic Art.* Oxford: Clarendon Press (reprinted with corrections 1969)

Jerem, E., 1984. An early Celtic pottery workshop in northern Hungary: some archaeological and technical evidence. *Oxford Journal of Archaeology* 3, 57–80

Jope, E.M., 1987. Celtic art: expressiveness and communication through 2500 years. *Proceedings of the British Academy* 73, 97–124

Kaul, F., 1991a, The Gundestrup cauldron, in *The Celts*, ed. S. Moscati. Milan: Bompiani/London: Thames and Hudson, 538–9

Kaul, F., 1991b. *Gundestrupkedelen.* Copenhagen: National-museet/Nyt Nordisk Forlag

Kaul, F., *et al.* 1991. *Thracian Tales on the Gundestrup Cauldron.* Amsterdam: Najade Press

Klindt-Jensen, O., 1959. The Gundestrup bowl: a re-assessment. *Antiquity* 33, 161–169

Kruta, V., 1982a. L'Italie et l'Europe intérieure du Ve siècle au début du IIe siècle avant notre ère. *Savaria* 16 = *Nemzetközi Kollokvium 1982 Boszok-Szombathely* (1983), 203–21

Kruta, V., 1982b. Aspects unitaires et faciès dans l'art celtique du IVe siècle avant notre ère: l'hypothèse d'un foyer Celto-Italique, in *L'Art Celtique de la Période d'Expansion: IVe et IIIe Siècles avant Notre Ere*, eds P.-M. Duval & V. Kruta = *Actes du Colloque au Collège de France à Paris du 26 au 28 Septembre 1978.* Paris: Librairie Droz, 35–76

Kruta, V., 1986. Le corail, le vin et l'arbre de vie; observations sur l'art et la réligion des Celtes du Ve au Ier siècle avant J.-C. *Etudes Celtiques* 23, 7–32

Luschey, H., 1983. Thrakien als Ort der Begegnung der Kelten mit der iranischen Metallkunst, in *Beiträge zur Altertumskunde Kleinasiens: Festschrift für Kurt Bittel*, eds R.M. Boehmer

& H. Hauptmann. Mainz: Philipp von Zabern, 313–29

Megaw, J.V.S., 1970a. *The Art of the European Iron Age*. Bath: Adams & Dart

Megaw, J.V.S., 1970b. Cheshire Cat and Mickey Mouse: problems in the analysis of the art of the European Iron Age. *Proceedings of the Prehistoric Society* 35, 261–79

Megaw, J.V.S., 1971. An unpublished early La Tène Tierfibel from Hallstatt, Oberösterreich. *Archaeologia Austriaca* 50, 176–84

Megaw, J.V.S., 1975. The orientalizing theme in early Celtic art: east or west?, in *The Celts in Central Europe: Papers of the II Pannonia Conference, Székesfehérvár 1974*, ed. J. Fitz = *Alba Regia* 14, 15–33

Megaw, J.V.S., & Megaw, M.R., (eds.), 1990a. *The Basse-Yutz Find: Masterpieces of Celtic Art*. London: Reports of the Research Committee of the Society of Antiquaries 46

Megaw, J.V.S., & Megaw, M.R., 1990b. 'Semper aliquid novum...' Celtic dragon-pairs re-reviewed. *Acta Archaeologica Academiae Scientiarum Hungaricae* 42, 55–72

Megaw, J.V.S., & Megaw, M.R., 1993. The earliest insular Celtic art: some unanswered questions. *Etudes Celtiques* 28, 283–30

Megaw, J.V.S., Megaw, M.R., & Neugebauer, J.-W., 1989. Zeugnisse frühlatènezeitlichen Kunsthandwerks aus dem Raum Herzogenburg, Niederösterreich. *Germania* 67, 477–517

Megaw, R., & Megaw, V., 1989. *Celtic Art from its Beginnings to the Book of Kells*. London: Thames & Hudson (reprinted with corrections 1990)

Megaw, R., & Megaw, V., 1992. The Celts: the first Europeans? *Antiquity* 66, 254–60

Morrice, R., 1992. Art history and archaeology. *The Field Archaeologist* 16, 301

Moscati, S., (ed.) 1991. *The Celts*. Milan: Bompiani/London: Thames & Hudson

Musée en Herbe 1985. *Un Village Gaulois au Temps d'Astérix: Catalogue*. Paris: Musée en Herbe

Neugebauer, J.-W., 1992. *Die Kelten im Osten Österreichs = Wissenschaftliche Schriftenreihe Niederösterreich* 92–4. St Pölten/Wien: Niederösterreichishes Pressehaus

Nicholson, P., 1989. *Iron Age Pottery Production in the Hunsrück-Eifel-Kultur of Germany: a World-System Perspective*. Oxford: British Archaeological Reports International Series 501

Olmstedt, G.S., 1976. The Gundestrup version of the Táin Bó Cuailnge. *Antiquity* 50, 95–103

Pare, C., 1991. *Fürstensitze*, Celts and the Mediterranean world: developments in the West Hallstatt culture in the 6th and 5th centuries BC. *Proceedings of the Prehistoric Society* 57(2),183– 202

Pauli, L., 1974. Der goldene Steig: Wirtschaftsgeographisch-archäologische Untersuchungen im ostlichen Mitteleuropa, in *Festschrift für Joachim Werner* eds G. Kossack & G. Ulbert = *Münchner Beiträge zur Vor- und Frühgeschichte* Ergänzungsband 1, 115–39

Pauli, L., 1985. Early Celtic society: two centuries of wealth and turmoil in central Europe, in *Settlement and Society: Aspects of West European Prehistory in the First Millennium B.C.*, eds T.C. Champion & J.V.S. Megaw. Leicester: Leicester University Press, 23–44

Peschel, K., 1984. Kriegergrab, Gefolge und Landnahme bei den Latènekelten. *Ethnographische-Archäologische Zeitschrift* 25, 445– 69

Piggott, S., 1959. A late Bronze Age wine trade? *Antiquity* 33, 122–3

Piggott, S., 1975. *The Druids* (revised edition). London: Thames & Hudson

Podro, M., 1982. *The Critical Historians of Art*. New Haven and London: Yale University Press

Powell, T.G.E., 1971. From Uratu to Gundestrup, in *The European Community in Later Prehistory*, eds J. Boardman, M.A. Brown & T.G.E. Powell. London: Routledge & Kegan Paul, 183–210

Raftery, B., 1991a. The Celtic Iron Age in Ireland: problems of origin. *Emania* 9, 28–32

Raftery, B., 1991b. Irland und der Kontinent während die Latènezeit, in *Marburger Kolloquium 1989: Wolfgang Dehn zum 80 Geburtstag*, ed. O.-H. Frey = *Veröffentl. d. Vorgeschichtl. Seminars Marburg* Sonderband 7, 49–64

Rausing, G., 1990. *Vitis* pips in Neolithic Sweden. *Antiquity* 64, 117–21

Renfrew, A.C., 1972. *The Emergence of Civilisation: the Cyclades and the Aegean in the Third Millennium BC*. London: Methuen

Rowlands, M.J., forthcoming. From the gift to market economies: the ideology and politics of European Iron Age studies, in *Europe in the 1st Millennium BC*, eds J. Jensen & K. Kristiansen. Sheffield: University of Sheffield Department of Archaeology and Prehistory

Rowlands, M.J., Bradley, R. & Gosden, C., 1987. The concept of Europe in prehistory. *Man* n.s. 22, 558–61

Sandars, N.K., 1971. Orient and orientalizing in early Celtic art. *Antiquity* 45, 103–12

Sandars, N.K., 1976. Orient and orientalizing: recent thoughts reviewed, in *Celtic Art in Ancient Europe: Five Protohistoric Centuries*, eds P.-M. Duval & C.F.C. Hawkes. London/New York: Seminar Press, 41–60

Schaaff, U., 1990. *Keltische Waffen*. Mainz: Römisch-Germanishes Zentralmuseum

Shefton, B.B., 1988. 2. Der Stamnos, in *Das Kleinaspergle* by W. Kimmig, = *Forschungen und Beiträge zur Vor- und Frühgeschichte in Baden-Würtemberg* 30. Stuttgart: Theiss, 104–52

Stead, I.M., 1984. Celtic dragons from the river Thames. *Antiquaries Journal* 64, 269–79

Stead, I.M., 1991a. *Iron Age Cemeteries in East Yorkshire = English Heritage Archaeological Report* 22. London: English Heritage & British Museum Press

Stead. I.M., 1991b. The Snettisham treasure: excavations in 1990. *Antiquity* 65, 447–64

Szabó, M., 1989. Beiträge zur Geschichte des keltischen Drachenpaarmotivs. *Communicationes Archaeologicae Hungaricae*, 119–28

Taylor, T.F., 1991. Celtic art [review of Megaw & Megaw 1989]. *Scottish Archaeological Review* 8, 129–32

Taylor, T.F., 1992. The Gundestrup cauldron. *Scientific American* 266(3), 66–71

Venclová, N.,1993. Habitats industriels celtiques du IIIe siècle en Bohême. *Etudes Celtiques* 28, 435–50

Verdery, K., 1992. Hobsbawm in the east. *Anthropology Today* 8, 1–10

Vitali, D.,1988. Elmi di ferro e cinturoni a catena: nuove proposte per l'archeologia dei Celti in Italia. *Jahrbuch des Römisch-germanischen Zentralmuseums, Mainz* 35, 239–84

Wallerstein, I., 1974. *The Modern World System*, second edition. London: Academic Press

Wells, P.S., 1980. *Culture Contact and Culture Change: Early Iron Age Central Europe and the Mediterranean World*. Cambridge: Cambridge University Press

23

Ethnicity and Exchange: Germans, Celts and Romans in the Late Iron Age

A. P. Fitzpatrick

The assumptions of imperialism, trade and a balance of trade which underlie the popular usage of the core-periphery model to explain changes in Celtic societies of western Europe are reviewed. The contrasting attitude of German societies to contact with the Roman world is also examined, and attention is drawn to links between Celts and Germans and to the major Germanic settlements of central Europe which have been almost entirely overlooked in the preoccupation with core-periphery models.

Les suppositions d'impérialisme, de commerce et d'équilibre commercial qui sont à la base de l'usage populaire du modèle centre-périphérie pour expliquer des changements dans la société celtique de l'Europe occidentale sont passées en revue. L'attitude distincte des sociétés germaines à l'égard du contact avec le monde romain est examinée. Finalement on signale les liens entre celtes et germains et l'importance des habitations germaines de l'Europe centrale, que la préoccupation avec les modèles centre-périphérie a presque fait oublier.

Introduction: two tribes, one world

Relations between the Celts and the classical world have fascinated scholars of the Iron Age for over a century, and recently core-periphery models have made them *the* focus of studies of the European Iron Age. Of equal interest, although usually to a different group of scholars, have been the transformation of the Roman Empire, the rise of the northern barbarians, and the beginning of the Dark Ages.

Although frequently taking different approaches, both groups of scholars share some assumptions, two of which are of especial interest here. The first is that trade between the classical world and the barbarian peoples was 'natural', and the second that liaisons between core and periphery are inevitable. At the risk of applying ethnic labels uncritically, the terms 'Celts', 'Germans' and 'Romans' are used here as shorthand for the purposes of argument, without prejudice to the many peoples subsumed by the groupings. It is these peoples and the ways in which they defined themselves and others who are the subject of our study. It is a subject both lesser and larger than the two scholarly traditions, yet it is a subject neglected in recent studies of the prehistory of Europe(s).

As usually constructed by French and English speaking archaeologists the Iron Age of Europe is an Iron Age of 'Celtic' Europe. It is a Europe in which Celt-

iberians may have a tenuous place, but in which Germans, Thracians and the peoples of much of Eurasia have no place. It is a Europe which looks to the south. Research has traditionally focused on two themes: 'Celticity' and links with the classical world (de Navarro 1936; Frey 1984). Within this tradition perceptions of links with the classical world have changed many times. Some older works uncritically accepted the Mediterranean world as the fount of civilisation and in some respects, despite the sophistication of their analyses, the acceptance of the Mediterranean world as the 'core' in recent studies of core-periphery relationships does the same.

Many studies of the Celts link the ultimate incorporation of Celtic peoples within the Roman Empire to the organisation and sophistication of Celtic societies (e.g. Roymans 1990, 261–70). A particularly clear index of this sophistication is seen in trade with the Roman world before the conquest. In contrast 'Germanic' contact with the Roman world is often seen as indicating both growing social organisation and greed, leading to a barbarism which transformed the civilised world (cf. Randsborg 1991).

In many respects these approaches to the roles of relations between the barbarian and classical Europes are very different, but they are united by a belief in the role of trade as a stimulus to social hierarchisation. Surprisingly, the character of the Mediterranean core is rarely considered, despite the similar importance ascribed to it in interpretations of later periods when it was clearly of a different character (e.g. Hodges & Whitehouse 1983).

Studies of the later pre-Roman Iron Age share a widely held, but rarely defined, assumption about the nature of Roman imperialism. Roman expansion in the later Republic is seen to be imperialist, entrepreneurial and capitalist, and these beliefs are taken to be sustained by a coherent and similarly informed foreign policy.

Relations between Celts and Romans and Germans and Romans are often considered to be successive, belonging to the pre-Roman and Roman Iron Ages respectively. However, the first century BC saw an overlap between Celtic and Germanic exchanges with the Roman world (Fig. 23.1). The areas participating in these relations encompass a 'Europe' which is rather greater than that often presented in core-periphery studies (cf. Fitzpatrick 1989).

Roman imperialism and economy: current orthodoxies

The later Roman Republican period, broadly the second and first centuries BC, saw a tremendous expansion of Roman influence, both in the Empire and in trades beyond its frontiers. Current interpretations of imperialism and exchange share a number of common beliefs.[1]

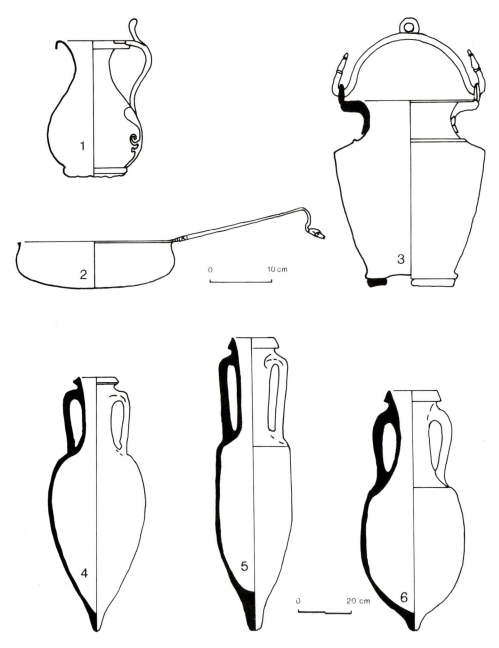

Figure 23.1 A selection of Roman goods admitted into the Germanic and Celtic worlds in the Late (Pre-Roman) Iron Age: 1. Kjaerumgaard type jug, 2. Aylesford type pan, 3. Fällanden type bucket, 4. Graeco-Italic wine amphora, 5. Dressel 1A wine amphora, 6. Lamboglia wine(?) amphora.

Setting aside Badian's (1958) thesis of defensive imperialism, Hopkins' new orthodoxy of Roman historical studies would accept the imperialist character(s) of Roman expansion (Hopkins 1978). Whether it was entrepreneurial or capitalist is more contentious (Dyson 1985) but there is general agreement on the character of the political economy (Garnsey & Saller 1987; Woolf 1992).

There is less consensus on the character of the Roman economy. It has been argued that Rome was an island of capitalism in the ancient world, and that the Roman world comprised an integrated economic system (Carindini 1980; 1986). It is a view which is not widely accepted and the substantivist view of Finley (e.g. 1985), that regional economies were linked by the political economy of the Empire, constitutes the current orthodoxy (e.g. Hopkins 1978; Duncan-Jones 1990).

Despite these orthodoxies, students of the European Iron Age have been keen to view core-periphery relations either explicitly (e.g. Nash 1987) or implicitly (e.g. Cunliffe 1988) in terms of world economies. It is rarely considered why Rome or her provinces should require these 'barbarian' imports of people or raw materials, or why there is an apparent absence of the rapid industrialisation which might require them. How such an integrated ideology, policy and strategy of economic imperialism could have been sustained across the Empire and its periphery is simply not addressed.

Nor do archaeologists explain how there was a much closer integration of the 'economies' of the Roman core and periphery than is evident when the provinces were subsequently established. While the character of the Empire undoubtedly changed, it is doubtful if it did so to such an extent as to fundamentally alter the integration of economies (Woolf 1990).

If the assumptions of archaeologists are out of step with the interpretations of historians in this respect, three other assumptions by archaeologists about the importance of exchange are also noteworthy.

The first assumption is that foreign contact is synonymous with change, and in particular rapid change. This reflects both 'traditional', diffusionist ideas and an interest in the extent of Romanisation before the conquest. Urbanism and exchange are often linked in this analysis, yet, whatever urban characteristics oppida may have had, they appeared first in central Europe, unencumbered by extensive exchanges with the Roman world (cf. Haselgrove 1988).

The second assumption is that Roman goods indicate a trade with Rome. There is no doubt that Roman merchants operated beyond the 'frontiers', but they are often mentioned in situations where they may be associated with military supply (Fitzpatrick 1989, 38). If Roman goods arrived beyond the frontiers as secondary exchanges, there is no immediate reason to assume that they did not travel alongside indigenous objects, such as querns, within internal exchange networks. The analytical separation of internal and external exchange

may be misleading. Stated simply, the arrival of Roman goods need not indicate Roman influence.

The third assumption is that there must be a 'balance of trade' This is commonly formulated as 'what can be set against these "Roman" imports?' (Fitzpatrick 1989, 40–2).

The extent to which these assumptions have dominated research can be seen in the context of relations between both Celts and Romans and Germans and Romans.

Celts and Romans

Whilst some aspects of trade were undoubtedly significant, these reservations have forced a reassessment of some interpretations of the ancient economy (e.g. Greene 1986). For our purposes the most notable example is the well rehearsed trade in Italian wine with the Celts (Tchernia 1983; 1986; Fitzpatrick 1987a; Hesnard 1990). This wine seems to begin to arrive in central and north-western Europe in the late third or early second century BC (Will 1987; Bats 1986, 399, 403; Fitzpatrick 1989, 33–4). The exchanges within France and the north expanded throughout the second century BC (Fig. 23.2), and were intensified in turns by the annexation of the *Provincia* in the 120s and by the conquest of Gaul in the 50s BC (Fitzpatrick 1985, 316–19; 1989, 33; Stevens 1980).

Accompanying this trade from the first century BC was a trade in bronze vessels, most notably of jugs and pans but in other vessels also (Werner 1954; 1978; Feugère & Rolley 1991). Campanian pottery fine wares are also found but their distribution is not as widespread (Fitzpatrick 1985, 333, n. 2; 1989, 36; Morel 1985; 1991, Roymans 1990, 150), while other imports, such as coins, are even rarer. The wine and the bronze vessels appear to have been used by the peoples of modern north-west Europe in traditional spheres of prestation and prestige such as feasting.

The commodity argued most frequently to have been 'exported' by the barbarian peoples is slaves, and this trade has been seen as a cause of increased hierarchisation within Celtic society (e.g. Nash 1978). There are a number of literary references to exchanges of Celtic slaves which have encouraged this view (Tchernia 1983, 97–9), but a sustained analysis does not support it. The references are often anecdotal and set in the encyclopedic context of geographies. Prosographical studies endorse the view that the majority of Roman slaves came from the east, and that warfare and trading were the principal sources of them (Harris 1980). While the scale of the exchange of slaves may have been significant within Celtic societies, it is difficult to accept that it was significant in the context of the classical world.

The argument for a trade in slaves neatly encapsulates the three assumptions identified earlier: (i) that trade causes change, (ii) that contact was directly with

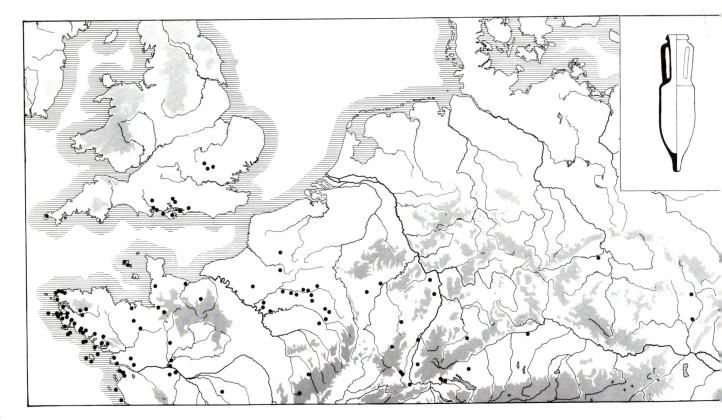

Figure 23.2. A distribution map of Dressel 1A wine amphorae in northern Europe (after Fitzpatrick 1985, figs. 4–5 with additions). Outwith Armorica and, to some extent, to the north of the Seine, the distribution of finds from France is very probably grossly underepresented. This is particularly so for the Orélanais, Bourgogne and Nivernais (see Fitzpatrick 1987a)

Roman rather than with other Celtic peoples, and (iii) that this effectively demanded the balancing of visible imports with 'invisible exports'.

The expansion of the Roman empire and trade beyond its frontiers seem likely to have been closely linked. In western Europe, the supply of the Roman armies in Spain during the Punic wars provided the opportunity for the wider distribution of Roman goods in a secondary trade to, and through, France. The movement of peoples, animals and foodstuffs was primary, and what archaeologists characterise as a trade in objects was secondary to it (Fitzpatrick 1985, 315–16; 1989, 41; Bats 1988, 405–11).

If this argument is accepted then a range of other forms of contact merits greater consideration. Of these, diplomacy and military alliances may be thought to be particularly important, although the absence of the award of citizenship may be noted. The potential impact of other less tangible exports such as conditional literacy has also been underestimated (Fitzpatrick 1989, 34–8).

The unrivalled opportunities for personal aggrandizement presented to the Italian elite by overseas expansion in the late Republic may account for the widespread distributions of exported goods. When areas closer to the frontiers (i.e. the provinces) became able to supply the armies with staples, the opportunities presented to producers in western Italy by the servicing of an administered trade altered dramatically. This does not mean that the Italian elite ceased to enjoy the benefits of an administered trade, only that Italian produce did (cf. Hopkins 1978, 37–47; Miró 1989, 248–52).

In assessing these assumptions, it must be questioned if in either scale or *kind*, ancient world systems were similar to modern ones, or that inter-regional trade could create the dependency suggested by core-periphery models. Instead it has been argued that the exchanges should be seen in the context of imperialism and the political economy, not in that of an integrated inter-regional economy or world economy (Fitzpatrick 1989; Woolf 1990; 1992).

Although the exchange in Roman goods is perceived of as largely, if not exclusively, between the Roman and Celtic worlds, at least some Roman goods arrived in the Germanic world during the later Republic.

Germans and Romans

Many works treat German trade with the Roman world as effectively dating from the Christian era (e.g. Cunliffe 1988, 171–7), and there is no doubt that the Roman Iron Age witnessed significant change and extensive exchange with the Roman world. However, a small range and quantity of Roman goods arrived in what became Free Germany during the pre-Roman Iron Age (Hachmann 1960; Kunow 1983, 66).

The imports are almost exclusively restricted to a

series of copper alloy vessels of which the best known are the Aylesford pans and the range of jugs once subsumed under the generic name of Kelheim (Fig. 23.3; Boube 1991; Feugère & de Marinis 1991). Although many copper alloy cauldrons with iron rims have been considered to be Roman or even Celtic imports, there is no obvious reason why they should not be considered to be local products (below). It is also uncertain whether some vessels belong to the pre-Roman Iron Age or shortly after (e.g. Eggers' type 18), while some may well be much later (e.g. Eggers' type 67; Kunow 1983, 20). The recorded distribution of buckets of Eggers' type 19 (Bolla *et al.* 1991, 18, fig. 9) might also suggest that it was made in northern Germany and was broadly contemporary with the fine Germanic copies of Roman silver cups (Künzl 1988, 40–9).[2] Although some new types of Roman imports have been identified, such as the Fällanden and Zubowice type buckets (Fitzpatrick 1987b; Wielowiejski 1985, 157, Abb. 2), the trend of recent research has been to reduce the range and number of imports. It is uncertain therefore whether Roman goods arrived in modern Norway and Sweden in the last centuries BC (*pace* Lund-Hansen 1987, 126).

Although bronze vessels such as Aylesford pans, Kelheim jugs and Fällanden buckets are often asserted to be associated with wine drinking, this is unsubstantiated. In the Roman world they were used for washing and bathing (Kunow 1983, 95–7) and were made either

in Roman Italy or in Roman colonies beyond it (Fitzpatrick 1987b, 107–8; Castoldi 1991). There is little to support the idea of the existence or export of services, although, *pace* Kunow (1983, 95–7), Aylesford pans and Kelheim jugs are associated frequently enough to suggest that they were originally a set used for the washing of hands at table (Fitzpatrick 1987b, 108; Bolla 1991, 148).

To an extent the narrow range of Roman imports results from the structure of formal deposition. All the vessels suggested to be imports dating to Eggers' Phase A are from burials, and with a single exception were the only imports in the graves (Kunow 1983, 35). However, to a greater extent the restricted range is due to precise selection, decisions which are emphasised by what was excluded; the most conspicuous absence is of wine amphorae. Julius Caesar's comments on the utter exclusion of wine by the Suebi for fear of their becoming 'soft and effiminate' (*B.G.* IV, 2) may seem to be a cliché of the pastoralist myth and the noble barbarian, but in this case it also appears to be true. This absence is underlined by recent finds of wine amphorae from the Celtic areas of central Europe.[3] As yet Campanian fine wares have not been recorded, although this might be due to the value(s) ascribed to fine pottery table wares in relation to amphorae (Fitzpatrick 1989, 36).

Of course it is unlikely that Roman goods were equally available across all of western and central Europe. An important factor in the availability of

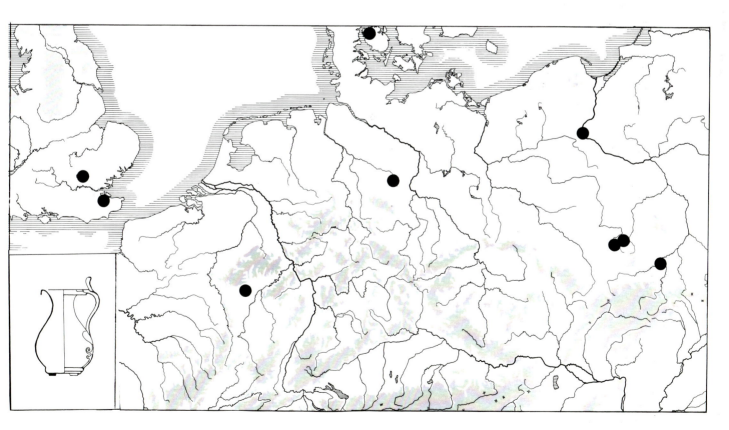

Figure 23.3. Distribution of Kjaerumgaard type jugs in northern Europe (after Boube 1991, fig. 15)

Italian wine north of the Alps may have been the relative lack of opportunities for the Roman elites of eastern Roman Italy in comparison with those in the west, notably Campania, to supply wine, and perhaps olive oil, to the Roman armies. The Roman goods which the German peoples did admit are likely to have arrived by different routes from those used in exchanges in the western Celtic world where the Garonne or the Rhone-Sâone axis would, *prima facie*, appear to have been the major arteries. It seems plausible that the goods in Germany arrived via the Celtic regions of central and eastern Europe, particularly over, or to the east of the Alps.

Trans-Alpine routes have been plausibly suggested for some Campanian fine wares in Switzerland, and at the oppidum of Manching in Bavaria (Fitzpatrick 1989, 36; Stöckli 1979, 195). The typological variation in some types of copper alloy vessels, for example Kelheim jugs, has usually been taken to be primarily chronological (e.g. Ulbert 1985, 81-7) but it also could be geographical, due to their manufacture in different regions (Wielowiejski 1985; Boube 1991).

However, hesitancy in interpreting the modest data in parts of central Europe which were at some stage Celtic, which has led to the authenticity of finds being doubted (cf. note 3), is also reflected in interpretations of Roman goods in Germanic areas in the pre-Roman Iron Age. Many scholars hesitate to accept the small number of finds as indicating a trade with Rome rather than with Celtic 'middlemen' or occasional trading

expeditions by Roman merchants (Eggers 1951, 20; Kunow 1983, 36, 50-1, Anm. 396).

Underlying these hesitations over the importance of these early imports are similar attitudes to Roman imperialism and exchange to those which have structured interpretations of relations between Celts and Romans. This has been emphasised by a tacit assumption that the frontiers of the Roman empire were static, often physical barriers beyond which trade was 'natural', reflecting the view that after the death of Augustus frontiers stabilised and 'foreign policy' became more cautious, switching from military to political intervention. This fails to recognise both the fluidity of frontiers under the principate and the *volte face* from the ideology of the later Republic which this policy would represent (Wells 1972, 1-13). At that time not only was an ambition to conquer the world believed to be just, it was considered to be achievable, and divinely sanctioned (Harris 1979).

In assessing the character and importance of trade beyond the frontiers it is what is thought to be the unusual character of these early imports, the exception rather than the rule, which requires explanation. Therefore, in contrast to interpretations of Celtic contact with Rome, it is the indigenous context of alliances and the context of votive deposition that have been emphasised when considering contact with Rome (Hedeager 1988, 130; 1992, 80, 156-7, 242-4).

In the 'balance of trade' proposed by Hedeager for this, and later phases of the Roman Iron Age (e.g.

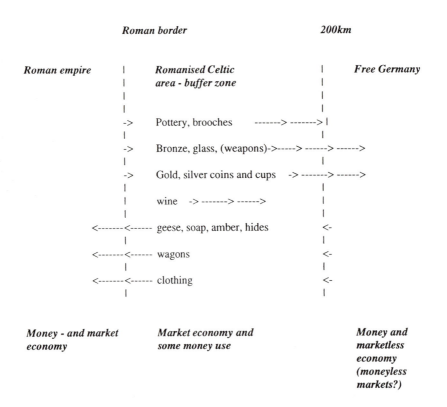

Figure 23.4. A 'balance of trade' between the Roman and German worlds in the Roman Iron Age (after Hedeager 1987). Note the 'balancing' of visible imports with 'invisible exports'.

1987, fig. 11.1, Fig. 23.4 here), amber and other commodities are to Germany (and to central Europe) what Celtic slaves are to western Europe. Slaves are sometimes also suggested, but the evidence for a German slave trade in the later Republic is no better than that for Gaul. Assertions that Germany was important source of slaves at this time (e.g. Nash 1987, 101 and *passim*, fig. 9.1) are unsubstantiated. Amber has been widely considered to have been an important commodity in exchanges (e.g. Redlich 1980, 330–1; Jensen 1982, 242–4). It does seem to occur more widely on settlements during the first century BC, and in some cases, such the oppidum of Staré Hradisko, it is found in large quantities (Beck *et al.* 1978).

However, the distribution of amber suggests a network as much as any single route and it is difficult to envisage the requirement of Roman world for either amber on such a scale or for the other raw materials exported (Wild 1976–77, 61), let alone how this might contribute to the development of a world economy. Instead a series of exchanges between, for example, the Roman colonies of northern Italy and the Celts of central Europe, seems more plausible than a direct trade between Italy and Germany.

Roman merchants operating at Aquileia and in Noricum, where the Madgdalensberg appears to have been particularly important, are likely to have figured prominently. In the same way that the conquest of Spain and the founding of colonies in France may have been catalysts for the arrival of greater quantities of Roman goods in north-western Europe, so the founding of colonies in northern Italy and subsequent increasing contact with Noricum through the first century BC may have had an equally important effect. The greater access to central Europe which this provided may have enabled the ready distribution of Roman goods there.

Direct and sustained political contact between Germans and Romans (other than Ariovistus) seems to date to the German campaigns of Augustus. It is demonstrated most notably by the Hoby burial which contained a service of silver plate likely to have been once owned by C. Siluis, the legate of Upper Germany and which was probably a diplomatic gift (Künzl 1988, 38). Direct, and differing attitudes, to Rome are perceived as emerging at this time (e.g. Hedeager & Kristiansen 1981, 160).

Celts and Germans

Although the core-periphery model and the assumption that the arrival of Roman goods indicates exchange with 'Rome' have dominated recent western European work, consideration of a range of other contacts continues to characterise work in central and eastern Europe. This is important, for what is at issue is not a codicil to the distribution of Roman goods but the recognition of other facets of the external relations of the Germans and Celts, not only with the Romans, but

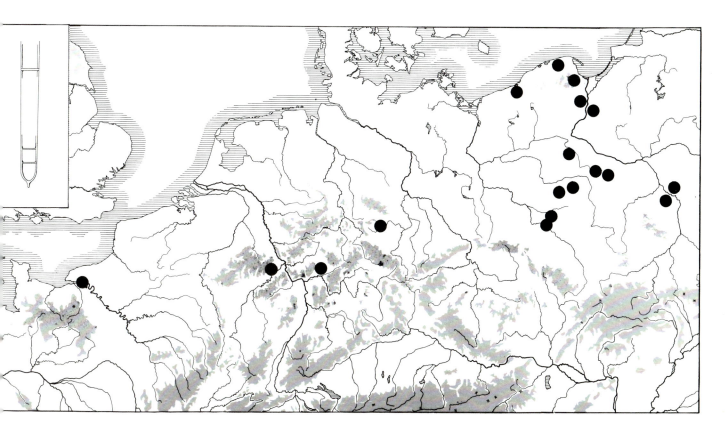

Figure 23.5. Distribution of Late (Pre-Roman) Iron Age 'Celtic' swords with 'spur-shaped' chapes (after Frey 1986, Abb. 6)

with each other. This is a much more important issue than such old questions as whether the Rhine was a boundary between them (e.g. Kossina 1907).

Amongst central and eastern European scholars there is a debate as to why certain elements of material culture are widely distributed. These materials have been taken to represent the 'Celticisation' of several archaeological 'cultures': Jastorf, Przeworsk, Oksywie and Zarubintsky, which Schukin would call the 'North European La Tène' (Schukin 1989, 18–77). Similar interpretations have also been offered for eastern Europe (e.g. Sulimirski 1976).

The archaeological evidence for this 'Celticisation' is essentially for the widespread distribution of brooches of mid-La Tène type, but belt hooks and looped belts are also found. There are also quantitative if not qualitative changes in burial practices and in some areas, notably Lower Silesia, the assemblage bears comparison with those from regions traditionally accepted as 'Celtic'.

The interpretation of these Celtic elements in eastern Europe has often been couched in terms of ethnicity and migrations, but while similarities have been stressed there are also absences, perhaps the most notable of which are Celtic coinage and Celtic 'art'. These interpretations are essentially culture historical, making an equation between distinctive types of material culture and particular peoples (Veit 1989). The assumption is weak, particularly as indexes of what a Celtic material culture is are not systematically propounded. Instead the evidence is in many ways comparable with

Hachmann, Kossack and Kuhn's *Völker zwischen Germanen und Kelten* in north-western Europe (1962). There are elements which may be characterised as 'Celtic' but there are also other elements sufficiently different as to make any correlation with a perceived homeland difficult. But in constituting the argument as 'either/or', the importance of small quantities of material in signifying links between very different peoples should not be overlooked.

In contrast to this migratory, seemingly collective, 'Celticisation' in north-eastern Europe, what might be characterised as alliances or other contacts between Celtic and German peers has been argued for northern Germany and parts of Denmark.

Some late La Tène weapon types are found across much of the Celtic and Germanic worlds (e.g. swords with 'spur-shaped' scabbard chapes; Schaff 1984, 623, Abb. 15; Frey 1986, Abb. 15, or swords with composite disc handles, Frey 1986, 54, Abb. 6). Although it is likely that some types were manufactured in a variety of places, others are considered to have been imported into Germany where, in comparison to the other weapons available, their users would have been heavily armed. On the simple basis of the discovery of swords in well-furnished burials and of more sophisticated association analyses it is suggested that the swords were used by people of a distinct social status (Frey 1986, 54–6; Hedeager 1992, 93–162).

Other suggested Celtic imports are less convincing. Copper alloy cauldrons and situale of Eggers' types 4–

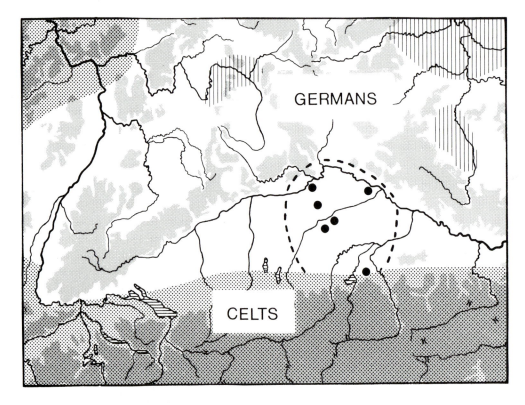

Figure 23.6. Late (Pre-roman) Iron Age groups in modern southern Germany c. *30 BC. Key: Stippled: population of the 'Celtic civilization'; Hatched: population of the 'German tradition'; Cricles within broken line: the apparent region of Celtic population of central German origin (after Christlein 1982, Abb. 5)*

8 and 15–16 have been thought to be both Roman or Celtic traded goods, or even booty from the Celtic world (Eggers 1951, 159; Kunow 1983, 17; Redlich 1980, 336, 358). A Celtic origin is possible, but the case has never been demonstrated convincingly, and many of the simple vessels could be local products. The silver Gundestrup cauldron has a specific eastern context (Taylor 1992), while the Brå cauldron is one of the few vessels for which a strong case can be made for Celtic manufacture (Klindt-Jensen 1953; Krämer 1979, 378–82).

The suggestion that a series of often elaborately decorated four-wheeled carts found in Denmark, Schleswig and Pommern are Celtic (Raddatz 1967) is less convincing. The vehicles are not paralleled amongst contemporary two-wheeled chariots found in burials in Celtic areas (Joachim 1969; van Endert 1987; vii–viii, xvii; Roymans 1990, 247–51), and the case for local manufacture is strong (Frey 1986, 60; Abb. 101; Hedeager 1992, 43, 82, n. 2). The same may be said for the supposedly 'Celtic' torques (Todd 1987).

These 'Celtic' goods, particularly the weapons, have been seen as being made by specialist smiths and/or workshops in southern Germany (Frey 1986, 65), and their acquisition interpreted in the evocative concept of *Gefolgschaft*. While the extent to which these goods really are Celtic is debatable, similarities between weapons emphasise contacts between Celts and Germans which the concept of *Latènesierung* (Frey 1986, 65) does nothing to explain. The circumstances of historically attested migrations such as that of the Cimbrii, Teutones and their associates (Champion 1980, 37–9), and of warlords such as Ariovistus in the service of Celts makes the case for military service, as well as raiding, plausible (cf. Redlich 1980, 358).

Alongside these contacts, which have been perceived largely as being between Celts and Germans, there was also contact initiated by the Germans. The migration of the Cimbrii has been mentioned, and the declared German origin of some of the tribes of Belgic Gaul may be relevant (*B.G.* II, 4). At a later date in central Europe 'Germanic' pottery and belt hooks in Moravia are interpreted as signs of increasing Germanic influence, usually implicitly seen as a prelude to migration (e.g. Čižmár 1990, 313). Ultimately 'Germanic' settlement does takes place in the later first century BC. These settlements are demonstrated perhaps most strikingly by the distribution of material ascribed to the '*Elbgermanen*', but there is also contemporary, if more subtle, evidence in Thuringia (Peschel 1978; 1988; Fischer 1988, 242–50) and other areas, such as Bavaria, with the appearance of the 'mixed' cemeteries of the Uttenhofen-Kronwinkl-Hörgertshausen horizon, which contain German pottery and other objects (Christlien 1982; Rieckhoff-Pauli 1983). The intermingling of German and Celtic objects is interpreted as the 'Germanisation' of some of the material culture of Celtic peoples. 'Celtic' material

culture gradually disappears and sites such as oppida were given up.

Everyday exchanges

What is perhaps most striking about these arguments over 'Celticisation', *Latènesierung* and Germanic settlement, is the extent to which they have been ignored in recent western literature. In part this reflects the late appearance of the German peoples in the twilight world which survives from the classical writers, allowing them little opportunity to influence a modern scholarly tradition concerned with 'Celticity' and classicism. It also reflects a recent emphasis on trade, for while military contact and service with Rome are recognised to have caused major changes in the Roman Iron Age (e.g. Hedeager 1992), earlier Germanic contacts with the Celts through migration or mercenary service are not considered as potentially having the same importance.

We have argued that our understandings of the nature of Roman imperialism in the later Republic must be located in the context of Roman society. Assumptions as to the universal applicability of ideas of imperialism, commerce and capitalism are just that: assumptions. That they have been so influential is in part because they draw on presumptions of 'Celticity' and classicism, and a certain view of Europe (cf. Rowlands 1990). Yet this has resulted in the neglect of the contacts between Germans and Rome, and in the clear manners in which these barbarian peoples precisely and positively used material culture being overlooked. In prohibiting Italian wine the Germans excluded the most widely distributed and accessible Roman commodity of the time. In using material culture these peoples helped to give structure and value to their worlds and in doing so they constantly renewed and reworked their knowledges. Material culture contributed to the constant redefinition of ethnicity. But in making themselves, for example, German they also defined the other, in this case, Celtic or Roman. It is these actions which are seen so clearly in the archaeological evidence for Germanic migrations.

The structural-Marxism deployed in many studies of core-periphery casts the barbarian peoples of the late (pre-Roman) Iron Age as unwitting actors in seemingly inevitable and inextricable processes of commerce and imperialism. Many interpretations are dominated by the assumed 'natural' and inevitable characters of trade and imperialism. This is so persuasive that interpretations of Germanic contacts with Rome either focus on the later Roman imports and ignore the precise choices in the pre-Roman Iron Age, or alter the emphasis of interpretation from a prestige goods economy to the maintenance of power through long-distance alliances.

The situation is both more complex and more subtle. Trade and exchange were defined in many ways and between many parties. Other external relationships of a seemingly smaller scale, and in which Rome had little or no part, were of equal importance but external exchange is as much about internal exchange. Trade is only one form of external contact, and not necessarily the most influential one.

Notes

1. Aspects of this section are elaborated on in Fitzpatrick 1989.
2. Hedeager's suggestion that imported Roman goods were not imitated (1992, 121, 156) is not supported by the evidence of the silver cups.
3. Although it has been assumed that the amphorae from central Europe are Dressel 1 from western Italy (Svobodová 1985, 664–5), on the evidence available they could equally be the contemporary Lamboglia 2 from eastern Italy (Fitzpatrick 1985, 307; Cipriano & Carre 1989, 80–5). The rarity of these finds in Bohemia and Moravia is such that their authenticity has been doubted (Meduna 1982), and this might be thought to question the degree to which their absence from Germany was by choice. However, more recent finds from Moravia are undoubtedly genuine (Čižmár 1989, 266; 1990, 313).

References

Badian, E., 1968. *Roman Imperialism*. Oxford: Oxford University Press

Bats, M., 1986. Le vin italien en Gaule aux IIème – Ier S. av. J.-C.: problèmes de chronologie et de distribution. *Dialogues Histoire Ancienne* 12, 391–430

Beck, C.W., Greenlie, J., Diamond, M.P., Macchiarulo, A.M., Hannenberg, A.A., & Hauck, M.S., 1978. The chemical identification of Baltic Amber at the Celtic oppidum of Staré Hradisko in Moravia. *Journal of Archaeological Science* 5, 343–54

Bolla, M., 1991. Considerazioni sulla funzione dei vasi in bronzo tardorepubblicani in Italia settentrionale, in *La Vaisselle Tardo-Républicaine en Bronze. Actes de la Table-Ronde C.N.R.S., Lattes, Avril 1990*, eds M. Feugère & C. Rolley. Dijon: Université de Bourgogne, Publications du Centre de Recherches sur les Techniques Gréco-Romaines 13, 143–53

Bolla, M., Boube, C., & Guillaumet, J.-P., 1991. Les situles, in *La Vaisselle Tardo-Républicaine en Bronze. Actes de la Table-Ronde C.N.R.S., Lattes, Avril 1990*, eds M. Feugère & C. Rolley. Dijon: Université de Bourgogne, Publications du Centre de Recherches sur les Techniques Gréco-Romaines 13, 7–22

Boube, C., 1991. Les cruches, in *La Vaisselle Tardo-Républicaine en Bronze. Actes de la Table-Ronde C.N.R.S., Lattes, Avril 1990*, eds M. Feugère & C. Rolley. Dijon: Université de Bourgogne, Publications du Centre de Recherches sur les Techniques Gréco-Romaines 13, 23–45

Carandini, A., 1980. Roma imperialistica: un caso di sviluppo precapitalisticio, in *The Seaborne Commerce of Ancient Rome*, eds J.H. D'Arms & E.C. Kopff. Rome: Memoirs of the American Academy at Rome 36, 11–20

Carandini, A., 1986. Il mondo della tarda antichità vista attraverso le merci, in *Società Romana e Impero Tardoantico III. Le Merci, gli Insediamenti*, ed. A. Giardina. Rome: Editori Laterza, 3–19

Castoldi, M., 1991. Origini e officine del vasellame in bronzo tardorepubblicano, in *La Vaisselle Tardo-Républicaine en Bronze. Actes de la Table-Ronde C.N.R.S., Lattes Avril, 1990*, eds M. Feugère & C. Rolley. Dijon: Université de Bourgogne, Publications du Centre de Recherches sur les Techniques Gréco-Romaines 13, 139–42

Champion, T.C. 1980. Mass migration in later prehistoric Europe, in *Transport, Technology and Social Change*, ed. P. Sorbem. Stockholm: Teknista Museet, 31–42

Christlein, R., 1982. Zu den jüngsten keltischen Funden Südbayerns. *Bayersiche Vorgeschichtsblätter* 47, 275–92

Cipriano, M.T., & Carre, M.-B., 1989. Production et typologie des amphores sur la côte adriatique de l'Italie, in *Amphores Romaines et Histoire Economique: Dix Ans de Recherches*, eds M. Lenoir, D. Manacorda & C. Panella. Rome: Collection de l'École Française de Rome 114, 67–104

Čižmár, M., 1989. Erforschung des keltischen Oppidums Staré Hradisko in den Jahren 1983–1988 (Mähren, SSR), *Archäologisches Korrespondenzblatt* 19, 265–8

Čižmár, M., 1990. Die Erforschung der spätlatènezeitlichen Siedlung in Bo itov, Bez. Blansko (Mähren, SSR), *Archäologisches Korrespondenzblatt* 20 (3), 311–15

Cunliffe, B.W., 1988. *Greeks, Romans and Barbarians: Spheres of Interaction*. London: Batsford

De Navarro, J.M., 1936. A survey of research on an early phase of Celtic culture. *Proceedings of the British Academy* 22, 297–341

Duncan-Jones, R.P., 1990. *Structure and Scale in the Roman Economy*. Cambridge: Cambridge University Press

Dyson, S.L., 1985. *The Creation of the Roman Frontier*. Princeton: Princeton University Press

Eggers, H.-J., 1951. *Der römische Import im freien Germanien*. Hamburg: Atlas der Urgeschichte 1

Feugère, M. & de Marinis, R., 1991. Les poêlons, in *La Vaisselle Tardo-Républicaine en Bronze. Actes de la Table-Ronde C.N.R.S., Lattes, Avril 1990*, eds M. Feugère & C. Rolley. Dijon: Université de Bourgogne, Publications du Centre de Recherches sur les Techniques Gréco-Romaines 13, 97–112

Feugère, M., & Rolley, C., (eds) 1991. *La Vaisselle Tardo-Républicaine en Bronze. Actes de la Table-Ronde C.N.R.S., Lattes, Avril 1990*. Dijon: Université de Bourgogne, Publications du Centre de Recherches sur les Techniques Gréco-Romaines 13

Finley, M.I., 1985. *The Ancient Economy* (2nd edition). London: Hogarth Press

Fischer, F., 1988. Südwestdeutschland im letzen Jahrhundert vor Christi Geburt: Anmerkungen zum Forschungsstand der Spätlatènezeit, in *Archaologie in Württemberg. Ergebnisse und Perspektiven archäologischer Forschung von der Altsteinzeit bis zur Neuzeit*, ed. D. Planck, Gesellschaft für Vor- und Frühgeschichte im Württemberg und Hohenzollern. Stuttgart: Konrad Theiss Verlag, 235–50

Fitzpatrick, A.P., 1985. The distribution of Dressel 1 amphorae in north-west Europe. *Oxford Journal of Archaeology* 4 (3), 305–40

Fitzpatrick, A.P., 1987a. The structure of a distribution map: problems of sample bias and quantitative studies. *Acta Rei Cretariae Romanae Favtorvm* 25/26, 79–112

Fitzpatrick, A.P., 1987b. Die Eimer vom Typus Fällanden: Ein italischer Bronzegefässtyp des 1. Jh. v. Chr. *Jahrbuch der Schweizerischen Gesellschaft für Ur- und Frühgeschichte* 70, 101–12

Fitzpatrick, A.P., 1989. The uses of Roman imperialism by the Celtic barbarians in the later Republic, in *Barbarians and Romans in North-West Europe from the later Republic to late Antiquity*, eds J.C. Barrett, A.P. Fitzpatrick, & L. MacInnes, Oxford: British Archaeological Reports International Series S471, 27–54

Frey, O.-H., 1984. Die Bedeutung der Gallia Cisalpina für die Entstehung der Oppida-Kultur, in *Studien zu Siedlungsfrägen der Latènezeit*, ed. S. Schieck. Marburg: Veröffentlichung der Vorgeschichtliches Seminars Marburg Sonderband 3, 1–38

Frey, O.-H., 1986. Einige Überlegungen zu den Beziehungen zwischen Kelten und Germanen in der Spätlatènezeit, in *Gendenkschrift fur Gero von Merhart*. eds O.-H. Frey, H. Roth, & C. Dobiat. Marburg: Marburger Studien zur Vor- und Frühgeschichte 7, 45–79

Garnsey, P.D.A., & Saller, R.P., 1987. *The Roman Empire: Economy, Society and Culture*. London: Duckworth

Greene, K.T., 1986. *The Archaeology of the Roman Economy*. London: Duckworth

Hachmann, R., 1960. Die Chronologie der jüngeren vorrömischen Eisenziet. *Berichte Römische-Germanischen Kommission*, 41, 1– 276

Hachmann, R., Kossack, G., & Kuhn, K., 1962. *Völker zwischen Germanen und Kelten*. Neumünster: Karl Wachholz

Harris, W.V., 1979. *War and Imperialism in Republican Rome 327–70 B.C.* Oxford: Oxford University Press

Harris, W.V., 1980. Towards a study of the Roman slave trade, in *The Seaborne Commerce of Ancient Rome*, eds J.H. D'Arms & E.C. Kopff. Rome: Memoirs of the American Academy at Rome 36, 117–40

Haselgrove, C. C., 1988. Coinage and complexity: archaeological analysis of socio-political change in Britain and non-Mediterranean Gaul during the later Iron Age, in *Tribe and Polity in Late Prehistoric Europe: Demography, Production and Exchange in the Evolution of Complex Social Systems*, eds D.B. Gibson & M.N. Geselowitz. New York & London: Plenum Press, 69–96

Hedeager, L., 1987. Empire, frontier and the barbarian hinterland: Rome and northern Europe from AD 1–400, in *Centre and Periphery in the Ancient World*, eds M. Rowlands, M. Larsen & K. Kristiansen. Cambridge: Cambridge University Press, 125–40

Hedeager, L., 1988. The evolution of Germanic society 1–400 A.D., in *First Millennium Papers*, eds R.F.J. Jones, J.H.F. Bloemers, S.L. Dyson, & M. Biddle. Oxford: British Archaeological Reports International Series S401, 129–44

Hedeager, L., 1992. *Iron-Age Societies: From Tribe to State in Northern Europe, 500 BC to AD 700*. Oxford: Blackwell

Hedeager L., & Kristiansen. K., 1981. Bendstrup – en fyrstegrav fra den roemerske jernalder, dens sociale og historiske miljø, *Kuml* 1981, 81–164

Hesnard, A., 1990. Les amphores, in *Gaule Interne et Gaule Méditerranéenne aux IIème et Ier Siècles avant J.-.C.: Confrontations Chronologiques*, eds A. Duval, J.-P. Morel, & Y. Roman. Paris: Revue Archéologique de Narbonnaise Supplément 21, 47–54

Hodges, R., & Whitehouse, D., 1983. *Mohammed, Charlemagne and the Origins of Europe: Archaeology and the Pirenne Thesis*. London: Duckworth

Hopkins, K., 1978. *Conquerers and Slaves*. Cambridge: Cambridge University Press

Jensen, J., 1982. *The Prehistory of Denmark*. London: Methuen

Joachim, H.-E., 1969. Unbekannte Wagengraber der Mittel- bis Spätlatènezeit aus dem Rheinland, in *Marburger Beiträge zur Archäologie der Kelten: Festschrift W. Dehn*. Bonn: Fundberichte aus Hessen Beiheft 1, 84–111

Klindt-Jensen, O., 1953. *Bronzekedelen fra Brå*. Aarhus: Iysk Arkæologisk Selskabs Skrifter 3

Kossina, G., 1907. Der Grenze der Kelten und Germanen in der La Tène-Zeit. *Korrespondenzblatt Deutschen Gesellschaft für Anthroplogie, Ethnologie und Urgeschichte* 38, 57–62

Krämer, W., 1979. Zwei Achsnägel aus Manching. Zeugnisse keltischer Kunst der mittellatènezeit. *Jahrbuch des Deutschen Archäologischen Instituts* 94, 366–89

Kunow, J., 1983. *Der römische Import in der Germania libera bis zu den Markomannenkriegen*. Neumünster: Gottingen Schriften zur Vor-und Frühgeschichte 21

Künzl, E., 1988. Germanische Fürstengraber und römisches Silber. *Jahrbuch Lauenburgische Akademie für Wissenschaft und Kultur* 1988, 31–53

Lund-Hansen, U., 1987. *Römischer Import im Nordern: Warenaustausch zwischen dem Römischen Reich und dem freien Germanien*. Copenhagen: Nordiske Fortidsminder Serie B, 10

Meduna, J., 1982. Review of *Die Groß- und Importkeramik von Manching* by W.E. Stöckli. *Prähistorisches Zeitschrift* 57, 150–6

Miró, J., 1989. *La Producción de Ánforas Romana en Catalunya: un Estudio sobre el Comercio del Vino de la Tarraconense (Siglos I a.C. – I d.C.)*. Oxford: British Archaeological Reports International Series S73

Morel, J.-P., 1985. La céramique campanienne en Gaule interne, in *Les Ages du Fer dans la Vallée de la Sâone. Paléometallurgie du Bronze*, eds L. Bonnamour, A. Duval & J.-P. Guillaumet, Paris: Revue Archéologique du l'Est et Centre-Est, Supplément 6, 181–7

Morel, J.-P., 1990, Aperçu sur la chronologie des céramiques à vernis noir aux IIième et Ier siècles av. J.-C., in *Gaule Interne et Gaule Méditerranéenne aux IIe et Ier Siècles avant J.-.C.: Confrontations Chronologiques*, eds A. Duval, J.-P. Morel & Y. Roman. Paris: Revue Archéologique de Narbonnaise Supplément 21, 55–71

Nash, D.E.M., 1978. Territory and state formation in central Gaul, in *Social Organisation and Settlement*, eds D.R. Green, C.C. Haselgrove & M. Spriggs. Oxford: British Archaeological Reports International Series S47, 455– 75

Nash, D.E.M., 1987. Imperial Expansion Under the Roman Republic, in *Centre and Periphery in the Ancient World*, eds M. Rowlands, M. Larsen & K. Kristiansen. Cambridge: Cambridge University Press, 87–103

Peschel, K., 1978. *Anfänge germanischer Besiedlung im Mittelgebirgsraum: Sueben – Hermunduren – Markomannen*. Berlin: VEB Deutscher Verlag der Wissenschaften

Peschel, K., 1988. Kelten und Germanen während der jüngeren vörromischen Eisenzeit (2.-1. Jh. v.u.Z.). *Frühe Völker in Mitteleuropa*, eds F. Horst & F. Schlettte. Berlin: Akademie-Verlag, 167–200

Raddatz, K., 1969. *Das Wagengrab der jüngeren vorrömischen Eisenzeit von Husby, Kreis Flensburg*. Neumünster: Offa Bucher 20

Randsborg, K., 1991. *The First Millennium AD in Europe and the Mediterranean: An Archaeological Essay*. Cambridge: Cambridge University Press

Redlich, C., 1980. Politische und wirtschaftliche Bedeutung der Bronzegefässe an Unterelbe und Saale zur Zeit der Römerkriege. *Studien zur Sachsenforschung* 2, 329–74

Rieckhoff-Pauli, S., 1983. Spätkeltische und frühgermanische Funde aus Regensburg. *Bayerische Vorgeschichtsblätter* 48, 63–128

Rowlands, M., 1990. Repetition and exteriorisation in narratives of historical origins. *Critique of Anthropology* 8 (2), 43–62

Rowlands, M., Larsen, M., & Kristiansen, K., (eds) 1987. *Centre and Periphery in the Ancient World.* Cambridge: Cambridge University Press

Roymans, N., 1990. *Tribal Societies in Northern Gaul: An Anthropological Perspective.* Amsterdam: Cingvla 12

Schaff, U., 1984. Studien zur keltischen Bewaffnung. *Jahrbuch des Römisch-Germanisches Zentralmuseums Mainz* 31, 622–5

Schukin, M.B., 1989. *Rome and the Barbarians in Central and Eastern Europe: 1st century B.C. - 1st century A.D.* Oxford: British Archaeological Reports International Series S542

Stevens, C.E., 1980. North-west Europe and Roman politics (125–118), in *Studies in Latin Literature and Roman History II*, ed. C. Deroux, Brussels: Collections Latomus 168, 71–97

Stöckli, W.E., 1979. *Die Groß- und Importkeramik von Manching.* Wiesbaden: Die Ausgrabungen in Manching 9

Sulimirski, T., 1976. The Celts in eastern Europe, in *To Illustrate the Monuments*, ed. J.V.S. Megaw, London: Thames & Hudson, 182–90

Svobodová, H., 1985. Antické importy z keltsých oppid v Čechách a na Maravě. *Archeologické Rozhledy* 37, 653–67

Taylor, T.F., 1992. The Gundestrup cauldron. *Scientific American* 266 (3), 66–71

Tchernia, A., 1983. Italian wine in Gaul at the end of the Republic, in *Trade in the Ancient Economy*, eds P.D.A. Garnsey, K. Hopkins & C.R. Whittaker. London: Hogarth Press, 87–104

Tchernia, A., 1986. *Le Vin d'Italie Romaine - Essai d'Histoire Economique d'après les Amphores.* Paris: CNRS

Todd, M. 1987. *The Northern Barbarians 100 B.C. - A.D. 300*, revised edition. Oxford: Blackwell

Ulbert, G., 1985. *Cáceres el Viejo. Ein spätrepublikanisches Legionslager in Spanisch-Extramadura.* Mainz: Madrider Beiträge 11

van Endert, D., 1987. *Die Wagenbestattungen der späten Hallstattzeit und der Latènezeit im Gebiet westlich des Rheins.* Oxford: British Archaeological Reports International Series S355

Veit, U., 1989. Ethnic concepts in German prehistory: a case study on the relationships between cultural identity and archaeological objectivity, in *Archaeological Approaches to Cultural Identity*, ed. S.J. Shennan. London: One World Archaeology 10, 35–56

Wells, C.M., 1972. *The German Policy of Augustus: An Examination of the Archaeological Evidence.* Oxford: Oxford University Press

Werner, J., 1954. Die Bronzekanne von Kelheim. *Bayerische Vorgeschichtblätter* 20, 43–73 (reprinted in Werner 1979)

Werner, J., 1978. Die Bronzekanne von Kelheim. Ruckblick und Ausblick. *Bayerische Vorgeschichtsblätter* 43, 1–18 (reprinted in Werner 1979)

Werner, J., 1979. *Spätes Keltenum zwischen Rom und Germanen* (ed. L. Pauli). Munich: Münchener Beiträge zur Vor- und Frühgeschichte Erganzungen Band 2

Wielowiejski, J., 1985. Die spätkeltischen und romischen Bronzegefässe in Polen. *Berichte der Römische Germanisches Kommission* 66, 126–320

Wild, J.-P., 1976–77. Loanwords and Roman expansion in north-west Europe. *World Archaeology* 8 (1), 57–64

Will, E. L., 1987. The Roman Amphoras from Manching: A Reappraisal. *Bayerische Vorgeschichtsblätter* 52, 21–36

Woolf, G.D., 1990. World-systems analysis and the Roman empire. *Journal of Roman Archaeology*, 3, 44–58

Woolf, G.D., 1992. Imperialism, empire and the integration of the Roman economy. *World Archaeology* 23 (3), 283–93

24

'Who are you Calling Peripheral?':
Dependence and Independence in European Prehistory

Andrew Sherratt

As at many conferences, there just wasn't time at the Bristol meeting to have a full public discussion of some of the issues raised in the papers. As usual, the most useful exchanges took place in the bar. This isn't a transcript of those discussions, more a version of what I would have liked to say if I had been fully sober and alert. The questions came from several quarters, but the first one was asked by a well known peer-politician ...

Comme à beaucoup de colloques, il n'y avait pas de temps, pendant les séances de Bristol, pour discuter pleinement quelques-unes des questions soulevées par les conférenciers. Comme d'habitude, les discussions les plus utiles eurent lieu au bar. Ce qui s'ensuit n'est pas une transcription de ces discussions, mais plutôt une expression de ce que j'aurais voulu dire si j'avais été totalement sobre et alerte. Les questions vinrent de plusieurs côtés, mais la première fut posée par un pair-politicien bien connu ...

I'd rather like to know, and I haven't yet had a satisfactory answer, just what a core-periphery system is, please?

To be useful, I think it really ought to be confined to economic networks that include cities and the division between raw-material producers and manufacturers.

So it's not a very useful concept for prehistorians, then, is it?

Not in the French sense of *la préhistoire*, no, since that ends with the appearance of the first cities; but the English sense applies right up to the arrival of the Romans, so that it's very much relevant to the later parts of prehistory. Actually, I quite like the French usage, since I believe that the first appearance of cities really was relevant to 'prehistoric' Europe; but I wouldn't want to use 'protohistory', because of its evolutionary overtones. I'd quite like 'parahistory', though.

Well I wouldn't, because it has equally objectionable overtones of diffusionism, and if you are limiting 'cores' and 'peripheries' to urban societies and their neighbours then you don't have a respectable concept to put in its place.

I'd like to use the phrase 'nuclear-margin system'.

And what is that, please?

In general terms, it is one of the features which followed the spread of modern humans, and became common in the post-glacial: the emergence of 'hot spots' of cultural and ecological development, like the Near East or Mesoamerica.

Well, of course, if we are talking about the beginnings of farming then I can see that these areas are centres of demographic growth that were probably very important for things like the spread of language groups. So you are really talking about Jack Harlan's crop centres?[1]

Yes, at least initially — though some were more nuclear than others, as Harlan himself pointed out, and the Near East was one of the most 'nuclear' of all.

So a 'margin' is the limit of diffusion of a particular crop complex?

No, not quite; because some of the effects of farming spread beyond the limits of farming itself, like pottery and polished axes. And although these have *sometimes* emerged among sedentary non-cultivators (like Jōmon), nevertheless their global distribution does tend to be on the edge of expanding farming systems — like Ertebølle or Dnepr-Donets — or when farming groups reach a temporary limit, like the 'sub-Neolithic' groups of north-east Europe. These features are what Phil Kohl would call 'transferable technologies', which were logically developed in one context but were quite easily capable of spreading beyond it.[2] The word 'margin' seems a rather useful one to describe the area where this is happening.

Yes, I can see that, though I'm not quite sure where it's taking us: it seems to need rather a lot of new words. What would you call the Neolithic Balkans or central Europe, for instance — they are neither 'nuclear' in terms of the beginnings of farming, nor 'marginal' in the sense you've just defined — so how do they fit in?

Er, yes, that's a problem, though it's certainly a distinction worth making. You could see those two areas as being an extension of the nucleus, in that they both represent a transplantation of the original, village-based, pattern of farming into a new area, with minimal adaptation and probably with a large measure of migration involved in the spread. Then we might want to distinguish western Europe and the North European Plain as something different again, involving a much greater degree of demographic fusion and cultural innovation to produce quite a new pattern, with megaliths rather than villages as the social foci. You might describe it as an outer rim to the nuclear extension. I don't want to proliferate terminologies just for the sake of it, but the picture I'm proposing is quite the opposite of diffusionism: it suggests continuous innovation, even if under the stimulus of an original event which happened elsewhere. It wasn't just a 'package' which was 'spreading', and was 'accepted' or 'rejected' in different areas: it was more like a chain reaction, creating certain zones of similarity because of the logic of their position in the chain.

Yes, I can see that it has a certain descriptive value, but is it anything more than a static description of the pattern of roughly concentric zones that resulted from the spread of farming?

I don't think that it's ever static, because the initial set of farming technologies introduced their own potential for change, which took some time to work through. I'm thinking of the way in which rectangular houses and flat-based pottery gradually caught up with the forms of pioneer simplification which characterised the spread of farming to the outer parts of Europe. This would indicate some growing formalisation of patterns of social life — things like communal eating and the elaboration of cuisine — which were part of the original, village-based, Neolithic way of life but which only reached the outer extensions of farming at a later time. These do, I think, show that the more 'sophisticated' parts of south-east Europe continued to act as a model for their neighbours — much as Italian table-manners

spread northwards during the Renaissance period.[3] To understand the changes which were taking place in Neolithic Europe we have to bear these regional disparities in mind.

So are you trying to say that this is core and periphery in action?

No, that's precisely what I'm trying to avoid saying. There are lots of examples of consistent patterns of spatial extension, broadly from the nuclear area of farming to its outer edges, which are not in any way the result of structural interdependence between economically complementary zones, but which it is useful to recognise — especially since diffusionism became a dirty word, and we almost gave up thinking on this scale. It's worthwhile being so systematic about describing them so that we can clearly differentiate such patterns from what happens later on.

But are they anything more important than the spread of table manners?

I wouldn't consider table manners unimportant, but I think that you can see a spatial logic to all sorts of things that have been seen as fundamental to the Neolithic way of life. Take stone axe manufacture, for instance, or the exploitation of obsidian. It's very characteristic that both of these reach a peak of activity, with intensive extraction and widespread circulation, and then die away again. This is a pattern that is repeated in area after area, from Çatal Hüyük onwards. When Neolithic societies got going, they had a tremendous appetite for certain types of raw materials — mostly concerned with tools for everyday activities like forest clearance or cutting tools — useful things, but ways of showing off at the same time, that were as essential to social reproduction as to physical survival. Then the peak of production and circulation passed. It seems to me that this whole material complex was generated by the conditions which obtained when farming was relatively new, and there were still large contrasts between adjacent areas in their capacity, say, for livestock rearing and their opportunities to employ labour, and that this intensive exchange was an institutionalisation of these conditions — with opportunities to participate where there was differential access to supplies of desirable types of stone.[4] When these conditions no longer obtained, then this whole cycle of exchanges lost its relevance; so that one can see a whole series of such short-lived but very intense episodes of exchange following some time after the arrival of farming — in Bulgaria, Hungary, Poland, Denmark, Britain and France. Together, they constitute a 'wave of exchange' following the 'wave of advance' of farming itself.

But surely it was metallurgy that created new needs, and simply replaced stone tools with new prestige goods?

It's not quite so simple, because although the succession works that way round in Hungary, it is inverted in the North European Plain. Lengyel copper ornaments and axes reached central Poland and Denmark around 4000 BC, in the Danish Early Neolithic, but were then replaced by the massive local circulation of stone axes.[5] Similarly in Poland at the same period, in the Globular Amphora culture: this is the time of the Krzemionki mines, and the massive transfer of their banded flint axes to Kuyavia, 600 years after the copper finds from Brześć Kujawski. The large quantities of flintwork were more appropriate to these sorts of circulation system than small quantities of metals — much as bronze was to be the prime material to circulate in Bronze Age Europe, rather than the rarer medium of silver. The system chooses its own commodities. Later on, northern and western Europe followed central Europe in promoting a few, specialised stone and metal forms, like battle-axes and flint daggers (supported by the Grand Pressigny quarries, for instance), and in this context copper became important again. It is almost as if each zone had to work its way through these stages, and follow through the cycle, and only took up metallurgy when it was ready for it.

Can you quantify these cycles? What sort of scale are we talking about?

Oh, something of the order of a few hundred years, and with stone axes circulating over an area something like 300 km across. Better to see them as echoes of the invention and spread of farming, rather than reflections of the economic fortunes of Mesopotamia!

But there were some connections, I think you said?

Yes, if I'm right, by the time that the stone axe boom was hitting northern and western Europe, the first spin-off from Near Eastern urbanisation was also arriving. Ploughs, wheels, that kind of thing. Alcohol, too — hence the globular amphorae.[6]

So Europe is a periphery at last, is it?

No, in terms of the distinction I'm trying to make, it's actually a margin to the nuclear areas of urbanisation. This is where the term becomes really useful. There *is* a periphery in the later fourth millennium, but it is restricted to the Near East — the territory reached by Uruk colonies in Syria and Anatolia. These were the areas which were persuaded to yield up their raw materials in exchange for manufactured products from Mesopotamia.[7] This was a real core, with substantial manufacturing capacity, drawing in supplies from a hinterland that was soon to reach as far as the Iranian Plateau and Afghanistan in one direction, and western Turkey and the Aegean in the other.

So in what sense was Europe a margin?

In the same sense that the sub-Neolithic cultures were a margin to the nuclear and surrounding areas which were directly affected by the emergence of agriculture: it was a zone whose development was profoundly affected by technologies and social practices which were developed in more central regions. Phil Kohl's transferable technologies.

I can see that it might be a useful concept, if you could convince me that it actually happened: but what can you point to in Europe that was actually transferred, rather than emerging in parallel from a common Old World background?

I must confess that quite a lot of it requires the eye of faith, and the whole reconstruction reads rather like a 'Just So' story, but I think there are enough concrete examples to make the rest of it plausible, at least. John Chapman doesn't like my plough horizon, but we've argued that out in print.[8] The case for wheeled vehicles is very much less ambiguous, and I don't know anyone who has seriously controverted it. Stuart Piggott has set out the evidence in detail,[9] and my only point of disagreement would be to see wheeled vehicles as spreading through Anatolia to south-east Europe, as well as via the steppes — which is, after all, the same 'wave of advance' simply separated by the Black Sea, and being transmitted through rather different kinds of societies on either side of it. Anyway, if you accept the argument for wheeled vehicles, I don't see why it is so implausible for the plough, which is just another application of yoked traction. Of course it may have been taken up with such alacrity because it mechanised other hand cultivation systems which were already preparing something like parallel furrows, but I think that the whole notion of using animals for this kind of activity requires a conceptual change as well as just an intensification in subsistence technology: it's part of a whole new attitude to domestic animals. You can see the contrast on a global scale if you compare the use of irrigation to the use of yoked animal technologies: irrigation has appeared in many disparate areas, quite independently (on any reckoning! I mean in Africa, south Asia and the Americas), since it is a natural extension of cultivating well watered soils and can come about wherever it is ecologically advantageous; whereas traction has a much more coherent distribution, centred on the western Old World, and didn't occur at all in the indigenous technologies of sub-Saharan Africa and the Americas. This suggests to me that it spread out as part of a coherent technical and ideological package, and wasn't constantly re-invented — just like the wheel, in fact.

Is that the hardest piece of evidence?

I would also point to metallurgy — the way that the Near Eastern technology of bivalve-mould casting and alloying replaced the impressive but technologically archaic pure copper metallurgy of the European Copper Age, which was largely based on hammering a simple blank into more complex shapes — hence the swift transition from axe-hammers and axe-adzes into shaft-hole axes with a deep blade.[10] This also spread by the same two routes, Anatolia and the steppes.

So it was essentially a technological and economic transformation?

Only in the sense that we naturally see material culture in those terms, and that the hardest pieces of archaeological evidence are those which relate to 'technology'. I may have been guilty of presenting the evidence in that way,[11] but you could also see it in a less nineteenth-century fashion, which would help to make sense of the nature of the archaeology. For instance the rather convenient concentration of wagon models and paired-animal graves in central Europe in the mid-fourth millennium BC, just at the point when we also have the first unambiguous ploughmarks in Denmark, could be seen as part of the social and ideological impact of the traction complex, as a new way of conceptualising domestic animals, which was perhaps not yet part of everyday life in terms of its routine application to transport and cultivation.

I don't quite see the link with urbanisation, though.

The argument here is essentially one of timing and geography: the routes by which I think these innovations spread to Europe lay precisely in the areas which were energised by the Uruk intervention — Anatolia and the Caucasus, leading to the steppes and south-east Europe. It was the spread of wheeled vehicles to the steppes which triggered off the series of vigorous cultures beginning with Pit Graves, that spread as far as the Urals and beyond. Western Anatolia and the Aegean were transformed from being rather sleepy backwaters to being dynamic centres of growth, largely — I would argue — through being linked up to a growing Mesopotamian core with its massive demands for raw materials. Although I don't see south-east Europe as being directly linked into these networks, it felt the spin-off from all this new activity. I'm sure that metallurgy received a decisive boost in this way.

Why?

Because it was increasingly becoming a medium of exchange, as well as a form of display, and was being accumulated and hoarded in quite a different way from its use during the Copper Age. Hoards as a feature of the archaeological record are one indication of this. This would suggest that a wider range of other materials were now entering the transaction circle, and that what we see are simply the durable parts which sur-vived. Copper Age trade seems to have been very much one like durable being exchanged for another, such as copper for flint, or amber for salt.

So what are these elusive organic commodities?

That is the other part of the argument for transferable technologies, and is much harder to demonstrate in a concrete way. But think about it like this: the urban revolution created a stratified society, with a true elite — people who had quite a different lifestyle from the rest of the population. This differentiation is obvious in terms of craft goods, and we can see it in the Troy treasures with their gold and silver cups and elaborate jewellery. Surely this was also expressed in terms of organic consumables — clothes and diet. As far as diet is concerned, it has long been accepted that wine formed part of it. The domestication of Mediterranean tree crops, from dates to vine, olive, fig and pomegranate, was one of the distinctive features of urbanising societies in the nuclear (now also core) area. These crops all require much more capital and labour than peasant farming, and their cultivation on any scale was closely linked to urbanisation. They didn't just spread around the Mediterranean because they had been domesticated, but only as part of the complex economies of scale which produced wheel-made pottery, for instance. Yet such a fundamental dietary change must have given rise to all sorts of experiments with fermentation techniques, which could well have become transferable technologies in their own right, even in a different culinary and social context. Similarly with clothing styles and the use of textiles.

Does any of this touch the archaeological record?

It certainly helps me to make sense of the series of ceramic changes, beginning in south-east and central Europe with Baden, where jugs and cups with metallic shapes — things like strap handles, omphalos bases, channelling, grey polished surfaces — are prominent features of precisely those 'elite' graves with wagon models and paired cattle burials. I don't imagine that Baden metalsmiths were capable of making silver vessels, but the style seems a clear imitation of elite drinking vessels in the areas with craft workshops which could make them.[12] And I imagine that it wasn't just empty show, and that they had something worth drinking from them. Then there is a whole series of European cultures which take their name from drinking vessels — Globular Amphorae, Corded Ware and Bell Beaker cultures . . . these would be the outer ripples of a dietary change that was essentially of Mediterranean origin, though of course locally interpreted in terms both of their social use and of the recipes used in preparing what was drunk. It wouldn't be the last time that elements of Mediterranean diet spread north, and usually at times of economic expansion in the south.

The same model could also apply to clothing, though here the steppe route was perhaps as important as the Anatolian one, and the archaeological correlate would be the spread of larger breeds of wool-bearing sheep that Sandor Bökönyi has talked about[13], and also certain clothing-related ornaments like knot-headed pins. The point I'm making is that the impact of all these things on temperate Europe was an indirect result of the larger scale of production and movement, and the innovations which came about, in the nuclear area of Bronze Age culture — which means the Near East.

Isn't this just a traditionally Old World way of looking at things? How would the Americas fit into this perspective?

American archaeologists have rather tended to avoid the issue since Lew Binford's strictures on reconstructing culture history;[14] but it is hard to account for what happened to North American cultures after the Archaic without mentioning Mesoamerica. Actually it's a rather interesting comparison with the Old World: because the major New World cultigens were largely of tropical origin, and domestic animals played such a minor role, the subsistence aspect came later than the 'ideological' features — earplugs, mirrors, figurines and 'cult' items in Adena and Hopewell, for instance.[15] This would be a margin created by 'escaped ideologies' as much as 'escaped technologies'. After AD 700 the connections are more explicit, and Puebloan communities supplied turquoise and other preciosities to north-west Mexico via Casas Grandes in Chihuahua, taking up cotton in return.[16] The Pueblo and Mississippian developments would have been unthinkable without inputs from complex societies further south.

This sounds very close to diffusionism!

In a way, yes; but why not? There is nothing automatic about the process I'm postulating. There were many features which didn't escape from the Old World urban core — I've mentioned wheel-made pottery, and you could add some of the other hallmarks of complex economies, which didn't arrive in north-west Europe until La Tène times, like the regular use of silver, or complex goldworking techniques, or ships with sails. All of these things required a different social context, with currencies, craft patronage and the need for bulk transport. Bronze Age urbanism provided its hinterland with an opportunity — a set of models that were selected and re-interpreted in very different social contexts. Rotary motion, for instance, wasn't applied in temperate Europe for pottery-making during the Bronze Age, because there was no context for mass production, but it seems to have been used for fancy items of woodwork like cups and furniture. This is precisely the kind of selective spin-off you might expect, which enriched European material culture without being part of a formal set of trading relationships which resulted in any kind of zonal economic specialisation related to the regular supply of raw materials. But it wouldn't have taken place unless there had been an urban revolution to re-nuclearise the nucleus, so to speak. That's why it was a world-system.

So after all that, Wallerstein is pretty irrelevant. All you've done is to pick out a word from the title of his book[17] and dress up Gordon Childe in a more fashionable terminology.

No, I think that both of them have made major contributions — in very different historical periods — to seeing how developments in different parts of the world were inter-related; but both need very major re-writing. In a way, they both suffer from the same deficiency, which is a suspicion of luxuries as things which people could have done without.[18] But in any case, they need to be brought together as partial descriptions of an evolving process. Isn't that what processualism was supposed to be about?

It certainly isn't about writing off half of European prehistory as something hardly worth studying because everything of importance was happening elsewhere. Not even a periphery, but only a 'margin'! That doesn't seem to me even to begin to explain what actually happened in Bronze Age Europe.

It isn't meant to explain everything, only to situate it in a real context. The point is that European cultures would have been different if they hadn't been exposed to it.

I don't deny the possibility that some cultural contacts may have taken place, but if you are talking about processes then surely this must imply something more fundamental.

Isn't this where the post-processualists have a point: the culture *is* important, and not just the decoration on top of a social process; and this is where the criticisms of Childe and Wallerstein are remarkably similar, and where archaeology may have something new to contribute. This is also where the idea of a margin comes in, and why Childe got the European Bronze Age wrong, even though he was very largely right about the Near East. Childe's description didn't have a margin: he saw Bronze Age Europe as what Wallerstein would call a periphery, opened up by Mycenaean prospectors and colonists — direct intervention. Everything was 'rooted in the Aegean market'.[19] Because he was working within a short chronology, he rather conflated the Bronze Age with the kinds of thing that happened in the Iron Age. That's why his descriptions ring rather false nowadays. Europe was much more independent than he imagined, not only in terms of its lack of direct economic articulation, but also in the way it used some of the new features of Bronze Age material culture. Childe didn't make his 'barbarians' sufficiently different: he saw bronze as meaning the same thing to Únětice chieftains and Syrian merchants. Because he saw bronzeworking simply as a technology, he tried to rationalise the way that European communities used it — for instance by explaining hoards as the stock in trade of wandering smiths, rather than as votive deposits in a system where gifts to the gods and gifts to other human actors were part of the same ideological-economic system. He didn't analyse it in terms of a value system in which bronze meant something different from the same material which circulated as a commodity in the Mediterranean. The margin doesn't value things in the same way. But the presence of bronze, and textiles, and a variety of local products such as fermented drinks, altered the kind of exchange system that was possible, simply because there were more materials and products circulating in it; and because bronze, in particular, had the 'prime value' of being convertible into a variety of different forms, and thus providing liquidity.[20] This allowed new forms of long distance trade to develop, though of a different kind from those in the Mediterranean. So the Bronze Age was different from the Neolithic; but it wasn't yet the Iron Age either.

Very profound. So what about Wallerstein?

In a way, he makes the same mistake.[21] On the face of it, he is saying quite the opposite of Childe, that capitalism and the world-system only began in the 16th century and certainly not in the Bronze Age. But in the way he looks at trade, he shares many of the same attitudes. He is really interested in the complementary specialisation in grain and manufacturing, and sees no role for the long distance trade in luxuries. He also stigmatises them as non-essentials, and therefore argues that before the Early Modern period the boundaries of political and economic units largely coincided. That's why the concept of a 'margin' would have no appeal for him. Archaeology gives quite a different picture: it was this high-value traffic which was often the precursor to the kinds of trade which involved bulk production and manufacturing, which typically arose at points where these routes entered the periphery, precisely so that local elites could retain the flows of precious materials and acquire more of the imported items which defined the nature of their power. Yet it is the independent mobility of these high-value items, without the intervention of urban markets, that is so characteristic of the kinds of development which took place within the margin. The transition to local manufacturing was relatively rare, even though the trade in high value items like amber and bronze crossed half the continent. If we are really interested in a world-system, and one that includes all the relevant elements, we have to describe the margin, too, because the development

of the periphery was intimately connected with the structures that developed beyond it.

*So you are really saying that Bronze Age Europe **was** in fact independent, even though it absorbed all these ultimately Near Eastern elements?*

Yes; culturally transformed, but structurally independent.

And that European trading networks effectively developed quite independently during the Bronze Age?

Yes, in the sense that the long-distance trade routes which we can identify, like those linking the Baltic and central Europe, came into existence *in parallel* to those between central Europe and the Mediterranean.[22] This is where calibrated radiocarbon dates really have changed our perception of what was happening. The Reinecke A2 link-up between the Carpathian Basin and Scandinavia took place in the first quarter of the second millennium, before any links are discernible between central Europe and Greece; and the Tumulus culture axis that developed in Reinecke B between Scandinavia and the north Alpine area — which I think must be seen as in some sense in competition with the earlier axis, and taking over from it — was generated by a similar complementarity. This is the old idea of an 'amber route'; but it was initially a link-up between central and northern Europe, not directly between the Mediterranean and the north (cf. Hopewell!). Central Europe had two advantages: its metal sources, and its steppe links with chariotry and horses. Where the northward routes crossed the Carpathians, in Slovakia, there was the opportunity to control the transfer of these resources and the result was the emergence of precocious 'hillforts' with complex fortifications and remarkable concentrations of wealth in metal and amber, as well as decorated antler horse-gear. This is a specifically European phenomenon, which developed at a major node in long-distance trade routes carrying a few high-value items. At the other end of this route, in Scandinavia, there was a more diffuse focusing of elite wealth which was gained by accumulating resources from a Baltic hinterland.[23] These inter-regional trade routes were powerful determinants of local prosperity and concentrations of power.

But how did these 'marginal' routes ever become relevant to core-periphery development?

Because at certain points the independent, 'marginal' trade routes came into articulation with the trunk routes linking the core and periphery, and created new nodes where power centres could form.

Like?

Troy, for one; Mycenaean Greece, on a small scale; or Etruria — and ultimately Rome — on a larger scale.

How do you mean?

Well, Mycenae in the Shaft Grave period — roughly Reinecke B — obviously did have a European hinterland, if only because amber was ultimately arriving there in small quantities. It seems likely that other high-value materials which at the moment we can't distinguish were also getting there in the same way; say, gold or tin. Some rare organic items, too, perhaps, that could travel long distances and were in great demand — like horses. These things weren't travelling just because Mycenaeans wanted them, as Childe imagined, but because they were already circulating in indigenous European networks. But having reached the Mediterranean, they could be funnelled into the palace-centred exchange systems focused on Crete. This would be why peninsular Greece came into the game at all, and had the opportunity to develop its own centres of power. On the other hand, because the Mycenaean links with central Europe were rather indirect (if only for geographical reasons), Bronze Age Greece never developed a temperate European periphery on any scale. Then came the collapse of the Late Bronze Age palatial economies, and the great expansion of the independent networks of temperate Europe in the Urnfield period, both in central Europe and the Atlantic area. By this time the 'amber route' really did reach all the way down to Italy, bringing back the bronze vessels and spreading the spectacle fibulae that so fascinated Montelius; so that when Phoenician and Greek urban-centred trade routes reached southern Italy in the 8th century, it was the intervening node of Etruria which played the same structural role as Mycenaean Greece had done in the Bronze Age world-system. And having easier access to central Europe around and across the Alps, the Etruscan cites really did begin to create a periphery: the area that we call the Hallstatt phenomenon, feeding metals, hides and salt to Italian manufacturing towns.[24]

And beyond the periphery?

Still the margin, though now largely iron-using and therefore rather different in its internal economy since it was no longer integrated by the circulation of bronze as a medium of prime value. There were rather stark contrasts between areas where the north-south routes were still operating, and those which were now even more isolated from the flows of valued materials. The amber route, now through Poland to the east Baltic rather than to Denmark, may well have carried a variety of valuable northern organic products like furs all the way to the Mediterranean. It was marked by fortified centres like Biskupin or Smolenice, which probably had a rather more similar character to the earlier Slovakian Bronze Age centres than to anything in the Mediterranean; and in fact this northern pattern persisted right down to the early Medieval centres like Gniezno, which formed one of the nuclei of the Polish state on a similar trading node. (It's quite near to Biskupin.) The difficulty in temperate Europe was always how to move from handling high-value, low-bulk goods into manufacturing products for more than local distribution, because of the problems of transport. The river systems were crucial in this. That is why the Rhineland became so important in the economic and political development of transalpine Europe in the Roman period and after.

So European economic development became increasingly independent of the old core region?

No: quite the reverse. As the core region expanded westwards along the Mediterranean, it created a periphery along the Rhône/Seine/Rhine corridors which eventually became part of the core itself, with its own periphery as far north as Scandinavia. The margin was thus increasingly incorporated within the core-periphery system, whose fortunes were linked to that of the whole urbanised oecumene as far as India — though of course there were rivalries for hegemony within it. When the focus of economic activity shifted to central and southern Asia, during the first millennium AD, most of temperate Europe was peripheralised again — even though in demographic terms it was much more densely settled than a thousand years earlier. 'In the Dark Ages, Europe was a colony of Islam: who then could see any future for it except to provide the rich Moslem cities of Baghdad, Cairo, Tunis and Cordoba with a regular supply of iron, skins and slaves?'

Which fashionable theorist wrote that?

Hugh Trevor-Roper![25] He was really trying to annoy the medievalists, but I think he was essentially right.

And that is 'dependency theory'?

Well, in a way. The whole 'world-system' idea was the result of the convergence two different areas of academic discourse, one empirical and one theoretical. The empirical one was the *Annales* school, represented by Fernand Braudel and Maurice Lombard. Braudel defined an 'économie-monde méditerranéenne'.[26]

Braudel convenait lui-même de l'imperfection de cette terme ... Il n'est pas facile en effet de désigner en français: 'un fragment de l'univers, un morceau de la planète économiquement autonome'. Ce 'système de Braudel' ... semble bien s'installer dès qu'il y a des villes. Celles-ci vont chercher de plus en plus loin les biens dont elles ont besoin.[27]

Thanks, Patrice. Yes, this *système-monde* came into being with the beginnings of urbanism, so Braudel himself was only talking about the last six percent of the process. He also didn't like formalising his view as a model, so he largely inspired by example, as did the great American historian, W. H. McNeill.[28] On the other hand there *was* a theoretical movement, led by our friend Andre Gunder Frank and Samir Amin[29], which was concerned with much more recent history and grew up in the late '60s as a critique of 'modernisation theory' in development economics (which was a essentially a sort of organic neo-evolutionism — the equivalent to Sahlins 'n' Service in anthropology). This movement did provide a relevant theoretical account, which pointed out that the reason why the third world didn't 'develop' along the classic lines laid down by Europe was that it had already been incorporated in the world-system, to its own disadvantage: it was trapped in a structure that kept it dependent on the West — hence 'dependency theory', or 'the development of underdevelopment'.

So how did fact and theory come together?

These two sets of insights were put together by Immanuel Wallerstein, who started out as an Africanist but made himself into a powerful and original modern historian. His 'modern world-system' began with the regional division of labour in Europe between the Baltic grain-producing areas and the growing mercantile states of the Atlantic seaboard, rather as the Third World is exploited nowadays for primary products, with the value being added elsewhere. This kind of structure was, in his conception, quite new because it involved 'an economic but not a political entity, unlike empires, city-states and nation-states ... It is a "world" system, not because it encompasses the whole world, but because it is larger than any juridically defined political unit.' It was the beginning of an international division of labour.[30]

And this is the current orthodoxy?

By no means: first of all, Jane Schneider made the point I mentioned above about luxuries — that these had always crossed political boundaries, and that this sort of long-distance trade was not just the icing on the cake, but a flow of convertible high-value commodities which often determined how the system developed.[31] So an appropriately modified world-system model ought to apply to earlier periods, too. She summed it up like this: 'it is possible to hypothesise a *pre-capitalist* world-system, in which core areas accumulated precious metals while exporting manufactures, whereas peripheral areas gave up these metals (and often slaves) against an inflow of finished goods'.[32] She also defined a margin: 'marginality is a concept distinct from periphery. In contrast to peripheral areas, marginal ones are disengaged from processes of struggle and competition, differentiation and specialisation in relation to much older and more developed centres of civilisation'.[33]

That rather appealed to me as a description of the European Bronze Age.

And has anyone described a world-system in detail before 1500?

Not for the ancient world, though a series of essays in one of the New Directions volumes gives a good idea of how archaeologists have sought to apply it to particular examples.[34] But a recent book by Janet Abu-Lughod gives a well worked example for the whole of the Old World in the thirteenth century AD, and shows that it consisted of several distinct yet overlapping and interlinked systems, from Europe to China.[35] It was the decline of the eastern part of this network, she argues, which allowed the rise of the west. And Andre Frank has now gone even further, in collaboration with Barry Gills, in describing the evolution of the world-system from the beginning of urbanism to the modern period.[36] They are particularly interested in tracing cycles of growth and contraction (A/B cycles, of capital accumulation and disaccumulation, or hegemony/rivalry — the terminology is that of François Simiand) which occur throughout the system. The collapse of Late Bronze Age palatial economies would be a good example of a B phase.

Do you agree with this?

Yes, as far as it goes, though I think that the margin has to be brought into it more significantly, not least because its oscillations are often conspicuously out of phase with those in the core-periphery: for instance the Mediterranean Bronze Age collapse was precisely the time of the Urnfield expansion — and not only in Europe but on the steppes, and in the Caucasus and highland Iran. And the margin was by far the largest component of the world-system(s) down to the early modern period, so that prehistoric Europe may not be atypical. What is also interesting, and why it is worthwhile to consider the process as a whole, is how new properties emerge at each stage. The change from household slavery to chattel slavery between the Bronze Age and the Iron Age, for instance, must have fundamentally affected the nature of the periphery. There was no second millennium equivalent to the slave gangs in the Laurion silver mines, and Daphne Nash's idea of 'warrior societies' in temperate Europe — living by slave-raiding to supply the Mediterranean[37] — would only have been possible in the Iron Age. In the same way, 'dependency' was a property which gradually emerged from the specialisation of economic zones within the system, as it became harder to escape from a position in the wider structure.

You clearly have an example in mind.

I'm thinking of Sicily. Its underdevelopment is clearly a major politico-economic problem in modern Italy.

There's a recent book by Stephan Epstein on late medieval Sicily, about whether it was already dependent and what was the cause of its economic backwardness.[38] From an archaeological point of view, Sicily and southern Italy always had a different role from northern Italy: as agrarian producers, rather than a metal supplier or a node in trade with the European hinterland, they received Mycenaean settlement and Greek colonies, growing grain rather than developing into an independent core area. Their role in the wider system remained similar from the Bronze Age onwards, but their dependency became gradually more absolute with each increase in scale. It seems a good example of continuity within the world-system, over three and a half thousand years.

Yes, OK; but isn't all this rather grindingly materialistic, with its constant reduction of everything to economics?

Only if you see economics as value-free. What we've been looking at have been flows of materials, but we've also seen how their uses and values have changed. The 'transferable technologies' actually increased the range of values and meanings, as innovations spread into new social contexts; it was the spread of core-periphery interactions into the margin that began to reduce them again. Indeed, you could equally well describe the process in ideological terms, as the growing hegemony of a restricted and partly arbitrary set of cultural values. If you want copper and I want gold — as was the case in the medieval trans-Saharan trade — then we both benefit from the exchange. It's when we both share a common value system that the inequalities arise. If we didn't all want manufactured goods then there wouldn't be a problem of foreign debt. Unfortunately elites all want to show off in similar ways, which end up by beggaring the rest of humanity. Solve that and you've solved half the world's problems. In my opinion ...

Hold on — Kristian Kristiansen has just sat down at the piano, and I think Sara Champion is going to sing 'The World-System Blues'.

The conversation breaks off as the music starts; glasses are refilled, and the participants settle in for a long night . . .

Notes
1. Harlan (1971).
2. Kohl (1987; 1989).
3. Braudel (1981); Mennell (1985), cf. Goldthwaite 1989.
4. Sherratt (1982).
5. Randsborg (1978).
6. Sherratt (1981; 1986b).
7. Algaze (1989).
8. Chapman (1982); Sherratt (1986a).
9. Piggott (1983).
10. Chernikh (1992).

11. Sherratt (1981); but cf. now Haudricourt (1988) and Bijker *et al.* (1987).
12. Sherratt & Taylor (1989).
13. Bökönyi (1987).
14. Binford (1972, 81-4).
15. Forbis (1975, 81-91). For even earlier connections, between Mesoamerica and the Andean region, note the distribution of Pacific *Spondylus* from Ecuador.
16. Griffin (1980, 380-1); map in Flon (1985, 335).
17. Wallerstein (1974).
18. Compare Childe (1951, 35): 'But the objects of Stone Age trade were always luxuries — if not merely shells or similar ornaments at least things that men could easily have done without', with Wallerstein (1974, 20-1): 'long distance trade was a trade in luxuries ... which depended on the political indulgence of the wealthy ... not really what we mean today by trade'; or (1974, 41-2): 'I am sceptical that the exchange of preciosities ... could have sustained so colossal an enterprise as the expansion of the Atlantic world'.
19. Childe (1958, 166): 'In the early Bronze Age peninsular Italy, central Europe, the west Baltic coastlands, and the British Isles were united in a single system for the distribution of metalware, rooted in the Aegean market.'
20. cf. Renfrew (1986); note also the copper axe currency of Ecuador.
21. Schneider (1977).
22. Sherratt (1987).
23. Kristiansen (1987).
24. Manufacturing requires both raw material supplies and specific ingredients; in historical times, the Italian leather industry used bulk materials from its hinterland and tanning agents such as valonea from the east Mediterranean oak *Quercus aegilops*. This is a good example of the way in which a core uses its periphery for raw materials and adds value through contacts, expertise and capital investment. Hallstatt C leather fragments from Switzerland have been claimed to show valonea tanning, and were presumably obtained (as elite harness equipment) from northern Italy (Piggott 1983, 172).
25. Trevor-Roper (1956): cover blurb paraphrasing sentences on pp. 11, 90-3; cf. Lombard (1973).
26. Braudel (1972, 371, 387): 'The Mediterranean ... a world economy of sixty days' travel'. The French edition was first published in 1949.
27. Brun (1987, 196). The quotations are from Braudel, in a passage translated by Sian Reynolds as 'a fragment of the world, an economically autonomous section of the planet able to provide for most of its own needs, a section to which its external links and exchanges give a certain organic unity' (Braudel 1984, 22). Braudel was distinguishing a 'world-economy' from the world economy in general, following a usage established in German by Fritz Rörig in his book *Mittelalterliche Weltwirtschaft, Blüte und Ende einer Weltwirtschaftsepoche* (1933).
28. e.g. McNeill (1983, 24-62).
29. Frank (1966; 1967); Amin (1974; 1976).
30. Wallerstein (1974, 15).
31. Schneider (1977); cf. Lombard (1971, 120): 'Grâce à l'abondance de cet instrument privilégié des échanges, l'or, de grands centres urbains en plein essor ont pu faire appel à tous les produits, si lontains soient-ils, dont ils ont eu besoin ... '.

32. Schneider (1977, 25).
33. Schneider (1977, 210.
34. Rowlands, Larsen & Kristiansen (1987); cf. also Champion (1989).
35. Abu-Lughod (1989).
36. Gills & Frank (1991).
37. Nash (1992).
38. Epstein (1992).

References

Abu-Lughod, J., 1989. *Before European Hegemony: The World System A.D. 1250–1350*. Oxford and New York: Oxford University Press

Algaze, G., 1989. The Uruk expansion: cross-cultural exchange in early Mesopotamian civilisation, *Current Anthropology* 30 (5), 571–608

Amin, S., 1974. *Accumulation on a World Scale*. New York: Monthly Review Press

Amin, S., 1976. *Unequal Exchange*. Brighton: Harvester Press

Bijker, W.B., Hughes T.P., & Pinch. T., (eds) 1987. *The Social Construction of Technology Systems: New Directions in the Sociology and History of Technology*. Cambridge, Mass.: M.I.T. Press

Binford, L., 1972. *An Archeological Perspective*. New York: Seminar Press

Bökönyi, S., 1987. Horses and sheep in east Europe in the Copper and Bronze Ages, in *Proto-Indo-European: the Archaeology of a Linguistic Problem*, eds E. C. Polomé & N. Skomal. Washington: Institute for the Study of Man, 136–44

Braudel, F., 1972. *The Mediterranean and the Mediterranean World in the Age of Philip II*. London: Collins

Braudel, F., 1981. *The Structures of Everyday Life* (Civilisation and Capitalism 15th–18th Century, Vol. 1). London: Collins

Braudel, F., 1984. *The Perspective of the World* (Civilisation and Capitalism 15th–18th Century, Vol. 3). London: Collins

Brun, P., 1987. *Princes et Princesses de la Celtique*. Paris: Errance

Champion, T.C., (ed.) 1989. *Centre and Periphery: Comparative Studies in Archaeology*. London: Unwin Hyman

Chapman, J.C., 1982. The 'secondary products revolution' and the limitations of the Neolithic. *University of London Institute of Archaeology Bulletin* 19, 107–22

Chernikh, E., 1992. *Ancient Metallurgy in the USSR: the Early Metal Age*. Cambridge: Cambridge University Press

Childe, V.G., 1951. *Social Evolution*. London: Collins

Childe, V.G., 1958. *The Prehistory of European Society*. Harmondsworth: Penguin Books

Epstein, S., 1992. *An Island for Itself: Economic Development and Social Change in late Medieval Sicily*. Cambridge: Cambridge University Press

Flon, C., 1985 (ed.). *The World Atlas of Archaeology*. London: Mitchell Beazley

Forbis, R.G., 1975. Eastern North America, in *North America*, ed. S. Gorenstein (St Martin's Series in Prehistory). London: St. James Press, 74–102

Frank, A.G., 1966. The development of underdevelopment. *Monthly Review* 18, 17–31

Frank, A.G., 1967. *Capitalism and Underdevelopment in Latin America: Historical Studies of Chile and Brazil*. New York: Monthly Review Press

Gills, B., & Frank, A.G., 1991. 5000 years of World System history: the cumulation of accumulation, in *Core-Periphery Relations in Precapitalist Worlds*, eds C. Chase-Dunn & T.D. Hall. Boulder & Oxford: Westview Press, 46–67

Goldthwaite, R., 1989. The economic and social world of Italian Renaissance majolica. *Renaissance Quarterly* 42, 1–32

Griffin, J.B., 1980. Agricultural groups in North America, in *The Cambridge Encyclopaedia of Archaeology*, ed. A. G. Sherratt. Cambridge: Cambridge University Press, 375–81

Harlan, J.R., 1971. Agricultural origins: centers and non-centers. *Science* 174 (4008), 468–73

Haudricourt, A.-G., 1988. *La Technologie, Science Humaine: Recherches d'Histoire et d'Ethnologie des Techniques*. Paris: Editions de la Maison des Sciences de l'Homme

Kohl, P., 1987. The ancient economy, transferable technologies and the Bronze Age world system: a view from the northeastern frontier of the Ancient Near East, in *Centre and Periphery in the Ancient World*, eds M. Rowlands, M.T. Larsen, & K. Kristiansen. Cambridge: Cambridge University Press, 13–24

Kohl, P., 1989. The use and abuse of world systems theory: the case of the 'pristine' West Asian state, in *Archaeological Thought in America*, ed. C.C. Lamberg-Karlovsky. Cambridge: Cambridge University Press, 218–240

Kristiansen, K., 1987. Center and periphery in Bronze Age Scandinavia, in *Centre and Periphery in the Ancient World*, eds M. Rowlands, M.T. Larsen, & K. Kristiansen. Cambridge: Cambridge University Press, 74–86

Lombard, M., 1971. *L'Islam dans sa Première Grandeur (VIII-XI Siècle)*. Paris: Flammarion

McNeill, W.H., 1983. *The Pursuit of Power*. Oxford: Blackwell

Mennell, S., 1985. *All Manners of Food*. Oxford: Blackwell

Nash, D., 1985. Celtic territorial expansion and the Mediterranean World, in *Settlement and Society: Aspects of Western European Prehistory in the First Millennium BC*, eds T.C. Champion & J.V.S. Megaw. Leicester: Leicester University Press, 45–68

Piggott, S., 1983. *The Earliest Wheeled Transport: from the Atlantic Coast to the Caspian Sea*. London: Thames & Hudson

Randsborg, K., 1978. Resource distribution and the function of copper in Early Neolithic Denmark, in *The Origins of Metallurgy in Atlantic Europe*, ed. M. Ryan. Dublin: Stationery Office, 303–18

Renfrew, A.C., 1996. Varna and the emergence of wealth in prehistoric Europe, in *The Social Life of Things: Commodities in Cultural Perspective*, ed. A. Appadurai. Cambridge: Cambridge University Press, 141–68

Rowlands, M., Larsen, M.T., & Kristiansen, K., (eds.), 1987. *Centre and Periphery in the Ancient World*, Cambridge: Cambridge University Press

Schneider, J., 1977. Was there a pre-capitalist world system?. *Peasant Studies* 6, 20–9. Reprinted 1991 in *Core-Periphery Relations in Precapitalist Worlds*, eds C. Chase-Dunn & T.D. Hall. Boulder & Oxford: Westview Press, 45–66

Sherratt, A.G., 1981. Plough and pastoralism: aspects of the secondary products revolution, in *Pattern of the Past: Studies in Honour of David Clarke*, eds I Hodder, G. Isaac & N. Hammond. Cambridge: Cambridge University Press, 261–305

Sherratt, A.G., 1982. Mobile resources: settlement and exchange in early agricultural Europe, in *Ranking, Resource and Exchange*, eds C. Renfrew & S. Shennan. Cambridge: Cambridge University Press, 13–26

Sherratt, A.G., 1986a. Wool, wheels and ploughmarks: local developments or outside introductions in Neolithic Europe?. *University of London Institute of Archaeology Bulletin* 23, 1–15

Sherratt, A.G., 1986b. Cups that cheered, in *Bell Beakers of the West Mediterranean: Proceedings of the Oxford International Conference* eds W. Waldren & R. Kennard. Oxford: British Archaeological Reports International Series S331, 81–106

Sherratt, A.G., 1987. Warriors and traders: Bronze Age chiefdoms in central Europe, in *Origins: the Roots of European Civilisation*, ed. B.W. Cunliffe. London: BBC Books, 54–66

Sherratt, A.G., & Taylor, T., 1989. Metal vessels in Bronze Age Europe and the context of Vulchetrun, in *Thracians and Mycenaeans: Proceedings of the Fourth International Congress of Thracology, Rotterdam 1984*, eds J.G.P. Best & N.M.W. de Vries. Leiden: Brill, 106–34

Trevor-Roper, H. 1965. *The Rise of Christian Europe*. London: Thames & Hudson

Wallerstein, I., 1974. *The Modern World-System: Capitalist Agriculture and the Origins of the European World-Economy in the Sixteenth Century*. New York: Academic Press